Lisa G.
435-4886

Applied
Business
Law

Tenth Edition

*Business Law
Applied to the Problems
of the Individual
as Citizen, Consumer,
and Employee*

Based on the Uniform Commercial Code

McKee Fisk

Professor of Business Administration
Graduate School of Business
University of Santa Clara
Santa Clara, California

Norbert J. Mietus

Professor of Business Law
School of Business Administration
Sacramento State College
Sacramento, California

James C. Snapp

Professor of Business Law
Southwest Missouri State College
Springfield, Missouri

Published by

L81 **SOUTH-WESTERN PUBLISHING CO.**

CINCINNATI   WEST CHICAGO, ILL.   DALLAS   NEW ROCHELLE, N.Y.
BURLINGAME, CALIF.   BRIGHTON, ENGLAND

ISBN: 0-538-12810-0

Library of Congress Catalog Card Number: 76-184776

5 6 7 8 K 9 8 7 6 5 4

Printed in the United States of America

Preface

At a time when important human institutions are being re-examined and are changing, the law is also changing. Serving the needs of society and reflecting the changes in ideals, values, and goals of our society, the law tries to keep pace with these changes. Legislative bodies enact new statutes, and courts interpret them according to present-day standards and needs. Even constitutions are amended. This, the Tenth Edition of *Applied Business Law*, incorporates many of these changes.

The enactment of the Uniform Commercial Code by all states, except Louisiana, has resulted in many changes being made in this edition, without reference to former or conflicting provisions which are now obsolete. In recognition of renewed interest in the rights and obligations of citizenship, in the historical development of our system of law, in court structure and procedure, and in criminal law, the first two units have been completely revised. Because of the obvious interest of young people in their rights and responsibilities, a chapter on the law as it relates to minors has been included. Increased significance of administrative law and regulation of business by government has resulted in the inclusion of a new chapter dealing with these important subjects. More emphasis has been placed on consumer law, and recent social legislation has been given attention.

Other changes have also been made. Based on a questionnaire returned by approximately 4,000 business law teachers giving their judgments and suggestions regarding course content and teaching methods, new materials have been added and changes made in organization and supplementary teaching aids. An abridged version of the text has been provided for those schools that wish it. Preventive law has been expanded to all appropriate chapters in an attempt to give advice on how to avoid some of the legal pitfalls that lie ahead. In recognition of the increased use of standardized legal forms, more such forms have been illustrated, especially in the workbook. In short, this Tenth Edition reflects the suggestions of experienced teachers.

The teaching-learning features of the book which have proven to be so successful in the past have been retained and updated:

(1) Opening interest-arousing situations—"teasers"—for each chapter.
(2) A descriptive leading question as the title for each section.
(3) A thought-provoking real-life problem at the beginning of each section, with the solution included in the discussion which immediately follows.
(4) Additional explanatory examples.
(5) Vocabulary review in self-test form.
(6) Summaries of highlights to be remembered and used for review.
(7) Hypothetical cases and actual court cases carefully chosen for student interest and useful for class discussion or outside study.
(8) Line drawings to emphasize selected concepts and rules, often with a gentle touch of humor.

Experienced teachers know that because our laws are made by fifty different sovereign states as well as by the federal government, because every law is subject to judicial interpretation which may vary with changing facts, and because man engages in an infinite variety of activities under the law, it is impossible to cover every possibility with precision. Exceptions, distinctions, and variations exist in the seemingly most simple rules. Where differences exist, an attempt has been made to present the generally prevailing or preferred view, including important exceptions. But a text of this nature is not intended to be definitive nor to take the place of professional legal counsel for the resolution of specific legal problems.

Nevertheless, the student who conscientiously reads this textbook and successfully does the assigned work will better understand the world in which he lives. He will expand his vocabulary and sharpen his ability to think analytically and systematically. He will be better equipped than most citizens to recognize legal problems.

To those many dedicated teachers who have worked with our book in the past, and to those teachers and other friends who have been so generous with suggestions for its continued improvement, we express our sincere gratitude.

McKee Fisk/Norbert J. Mietus/James C. Snapp

Consulting Editor: **Ronald A. Anderson**
Professor of Law and Government
Drexel University

Author of *Anderson on the Uniform Commercial Code;*
Anderson's Uniform Commercial Code Legal Forms

Contents

Introduction

"STUDY BUSINESS LAW?

WHO, ME?!"

—A Drama In One Act

You are seated outside the high school counseling office. With you are Betty Burke and Hank Crowell. Both of them have already taken the course in business law. Now they are trying to persuade you to add it to your program. You are not enthusiastic about the prospect.

YOU: Why should I take business law? I don't want to become a lawyer. I'm not even sure I'll end up in business.

BETTY: But it's not supposed to make you into a lawyer. A person goes to college and then on to a law school for that. As for business, the law affects almost everything you do, whoever you are and wherever you go.

HANK: Right! I remember our teacher quoting a Supreme Court judge. Felix Frankfurter—a smart man and I'll never forget his name. Anyway—Judge Frankfurter said our society is a legal state because everything, but everything, that takes place sooner or later raises legal questions.

YOU: He's putting you on. Sure, lots of people violate traffic laws, but that's routine and I've had the driver's ed. course. Maybe some people commit crimes, but not me. Let the police and the T.V. detectives worry about murder.

BETTY: You're foolish if you think that's all there is to law— parking tickets and T.V. detective shows . . . Look. This morning you got up, right? And you turned on the lights and your favorite radio station, right? Well, your folks had to make contracts for both of those little comforts. And both are regulated by law. You got dressed and ate breakfast. Everything you ate and wore and used was made and sold under a whole string of legal agreements. Then you came to school in a bus the district leases from a bank. And you came because a law says everyone our age must come. Law. Law. Law.

HANK: Right! Here's something else to think about. This school is on land held under legal title. It was bought with money raised by selling bonds. Your father works under an employment contract. He works for a corporation—a legal being. He's a salesman—and an agent. All law, man, all law. You can't avoid it.

BETTY: Sure. And our school is paid for by taxes collected under law. The teachers and other workers are covered by workmen's compensation laws in case they're hurt on the job. Almost everybody who works is covered by social security laws. Even you have a social security number, don't you?

YOU: Yeah. But I still say a guy doesn't have to know all those fancy technicalities to get by.

HANK: Of course you don't—but who wants to just get by? Besides, the class covers basics—not just a lot of technicalities. And everything comes alive with real court cases and examples from daily life, of guys just like us . . . After a few weeks in class we could tell how people in trouble could have avoided a lot of grief and expense if they'd only known and followed the law.

BETTY: That's true and I can prove it. I know I've helped my folks with ideas I've learned about sales warranties and buying on credit. And I know how to open a bank account and how to use commercial paper. Do you?

YOU: No—but . . .

HANK: I do. And I've had fun talking with my dad about his union and the Taft-Hartley Act. 'Bet you never even heard of that. He thinks I'm pretty smart . . . When I got my car I knew what kind of insurance I should get and what it covered. I'll bet you don't know these things.

BETTY: Something else too. Pretty soon we'll all be finding jobs, and getting married, and renting apartments or buying houses. These are legal relations, every one. We ought to know at least the fundamentals about the law on each.

YOU: It all sounds so complicated.

HANK: Only because you haven't had the course. The book is really easy to read because it has all sorts of interesting examples from real life. There are even some cartoons and fascinating stuff on crimes and torts.

BETTY: I'll bet you still think a tort is a fancy cake! Well, it isn't. And I'll bet you don't even know the difference between a felony and a misdemeanor. Or between state and federal courts.

HANK: Or between a summons and a subpoena. Man, you'll be in hot water if you ever get sued.

YOU: No I won't. I'll take the course . . . Now are you happy?

BETTY: You should be happy.

HANK: You're getting smarter all the time.

* * * *

A course in business law has many values. Like Betty and Hank, you will learn about the legal environment in which you live, and about the laws which govern human conduct in civilized society. You will also learn how to avoid many legal difficulties, and how to cooperate more effectively with a lawyer if and when that proves desirable or necessary.

HOW TO STUDY BUSINESS LAW

These suggestions are made to help you understand the material in your assignments thoroughly and in the shortest time. They supplement any how-to-study directions which your instructor may provide.

1. The law is about people. People make the laws, use them to get things done in an orderly way, and sometimes break them. In reading the problems and examples, imagine you are one of the parties.
2. Each chapter is introduced with three simple questions that you should be able to answer from what you already know or what you think is fair or reasonable. Answer each of these questions before you read the chapter.
3. After you have answered the three introductory questions, scan the topic headings to see whether your reasoning was sound and to get a general idea of what is included. You can do this by reading the chapter rapidly, checking items that are difficult or puzzling.
4. After you have read the chapter rapidly, read it a second time more slowly and carefully, making notes of the important points in your notebook. Each topic heading is stated in the form of a question; try to answer it before you study the next topic. Be sure that you understand its meaning before you continue. If in doubt, read the topic again and, if necessary, ask someone to help you with it. If you do not know the meaning of a legal word, look it up by referring to the index or the glossary.
5. As you read the paragraphs, try to apply the rules to yourself or to your family and friends. Recall, if you can, situations within your own experience to which the rules apply.
6. Examples of legal problems from real life ("Law As People Live It") and actual case problems ("Law As Courts Decide It") appear at the end of each chapter. All are covered in the text, and you can sharpen your wits by being the judge and solving them. Make a note of the page on which you think the answer to each is found.
7. Before you begin your study of a new chapter, review the sections entitled "Your Legal Vocabulary" and "Remember These Highlights" of the preceding chapter to refresh your memory. Just before you go to class, if you have time, review the similar sections of your new chapter.

HOW YOU CAN SOLVE LEGAL PROBLEMS

Following each chapter you will find a number of real-life problems under the heading "Law as People Live It." You will also find actual cases that have been decided by courts, headed "Law As Courts Decide It," which contain more details and sometimes will be more difficult to understand. The method of solving is essentially the same in both problems and cases.

To answer the question raised in a problem or case, first read it carefully. Be sure you understand the question. Then analyze the situation, determine the rule of law involved, and reach a decision. The basic rule will always be found in the same chapter in which the problem appears.

You will find it helpful to follow these five steps:

1. What are the facts? Restate in your own words the important facts. Read the problem or case more slowly and possibly make a simple diagram showing the various parties and relationships. You can identify the party who is suing or seeking relief as the P or plaintiff, and his opponent as the D or defendant.

2. What is the disputed point?

3. What rule of law is involved? Sometimes more than one rule may be involved.

4. How does this rule apply to the facts?

5. What is the answer or decision?

In oral reports to the class or in written assignments, your instructor may prefer that you use only three of the above steps; in this order:

1. State your answer or decision.
2. Give the rule of law that supports your answer.
3. Explain how the rule of law applies to the facts.

LEGAL ADVICE

1. Consult a qualified lawyer if you have any doubts about your rights or duties when your property, life, or liberty is endangered or significantly changes. If you don't know a lawyer, ask your banker, relatives, friends, or local lawyers' reference service for suggestions.

2. Obtain advice from your lawyer before making a major move, such as buying or selling real property, preparing a will, entering into a business, or making any important agreement. It costs comparatively little and will help you to avoid costly errors.

3. Ignorance of the law is normally no excuse if you have committed a crime or invaded the personal rights of another. Make yourself familiar with local, state, and federal laws.

4. Remember that a minor is generally liable for his crimes and torts and may also be bound by his contracts.

5. There is always more than one side to a legal dispute. Try to learn the other fellow's version of the situation and honestly seek a friendly solution out of court. Remember that in every court action, at least one party loses.

6. If you are convinced that you have a good cause of action against another person but your attorney disagrees, the chances are good that your attorney is right.

7. If someone injures you or your property in a tort, such as an automobile accident, don't rush to sign a statement releasing him from liability in exchange for some payment of money. The damages may be greater than first determined. On the other hand, don't delay in consulting an attorney and in taking an action if appropriate—you may lose your rights if you do.

8. Although oral agreements can be legally binding, it is prudent to spell out in writing all contracts which involve relatively much time, money, or detail, and to have both parties sign and receive copies.

9. Keep important papers secure in a safe place, such as a safe-deposit box. But also keep copies of these important papers in a safe place at home so that in case of your death, your survivors know what provisions have been made for them since your safe-deposit box will be kept sealed until a court order is given to open it.

UNIT ONE

You and the Law

UNIT ONE

For people to live and work together in harmony, rules of conduct—law—must be made and obeyed. It sometimes seems that there are rules for everything—rules at home, rules at school, rules at work, and rules at play—but these rules protect each person's rights and are essential if we are to get along with each other, be productive, and enjoy life.

Law consists of the rules of conduct that can be legally enforced. Without law, men would probably still be fighting each other to settle disputes, expecting no help from society and getting none. Since in your lifetime you will be engaged in countless thousands of activities regulated in some manner by law, it is essential that you know and understand the law.

In this unit we shall trace the development of our system of law and see what forms it takes today. We shall also discuss the rights and responsibilities of citizenship and shall see that the "good" citizen helps to shape laws through participation in government to meet the changing needs of society.

As part of the change, the role of the minor is expanding as evidenced by recent passage of the 26th Amendment allowing 18-year-olds to vote. As a result, young people are gaining additional rights and assuming more responsibilities. We shall take a careful look at the role of the minor as a citizen, student, and driver.

Finally, we shall study our laws as they relate to the consumer. As a result of changing attitudes, consumer protection is very important in today's market place. We shall see what specific legal protections are afforded the consumer as a result of this greater interest and concern.

CHAPTER **1** Law and Society

1. *In a game of football or basketball, why do we have rules and a referee?*

2. *Some customs, like driving on the right side of the road, have been enacted into law; some, like women wearing dresses, have not. How do you account for the difference?*

3. *While boating, you observe a boy topple from a wharf into the water. Are you under any legal duty to try to rescue him?*

WHY DO WE HAVE LAW?

Problem: A small child was lost in the mountains while on a camping trip with his family. Other campers were asked to join in the search. Some refused. Did they violate any law?

This is a free country. So why can't we do anything we please? Possibly we could if each of us lived entirely alone and had no contact with anyone else. Or perhaps it would be possible if each person's actions were guided by the "Golden Rule"—treating others as he would want to be treated himself. But since man is naturally social, and since each individual is unique and unpredictable, men have found it necessary to develop rules and regulations to govern their relations. These rules—known as laws—establish and enforce certain standards of conduct. In doing so, they provide guidelines and make behavior more predictable. Thus, they help to protect every individual's freedom and rights.

> "We hold these Truths to be self-evident, that all Men are created equal, that they are endowed by their Creator with certain unalienable Rights, that among these are Life, Liberty and the Pursuit of Happiness."
>
> —The Declaration of Independence

Freedom and rights, however, are coupled with limits and duties. A famous judge once said, "Your right to swing your fist ends at the point where the other fellow's nose begins." If others are to respect your rights, you must also respect theirs. Thus, your right to drive a car is limited by a duty to abide by the "rules of the road," and to respect the rights of other drivers. If you buy a meal in a restaurant, you have the obligation to pay for it; and if you borrow a lawnmower from a neighbor, you have a duty to return it. As you see, most legal duties arise from the rights of other persons.

Inevitably, in any society, some people misbehave. While some of this misbehavior is intentional (a thief steals your color TV), much of it is also due to carelessness (a trash fire spreads from your yard to a neighbor's house), or even to ignorance of the rules (you're caught doing what you thought was a lawful 45 in a 25 m.p.h. zone). Often, honest and well-intentioned persons become involved in disputes and are unable to determine who is in the wrong. Whatever the cause of conflict, law may be invoked to deal with it— to protect the innocent, to discipline the wrongdoer, and to settle disputes and differences without violence.

The purposes of law can be said to be:

(1) To influence, establish, and enforce standards of conduct, including rules for orderly conduct of business transactions;

(2) To provide for the protection of individual rights;

(3) To provide ways of avoiding and, if necessary, of settling conflicts;

(4) To promote justice and provide for the general welfare.

Law consists of the rules of conduct that society will enforce through its system of law enforcement, courts, and regulatory agencies. Much of it is a reflection of present-day social and business standards and customs. As those standards and customs change, the law changes. For example, within your lifetime and experience many laws have been changed in response to our changing values and moral standards, our beliefs regarding justice, the rights and relationships of individuals, and the importance of the quality of human life.

Not all customs or ethical and social standards have the force of law. Only those that society will enforce through its legal system have legal standing. In the problem on page 3, the campers were within their legal rights in refusing to aid in the search for the lost child. Although their refusal may have been a breach of a moral duty, they violated no law, hence no legal duty; and there was no legal penalty to which they were subject.

HOW DID OUR LAW DEVELOP?

Problem: In a certain state a custom developed among those who drove on narrow roads in the mountains that when a driver going up met a driver coming down, the driver going up had the right of way. Would this custom have the force of law?

Since the time when people first lived together in groups, tribes, or communes, rules have been adopted to protect group members and to govern their relationships with each other. In early Medieval England, there was no formal body of written law, and each feudal lord or baron administered his own law in his own court. Although these barons' courts showed some similarities, the laws tended to be local or regional, and disputes were settled on the basis of local customs and the judgment of the baron. As the country became unified, communications among judges improved and the law became common to the whole country. The decisions in individual cases became the precedents for settling future, similar cases. Originally few decisions were recorded, and so the early common law was sometimes known as "unwritten law." Eventually the principles and rules announced by the courts were preserved in writing. The particular rules thus became fixed and people knew what to expect if similar circumstances arose in the future. Thus developed what has come to be known as the customary or *common law*—law which has its origin in the traditions, customs, and trade practices of the people. Common law operates through the *rule of precedent*. This rule means that like cases in the future are to be decided in a like manner.

In 1215 the English barons forced the adoption of the *Magna Carta* which provided in writing certain guarantees and protection against arbitrary acts of the king. Later the Magna Carta was revised and other documents, such as the English Bill of Rights (1689), were adopted. When the American colonies were settled, the colonists adopted the principles of the Magna Carta and the common law primarily as a body of unwritten legal principles. This early English law thus became the foundation of the legal system of our federal government and of all the states except Louisiana, where French influence and law prevailed.

Many of the common law principles and rules have now been written into law by legislative bodies; however, those which appear in decided cases or even remain unwritten are enforced just as strictly by the courts. In the problem on page 5, the custom establishing the right of way was common law, and although it was not in writing it had all the force of written law.

In the course of time, certain limitations of the common law were recognized. Thus, there developed a supplementary system of law known as *equity*. Equity attempts to protect a person or his property when there is no adequate remedy at common law. In the United States, law and equity have in many respects become one, and the same court will give both types of remedy.

Today, there are two great systems of law in the western world: the common law, and the Roman civil law. Both systems have the same objective, the safeguarding of life, liberty, and property of the people. Louisiana follows the Roman civil law that was in effect when the Louisiana Territory was ceded to this country by France. The difference is chiefly in procedure or methods by which a legal action is instituted and conducted. Also, under the civil law, the main rules are written into legislative codes rather than being defined by judges.

WHAT ARE THE FORMS OF LAW TODAY?

Problem: Congress enacted a law that requires pre-packaged food products to be labeled to show the weight of the contents. What kind of law is this?

There are 51 basic legal systems in the United States—that of the federal government and those of the 50 states. Although these systems are similar in many ways, they also have important differences. The law is found in four forms: (1) the constitutions of the United States and of the 50 states; (2) the statutes enacted by our elected representatives, as in the above problem; (3) case law, as expressed in court decisions; and (4) administrative law. Treaties made with other countries also have the force of law.

(1) CONSTITUTIONAL LAW

A *constitution* is a body of basic principles stating the powers and limitations of a government and the way those powers are to be exercised. Most constitutions in democratic societies establish not only the form and powers of government, but also limit those powers and define the rights of individual citizens. For example, the Constitution of the United States and the first ten amendments (Bill of Rights) adopted many of the principles of the Magna Carta and later documents relating to the rights of individuals. Included are the right to: trial by jury of one's peers (equals); a speedy trial under due process of law; equal justice for all; freedom of speech, assembly, and worship; and fair compensation for the taking of private property for a public purpose.

> "This Constitution and the laws of the United States which shall be made in pursuance thereof; and all treaties made, or which shall be made, under the authority of the United States shall be the supreme law of the land . . ."
>
> —Article VI, Section 2, U. S. Constitution

The Constitution of the United States is the supreme law of the land within the scope of its stated powers; each state constitution is the supreme law within the particular state as to the other powers of government.

> "The powers not delegated to the United States by the Constitution, nor prohibited by it to the States, are reserved to the States, respectively, or to the people."
>
> —Tenth Amendment, U. S. Constitution

Neither the federal nor state government is permitted to conflict with the other's area of power of jurisdiction. However, the Federal Constitution limits the powers not only of the federal government but also of the states in order to protect the rights of its citizens.

> "No State shall make or enforce any law which shall abridge the privileges or immunities of citizens of the United States; nor shall any State deprive any person of life, liberty, or property, without due process of law; nor deny to any person within its jurisdiction the equal protection of the laws."
>
> —14th Amendment, U. S. Constitution

State constitutions recognize these limitations and their relations with the federal government.

> "The Constitution of the United States, and the laws made, or which shall be made, in pursuance thereof,

and all treaties made, or which shall be made, under the authority of the United States, are, and shall be the Supreme Law of the State and the judges of this State, and all the people of this State, are, and shall be bound thereby . . ."

—Constitution of Maryland, Article II

(2) STATUTE LAW

Many of our laws, especially those we read about in the daily newspapers, are created by legislative bodies. The laws enacted by Congress, as in the problem on page 6, and by the state legislatures are *statutes*. Acts of Congress become part of the law of the land by virtue of the Federal Constitution which gives Congress the power:

"To make all Laws which shall be necessary and proper for carrying into Execution the foregoing Powers, and all other Powers vested by this Constitution in the Government of the United States, or in any Department or Officer thereof."

—Article I, Section 8, U. S. Constitution

Statute law also includes *ordinances,* which are enacted by local bodies such as city councils and county governing boards. Statutes include such laws as those that specify the speed limits of motor vehicles, the taxes one must pay, and the minimum wages a worker is entitled to receive.

Each state may enact such statutes as it wishes as long as they are in harmony with its own constitution and the Federal Constitution. Similarly, each local government may enact such ordinances as it chooses if they are in harmony with the city charter as well as with the state and federal constitutions and statutes. Statutes or ordinances that conflict with either the federal or state constitutions are said to be *unconstitutional.* Laws declared to be unconstitutional by the U. S. Supreme Court are void and have no effect.

Because of the differences among the laws of the several states, especially as applied to business, confusion may arise when persons accustomed to the laws of one state do business in others. To minimize such difficulties, many states have adopted certain "uniform laws," which are essentially the same from state to state. One such uniform law is the Uniform Commercial Code, which will be discussed later.

(3) CASE LAW

Case law is found in the form of decisions and opinions of judges of the U. S. Supreme Court and other high federal and state courts. The term "case law" is often used to mean the same thing as common law.

Legislative bodies can modify or suspend common-law rules as announced by courts. Until or unless such rules are changed by statute, however, they are just as binding upon the people as law in any other form.

(4) ADMINISTRATIVE LAW

Because of the complexity of society and of government, legislative bodies have, by statute, created a large number of *administrative agencies* to carry out some of the many and diverse functions of government. Although these agencies vary greatly in name, purpose, and power, they generally have in common the right to make rules, establish rates, and determine the rights of parties. Their general regulations and specific rulings have the force of statute, and are known as *administrative law*.

Each agency regulates a specific area of activity. For example, the Interstate Commerce Commission deals with trade that crosses state boundaries; and the National Labor Relations Board governs union and management activities in the field of employment. The Veteran's Administration regulates such matters as the following:

> "Basic eligibility for educational assistance is subject to the following requirements: (a) Service. The veteran must have served on active duty for a continuous period of 181 days or more, any part of which occurred on or after February 1, 1955, or if he served less than 181 days, must have been discharged or released on or after February 1, 1955, because of service-connected disability."—21.1040, Chapter 1, Title 38, Code of Federal Regulations (Veterans' Benefits), as prescribed by the Veterans Administration

Many agencies operate in much the same manner as courts do, but an appeal may usually be taken to the courts from an action of an administrative agency.

 The Insurance Commissioner of a state, with the legal right to approve or disapprove rates charged for insurance, refused to approve an increase in the charge for fire insurance requested by the Triple Safety Insurance Co. The company appealed the Commissioner's decision to the Court of Appeals, which reversed the decision.

WHAT IS BUSINESS LAW?

Problem: Werner, a school teacher, agreed to buy a used automobile from Franich Motors on a time payment plan. He was asked to sign a lengthy printed form that had the details of the transaction typed in. Uncertain about the contents but knowing that if he were to buy the car he would have to sign the contract, Werner signed. How would a knowledge of business law have helped him?

Business law, sometimes known as commercial law, is concerned with the rules that apply to business situations and transactions. A look at the table of contents of this book should make it clear that the scope of business law is very broad, and that most of the topics covered are of importance to all citizens, not just "businessmen." Everyone engages in activities governed by business law. For instance, Werner, in the problem, would be able to deal more effectively with Franich if he had a knowledge of business law.

Business law has been developing even longer than common law, for it had its beginnings when Phoenician merchants began sailing the waters of the world. About a thousand years later, early English merchants recognized a special common law for traders called the *law merchant.* Eventually the law merchant became part of English common law and then part of our law. Today, however, much of our business law—including the law merchant—is undergoing change.

Each state has its own laws, and while similar, there are many state-to-state differences. With the growth of interstate commerce and large business firms, and with the speed of modern-day transportation and communication, uniformity of laws governing business and commercial transactions became a necessity. The adoption of the *Uniform Commercial Code* in all states but one,[1] and in the District of Columbia and the Virgin Islands as well, was a major step towards achieving that uniformity. In addition, the UCC has simplified, clarified, and modernized many laws relating to commercial transactions

[1] Louisiana, which follows the civil law, is the only non-Code state.

such as sales, and has made them more flexible and responsive to modern conditions by permitting wider use of custom and usage in the areas covered by the Code. With certain exceptions, it also recognizes agreements between the parties if they are reasonable even though they do not conform absolutely and rigidly to generally accepted legal principles. The Code also applies a higher standard of conduct to merchants than to those not engaged in business. "Good faith" is required in all dealings covered by the Code, and "unconscionable" provisions may not be enforced by the courts.

YOUR LEGAL VOCABULARY

administrative agency
administrative law
business law
case law
common law
constitution
equity
law

law merchant
Magna Carta
ordinances
rule of precedent
statutes
unconstitutional
Uniform Commercial Code

Write the numbers 1 to 10 in a column to represent the following definitions and explanations. Then after each number write the term in the list above which matches that definition or explanation.

1. Like cases are to be treated in like manner.
2. Rules of conduct that can be enforced by court action.
3. The customs and the practices of the people that have the force of law.
4. A statute that simplifies, clarifies, and modernizes the law of commercial transactions.
5. Rules and regulations of government agencies having the force of law.
6. Body of basic principles stating powers and limitations of government.
7. Enactments of Congress and state legislatures.
8. Enactments of local governmental bodies.
9. Rules of law that apply to business situations and transactions.
10. Law found in the decisions and opinions of courts.

REMEMBER THESE HIGHLIGHTS

1. Law consists of the rules of conduct that can be enforced by society through its courts and through government administrative agencies.
2. The law provides for settling conflicts peacefully, protecting individual rights, and promoting justice.
3. The two great systems of law in the western world are common law and Roman civil law. All states but Louisiana follow the common law.

4. The common law finds its authority in the customs and practices of the people. It operates through the rule of precedent.
5. When no adequate remedy is available to a person through the common law, he may obtain relief through a supplementary system of law known as equity.
6. Law is found in four basic forms: constitutions, statutes, case law, and administrative law.
7. Business law is concerned with the rules that apply to business situations and transactions. The Uniform Commercial Code is an important part of business law.

LAW AS PEOPLE LIVE IT ⚔

Be prepared to state the reason for your answer to each question raised in the following problems. (See page xi for suggestions.)

1. Douglas invited Marcum to attend a football game and agreed to call for her at one o'clock. Marcum had other plans for that afternoon but canceled them to accept Douglas' invitation. Douglas failed to show up and did not notify Marcum. Did Marcum have a right of legal action against Douglas?
2. In a certain section of a city the houses were set back 75 feet from the street. Lent wanted to build a home in that neighborhood but planned a setback of only 50 feet. In the absence of an ordinance, could Lent be required to conform to the custom of a 75-foot setback?
3. Gomez was stopped from publishing a paper under an ordinance that provided no papers could be published that found fault with local officials. Would federal law guaranteeing freedom of speech allow him to continue in spite of the local ordinance?
4. A state statute authorized the State Highway Commission to establish speed limits in accordance with traffic and road conditions. The maximum speed permitted by statute was 65 miles per hour. The Commission set a limit of 45 miles on a certain stretch of road. Yandell was cited for exceeding that limit. He contended that the State Highway Commission had no power to set a speed limit less than 65 miles per hour. Was he correct?
5. Gregory and Blech were discussing the common law. Gregory maintained that a legislature had the power to enact a statute that changes a common-law rule. Was he correct?
6. In what ways would the following people find the study of business law helpful: (a) an apartment house owner, (b) a physician, (c) the operator of a beauty shop, (d) a farmer, and (e) a housewife?
7. Rinehart wished to construct a service station on certain land that he owned, but Fiala, who lived next door to Rinehart's property, and other neighbors objected. They claimed that the zoning regulations as

imposed by an administrative agency did not permit a service station at that location. Does the law protect both the rights of Rinehart and of Fiala in a conflict of this kind?

8. Vincent obtained a court judgment prohibiting a pipeline from being run across his property without payment. Can Catuzzo, Vincent's neighbor, who is similarly concerned, rely on this court decision in his dealing with the pipeline company?

9. Weems applied to the State Board of Accountancy for a license to practice accounting. Even though he believed that he met all the qualifications, Weems' application was denied. Does he have any rights?

10. The city of Moderna wished to develop a park along a river on property owned by Haley. Can the city require Haley to give the property to the city?

LAW AS COURTS DECIDE IT

Be prepared to state the reason for your answer to each question raised in the following cases. (See page xi for suggestions.)

1. George Andrews was arrested on the street in an area where a murder had been committed a few hours earlier. The arresting officer had no search warrant, but arrested Andrews for carrying a concealed weapon —a .38 caliber Cobra revolver. The officer relied on a clause in the Michigan Constitution that exempted from the requirement of a search warrant "any criminal proceeding, any . . . firearm . . . seized by a peace officer outside the curtilage (yard) of any dwelling house in this state." The United States Supreme Court had earlier held that the Fourth Amendment to the Constitution of the United States prohibiting unreasonable search and seizure applied to the states through the 14th Amendment. Also, a United States Court of Appeals had previously held in another case that the clause in the Michigan Constitution relied on by the officer was in conflict with the U.S. Constitution. Must the Michigan courts recognize the superior authority of the United States Supreme Court and the Constitution of the United States? (People v. Andrews, 21 Mich. App. 731, 176 N.W. 2d 460)

2. Harris, a bookkeeper for Bolden, the owner of a service station, was injured in a fire that killed a customer, Barnes. In an earlier lawsuit, Barnes' widow had sued Bolden, claiming his negligence had caused her husband's death; however, the court had held that Bolden was not negligent and that the cause of Barnes' death was his own negligence. In this action, Harris sued Bolden and Standard Oil Company for her injuries, likewise claiming negligence by Bolden in the accident that caused the fire and by Standard Oil Company in designing the building. Should Harris win the case? (Standard Oil Company v. Harris, 120 Ga. App. 768, 172 S.E. 2d 344)

3. Adams was cited by a Dayton police officer for operating a motor vehicle at 35 miles per hour in a 25-mile zone. The speed of Adam's vehicle was checked by use of radar. One cooperating officer operated an unmarked motor vehicle owned by the city of Dayton which carried the radar equipment. The arresting officer operated a properly marked police car. The Ohio Revised Code provided that "any motor vehicle used by a member of the state highway patrol, or by any other peace officer, while said officer is on duty for the exclusive or main purpose of enforcing the motor vehicle or traffic laws of this state . . . shall be marked in some distinctive manner or color." Upon being found guilty, Adams appealed his conviction, claiming the City of Dayton was bound by state statutes even though its local ordinance did not require police cars on traffic patrol to be marked. Do you agree that the word "ordinance" is included within the meaning of the term "law," and the word "state" in the statute includes "city"? (City of Dayton v. Adams, 9 Ohio St. 2d 89, 223 N.E. 2d 822)

4. Smith signed a contract purchase order for a new automobile from Zabriskie Chevrolet, Inc., making a down payment. While driving his car home from the dealer's showroom it developed such mechanical trouble in the transmission that the car could not move. Smith immediately notified the dealer that he was canceling the agreement to purchase the car because it was defective. Zabriskie thereupon repaired the car and offered it to him again. Upon Smith's refusal to carry out the contract, Zabriskie sued him for the balance due, claiming, among other things, but submitting no evidence, that it was the usage and custom of the automobile trade that a buyer accept a new automobile, although defective, if such defects can be and are cured by the seller. Under these circumstances could Zabriskie enforce the agreement and collect the balance due? (Zabriskie Chevrolet, Inc. v. Smith, 99 N.J. Super. 441, 240 A. 2d 195)

5. Peterson, an experienced feed lot operator, purchased 348 feeder heifers from Lowrance at a cost of $4,589 plus commission. Before accepting delivery he inspected the cattle, rejecting four head costing $526. Soon after the heifers were delivered to the feed lot, a serious disease known as "red nose" developed and 81 of the heifers died. Peterson refused to pay, claiming breach of an implied warranty that the cattle were merchantable and fit for sale. Lowrance contended that it was the custom and usage of the trade that after a buyer's inspection of cattle and rejection or cutting out, his acceptance is irrevocable and without recourse. Peterson did not deny this. Lowrance also claimed that under the UCC, an implied warranty can be excluded or modified by usage of the trade. If this is the case, must Peterson pay for the heifers? (R.D. Lowrance, Inc. v. Peterson, 185 Neb. 679, 178 NW 2d 277)

CHAPTER 2 Law and the Citizen

1. *A friend of yours was born in this country while his parents were citizens of France. Is your friend a citizen of the United States?*

2. *Your next door neighbor owns a trumpet. May he play or practice it any time without regard to his neighbors?*

3. *What rights do you have if you are arrested and taken to a police station?*

WHAT IS CITIZENSHIP?

Problem: Hensley, who was a pacifist, refused to pay the percentage of his income taxes which he said would be allotted by the government to war expenses. Can he be required to pay?

Citizenship is membership in the civil and political community— the nation and state of one's residence. It is a give and take relationship between an individual and a government: the *citizen* gives his allegiance to and accepts the benefits of the government; in return for the allegiance of its citizens, the government protects them both individually and collectively.

Allegiance is the bond of loyalty and obligation of the citizen to his government. It requires the giving of support and cooperation— rendering service when called upon, and accepting a duty to abide by existing laws. Where the law requires certain positive acts, such as the payment of legally levied taxes, the citizen has a duty to do as required. Thus, the government can require Hensley to pay his income tax.

HOW DOES ONE GAIN OR LOSE HIS CITIZENSHIP?

Problem: Sakai was born in the United States while his parents, Japanese citizens, were students at a university in this country. Is Sakai a citizen of the United States?

Most of us take our citizenship for granted. Have you ever considered what makes you a citizen? The 14th Amendment to the

Constitution states, "All persons born or naturalized in the United States, and subject to jurisdiction thereof, are citizens of the United States and the States wherein they reside." Thus, by virtue of the fact that one is born in the United States, he is a citizen. In the problem, Sakai is a United States citizen even though his parents are not.

Congress has also provided that certain other persons are citizens of this country by virtue of their parentage. Included are those born outside the limits of the United States while one or both parents are U. S. citizens.

 Craiker was born in London while her parents, who were United States citizens, were residing there. Because of her parents' United States citizenship, she was a citizen of the United States.

The United States Constitution (Article I, Section 8) gives Congress the power "to establish a uniform Rule of Naturalization." *Naturalized persons* are former aliens or foreigners who have been granted the same rights and privileges as native citizens. Naturalization therefore is under the jurisdiction or control of the federal government.

Note, also, that a citizen is subject to the jurisdiction of both the United States and the state in which he lives. Thus, one holds a double or dual citizenship in that he is a citizen of the state in which he lives and also of the United States. Furthermore, the U.S. Constitution provides that a state may not discriminate in favor of its own citizens against the citizens of another state.

By both the common law and statute a person may voluntarily renounce his citizenship and allegiance to the United States. This act of abandoning one's country and citizenship is known as *expatriation*. It may be done in one of several ways, but only after the citizen has actually moved from the United States and after he has become twenty-one years of age.

 McDonald, a native-born United States citizen, voluntarily enlisted in the armed services of another country without prior approval of the Secretary of State, as required by statute. The court held that by so doing he voluntarily gave up his citizenship in the United States. The only way he could regain it would be through the process of naturalization.

HOW DOES THE CITIZEN SHOW HIS ALLEGIANCE?

Problem: The city of Danville had an ordinance that prohibited open burning of trash. Morris was cited for violating the ordinance. He claimed that he did not know of the law, and therefore should not have to pay the fine. Do you agree?

As you recall, allegiance is the primary obligation of citizenship. In addition to loyalty and obedience to the law, allegiance implies a duty to keep oneself informed of the law. Indeed, the courts have repeatedly held that ignorance of the law is no excuse for violating it. Thus, Morris' ignorance did not prevent his having to pay a fine.

An important obligation of able-bodied male citizens, recognized from the earliest days of our country, is to serve in the armed forces during war or a time of national emergency. Similarly, every properly qualified citizen is obliged to serve as a juror if called on.

There are other obligations of a citizen, however, that are not enforceable by law. Voting is an example. One is not punished if he fails to vote, yet voting is an important right and obligation of citizenship. Similarly, it is an obligation of citizenship to keep oneself informed on the issues of an election and of government generally.

Being a "good" citizen means exercising the duties of citizenship, as by running for public office and expressing one's opinions on problems and issues of the day, even though there is nothing compelling or forcing one to do so. Perhaps one of the most important of such obligations is the duty to accept the decisions of the majority even when we disagree, and then to work peacefully with other like-minded individuals for the change we desire. Likewise, if we are part of the majority we have the obligation to protect the rights of the minority of those who disagree with us. Indeed, as a court stated, the purpose of protecting speech is to invite dispute.

> "I disapprove of what you say, but I will defend to the death your right to say it."
>
> —Voltaire

HOW DOES GOVERNMENT PROTECT THE CITIZEN?

Problem: Nunes lent Horn $500, but Horn would not repay when it was due. Does the law give Nunes any right to try to collect the amount owed him?

In return for its citizens' allegiance and support, government provides protection on both an individual and a collective basis. This function of government was established in the Preamble to the Constitution, which declares that the purpose of the founders is "to establish Justice, insure domestic Tranquility, provide for the common defense, promote the general Welfare, and secure the Blessings of Liberty . . ."

In a general way, the Preamble defines the collective rights of the people. More specific rights are stated in other parts of the constitutions and in the statutes and other laws both of the federal government and of the states. It is government's role to protect these rights and to enforce them under what is known as the police power of the government. *Police power* is the authority granted by the constitutions to govern and to use legislative power for the protection of the health, safety, and morals of citizens, and the advancement of their "general welfare."

Providing "for the common defense" means more than establishing and maintaining armed forces and declaring war. It includes protection of U. S. citizens in other countries when necessary, and of the economic interests of the country and its citizens on foreign soil. These rights are often recognized in treaties or other international agreements.

In addition, government provides agencies for the administration and enforcement of the law on all levels—national, regional, state, and local. These agencies act to protect the person and property of individuals and to provide a means of avoiding and settling disputes. If the rights we have by virtue of constitutional or statutory law are violated, we have the right to appeal to the courts for protection or redress. Thus, Nunes in the problem, could expect help in enforcing his rights against Horn. At other times, we may call upon law enforcement agencies for assistance: the sheriff or police department or state highway patrol, for example, may always be called upon for protection of person, and in certain situations, property.

WHAT ARE YOUR RIGHTS AS AN INDIVIDUAL?

Problem: In a class discussion, Moody stated that the term "civil rights" referred only to the movement to eliminate racial discrimination in our society. A fellow student disagreed, saying that the term actually had a much broader interpretation. Who was correct?

The usual abbreviations for sections of the country are A. or Atl. (Atlantic), N.E. (Northeastern), N.W. (Northwestern), P. or Pac. (Pacific), So. (Southern), S.E. (Southeastern), and S.W. (Southwestern). Federal cases are abbreviated U.S. (United States Reporter), S.Ct. (Supreme Court), F. (Federal), and F. Supp. (Federal Supplement). There are also other collections of cases. N.Y.S. (New York Supplement) consists of New York cases.

Occasionally some of the reporters and codes or statutes can be found in public libraries, but the most likely place will be a law library such as many counties maintain for use of judges and attorneys or in university law schools. Many attorneys and law firms also maintain their own libraries.

AS A CITIZEN...

You have certain rights set forth in the Constitution and protected by law. These individual rights distinguish our free society from totalitarian systems.

Your rights under law include:

1. The right to equal protection of laws and equal justice in the courts;
2. The right to be free from arbitrary search or arrest;
3. The right to equal educational and economic opportunity;
4. The right to choose public officers in free elections;
5. The right to own property;
6. The right of free speech, press, and assembly;
7. The right to attend the church of your choice;
8. The right to have legal counsel of your choice and a prompt trial if accused of crime.

With your rights as a citizen go individual responsibilities. Every American shares them. Only by fulfilling our duties are we able to to maintain our rights.

Your duties as a citizen include:

1. The duty to obey the laws;
2. The duty to respect the rights of others;
3. The duty to inform yourself on issues of government and community welfare;
4. The duty to vote in elections;
5. The duty to serve on juries if called;
6. The duty to serve and defend your country;
7. The duty to assist agencies of law enforcement;
8. The duty to practice and teach the principles of good citizenship in your home.

—Adapted from *Law Day USA*
American Bar Association

YOUR LEGAL VOCABULARY

allegiance
citation
citizen
citizenship
civil rights
double jeopardy
due process

expatriation
natural rights
naturalized person
police power
political rights
reporter

1. The reference used to locate volume and page on which a particular case may be found.
2. A citizen's act of voluntarily forfeiting or renouncing his citizenship.
3. Being placed on trial more than once for the same offense.
4. Membership in the civil and political community.
5. Authority of government to make such reasonable rules, within constitutional limits, as are necessary for the health, safety, morals and general welfare of the people.
6. A foreigner who has been granted rights and privileges of a natural citizen.
7. All individual rights which are not political in nature.
8. One who gives allegiance to and accepts protection from a state or country.
9. The bond of loyalty and obligation which ties a citizen to his government.
10. Powers and privileges which arise from the nature of man.

REMEMBER THESE HIGHLIGHTS

1. All persons born in the United States or of U.S. citizens in foreign countries are citizens. Foreign-born persons may become naturalized citizens. Citizens, whether natural-born or naturalized, have essentially the same rights. One has citizenship in both the nation and the state in which he resides.
2. Citizenship is a two-way process — the citizen gives his allegiance to the government; the government gives protection to its citizens.
3. Allegiance requires: loyalty to the government, knowledge of and obedience of its laws, and serving on juries and in the armed forces when called upon to do so.
4. Being a good citizen means: exercising the duties of citizenship, accepting the decision of the majority, and protecting the rights of the minority.
5. Rights of the individual may be classified as: natural rights, civil rights, and political rights.
6. Natural rights arise from the nature of man and are enforced by law.

7. Civil rights are nonpolitical rights and include: (1) freedom of self-expression, (2) personal security, (3) equality before the law, and (4) ownership and protection of private property.

8. Political rights enable a citizen to participate in government by voting and holding public office.

9. Rights are not absolute. Both personal and property rights are subject to the rights of others and to the social good.

10. Law is a constantly changing process, adapting to new needs and conditions. These changes occur because of new inventions, social conditions, and changes in the attitudes, morals, and personal values of the people.

LAW AS PEOPLE LIVE IT

1. Herman Wage, a native of Belgium, came to the United States on an approved visa. After living here the required period of time, he applied for citizenship, met the other requirements, and became naturalized. Does he have all the rights and obligations of citizenship that a person born in this country has?

2. Gorsche, an American citizen, renounced his U.S. citizenship and went to Canada to avoid the draft. He later decided he wished to become a citizen of the United States again. May he?

3. An ordinance of Brown County provided that all dogs must be vaccinated and licensed. Martin's dog was picked up because it had no license. Martin refused to have the dog vaccinated, and the County refused to issue him a license until he did so. Martin claimed the requirement was an invasion of his personal rights and that he had no obligation to obey such laws. Do you agree with him?

4. Pitts, a citizen of one state, held a job across the river in another state. He was required to pay an income tax to the state in which he worked even though it was not levied on citizens of that state. He claimed that he was entitled to work in the state without paying the tax. Is that correct?

5. Packard wanted his 14-year-old son to learn a trade by working as a cement finisher instead of attending school. He maintained that the state could not require his son to attend school, and to do so infringed on his and the boy's rights. Is that correct?

6. Clemons, a citizen of Missouri, went to the polls on election day to cast her ballot in the state election. She had met all the qualifications for voting but had not registered as required by state law. Can she vote?

7. In a dispute with Collins over the repayment of money loaned to him by Bevans, Bevans claimed that if Collins did not repay the money she had lent him when it was due, the courts could authorize the seizure and sale of his property to pay his debt. Is that correct?

8. Thomas was arrested and charged with driving while intoxicated. The prosecuting attorney suggested to Thomas that if he would plead guilty to reckless driving, a lesser crime, he would request the court to dismiss the more serious charge of driving while intoxicated. Thomas claimed that this was putting him in double jeopardy. Do you agree?

9. Because of frequent brawls and other disorders, the City Licensing Board revoked the license of Dreamland Dance Pavillion, causing it to cease operations. This action was taken without a hearing and without giving Knutson, the owner, an opportunity to defend his right to the license. Knutson appealed to the courts, claiming his right to due process had been denied. Was it?

10. Explain the meaning of the following:
    (a) American Football League v. National Football League, 323 F. 2d 124
    (b) Zimmerman v. Holiday Inns of America, Inc., 438 Pa. 528, 266 A. 2d 87
    (c) Hemingway's Estate v. Random House, Inc., 296 N.Y.S. 2d 771, 244 N.E. 250, 23 N.Y. 2d 341
    (d) Swenson v. File, 90 Cal. Rptr. 580, 475 P. 2d. 852

LAW AS COURTS DECIDE IT

1. Sheppard, who was accused of murdering his wife, was arrested and brought to trial. Before the trial and during it, the police, coroner, and prosecuting attorney talked freely with the press and allowed reporters, TV cameramen, and commentators access to much of the information they had used in developing the case. Many sensational newspaper stories implying Sheppard's guilt were released; editorials on several occasions demanded that steps be taken against the accused man. During the trial, most of the space in the courtroom was set aside for reporters, commentators, and cameramen. Jurors were allowed to read the papers and listen to the broadcasts. Despite repeated requests from Sheppard's attorney to get the court to control the news media, to stop the prosecutor from giving out information, and to insist that the news reports not be available to the jurors, the court allowed these practices to continue. Sheppard claimed that he was deprived of his right to due process and did not have a fair trial because of the publicity which prejudiced the community and the disruptive influences of the news media in the courtroom. Was that claim valid? (Sheppard v. Maxwell, 384 U.S. 333, 86 S.Ct. 1507)

2. Miranda was arrested at his home and taken to the police station where he was accused of kidnapping and rape, and identified by the party who made the complaint. Miranda was then taken into "Interrogation Room No. 2" where he was questioned by two police officers. During the two hours of questioning, Miranda orally confessed to the

crimes and later signed a confession which stated that the confession was made voluntarily, "with full knowledge of my legal rights, understanding any statement I make may be used against me." At the trial, the officers stated that they had not told Miranda that he was entitled to have an attorney present while being questioned or that under the Fifth Amendment to the Constitution he had the right to remain silent and not incriminate himself. Miranda claimed that failure to tell him of his constitutional rights deprived him of due process and that the confession he had made could not be used against him. Do you agree? (Miranda v. State of Arizona, 384 U.S. 436, 86 S.Ct. 1602)

3. Harris was arrested for making two sales of narcotics and, in violation of his constitutional rights, was not advised of his right to remain silent and have an attorney. During the police questioning, Harris confessed to selling heroin and did not claim that the confession was coerced or forced from him. This confession was not introduced as evidence at his trial, but Harris did testify on his own behalf and denied having made one sale of heroin, as alleged. He claimed the other sale was baking soda to defraud the buyer. Another witness had previously testified that a chemical analysis of the contents of the bags sold showed they contained heroin. On cross-examination, to demonstrate to the jury that Harris' testimony could not be believed, the defendant was asked whether he had made certain statements to the police at the time of his arrest. He claimed he could not remember. The question in the case is whether the statements which could not be used directly as evidence by the prosecution because they violated the defendant's constitutional rights could be used indirectly to attack the credibility of the defendant's testimony. What is your opinion? (Harris v. New York, 91 S.Ct. 643)

4. Poppy Construction Company was engaged in the business of developing, building, and selling a tract of houses in San Francisco. Burks and his wife, who were Negro, offered to purchase one of the houses for $27,950. Poppy had a policy and practice of refusing to sell housing in the tract to Negroes on the same conditions as to others. Burks claimed this was racial discrimination which was contrary to the laws of California and the Constitution of the United States. If such was the case, should Poppy be required to accept Burks' offer to purchase the house? (Burks v. Poppy Construction Company, 57 Cal. 2d 463, 20 Cal. Rptr. 609, 307 P. 2d 313)

5. Dr. Manuel Mendez and his wife and son, Mexican nationals, were admitted to the United States for two years as exchange visitors. While the couple was residing in Baltimore, a second son was born to them. In defending the Mendez family from deportation it was contended that the second son was a citizen of the United States. Is that correct? (Mendez v. Major, 340 F. 2d 128)

CHAPTER 3 Law and the Minor

1. *A buddy of yours, age 18, borrowed the driver's license of a friend, age 22, to use as an I.D. card in gaining admittance to a bar. If the deception was recognized, what could be the result?*

2. *As a minor you work part time for Deluxe Supermarket. Are your parents entitled to your wages?*

3. *Your 16-year-old cousin wishes to date a boy of whom her parents disapprove. Can they prevent her from going out with the boy?*

WHAT IS THE LEGAL STATUS OF A MINOR?

Problem: Juan, age 17, maintains that as an American citizen he has the same rights as his friend Keith, age 21, and therefore could legally do anything Keith could do. Is that correct?

A *minor* (or infant, as he is sometimes referred to by the law) is one who has not yet reached the legal age of adulthood. By common law, and statute in most states, this means anyone under 21 years of age. The concept and problems of minority have been recognized for centuries. It has long been acknowledged that children and youth need protection against their own immaturity and lack of experience as well as against those who would take advantage of them. Therefore, the young are given many special privileges and legal rights not accorded to adults. They are also under certain restrictions and do not have all rights of adults. In the problem, for instance, 17-year-old Juan could not claim the same rights as his friend, Keith, who was a legal adult.

In some circumstances—driving an automobile, for example, and being held to respect the rights of others—minors are treated as adults. They are held responsible if they commit crimes after a certain age. If they are negligent and thereby injure someone or damage his property, they are usually liable for the loss (in some cases the parents are also held liable). For many purposes, an adult must represent or act for a minor. Indeed, minors who have no parents, and in some cases even those who do, will have a *guardian* appointed for them by a court to act in place of the parents or for some special purpose.

> The parents of Keema, age 15, were killed in an airplane accident. A court appointed his paternal grandparents as guardians to take care of him, act in the capacity of parents, and be responsible for his estate. This guardianship will last until Keema reaches adulthood.

It has been pointed out that the law changes as social conditions change. Such has been the case with the law governing minors. As the amount and extent of education have increased, parental control decreased, and greater freedom, mobility, and buying power been acquired by young people, laws have lowered the age at which minors assume certain adult rights and responsibilities. Recent examples of law following social changes are: the 26th Amendment to the U. S. Constitution lowering the voting age to 18 in both state and federal elections, liberalized curfew ordinances and, in some states, the legalizing of the purchase and consumption of alcoholic beverages at age 18.

> "The right of citizens of the United States, who are eighteen years of age or older, to vote shall not be denied or abridged by the United States or by any State on account of age."
>
> —26th Amendment, U. S. Constitution

State laws vary with respect to minority as they do on other matters. In some states, minors reach their *majority* (the age at which one ceases to be a minor) at age 18.[1] In a few states, one or both sexes reach their majority upon marriage, and in most states veterans and those in the armed forces are given special rights. A minor may in some states be given certain adult rights by court order.

All persons, minors and adults, are required to respect the legal rights of others, and to obey certain laws which protect society as a whole. These laws and their violations, torts and crimes, are discussed in Chapter 5. In addition, there are also special laws affecting only minors. Many of these you are familiar with—required

---

[1] Michigan, North Carolina, Tennessee, and Washington. California, New Hampshire, New Mexico, Oregon, and Vermont place certain limitations on 18-year olds. Other states are considering changes in laws affecting minors.

attendance at school, parental and school control of children, exclusion from specified places like bars, and curfews. A *curfew* provides that during designated hours people, usually those under age 18, must not be on the public streets or in semi-public places like dance halls and drive-ins, unless accompanied by an adult.

Minors age 18 or over are usually treated as adults if they commit a crime and are arrested. In most states if a minor is jailed, he must be segregated from adults. Also, if the court believes a minor over 18 (in some states, 16) is immature for his age, he can be tried in juvenile court, as discussed in Chapter 6.

> Greene and other students, all 17 and 18 years of age, were arrested for rioting and destroying school property. The state law provided that minors 16 years of age and older charged with criminal offenses can be tried in criminal court rather than in juvenile court. The students were so tried and convicted, but received suspended jail sentences.

From a very early age, children buy things and enter into contracts. The inexperience of children and youth create some special problems and their contractual liability is limited, as discussed in Chapter 9. Under certain conditions a minor's contracts cannot be enforced against him. Nevertheless, he has a right to enforce contracts against adults provided, of course, he carries out his part of the bargain.

Like all persons, minors have constitutional rights. Only recently has it been determined that minors have the same protection on arrest as adults (Chapter 2) and that they are entitled to a jury trial if their cases are not held in juvenile court. Minors whose hearings are in juvenile court are not entitled to jury trials because they are not being tried for committing a crime. Even in juvenile court, minors are entitled to due process except for the jury trial.

Minors have other rights upon attaining ages specified by statute; for example, usually at age 16 or 18 they may be employed full time (Page 425), although there may be restrictions as to hours and kinds of work. When younger, a minor may be employed part time when it does not interfere with required attendance at school. Often a permit is required. Minors also have the right to operate motor vehicles upon meeting statutory requirements.

The legal age for marriage also varies by state. In most states girls can marry at age 18 without parents' consent. For boys the usual age is 21. However, in most states girls can marry at age 16 and boys at 18 with parental consent. Some states require authorization of a judge as well as parental consent.

 Jane Williams and Bob Wilson, both under the legal age, were married without their parents' consent. The parents of either of the individuals involved can probably have the marriage annulled—that is, dissolved or ended without divorce—before the parties become of age.

WHAT RIGHTS AND DUTIES DO PARENTS HAVE?

Problem: Macintosh, age 16, preferred to live with his maternal grandparents on their ranch rather than at home in the city. His parents insisted that he live with them and that they had a legal right to require him to do so. Must Macintosh live with his parents?

By statute, all states routinely allow qualified parents to have custody and control of their natural and adopted children. This means the parents have authority to restrain them, administer reasonable punishment if necessary, and compel obedience to reasonable and necessary directions. These rights continue until the children reach their majority or until the parents give up or are denied their rights. Parents also have the right to determine the residence of their children. Thus, Macintosh's parents have the legal right to decide whether he must live with them or with his grandparents. Parents, of course, have obligations to their children. Included are the duties to protect and take care of them, to provide support according to the parents' financial means, and to see that they are educated. Less tangible, but equally important, are the parental obligations of affection, moral support, and guidance.

Penalties may be imposed on parents who fail in certain of these duties. For example, willful failure to support one's children is a misdemeanor, and desertion is a felony in most states. Parents who do not require their children to attend school during the years prescribed by statute are subject to fine or imprisonment. And children who are illegally abused or mistreated may be taken from their parents by the courts. Under certain circumstances parents are liable for damage caused by their minor children to others, because parents are supposed to exercise proper control. This liability may be unlimited if a child is entrusted with a dangerous instrument, such as a car or a gun, which the parents know he cannot handle with care.

Parents are also entitled to the services of their children. This means children who live at home are expected to assist their parents as requested and to do so without payment. Of course, by agreement children may be paid for work done, but this is usually on a voluntary basis. Normally minor children working for their parents are exempt from most child labor laws. (Chapter 30) If a child is earning wages, the wages belong to his parents, and statutes usually provide that employers must pay the wages earned to the parent if he so requests; otherwise they are paid to the minor. This right to the services of children makes it possible for a parent to claim damages when he is wrongfully deprived of the child's services.

Parents are entitled to the services of their children.

Parents may, under certain circumstances, lose custody and control of their children. Normally parental rights are shared, but the law recognizes that the father's authority is superior to that of the mother while they are living together as husband and wife (the father, by law, is "head of the house"). Upon the death of the father or mother, the surviving parent is entitled to the full parental rights. In addition to the loss of custody by court order, as when parents are declared unfit, one or both parents will lose custody by divorce or legal separation. Other ways are by adoption and emancipation.

Emancipation involves the voluntary surrender by the parents of the care, custody, control, and earnings of a minor child. A minor naturally becomes emancipated when he reaches his majority, but he may also be emancipated before that time if he legally marries, or (with parental consent) becomes self-supporting. Generally in the last case, he is not living with his parents, and is otherwise free from parental authority. Some states recognize partial emancipation which may consist of allowing a child to retain his earnings and spend them as he pleases. This is becoming more common because "at some point," as stated in a recent court decision, "minors must have some right to their own views and needs for their independent and painful transition from minority to adulthood."

WHAT ARE THE RIGHTS AND DUTIES OF STUDENTS?

Problem: Welch, age 13, was frequently absent from school because his parents needed him to work in their store. Is Welch a truant?

In the United States one of the basic rights of a minor is the right to a free education through high school, or in some states through age 14. Reciprocally, courts have held that one of the most important obligations of a parent—not only to the child, but also to society—is to see that his children receive an education. This attitude has not always existed, but has developed as the nation has become more affluent and the need for child labor has decreased. Today, all states but one require attendance at either a public, parochial, or other private school until a specified age.

As pointed out earlier, parents are required to send their children to school and penalties are provided for those who fail to do so. Students who do not attend school when lawfully required are *truants,* and their parents are responsible. Accordingly, in the problem, Welch is a truant and his parents can be fined or jailed for failing to see that the boy attends school. If truancy is habitual, the parents can be charged with child neglect and the child can be declared delinquent and placed under the jurisdiction of the juvenile court. School authorities and the courts are usually lenient in enforcing these statutes unless the breach of duty is willful and deliberate. Habitual run-aways and those who leave home without parental consent, like truants, may be detained by the police and returned home or placed under the jurisdiction of a juvenile court.

Although schools do not have the same rights of control and discipline that parents have, they are given special rights by law. To enable them to fulfill their educational function, statutes authorize school authorities to adopt reasonable rules and regulations and provide penalties for disobedience. Schools are required to protect the rights of students to study, learn, and participate in the various activities of the school. They must also provide reasonable supervision to assure the physical safety of students and are liable if a student is injured because of lack of such supervision.

Legally, students have no right to determine curriculum or school regulations or to control school property. As a practical procedure and as a learning experience, however, most schools provide for student government and for student participation in many other activities. From these experiences, it is hoped that students will learn the wisdom of compromising differing points of view, and gain an understanding of the importance of obeying rules and agreements democratically decided even when they disagree with them. Although schools may permit students to establish rules for their own conduct, including the use of student courts to discipline fellow students who violate the rules, school authorities are still legally responsible.

Nevertheless, there are legal limits to which school authorities may go in establishing rules. Under the due process clause of the 14th Amendment to the U. S. Constitution, regulations cannot be arbitrary or capricious. This means that the regulations cannot just reflect the personal prejudices, likes, or dislikes of those who make them. For example, students are entitled to the right of free speech, and regulations may not deprive them of this right unless it is evident that a particular incident will cause "a material and substantial disruption" and interfere with the work of the school. The U. S. Supreme Court has held that free speech is subject to reasonable restrictions as to time, place, manner, and duration in the light of the special environment of the school. Likewise, there must be good reason for adopting a rule prohibiting extreme styles of dress or hair—something more than the fact that those who make the rules do not like the styles. If there is reasonable evidence in a particular school that long hair is "disruptive" or interferes with the work of the school, it can be banned.

 In a California city with a rule forbidding beards on students, one bearded student was told he must shave before he would be admitted to the school. Because there was no religious reason for the beard, the court held that a rule against beards was reasonable because beards distracted others from their study.

Just as one has a duty to obey the laws of a state, so a student must obey the regulations of a school. As with criminal statutes,

Unit I □ YOU AND THE LAW

disobedience results in punishment, but the punishment must be reasonable. The most serious punishment is suspension for a specified period or expulsion from school, which usually must be acted on by the school board. One who is expelled may be entitled to due process and review of the decision by the courts.

WHAT ARE A MINOR'S RIGHTS AND RESPONSIBILITIES AS A DRIVER?

Problem: Bailey had received his father's permission to drive the family station wagon on a biology class field trip. Can he legally do so?

In owning and driving a motor vehicle, a minor is generally treated as an adult. There is no legal restriction on owning a motor vehicle. Motor vehicles include automobiles, trucks, motorcycles, motor bikes, motor scooters and, in some states, snowmobiles. As discussed later, it is necessary for the owner to have a certificate of title and, before the vehicle can be operated on the highway, a certificate of registration. To drive an automobile, one must only have a license. Accordingly, Bailey in the problem would need a driver's license to drive his father's car. Of course, his father must also have a valid certificate of registration.

Every state requires the operator of a motor vehicle to hold a valid driver's license and usually to have it in his possession while driving the vehicle. A *driver's license* is a permit to operate a motor vehicle on the highways of the state. To obtain such a license, all states require that the applicant be of a certain age, generally 16, and that he pass one or more examinations. These examinations, which vary from state to state, usually include a driving test, a test of vision, a test on motor vehicle laws, and a road sign recognition test. Some states require a photograph or fingerprints. A fee must also be paid.

To prepare high school students to pass the test required for operator's licenses, most schools offer driver education courses. Some states require such courses for high school graduation. In a few states, special licenses are issued to students enrolled in driver's training; in others, students who successfully complete approved courses in driver training are issued their licenses without taking all or part of the required tests. Students successfully completing courses in driver education are sometimes eligible for lower automobile insurance rates. Regular licenses are generally issued to persons over 16 years of age who pass the tests and pay the required fees. Several states issue a provisional or probationary license to minors under ages 18 or 21. These licenses usually must be renewed each year, whereas regular licenses may need to be renewed less frequently. Some states issue permanent licenses or licenses "good until revoked."

Restricted, junior, or "learner's" licenses may be issued to younger and inexperienced drivers. (Some states also issue restricted licenses to elderly persons or those with physical defects.) The holder of a restricted license may be limited in his driving; for example, driving only to and from school by the most direct route. A person with a regular license may have to accompany him. Many states require the signature of one or both parents, or a guardian, before issuing a license to a minor under age 18 or 21. In many states the parents must agree to be responsible for damage caused by the minor's negligence while driving.

Most states require special licenses of persons who are employed to drive trucks, buses, or cars for others. Often stricter tests are required for a chauffeur's license. Generally one who drives passengers for hire, such as a bus driver, must be at least 21 years of age. Many states have special rules governing those who operate motorcycles, scooters, and farm vehicles.

Under some circumstances drivers' licenses may be suspended for a certain length of time or revoked entirely. In general, you may lose your license if you:

1. are convicted of reckless driving three times within 12 or 18 months;
2. kill someone while driving negligently;
3. drive your car while intoxicated or under the influence of narcotics;
4. commit a felony while using a car;
5. fail to report an accident that resulted in death or injury to some other person;
6. make false statements under oath involving the registration or operation of an automobile;
7. become physically or mentally disabled;
8. habitually or persistently violate traffic ordinances or regulations.

In most states two certificates are issued to the owners of motor vehicles. One is a *certificate of registration,* a license permitting a described motor vehicle to be operated on the highways of the state. The other is a *certificate of title,* a document showing the ownership of the vehicle.

To exercise control over the use of the highways and to identify vehicles and their owners, all states require annual registration of motor vehicles. License plates or tabs showing the year of registration are issued to be attached to the vehicle. Driving without a valid driver's license and a current certificate of registration is a misdemeanor and subjects the driver or car owner to a fine.

Driving an automobile is sometimes a pleasure, sometimes a necessity. In either case, it is also a great responsibility. Careless driving can cost the driver his license, his car registration, his fortune, his liberty, and even his life. It is no secret that the accident rate for drivers who are minors is much higher than for older drivers. (Automobile insurance costs tell us this!)

Although the states differ widely on many specific traffic regulations, such as maximum speed limits, the "rules of the road" do not vary greatly. Many of the rules of the road have been enacted as statutes in all states. Some of these rules have exceptions or have been modified by statute. For example, stop signs at intersections mean that the usual right-of-way rule does not apply. Also, pedestrians at intersections controlled by signal devices are required to observe the signals.

All states require that applicants for driver's licenses pass an examination.

A motorist may ordinarily assume that others will obey the rules of the road. Even so, most experienced drivers drive defensively, always alert for unexpected action by others. The driver of a motor vehicle is required to exercise reasonable care to avoid injury to persons or to the property of others. What constitutes reasonable care depends largely upon the circumstances, such as speed, visibility, amount of traffic, weather, and condition of the road.

Failure to exercise such care renders the driver liable in a civil action for damages because of his negligence; it may also make him liable in a criminal action for violation of one or more traffic laws. The alertness and attention of the driver, as well as his consideration of others, must be much greater to constitute reasonable care when children or persons obviously under a physical disability—such as the aged, the blind, or the crippled—are on the road.

IMPORTANT RULES OF THE ROAD

1. The operator of a vehicle must—

    (a) use reasonable care to avoid accidents;
    (b) give signals to warn other drivers when he intends to reduce speed or change direction;
    (c) drive to the right of the center of the road;
    (d) pass on the left in overtaking another vehicle, except in one-way or multiple-lane traffic;
    (e) give way to a vehicle wishing to pass;
    (f) keep to the right when driving slowly.

2. When two vehicles reach an intersection at the same time, the one on the left shall yield the right of way to the vehicle on his right.

3. Pedestrians crossing at an intersection have the right of way.

4. Vehicles traveling on a public roadway have the right of way over vehicles entering from a private driveway.

5. Emergency vehicles with proper lights and signals have the right of way over other traffic.

When one does not exercise reasonable care, or unreasonably interferes with the use of a public road by others, or disregards the safety of himself and others, he may be prosecuted for *reckless driving*.

There is often a great temptation to take chances, to show off, or to take dares. For some persons it is a thrill to drive at excessive speeds, to beat the lights, and to pass all others, but such conduct is usually a sign of immaturity and inexperience in driving. The wrong split-second decision, under such circumstances, may cause an accident, and affect the health, happiness, and prosperity of the careless driver for the rest of his life.

In addition to careful driving, other laws may require inspection of the vehicle and correction of any defects, and installation of safety equipment. Most states do not require car owners to carry liability insurance but they do require drivers who cause damage to others to have financial responsibility. The usual way of demonstrating this is with liability insurance, but it may not completely cover a court judgment. For young car owners, liability insurance is sometimes difficult to get except on assigned risk (Page 515), and the high accident rate of such drivers also makes it very costly.

IN CASE OF ACCIDENT...

1. Stop your car no matter how trivial the damage may seem. If no one is present and you have damaged another's property, leave a note with your name, address, and phone number. If the accident is serious and you are not injured, call the police and do not leave the scene of the accident until they arrive.
2. Give aid to injured persons.
3. Clear the road if possible and warn approaching traffic.
4. Notify police or state highway patrol of the accident.
5. Keep vehicles involved in the accident at the scene until the police arrive.
6. Exchange identification with the other driver and get license number and description of each car involved.
7. Get names and addresses of all witnesses.
8. As soon as possible make specific notes and a diagram of what happened.
9. Give your statement of what happened only to the proper authorities.
10. Report the accident to the proper police or state authorities promptly if required by the financial responsibility law of the state.
11. If you have insurance, report the accident to your agent as soon as practicable.
12. Do not say anything or sign any statement regarding responsibility for the accident until you have consulted your attorney or insurance agent. Do not admit fault to the other driver, to any witness, or even to the police. You may not know or understand all the facts, and such admission could later be held against you in court.

YOUR LEGAL VOCABULARY

certificate of registration	guardian
certificate of title	majority
curfew	minor (or infant)
driver's license	reckless driving
emancipation	truant

1. A person who is not 21 years old or has not reached the legal age for adulthood.
2. The age at which one ceases to be a minor.
3. A document showing ownership of a vehicle.
4. An adult who is appointed to have the custody and care of a minor or his estate or both during his minority.
5. The hours between which minors below a specified age are not allowed on public streets or in semi-public places unaccompanied by an adult.
6. A minor who fails to attend school when he is legally required to do so.
7. A license permitting a vehicle to be operated on the highway of a state.
8. A permit to operate a motor vehicle.
9. The voluntary surrender by the parents of the rights to custody, control, and earnings of a minor child.
10. Disregard for the safety of himself and others by the driver of a vehicle who drives without exercising reasonable care.

REMEMBER THESE HIGHLIGHTS

1. A minor is a person who has not reached the legal age of adulthood. In most states this is 21.
2. As a protection against their own immaturity, minors have many restrictions placed on their conduct. On the other hand, they also have privileges and legal rights not accorded adults.
3. All persons, including minors, are required to obey the law and are responsible for failure to do so.
4. Minors acquire many adult rights, with corresponding obligations, before they reach the age of majority.
5. Parents have custody and control of their children and the right to their services and earnings until they become of age or are emancipated.
6. Emancipation occurs when a minor becomes of age, or is legally married, or when his parents voluntarily surrender their parental rights.
7. One of the basic rights of a minor is a free education through high school. Schools have special legal rights to control the conduct of students, but these rights cannot be used to deny students' constitutional rights.
8. In owning and driving a car, minors are treated as adults and have the same duties to obey traffic regulations as adults.
9. Drivers' licenses may be revoked and the privilege of driving withdrawn if a driver is reckless, fails repeatedly to comply with the rules of the road, or commits other acts that make him a menace on the highway.
10. Because most minors are inexperienced in driving, they need to be especially alert and careful in driving and avoid taking chances or showing off.

LAW AS PEOPLE LIVE IT

1. John Clark, age 17, came into possession of a credit card made out to Don Clark. He used the card to purchase $190 worth of clothing, and was later arrested for obtaining property under false pretenses — a crime. Does the fact that Clark is a minor excuse him?

2. Kirker, age 19, was induced by Brown to marry her. Kirker by law was required to have the consent of his parents, but they refused to give it. Kirker and Brown then went to a neighboring state and were married. Several months later, but before reaching 21, Kirker filed suit for annulment. Will it be granted?

3. Foss, a minor 18 years of age, worked as a transistor assembler and was paid $80 per week. She lived at home and did not pay for her board or room or for the use of the family car. Her parents insisted that her pay belonged to them. Is that correct?

4. Vaught disliked the "hippie" life-style adopted by his 19-year-old daughter, Karen. She was attending college in a distant city, and he was supporting her. When she moved out of the college dormitory and into a commune in spite of his expressed objections, Vaught cut off her support, including her tuition. Was Vaught within his right?

5. While the teacher was out of the room, Zavattari was injured during some horseplay in the school's chemistry laboratory. Zavattari had not been a participant in the disorder. Do he and his parents have a right of action against the school?

6. Peck and Muller, students, published an underground newspaper that was critical of some things that went on in the community. School officials arbitrarily banned the paper and prohibited its distribution at the school because, they said, students should not be concerned with such matters but should devote themselves to their studies. Was the banning of the paper a reasonable exercise of the school's authority?

7. In violation of a school regulation prohibiting the wearing of buttons or other insignia of a controversial nature, Myers and some other students wore buttons proclaiming "No Busing." This rule was adopted after there had been many disturbances, including fights, sit-ins, and destruction of property at various times and on various issues. The students were suspended and claimed their right to freedom of speech was denied. Do you agree?

8. Ingram bought an automobile from Mason Motor Sales. He paid the necessary license and registration fees and within a few days received a certificate of title and a certificate of registration. Ingram then contended that the legal effect of the two certificates was the same, that in essence they were duplicates. Is he correct?

9. Blake received the highest grade of anyone in his driver education course and easily qualified for a regular operator's license upon reaching the

minimum age. Because of his rare ability as a driver, Blake liked to show off and was frequently apprehended for reckless driving even though he never touched another car or hit a pedestrian. Could Blake's operator's license be suspended or revoked?

10. Childs, driving on the open highway where the speed limit was 65 miles an hour, came upon a sign stating "Men and equipment working." Does this require him to reduce his speed?

LAW AS COURTS DECIDE IT

1. Gault, 15 years of age, was taken to the children's Detention Home on the complaint of Cook, who claimed Gault telephoned her making lewd, indecent, and obscene remarks, which is contrary to law in the state of Arizona. Gault's parents were not notified of this but learned of it through a friend. At the time he was taken into custody, Gault was on probation as a result of being in the company of another boy who had stolen a wallet from a woman four months earlier. A hearing date was set, but Gault's parents were not notified of the date of the boy's hearing until two or three days before it was scheduled. At the hearing Gault was found to be delinquent even though he did not admit to the charges, and was committed to the State Industrial School "for the period of his minority" unless discharged sooner. The hearing was conducted in an informal manner. No attorney was present to represent Gault. Nor was Cook, the complaining witness, present. The judge found Gault delinquent because he was "habitually involved in immoral matters." Under Arizona law there is no appeal from the decisions of a juvenile court. Gault claimed that he was denied due process, and granting that hearings for juvenile offenders are more informal than those for adults, he is entitled to the same constitutional rights as other citizens. Is that correct? (Application of Gault, 87 S. Ct. 1428, 387 U.S. 1)

2. Kallio, age 18, had purchased a car out of his part time earnings and was personally paying for its operation and maintenance, including insurance. About 4 a.m. one morning he crashed into the rear of Foran's car while Foran, who had run out of gas, was refueling it. Foran sued for damages and included Kallio's parents as defendants. Foran claimed that Kallio was an unemancipated minor, living at home while attending college, and therefore under the control of the parents who were entitled to his earnings, thus making the parents liable for his acts. The senior Kallio presented evidence that his son had been allowed to keep his earnings, that he had not only purchased and maintained his car out of those earnings but also was paying for his college education and therefore was partially emancipated. Do you agree? (Foran v. Kallio, 56 Wash. 2d 769, 355 P. 2d 769)

3. Crews, a 17-year-old high school student, was refused admission to the high school solely because the length of his hair did not conform to the unpublished standards of the school. These regulations left it up to the individual teacher to decide on the acceptable length of hair. The only notice of "standards" was a letter of a very general nature, sent to the parents of all high school students, regarding dress and appearance. Crews maintained that the rules were not substantially justified, and that by using them to deprive him of his education, the school was violating his constitutional rights. The principal of the school maintained that the work of the school was disrupted, and that the students' health and safety were endangered by long hair; he admitted, however, that the long hair of girls did not create disruption or endanger them. Was the school within its rights in refusing to admit Crews? (Crews v. Cloncs, 432 F. 2d 1259)

4. Sessions and Hartley were engaged in racing their automobiles on a state highway in South Carolina. Sessions' car struck another car in which Johnson was riding. Johnson was killed, and the administrator of her estate sued Hartley. A South Carolina statute made racing on a state highway a crime. Hartley contended that he was not liable since his car was not involved in the accident. Who should win? (Skipper v. Hartley, 242 S.C. 221, 130 S.E. 2d 486)

5. The school authorities of Des Moines Public Schools, fearful of disturbance and disruption of school discipline, adopted a regulation prohibiting students from wearing armbands to school and stipulated that if any student did so, and refused to remove it when requested, he would be suspended until he returned without the armband. The regulation did not prohibit the wearing of all symbols of political or controversial significance, and many students from time to time did wear such symbols. Tinker and Eckhardt, aware of the regulation, wore black armbands to school to show their disapproval of the Vietnam hostilities. They were suspended and thereafter filed this action, claiming that the right of free speech as guaranteed by the First Amendment of the U.S. Constitution had been denied. The school authorities claimed they were responsible for controlling the conduct of the students to protect the rights of other students and ensure that the work of the school was not interfered with. It was their opinion that wearing the armbands would substantially interfere with the normal operation of the school and infringe upon the rights of other students. The students wearing the armbands went about their usual duties and did not disrupt or interrupt the school's operations. Their only deviation was wearing the armbands to make their views known. Do you agree that the students were denied their right of freedom of speech? (Tinker v. Des Moines Independent Common School District, 393 U.S. 503, 89 S.Ct. 733)

CHAPTER 4 Law and the Consumer

1. *Square Deal Mail-Order House advertised a free thermometer with the purchase of a barometer. Is this an unfair trade practice?*

2. *Sweaters that are seconds or "irregulars" are advertised at the regular price for standard merchandise. Is this an unfair trade practice?*

3. *The label on a loaf of bread states that the weight is 16 ounces. Is any law violated if the weight is only 15 ounces?*

WHY DOES THE LAW PROTECT THE CONSUMER?

Problem: Thrifty Department Store advertised it would add a new storage closet to a home for $119.00. A picture in the ad showed a closet that cost $250.00 not including installation fees. Ainsworth purchased one and received only the unassembled items which she would have to put together and install herself. She complained to the store, but they refused to accept return of the goods or refund the price. What other steps might Ainsworth take?

For centuries, the relation between buyer and seller has been best expressed by the legal maxim, caveat emptor—"let the buyer beware"—but caveat emptor is changing. As the marketplace has become more and more complex, society has in turn become more and more concerned with the plight of the consumer. In an affluent and modern society such as ours, the sheer abundance and variety of goods can be overwhelming. The average consumer can no longer be expected to be a competent judge of quality—many products are new and unfamiliar, others are so complex that the average person has no way of knowing if they are defective or of repairing them if they are. Modern packaging techniques often make it impossible for the consumer to examine a product before he buys. In addition, sales have become less personal. Where the seller was once typically a friend or neighbor, he is now usually a stranger to the buyer. The two may never meet face-to-face; communication may be entirely by phone or letter. With the aid of modern transportation, products are sold far from the point of their manufacture, and the salesperson may actually know little more about the product than the consumer. All of these problems of the consumer have been

---

BUYER'S BILL OF RIGHTS

1. The right to make an intelligent choice among products and services.

2. The right to accurate information on which to make his free choice.

3. The right to expect that his health and safety are taken into account by those who seek his patronage.

4. The right to register his dissatisfaction and have his complaint heard and weighed when his interests are poorly served.

This "Buyer's Bill of Rights" will help provide greater personal freedom for individuals as well as better business for everyone engaged in trade.

—excerpts from an address to the Congress of the United States, by President Richard M. Nixon, October 30, 1969

---

intensified by more aggressive and sophisticated marketing techniques. Advertising is big business. Consumers today must deal with such sales gimmicks as trading stamps, one-cent sales, "free" merchandise, games, discounts from listed prices, and prizes packaged with the products. A constant barrage of competitive sales efforts—including billboard advertisements, television commercials, and a flood of direct mail—is aimed at the consumer. All of this has created legal problems our forefathers did not experience or expect.

It was formerly thought that consumers would best be protected under our system by simply keeping business competitive and by protecting honest businessmen against the dishonest ones. Many statutes have been enacted both by the states and the federal government for this purpose; anti-trust or monopoly laws, as discussed in Chapter 10, are an example. Also, numerous regulatory, administrative agencies have been established, such as the Federal Trade Commission, and state departments and boards of real estate, insurance, and banking. And of course, the basic law of contracts, torts, and crimes has provided much protection against certain kinds of violations. For example, anyone defrauded (cheated) in a contract has a right to the aid of a court in an action against the other party to the contract. Laws on bailment, sales, and agency include remedies for those whose rights are disregarded.

The consumer's remedies under these laws may be too expensive for him to enforce, however, and they are usually not worth enforcing unless large sums of money are involved. Similarly, getting redress through administrative agencies, largely oriented to business, was often difficult, frustrating, and futile. Accordingly, if consumers were to be protected adequately, additional safeguards were needed. Reflecting the social changes that have occurred and are still taking place, and a new concern for human life and environmental quality, special statutes have been enacted by cities, states, and the federal government for the specific protection of the consumer. Some states have established special offices for the protection of consumer interests, as in the Department of Law of the State of New York, the Department of Justice of Pennsylvania, and the Attorney General's offices in Ohio and California. Courts have recognized new social needs and are holding manufacturers as well as others to greater accountability to consumers. *Class actions* have made recovery easier by permitting one or several persons to sue on behalf of themselves and all other similarly affected persons.

Some laws designed for consumer protection are discussed in this chapter. In some cases, violation is a criminal offense and subjects the offender to fine or imprisonment, or both. In other cases, the improper conduct may be ordered stopped by a government official, agency, or commission. Usually consumers who wish protection of these laws must report violations to the proper authorities, as Ainsworth should do in the problem, although government agencies may also take the initiative in identifying and prosecuting violators. A consumer should remember, however, that laws cannot take the place of individual alertness and care in buying goods and services.

WHAT LEGAL PROTECTION IS AFFORDED CONSUMERS?

Problem: McKittrick agreed to allow a contractor to install aluminum siding on his home. The materials and service were to be free if he would allow his home to be used as a "model." McKittrick would receive $100 commission for every person to whom he showed the siding provided such person also purchased the siding for his home. McKittrick had to sign a contract obligating him to pay $3,000 even though the cash price would have been $1,400. The contractor said the cost would be made up "in no time" when the commission checks came in. None ever did. Is there anything McKittrick can do?

Consumer laws provide protection in four ways:

(1) By prohibiting unfair, deceptive, or unconscionable trade practices, including misleading advertising and practices such as the one in the problem;

(2) By defining and setting minimum or required standards in such areas as credit agreements and finance charges, packaging and labeling, weights and measures, quality, safety, and merchantability of many kinds of goods;

(3) By establishing procedures to assure that the laws are complied with; for example, licensing and inspection services; and

(4) By providing redress for injuries suffered.

The number and variety of unfair, deceptive, and unconscionable trade practices are remarkable. Failure to meet minimum or prescribed standards is frequently recognized as an unfair trade practice; common examples are discussed in the next topic. Deceptive, fraudulent, and unconscionable practices are more difficult to identify and prove. For this reason some cities have established independent offices of consumer protection, and some states have consumer specialists within the office of the Attorney General. Thus, McKittrick, in the problem, could report his experience to the proper authority if his state has such a service. He would probably obtain some relief, but more important he might be able to protect others by forcing the contractor out of business through revocation of his license.

Many statutes have been enacted and many agencies have been authorized to provide service as well as protection to consumers. On the federal level these include the Department of Agriculture, the Transportation Department, the Federal Housing Administration, the Federal Deposit Insurance Corporation and Federal Home Loan Bank Board, the Department of Housing and Urban Development, the Postal Service, the Securities and Exchange Commission, and the Office of Economic Opportunity. Many states have other services available for the knowledgeable consumer.

Many organizations of businessmen and other private organizations such as Consumers' Research and Consumers' Union provide information and assistance. One businessmen's organization, the

Better Business Bureau, has offices in principal cities and is helpful with information and assistance to consumers who have difficulties in business dealings in their communities.

WHAT ARE UNFAIR TRADE PRACTICES?

Problem: The Silk Shop sent an unordered necktie through the mail to Lindsay with an invoice for $4.00 stating if it were paid within ten days a $1.00 discount would be allowed. When Lindsay did not pay he received letters demanding payment and threatening action if he did not pay or return the tie. Is this an unfair trade practice?

The Federal Trade Commission (FTC) has been established to prevent unfair trade practices. Generally any method of business that is fraudulent (deceitful) or that lessens or destroys competition by any means other than efficiency is an *unfair trade practice*. Such practices are prohibited because they are opposed to good morals and fair dealing. Sending unordered merchandise and demanding payment for it or its return, as in the problem, is an unfair trade practice. Indeed, federal law prescribes that when someone deliberately sends unordered merchandise through the mails, the recipient is under no obligation to return or to pay for it even if he uses it. The FTC has authority to order persons engaged in unfair trade practices to "cease and desist" if they do not do so voluntarily. Various state agencies have similar authority with respect to state laws.

Unfair trade practices take many forms. Some of the more common ones are as follows:

(1) USING FALSE AND MISLEADING ADVERTISING

Problem: Ziermer read an ad in a newspaper advertising "new, famous-name, automatic washing machines for sale at $99.50, limited time only." Ziermer, who needed a new washing machine, went to the store and found that the machines advertised were not a famous brand nor were they really automatic machines. The salesman attempted to sell another "fully automatic" machine for $175. Do you agree with Ziermer that this was misleading advertising?

The federal government and most of the states have enacted laws relating to false or misleading advertising, not only in newspapers and magazines but also in handbills, posters, circulars, pamphlets,

A person
who receives
unordered goods
need not keep nor
pay for them.

WHATEVER THAT IS I DIDN'T ORDER IT.

and even letters. The FTC is also responsible for enforcing the law relating to misleading advertising on radio and television. TV advertising causes peculiar problems because of the ease with which demonstrations can be faked, as for example, shaving "sandpaper" which is really loose sand on glass. Such faking is false advertising. *False advertising* makes untrue claims of quality or effectiveness, fails to reveal important facts, or makes suggestions or representations by statements, designs, or sounds that are untrue. It is not necessary to prove an injury to a competitor to stop misleading advertising; it may be stopped merely because it is unfair and deceptive. *Bait and switch advertising,* as in the problem, is also prohibited. This is a type of "come-on" advertising designed to lure prospective customers into a store by concealing the true purpose of the ad. Once he is in the store an attempt is made to "switch" the customer to another, more attractive but costlier product.

It is also an unfair trade practice for food chains and grocery stores to advertise sale items that are not in stock nor available in sufficient quantities at their stores.

(2) CONDUCTING GAMES OF CHANCE AND LOTTERIES

Problem: At The Candlelight, a campus hangout, whenever a customer received a cash register receipt with a red star on it, his money was returned. Is this a lottery?

A *lottery* is any scheme for the distribution of goods that involves the three elements of payment of consideration (Page 157), chance, and a prize to some but not all of those who give the consideration. Examples of lotteries are games of chance, punch boards, raffles, and drawings. The use of lotteries to market goods is unfair competition. The problem above is an example of a lottery. The prize was return of the purchase price to a winner who won by chance. The consideration was payment made for the purchase.

The United States postal laws and regulations prohibit the sending of any matter through the United States mail that is in the nature of a lottery.

(3) PRICE CUTTING AND UNFAIR PRICING METHODS

Problem: Clark advertised a set of non-stick cookware at "fabulous savings, regularly $39.95, now $19.95." In fact, these sets were marked at the factory with the inflated price of $39.95; Clark paid only $12.50 for each set and regularly sold them for $19.95. Is this an unfair pricing method?

Five unfair trade practices exist in connection with the pricing of articles for sale:

(a) Representing goods as being sold at a considerable discount when that is not true, as in the problem.

(b) Representing goods or services as being "free" provided a customer purchases something else, when in fact the price is higher than it would be without the "free" goods or service. The use of trading stamps and other give-aways is sometimes prohibited when they are advertised as "free."

(c) Representing prices to be wholesale prices when they are actually retail prices.

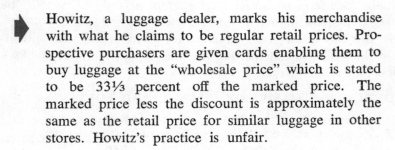

Howitz, a luggage dealer, marks his merchandise with what he claims to be regular retail prices. Prospective purchasers are given cards enabling them to buy luggage at the "wholesale price" which is stated to be 33⅓ percent off the marked price. The marked price less the discount is approximately the same as the retail price for similar luggage in other stores. Howitz's practice is unfair.

(d) Price cutting in violation of fair trade acts. To discourage price cutting, many states have enacted *fair trade laws*. Such laws require that trademarked goods and brand merchandise may not be sold by any retailer below prices set by the manufacturer if an agreement to that effect is made between the manufacturer and the wholesaler or retailer. This is designed to prohibit retailers from using well-known brands as *loss leaders* or "bait" to attract customers. It also tends to protect the small or inefficient retailer.

(e) Price cutting below cost. Some states have enacted "Unfair Sales Acts" in addition to fair trade laws. These acts forbid persons engaged in business to sell goods at prices less than the cost to themselves plus some minimum markup with intent to harm competition.

(4) MISBRANDING AND MISLABELING GOODS

> **Problem:** The gasoline pumps at Estee service station were labeled "Premium," "Regular," and "Standard," respectively, and the prices varied by two to three cents per gallon between grades. An investigation revealed that the gasoline from the three pumps had identical octane ratings and was the same in other respects. Was this misleading?

Misbranding and mislabeling occur frequently. For example, the use of the initials "M and J" on a cheap coffee that was not a blend of Mocha and Java coffee has been held to be unfair competition. The use of "super" in the brand names of second-line tires was held to confuse and mislead the public into thinking these tires were superior to the first-line tires named "deluxe." Similarly, the different labeling of the gasoline pumps when there was no difference in the product was misrepresentation.

Misrepresentation of composition includes the imitation of well-known terms and descriptive words by words that have been invented and made to look like the original. For example, "Camel spun" conveys the idea that the fabric is camel's hair, and "shammy" imitates chamois.

In addition to labeling provisions that are deemed to constitute an unfair trade practice and those included in the Federal Food, Drug and Cosmetic Act, Congress has enacted a Hazardous Substances Labeling Act and, more recently, a Fair Packaging and Labeling Act. Both the Federal Trade Commission and the Food and Drug Administration (FDA) have authority to enforce the provisions of the Fair Packaging and Labeling Act that covers all commodities not covered by other acts. Except for those under the jurisdiction of the FDA, violations are deemed to be unfair trade practices.

(5) SELLING USED ARTICLES AS NEW

> **Problem:** AAA Typewriter Sales represented that used electric typewriters were "completely rebuilt at the factory." In fact, they had been cleaned and overhauled in its own repair shop. Did this misrepresentation result in unfair competition?

Many misrepresentations involve the sale of used, secondhand, or rebuilt articles as if they were new. The most common misrepresentation occurs when no indication is given that the goods are secondhand. Others refer to the condition or quality of secondhand or rebuilt articles. In used cars, for example, odometers may be turned back. In many states this is illegal and prohibited. However, at least one court has held that this is not an unfair practice if the odometer is turned back to zero because a prospective buyer should know that this would not represent the correct mileage. In the problem, unless the typewriters were actually rebuilt at the factory, the representation constituted unfair competition.

(6) OTHER UNFAIR TRADE PRACTICES

Problem: Blazon, Inc., a manufacturer of toys and sports equipment, sued Blazon Mobile Homes, makers of trailers and campers, asking the court to prohibit Mobile Homes from using the same name and trademark, claiming it was an unfair trade practice. Is that correct?

There are numerous other forms of unfair trade practices. One type is the use of the same or similar brand name or trademark as a competitor when such use tends to cause confusion, deceive the public, or have a unique relation to the product. In the problem, however, the court held that no confusion or deception resulted from the use of the same brand name because the products were so different and non-competitive. Hence, there was no unfair practice involved.

Other such practices include commercial bribery. This involves payment to the employee of another, without the latter's consent, to buy information, favors, or other conduct relating to the other business for the benefit of the briber, particularly where he is a competitor with such other employer. Also, it is an unfair trade practice for a manufacturer to pay a retailer's salesperson "push money" for greater effort in promoting the manufacturer's product.

Numerous other consumer laws help to protect the consumer, such as the Fair Credit Reporting Act, the Truth-in-Lending Act (Chapter 22), and the Occupational Safety and Health Act of 1970. (Chapter 31) Of special interest are new requirements for automobile safety and the regulation requiring the posting of the octane ratings of gasoline.

WHAT FEDERAL LAW REGULATES FOOD, DRUGS, AND COSMETICS?

Problem: Beckett developed a drug designed to relieve acne. Without getting government approval for his new drug, he sold several cartons of it and shipped them from his factory in Massachusetts to a drug wholesaler in Colorado. Could he legally do so?

The Federal Food, Drug, and Cosmetic Act, administered by the Food and Drug Administration (FDA), prohibits the manufacture or introduction into interstate commerce of any food, drug, medical device, or cosmetic that is adulterated or misbranded. To "promote honest and fair dealings in the interests of consumers," the act also authorizes the establishment of reasonable standards of quality for foods, prohibits certain deceptions, and requires products to be

---

LABELING REQUIREMENTS OF THE FEDERAL FAIR PACKAGING AND LABELING ACT; FEDERAL FOOD, DRUG, AND COSMETIC ACT; AND FEDERAL HAZARDOUS SUBSTANCE LABELING ACT:

All Products Must Show:

(1) Name and address of the manufacturer, packer, or distributor;

(2) Quantity, such as the weight, measure, or numerical count of the contents;

(3) Usual name of each ingredient in descending order of volume;

(4) The package must be labeled "caution," "warning," or some other term if its contents are of a hazardous nature. If appropriate, first aid instructions must be included.

Labels on Packaged Food Products Must Also State:

(1) Any artificial flavoring, coloring, or chemical preservative;

(2) Usual name of the ingredients if different from the product;

(3) Any directions necessary if the food is for special dietary use;

(4) Whether it is an imitation of a standard food, as a coffee substitute;

(5) Quality, if substandard.

Labels on Drugs Must Also Give:

(1) Adequate directions for use;

(2) Warnings against unsafe use by children;

(3) If habit-forming: "warning — may be habit forming";

(4) Warnings against use that may be dangerous to health;

(5) Usual name of the drug if a trade name is used;

(6) Amount of certain ingredients, as alcohol, ether and arsenic.

Failure to state these facts on the label is misbranding or mislabeling.

---

prepared under sanitary conditions. The FDA also administers the Federal Hazardous Substances Labeling Act which provides that labels must warn of the hazards of using products such as furniture polish, cleaning fluids, and other substances which may cause illness or death if improperly used.

To assure that they are safe and effective, no new drugs may be sold in interstate commerce without approval of the FDA. After a new drug receives marketing approval, the law requires continued careful observation including the reporting of all adverse effects and new clinical experiences. If the added experience shows the drug to be unsafe, marketing approval will be withdrawn. Thus, Beckett, in the problem, must submit his product to the FDA for approval before it can be marketed legally in interstate commerce.

(1) SANITATION

Foods, drugs, and cosmetics must be prepared under sanitary conditions. This means that ingredients must not be filthy, decomposed, or otherwise unfit for use, nor may they come from diseased animals. Factories or laboratories used for production must be clean.

(2) ADULTERATION

If a product is *adulterated,* meaning that it does not meet minimum standards of purity and quality as set by the FDA, it may be confiscated. In general, a food, drug, or cosmetic is adulterated if any substance has been mixed or packed with it so as to reduce its quality or strength below the prescribed standards.

 A meat packer made hot dogs that contained 30 percent cereal and labeled them "all meat." The hot dogs were adulterated and misbranded as they did not meet standards set by the FDA.

(3) MISBRANDING

All foods, drugs, and cosmetics must have labels stating (a) the name and address of the manufacturer, packager or distributor; and (b) the quantity, such as the weight of the contents. In addition, certain special items of information must be included on labels for packaging food products, drugs, and cosmetics. For example, the label on a packaged food product must include any directions that are necessary if the food is for special dietary use, and a label on a drug or cosmetic product must warn against use that may be dangerous to health. Proper labeling of products is required not only for the physical well-being of the consumer, but also for his economic well-being; that is, to assure the consumer that he is not paying for something that he is not getting. Failure to state the required facts on the label is *misbranding*.

Under both the Food, Drug, and Cosmetic Act and the Fair Packaging and Labeling Act, containers must be made in such a manner that neither their form nor the manner in which they are filled will be misleading. When the container is much too large for the contents, giving the impression it contains much more than it does, it is said to be *slack-filled*. However, some space may legitimately result from settling of the contents after the initial filling.

 A manufacturer of cereal was required to change the method of packaging his product because the food occupied only 40 percent of the capacity of the carton in which it was packed and thus gave a false impression of the quantity it contained. The cereal carton was slack-filled.

HOW MUST TEXTILES AND FURS BE LABELED?

Problem: Charlesworth purchased a shirt that was labeled "wash and wear, permanently pressed." There was no other label or tag attached. Does this meet the labeling requirements of the law?

Labeling of textile and fur products is required by three federal laws: the Textile Fiber Products Identification Act, the Wool Products Labeling Act, and the Fur Products Labeling Act. Fur-trimmed garments are subject to the Fur Act. These laws are administered by the FTC.

In general, these acts require that any garment containing a textile, wool, or fur product sold in interstate commerce must be labeled or marked to show the kind and proportion of each fiber used in the article. It is a violation of the Wool Act to understate or overstate the wool content.

The shirt in the problem should be labeled to show the proportion of polyester and other textile products it contains. Certain articles are excluded; but if any exempt article is labeled, the label must be accurate.

The FTC is also charged with enforcing the "Flammable Fabrics Act" which is designed to prevent the sale of wearing apparel that is easily set on fire.

The penalty for violation of these acts varies, depending upon whether the violation is willful or without criminal intent.

WHAT IS THE EFFECT OF GOVERNMENT STANDARDS?

Problem: Thornburg purchased some beef at Markle's Meat Market that had been produced on a local farm and was labeled "Cavett's Choice" grade. Does this mean that Cavett's Choice is the same as U.S. Choice?

Congress has passed several laws authorizing the use of quality standards for various commodities. For the most part, use of these standards is not required. However, if the standards are used for goods in interstate commerce (and many are), they must conform to the government definition. Thus, if Markle's beef in the problem had been labeled U. S. Choice, it would have had to conform to U. S. standards for that grade. Because it was labeled in the name of the meat packer and was not sold in interstate commerce, the beef may or may not have met U. S. Choice standards.

Federal standards have been set up not only for meats but also for poultry, eggs, dairy products, fruits, vegetables, honey, and many other foods. Standards for many other goods are set by trade associations, as in the case of mirrors; by national organizations, such as the American Standards Association or American Society for Testing Materials; and by various governmental agencies. Often these voluntary quality standards have the force of law when they are approved and adopted by a governmental agency such as the FTC. Occasionally states require quality standards for certain dairy products and eggs.

Another source of legal protection of consumers is in the inspection service of the United States Department of Agriculture to canners, packers, and processors. A seal is placed on the product to indicate that it was inspected. In most cases, the inspection is voluntary and paid for by the processor. In other cases, as for poultry and meat entering interstate commerce, the inspection is required by law and has the effect of requiring the states to meet federal standards. About all the seal means is that the product was disease free and was processed under clean and sanitary conditions. Voluntary organizations, such as the American Medical Association and Underwriters Laboratory, also provide seals of approval for various products. Such seals, of course, have no legal significance but are a helpful guide for the consumer.

Many states and cities have adopted the standards set up by the federal government or have set up their own. For example, most states recognize three grades of gasoline and require all gasoline sold to meet the minimum standards of the grades recognized.

WHAT ARE THE STANDARDS FOR WEIGHTS AND MEASURES?

Problem: The laws of a certain state require that any loaf of bread being offered for public sale weigh no less than 16 ounces. The Square-Deal Bakery made loaves that were short weight by two ounces and sold them as standard loaves. What action could be taken against the bakery?

The United States Constitution gives Congress the power to fix standards of weights and measures. In exercising this right, the federal government has set standards for such things as the containers for fruits and other dry commodities, units of electrical measurement, and the standard legal weight of a bushel of certain products. Most other standards of weights and measures are left for regulation by the states and vary from state to state.

In the case of universally used food such as bread, many different sizes of standard loaf are found among the states. A person who buys a bushel of sweet potatoes will receive from 46 to 60 pounds, depending on the state in which he buys it. The weight of a bushel of apples varies in the different states from 44 to 50 pounds.

Weights and measures laws, except as to mislabeling if in interstate commerce, are enforced by state or local government agencies. Violation is punishable by fine or imprisonment or both. Also, the goods may be confiscated or released under bond after confiscation to be reworked so as to comply with the law. In the problem, the bakery would probably be fined and required to comply with the law.

Most states provide for the inspection and testing of weighing and measuring devices such as gasoline pumps, scales, and taxicab meters at least once or twice a year. The testing is ordinarily done by a local sealer of weights and measures. Seals certifying to the accuracy of the devices are usually placed on them. Penalties are imposed for tampering with the scales, pumps, or meters after they have been sealed. Devices that are inaccurate and cannot be corrected by adjustment may be confiscated and destroyed.

WHAT STATE AND LOCAL LAWS PROTECT CONSUMERS?

Problem: McCormick was having difficulty with his car and took it to Five Corners Garage to have it checked. After looking over the car, the owner gave him a list of parts that should be replaced and other work to be done that amounted to $179.00. McCormick had the work done and later found that all that was needed was a new distributor, costing less than $25. All the other parts installed by the garage were not really necessary for the proper functioning of the car. What rights, if any, does McCormick have against the garage owner?

Most states and many cities have enacted laws similar to the Federal Food, Drug, and Cosmetic Act within recent years. They also have laws that protect consumers in many other ways. Indeed, the legal protection available to consumers is suprisingly extensive. In New York State, for example, nearly 20 state agencies are concerned in one or more ways with administering and enforcing laws designed to protect consumers. California has 61 such agencies. Some of the ways states and cities look after consumer interests follow.

(1) CONSUMER PROTECTION LAWS

Many states have enacted statutes designed to provide consumers with protection against fraudulent and unfair practices. These are variously titled and give consumers, individually or in a class action, rights against those who take unfair advantage or cause damage. The consumer may sue for damages and get a court order stopping such practices. Thus, if McCormick, in the problem, lives in a state having such a statute, through court action he can obtain damages to reimburse him for his loss and enjoin the garage owner from inflating the repair costs of any car owner who may come to him. He may also be able to get punitive damages—a penalty assessed by the court against the garage owner for his fraudulent act. Unfortunately the consumer may not know that he has been victimized.

(2) LICENSING

Consumer protection in many areas begins with legal standards and licensing for both practitioners and establishments. This is particularly true for those who render personal service related to health, such as physicians, dentists, nurses, laboratory technicians, and pharmacists. Licenses may also be required of others, such as beauticians, barbers, morticians, accountants, psychologists, contractors, plumbers, electricians, and certain salespeople, such as real estate and insurance agents.

Institutions and business establishments may also be required to meet minimum standards before they are licensed, for example, hospitals, rest homes, clinics, private schools, and money-lending and check-cashing agencies. Statutes generally provide that a person or institution that fails to meet the standards set will have its license revoked by the regulatory agency.

(3) SANITATION AND SAFETY

Statutes providing for inspection of businesses handling foods, such as meat markets, bakeries, hotels, camps, and restaurants, have been enacted in all states and in many cities. Certain standards of cleanliness and sanitation are prescribed, and periodic health examinations may be required of food handlers. Establishments not meeting the standards may be closed. Enforcement of these and other similar laws depends upon local interest and consumer concern.

Safety laws apply to buildings and places open to public gatherings. They relate not only to required types of construction but also to such things as location, use, sanitary facilities, fire escapes, sprinkler systems, the maximum number of persons who are allowed in the place, and the number, marking, and lighting of exits.

(4) FOOD ADULTERATION

Laws prohibiting the sale of tainted meat and unclean milk have been on the statute books of some states and cities since 1850. Now all states regulate the purity and quality of these products. The Standard Milk Ordinance requires milk to be graded and labeled properly. Some states require that milk, when served in a public eating place, be opened and poured from an individual carton or bottle in front of the patron. This is to prevent adulteration and to help assure cleanliness.

Most states also provide for inspection of poultry, meat, and sea foods. Some states regulate the amount of insecticides that can be left on fresh fruit and vegetables when they are marketed. **Penalties are provided for violation of pure food laws.**

(5) BEDDING LAWS

Bedding and upholstery laws are in force in most states. They govern the use of secondhand or shoddy material in the manufacture for sale of such products as mattresses, comforters, quilts, cushions, pillows, and upholstered furniture. Some states prohibit the use of secondhand or shoddy material, but most states will allow its use if it has been sterilized and properly labeled.

Many other statutes protect consumers. Several states have recently enacted statutes that provide for a "cooling off" period for consumers who purchase something from a door-to-door salesman. Such a law typically gives the consumer three days to reflect over his decision and to change his mind if he wishes to do so. He may then rescind the contract and get back all or most of any money he has paid. Most states have laws regulating "going-out-of-business" and bankruptcy sales that are often used to bilk and defraud consumers who believe they may get a bargain when in fact the merchant is just selling old merchandise that was hard to sell or bought for that purpose. Frequently a license must be obtained for permission to advertise a sale as a "bankrupt sale."

TO AVOID BEING VICTIMIZED . . .

1. Know your merchandise and know your rights. Compare values and prices, and shop around. The best protection for the consumer is self-protection.
2. Beware of bait and switch advertising; and don't forget that "loss leaders" are designed to lure you into the store so that you will buy other items that produce a profit — sometimes far greater than any loss caused to the dealer by the "bait."
3. Be suspicious of excessive price-cutting and special sales. They may be genuine. On the other hand, they may be designed to unload old and discontinued merchandise, or goods of inferior or substandard quality.
4. Don't be taken by lotteries or "free" offers. When one person gets something for nothing, others get nothing for something.
5. Never sign anything you have not read or cannot understand.
6. Develop the habit of reading the label. This will pay substantial dividends over the years.
7. Check purchases that are weighed or packaged at the store. Look for a seal on weighing and measuring devices. The Council on Consumer Information reports that more money is lost through short weights and measures than through burglary and theft.
8. Report business practices you believe to be unfair to the appropriate governmental agency.

YOUR LEGAL VOCABULARY

adulterated
bait and switch advertising
class action
fair trade laws
false advertising

loss leaders
lottery
misbranding
slack-filled
unfair trade practice

1. Partly filled, giving the impression that a package contains more than it does.
2. Opposed to good morals and fair dealings in business.
3. Goods, usually well-known brands, sold at a discount to attract buyers into a store.
4. Legal suit brought by one or several persons on behalf of themselves and others similarly situated.
5. Untrue claims of quality or effectiveness of goods or services offered for sale.
6. Statutes which require that trademarked goods and brand merchandise cannot be sold below prices set by the manufacturer.
7. A product in which another substance has been added thus reducing its purity and quality.
8. Failure to state required facts on a label.
9. "Come-on" advertising to lure prospective customers into a store in order to persuade them to buy more attractive but costlier goods.
10. A scheme that involves consideration, chance, and a prize to some who pay the consideration and win.

REMEMBER THESE HIGHLIGHTS

1. The federal government has enacted laws administered by the Federal Trade Commission prohibiting certain unfair trade practices in interstate commerce. Many states have similar laws.
2. Some trade practices that are held to be unfair are (a) false and misleading advertising, (b) use of lotteries, (c) price cutting and unfair pricing methods, (d) misbranding and mislabeling, and (e) selling used or rebuilt articles as if they were new.
3. The Federal Food, Drug, and Cosmetic Act prohibits the manufacture or the introduction into interstate commerce of any food, drug, medical device, or cosmetic that is adulterated or misbranded. This act requires that certain information be given on the labels of all foods, drugs, medical devices, and cosmetics, and that special information be included on the labels of foods and drugs. Most states have similar laws.
4. Asserting that informed consumers are essential to the fair and efficient functioning of a free-market economy, Congress has enacted a Fair Packaging and Labeling Act to supplement the labeling requirements of the FTC, FDA, and the Hazardous Substances Labeling Act.

5. For the benefit of the consumer, the federal government and many states have set up standards of quality for numerous food products.
6. Most states provide for regulating and enforcing standards of weights and measures.
7. All states and many cities have enacted laws that protect consumer health by providing standards, licensing, and inspections.
8. Federal laws provide for labeling of fur and textile products to show the kind and proportion of each natural or manufactured fiber included in a product.

LAW AS PEOPLE LIVE IT

1. Giannini was a licensed nurseryman but was not licensed as a landscape contractor. He sold $450 worth of seed, plants, and shrubs to McConnell who was putting in a new lawn and garden. She asked Giannini for suggestions and he did much of the arranging and planting. He recommended some other shrubs and plants. When he billed McConnell $1,100 and she refused to pay, he sued her. Do you believe McConnell's claim that Giannini needed a landscape contractor's license is correct?
2. Madwin and a hundred other students paid a travel agency in advance for charter flights to Europe. The flights did not take place and the students could not get a refund. What could Madwin and the other students do?
3. Wolfrum Watch Company represented that its watches using the brand names of "Seventeen" and "Twenty-One" contained 17 and 21 jewels respectively and that the jewels were genuine rubies. If these claims were not true, could Wolfrum be required to stop such advertising?
4. The manufacturer of candy bars placed a number on the inside of each wrapper. Buyers who found a number ending in two nines were entitled to receive a large box of candy. Does this scheme constitute a lottery and, therefore, an unfair trade practice?
5. Durham Drug received two unordered cases of Quik-Relief Pain Kill from Safe-T Manufacturing Company along with a bill for the cost of the merchandise. An enclosed letter explained that advertisements had been placed in the local newspaper announcing that the product was available at Durham Drug. Did these acts constitute unfair trade practices?
6. Vail Vending Corporation mixed candy, gum, and a variety of metal and plastic trinkets together and placed the mixture in vending machines. Portions of the mixture could be purchased by inserting a coin and turning the crank. Does the mixing of trinkets with gum and candy constitute an adulteration under the Federal Food, Drug, and Cosmetic Act?

7. The label on Tru-Flavor brand of orange juice stated it was made of "pure sun-ripened Florida oranges." In fact it consisted of a mixture of citric acid, artificial color and flavor, and 25 percent orange juice. Would the FDA be justified in seizing this product?

8. A truck loaded with frozen pizzas was involved in an accident and ran into a lake. The pizzas were submerged and absorbed some of the lake water. The owners endeavored to salvage the pizzas. Did the lake water cause the pizzas to be adulterated so that they could be seized and destroyed?

9. Alexander Pharmaceutical packed mineral oil into bottles labeled, in part, "Castor Oil . . . Dose: Children, one to two teaspoonfuls. Adults, one to two tablespoonfuls." Did this label meet the requirements of the Food, Drug and Cosmetic Act?

10. Headington operated a chicken processing plant, shipping dressed poultry to neighboring states. Was he required to arrange for United States Department of Agriculture inspection of his products?

LAW AS COURTS DECIDE IT

1. Best paid $5,000 in advance for 200 hours of dancing lessons from an Arthur Murray franchised dancing studio. After using a few hours of instruction, Best sued for the return of her money claiming the contract was in violation of a state law requiring that all contracts for dancing instruction for more than $500 must be for "a precisely measured period of years or part thereof," and that 200 hours of instruction did not meet that requirement. Should Best recover the amount owed for the unused dancing lessons? (Best v. Arthur Murray Town & Country Dance Club, 60 Misc. 2d 66, 303 N.Y.S. 2d 546)

2. Del Spina, on behalf of himself and other service station owners, sued several oil and refining companies to prohibit the companies from operating games of chance in connection with the sale of motor fuel. Del Spina claimed that the sale price was increased as a result of the games and that this violated the state law which provides that it is "unlawful for any retail dealer to use lotteries, prizes . . . or other games of chance in connection with the sale of motor fuel." The oil companies claimed that it was not necessary to purchase motor fuel in order to participate in the games. Thus, no one had to pay to participate, an essential element in a lottery or game of chance under the statute. Should the oil companies be prohibited from sponsoring these games? (United Stations of New Jersey v. Kingsley, 99 N.J. Super. 574, 240 A. 2d 702)

3. Arrow Metal Products Corporation manufactured an awning which it described in its sales and advertising material as "porcenamel." The awnings were not coated with porcelain enamel, but with a plastic resin.

The Federal Trade Commission claimed the use of "porcenamel" had a tendency to deceive the public and issued a cease and desist order. Should the order be upheld? (Arrow Metal Products Corporation v. Federal Trade Commission, 249 F. 2d 83)

4. Meddin Bros. Packing Company was engaged in slaughtering animals and packing meat for human consumption. Portions of the animals slaughtered considered not suitable for human consumption were packed in old cartons, sold, and shipped to Allen Products Company for use in making dog food. The inedible meat products shipped to Allen Products were not inspected and passed as required for meat products designed for human consumption. The containers, however, were labeled "inedible food." In a dispute over the labeling of the containers used for shipping the left-over meat products, it was contended that the labeling requirements of the Food, Drug, and Cosmetic Act applied only to meat products designed as human food, not to dog food. Is that correct? (Meddin Bros. Packing Co. v. United States, 417 F. 2d 17)

5. The Food and Drug Administration seized 906 packages of Vitasafe food supplement capsules claiming that as an article of food it was mislabeled and misbranded. The manufacturer's label implied and suggested that women had different nutritional needs than men and that "Vitasafe Formula W" would satisfy these special requirements while "Vitasafe Formula M" would satisfy the special needs of men. It was also claimed by the manufacturer that the nutritional value of Vitasafe capsules was enhanced by the presence of added ingredients. Moreover the label listed many health conditions for which the capsules supposedly provided effective treatment. The FDA presented evidence showing that there are no essential differences in the nutritional requirements of men and women except for iron, which was in the same quantity in both formulas, M and W. Evidence was also introduced showing that normal diets supply the amounts of the listed ingredients greatly in excess of those needed. Accordingly, the representations on the labels were false and misleading. Was the labeling law violated? (United States v. Vitasafe Formula M, 226 F. Supp. 266)

Our Legal System

UNIT TWO

As we have learned, law imposes certain obligations and responsibilities on individuals in return for certain rights and protections. If everyone obeyed the law and met his legal and moral obligations, there would be few law violations and, therefore, little need for courts and other law enforcement agencies. However, in any human society, there always are individuals who for one reason or another break the law. This unit discusses various kinds of law violations, how the law is enforced, and the role of the courts in dealing with law violators.

Law violations differ in severity and in who is affected by the violation. We are all familiar with some of the more serious crimes. Federal law lists almost 3,000 crimes, and state and local law even more. Civil law relates to violations committed against individuals, while criminal law relates to violations committed against society as a whole. Because business crimes are especially important to us in our study, we shall take a careful look at them.

Law includes not only rules for proper conduct, but also the means for enforcing these rules. We shall take a look at our various law enforcement agencies and study the role of the courts in administering justice. You will see that procedures vary in dealing with civil cases, criminal cases, and cases involving juveniles.

CHAPTER 5 Crimes and Torts

1. *Your neighbor sees a burglar breaking into your home but does not notify the police. Has the neighbor committed a legal wrong?*

2. *A bicycle rider deliberately rides into a group of people standing on a sidewalk. A girl is struck and injured. What kind of wrong is this?*

3. *Two small boys break into a public school building one weekend and cause $500 damage by breaking windows and overturning furniture. Have they committed a crime?*

HOW DO CRIMINAL LAW AND CIVIL LAW DIFFER?

Problem: Observing that the driver had left his wallet on the seat of a parked car, a high school student took the wallet and spent the money. Did he commit a crime?

We have learned that the law gives each person certain personal rights that he may expect both the Government and other persons to respect. We have also learned that the law imposes certain obligations on all persons. When the legal rights of an individual are violated, the matter is governed by civil law. *Civil law* in this sense differs from the system of law discussed on page 6 and refers to the branch of law concerned with wrongs against individuals. When a person fails in his obligation to society as represented by government, and violates a public duty rather than an individual right, the wrong is governed by *criminal law*.

Criminal law is concerned with such relatively minor wrongs as littering, disturbing the peace, and disorderly conduct as well as with more serious ones such as murder, robbery, and bribery. In the problem, the taking of the wallet was the crime of theft or larceny. In a criminal action the state (or "the people" as it is sometimes called) prosecutes the wrongdoer. Civil law is concerned with situations in which one person may have a right of legal action against another person. For example, legal actions for damages when one is wrongfully injured in an automobile accident, or when a seller fails to fulfill the terms of a contract, are governed by civil law.

Chapter 5 □ CRIMES AND TORTS

Business law is largely concerned with civil law, much of it with contracts. Some of business law is concerned with torts, as for example the negligence of a manufacturer in distributing faulty products, causing injuries. Criminal law affects business in many ways, as when an employer violates minimum wage laws or a customer is caught shoplifting.

WHAT ARE TORTS AND CRIMES?

Problem: Collier, a bookkeeper for McBride, juggled the books over a period of years in such a way that he was able to take for himself about $10,000 belonging to his employer. If Collier repaid the money, would the wrong still be considered a crime?

When a person causes injury to another by failing to do something required by law (as distinguished from a duty imposed by contract), he commits a *tort*. For example, a seller may commit the tort of fraud if he intentionally lies about his product to a customer who believes him and buys in reliance on the false information.

In addition to the duties which the law imposes upon persons in respect to the rights of individuals, it prescribes certain other things that persons must do or must not do in respect to the rights of society. For a breach of the duty to observe such laws, the law provides a punishment. When a person does not obey a law for which a punishment is provided, he commits a *crime*. A crime consists of an act that (1) violates the social standards of the time and offends society as a whole, (2) injures public institutions or property, or (3) injures a person. In addition, for an act to be a crime there must be criminal intent, which is usually indicated by one's actions.

Accordingly, in the problem, Collier was guilty of a crime known as *embezzlement*, which is the fraudulent taking or use of money or other property of another entrusted to one's care. The fact that Collier repaid the money to McBride did not offset his earlier commission of the crime.

Note that a tort and a crime are similar in that they are both breaches of duties imposed by law. They differ in that a crime has social consequences and is punishable by the State, whereas a tort has individual consequences for which only the injured party has a right of action. Some acts are both torts and crimes.

HOW ARE CRIMES CLASSIFIED?

> **Problem:** Gordon was a witness at a trial of a friend. He took an oath "to tell the truth, the whole truth, and nothing but the truth." While being questioned by one of the attorneys, he deliberately lied to help his friend. Did he commit a crime in doing so?

Crimes are classified in terms of their seriousness as (1) felonies, and (2) misdemeanors. Each state has its own criminal law distinguishing between felonies and misdemeanors and stating the punishment. Thus, a felony in one state may be a misdemeanor in another state.

In addition, the federal government identifies a special category of crime known as treason. The United States Constitution declares:

> "Treason against the United States shall consist only in levying war against them, or in adhering to their enemies, giving them aid and comfort."
>
> —Article III, Section 3, U. S. Constitution

(1) FELONIES

A *felony* is a crime of a serious nature. The test of whether a crime is a felony generally is whether the act is declared by law to be such or when it is punishable by death or imprisonment in a state prison. Murder, kidnapping, arson, embezzlement, forgery, theft or larceny, perjury, and the like are classified as felonies. When a person is under oath, as in the problem, and willfully does not tell the truth, he commits *perjury* and may be punished.

(2) MISDEMEANORS

A *misdemeanor* is a crime of a less serious nature, usually punishable by a fine or confinement in a county or city jail, or by both. Drunkenness, driving an automobile at excessive speed, and the like are usually classified as misdemeanors. Some states have adopted a new classification of minor misdemeanors, known as *infractions*. Such things as overtime parking, failing to clear snow from sidewalks, and littering are classified as infractions. Ordinarily no jury is allowed for trying cases involving infractions and the punishment is usually a fine.

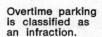
Overtime parking is classified as an infraction.

WHAT ARE BUSINESS CRIMES?

Problem: Gateway Market, as required by law, withheld income and social security taxes from the wages paid to its employees and paid the money to the federal government by specified dates. Being short of money when the withheld taxes were due one month, Gateway did not make the payments. Was it guilty of a crime?

A business, like any person, is subject to all crimes. Some, however, are found more frequently in the business world than elsewhere, and others are peculiar to business. Although not commonly thought of as such, even violations of administrative regulations are crimes. For example, an employer who violates the child labor regulations, or who deliberately fails to file his income tax return by the date specified by law, is guilty of a crime. Thus, Gateway Market in the problem, was guilty of a crime. Likewise, violations of state laws regarding weights and measures or federal laws governing packaging and labeling are business crimes. Some of the more common business crimes are discussed below.

(1) LARCENY

The crime of *larceny* is commonly known as theft and includes the wrongful taking of personal property belonging to someone else with intent to deprive the owner of possession. Thus, larceny, a broad technical term, includes such crimes as embezzlement (Page 74), *robbery* (which is taking property of another against his will and by force or by putting him in fear), *burglary* (which is taking the property of another by breaking into and entering a building with intent to steal), and shoplifting. In most states robbery and burglary, as well as other forms of larceny including shoplifting, are designated as separate crimes. Depending on the value of the property stolen and the seriousness and circumstances surrounding the act itself, larceny may be either a felony or a misdemeanor. Burglary is always a felony.

(2) FALSE PRETENSES

When one obtains money or other property from another by making false representation of a past or existing fact, he is said to be guilty of *false pretenses* or false representation. This crime differs from larceny because the victim parts with his property voluntarily. It is held by some courts to be similar to *swindling* when one gains an advantage by trickery and cheating. False pretenses is a type of fraud (Page 124) and is also a tort.

 Klassen was arrested for speeding on his motorcycle. A friend, Marquis, said he had just been fined for a similar offense and that the fine was $75. Actually it was $12. Because Klassen was busy, Marquis offered to pay the fine for him. He accepted the $75, paid the $12 fine, and pocketed $63. Marquis was guilty of obtaining money under false pretenses.

(3) FORGERY

Forgery is a type of fraud which involves falsely making or maliciously altering any writing such as the signature of another person. There must be intent to defraud either the person whose name is signed or someone else. The most common forgeries are found on checks. In some states it also includes altering the check or instrument. False pretense enters into forgery because the signer pretends he is someone else. Forgery is usually a felony. Of course if one is directed by another person to sign that person's name there is no forgery.

(4) BRIBERY

Bribery is the crime of voluntarily giving or receiving money or anything of value with the intention of influencing someone in the discharge of his official duty. In many states, special crimes have been declared which are similar to that of bribing an official, such as bribing a purchasing agent or an athlete.

(5) EXTORTION

The crime of *extortion* involves unlawfully demanding or taking money or other property from a person by force, compulsion, or threat of force. Usually the one extorting the money agrees to do or not to do something that affects the victim. Blackmail is a form of extortion.

 The attorney for a labor union threatened to foment a strike among the employees of a company unless he was paid $10,000. The attorney was guilty of extortion.

(6) CONSPIRACY

Conspiracy is an unlawful agreement between two or more persons to do by common action an unlawful or criminal act, or do a lawful act by unlawful means. Usually the agreement is secret.

WHAT ARE SOME COMMON TORTS?

Problem: Martinelli was erecting a scaffold in preparation for painting a building when the head flew off his hammer, hitting and injuring Bott, a passerby. Did Martinelli commit a tort?

A tort may be the result of a deliberately harmful act or an act that is done unintentionally, or, as in the problem, it may result from doing a legal act in a manner that is harmful to someone else. Since a tort is any invasion of a private right, some of them are discussed later in connection with other topics. A few of the more common torts are as follows:

(1) ASSAULT

A person has the right to be free from reasonable fear that he will suffer personal injury from another person. A breach of the duty or failing to observe the right is an *assault*. It consists of a threat to inflict physical injury upon another causing a reasonable fear that it will be carried out. Mere words do not constitute an assault; threat of violence must also be displayed. The threat must be accompanied also by an apparent ability to carry it into execution.

 Anderson, an elderly and totally blind person, thought Pratt, who was not blind, was taking advantage of him. He threatened to "beat Pratt's face to a pulp." Because it was obvious that Anderson could not carry out his threat there was no assault.

(2) BATTERY

A person has the right to be free from unlawful physical mistreatment. A breach of the duty to observe this right is a *battery*. It consists of the unlawful touching of one person by another. For example, injuring another in anger, violently jostling another, or throwing water upon him in a spiteful, rude, or insolent manner constitutes a battery. A battery is usually preceded by an assault, hence the common phrase, assault and battery. Where a victim is not aware that he is going to be struck, there is no assault, only a battery.

(3) TRESPASS

A person has the right to the possession of his property without unlawful interference by others. Failure to observe this right is known as *trespass*. It may consist of any one of the many forms of interference with the possession of property. Dumping rubbish on the land of another, breaking windows of a neighbor's house, or puncturing the tires of another's automobile are trespasses. The fact that the trespass is unintentional is immaterial.

(4) NUISANCE

A person has the right to the use and enjoyment of his property without unreasonable interference from others. This means that one must use his property so that it does not injure others. To use one's property in a manner that unreasonably interferes with others' use and enjoyment of their property is a *nuisance*.

 Channel operated an asphalt plant near the homes of Mirande and Roland who had lived there before the asphalt plant was opened. They claimed the fumes, odors, smoke, dirt, and dust caused by the plant and blown by the wind over their homes created a nuisance. The court agreed and held that Channel must modify the plant to eliminate the nuisance.

(5) CONVERSION

A person has the right to own, possess, and use personal property free from interference by others. When one person's right to his personal property is interfered with by another, as by carrying away or destroying his goods or using them in a manner inconsistent with the owner's rights, the wrongdoer is guilty of *conversion*. A thief converts goods when he steals them. Conversion does not depend, however, upon the intent to do a wrongful act. Thus, a person who innocently purchases a stolen automobile from a thief is guilty of conversion and is liable to the owner for its value.

> Ayala, a truck driver for Stein, returned the truck to the company yard at the close of business each day. He had keys to the yard and the truck. Regularly on weekends, without Stein's knowledge or consent, Ayala went to the yard, took the truck and used it to haul things for others, pocketing the income. He returned the truck to the yard before it was needed on Monday. Ayala was liable to Stein for conversion.

(6) DEFAMATION

A person has the right to be free from malicious gossip and unjustified attempts to undermine his reputation. A breach of the duty to observe this right is *defamation*. If the defamation is spoken, it is *slander*. If it is written or printed, it is *libel*. To provide a basis for legal action, the idea must be (a) communicated to another person, (b) be untrue, and (c) bring the person into disrepute, contempt, or ridicule by others.

> A news commentator reported on a radio program that an officer of a prominent corporation had a conflict of interest because a small company he owned secretly was selling goods to the corporation at a high profit to the officer. This was true. Therefore the news commentator was not guilty of defamation.

(7) NEGLIGENCE

A person has the right to be free from injuries to himself and his property caused by others who do not exercise the proper degree of care. This means that one must conduct himself in his relations to others as a reasonably prudent person would under the circumstances at the time. Failure to use reasonable care is *negligence,* and there is liability if damage results. This is probably the most common tort.

> McMillan did not look where she was going while parking her car. The car leaped the curb, crashing into Sarlotte's window. McMillan was liable for negligence.

WHO IS RESPONSIBLE FOR CRIMES AND TORTS?

Problem: As a favor to two of his friends, Watson agreed to drive them in his car to a store, wait in the car while they robbed the storekeeper, and drive them away. The three men were caught while making the getaway. Watson declared he was not guilty of a crime because he did not take part in the robbery and was not going to get any of the loot. What is your judgment?

Any person who is capable of distinguishing right from wrong and voluntarily does an act punishable by the state commits a crime. Under the common law small children under 7 years of age are not held liable for crimes. Usually those over 14 years old are presumed to know the difference between right and wrong, and are therefore accountable for their acts. For children between 7 and 14, such knowledge must be shown. Many states have statutes fixing the age of criminal liability. Ignorance is generally no excuse for violating a law; a person is presumed to know what the law is. Insane persons are not held liable for their criminal acts because one must have sufficient mental capacity at the time of the crime to realize the difference between right and wrong to be guilty of committing it. A person is generally responsible for his crimes even though he may be weak-minded or have a sub-normal mental capacity.

When one person aids another in the commission of a crime, he is also guilty of criminal wrongdoing. For example, a person who acts as a lookout to warn a robber of the approach of an officer or drives the getaway car, as Watson did in the problem, is recognized by law as a partner in the robbery. Similarly, a person who gives advice to another person or otherwise aids and abets him in the commission of a crime is guilty of the same crime even though he is not present. The person who knowingly receives and sells stolen goods is guilty of a separate crime.

When one person aids another in the commission of a crime, he is also guilty of a wrongdoing.

In general, all persons may be held liable for their torts. Thus, even children may be responsible for injuries they cause others. In some states statutes provide that parents are liable up to a specified maximum amount of money for the torts of their children under certain ages. Many states also provide that parents are liable for damages negligently caused by their children while operating an automobile. In certain other cases one person may also be responsible for the tort of another person, as for example, an employer for the act of an employee committed within the scope of employment. This, however, does not relieve the employee of his liability.

WHAT IS THE LIABILITY FOR CRIMES AND TORTS?

Problem: An ordinance required that water not be wasted by allowing it to run into the street and sewers. Lapper was watering his lawn and irrigating his garden and forgot to turn the water off. The water ran into the street all night, making a considerable stream. He was cited for wasting water. What was Lapper's liability for violating the ordinance?

We have learned that a crime results from failure to obey a law for which punishment is provided. The liability imposed for a crime is punishment by imprisonment or fine or both. Lapper was guilty of a misdemeanor and was subject to such punishment as the court would decide under the law. Criminal statutes ordinarily set maximum limits for punishment but allow a judge considerable freedom in determining the appropriate punishment. A court may impose and then suspend punishment, subject to the good behavior of the guilty party who may be placed on probation for a prescribed period of time.

The state does not punish a wrongdoer for a tort. The one who suffers injury must seek relief in a civil action. As explained earlier in this chapter, this is an action between persons, as distinguished from a criminal action in which the government ("the people") prosecutes the case. The liability for tort is in the form of money damages awarded to the injured party. Note, however, that in most states, in the case of negligence on the part of the defendant, the injured person in order to collect damages must not have failed to exercise proper care himself. Failure to exercise such care is known as *contributory negligence*.

► Schmidt came running up to an automatic elevator just as the doors were closing. Not wishing to wait for the next elevator, he negligently put his arm into the door to stop it from closing. In so doing, his arm was broken. Schmidt would not be able to recover damages because of his own contributory negligence.

IN TIME OF LEGAL TROUBLE, REMEMBER THAT . . .

1. You should consult a lawyer who is qualified to handle the kind of case in which you are involved.
2. Ignorance of the law is no excuse if you have committed a crime or invaded the personal rights of another person.
3. Although one may have a right of legal action, it is usually better in terms of costs, time, worry, and personal relations to settle the dispute out of court if possible.
4. If you believe that you have a good right of action against another person but your attorney thinks not, your attorney is probably right.
5. A minor may be just as liable for his crimes and torts as an adult. The fact that a minor who is accused of a crime may be tried in a juvenile court does not change the liability.
6. If you are injured by a tort, don't be hurried into signing a statement releasing the one who committed the tort from liability. On the other hand, don't delay too long in taking action — you may lose your rights if you do. Commonly after a year you are barred from suing, although for minors the time generally does not begin to run until majority.

YOUR LEGAL VOCABULARY

assault	felony
battery	forgery
bribery	infraction
burglary	larceny
civil law	libel
conspiracy	misdemeanor
contributory negligence	negligence
conversion	nuisance
crime	perjury
criminal law	robbery
defamation	slander
embezzlement	swindling
extortion	tort
false pretenses	trespass

1. The wrongful taking of personal property belonging to someone else.
2. A breach of duty imposed by law causing injury to another.
3. A breach of duty imposed by law for which punishment is provided.

4. The crime of giving or receiving money with the intention of influencing one in the discharge of his official duty.
5. The unlawful touching of one person by another.
6. The signing of the name of another person with intent to defraud.
7. A crime of a serious nature punishable by death or imprisonment in a state prison.
8. Defamation by the spoken word.
9. A secret and unlawful agreement between two or more people to do an unlawful act or to do a lawful act by unlawful means.
10. A crime of a minor nature punishable by fine or imprisonment in a county or city jail, or by both.

REMEMBER THESE HIGHLIGHTS

1. Every person has certain rights in respect to the conduct he may expect of others. He has corresponding duties to refrain from violating the rights of others. He is generally liable for any such violations.
2. Violation of a duty imposed by law is generally a crime or a tort. Criminal law governs crimes and civil law governs torts.
3. A crime has social and public consequences and is punishable by the state; a tort has individual consequences for which only the injured party has a right of legal action. Some acts are both torts and crimes.
4. Crimes are divided into felonies and misdemeanors. The federal government also recognizes treason as a special category.
5. Some business crimes are larceny, forgery, burglary, robbery, false pretenses, conspiracy, extortion, and bribery.
6. Some examples of torts are assault, battery, trespass, nuisance, conversion, defamation, and negligence.
7. Anyone of sufficient capability of knowing the difference between right and wrong is responsible for his crimes and torts.
8. Crimes are punished by fine, imprisonment, or both. In some states, capital punishment is still imposed for the most severe crimes.
9. Tort liability is determined in a civil action and may be settled by an award of money damages.

LAW AS PEOPLE LIVE IT

1. Rodriguez owned some vacant land. He was given a citation and fined for allowing weeds to grow and become a fire hazard on the land in violation of a city ordinance. Is this a crime?
2. Dalberg and Murphy, next door neighbors, had an argument over a tree Dalberg planted on his land. Murphy objected to the location of the tree and chopped it down one weekend. Is this wrong against Dalberg governed by criminal law?

3. South-Central Power Company constructed a transformer and sub-station on a lot next to Alford's home. The transformers were about 20 feet from his home, and the humming and vibration interfered with conversation and rest in the home. Did Alford have a right of action against the power company?
4. Dodson and Durio Manufacturing Company was cited and charged with dumping refuse in a navigable river and polluting it. Some employee had accidentally left a valve open and the refuse flowed into the river. The company said it was not guilty because it didn't know it was violating the law. Is this a good defense?
5. Roberts entered a gift shop at night and stole several valuable items. Wheele stood outside the shop to whistle a warning to Roberts in case a policeman approached. Did Wheele commit a crime?
6. Nethercutt had his pocket picked. He reported to the police that he had been robbed. Is that correct?
7. Barton was arrested and charged with being a "fence" because he received stolen property and disposed of it by selling it through his store. Barton claimed that he did not take part in the burglaries and robberies and therefore had committed no crime. Is Barton right?
8. Hagar, when asked about Holfey's qualifications as an attorney, said, "That guy is a shyster lawyer." Was such a statement slander or libel?
9. Lynch hauled a box of junk to the edge of town and tossed it onto land belonging to Haines without ever touching the land himself. Haines, standing nearby, contended that Lynch had trespassed. Was Haines correct?
10. Morris, age 17, threw a stone and shattered the large neon sign belonging to the New World Savings and Loan Association. When confronted by the owner, he contended that he was not liable for the tort because he was a minor. Was Morris correct?

LAW AS COURTS DECIDE IT

1. Two police officers observed an unlighted automobile about midnight with its motor running and its rear trunk lid open near the gasoline pumps of a service station. The service station was not open, although there were lights in the office. The officers stopped to investigate and questioned Smith and a companion who were standing beside the car. One of the officers leaned over to examine the contents of the trunk, and as he did so both men grabbed the trunk lid and pushed it down on the officer, injuring him. The other officer arrested the two men and charged them with committing criminal assault. Smith and his companion claimed they did not intend to commit a crime or injure the officer but merely wished to frighten the officers. Moreover, Smith claimed the officers needed a warrant to arrest him. Were these defenses good? (State of Connecticut v. Smith, 157 Conn. 351, 254 A. 2d 447)

2. John and Jimmie Fowler, man and wife, owners of a motel and restaurant, were charged with income tax evasion. They claimed that their lack of education, having only a third and eighth grade education respectively, made them not capable of intentionally deciding to evade income taxes. Also, they claimed they were unable to understand what their constitutional rights were when the investigating agent of the Internal Revenue Service explained them. The government introduced evidence showing that the Fowlers had operated their business profitably for several years and that they owned other rental properties. Is the claim that the lack of education made them incapable of intentionally avoiding their income taxes good? (Fowler vs. United States, 352 F. 2d 100)

3. Jackson was found guilty by a jury of the possession and sale of narcotics and sentenced to life imprisonment for the sale, and ten years, to run concurrently, for possession. He had a prior conviction for a narcotics offense and the life sentence was mandatory under Illinois law. Upon being approached to buy the drugs, Jackson, accompanied by the purchasers, went to two different places before he obtained the drug. He admitted possessing and selling the narcotic but claimed he was not guilty. His reason was that he had been a narcotics addict for more than 20 years and was suffering and ill because he had had no drugs for three days and needed some for himself. He claimed that as a narcotics addict he should not be convicted for acts that were impelled by that addiction. He also claimed that he was legally insane at the time of the crime because he was suffering from a mental defect caused by withdrawal symptoms which so overwhelmed him that he did not have capacity to appreciate that his conduct was criminal. Hence this should be a good defense against the possession and sale of narcotics. Do you agree? (People of the State of Illinois v. Jackson, 253 N.E. 2d 527, Ill.)

4. Sanders had finished shopping in a Safeway supermarket. After leaving the checkout stand, she placed her bag of groceries on a counter to straighten out the items in the bag. Finishing this task, she turned to leave the store and tripped over a lawn chair that was being displayed for sale. The aisle was 80 inches wide and the chair, which was in plain view, occupied 24 inches, leaving 56 inches of clear walking space. Sanders sued Safeway for injuries sustained in tripping over the chair. Was Safeway liable? (Safeway Stores, Inc. v. Sanders, 372 P. 2d 1021, Oklahoma)

5. A 7-Eleven store in Washington, D.C., had been burned and merchandise stolen. A police officer observed a man by the name of Short standing near a car which was close to the store. In the trunk of the car were some beer and wine of the brands carried by the store. There was no evidence that Short knew any of the other men in the car. Short was arrested and charged with aiding and abetting the looting of the store. Was he guilty? (Williams v. United States, 254 A. 2d 722)

6 Law Enforcement and the Court System

1. *A car which failed to stop at a stop sign collided with your car and caused injury to you and $600 in damages to your car. After a legal action the court awards you $4,500 in damages. If the owner of the other car fails to pay, how can you get the money?*

2. *You lend a friend $1,000 to be repaid in a year. If he fails to repay you, what legal steps can you take?*

3. *Your mother is notified to appear in court for jury duty. What is her obligation?*

HOW IS THE LAW ENFORCED?

Problem: Voorhees contracted with Stewart to construct a building to his specifications to be occupied by one of Stewart's Worthmore Supermarkets. When the building was about finished, Stewart wrote Voorhees that he had decided not to open the store and canceled the contract. Voorhees had invested about $100,000 in the building. What should Voorhees do to recover his loss?

Law not only includes rules of conduct, but also the ways of enforcing those rules. Even if we had a perfect set of legal rules they would be meaningless without machinery for their enforcement. Under the civil law any enforcement of rights must generally be initiated and undertaken by the injured party through the courts. In the problem, Voorhees suffered a financial loss because Stewart refused to perform as agreed. This loss should fall on Stewart, not on Voorhees, but Stewart might refuse to pay for the loss unless compelled to do so by a court. Furthermore, the amount of money to be paid as damages would need to be determined. Thus, the means of enforcing the civil law and of insuring justice to persons whose rights have been violated is as important as the law itself. As discussed later, courts have been established for this purpose.

The steps in enforcing criminal law are somewhat different because crimes are considered to be offenses against the public or society. The injured party must appeal to the police or to the government office or agency with authority to take appropriate steps under the circumstances. Court action is then initiated and undertaken by the designated government officer. Government officers may also take steps in their own right to enforce the criminal law.

 Harvey telephoned the sheriff's office reporting that there was a prowler around his home in the country. Two officers were sent to Harvey's home and apprehended a man trying to break in. The man was arrested and taken to the county jail. Since this involved a crime, the district attorney's office would have to take the necessary steps to have him brought before a court for trial.

In the field of criminal law the three agencies concerned with law enforcement are the police officers, the prosecuting attorney's office (variously known as the district attorney or state attorney), and the courts. Their purpose is to maintain an environment of lawful order, to protect individuals from those who are either careless, negligent, or lawless, and generally to enforce the laws.

The structure of law enforcement agencies varies from state to state. The federal government has its own law enforcement agencies which include the F.B.I. (Federal Bureau of Investigation) and United States Marshalls, as well as other officers with specialized duties such as military police, customs officers, mail inspectors, narcotics officers, and immigration officials with limited police power. All federal officers enforce only federal laws but cooperate with each other and with state and local officials on request. The office of the U. S. Attorney General with U. S. District Attorneys throughout the country is responsible for prosecuting in federal courts those charged with violating federal law.

All states have a system of state police variously called state troopers, highway patrol, constabularies, rangers, or just state police. In addition, there are specialized officers, as in the federal government, with limited authority, such as fish and game wardens, park and forest rangers, and investigators for various agencies. State police officers enforce state laws although they may also have authority to enforce local laws and to cooperate with local authorities. Often state statutes and local ordinances are identical. Each state has an attorney general who has the responsibilities delegated to him by the state constitution and statutes.

At the local level there are two or three groups of police officers. Each county has a sheriff with deputies. A county sheriff normally

Unit II □ OUR LEGAL SYSTEM

has authority to enforce county ordinances and state statutes within the county, including the cities with their own police officers. By agreement they commonly leave all law enforcement within the cities to local police except when asked to cooperate. In some states all local jail facilities are operated by the sheriff. City police have authority to enforce state, county, and city laws only within the city limits. In some states, counties have other law enforcement officers known as constables whose authority is limited to enforcing all state and county laws within specified districts. Counties also have prosecuting attorneys, sometimes known as county or district attorneys, responsible for the prosecution of criminal cases. The local law enforcement officials are responsible for enforcing the state criminal statutes as well as the local ordinances. In some states there are city prosecuting attorneys as well as county or district attorneys, but their power and authority, like that of the city police, is limited to crimes committed within the city limits.

 On the complaint of a resident, Dainow was arrested by a city police officer who lived nearby for dumping garbage and rubbish beside a county highway, outside the city limits. In court, Dainow was found not guilty because he was arrested by an officer who had no power or authority outside the city limits.

Because many local officers are generally responsible for protecting people in their communities against all state and local crimes committed in their jurisdictions, close cooperation among law enforcement officials on the federal, state, and local levels is essential. The ease with which a criminal can flee beyond the jurisdiction where he committed the crime, even to another state or country, requires fast and efficient cooperation and communication among all law enforcement agencies. Telephone, teletype, and radio broadcasting networks link agencies together so that dangerous criminals can be quickly apprehended. Law enforcement officers at all levels and in different states also work together and exchange information in investigating crimes. As a result, when someone suspected of a crime in one state is apprehended in another state, it is usually possible to have him returned for trial by a process called *extradition*.

 Walker escaped from prison in Kansas and fled to Missouri. After the officers in that state were notified by the Kansas authorities, Walker was arrested. He could be returned to Kansas by an extradition proceeding.

WHY DO WE HAVE COURTS?

Problem: Leslie was cited by a police officer for making an improper U-turn at a street intersection. Leslie claimed there was no sign forbidding a U-turn at that intersection. The officer replied, "Sorry, you can tell it to the judge in court." Why is a court necessary?

A *court* is a tribunal established to administer justice. It may decide controversies properly brought before it, award damages, impose punishment for crimes, or grant other appropriate relief. It is obvious why we have courts to decide controversies in civil cases. In criminal cases, unless a person pleads guilty, it is always necessary for a court to decide whether the law has been violated, as in the problem. And, of course, if a person is found guilty or pleads guilty, the court must determine in the light of all the circumstances what punishment should be imposed. But equally important, it is essential that the rights of an accused party be protected.

A court consists not only of one or more judges, but also of attorneys, who are officers of the court, and others who are necessary for its operation. In legal writing the words "court" and "judge" are often used synonymously. While presiding over a legal action, the judge is usually referred to as "the court."

Courts vary in power and authority from justice of the peace and small claims courts to the supreme courts of the various states and the Supreme Court of the United States. State courts have power to hear cases involving violation of the state laws and between citizens of the state and, under certain circumstances, between citizens of that state and some other state. Federal courts have power to hear civil and criminal cases involving federal law, proceedings specifically referred to in the Constitution, and actions such as those brought by citizens of one state against those of another when the amount involved is $10,000 or more.

Gulaskey had a right of action against Bathgate for $15,000 for a breach of contract. Both were residents of Florida. Gulaskey would have to sue Bathgate in a Florida court.

Jurisdiction is the power of a court to hear controversies, to determine the rights and obligations of parties, and to enforce its orders. The jurisdiction of a court is always limited in territory, and it may be limited to controversies of a particular kind. Some courts have jurisdiction to review cases that are appealed. Most have original jurisdiction only, that is, they have authority only to hear a case when it is first brought into court.

WHAT IS OUR SYSTEM OF COURTS?

Problem: Dukes imported some antiques which he claimed were over one hundred years old and therefore were exempt from import duties. The Collector of Customs disagreed and refused to admit them without payment of the assessed duty. Did Dukes have any recourse from the Collector's ruling?

As stated on page 6, there are 51 legal systems in our country. Each state has a system of courts for the enforcement of its laws, and the federal government (including the District of Columbia) has a system of courts to enforce its laws.

(1) FEDERAL COURTS

The United States Constitution (Article III, Section 1) provides: "The judicial power of the United States shall be vested in one Supreme Court, and such inferior courts as the Congress shall from time to time ordain and establish." The Supreme Court's decisions with respect to federal law are final, and such decisions may affect the powers of government and rights of the people. This court

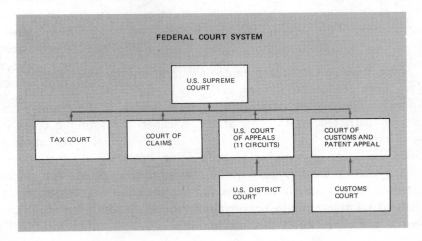

FEDERAL COURT SYSTEM

consists of nine judges, called justices of the Supreme Court. The presiding judge is the Chief Justice.

Congress has from time to time created other federal courts subordinate to the Supreme Court. In addition to the Supreme Court, the present federal court system includes district courts, courts of appeal, the customs court, the court of customs and patent appeal, the court of claims, and the tax court. In the problem, Duke could appeal the ruling of the Collector of Customs to the customs court.

(2) STATE AND MUNICIPAL COURTS

The systems of courts in the different states are organized along similar lines. Each state ordinarily has (a) a supreme court; (b) county, circuit, superior, or district courts having original jurisdiction over important cases; and (c) justice of the peace courts with original jurisdiction over minor cases. Many states also have intermediate courts of appeals.

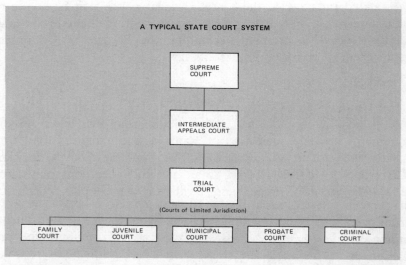

A TYPICAL STATE COURT SYSTEM

SUPREME COURT

INTERMEDIATE APPEALS COURT

TRIAL COURT

(Courts of Limited Jurisdiction)

FAMILY COURT — JUVENILE COURT — MUNICIPAL COURT — PROBATE COURT — CRIMINAL COURT

Some states use different names for their courts. For example, in New York the court of final authority is the New York Court of Appeals; whereas the original trial court, which is the county, circuit, or district court in other states, is called the supreme court in New York. The trial court or the court of original jurisdiction is called the court of common pleas in some states.

Many cities have police, traffic, or municipal courts for minor offenses. Some states have courts for special cases, as, for example, criminal courts, probate or surrogate courts, juvenile or children's courts, and courts of domestic relations.

Cline owed Bollum $75 for some bricks Bollum had sold him, but Cline failed to pay him. The state Bollum lived in has a small claims court in which actions for $300 or less can be filed. The cost of filing is nominal, each party may represent himself, and the proceedings are conducted informally. Bollum, therefore, filed his suit against Cline in a small claims court.

An action is usually filed in the lowest court of original jurisdiction available for the action. The decision in most cases may be appealed to the next higher court and, unless the state supreme court has already ruled on the issues involved, an appeal may be taken to that court. The decision of the supreme court of a state is final in all cases not involving the Federal Constitution, federal laws, or treaties. Cases that involve these rights may be reviewed by the Supreme Court of the United States.

HOW DOES A JUVENILE COURT DIFFER FROM OTHERS?

Problem: Scott, age 15, was detained by the police for shoplifting and referred to the juvenile court. Would he be treated differently there from the way he would be in a criminal court for adults?

All states have provided by law for juvenile courts to assume special jurisdiction of minors—persons under the age of 21. They are often called *juveniles*. In most states the jurisdiction extends only to persons under age 18, and all states provide that for certain crimes and under certain conditions the juvenile court may transfer a minor or juvenile of specified age, such as 16 or 18, to the jurisdiction of a criminal court to be tried as an adult. This is usually done when it is determined that the minor has the intelligence and moral perception to distinguish between right and wrong and to understand the legal consequences of his acts sufficiently to be treated, prosecuted, and convicted as an adult. However, a criminal court usually has jurisdiction of a minor accused of murder. Regular courts are used when a minor is involved in a tort or other civil action.

The juvenile court is a court of special and limited jurisdiction designed to look after the interests of minors who get into trouble or do not have parents to take care of them. The court protects minors generally from the results of their own immaturity and may serve as the guardian of children who are abandoned, orphaned, or incapable of self-support. They are not treated as criminals unless transferred to another court. A major function of the juvenile courts is to treat a minor in trouble with the law as a delinquent child. Its purpose is to provide guidance, rehabilitation, and reform rather than fix criminal responsibility, guilt, and punishment. Accordingly, in the problem, Scott would not be treated as an adult but would be entitled to a hearing that would take his age and immaturity into consideration. A *delinquent* child is variously defined by statute, but in general this means he is a child under a specified age who violates any law, is *incorrigible* (meaning ungovernable or uncontrollable), immoral, repeatedly runs away from home, is truant from school, or is growing up in idleness and crime. He may be an "abused" child but not necessarily neglected or dependent.

 A juvenile court decided that a ten-year-old girl was abused and delinquent because she was growing up in a home where narcotic drugs were regularly used and "pot" parties were frequently held. In accordance with the law the court brought the girl under its jurisdiction and placed her in a foster home.

For a minor or juvenile who is in trouble for violating the law there are many advantages in being under the jurisdiction of a juvenile court rather than a regular criminal court. The juvenile normally is not "arrested" and "booked" and "jailed"; he is "detained" or "taken into custody" and "confined." Under the laws of most states, if he is under age 17 or 18, he is supposed to be taken to a detention facility rather than a jail. Some states provide that juveniles 16 to 18 years of age taken into custody are not to be confined with persons convicted of a crime or awaiting trial on criminal charges. If the juvenile is declared delinquent, the record is not open to the public. As pointed out in Chapter 3, certain laws apply to minors only—and these are in addition to the laws all people must obey.

Hearings in juvenile courts are much different from those in other courts. There is no "trial" in the usual sense, and the proceedings are very informal, not open to the public, and usually held in the office of the judge or in a conference room. The parents are required to be present and an attorney may or may not be in attendance. The juvenile, as an accused person, is entitled to an attorney and all other constitutional rights as discussed earlier. The purpose of the hearing is to determine whether the juvenile is guilty of the offense, why the law was violated, and what should be done so such acts will not occur in the future. Accordingly, specialists such as a psychologist, social worker, and physician may be in attendance.

The hearing includes presentation of the evidence and discussion with the accused minor, his parents, and others concerned. If the minor is found guilty of the offense, the judge will decide what should be done. Statutes give the court wide discretion and considerable latitude in making its determinations. If the court declares the juvenile to be delinquent, it will either place him on probation or order him to be confined in a detention home or other facility. *Probation* allows a person to be at liberty under supervision with an opportunity to prove that he can be trusted to obey the law and not get into further trouble. A minor may be released to his parents if it is a first offense, or he may be placed under the supervision of a probation officer or the care of a social agency. If the offense is serious or the offender has been in trouble before or is incorrigible, the court may order him confined in a local detention home for a certain length of time or placed in a state school under closer supervision. When a court determines that a minor is delinquent, it may retain jurisdiction over him until the minor reaches his majority. If the minor is sent to a state school, the court usually transfers jurisdiction to the state authority that operates the school. This authority then has the power to release the offender on probation when it believes he is ready to be returned to his home and given his liberty.

WHAT IS THE PROCEDURE IN A CRIMINAL ACTION?

Problem: Holt was suspected of failing to file and pay his income tax, a criminal offense. What steps must the government take to determine whether Holt committed a crime?

As we have learned, a *criminal action* refers to a court proceeding by the state, or "people," against a person accused of a crime. Under our system of law a person is presumed to be innocent until guilt is proven in a competent court, or is admitted. Thus, in the problem, if Holt does not admit failing to file and pay his income tax, the government must prove him guilty in a court.

Codes or laws of procedure specify in detail the conduct of a trial to assure fairness and the protection of the rights of the person accused—in short, due process. Each state has its own system, and the procedures vary.

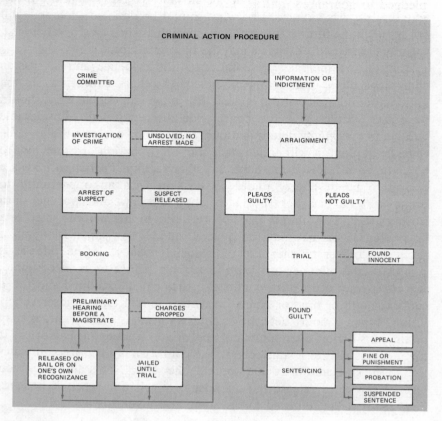

CRIMINAL ACTION PROCEDURE

Unless an arresting officer apprehends a person committing a crime, the first step is an investigation to determine who is believed to have committed the crime that has been reported. Such investigation continues to obtain evidence to present in court. Under some circumstances a warrant must be issued by a court for the suspected person to be placed under arrest. Upon his arrest, he is supposed to be advised of his constitutional rights, "booked" (fingerprinted and photographed), and the police record is checked to determine whether he has been in trouble with the police before. As part of the investigation the arrested person may then be questioned by both the police and prosecuting attorney, but he is advised that he has the right to keep silent, that if he does speak, anything he says may be held against him, and that he may have an attorney present during the questioning. After booking, the suspect appears before a judge who determines whether he shall be kept in jail or released on a bail bond. _Bail_ is a sum of money or property deposited or pledged to guarantee that the arrested person will appear for a preliminary hearing or trial. If he cannot put up bail or find a friend to do so, a professional bondsman may put up the bail for a fee. Otherwise the accused person must remain in jail. Except for the most serious cases, judges usually release suspects on bail. If the person does not appear for trial, the bail is forfeited to the state and a warrant is issued for his arrest. In some cases, the accused is released on his own _recognizance_, meaning that he promises to appear as scheduled without putting up bail.

For many misdemeanors, including most traffic violations, the arresting officer may give the offending person a summons. This is a notice specifying the offense and directing the person to appear in court at a specified time or to pay a prescribed fine.

A formal accusation, known as a _complaint_ (or information), is then filed by the prosecutor. In some states and the federal government an _indictment_ is required by a _grand jury_ (a group of citizens selected to hear the evidence of the prosecution) before a person can be brought to trial for a felony or a capital crime such as murder. An indictment declares there is good reason to try a certain person for a specified crime. If a person is held on an information or complaint, he is given a preliminary hearing before a judge to determine from the evidence whether he should be held, "bound over," for trial as charged. The accused person after the filing of the formal charge is the _defendant_—the person against whom the action is brought. The state in a criminal action is known as the _prosecution._

Before the trial the defendant is brought before the court to hear the formal charges or indictment and required to plead guilty or not guilty. This is known as _arraignment._ If the defendant pleads guilty, the prosecution ends and the defendant is sentenced. If he pleads not guilty, he must stand trial.

WHAT IS THE PROCEDURE IN A CIVIL ACTION?

> **Problem:** Paulson owed Turner $15,000 which he did not pay when it was due. How would Turner go about getting payment?

When a person has been injured by the wrongful conduct of another, he must be able to obtain relief afforded through the courts. He may set the machinery of law in motion by having a lawyer bring a civil action or suit as Turner could do in the problem. A *civil action* is a proceeding by one party against another for the purpose of enforcing the former's rights in a court.

A civil action involves two parties. Each of these parties may consist of one or more persons. The one who brings the legal action is the *plaintiff;* the one against whom it is brought is the defendant.

> Baird and Hayes negligently ran their motor boat near a beach area and injured Moon who was swimming. Moon brought an action to collect for personal injuries and for doctor and hospital bills. Moon was the plaintiff, Baird and Hayes, the defendants.

In state courts a civil action is commenced by the filing of the plaintiff's complaint or petition with the clerk of the court. This is usually done by the attorney for the plaintiff. The complaint sets forth the cause of the action, and states the claims of the plaintiff. In order for the court to have the right and power to act, it must have jurisdiction and the defendant must be properly served with a *summons* or court order and a copy of the complaint. In some states, the complaint itself is served on the defendant thereby eliminating the summons. The summons directs the defendant or his attorney to answer the complaint, or to appear and show why judgment should not be rendered against him. If the defendant does not answer the complaint within the time allowed (generally not more than 20 days), the plaintiff may win the case by default and a judgment is entered in his favor.

In the problem at the beginning of this topic, Turner, the plaintiff, must file a complaint with the appropriate court. A summons would then be issued directing Paulson to answer the complaint.

After an action has been started, the parties must reduce the controversy to definite issues that are to be tried. This is done by filing with the court a series of statements, called *pleadings,* seeking to support the cause of the action or to defeat it.

The first statement of the facts is in the plaintiff's complaint. The defendant files his *answer,* a statement in reply, in which he may do any one of several things:

(1) Declare that the facts alleged, if true, do not constitute a wrong for which he has any liability. This is an issue of law.

(2) Deny the truth of the facts stated in the complaint. This raises an issue of fact.

(3) Admit the facts alleged, but set up other facts that excuse him from liability.

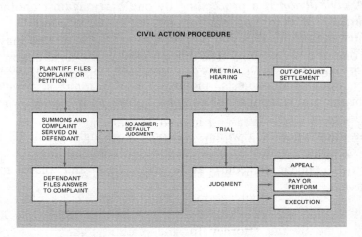

CIVIL ACTION PROCEDURE

After the parties have reduced their controversy to one or more issues by means of the pleadings as above, a pre-trial hearing is held in an attempt to resolve the differences without going to court. Should this prove to be unsuccessful, a date is set for the trial. If the defendant does not appear or answer, the plaintiff must prove his complaint to the satisfaction of the court before receiving judgment.

HOW IS A CASE TRIED?

> **Problem:** McCorkle was given a citation by the State Highway Patrol for reckless driving. During the legal proceedings, he pleaded not guilty. How would the facts and McCorkle's guilt or innocence be determined?

Issues of fact in a case are normally determined by a jury unless there has been a waiver of a right to trial by jury. Issues of law are decided by the judge. *A trial jury* is a body of disinterested citizens (usually 12) selected to determine questions of fact. The jury is usually selected from lists of voters or tax rolls. The method of selection varies from state to state, but usually involves a three-step process. Lists of prospective jurors are prepared, and from these lists a panel of prospective jurors is selected, generally by lot or at random. For the panel the attorneys for the plaintiff and defendant have the right to examine prospective jurors and to reject any number for good cause such as close relationship by birth or marriage to one of the parties. The attorneys may also reject a limited number of prospective jurors without good cause. Jurors are sworn to render their verdict fairly, impartially, and without bias.

After the jury has been selected and sworn, the attorneys outline briefly what each side intends to prove and the important parts of the evidence to be offered. Evidence is then presented to the jury first by the plaintiff and then by the defendant. *Evidence* includes any means used to prove or disprove the alleged facts. It may consist of written documents, objects, pictures, or of *testimony,* which consists of the oral statements of persons, known as *witnesses,* who have knowledge of the facts.

The attendance of a witness in court is brought about by means of a *subpoena,* which is a written order commanding the named person to appear in court at a given time and place to give testimony.

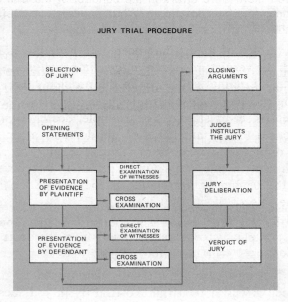

JURY TRIAL PROCEDURE

SELECTION OF JURY

OPENING STATEMENTS

PRESENTATION OF EVIDENCE BY PLAINTIFF

DIRECT EXAMINATION OF WITNESSES

CROSS EXAMINATION

PRESENTATION OF EVIDENCE BY DEFENDANT

DIRECT EXAMINATION OF WITNESSES

CROSS EXAMINATION

CLOSING ARGUMENTS

JUDGE INSTRUCTS THE JURY

JURY DELIBERATION

VERDICT OF JURY

Summers, waiting for a bus, observed a two-car collision in which Wiffler made a left turn without signalling and was struck by a pick-up truck driven by Talley. If there should be a legal action as a result of this accident, Summers could be subpoenaed as a witness by either side and required, under oath, to tell the truth as to what he observed.

Following presentation of the evidence, the attorneys summarize and argue the case before the jury, if there is one, and the judge.

The judge then instructs the jury with respect to the rules and principles of law governing the issues before them. The jury retires for private discussion and deliberation in order to reach a verdict. The *verdict* is the decision of the jury with respect to the facts, and it requires an unanimous vote in criminal cases. In some states, under certain conditions, a verdict can often be brought in if most of the jurors agree, for example nine. In the problem, McCorkle's guilt or innocence would be determined using the above procedures.

WHO RENDERS THE JUDGMENT?

Problem: Bettencourt was tried on a charge of conspiracy and found guilty by a jury and sentenced by the judge. He believed there were errors in the conduct of the trial and that the verdict was not proper. What recourse does Bettencourt have?

After the verdict of a jury has been returned, the judge, in accordance with the verdict, renders a *judgment,* which is the final result of the trial. In a criminal action, as in the problem, the judgment is the sentencing or other punishment, such as a fine. For some crimes the punishment is set by statute. For example, death (*capital punishment*) is decreed for certain kinds of murder and other crimes, although in a diminishing number of states. Flogging or whipping is still a punishment in one state. Other penalties include revoking a license that the defendant may hold, as to practice medicine or to engage in the sale of alcoholic beverages. Forfeiture of the right to vote or hold public office is generally part of the punishment for a felony. The judge may use considerable discretion in determining the punishment and will take into consideration any recommendations that a jury may make. In a few states the jury determines the punishment. A convicted person may be ordered confined for a specified time in prison, or in jail for misdemeanors, or fined, or both. Under some circumstances the judge may suspend the sentence and place the convicted person on probation. The suspended sentence may be revoked and the punishment carried out if the convicted person does not conduct himself properly.

In a civil action the judgment usually requires the loser to pay the costs of the trial, but ordinarily each party pays his own attorney's fees.

Generally a judgment of a lower court is not final as to the rights of the parties. Either of the parties is ordinarily entitled to have the case reviewed for errors by a higher court. You recall that issues of law are decided by the judge. If either party believes the judge did not rule properly on such issues, he may appeal to a higher court claiming errors. Thus, Bettencourt, in the problem, can appeal the decision to a higher court.

When an appeal is made, the higher court may find that an important material error was made during the trial in the lower court, such as incorrect instructions to the jury or the admission of evidence that should have been rejected. In such an event the court may modify or reverse the judgment of the lower court or order a new trial. If there is no error in the record, the reviewing court will affirm the judgment of the lower court, in which event the rights of the parties are decided. If the reviewing court is not the highest court, either party may again appeal the case. If the case involves a U. S. Constitutional problem, it may be appealed to the federal courts after the the remedies in the states courts have been exhausted.

HOW IS A JUDGMENT SATISFIED?

Problem: The Internal Revenue Service and Jenkins disagreed regarding the amount of income tax Jenkins owed. After I.R.S. assessed the amount due and the agency appeals board affirmed the tax assessed, Jenkins appealed to the Tax Court which gave judgment to I.R.S. What steps must the I.R.S. take to collect on the judgment?

Ordinarily, when judgment becomes final, the loser will pay or arrange to pay the amount or perform any other requirements of the judgment. If he does not pay, the plaintiff may obtain a writ of execution. *Execution* is the process by which a judgment for money is enforced. The court commands the sheriff, or other officer, to seize and sell the defendant's property and to apply the proceeds, after deducting the costs of the sale, to the satisfaction of the judgment. Certain property, however, is exempt. Thus, in the problem I.R.S. could get a writ of execution if Jenkins did not pay.

If the defendant has no property over and above the amount that is exempt, nothing will be obtained and the judgment will remain unsatisfied. The judgment remains in force, however, for a period of time fixed by statute. If within that time the debtor acquires any property above that which is exempt, it is subject to seizure and sale for the purpose of satisfying the judgment.

In felony criminal actions the punishment is confinement in a state prison or other similar institution. The statutes of most states provide for variable sentences, for example, one to ten years or five years to life. Thus, if a prisoner is making good progress toward rehabilitation, a recognized function of most penal institutions, he may be placed on *parole* or released before the maximum sentence is completed. When one is paroled he is released conditionally and placed under the supervision of a probation officer, and if he gets into trouble again or violates the conditions of his parole during the life of his sentence, he is returned to prison. If he is released because of a reduction in sentence, the sentence cannot be restored because of misconduct. All states have provisions for the governor to grant pardons to a convicted person or to commute the sentence by making it less severe, as, for example, reducing a death sentence to life imprisonment. The President has the same power for federal offenses.

IF STOPPED BY THE POLICE . . .

1. Stay calm; never argue or physically resist. There should be no resistance by word or force.
2. Ask what the charge is.
3. Get names and addresses of witnesses if any are present.
4. Get the names and badge numbers of the arresting officers.
5. After identifying yourself, if the charge is serious and the officer plans to arrest you, talk only to your attorney about your case.
6. Remember that you are entitled to make a limited number of telephone calls within a few hours after your arrest.
7. If you are under 21, telephone your parents first. If you can't reach them, call an attorney or a close adult friend.

YOUR LEGAL VOCABULARY

answer	execution	pleadings
arraignment	extradition	probation
bail	grand jury	prosecution
capital punishment	incorrigible	recognizance
civil action	indictment	subpoena
complaint (or information)	judgment	summons
court	jurisdiction	testimony
criminal action	juvenile	trial jury
defendant	parole	verdict
delinquent	plaintiff	witness
evidence		

1. The decision of a jury with respect to the facts of a trial.
2. A series of statements seeking to support a cause of action or to defeat it.
3. Oral statements of witnesses.
4. A tribunal established to administer justice.
5. A person who has knowledge of the facts.

6. The power of a court to hear and decide controversies.
7. Incorrigible; a child under a specified age who violates any law.
8. A written order commanding a person to appear in court and give testimony.
9. The one who brings a legal action against another.
10. After conviction, the privilege of being at liberty conditionally under supervision rather than serving the sentence.

REMEMBER THESE HIGHLIGHTS

1. Law not only includes rules of conduct, but also provides the ways of enforcing those rules. Any set of rules would be meaningless without machinery for their enforcement.
2. Civil law is enforced through the courts on the initiative of an injured party. The criminal law is enforced through the courts by the police or the district or prosecuting attorney on their initiative, usually on request of a victimized individual.
3. The federal government and each state have separate court systems. A court has no power over matters outside of its jurisdiction.
4. Legal actions are either civil actions in which one party brings suit against another, or criminal actions in which the state brings the action.
5. All states provide for juvenile courts with special jurisdiction limited to those under the age 18 or 21. These courts are conducted with less formality than other courts and emphasize rehabilitation of offenders.
6. Juvenile courts treat minors, who commit offenses that would be crimes if they were adults, as delinquents. Delinquency is not a crime. Delinquent children are deemed to be in need of rehabilitation and guidance rather than punishment.
7. A criminal action is started by filing an information or indictment by the prosecuting attorney. The defendant must plead guilty or not guilty to the charges. A civil action is commenced by filing a complaint. The controversy must be reduced to issues by means of pleadings.
8. Members of a trial jury should be disinterested, should not be biased or prejudiced, and should be able to vote impartially in reaching a verdict.
9. Evidence may include documents, objects, pictures, or testimony.
10. Witnesses who have knowledge of the facts in a case may be commanded by subpoenas to appear in court and give testimony.
11. A judgment may ordinarily be appealed to a higher court. Judgment in a criminal action is sentencing by the judge. In a civil action, if a judgment for money is not satisfied, the defendant's non-exempt property may be seized and sold to pay it. If any party to a legal action is dissatisfied with the verdict or judgment and can show errors in the trial, he may appeal to a higher court.

LAW AS PEOPLE LIVE IT

1. Allen was suspected of committing a crime in the state of Connecticut. A bulletin was sent to neighboring states, and Allen was apprehended in Massachusetts. Could he be returned to Connecticut?
2. Wadleigh, on what he thought would be a short errand, left his car in a fifteen-minute zone. He was away longer than the zone allowed and received a citation ordering him to appear in court. Will this be a state or municipal court?
3. Flaherty entered into a contract with Schuett to paint an apartment building owned by Flaherty. Schuett refused to perform and it cost Flaherty $4,000 more to have the building painted, so he brought an action against Schuett. Was this a civil or criminal action? What would be the result if Schuett ignored the complaint?
4. Jager was habitually running away from home and was continuously truant from school. Can he be placed under the jurisdiction of a juvenile court as a delinquent child?
5. Kinsey, a seven-year-old-girl, was neglected by her parents, both of whom worked. Can she be declared a delinquent child and taken away from her parents by being made a ward of the juvenile court?
6. Cleaver was arrested for bribery. What were his rights at the time of his arrest and booking?
7. Kahn was arrested for disturbing the peace. Must he remain in jail until his trial?
8. Bennett was found guilty by a jury of commiting a felony. What choices would the judge have in passing sentence on him?
9. Yost, plaintiff in a civil action, was denied judgment. He believed that several errors had been made during the trial. Was the judgment final?
10. Corder was awarded a judgment of $4,500 against Monson. If Monson failed to pay it, what could Corder do?

LAW AS COURTS DECIDE IT

1. This is an action to recover $6,837.50 paid by Allstate Insurance Company to the owners of a store building for damage caused by fire. The fire was set to some boxes and cartons piled close to the building by two boys 13 and 14 years of age. The fire spread to the building and damaged it. The defendant boys claimed they were not liable for the damage because they were too young to have intent to do wrong and that their conduct was that of teenagers of the same age, education, and experience. Is that a good defense? (Allstate Fire Insurance Company v. Singler, 9 Ohio App. 2d 102, 233 N.E. 2d 65)
2. McAlpine, a minor, was found by the Juvenile Court to be a delinquent child and was committed to the Texas Youth Council. He was then

placed on probation with an uncle. Several months later the Juvenile Court revoked the probation and ordered the boy to be transferred to the Gatesville School for Boys. Texas law provides that when a child has been committed to the control of the Texas Youth Council, the Juvenile Court has no authority to modify or revoke its previous orders. Under these circumstances did the Juvenile Court act within its rights in revoking McAlpine's probation and committing him to the Gatesville School for Boys? (McAlpine v. State, 457 S.W. 2d 426, Texas)

3. Kent, a 16-year-old boy, was taken into custody by the police of Washington, D.C., held, and questioned about breaking into an apartment, stealing a wallet, and raping the occupant. He admitted the offenses and volunteered information as to several similar offenses. At the time he was on probation for housebreaking and attempted purse snatching. Under the Juvenile Court Act any child 16 years of age or older who is charged with an offense which in the case of an adult would be a felony may have his case transferred to the District Court after full investigation by the Juvenile Court judge. The Juvenile Court waived its jurisdiction in the case of Kent, and he was properly tried and found guilty by a jury in the District Court. Kent, admitting through his attorney that the court had the right to waive its jurisdiction after a full investigation, claimed nevertheless that the Juvenile Court had acted in an arbitrary manner and denied him due process by transferring him to the jurisdiction of the District Court without a hearing at which he was present and without stating its reasons for so doing. Was the court within its rights in waiving jurisdiction after full investigation without a hearing? (Kent v. United States, 86 S. Ct. 1045, 383 U.S. 541)

4. Everly, a citizen of the United States and of West Virginia, was summoned to serve on the grand jury being empaneled by the Circuit Court. He refused to serve and announced in open court that he had "personal conscientious objections" to such service. At a later hearing the judge found Everly guilty of contempt of court for refusing to serve on a grand jury and sentenced him to ten days in jail. At the hearings he testified that his objections were religious, that he was an ordained minister, and that he felt that as an ambassador of God he was violating his religious convictions by serving as a juror. Everly declared he would rather go to jail than serve as a juror. Under these circumstances was Everly in contempt of Court? (State v. Everly, 146 S.E. 2d 705, W. Va.)

5. Defendant Castone was convicted of forgery, given a suspended sentence, and placed on probation under a condition that he leave the county. Later Castone returned to the county and attempted to pass another bad check. Upon being arrested the court revoked Castone's probation. He claimed the court had no authority to "banish" him from the county as a condition of probation. Did the court abuse its discretion? (State v. Castone, 10 Ariz. App. 411, 459 P. 2d 328)

UNIT THREE

Contracts

UNIT THREE

In our relations with other people we frequently make agreements. Most of these pertain to matters that are not very important or involve social obligations that are not enforceable by law. Other agreements are made with the mutual intention of creating legal obligations which may require payments of money extended over long periods of time. Agreements made with a mutual intent to create legal obligations are called contracts.

To be binding, a contract must be the result of a genuine offer and acceptance by competent parties made freely and voluntarily in an atmosphere of honesty and fair dealing. There must also be consideration, which is what one person asks another to give or do in return for the former's promise. Even if the parties reach a mutual agreement, it does not necessarily follow that a contract results. Certain kinds of agreements are illegal or unenforceable.

Although most contracts are discharged when the parties fulfill their obligations as agreed, some are discharged because of special events and circumstances. If the obligations of the contract are not met, the injured party may seek certain remedies prescribed by law.

Almost everyone enters into contracts in the course of everyday life. Business can be conducted as it is today only because contractual promises are carried out. Because everyone enters many business transactions involving contracts, the related rights and obligations should be understood in order to avoid trouble.

As you study the units which follow, observe that almost all business law consists of rules which govern contracts.

CHAPTER 7 How Contracts Are Made

1. *You write a letter asking the price of a build-it-yourself motor scooter kit; Zip-by Motors sends you the kit and a bill. Must you pay for the kit?*

2. *Your neighbor tells you that a friend of his has lost his dog and is publicly offering a reward for its return. If you find the dog, can you collect the reward?*

3. *Without reading it, your father signs a contract to buy a car. Later he finds that he has agreed to buy more accessories than he had intended. Can he be held to the contract?*

HOW ARE CONTRACTS MADE?

Problem: Herbert phoned Young, saying, "I hear you want a business law book. I'll sell you mine for $4.00." Was a contract made?

A *contract* is a legally binding agreement—one that is enforceable by law. This agreement results from an exchange of acts, or of promises to do or not to do certain things. In many contracts, one person makes a promise in return for a counter-promise; a home-owner may offer to pay a painter in exchange for the painter's offer to paint the house. In other cases, a promise is made to do something in return for the performance of an act; a person may promise a reward for the return of lost property. In each case, the *offeror* must make a definite offer; the one to whom the offer is made, the *offeree,* must accept the offer exactly as it was made to him. Without both offer and acceptance, there is no agreement; when there is no agreement, as in the problem, there is no contract.

▶ Clayton and Tidyman were admiring Tidyman's sailboat one day when Clayton asked Tidyman how much the boat was worth. When Tidyman replied, "Nine hundred dollars," Clayton immediately said, "I'll take it at that price." No contract was formed because

Tidyman was merely stating his estimate of the boat's value; he was not making an offer. Actually, Clayton was the offeror and Tidyman the offeree. If Tidyman accepted Clayton's offer to buy the boat for $900, there would have been the necessary agreement.

WHAT ARE THE REQUIREMENTS OF AN OFFER?

Problem: Bolt's Bootery advertised a sale of "name brand" suede shoes. Mooradian offered to purchase two pairs of the shoes at the advertised price but Bolt refused to sell them to him, claiming that the ad was not an offer. Do you agree?

An _offer_ is a proposal that expresses, or appears to express, the willingness of the offeror to enter into a legally binding agreement. Generally, to be an offer, a proposal must be:

1. Intended to create a legal obligation;
2. Definite and certain; and
3. Communicated to the offeree.

(1) AN OFFER MUST BE INTENDED TO CREATE A LEGAL OBLIGATION

The offeror must intend, or must appear to a reasonable man to intend, that his proposal will create a legal obligation if it is accepted. People often make agreements that are not expected to be legally enforced. For example, if two persons agree to attend a party together on a certain evening, no contract is intended or formed. If one of the persons does not keep the date, the other may be offended but he can not sue. He has no legal remedy—that is, courts will not enforce his right to have the other person do as he promised—because a social invitation is not intended to create a legal obligation.

Even some things which appear to be offers are not. Before making a contract, the parties will often discuss or negotiate to reach acceptable terms; one party may indicate a willingness to consider certain terms without making a legal offer. For example, newspaper and magazine advertisements, advertisements sent by mail, form letters, radio and TV ads, and similar announcements are all generally held to be in the nature of preliminary negotiations. They are invitations to others to make offers, and not offers in themselves.

A person who advertises something for sale cannot be expected to sell to everyone who replies to the advertisement; perhaps he has only one or a limited number of items for sale. Thus, when Mooradian answered the advertisement and proposed to buy the shoes at the advertised price, he was the offeror, not Bolt.

If an advertisement is sufficiently definite and clear, however, and is worded in such a way as to give a reasonable man cause to believe it is an offer rather than a mere invitation to make an offer, it may be held that acceptance forms a contract.

When a reasonable man would recognize that a certain statement is made in jest or in the heat of anger, the statement cannot be turned into a contract by an acceptance. This is because: (a) the person making the statement does not intend to be bound by it; and (b) the person to whom the statement is made should know that an offer is not intended—that the person making the statement is joking or "blowing off steam."

A statement made in jest or anger can, however, be an offer that is binding on the person making it if the other person reasonably believes that it is intended to be an offer.

(2) AN OFFER MUST BE DEFINITE AND CERTAIN

Problem: Embree wired Piersol "Offer 1000 boxes No. 1 Elberta peaches. Immediate delivery. Wire reply." Was this offer sufficiently definite to make a contract if Piersol accepted?

If a proposal is vague or incomplete, a court may not enforce it. Terms must be definite enough to allow the court to determine what was intended by the parties, and to fix their legal rights and duties. However, all the terms need not be stated in the offer. Some may be implied, as were those in the problem. Embree's offer implied that the price was the market price, and that payment would be made according to the custom of the trade or by law.

(3) AN OFFER MUST BE COMMUNICATED TO THE OFFEREE

Problem: McColm, the circulation manager of *Dawn,* a weekly magazine, frequently conducted contests to encourage independent subscription solicitors to greater production. On November 15, he posted a notice announcing a 10-day all-expense-paid trip to Hawaii for the solicitor selling the most subscriptions in the next 60 days. Eichen, who had not heard about the contest, turned in the most subscriptions during that time period. Was he legally entitled to the trip?

A person cannot accept an offer without knowing about it; obviously there is nothing he can accept. For instance, the offer of a reward that is made to the general public generally cannot be accepted by a party who has not heard or seen the offer. Another example is shown in the problem. Most courts require that anyone carrying out the terms of such an offer must know of the offer in order to make an acceptance and claim the reward. Accordingly, Eichen was not entitled to the prize because he had not known of the offer before he turned in the subscriptions.

A few states make an exception in the case of reward offers, and hold anyone fulfilling the offer's terms may claim the reward.

HOW IS AN OFFER ENDED?

Problem: On June 3, Posey sent a letter to Mortimer offering to lend him $10,000 and stating that the acceptance must be received no later than 5 p.m., June 10. Mortimer posted his acceptance on June 9, but the letter was delayed and did not arrive until June 12. Did it still operate as an acceptance?

A valid acceptance will naturally end an offer because a contract has resulted. But an offer may also be terminated without any contract arising:

1. At the time stated in the offer;
2. At the end of a reasonable length of time if the offer does not state how long it will remain open;
3. By a rejection of the offer by the offeree;
4. When the offeree makes a counteroffer;

5. If it is withdrawn by the offeror before the offeree has accepted;
6. By the insanity or death of the offeror or offeree.

(1) AN OFFER ENDS AT THE TIME THAT IS STATED IN THE OFFER

In making an offer, the offeror may state how or when the offer must be accepted. Since Posey, in the problem, did not receive Mortimer's reply by the time specified, it did not constitute an acceptance.

(2) IF THE OFFER DOES NOT STATE HOW LONG IT WILL REMAIN OPEN, IT TERMINATES AT THE END OF A REASONABLE LENGTH OF TIME

Problem: Schramm telephoned Kruger one morning and offered to sell him 40 crates of asparagus at a certain price. Kruger said he would let Schramm know. Schramm then phoned Coffey and made an offer to sell him a used tractor. Like Kruger, Coffey replied he would have to let him know later. How long would these offers remain open?

What is considered to be a reasonable length of time depends entirely upon the circumstances. In the problem, if the offer to sell the asparagus was not accepted quickly, it would terminate because of the perishable nature of the produce. The offer to sell the used tractor would be effective for a longer time.

(3) AN OFFER ENDS WHEN IT IS REJECTED BY THE OFFEREE

Problem: Irving offered to sell Davis some skis for $80, but Davis replied, "No, too much." The next day Davis called Irving and said he had changed his mind and would accept the offer. Was a contract formed?

If the offeree rejects the offer, it is terminated even though the time the offeror agreed to keep the offer open has not expired. Thus, Davis' refusal to accept Irving's offer ended it. When Davis changed his mind, he became the offeror in a new offer.

(4) THE ORIGINAL OFFER ENDS WHEN THE OFFEREE MAKES A COUNTEROFFER

Problem: Pardee offered to sell Dodd six acres of land for $5,000. Dodd said he'd pay $4,000. When Pardee refused, Dodd said, "O.K. I'll pay $5,000." Did this create a contract?

When an offeree accepts an offer, he must accept it exactly as it was made. If he varies or qualifies the offeror's proposal in any way, the result is a _counteroffer_. In making a counteroffer, as in the problem, the offeree says in legal effect, "I refuse your offer; here is my counteroffer." Thus, a counteroffer not only terminates the original offer; it also immediately becomes a new offer. The original offer cannot be accepted by the offeree after a counteroffer has been made unless the original offer is renewed by the offeror. Thus, no contract was made in the problem.

(5) THE OFFER IS USUALLY ENDED IF IT IS REVOKED BY THE OFFEROR BEFORE THE OFFEREE HAS ACCEPTED

> **Problem:** McNeil offered to sell to Haller ten tons of first quality raisins. Before Haller had accepted the offer, McNeil found that half of the raisins were damaged by mildew. He thereupon telephoned Haller and told him he would be able to sell only five tons. Was McNeil entitled to change his offer without liability?

An offeror may ordinarily revoke or modify his offer at any time before it has been accepted even though he may have stated that the offer would remain open for a definite longer time. Thus McNeil, in the problem, could modify his offer to Haller. Withdrawing an offer before it is accepted is known as the right of _revocation_. A modification or revocation is not effective until it is communicated to the offeree or received at his mailing address.

(6) THE INSANITY OR THE DEATH OF THE OFFEROR OR OFFEREE TERMINATES AN OFFER

> Wilkinson offered to sell Nelson his cabin cruiser for $3,500. Before he could accept the offer, Nelson was killed in an automobile accident. The offer was thus terminated.

HOW CAN AN OFFER BE KEPT OPEN?

> **Problem:** Falk offered to sell his stereo system to Plimpton for $400 cash, but Plimpton wanted a few days to see if he could arrange to get the money. He gave Falk $25 to keep the offer open for three days. Must Falk do so?

The offeree may give the offeror something of value in return for the latter's promise to keep the offer open a certain length of time. This agreement is in itself a contract and is called an _option_.

The offer cannot be withdrawn during the period covered by the option without the offeror becoming liable for breaking the contract. In the problem, Plimpton held an option to buy the stereo and Falk could not withdraw the offer or sell to anyone else during the three-day period without becoming liable to Plimpton. The offeror may keep the consideration paid for an option if the offer is not accepted within the time allowed.

An offer may also be kept open when state statutes provide that a *firm offer*—an offer in writing—cannot be revoked within the stated period. The UCC applies this rule to merchants selling or buying goods who agree in writing to keep an offer open for a definite time (not in excess of three months). The offer cannot be revoked during that period.

 On January 9, Willson, a supplier, offered in writing to sell Wawona Farms 100 tons of fertilizer at a certain price. He stated, "This price is firm for thirty days." A week later, and before the offeree accepted, the market price was raised and Willson attempted to revoke his offer. He could not do so; it would remain in effect until February 8.

WHAT ARE THE REQUIREMENTS OF AN ACCEPTANCE?

Problem: Agnew offered to sell his guitar to Allen. Parker, who overheard the offer, said he would take it. Did Parker's acceptance make a contract?

Acceptance occurs when a party to whom an offer has been made agrees to the proposal or does what is proposed. If the acceptance is to result in an enforceable agreement, it too must meet certain requirements. An acceptance must be:

1. Made only by the person or persons to whom the offer was made;
2. Unconditional and identical with the offer; and
3. Communicated to the offeror by appropriate word or act.

(1) AN ACCEPTANCE MAY BE MADE ONLY BY THE PERSON(S) TO WHOM THE OFFER WAS MADE

An offer made to one person cannot be accepted by another. Accordingly, no contract was made in the problem.

An acceptance may be made only by the person to whom the offer was made.

There are instances, however, when an offer is made to a particular group and not to an individual—a form letter may be sent to many persons, or an offer of a reward may be made to the general public. In such cases, any member of the group or general public who knows of the offer may accept it.

REWARD for return Cupertino class ring 1971. Initials TAP. Lost near Calabazas Park. Phone 369-8407

Wight saw this ad in the newspaper and, having found the ring, returned it. She was entitled to the reward because she accepted an offer that had been made to the general public.

(2) THE ACCEPTANCE MUST BE UNCONDITIONAL AND IDENTICAL WITH THE OFFER

Problem: Whitney offered to sell Singer his cabin in the mountains for $3,000, but specified that the entire amount was to be paid within 30 days. Singer accepted the offer but changed the time of payment to 90 days. Did this change affect the acceptance?

As stated on page 113, if the offeror specifies the time or the manner in which the acceptance is to be made, it must be so made in order to complete the agreement. Any change in the terms of the offer by the offeree, as in the problem above, results in a counter-offer which, as you recall, terminates the original offer. However, suggestions as to methods of carrying out the contract or other immaterial matters do not make the acceptance conditional.

(3) THE ACCEPTANCE MUST BE COMMUNICATED

Problem: Karber wrote Warton, saying: "I have a buyer for your forty acres at the edge of town, $16,000. Unless

Unit III □ CONTRACTS

I hear from you to the contrary, I shall sell it for you at that price." Warton did not reply, and Karber tried to hold him to the proposal. Was Warton bound?

As a general rule, an acceptance must be more than a mental decision. It must be communicated. Moreover, a person is normally under no duty to reply to offers made by others. This means the offeror cannot usually frame his offer so that silence is acceptance. Thus, Warton, in the above problem, would not be bound by Karber's offer to sell his land.

In certain transactions, known as *unilateral contracts*, only one of the parties makes a promise. Usually, it is the offeror who promises something in return for the performance of a certain act by the offeree. For example, he may promise a $20 reward for the return of his lost wallet. To accept such an offer, the offeree must perform the act as requested. When the act will take a substantial time to perform, it is usually held that the offer cannot be revoked until an offeree who has begun performance has had a reasonable time to complete it.

In other cases, the contract will be *bilateral*; that is, both parties will make promises. For example, a seller may promise to deliver requested goods in exchange for a buyer's promise to pay the agreed price. Bilateral contracts require that the offeree make and communicate the requested promise to the offeror. Until he does so, there is no acceptance.

An acceptance may be communicated orally, in person or by telephone, or it may be in writing, and sent by mail or telegraph. The offeror may state which method the offeree is to use. If he does not, and if business custom does not govern, the modern trend is to regard acceptance made in any reasonable manner as valid. Indeed, the UCC provides that an acceptance of an offer to buy or sell goods may be made "in any manner and by any medium reasonable in the circumstances."

It sometimes becomes important to determine exactly when acceptance is made and the contract formed. Oral acceptances are made at the moment the words are spoken. Acceptances sent by mail generally take effect when properly mailed. A telegram takes effect as an acceptance when handed to the clerk at the telegraph office. The offeror can rightfully stipulate that an acceptance will not be effective until it is received. This protects him from the possibility that the acceptance will be effective even if it does not reach him.

WHAT IS THE EFFECT OF ACCEPTANCE?

> **Problem:** Ramirez offered to purchase Jessee's appliance business and gave Jessee a check for $5,000 as a good faith deposit. The agreement provided that if the offer was not accepted by May 1, the check "shall be returned." Prior to May 1, Jessee cashed the check but did not otherwise notify Ramirez. What effect did cashing the check have on the offer?

A valid acceptance of a valid offer results in a contract—an agreement enforceable at law. *Valid* means legally effective. Thus, cashing of the check in the problem indicated assent to the offer; the check could not thereafter be returned and there was a valid acceptance of the offer. A *void agreement* (or an invalid one) cannot be enforced in the courts; it has no legal force or effect.

Under certain circumstances the courts will enforce a contract against one of the parties but not against the other. Such agreements are *voidable contracts*. For example, when one party persuades the other to enter into the contract by means of fraud, such as representing a used car as new, the contract is voidable by the buyer.

The difference between a void agreement and a voidable contract is important. A voidable contract can be enforced by the injured party, but usually it cannot be enforced against him. An agreement that is void, on the other hand, cannot be enforced by either party.

WHEN YOU ENTER INTO A CONTRACT . . .

1. Retain a copy of any documents you sign. If you are the offeror, keep a copy of any written offer you make.
2. Be sure that the terms of the offer and acceptance are sufficiently clear and complete. Vague or incomplete terms may mean confusion and possibly lead to legal action. Moreover, courts will not enforce an agreement if they cannot determine what the parties intended.
3. Remember that an offer must normally be accepted in the exact form in which it was made, and in the time or manner specified. If it is not, the offer is terminated.
4. Arrange for an option contract if you want to be assured that an offer will be kept open for a specific length of time.
5. To have evidence of proper mailing of the acceptance of an offer, send it by certified or registered mail. However, a carbon copy of a letter supported by testimony of proper posting of the original (with correct address and sufficient postage) may be proof of acceptance of an offer made by mail.

YOUR LEGAL VOCABULARY

acceptance	offeror
bilateral contract	option
contract	revocation
counteroffer	unilateral contract
firm offer	valid
offer	void agreement
offeree	voidable contract

1. A legally binding agreement.
2. A proposal that expresses the willingness of the offeror to enter into a legally binding agreement.
3. The party to whom an offer is made.
4. A contract that the courts will enforce against one of the parties but not against the other.
5. The party who makes an offer.
6. A contract in which both parties make promises.
7. An agreement that is not enforceable.
8. Withdrawal of an offer before its acceptance.
9. An acceptance that varies or qualifies the offeror's proposal.
10. A contract to keep an offer open a certain length of time.

REMEMBER THESE HIGHLIGHTS

1. There can be no contract without an agreement between two or more parties, resulting from an offer and an acceptance.
2. An offer must be (a) made with the offeror's apparent intention to be bound thereby, (b) definite, and (c) communicated to the offeree.
3. If not accepted, an offer is ended at the time stated, at the end of a reasonable time, by rejection, by counteroffer, by the offeror's revocation, or by insanity or death of one of the parties.
4. The offeree must accept the offer unconditionally—in the exact form and manner indicated by the offeror.
5. An acceptance must be communicated to the offeree. If it is sent by mail or wire, it is effective at the time it is properly sent unless the offeror requires other action.
6. Agreements which are enforceable by the courts are valid contracts; those which are unenforceable are void. Contracts enforceable only by the injured party are voidable at his option.

LAW AS PEOPLE LIVE IT

1. Exasperated because his car would not start, Lindquist said to his friend, Arnold, "I'll sell this lemon for $5!" Arnold readily agreed to buy. Did a binding contract result?

2. A commission merchant wired a dealer: "Have 24 crates of strawberries which will sell you at market price." Four days later the dealer wired that he accepted the offer. Was a contract formed?

3. Bell Construction Company advertised that it would hire qualified workers to build a dam at a certain location. When Clauson, who was qualified, showed up but was not hired, he claimed the ad was an offer of employment which he had accepted, creating a contract. Do you agree?

4. Gordon's saddle horse was lost and Gordon advertised a reward of $50 to anyone who returned it. Scott, a neighbor, who had no knowledge of the reward, found the horse and returned it to Gordon. Was he entitled to the reward?

5. Bemis offered to sell 50 bales of cotton on certain terms with "immediate delivery" to Vallems. Vallems accepted the offer but said "Suggest delivery in thirty days." Did this suggestion make Vallem's acceptance void?

6. Neil notified several contractors that he was going to pave a parking lot and requested bids. Rasmussen submitted the lowest bid but Neil gave the contract to Jolly. Rasmussen claimed the lowest bid must be accepted. Is he right?

7. Stevens offered to sell Espinosa a painting for $700. Espinosa put up a deposit of $50 in exchange for which Stevens gave him ten days to decide. Meanwhile, Riffe saw the painting and offered $1,200 for it. Stevens, eager to sell to Riffe at the higher price, notified Espinosa that he would return the $50 since the $700 price was no longer acceptable. Could he do this?

8. Aris offered in writing to sell his car to Hayes for $400, and stated that if he did not receive a reply within ten days, he would consider the offer accepted. Hayes made no reply. Was there a contract?

9. Warren orally offered to sell his radio to Haynes for $45 cash and gave him one week in which to accept. Three days later, Warren notified Haynes that he had decided to keep the radio himself. Was he within his rights in doing so?

10. Kaulbach offered to sell his St. Bernard puppy to Bright. Bright was not interested, but knew that his friend, Vance, would be. Vance loved dogs and notified Kaulbach that he accepted the offer. Was a contract formed?

LAW AS COURTS DECIDE IT

1. In February, Crouch asked the Purex Corporation for its lowest selling price on an old mining building and its equipment in Meade, Kansas. Purex replied $500. On March 19, Crouch countered with an offer of $300 but received no reply. On April 16, Crouch wrote

accepting the $500 offer, enclosing his check for that amount. This check was cashed by Purex on April 23. On April 17, Purex offered to sell the building and equipment to one Asche, and on April 24, Asche accepted the offer enclosing a check for $500. On April 27, Purex telegraphed Crouch that his offer was "unacceptable" and stated that his check had been "mistakenly deposited." On May 6, Purex returned the $500 to Crouch in a letter which explained that the reason his offer could not be accepted was that the corporation had received and accepted another offer "prior to receipt of yours on April 23." In the meantime Asche had contracted to sell the building to Marrs for $500 and the equipment to another party for $800. Crouch claimed that cashing his check constituted acceptance of his counteroffer and formed a contract. Do you agree? (Crouch v. Marrs, 199 Kan. 387, 430 P. 2d 204)

2. Epton orally entered into an option to buy the defendant CBC Corporation's 54 percent share of the ownership of the Chicago White Sox baseball club for $4,800,000. The option, which was to have been reduced to writing, was for a period of one week in return for payment of $1,000. It provided that, to accept, Epton must give CBC a certified or cashier's check for $99,000 and notify the corporation in writing that he was exercising his option. Twice during the week Epton orally assured CBC of his intent to exercise the option and offered to deposit $99,000 as soon as the option agreement was signed by CBC. This was never done. Epton claimed that the oral notice of intent to exercise the option was sufficient, and that failure of CBC to sign the written option agreement excused both the written requirement and the necessity of the $99,000 deposit. Do you agree? (Epton v. CBC Corporation, 48 Ill. App. 2d 274, 197 N.E. 2d 727)

3. Schlanger, trading as Miami Knitting Mills, purchased some textiles from Tanenbaum and a controversy arose concerning the sale. Tanenbaum sent Schlanger an invoice describing the goods with the price. Also stamped on the invoice in red ink were the words, "All controversies arising out of the sale of these goods are to be settled by arbitration." Tanenbaum claimed this statement was part of the contract although in making the sale no mention was made of it. Schlanger denied that arbitration of differences was part of the contract and refused to submit it to arbitration. Tanenbaum asks the court to require that the dispute be submitted to arbitration. The law of the state of New York provides that "A contract to arbitrate a controversy thereafter arising between the parties must be in writing." The questions in this case are whether the invoice is a contract and, if so, whether Schlanger agreed to the arbitration of the differences. Must the controversy be submitted to arbitration?

(Tanenbaum Textile Company v. Schlanger, 287 N.Y. 400, 40 N.E. 2d 225)

4. On March 6, Gillespie offered to sell a 600-acre tract of land under certain conditions to Post for $550,000. The agreement provided that the purchaser should comply with the terms of the offer within 90 days. On May 23, Post accepted the offer conditionally. The condition was not satisfactory to Gillespie, and he declined to accept. On June 12, Gillespie notified Post that his offer was revoked. Would Post's claim that Gillespie had accepted the offer be upheld? (Post v. Gillespie, 219 Md. 378, 149 A. 2d 391)

5. An action was brought to recover $2,500 from Peerless Insurance Company, under an accident insurance policy issued to William W. Gorham, who was killed in an automobile accident on December 11. Gorham had received an ad soliciting an offer for insurance, and submitted his application on November 12 along with the first month's premium of $1. The ad stated, "Your policy will be mailed to you as soon as your application is approved"; and "Your application is expected to reach our office not later than November 20." The application also stated, "Send only $1.00 for your first month's premium, during which time you will be completely insured." Following receipt of Gorham's application, Peerless kept the premium and returned the application with a request that Gorham answer certain questions that had been left unanswered. The completed application was received by Peerless on December 1. The contract was finally issued on December 19 without knowledge of Gorham's death. Gorham's father, plaintiff in this action, claimed that in light of the advertising and retention of the premium the insurance policy was effective no later than December 1, and the delay in issuing it was unreasonable. The company claimed the policy was not effective until it was issued. Decide. (Gorham v. Peerless Life Insurance Company, 368 Mich. 335, 118 N.W. 2d 306)

CHAPTER 8 Void and Voidable Agreements

1. *You buy a typewriter in a department store that the young stationery department salesman claims is "the best one made." If you later find that this statement is false, can you avoid the contract?*

2. *Your father offers to sell an antique desk for $190, but in typing the offer he carelessly writes $109. A buyer says "I accept." Can your father later avoid the sale when he realizes that he made a mistake?*

3. *You buy a set of encyclopedias having been told the price is $120. You sign the order blank without reading it and later learn the total price as stated therein is $220, including carrying charges, credit insurance, packing and shipping, and state and local sales tax. Is the contract enforceable?*

WHAT MAKES AN AGREEMENT VOIDABLE?

Problem: Wilbur offered to sell Benson a motorbike which he dishonestly claimed was new and had been driven only 5,000 miles. Relying on these statements, Benson accepted the offer. Later, when he learned that the machine was rebuilt and had gone 50,000 miles, Benson refused to go through with the deal. Was he bound by the purchase contract?

Every contract is based on an offer and an acceptance. However, the offer and the acceptance must be real and genuine; they must be given freely and voluntarily in an atmosphere of honesty and fair dealing. If one enters a contract because he has been deceived, misled, or forced, he may avoid the contract if he chooses. In the problem, there was an offer and an acceptance but the agreement was voidable because Benson was deceived by Wilbur's false statements.

Usually, before a contract is found voidable, a court must determine that the party who claims he was tricked or coerced was exercising reasonable care and judgment at the time. If he was, the court may find that the promise was induced by fraud, duress, or undue influence, and cannot be enforced against the victim. There are also cases where contracts are held void or voidable because of certain types of mistakes.

WHAT IS FRAUD?

> **Problem:** Herschell bought a house from McNabb, relying on McNabb's statements that it was in good condition and well constructed. Soon after, rain caused the house to leak badly, and investigation showed the cause to be faulty construction which had been cleverly concealed by patching and painting. Could Herschell avoid the contract?

The basis of *fraud* is false representation or concealment. However, not every misrepresentation or concealment amounts to fraud. All of the following five circumstances must be present for fraud to exist:

(1) THERE MUST BE A FALSE REPRESENTATION, OR DELIBERATE CONCEALMENT, OF A PRESENT OR PAST FACT

Fraud can result from the making of false statements. It can also be found in the concealment of facts which otherwise could be recognized by a prudent person. Generally a seller is not obligated to reveal all he knows about a product; however, he must not act so as to prevent the other party, acting as a reasonable person, from learning the relevant facts. In the foregoing problem, the buyer entered into the contract believing the house to be in good condition. If McNabb had not deliberately concealed the faulty construction, it could have been discovered upon inspection. This intentional trickery amounted to fraud, and Herschell could avoid the contract.

To constitute fraud, the concealment or misrepresentation must be deliberate. It may be active, as in the problem, or it may arise because one has a duty to speak and fails to do so.

A present or past fact does not include an opinion, a judgment, or a prediction of the future. If someone tells you that a certain article "will pay for itself," "is a bargain," "is the best on the market," or "is of great value," you have no right to rely upon such remarks. They are usually statements of *opinion* or belief only, not statements of fact. Hence, opinions which prove to be wrong normally do not constitute fraud.

During negotiations for the sale of a star sapphire ring, Horne honestly told Laughlin he had paid $250 for it ten years ago. He also stated that it was worth "at least $500 now." The first statement was one of fact; the buyer could rely upon it to be true and claim fraud if it was false. But the present value was a statement of opinion, and would not be fraudulent even if false. Laughlin had no right to rely upon it.

(2) THE MISREPRESENTED OR CONCEALED FACT MUST BE MATERIAL

In order to be fraudulent, a statement must be a false representation of a present or a past *material fact*. A fact is material, regardless of its apparent importance, if its misrepresentation or concealment influences the other person's decision to enter into the agreement. Usually the situation is such that, had the party known the true facts, he would not have made the contractual agreement.

(3) THE PERSON WHO MAKES THE FALSE REPRESENTATION MUST KNOW IT TO BE FALSE OR MAKE IT RECKLESSLY WITHOUT REGARD TO ITS TRUTH

Problem: Stewart, a salesman for Buy-Rite Used Cars, represented to Fulbright that a certain car was a "one owner vehicle" and had never been in a wreck. Stewart did not know that it had been in a serious wreck and had been owned by three people, but he was anxious to make the sale and said what he thought his prospect wanted to hear. Fulbright bought the car relying on Stewart's statement. When he discovered the facts, he sought to have the sale set aside on grounds of fraud. Would he succeed?

Fraud clearly exists when a person deliberately makes a false statement or conceals a material fact, or intentionally acts in such a way as to mislead another into entering a contract. Fraud also exists, however, if a person makes a statement of fact rashly, without determining its truth or falsity, especially if he should know the facts.

In the problem, Stewart made the statements concerning the car with reckless disregard of the truth. In his position as a car salesman, Stewart is expected to know the facts. Hence, Fulbright was justified in claiming fraud.

(4) THE MISREPRESENTATION MUST BE MADE WITH THE INTENTION OF INFLUENCING THE OTHER PERSON TO ACT UPON IT

Problem: Giffin was having financial difficulties and needed credit. He gave the Reliable Credit Bureau a false report showing his financial condition as satisfactory. Olsen got a report from RCB on Giffin and, relying on it, sold him a new electronic calculator. Soon thereafter Olsen learned the truth and, claiming fraud, sued to repossess the calculator. Should he succeed?

For a statement to be fraudulent, there must be an intention on the part of the person making it that it should be relied and acted upon. Generally the statement is made directly to the person who is to be influenced. However, this is not necessary. A person may, like Giffin in the problem, tell a third party with the expectation that the statement will be passed on to the one whose conduct he intends to influence. Accordingly, Olsen should be allowed to repossess the calculator.

(5) THE MISREPRESENTATION OR CONCEALMENT MUST INDUCE ACTION AND CAUSE INJURY TO THE OTHER PARTY

Problem: Clark, in bargaining with Myers to sell his sailboat, said it was a "Mariner." Myers knew it was an "Islander" but bought it anyway. When he became dissatisfied with the boat, Myers claimed fraud, returned the boat to Clark, and demanded his money back. Should he succeed?

A misrepresentation or concealment does not constitute fraud unless it actually deceives the person who is intended to be misled by it. Unless the wrongful concealment or misrepresentation is a factor in the person's decision to enter into the contract, there is no fraud. Moreover, if the result does not cause injury to the defrauded party, he has no legal right or need to recover damages. Accordingly, Myers' claim of fraud would not be upheld.

WHAT ARE THE RIGHTS OF THE DEFRAUDED PARTY?

Problem: Erickson was fraudulently induced by Sessions to buy a set of what he thought to be authentic Queen Anne dining room chairs. Immediately upon discovering the fraud and before paying, Erickson notified Sessions that he would not perform the contract. Was Erickson within his rights?

Contracts entered into as a result of fraud are voidable by the injured party. Thus, a defrauded party may choose to repudiate, or disaffirm, the agreement. *Disaffirmance* is a refusal to carry out or abide by the terms of a contract. Normally when one decides to exercise his right to disaffirm, he must return anything he has received. If he has performed his part of the contract, he may recover what he has paid or given under its terms. If he has done nothing, like Erickson, he may simply be released from his obligation to perform. If he is sued on the contract, he can plead fraud as a defense; or he may himself sue and collect damages caused by the fraud.

A defrauded person may also choose to ratify the agreement; either party may then enforce it. *Ratification* is an approval or confirmation of an otherwise voidable act or contract. Silence or failure to disaffirm within a reasonable time after discovering the fraud will usually be considered ratification and the contract may then be enforced against the defrauded party. Ratification, once made, cannot be withdrawn. Even if the defrauded party decides to ratify the agreement, however, he may obtain reimbursement for any loss or damage he has suffered.

 Coleman was induced by fraud to purchase an air conditioning unit for his office from Pinkston. Additional duct work costing $1,500 was necessary to make it effective. Coleman ratified the contract by bringing suit against Pinkston for the extra expense.

WHAT IS DURESS?

Problem: Joyce owned a valuable antique rolltop desk that George, without success, had offered to purchase. Joyce was induced to sell only after George threatened to "have someone burn your house because if I can't have that desk, no one will!" Joyce later repudiated the contract and George sued. Would he win?

If one person compels another to enter into an agreement by threat of force or by an act of violence, the agreement is said to be obtained under *duress*. Duress makes an agreement voidable. In instances of duress, a person is denied the exercise of his free will in entering into contracts. The threatened or actual violence may be to the life, liberty, or property of the given person, his immediate family, or his near relatives. In the problem, if Joyce acted under duress in making the contract with George, he could avoid it.

Duress makes an agreement voidable.

A person is usually not guilty of duress when he does or threatens to do something he has a legal right to do.

WHAT IS UNDUE INFLUENCE?

Problem: Robie was an elderly woman lacking in knowledge and business experience, who after investing an inheritance in a home for herself, took in Peacock, 28 years of age, as a boarder. During the two months he lived in her home, Peacock was very attentive to Mrs. Robie who was quite ill and easily influenced. Four weeks before her death Mrs. Robie deeded the house and sold her car to Peacock for ridiculously low prices. After her death, her children sued to have the deed and gift set aside, claiming Peacock had used undue influence on their mother. Should they succeed?

When a relationship of such trust and confidence exists that it is clear that one party could overpower the other's free will, *undue influence* is presumed to exist in contracts between the parties. Relationships involving this possible presumption of undue influence include those between husband and wife, parent and child, guardian and ward, attorney and client, physician and patient. Undue influence may arise out of family relationships, mental weakness, or business relationships involving trust and confidence. When a person makes a contract under undue influence, the contract is voidable by the victim if it can be shown that unfair advantage has been taken of him.

In the problem, although the relationship between Mrs. Robie and her boarder, Peacock, was one not normally considered as close and trusting, the evidence showed that such a relationship did exist in this case. In setting aside the deed, the court said "it is repulsive to every rule of law and love of justice to argue that Mrs. Robie would uninfluenced deed this property to a young man whom she had known for hardly two months, thereby disinheriting the children whom she had mothered and to whom she was bound by ties of love and affection."

WHAT IS THE EFFECT OF MISTAKE?

> **Problem:** Herrick signed a written contract to pay Mc-Kinney $200 for installing lightning rods on his house. When he was sued on the contract, Herrick pleaded mistake, claiming that he believed he was to pay only $30 and that he had not read the contract before he signed it. Was that a good defense?

In the course of making a contract, it is very easy to make a mistake. However, an error made by one party without the knowledge of the other generally has no effect on the agreement.

A man may intend to sell for one price but quote another. In filling in blanks or writing letters, wrong figures may be inserted. Failure to read a contract before signing, or a hurried or careless reading of a contract, may result in a person's assuming obligations that he had no intention of assuming. All of these things are mistakes, but they do not affect the validity and enforceability of the contract. Mistake as used in contract law should not be confused with carelessness, ignorance, poor judgment, or lack of knowledge or ability. In the problem, mistake was not a good defense.

In making contracts, persons are ordinarily bound by what they do and say, regardless of other intentions. Thus, many mistakes do not affect contractual agreements. However, under certain circumstances, mistake does make an agreement void or voidable.

WHAT MISTAKES MAKE AGREEMENTS VOID OR VOIDABLE?

Problem: Bernard agreed to sell Hall a lot on a street known as Highland. Unknown to either party, there were two streets with that name in the city. One was Highland Drive, the other was Highland Avenue. Bernard's lot was on Highland Drive, whereas Hall thought it was on Highland Avenue. Is their contract enforceable?

Agreements are void when there is a mutual mistake of material fact. Thus, in the problem, the parties' mutual mistake as to the identity of the subject matter made the contract unenforceable. Existence of the subject matter is another material fact which, if mutually mistaken, can make the contract void.

 Lyman, who lived in Tulsa, sold Porter his Offy racing car which was stored in Milwaukee. Unknown to either party, the car had been destroyed by fire two days before the sale. There was no contract.

When only one party is mistaken as to the existence of a material fact, courts may or may not grant relief. If the error arises from the negligence of the mistaken party, courts will generally hold him to his contract. However, where the mistake was recognized but not disclosed by the other party, who apparently hoped to gain an advantage by remaining silent, courts will grant relief by making the contract void.

There may also be a mistake on the part of one party as to the identity of the other. Suppose, for example, that a wholesaler in Detroit had a steady customer, John Jones of Chicago. Then he receives a letter from a John Jones in Seattle. If the seller contracts with this John Jones under the mistaken impression that he is dealing with his steady customer, the contract will be voidable. When the parties deal face to face, however, the contract is not affected by mistaken identity.

TO PROTECT YOURSELF AGAINST FRAUD . . .

1. In an important deal, always investigate first. Rely on yourself or, better, consult trustworthy independent counsel. It may be unwise to believe the representations of the other party; he is primarily concerned with his interests, not yours. Moreover, he is generally not obliged to volunteer information or tell all he knows.
2. Don't be rushed into a decision. Legitimate proposals bear careful investigation; almost all of them will survive an overnight or longer delay.
3. Learn to distinguish between fact and opinion. Don't rely on the other party's opinion unless he is an expert and you request his expert advice.
4. If you suspect or know of fraud or improper concealment, don't enter into the contract.
5. When fraud is discovered, act promptly to disaffirm the contract or take other steps to protect your rights. "Sleeping on your rights" may cause you to lose them.

YOUR LEGAL VOCABULARY

disaffirmance	opinion
duress	ratification
fraud	undue influence
material fact	

1. A belief or judgment; not a fact.
2. Intentional false representation or concealment of a material fact meant to and which does deceive and cause legal injury to another.
3. An influence one person has over another which is so great as to overpower the latter's freedom of will.
4. A fact which has a substantial influence on a person's decision to act.
5. Threat of force or act of violence which causes a person to do something he otherwise would not have done.
6. An approval of an otherwise voidable act.
7. A refusal to abide by or carry out the terms of a contract.

REMEMBER THESE HIGHLIGHTS

1. An offer and its acceptance must be real and genuine, given freely and voluntarily in an atmosphere of honesty and fair dealing.
2. Fraud exists when false representation or concealment of a past or present material fact is intended to and does influence the action of another, causing him legal injury. Contracts induced by fraud are voidable by the defrauded party.
3. Duress consists of actual or threatened violence to the life, liberty, or property of a person (or that of his family or near relatives) which causes him to do some act which he would not otherwise have done. Contracts obtained under duress are voidable by the victim.
4. Undue influence exists when one party has such an overpowering influence over the other as to deprive him of his freedom of will. If this influence is used to take unfair advantage in a contract situation, the agreement is voidable by the victim.
5. As a general rule, mistake does not affect the validity of an agreement. However, an agreement is void if there is mutual mistake as to the identity or existence of the subject matter.

LAW AS PEOPLE LIVE IT

1. Relying on statements by Thomas that a new, small computer would do the work and save the expense of three employees, Graves bought the machine. When Graves found that he could not eliminate these employees, he claimed fraud. Do you agree with him?

2. Kaufman, shopping for an antique automobile, was told that a certain vehicle was a 1907 EMF. Kaufman, an antique car buff, knew the car was a 1911 model but purchased it anyway. Later, deciding it was not a good buy, he sought to avoid the contract by claiming fraud. Would he be successful?

3. After examining the exterior of several bales of wool and being assured that all contained top quality and clean wool, Kinney purchased 100 bales. When Kinney received the wool, he discovered that it had been cleverly packed so that the outside layers were clean and of good quality, but the inside layers were of poor quality and mixed with leaves and dirt. He attempted to avoid his contract, claiming fraud. Was there fraud?

4. During negotiations for the sale of a certain salt well, Hutton stated that it was free of gypsum and that the brine was 90 percent in strength. In fact, the well contained gypsum and was deficient in strength. Curry, the purchaser, defending a suit for the purchase price, claimed the contract was void because of fraud. Was it?

5. MacTavish owned a farm worth about $200 an acre. By making false representations, he induced Amling to buy it for $400 an acre. Shortly thereafter, oil was discovered under the land. When MacTavish learned of the discovery, he sought to have the conveyance set aside on grounds of fraud. Should he succeed?

6. Ossian, an orphan, had been left some land as an inheritance which was to be deeded to her at age 21. She lived with MacKenzie, an uncle, who was her guardian. MacKenzie persuaded Ossian to sell the land to him at half its true value. When Ossian learned of this she sued, offered to return the money and to recover the land. Would she be successful?

7. Newman's wife became ill and was admitted to the Community Hospital. After several attempts to get Newman to pay the bill, Community Hospital threatened to sue. Newman consulted an attorney and then promised to pay the bill in installments. When he failed to pay, the hospital sued him. He claimed that his promise was not binding because it was obtained under duress. Was it?

8. Ramon fraudulently induced Wilkins to purchase an engagement ring which he said had a "full carat, blue-white diamond" in its setting. Wilkins had a jeweler appraise the ring before sending the payment for it. The jeweler informed Wilkins that the diamond was a fake. Wilkins returned the ring and refused to pay for it. Was he within his rights?

9. Gundar sent King a letter offering to supply King with 150 gallons of propane per week at a cost of 16.9 cents a gallon. King accepted the offer and then Gundar discovered he had made a mistake, intending to quote the price at 19.6 cents a gallon. Could he have the agreement declared void?

10. Hyatt agreed to sell Johnson a house and some property located at 114 South Street, Kansas City. Unknown to Johnson, Hyatt's property was in Kansas City, Kansas; Johnson thought the property was in Kansas City, Missouri. Is the contract enforceable?

LAW AS COURTS DECIDE IT

1. Vaughn Turner, the father of Clifford Turner, age 17, filed suit to have the marriage of his son to Marcella E. Gilbert Turner annulled and the consent he had previously given canceled. He claimed that he was induced to give his parental consent to the marriage by fraud. Clifford and Marcella represented to him that they had already been married in Tijuana, Mexico, that Marcella was pregnant, and that "Clifford was the father." Because of these representations the father gave his consent. This was required by law because his son was under age 18. Both the marriage in Tijuana and the representation that Clifford was the father were false. Marcella had been pregnant about seven months when Clifford met her. Indeed when the child was born, the birth certificate listed the name of the mother as Marcella E. Belden and the father as James Taylor Belden. Could the consent be canceled and the marriage annulled? (Turner v. Turner, 167 Cal. App. 2d 636, 334 P. 2d 1011)

2. Richard purchased a lot and model home from the defendant, a developer of residential real estate. The sales agreement provided that the sale was subject to zoning ordinances. At the time of the sale, the defendant delivered a plot plan to Richard showing a twenty-foot side yard which complied with minimum requirements of the zoning regulations. After taking possession of the house, however, Richard discovered that the building was in fact only 1.8 feet from the property line. Richard claims that he relied on the representations of the developer, who should have known that the property did not meet the zoning requirements. He seeks damages for the misrepresentation. Should he recover? (Richard v. Waldman and Sons, Inc., 155 Conn. 343, 232 A. 2d 307)

3. On June 26, Dan Spencer applied for insurance on his automobile through the "Arkansas Automobile Assigned Risk Plan." He made a down payment of $15. The application stated that "Coverage becomes effective only in accordance with the terms of the Plan," but neither Spencer nor the insurance agent read this statement. According to the terms of the plan, coverage did not become effective in Spencer's case until July 2. On June 27, Spencer's car became involved in an accident which killed Charles Hughes.

Hughes' widow thereupon sued the insurance company for damages. Spencer testified that he believed he was covered by insurance. Was the company liable? (Manufacturers Casualty Insurance Co. v. Hughes, 229 Ark. 503, 316 S.W. 2d 827)

4. George H. McDonnell, a widower, died without making a will. His estate included some cash, a small amount of personal property, and a one-fourth interest in some real estate. The other interests in the real estate were held by McDonnell's three stepchildren. In settling the estate, one of the stepchildren, Monica Williams, told McDonnell's sister, Mary, that the estate consisted of cash and personal property. She made no mention of the real property. Monica then asked Mary to sign a release so that funeral expenses could be paid. Mary agreed and, relying on Monica's representations, signed the document without reading it or having it read to her. The document included a quitclaim deed to the real property and an assignment of Mary's interest in the estate to the three stepchildren in exchange for certain consideration. In this action, Mary is seeking to have the quitclaim deed and assignment set aside, alleging that concealment of the existence of the real property was fraud. Should Mary succeed? (In re McDonnell's Estate, 65 Ariz. 248, 179 P. 2d 238)

5. Mitchell, a truck driver, had signed a release settling all claims for personal injuries sustained in an accident between two trucks. Now he sues to recover damages and to set aside the release. In order for Mitchell's employer, Herrin Transportation Company, to be paid for damage to the truck and medical service for Mitchell, both the Company and Mitchell had to sign the release prepared by the insurance company. When Mitchell refused to sign, the employer, anxious to be reimbursed the $389 it had expended, put pressure on him. After several discussions, the company informed Mitchell that if he did not sign the release he would not have a job. Mitchell testified that he signed rather than lose his job. He contends that he signed under duress. Do you agree? (Mitchell v. C. C. Sanitation Company, 430 S.W. 2d 993, Texas)

CHAPTER 9 Competent Parties

1. *A 15-year-old girl purchased a coat for $175 in a department store and charged it to her mother's account. Must the mother pay for the coat?*
2. *A high school student trades his trumpet for a set of drums owned by a fellow student. If he decides a few months later that he prefers his trumpet, can he get it back?*
3. *If a minor decides to leave home where his board and lodging are provided, must his parents pay the costs away from home?*

WHO MAY ENTER INTO CONTRACTS?

Problem: Paterni sold an expensive painting to a woman who was generally known to be mentally unbalanced. Later, after treatment in a mental hospital, the woman regained her reason. Realizing that her art purchase had been a foolish one, she returned the painting to Paterni and demanded a refund of the money she had paid. Was Paterni obligated to do so?

Each of the two or more persons who enter a contract must have capacity and be competent to contract. *Capacity to contract* is the ability to make legally binding agreements. Unless declared by law or a court to lack this ability, all persons are presumed to have it.

Persons who have capacity to contract are known as *competent parties.* Contracts made by competent parties may be enforced against them. On the other hand, persons whose contracts cannot be enforced against them are said to be incompetent. Incompetents include those who are under legal age, those who are mentally ill or insane, those who are seriously intoxicated by liquor or drugs, and under certain conditions in certain states, convicts, and aliens from countries with whom the United States is then at war.

Generally to have the competence required for capacity to contract, a person must have ability to understand the nature of the transaction and its consequences. This is why a contract entered into by a person so intoxicated as to be incapable of understanding that he is making an agreement is ordinarily not enforceable against him.

For the same reason, contracts are not enforceable against an *insane person*—one who is mentally ill or whose mind is unsound, deranged, or otherwise seriously defective so that he cannot understand the nature or consequences of his acts. In the problem, Paterni was obligated to refund the woman's money as requested. She was an incompetent at the time she bought the painting, and her contract was not enforceable against her.

The general rule is that one who does not have the ability to understand the agreement and its consequences may avoid his contract. A minor has this same right to disaffirm, but for different reasons.

HOW DOES THE LAW PROTECT CONTRACTING MINORS?

> **Problem:** Lange, age 17, used most of his summer earnings to buy a scuba diver's outfit at Bremner's Sporting Equipment. When he learned a few days later that he had paid more than was being charged elsewhere, he returned all the equipment to Bremner and asked for a refund of his money. Lange claimed he was too young to enter into a contract and that he could disaffirm the sale if he wished. Would the seller be required to refund the amount Lange had paid?

The law assumes that young people, because of their limited experience in the business world, should be given protection against both their own immaturity and the possibility that older persons might take advantage of them. Thus, minors are given the right to disaffirm, or avoid, most of their contracts. In many instances, they may return what they have purchased and demand the return of their money. Lange was within his rights when he returned the scuba diving outfit and requested a refund. He was wrong, however, in claiming that he was too young to enter into a contract. If a businessman wishes to make an important contract with a person under legal age, he may require that some adult sign the agreement also. In such a case, the adult can be held liable for damages if the minor disaffirms. This is the reason parents are frequently asked to join in signing their children's contracts. Except for certain necessities of life, however, parents are not liable for the contracts of their children unless they agree to be liable.

 Harold wished to buy some skis from Sherman, but Sherman was not willing to sell them to him because he was a minor. Harold convinced his father to become a co-buyer on the contract, and Sherman sold them the skis. Sherman could now hold the father liable if Harold did not live up to the contract.

Generally a minor's contracts are voidable by the minor; while he can enforce them against others, others cannot enforce them against him. Neither does an adult have the right to avoid his part of a contract on the grounds that the other party is a minor and incompetent. If an adult refuses to carry out such a contract, the minor can enforce the contract against the adult in court.

Bedrosian, age 16, agreed to sell his sports car to Hagen, age 22, for $1,500. When Hagen found another car he liked better, he told Bedrosian that he was canceling their contract because of Bedrosian's minority. Hagen had no right to break the contract because Bedrosian was a minor. He could be held to his contract if Bedrosian wished to hold him.

When a minor does disaffirm a contract, he must return what he has received, if he still has it, or any part that he does have. He is then entitled to have returned to him what he has given the other party. In some states, however, a minor who is over the age of 18 must return everything that he received in as good a condition as it was when he received it. If he cannot, he must pay the difference in value, or have it deducted from the amount he has paid before any refund is made to him.

Jepsen, age 20, bought his fiancee, Porter, a diamond engagement ring and a necklace, paying for them in weekly installments of $10. On his 21st birthday they quarrelled, and Porter returned the ring but refused to part with the necklace. The next day, Jepsen returned the ring to the jeweler and demanded a refund of the money he had paid for both pieces of jewelry. Jepsen was entitled to the money he had paid on the ring. In some states he was even entitled to what he had paid on the necklace, since he returned everything that was still in his possession. In other states, he could be held for the price of the necklace.

Unless disaffirmance is prohibited by statute, a minor generally can disaffirm a contract whether or not it has been fully performed.

As in the case of fraud, disaffirmance may be accomplished by any act or statement showing intent to disaffirm.

 Swanson, age 17, contracted to purchase a motor scooter from Barnouti for $225 and rode it home to show his father. After talking with his father, Swanson decided not to carry out his contract. He returned the scooter to Barnouti. This act was clearly a disaffirmance.

WHAT CONTRACTS OF MINORS ARE ENFORCEABLE?

Problem: Upon graduation from high school, Costis, age 17, went into business as a photographer and bought the necessary equipment from Stephens. When Costis failed to make a success of the business, he returned the equipment to Stephens and attempted to avoid the contract. Could he do so?

Statutes in all states permit minors to enter into enforceable contracts for certain purposes and under specified conditions. For example, in most states a minor can enter into a binding contract to sell real property if the contract is approved by a court. Similarly, in California, minors who are employed as actors or actresses or as professionals in sports may not avoid court-approved contracts. In Iowa, Louisiana, Maryland, New York, Utah, and Virginia, a minor who engages in business or trade is not permitted under most circumstances to avoid an agreement entered into with respect to his business. Accordingly, Costis, in the problem, would not be able to avoid his contract if he lived in a state that prohibited minors engaged in business from avoiding contracts relating to the business. Also, as mentioned on page 137, in certain states a minor must return what he received in order to disaffirm a contract made after the age of 18.

More than half of the states provide that minors who are over a certain age may not avoid certain contracts of insurance. Practically all states permit minors to make deposits in banks and in savings and loan associations, and to make withdrawals as if they were adults, without any rights of disaffirmance.

WHEN MAY A MINOR DISAFFIRM A CONTRACT?

Problem: Elias, a minor, exchanged an expensive camera for some golf clubs owned by Benson. Soon after reaching his majority, he sold the golf clubs to Niswonger. Then he exercised his right of disaffirmance and demanded the return of his camera from Benson. Was he entitled to do this?

A minor may disaffirm his voidable contract while he is still a minor or within a reasonable time after he reaches his majority. In most states his failure to disaffirm, or silence, will be considered as ratification. If a minor has transferred real property, however, he usually cannot disaffirm the contract until he comes of age.

After reaching his majority, a person may affirm or ratify a contract that he made while he was a minor. In that case the contract becomes just as binding upon him as if it had been made after he had become an adult. Ratification may be an express promise to perform as agreed or an act that clearly indicates the adult's intention to be bound by his agreement. Ratification once made cannot be withdrawn. Elias' sale of the golf clubs in the above problem was an act of ratification. He could not later disaffirm the contract.

If a minor decides to avoid a contract, he must avoid the entire agreement. Likewise, after reaching his majority, he must avoid or ratify the entire contract. He cannot avoid one part and ratify another.

DOES MISSTATING HIS AGE BIND A MINOR?

Problem: Drummond, a mature-looking minor, stated that he was of age when he purchased a used car from Tri-City Motors for $1,500. Several months later, having paid $600, he claimed minority, disaffirmed the contract, returned the car with a crumpled fender, and demanded the return of what he had paid. Must Tri-City Motors comply?

In most states a minor who falsely states his age is not barred from disaffirming a contract. However, a minor who attempts to take unfair advantage of another by giving a false age may usually be held liable for the false representation. This is a tort. (Page 77) As we learned in Chapter 3, a minor is liable for his torts and crimes although he is usually not liable for his contracts. The other party to the contract can usually collect from the minor any damages that he suffered because of the minor's fraud even though he cannot hold the minor to his agreement. Thus, Drummond was within his rights in repudiating his contract, but Tri-City could probably hold back from the refund of money an amount equal to the cost of repairing the crumpled fender and the decrease in the value of the car. Moreover, because of his tort, Drummond could be held liable in damages for deceiving Tri-City.

MUST MINORS PAY FOR NECESSARIES?

Problem: Lowell, an emancipated minor, was living away from home. He rented an apartment from Chawner for a year at $105 a month, but after two months, moved. Could Chawner hold Lowell to the contract on grounds that lodging was a necessary?

Although the law permits a minor to avoid most of his contracts, it does not allow him to avoid all responsibility when he obtains things he really needs under an agreement to pay for them. If the minor could avoid all responsibility, businessmen might refuse to supply him with the necessities of life. However, one who supplies necessaries to a minor may collect only the reasonable value for them if the agreed price is unreasonable.

Which items are not classified as necessaries for minors?

Necessaries are things not already possessed or being supplied to a minor that are reasonably required and are suitable to his economic and social status. Courts have found such things as food, clothing, shelter, common school education, medical care, and tools with which to earn a living to be necessaries. The following items have been excluded: kid gloves, jewelry, liquor, tobacco, pleasure trips, automobiles, and expensive food for parties. An automobile is a necessary, however, when it is essential to a minor's earning a living.

An article must meet the following four requirements before a minor can be held responsible for payment:

(1) IT MUST BE REASONABLY REQUIRED WHEN FURNISHED

Lodging is clearly a necessary; Chawner's claim in the problem would meet this requirement.

(2) IT MUST BE ACTUALLY FURNISHED

Even though a minor may agree to purchase a necessary, he cannot be required to pay for it unless it is actually supplied to him. Thus, Chawner could not require Lowell to pay for the apartment for the months he did not occupy it.

(3) IT MUST NOT BE OTHERWISE FURNISHED

If Lowell's parents had arranged for his lodging or if it had been otherwise provided, his apartment would not have been a necessary.

(4) IT MUST BE REASONABLY SUITABLE TO THE AGE AND SOCIAL AND ECONOMIC STATUS OF THE MINOR

Under this rule, what is considered a necessary for one person is not always a necessary for another. Take, for example, a situation in which a merchant sells similar, expensive clothing to a girl whose parents are poor and to a girl whose parents are wealthy. Such expensive clothes cannot be considered a necessary to a poor girl because they are not customary and reasonable for her in light of her economic condition.

> ## MINORITY IS A SHIELD, NOT A SWORD . . .
>
> 1. The minor is given special rights as a protection against persons who might take advantage of his youth and inexperience. It is only fair, then, that minors not take advantage of honest dealers.
> 2. Because state laws differ considerably, minors and those who deal with them should check the local regulations.
> 3. If a minor who reaches his majority plans to disaffirm a contract, he should do so promptly. Delay or silence will result in ratification.
> 4. When one who deals with a minor wishes to be assured that someone will pay damages if the contract is not performed, he should obtain an adult's signature on the contract. Although the minor cannot be held, the adult can.

YOUR LEGAL VOCABULARY

competent party

capacity to contract

insane person

necessary

1. One whose mind is unsound, deranged, or seriously defective.
2. Ability to understand the nature of a transaction.

3. One who has capacity to contract.
4. That which is reasonable and proper for one's maintenance.

REMEMBER THESE HIGHLIGHTS

1. Generally all persons who can understand the nature of a contract and its consequences are competent to contract.
2. Contracts made by a minor are usually voidable by the minor.
3. An adult may not avoid a contract on the ground that the other party is a minor.
4. A minor may usually disaffirm a voidable contract any time before he becomes of age or within a reasonable time thereafter. In doing so, he must return what he has received if he still has it.
5. A minor may ratify a contract made during minority either by an express promise or by an act after reaching his majority. In most states silence will be considered as ratification.
6. A contract of a minor is binding when it is authorized by law.
7. A minor is liable for the reasonable value of necessaries supplied him.
8. Others who lack capacity to contract are insane persons, seriously intoxicated persons, and under certain circumstances, convicts, and certain aliens.

LAW AS PEOPLE LIVE IT

1. Wayne Brooks, 17 years of age, purchased expensive fishing eqiupment for cash. When his father learned of this the next day, he demanded that his son return the merchandise. May Wayne legally require the merchant to take the merchandise back and refund the price paid?
2. Clayton sold his used baseball mitt to Tydings, a minor. After trying out the mitt and finding it unsatisfactory, Tydings took it back to Clayton. When Clayton refused to take the mitt back, Tydings tossed it on a table and walked out. Was this act a disaffirmance?
3. Barr, a minor, purchased a motor scooter for $240 from Hurwitz, another minor. Claiming it was defective, Barr sought to return the motor scooter to Hurwitz and demanded the return of the purchase price. Assuming Hurwitz still had the money, could he be required to return it to Barr?
4. Three weeks before reaching his majority, Austin contracted to buy a stamp collection from Ellis and to make payment in 30 days. When payment became due, Austin refused to pay for the stamps and offered to return them. Ellis claimed that Austin, now having reached his majority, was guilty of breach of contract, and refused to accept the stamps. Must Ellis take back the stamp collection?

5. Pietrowski was 20 years of age, but her dress and appearance made her seem older. When she purchased the Modern Beauty Salon from Carr, in April, including the equipment and supplies, she represented herself as being 23. Each month thereafter, Pietrowski made payments of $200 to Carr. By the time of her 21st birthday, in October, Pietrowski decided she preferred to be an employee. However, she continued to make payments until December, when she notified Carr that she was disaffirming the contract. Will Carr's claim that she had ratified the contract by making a payment after becoming 21 be upheld?

6. Karen, a college freshman, age 17, bought a formal dress for a special occasion. After wearing it, she returned it to the store and demanded the return of her money. Will she succeed?

7. Kruger sold his trumpet for $85 to Rogan, age 16, who made a payment of $50. Unable to pay the balance, Rogan sold the trumpet to Taylor, age 17. Taylor did not like the instrument and returned it to Rogan. Was Kruger's claim that Rogan had ratified the contract by selling the trumpet to Taylor correct?

8. Charles was 19 and just married. He rented an apartment, but after six months he and his wife decided to obtain a divorce. Charles thereupon disaffirmed the rental contract and demanded the return of what he had paid. Was he entitled to do this?

9. Blankenship, 17 years of age, broke his ankle while playing touch football. Later, when he received a bill from the physician who set the ankle, Blankenship refused to pay and pleaded minority as a defense. Can the physician enforce payment?

10. Angelli, a minor, disliked the dresses her mother insisted she wear, and purchased two new ones at the Chic Shop. Mullennix, the owner of the shop, claimed the dresses were necessaries. Was he correct?

LAW AS COURTS DECIDE IT

1. When the plaintiff, Kruse, was employed by the defendant as a laborer, he was given the choice of accepting workmen's compensation benefits for any injuries incurred or of suing for damages. This choice was required by law in the state of Oregon. Kruse was handed a written form which was carefully explained to him in the presence of his wife, and he elected to accept the compensation. Later, after sustaining an injury, Kruse sought to repudiate the agreement on the ground that he did not understand it, and sued the company for damages. He claimed that he lacked capacity to contract because of mental retardation. He also claimed he was unable to read some of the more complicated words in the agreement,

was easily influenced, and had difficulty understanding abstract principles and complicated situations. Was this sufficient to make him incompetent to contract? (Kruse v. Coos Head Timber Company, 248 Ore. 294, 432 P. 2d 1009)

2. Lindsey was a minor, married, and attending college. He and his wife both had jobs, and he received no support from his parents. He contracted to buy a trailer home from Hubbard and paid $1,495 down. Later, he disaffirmed the contract and sought to recover his money. Hubbard claimed he was entitled to recover the reasonable value of the trailer home because it was a necessary to Lindsey. Do you agree with Hubbard? (Lindsey v. Hubbard, 74 S.D. 114, 49 N.W. 2d 299)

3. Rogers, age 19, needed a job and applied to the plaintiff, an employment agency, for help in finding one. The contract provided that Rogers would pay a fee, according to the schedule set out in the agreement, if he obtained employment as a result of a lead furnished by the agency. The agency referred Rogers to an employer in Charlotte, N.C., and he was employed. The fee for this service was $219. When Rogers did not pay, the employment agency sued him, claiming the service provided Rogers was a necessary to enable him to earn a livelihood for himself and his family. Do you agree? (Gastiona Personnel Corp. v. Rogers, 5 N.C. App. 219, 168 S.E. 2d 31)

4. Jerry Lee Camp erroneously believed that he became of age at 18. Eight months before he became 21, he signed a note for $3,000 payable at $125 a month. He regularly made payments for ten months, including three payments after he became 21. He then learned that he did not become of age until he was 21, and sought to disaffirm his contract. Could he do so? (Camp v. Bank of Bentonville, 230 Ark. 414, 323 S.W. 2d 556)

5. Representing himself as being 22 years of age, Schaeffer, age 19, borrowed $540 from Royal Finance Company. Before becoming 21 Schaeffer paid $40 on the loan; after reaching his majority, he repudiated the obligation. The plaintiff finance company thereupon sued for the balance due. Schaeffer pleaded his minority and claimed that the finance company knew or could have ascertained his true age by requiring evidence of his age. Should the finance company be given judgment? (Royal Finance Company v. Schaeffer, 330 S.W. 2d 129, Missouri)

CHAPTER 10 Legal Agreement

1. *If a neighbor offered you $50 to "get rid" of an annoying dog, would you have a right to collect the money if you complied?*

2. *You purchase a half interest in an Irish Sweepstakes lottery ticket from a friend, and the number is a winner. Can you require him to pay you half of what he receives?*

3. *You sign an agreement with the accounting firm for which you work, promising not to work for another accounting firm in your city for two years after leaving your present employer. Can this agreement be enforced?*

WHAT MAKES AN AGREEMENT ILLEGAL?

Problem: Clark, a candidate for county supervisor, promised to appoint Clifford as a road foreman if he were elected. For this promise, Clifford paid Clark $500. Was this agreement legal?

Although the parties are competent and reach a mutual agreement, it does not necessarily follow that they may contract entirely as they wish. The formation, purpose, and performance of the agreement must not be contrary to law or to the interests of society. Some types of agreements have been declared illegal by statute. Others have been judged by the courts to be contrary to the public good or to be injurious to the health or morals of the community. All such agreements are illegal. The agreement in the problem was illegal because it was contrary to the public good.

WHAT IS THE EFFECT OF ILLEGALITY?

Problem: Rozetta paid Smart, a quarterback on a professional football team, to "throw"—i.e. lose—an important game. Smart's team won. Would a court help Rozetta recover the money he paid?

Illegal agreements are usually void and therefore unenforceable. Accordingly, most courts would not give relief to Rozetta or aid him in recovering the money he had paid. If they did assist persons in enforcing such agreements or gave relief to persons who had performed under them, courts would seem to encourage the making of illegal agreements. In dismissing an action for illegality, one court said, "The law leaves the parties to an illegal transaction where it finds them; . . . and the law cannot be invoked to enforce an agreement which such law denounces as invalid."

A contract may contain several provisions, some of which are legal and some of which are illegal. If the legal part can be separated from the illegal part, courts will usually enforce the legal part.

WHAT TYPES OF AGREEMENTS ARE ILLEGAL?

Problem: Blank's son had been arrested for embezzling $10,000 from his employer, Cutler. Blank repaid the money. He also promised Cutler $2,000 if he would agree not to prosecute the son for the criminal offense. If Cutler agreed and Blank paid the money, would the agreement be enforceable?

Among the agreements which are illegal and unenforceable are:

(1) AGREEMENTS TENDING TO OBSTRUCT JUSTICE

Agreements that encourage lawsuits, that tend to corrupt justice, or prevent people from appealing to the courts for protection are illegal. Examples of agreements that tend to corrupt justice include promises by witnesses to give false testimony or not to testify at all, or agreements to pay a witness more than the regular fee or an additional fee in case a certain verdict is rendered. Another such agreement is *compounding a felony*, which is committed by a person who accepts money or property in exchange for his promise not to prosecute. Since the agreement in the problem involved compounding a felony, it was illegal and unenforceable.

(2) AGREEMENTS TENDING TO INJURE PUBLIC SERVICE

Problem: Holt, a building contractor, agreed to pay $1,200 to Everett, the building inspector, if he would "do a good job" (implying he would overlook certain requirements) in inspecting a tract of homes Holt was constructing. If Holt refused to pay the money, could Everett collect it through court action?

It is important for people to have confidence in the integrity of their governmental agencies and officials. Thus, agreements that tend to injure the public service are void and cannot be enforced. Actual corruption or injury does not need to result from such an agreement. If the agreement places the parties in a position where corruption might be the result, it is unenforceable.

Any agreement that tends to betray public trust and confidence, or to interfere with the proper performance of the duties of a public official is void. For example, a public official cannot collect a fee for promising to do something which he is already duty-bound to do, or for promising to violate his duty in some way. Accordingly, in the problem, Everett would not be able to force Holt to pay. It is also illegal to make agreements for the obtaining of an appointment to public office, the awarding of a public contract, or the signing of a pardon.

A common example of an agreement tending to injure public service is the *illegal lobbying contract,* in which it is agreed that bribery, threat of loss of votes, or other improper means will be used to influence a lawmaking body to pass or reject certain legislation. In most states, however, an agreement by which an attorney or an expert is promised compensation to appear before a committee or other public body to present facts and arguments in favor of or against certain official legislative action is valid.

(3) AGREEMENTS AFFECTING MARRIAGE

> **Problem:** Barr's twenty-two-year-old daughter was engaged to Rose. Barr disapproved and promised to set Rose up in a drive-in hamburger business if he would break the engagement. Rose broke the engagement but Barr refused to carry out his part of the bargain. Can Rose enforce Barr's promise?

Agreements that attack or undermine the freedom and security of marriage are illegal because they are contrary to public policy. Examples of such agreements are those in which a person promises never to marry, promises to pay to dissuade someone from marrying, or promises to do or not to do something in consideration of divorce. In the above problem, the court would not require Barr to perform his part of the bargain because the contract was antagonistic to marriage.

(4) AGREEMENTS TO COMMIT CRIMES OR TORTS

Obviously any agreement to commit a crime or a tort, or for that matter to violate any law, is illegal. It would be unthinkable for the law to prohibit something in one form and approve in another.

Any agreement to commit a crime or a tort is illegal.

(5) LOTTERIES, WAGERS, AND GAMBLING AGREEMENTS

Any agreement that involves gambling or a lottery is usually illegal. If you should win a *wager,* that is, a bet on any event whose happening depended upon chance, or if you should win a prize in a lottery, in most states the courts would not compel the payment of the money or prize. Both wagers and lotteries have the elements of an illegal gambling agreement: consideration paid, and a prize to be awarded as the result of chance or an uncertain happening.

Some states, including California, Colorado, Florida, Illinois, Maryland, Nevada, and New York, have legalized certain forms of gambling under specified conditions, including pari-mutuel betting under state supervision at approved race tracks. In some states, as for example New York, the loser, or someone with an interest in the transaction, may recover what has been paid as the result of a wager. Both this law and the one that prevents any recovery at all are based on the belief that they will discourage illegal gambling agreements.

(6) AGREEMENTS TO PAY USURIOUS INTEREST

Problem: Boylan was desperately in need of money to pay the hospital so that he could bring his wife and baby home. Because he had nothing to use as security for the loan and had established no credit, Boylan was forced to borrow the money from a loan shark. He borrowed $500 which he promised to repay in 12 monthly installments of $60 each. Was this agreement legal?

Most states have laws which provide that a lender of money may not charge more than a specified maximum rate of interest, as shown

in the table. The rate agreed upon by the parties, which is called the *contract rate,* may not lawfully exceed this maximum. To require the payment of a higher rate is *usury.* In the problem, the agreement made by Boylan would be usurious in most states because the interest rate was more than 50 percent on the unpaid balances. The penalty for usury is generally a civil penalty exacted for the benefit of the borrower, but some states also impose criminal penalties.

In making an agreement to borrow and lend money, the parties may agree upon any rate of interest so long as it does not exceed the maximum permitted rate. If, however, a person borrows money for which interest is charged but no rate is stated in the contract, the rate of interest to be paid is the *legal rate* specified by statute. In some states the maximum rate and the legal rate are the same.

Usury laws generally do not apply to the sale of goods on credit; however, at least one state (Wisconsin) says they do. Certain licensed businesses, such as pawnbrokers and personal finance companies, are regulated by small loan laws rather than usury laws. These exceptions are discussed in Chapter 22.

Legal and Maximum Contract Interest Rates

(Other than those governing small loans, which are shown in Chapter 22.)

State	Legal Rate (%)	Maximum Contract Rate (%)	State	Legal Rate (%)	Maximum Contract Rate (%)
Alabama	6	8 if in writing	Montana	6	10 if in writing
Alaska	6	8	Nebraska	6	9
Arizona	6	8 if in writing	Nevada	7	12 if in writing
		6 if oral	New Hampshire	6	any, if in writing
Arkansas	6	10 if in writing	New Jersey	6	6
California	7	10 if in writing	New Mexico	6	10 if in writing
Colorado	6	any, if in writing			12 if in writing
Connecticut	6	12			but no security
Delaware	6	6 [1]	New York	6	6 [2]
D.C.	6	8 if in writing	North Carolina	6	6 [3]
Florida	6	10 if in writing	North Dakota	4	7 if in writing
Georgia	7	8 if in writing	Ohio	6	8 if in writing
Hawaii	6	12 if in writing	Oklahoma	6	10
Idaho	6	8 if in writing	Oregon	6	10 if in writing
Illinois	5	7 if in writing	Pennsylvania	6	6 with certain
Indiana	6	8 if in writing			exceptions
Iowa	5	7 if in writing	Rhode Island	6	30 on amounts
Kansas	6	10 if in writing			over $50
Kentucky	6	6	South Carolina	6	7 if in writing
Louisiana	5	8	South Dakota	6	8
Maine	6	any, if in writing	Tennessee	6	6
Maryland	6	6	Texas	6	10
Massachusetts	6	any, if in writing	Utah	6	10 if in writing
Michigan	5	7 if in writing	Vermont	6	6
Minnesota	6	8 if in writing	Virginia	6	6
Mississippi	6	8 if in writing,	Washington	6	12 if in writing
		with certain	West Virginia	6	6
		exceptions	Wisconsin	5	10 if in writing
Missouri	6	8 if in writing	Wyoming	7	10

[1] On secured loans above $5,000, a bank may charge any rate if in writing.
[2] Secured demand loans above $5,000 may be at any rate if in writing.
[3] If the loan is for agricultural purposes, 10 percent of the loan may be charged in lieu of interest.

A lender of money cannot legally charge more than a specified rate of interest.

YES, WE CAN LOAN YOU THE MONEY, BUT OUR INTEREST RATE IS 50%!

SHADY LOAN CO.
WE LEND TO ANYBODY

(7) AGREEMENTS MADE WITHOUT A REQUIRED LICENSE

All states require that persons engaged in certain occupations and businesses have a license or permit. Physicians, dentists, plumbers, electricians, druggists, real estate brokers, and insurance agents are among these persons. Licensing laws are usually enacted in order to prevent incompetent or dishonest persons from harming the health, morals, or welfare of the community. When this is the purpose of the law, any agreement made by or with an unlicensed person is void.

(8) AGREEMENTS THAT ARE UNCONSCIONABLE

Problem: Frostifresh Corporation sold a refrigerator-freezer to Reynoso, a Spanish-speaking individual, on an installment payment contract. The written contract was entirely in English although the negotiations and sale were made in Spanish and the seller knew Reynoso could not read English. The freezer, which cost the dealer $348, was sold for $1,146 including a credit charge of $246. Was this unconscionable?

The Uniform Commercial Code provides that a court may find that a contract or a clause of a contract is *unconscionable*—that is, so one-sided that it is commercially unreasonable, harsh, and oppressive. Such was the case in the problem. When a court decides a contract is unconscionable, it may refuse to enforce the contract, enforce the contract without the unconscionable clause, or limit its application so that the contract is no longer unfair. The Code provision is not designed to relieve a person of a bad bargain, but only to determine whether the contract was, in the light of the circumstances at the time of its making, unconscionable or oppressive, and therefore unenforceable as such.

(9) AGREEMENTS RESTRAINING TRADE UNREASONABLY

Problem: Haggblade and Litzinger were in the restraurant supply business in a certain city. They agreed that Haggblade would sell only to restaurants located north of Main Street and Litzinger only to those south of Main Street. If one of them violated the agreement by moving into the other's territory, could he be stopped?

Agreements that unreasonably restrain trade are void and accordingly unenforceable. Competition protects businessmen and consumers alike. Hence, both state and federal law seek to prevent monopolies and combinations that restrict competition, as in the problem, or that deprive a person of the means of earning a livelihood and engaging in the work for which he is best suited. Unless expressly permitted by statute, contracts are illegal as unreasonable restraints on trade in the following cases:

(a) When the restraint tends to control prices, limit production, or create a monopoly.

> The City of Squamish advertised for bids to pave two streets. Andrews and McKenna, paving contractors, agreed that each would submit bids on both jobs, but that on one bid McKenna would be low bidder and on the other, Andrews would make the low bid. Because this agreement was in restraint of trade and designed to control prices, it was illegal and void.

(b) When the restraint limits competition unreasonably.

> Garner had for many years held a contract to take photographs for the Sunset Heights High School annual. Crabtree, a photographer in a neighboring town, decided to make a competitive bid for the school's business. When Garner learned of Crabtree's intentions, he agreed to pay Crabtree $500 if he would not compete for the Sunset business. This agreement was unenforceable because it limited competition unreasonably.

A restraint is also considered to be unreasonable when it produces undue hardship upon the person subject to the restraint, or if the restraint is greater than necessary to protect the person benefitting from the restraint.

(c) When the restraint unreasonably limits the transfer of property.

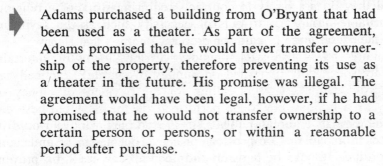 Adams purchased a building from O'Bryant that had been used as a theater. As part of the agreement, Adams promised that he would never transfer ownership of the property, therefore preventing its use as a theater in the future. His promise was illegal. The agreement would have been legal, however, if he had promised that he would not transfer ownership to a certain person or persons, or within a reasonable period after purchase.

ARE ANY AGREEMENTS IN RESTRAINT OF TRADE VALID?

Problem: Moss was employed as a dentist by Wise, who had an office in a small city. As part of his contract of employment, Moss agreed that for a period of two years after he left Wise's employment he would not practice dentistry within the city. If Moss failed to live up to the agreement, could Wise require him to do so?

Not all agreements that restrain trade are illegal, for some trade practices of this nature are believed to be socially and economically desirable if they are reasonable. For example, an inventor who holds a patent has the right to keep others from copying his invention. In some states a manufacturer of goods has the right to specify a price below which goods with his trademark may not be sold. Other examples of valid trade restraints include: (a) a contract in which one who sells his business promises not to compete with the buyer within a reasonable area or for a reasonable length of time; and (b) a promise of an employee to his employer not to work for a competitor for a reasonable time after termination of his employment. Thus, because the restraint placed on Moss in the problem was reasonable and necessary to protect Wise's dental practice, it was valid. Wise could prevent Moss from opening a competing practice within the area and time provided in the contract.

WHAT OTHER CONTRACTS ARE ILLEGAL?

Problem: Hodge borrowed $500 from Pengilly and agreed to repay her in 90 days. The due date fell on a Sunday. Does this have any effect on its legality?

Whenever a statute prohibits an act, it is illegal. Agreements made or to be performed on a Sunday are regulated by most states and some may be illegal and void. These "Sunday laws" vary, but in general they do not apply to contracts requiring work of a religious or charitable nature, or to acts of necessity such as the saving of life or the preserving of health or property.

In many states other acts, including various forms of entertainment, are specifically permitted on Sunday by statute. Practically all states provide that contracts calling for the payment of money on Sunday or a holiday are to be performed on the next business day after the Sunday or holiday. Thus, in the problem Hodge would be required to repay the loan on the next business day. Agreements made on a Sunday to be performed on a weekday are valid in most states provided they are ratified on a weekday.

Other agreements usually specified as illegal are those for the sale of certain drugs and narcotics except by a physician's prescription.

IN MAKING CONTRACTS...

1. Agreements made with unlicensed persons are generally void when licenses are required for that kind of service. Deal only with reputable, licensed, professional persons.
2. Most states impose penalties for charging excessive interest. Be aware of the legal rates of interest in your state.
3. Illegal agreements are unenforceable, and relief is generally not available to those parties to such agreements. Avoid entering such contracts.
4. Wagering is illegal in most states. Know the law in your state if you participate in wagering agreements.

YOUR LEGAL VOCABULARY

compounding a felony
contract rate
legal rate
illegal lobbying
  contract

unconscionable
usury
wager

1. A contract in which bribery, threat of loss of votes, or other improper means are used to influence legislation.
2. Unfair, oppressive, and commercially unreasonable.
3. The rate of interest specified by statute when no rate is stated in the contract.
4. The charging of interest on a loan beyond the maximum rate.
5. The rate agreed upon by parties to a contract for lending money.
6. A bet on any event the happening of which depends upon chance.
7. Accepting any money or property in return for a promise not to prosecute a felony.

REMEMBER THESE HIGHLIGHTS

1. The formation, purpose, and performance of an agreement must not be contrary to statutory or common law, contrary to public policy, or unconscionable.
2. Illegal agreements are usually void and therefore not enforceable by either party.
3. Among agreements violating law or public policy, and therefore unenforceable, are those which:
    (a) tend to obstruct justice;
    (b) tend to injure public service;
    (c) attack or undermine marriage;
    (d) involve gambling;
    (e) involve payment of usurious interest;
    (f) are made without a required license; or
    (g) restrain trade unreasonably.
4. Some agreements which restrain trade are valid and enforceable. These include agreements imposing reasonable limitations on competition in business or exercise of occupation.

LAW AS PEOPLE LIVE IT

1. Kane, defendant in a legal action, told Ling, a key witness for the plaintiff, that he would pay his expenses if he took a leisurely world cruise while the trial was in progress. Ling agreed, and upon his return presented his expense account to Kane. Can Ling collect?
2. Hardbeck caught his limit of trout but had no use for them. He sold them to Flewellen's Market despite a state law prohibiting the sale of fish and game caught by sportsmen without a commercial license. At the time of the agreement, Flewellen offered to let Hardbeck take out the value of the fish in trade. When Hardbeck later tried to do this, Flewellen refused. What rights does Hardbeck have?
3. Balko, owner of a grocery store, made application to the State Liquor Control Board for a $75 license to sell beer. When the application was denied, Vogt, a customer, told Balko he knew someone on the Board and could get a license for him for $300. Balko paid Vogt the money but never received the license. Can he recover the money?
4. Cox, who was old and lonely, feared that his daughter would leave him when she reached marriageable age. He therefore promised to pay her $10,000 if she would never marry, but stay with him as nurse and companion. His daughter agreed and accepted the $10,000. Five years later she married. Cox sued for breach of contract. Will he win?

5. Blum and Elias, each a road-building contractor, received information from the State Highway Commission that contracts for two state road projects would be let in their county to the lowest bidder. Blum and Elias agreed that Blum would not bid on the north project whereas Elias would not bid on the south project. However, Blum bid on and received the contracts for both projects whereupon Elias sued him for the profits on the north project. Should Elias win?
6. Sharp, who was experiencing serious financial difficulties, thought he could raise money quickly by having a fire and collecting on his fire insurance. He arranged to pay a character known as Droopy $10,000 to set fire to his business warehouse. Was this agreement void or voidable?
7. Clement lost a $200 bet with Dale and paid him the money. Later, when he learned that betting was illegal in his state, Clement attempted to have the agreement canceled and recover what he had paid. Will he succeed?
8. Lawrence, desperately in need of funds, borrowed $75 from Danton, promising to repay some of the principal each month and to pay interest at the rate of 10 percent a month on the unpaid balance. In your state would Danton be guilty of usury?
9. Weems, graduate of a recognized dental school in England, took up the practice of dentistry in a small town in the Midwest. He did not obtain a state license. Crowe, a patient, refused to pay his dental bill when he learned this. Can Weems collect?

LAW AS COURTS DECIDE IT

1. Melton purchased a truck from Prickett for $8,833 with a down payment and the balance due monthly. General Motors Acceptance Corporation assumed the contract and held a conditional title to the truck pending payment of the amount due. Melton was not given a certificate of title although a statute provided that "It shall be unlawful for any person to buy or sell in this state any vehicle . . . unless at the time of delivery thereof there shall pass between the parties a certificate of title . . . and the sale of any [such] vehicle . . . shall be void." Following a fire which practically destroyed the truck, Melton sued to recover the money he had paid; Prickett and GMAC filed a counterclaim for $3,806, the balance due. During the litigation that followed it was contended that the action should be dismissed because the contract was contrary to statute and void. Do you agree? (Melton v. Prickett, 203 Kan. 501, 456 P. 2d 24)
2. Robinson, assistant manager of a drugstore owned by the plaintiff, was implicated in and admitted the theft of cash and merchandise from the store. He signed an agreement to repay the store $2,000 and in fact did pay $741. He then refused to make further payments

and the store brought this action to require compliance with the contract. Robinson's defense is that he signed the agreement under duress, and he seeks recovery of the money paid. The agreement between Robinson and the store clearly indicates that the plaintiff agreed not to prosecute the defendant. Should judgment be given the plaintiff? (Gallaher Drug Company v. Robinson, 13 Ohio Misc. 216, 232 N.E. 2d 668)

3. Griffith commenced a suit for malpractice against a physician. To establish his case, he needed other physicians to testify that the defendant physician's conduct had not been in accord with sound medical practice. Griffith's attorney contacted Dr. Harris and Dr. Minton, both of whom agreed to testify favorably for Griffith. The doctors were to be paid as expert witnesses. When the time for the trial arrived, both Harris and Minton informed Griffith's attorney that they would not appear without being ordered to do so by the court, and that if they did testify, their testimony would not be favorable to Griffith. Because Griffith did not have any other medical testimony, his malpractice case was dismissed. He then sued the doctors for breach of contract. What result? (Griffith v. Harris, 17 Wisc. 2d 255, 116 N.W. 2d 133)

4. Lundstrom purchased a color television set on a time payment plan from Utah Electronics, Inc. The price was $995 although the recommended retail price was $695. The plaintiff now seeks to have the sale set aside, and claims the $300 between the recommended retail price and the time payment price was really interest and therefore constituted usury. Is he correct? (Lundstrom v. Radio Corporation of America, 17 Utah 114, 405 P. 2d 339)

5. A secret process known as TREAT-A-MATIC, developed by the plaintiff, Water Services, was designed to purify water for industrial purposes. As part of their contract of employment, all employees of Water Services were required to sign a statement promising that for two years after termination of employment the employee would not engage "in any business which reasonably [could] be considered competitive to Water Services in any territory in which he has performed services under this contract." Glad was employed for the territory in northern Georgia, where he learned the components, suppliers, and secret process of TREAT-A-MATIC. Two years later he resigned and was employed by the defendant, a competitor of Water Services who had been unable to develop a water purification system. Using the confidential information acquired from his previous employer, Glad helped to develop a competitive system known as TESTOMATIC. Water Services sued to enforce its agreement with Glad. Tesco claimed Glad's contract with Water Services was in restraint of trade. Judgment for whom? (Water Services, Inc. v. Tesco Chemical, Inc., 410 F. 2d 163)

CHAPTER 11 Consideration

1. Upon learning that you plan a trip to Europe, your grandmother promises to give you a movie camera. If she fails to do so, can you legally require her to keep her promise?

2. Your next-door neighbor offers to pay the rent for a nearby garage if you will stop parking your old car on the street in front of his house. If you agree, can you require him to pay?

3. You stop to help a stranded motorist and tow his car to his home. In gratitude, he then promises to send you $25. If he fails to keep his promise, can you compel him to do so?

WHAT IS CONSIDERATION?

Problem: When Craig heard that her 18-year-old nephew, Chuck Warmer, was planning to drop out of school, she wrote promising him a car if he would remain in school and graduate with his class. Chuck did so. Can he hold his aunt to her promise?

A contract is usually an agreement in which, in effect, one party says to another, "If you do this for me, I shall do that for you." The thing which one person asks another to do in return for his promise is the *consideration;* consideration may be the giving of another promise, or it may be an act. In the foregoing problem, Craig asked her nephew to act in a certain way—not to quit school but to remain and graduate with his class—in return for her promise to give him a car. His act was the consideration for her promise.

Consideration may also consist of *forbearance,* that is, refraining from doing what one has a right to do. You may, for example, refrain from practicing on your electric guitar for a month in return for the promise of a neighbor to pay you $10. Your forbearance is the consideration for his promise.

Thus, the consideration necessary to make a promise enforceable may consist of (a) a return promise, (b) an act performed, or (c) a forbearance.

Consideration must: (a) be lawful, and (b) require conduct that is not already required by law, or must prohibit conduct which is not already prohibited by law. If the consideration is a promise, the promise must also (c) be definite.

WHY IS CONSIDERATION REQUIRED?

Problem: Offen promised to give his girl friend, Lee, a ski outfit. Later, when they quarreled, he refused to carry out his promise. What, if anything, could Lee do to compel Offen to make good on his promise?

Consideration is required to make a promise binding. If no consideration is given, the agreement normally results only in a moral obligation which the courts will not enforce. Thus, in the problem, Lee would have no legal right to compel Offen to fulfill his promise because she gave no consideration for it. If a gift has actually been made, the courts usually will not require it to be returned. Also, if a promise is performed voluntarily without consideration, it is valid.

As you study other parts of this book you will find that consideration is presumed to exist in certain agreements, such as contracts under seal in some states. A *seal* may be an impression on paper, a "wafer" (round piece of paper) affixed to the contract, the word "Seal," or the letters "L.S." (an abbreviation for the Latin words meaning "place of the seal"). In the early days, when few people could read or write, a person who wished to bind himself to some act would affix his seal to the writing. In most states today, the seal is not a substitute for consideration.

In several states consideration will be presumed if the promise is in writing, and in other states certain written promises are binding even if there is no consideration given in exchange for the promise. For example, under the Uniform Commercial Code certain written agreements made by merchants need no consideration.

WHAT IS ADEQUATE CONSIDERATION?

Problem: While cleaning out her attic, Blum found an old glass lampshade. Oliver, recognizing it as an antique made of Tiffany glass, offered Blum $150 for it. Blum accepted the offer but before Oliver picked it up Blum learned that the shade was worth at least $350. She attempted to cancel the contract because the consideration was not adequate. Could she do so?

We all know that the value different persons place on the same property may vary. While a collector of rare old spoons may think that $150 is a very reasonable price to pay for an unusual piece, most of us would not think of paying that much for a spoon. Also, a person may place greater value on a thing at one time than another. A can of gasoline is worth more to someone stranded on a deserted highway than at a city service station. What is fair, reasonable, or adequate consideration is very difficult to determine. Therefore, unless it is required by statute or there is evidence of bad faith, fraud, or unconscionable dealing, courts do not inquire as to the adequacy of the consideration. A grossly inadequate consideration may, of course, be regarded with suspicion as possible evidence of fraud. But generally, how small or large the actual value may be is immaterial so long as the parties have agreed. Thus Blum, in the problem, could be held to her promise to sell the lamp for $150.

The adequacy of consideration generally does not concern the courts.

It is not uncommon in certain written contracts to refer to the consideration as one dollar or some other small amount which bears no relation to the real value of the contract. This is known as *nominal consideration.* Courts enforce contracts supported by nominal consideration if the relation of the parties and other circumstances indicate that, in fact, consideration was given. If it is clear, however, that the nominal consideration was stated to give the appearance of validity and that no consideration was actually given in exchange for the promise, most courts will not enforce the contract.

IS AN EXISTING OBLIGATION CONSIDERATION?

Problem: Bolt contracted to have Putney overhaul the engine of his car for $265 plus the cost of any parts. Before he delivered the car to Putney, Bolt asked Perry for an estimate. Perry offered to do the job for $225 plus parts. Thereupon Bolt talked with Putney, who agreed to meet Perry's price. Can Putney be held to the lower price?

If a person does or promises to do something that he is by law already bound to do, the act or promise does not constitute consideration and cannot be used as such in exchange for the promise of the other party. This rule applies in the case of Bolt and Putney. Bolt was already legally obligated to pay for the overhaul job. Thus, in order to bind Putney to his promise to reduce the price, Bolt would have to provide some new consideration. If he does not, he is obligated to pay the $265 as originally agreed.

The same rule holds true when a person demands further compensation for carrying out a contract he has made.

 Andreas contracted with the Chamber of Commerce to build a float at a cost of $10,000 for the parade celebrating the city's centennial year. Two weeks before the parade, Andreas refused to complete the float unless the Chamber would promise to pay him $12,500. The Chamber made the promise; but Andreas could not collect the additional money because he was already obligated to complete the float. The Chamber would receive nothing more for its promise to pay the additional $2,500.

This rule is usually also applied when a creditor (one to whom a debt is owed) agrees to accept less than the total amount due in full settlement of a debt. Thus, if one person owes another $200, a promise by the creditor to accept $100 in full payment is not binding; the creditor may change his mind because the debtor's partial payment is not consideration. In a few states, however, the debtor's payment of a lesser sum than due supports a creditor's promise to release the indebtedness in full.

 Fikes borrowed $500 from Baxter, but when payment was due he said he was able to pay only $350. Baxter agreed to accept that amount and release Fikes from paying the balance. According to the laws in most states, Baxter could not be held to his agreement because there was no consideration for his promise. Fikes did not promise to do anything he was not previously obligated to do.

When a debtor who pays or agrees to pay his creditor less than the amount due also gives or does something else, there is consideration for the acceptance of the smaller amount by the creditor. Thus, payment of a debt before it is due, or the giving of something extra—such as a pen and pencil set—is consideration for the release of the remainder of the debt.

Under the UCC, modification or change in a contract for the sale of goods needs no consideration to support the promise to change the terms.

HOW MAY FORBEARANCE BE CONSIDERATION?

> **Problem:** Peters' son had purchased an expensive suit on credit from the Toggery. When he did not pay, the store's owner, Martin, threatened to sue him. Peters promised to pay the amount due provided Martin would refrain from suing his son. Can Martin hold Peters to his promise?

We have seen that giving up or promising to give up a right to do what one is legally entitled to do may constitute consideration. In Peters' case the promise of Martin to refrain from suing his son constituted a forbearance and was consideration for his promise to pay the son's debt.

Forbearance is commonly the consideration in cases of compromise. To illustrate, if a person has been injured in an automobile accident, he may have a right to sue for damages. He may promise not to bring suit in return for the promise of the other party to pay him a specified sum of money.

Another example is the case of compromise between debtor and creditor. If there is an honest dispute between the parties as to the amount owed, payment of less than the claimed amount is consideration for the creditor's agreement to release the debtor in full. If the debtor contends in good faith that the debt is $50 and the creditor in good faith contends that it is $100, and if the parties agree respectively to pay and accept $75, the agreement is binding. The consideration for the promise of each is the other's refraining or promising to refrain from taking the matter to court. This is known as *compromise of a disputed claim.* Under the UCC, if the creditor accepts a check for part of a debt with the notation that it is intended as payment in full, the entire debt is released even if no dispute exists.

Creditors of a debtor may agree to accept a certain proportion of their claims in full satisfaction of the debtor's obligations. This is known as a *composition of creditors,* and it is binding on all who agree. Consideration for the promise of each creditor to release the debtor from full payment of his debts is the promise by the other creditors to refrain from bringing suit for the entire amount due them.

 Oberlin was in financial trouble. He owed Foley $10,000 and Roth $15,000 for merchandise he had bought. To enable Oberlin to stay in business, Foley and Roth agreed to accept 60 percent of their claims in full settlement. This agreement was a composition of creditors, and neither creditor could collect the unpaid 40 percent of his claim.

IS PAST PERFORMANCE CONSIDERATION?

Problem: Don and Nan Best named their baby Eric Durham after a boyhood friend of Don's. Durham, who was pleased with this, promised to give them a $1,000 savings bond to be used for Eric's education. If Durham failed to keep his promise, could it be enforced?

You recall that consideration is what one person asks of another in return for his promise. The consideration therefore must be given after the promisor states what he requests. An act performed or a promise given independently, before it is requested in exchange for another's promise, is a *past consideration* and legally is no consideration at all. Thus, the Bests' naming of the baby was no consideration and the promise of Durham is unenforceable.

If Durham should give Best the bond, as promised, he would be making a gift. A *gift* is the voluntary transfer of ownership of property without consideration. A gift that has been performed or transferred cannot be recovered by the donor; the one receiving it has good title to it. On the other hand, promises to make a gift cannot be enforced.

ARE CHARITABLE SUBSCRIPTIONS BINDING?

Problem: Hollowell pledged $5,000 to the building fund of the Community Hospital. Relying on this and other pledges, the Board of Directors of the hospital entered into a contract for construction of a new wing. Can Hollowell be held to his pledge?

Whenever a person makes a subscription or otherwise pledges to pay money to a church, a community chest or united appeal, a nonprofit college, or other charitable organization that depends on voluntary contributions, he may think he is simply promising to make a gift. As a matter of public policy, however, the courts generally hold that such subscriptions are binding obligations. Thus, Hollowell's subscription could be enforced even though he might argue that he received nothing in exchange for his promise.

FRANKLIN COLLEGE BUILDING FUND

To provide additional library space and facilities and in consideration of the gifts of others, I (we) subscribe to the FRANKLIN COLLEGE BUILDING FUND

the sum of _One hundred_ Dollars ($ _100.00_)

TOTAL SUBSCRIPTION	$100.00
AMOUNT PAID	20.00
BALANCE	80.00

Balance to be paid: _$20 quarterly_

Jan Jaffe
(Donor's Signature)

March 1, 19 – –
(Date)

Subscription to a Building Fund

TO PREVENT MISUNDERSTANDINGS ABOUT CONTRACTS, REMEMBER THAT . . .

1. Consideration is a necessity if a contract is to be binding.
2. Once a valid contract has been made, adequacy of consideration is generally considered unimportant. Be sure that you know and are satisfied with the true value of the consideration before entering into the contract.
3. Promises to make gifts cannot be enforced by the donee, and may be revoked without liability by the donor.
4. A pledge to pay money to a charitable institution is generally held to be a binding obligation. A pledge should not be made unless the pledgor intends to fulfill it.

YOUR LEGAL VOCABULARY

composition of
creditors

compromise of a
disputed claim

consideration

forbearance

gift

nominal consideration

past consideration

seal

1. A consideration which bears no relation to the real value of the contract.
2. Refraining from doing what one has a right to do.
3. Mutual promises of a debtor and creditor to refrain from going to court to litigate a disagreement regarding the amount of a debt.
4. An impression on paper, a word or letters other than a signature indicating intent to bind one to a contract.
5. The agreement of all creditors to accept a proportion of their claims in full satisfaction of a debtor's obligations.
6. What one person asks another to do or give in return for his promise.
7. A voluntary transfer of ownership of property without consideration.
8. An act performed or a promise given independently, before it is requested in exchange for another's promise.

REMEMBER THESE HIGHLIGHTS

1. A lawful consideration is necessary to make a promise binding. Such consideration may consist of a return promise, an act, or a forbearance.
2. The adequacy or fairness of the consideration is immaterial as long as the consideration is what the promisor requests in return for his promise.
3. Performing or promising to perform an existing obligation is not valid consideration.
4. Past performance or a past promise is not valid consideration for a promise given in the present or the future.
5. If the doing of an act is illegal, forbearing to do the act or promising to forbear is not valid consideration.
6. Agreements modifying contracts for the sale of goods need no further consideration to be binding.
7. Pledges to pay money to charitable enterprises are usually held to be enforceable promises.

LAW AS PEOPLE LIVE IT

1. Herbold was hoping to commute to college the following year but had no means of transportation. His brother promised to give him a

secondhand motorcycle, but he later refused to carry out his promise. Can Herbold legally require his brother to fulfill his promise?

2. Woodwick promised to pay $1,000 to his niece, who planned to quit her course in nursing, if she would continue and become a registered nurse. The niece complied, but Woodwick then refused to pay the $1,000 on the grounds that completion of the course contributed to her own success and there was no consideration for his promise. Can Woodwick's niece collect the $1,000?

3. Kirshen contracted to recover a sofa for Bohman for $295, including materials. When the work was partially completed, Kirshen discovered he had made a mistake and that the amount was inadequate. He refused to complete the work unless Bohman promised to pay him $400. Was Kirshen within his rights?

4. Paterni Paving Co. contracted to pave a driveway and parking lot for Mooradian Market. Mooradian accepted the contract price of $2,500 in good faith, but when the job was partially completed Paterni discovered that he had made an error in his bid. He informed Mooradian that he would be unable to complete the job unless he was paid an additional $600. Mooradian agreed to pay the additional amount but when the job was completed claimed all he owed Paterni was $2,500. Is that correct?

5. Gilliland owed Haskins $500 that was due and payable. Gilliland was expecting an inheritance, and so asked Haskins to extend the time of payment for six months. Haskins agreed, but shortly thereafter brought suit against Gilliland to collect the debt. Will the suit be successful?

6. Bashford's daughter bought an electric typewriter from Spangler on an installment plan. When she was unable to keep up the payments, Spangler came to repossess the typewriter in accordance with the terms of the contract. Bashford promised to make the payments if Spangler would allow the daughter to keep the typewriter. If Spangler agreed, could Bashford hold him to his promise?

7. On December 10, Petrucci contracted with Norton to paint both the interior and exterior of Norton's house for $750. Payment was due in 60 days. On January 5, Petrucci offered to accept $650 in full settlement of the debt if Norton paid that day. Norton agreed, and on that date paid the $650. Later Petrucci changed his mind and sued Norton for the $100 balance. Will Petrucci succeed in his suit?

8. Upon returning from a vacation trip, Biggerstaff found that his neighbor had mowed and watered his lawn during his absence. In gratitude, Biggerstaff telephoned the neighbor and promised to pay him $10. Is he legally bound to keep his promise?

9. Lease owed Goddard $1,000, Riniker $3,000, and certain sums to other creditors as well. Lease had only enough assets to pay each creditor sixty cents on each dollar he owed. All the creditors agreed

to accept that amount. After Lease paid all his creditors 60 percent of their claims, Goddard and Riniker filed suits for the 40 percent balance due them. Must Lease pay?

10. A dispute arose between Joyce and Littlejohn over Joyce's debt. In good faith, Joyce claimed he owed $1,400. Littlejohn insisted that his records showed it was $1,900 but finally agreed to accept $1,600, which Joyce paid. Later Littlejohn sued for the remaining $300. Will he be successful?

LAW AS COURTS DECIDE IT

1. The plaintiff, Glen Manufacturing, held a patent on a particular type of toilet tank cover and licensed the defendant, Perfect Fit Industries, to manufacture them. The agreement provided that Perfect Fit was to pay Glen Manufacturing ten cents for each toilet tank cover made or sold by them. Perfect Fit also manufactured other tank covers not licensed. No royalty payment had been made on the 157,400 covers produced. The plaintiff claimed that payment is due on all covers made or manufactured whether under the patent license or not. Defendant claimed payment is due only for covers manufactured under the patent license, and that the agreement to pay on all covers made is illegal because it was misuse of the patent and tended to promote a monopoly. Is the promise of Perfect Fit to pay royalties on all toilet tank covers manufactured by them enforceable? (Glen Manufacturing, Inc. v. Perfect Fit Industries, Inc., 299 F. Supp. 278)

2. McMillan was paid $1,000 when he granted to Carolina Power and Light Company a right of way for its power line to cross an extensive timber tract. The deed granting the right of way also gave the power company the right to cut down trees outside the right of way which might endanger the power line. McMillan sold the land to the Weyerhauser Company subject to the right of way. Weyerhauser now claims that it is entitled to damages for trees cut down off the right of way. In part, Weyerhauser's case is based on a claim that $1,000 was inadequate consideration for the valuable right of way and the continuous right to cut down valuable timber. Weyerhauser claims that because of this inadequacy it is not bound by the contract and should be paid for the trees cut down. Is Weyerhauser correct? (Weyerhauser Company v. Carolina Power and Light Company, 257 N.C. 717, 127 S.E. 2d 539)

3. Louis Dahn and his wife Mamie purchased a mobile home. The buyers financed the purchase through the Fourth National Bank and Trust Company, and the bank reserved the right to take possession of the mobile home upon any default of payment. After the death

of Louis, Mamie notified the bank that she was unable to keep up the payments, and stated that it could repossess the mobile home. After the bank took possession, Mrs. Dahn objected and filed this action, claiming there was no consideration for her promise to allow the bank to repossess the property. Do you agree? (In re Estate of Dahn, 204 Kan. 535, 464 P. 2d 238)

4. Skinner and Smith had a dispute regarding the value of certain real property in Atlanta. To settle the matter, they agreed to be bound by the appraisal of a real estate appraiser mutually acceptable and agreed upon by the two parties. The agreement also provided that if the appraisal exceeded $24,735, Smith would pay Skinner the difference in "full and final settlement." If the appraisal was less than $24,735, Skinner agreed to pay Smith the difference. The appraiser valued the property at $20,000. Skinner objected to the report, claiming errors in it. Must he abide by the appraisal? (Skinner v. Smith, 120 Ga. App. 35, 169 S.E. 2d 365)

5. Boston Redevelopment Authority, acting under its legal power, purchased the building in which the plaintiff, Graphic Arts, conducted its business. To induce the plaintiff to leave the premises "peacefully and expeditiously without requiring legal action" and "to relocate its business elsewhere and not liquidate," i.e. go out of business, the Authority promised to pay the "total certified actual moving expenses" of Graphic Arts. Graphic Arts agreed to move and complied with all conditions; its moving expenses amounted to $130,000. Boston Redevelopment Authority had paid all but $54,069 of this, and Graphic Arts seeks the balance due. The Authority claimed its promise was without consideration and sought to have the legal action dismissed. Should this be done? (Graphic Arts Finishers, Inc. v. Boston Redevelopment Authority, 255 N.E. 2d 793, Mass.)

6. Powell entered into a contract of employment with the plaintiff, Abalene, as a pest exterminator. He agreed, among other things, not to engage in the exterminating business himself or as an employee of any other firm within a specified five-county area for five years after terminating his employment. Later, in violation of the agreement, Powell organized his own exterminating business. Abalene claimed Powell had breached his contract and asked for an injunction to stop him. Powell claimed his promise not to compete with his employer was not supported by consideration. Is that correct? (Abalene Pest Control Service, Inc. v. Powell, 176 N.Y.S. 2d 6)

CHAPTER 12 Form of Agreement

1. *A dealer convinces you to buy an accordian when he promises to take it back if you cannot learn to play it. This promise is not in the written contract you sign. Can you legally hold the dealer to his promise?*

2. *A friend orally agrees to pay a sports shop for a $75 pair of skis you wish to buy. Can the shop owner collect from your friend?*

3. *Your father signed a printed note promising to pay $1,000 and interest at 7 percent. After signing, a typist had typed in "7" and did not delete the "8" printed on the note. What rate of interest must your father pay?*

MUST CONTRACTS BE IN ANY SPECIAL FORM?

Problem: Scholten orally agreed to sell 100 acres of his farm to Belden Brick Corporation. When Belden later asked Scholten to sign a contract, he said he had changed his mind and wouldn't sign or sell anything. Can Belden enforce the agreement?

Unless a particular form is required by statute, contracts may be oral or written. Most contracts are oral. Many are made by telephone. Others are made and carried out in a single face-to-face conversation; for example, in the sale of personal property, the payment and the delivery of the goods often occur at the time the agreement is made. A person may take a job, ride a bus, rent an apartment, and enter many other business agreements without the formality of a written contract. Business could scarcely be conducted on any other basis.

There are, however, certain kinds of agreements, described later in this chapter, which cannot be enforced in court unless there is some writing to prove their existence. The agreement in the problem, involving the sale of land, is one of these types. Because the agreement was not in writing, Belden could not require Scholten to fulfill his contract.

Even when a written contract is not required, there are many times when it is sensible and desirable to reduce an agreement to writing. This would be true when the agreement is complex and contains many details which could lead to later misunderstandings. It would also apply when large sums of money or long periods of time are involved, especially when one is dealing with strangers. In any of these cases, both parties will probably want to see and have the terms in definite, written form. They are thus assured that the other party cannot effectively deny ever having made the contract, and the chance of later confusion or disagreement is greatly reduced. In' the end, putting the contract in writing may even save the time and great expense that would arise from a legal action. Whenever possible or practical, prudent persons seek the aid of a lawyer in the preparation or review of important contracts.

HOW ARE CONTRACTS CLASSIFIED?

> **Problem:** Langley walked up to the ticket booth at a movie theater. He gave the cashier the price of admission and she gave him a ticket. No words were spoken. What kind of a contract was this?

Contracts may be classified in various ways, according to their various characteristics. A single contract may be classified in more than one of the following categories:

(1) EXPRESS AND IMPLIED CONTRACTS

(a) **Express contracts.** An *express contract* is one in which the agreement is stated in words, written or spoken.

An express contract is stated in words, written or spoken.

(b) **Implied contracts.** An *implied contract* is one in which the intent of the parties is shown by their conduct and actions. Langley, in the problem above, made an implied contract with the theater cashier.

(2) FORMAL AND SIMPLE CONTRACTS

(a) Formal contracts. A *formal contract* is a written contract that must be in some special form in order to be enforceable. Two kinds of formal contracts are: (a) commercial paper, and (b) contracts under seal. Commercial paper is a special contract, such as an ordinary check, that must be in writing and meet certain other requirements, such as the use of certain words, to be valid. Commercial paper is discussed in Unit VII. A *contract under seal* is a contract to which a seal is attached. In some states, certain contracts are required to be under seal in order to be valid.

(b) Simple contracts. All contracts which are not formal are *simple contracts,* whether oral, written, or based on conduct. Some simple contracts must be evidenced by a writing in order to be enforceable.

(3) EXECUTED AND EXECUTORY CONTRACTS

(a) Executed contracts. An *executed contract* is one that has been fully performed or completed by both parties.

> You order two hamburgers "to go" at The Hangout. The cashier takes your money and hands you a bag containing your order. This is an executed contract because it has been fully performed.

(b) Executory contracts. An *executory contract* is one that has not been fully performed—that is, the terms of the agreement have not been carried out by one or both of the parties.

WHAT IS THE STATUTE OF FRAUDS?

Problem: Boggs orally agreed to employ Elias for three years at a salary of $12,000 the first year, $14,000 the second year, and the third year salary would be negotiated at the end of the second year. At the end of the first year, Elias expected the pay increase, but Boggs claimed it was agreed to negotiate it. How could this difference have been avoided?

One important purpose of business law is to protect and aid persons in their business dealings. Requiring that certain types of agreements be in writing to be enforced is one way of providing this protection. A writing is more reliable proof of an executory agreement than oral evidence based on memory, and a writing is not affected by the death or absence of witnesses. It also prevents dishonest persons from intentionally misrepresenting the facts of an oral agreement. Thus, the differences between Boggs and Elias, in the problem, could have been avoided if the contract had been in writing.

Years ago, injustices arising from the failure of memory or intentional misrepresentation were found to be most frequent in certain kinds of oral contracts. To reduce these injustices, the English Parliament in 1677 enacted a statute which, among other things, required written evidence of certain agreements. This statute, because it was designed to prevent fraud, was called the *Statute of Frauds.* The name is now commonly used to designate statutes enacted by all states which require written evidence if certain contracts are to be enforced.

Agreements subject to the Statute of Frauds are enforceable only against those who have signed a statement containing the essential terms of the agreement. The act does not prevent the performance of oral agreements and does not affect oral agreements which have been fully performed.

WHAT CONTRACTS ARE SUBJECT TO THE STATUTE OF FRAUDS?

Problem: When Lawrence purchased a new car, he decided to sell his old one instead of trading it in. Zall agreed to buy the old car for $750. He promised to pay for it within six weeks and take delivery of it when he paid. To be enforceable, must this contract be in writing?

To be enforceable under the Statute of Frauds, the following six types of executory contracts (and, in some states, other types of contracts) require written and signed evidence of agreement. Unless otherwise provided by statute, these contracts must either be (a) in writing, or (b) evidenced by a memorandum. In either case, the writing must be signed by the party against whom the contract is to be enforced, although in good business practice both parties would sign.

Contracts subject to the Statute of Frauds include those:

1. To buy and sell goods for a price of $500 or more;[1]
2. To buy and sell real property;
3. That cannot be performed within a year;

[1] All states except Louisiana have adopted the $500 figure specified by the UCC. Also in Louisiana, there is no requirement for a writing.

4. To answer for the obligation of another person;
5. Having marriage as a consideration;
6. To be personally liable for a debt of an estate.

(1) A CONTRACT FOR THE SALE OF GOODS FOR $500 OR MORE

Although this type of contract must generally be evidenced by a writing to be enforceable, there are exceptions, as discussed in Chapter 18. However, in the ordinary situation, there would have to be written proof of an agreement like the one in the problem if it is to be enforced. The writing would need to be signed by the person against whom enforcement was sought. That is, if Lawrence refused to sell, Zall could enforce the agreement only if Lawrence had signed. Likewise, Zall must have signed in order for Lawrence to enforce Zall's promise to buy at the agreed price.

(2) A CONTRACT TO SELL OR A SALE OF ANY INTEREST IN REAL PROPERTY

Problem: Carr orally agreed to sell his house to Ellis at a price of $27,000. Soon thereafter, Carr was offered $35,000 for the property by Rogers. Can Ellis hold Carr to his agreement?

The transfer of, or promise to transfer, any interest in real property—that is, land, buildings, and other things permanently attached to land—must be in writing to be enforceable. Thus, there should be written evidence of transfers of title to and of contracts to sell or mortgage the entire property; likewise, transfers of lesser interests, such as the right to remove oil or timber from land, must be in writing. Although leases come under this classification, most states have special statutes which provide that oral leases for a period of one year or less may be enforced. In the problem, unless the agreement is evidenced by a writing and signed by Carr, Ellis cannot hold Carr to the oral contract. Similarly, if Ellis changes his mind, he cannot be held to the agreement unless he has signed it.

An agreement authorizing or employing an agent (see Unit IX) to buy or sell land must also be in writing in some states.

(3) A CONTRACT THAT CANNOT BE PERFORMED WITHIN ONE YEAR AFTER ITS MAKING

Problem: In April, Hobart telephoned his young friend, Sherman, and promised him a job in the computer department of Hobart Enterprises "for a year at the usual

> wages" beginning when Sherman graduated from school in June. Sherman accepted immediately. If Hobart later refused to employ Sherman, could Sherman enforce the agreement?

A contract which cannot be performed within a year from the time it is made will not be enforced by courts unless there is written proof of the agreement. Notice that the year is figured from the time the agreement is reached, not from the time performance is to begin. Accordingly, the agreement in the problem was not enforceable.

This provision does not apply to agreements that can be carried out within a year, even if such agreements are not actually carried out within that time. The test is not whether the agreement is actually performed within a year, but whether there is a possibility of performance within a year. To illustrate, one person's oral agreement to work for another "as long as the business exists" is binding. This is because the agreement might be performed within a year, even if the performance is expected to continue longer if the business succeeds. On the other hand, an agreement to support a three-year-old child until he attains his majority must be in writing to be enforceable because the contract will definitely require more than a year for its completion.

(4) A CONTRACT TO ANSWER FOR THE OBLIGATION OF AN-OTHER PERSON

> **Problem:** Sheldon wished to buy a color TV from Hayden, who was doubtful of his credit standing. Sheldon's friend, Lewis, who had accompanied him on the buying trip, said, "If Sheldon doesn't pay you, I will." Can Hayden enforce Lewis' promise?

This provision of the Statute of Frauds refers to a promise to answer for the debt or default of another person, a subject discussed in Unit VI. In the above problem, Lewis' promise is unenforceable because it is not in writing and signed by him.

(5) A CONTRACT FOR WHICH THE CONSIDERATION IS MAR-RIAGE

> **Problem:** During a telephone conversation, Sellers vowed to provide for the support of Sandra's mother if Sandra would marry him. Is Sellers' promise enforceable?

This provision of the statute applies only to agreements which have marriage as the consideration for a promise to pay money or transfer property to another, or to give some other valuable consideration. Mutual promises to marry do not come under this provision. In the problem, Sellers' promise is unenforceable.

(6) A CONTRACT BY AN EXECUTOR OR ADMINISTRATOR TO BE PERSONALLY LIABLE FOR CLAIMS AGAINST THE ESTATE OF A DECEASED PERSON

Problem: Woodward was executor of Giffin's estate. At the time of his death, Giffin owed Eaton $10,000. Woodward wrote Eaton that he was sure there were sufficient funds in the estate to pay him and that he would "see that you are paid from the estate." Can Woodward be held personally liable for the debt?

An executor or administrator is one who settles the affairs of a deceased person. (His duties are discussed in Chapter 42.) He pays the debts, carries out the terms of the will (if there is one), and distributes the rest of the personal estate. A personal representative of this kind is under a duty to pay the debts of the deceased person out of the latter's estate. He is not, however, personally liable for such claims unless he expressly agrees to pay them. Thus, in the problem, Woodward cannot be held personally liable for Eaton's debt; his letter stated only that the debt would be paid from the estate. If the executor or administrator promises to pay a claim made against the estate out of his own pocket, the agreement, in order to be enforceable, must be in writing and signed by him.

WHAT SHOULD A MEMORANDUM CONTAIN?

Problem: Smittcamp entered into an oral contract to sell his entire crop of peaches for five years at the market price to Wawona Cannery. Later he decided he did not want to sell his crop to Wawona and wrote, "Re my peach crop—I have changed my mind and do not wish to sell my peaches to you for five years as we discussed" and signed his name. Was this writing a sufficient memorandum to allow Wawona to enforce the contract against Smittcamp?

A memorandum is evidence of an agreement which, in most states, satisfies the writing requirement of the Statute of Frauds. Usually any wording that clearly states the material terms of the agreement will do. However, in the case of a sale of goods, the UCC provides that the memorandum need only state a quantity of described goods which are involved and indicate that there has been a sale relating to them. Thus, the letter Smittcamp wrote in the foregoing problem would actually prove the existence of the agreement to sell his peach crop to Wawona.

The memorandum need not be in any special form. Indeed, it does not have to be a single writing. A series of writings, such as an exchange of letters or telegrams, is sufficient if it is complete and if the writings refer to one another in such a way that they are clearly part of the same agreement. The memorandum may be printed, typed, or written by pen or pencil. The signature may be written, stamped, engraved, or printed. It may consist of any mark that is intended as a signature. An adequate memorandum includes:

1. Date and place of the contract;
2. Names of the parties;
3. All material terms of the agreement, usually including the subject matter, price, and any special conditions such as time or method of delivery and terms of payment;
4. The signature of the party who is being sued. This signature may be by an agent.

These items do not need to be in any particular order. If custom or business usage is well established, some items need not be included. For example, such items as terms of payment and delivery, even price, are often omitted from orders for goods because they are governed by custom.

WHAT IS THE EFFECT OF FAILURE TO COMPLY?

Problem: Poole wrote Mortimer, offering to sell his mountain cabin for a specified price and asking for an immediate reply. Mortimer telephoned Poole accepting the offer. If Mortimer defaulted on his promise to buy the cabin, what rights would Poole have?

One purpose of having written proof of certain contracts is to be able to establish the intent of the parties if the contract must be enforced through court action. It has nothing to do with the legality of the contract. Thus, an oral agreement which falls into one of the classes of contract subject to the Statute of Frauds is as legal as any other. The parties may fulfill their agreement by performing voluntarily. Failure to comply with the statute simply means that when complications arise—for instance, one party fails or refuses to perform as agreed—courts will not enforce the contract. This is true even though the agreement is a valid contract in every other way. If the writing or memorandum is signed by one party to the contract, as in the problem, it can be enforced against him (Poole) but not against the other party (Mortimer). If such a contract is carried out, however, neither party may thereafter complain of the contract's failure to comply with the Statute of Frauds.

WHAT IS THE PAROL EVIDENCE RULE?

Problem: Spaulding bought a new car from Wayne Motors, signing the usual contract which stated the terms completely. Later Spaulding alleged that as part of the bargain Wayne orally promised that, if within two months the factory list price was reduced, he would lower the price by the same amount for Spaulding. The factory list price was reduced, but Wayne refused to pass the savings on to Spaulding. What were Spaulding's rights?

When parties have put their agreement in writing, the *parol evidence rule* declares the writing to be the only allowable evidence of the terms of the contract. Parol evidence, which includes all prior oral or written agreements or other outside evidence, is generally not allowed to add to, subtract from, or otherwise change the written contract. The law presumes that, in reducing their agreement to writing, the parties have included (or intended to exclude) all previous oral or written agreements. Accordingly, the writing is held to be the best evidence of their intent. In the problem, therefore, it could not be proved in court that Wayne's promise was ever made. Spaulding should have included all of the terms of the agreement in the written contract.

Parol evidence may be used, however, to prove such things as mistake, fraud, illegality, customs and trade usage, clerical errors, and the meaning of terms. When a contract is obviously ambiguous, parol evidence may be used to clarify terms in order to determine the true intent of the parties. Such evidence does not change the writing but rather explains the meaning of the writing or shows that there never was any enforceable contract.

HOW ARE WRITTEN CONTRACTS INTERPRETED?

Problem: Piersol purchased a car on installments from Mikesell for $2,000. The written contract provided that monthly payments of $100 were to be made on the first of each month. Piersol explained he did not receive his paycheck until the tenth and would prefer to make the payments on that date. Mikesell agreed and crossed out the printed word "first," wrote in "tenth," and initialed it. During the first month, however, Mikesell sought to repossess the car when Piersol failed to make the payment on the first. Will he succeed?

Even though the parties put their contract in writing, something in it may not be quite clear or require interpretation. This is frequently the case when printed order blanks are used. It also occurs when partially printed contract forms are used, because in the completion of the forms some contradictory terms may be added. Moreover, words do not always have the same meaning to different persons. One person may use a term that seems perfectly clear to him, but which may mean something quite different to the party with whom he is dealing.

Because of these and other difficulties that arise between parties even when the contract is written, the courts have adopted a number of rules that are applied in interpreting the meaning of contracts.

(1) THE WRITING IS TO BE CONSIDERED AS A SINGLE, WHOLE DOCUMENT

For example, each clause must be interpreted in the light of all other provisions of the contract. Words are interpreted as they are ordinarily used unless circumstances indicate a different meaning. Technical terms or abbreviations are given their technical meaning unless the contract as a whole shows a different meaning is intended.

(2) WHERE A PRINTED FORM IS USED, TYPEWRITTEN PROVISIONS WILL PREVAIL OVER CONTRADICTORY PRINTED PROVISIONS, AND HANDWRITTEN ONES OVER BOTH PRINTED AND TYPEWRITTEN

Similarly, if the contract is typewritten, handwriting will prevail over the typing. Presumably, the writing is the latest expression of intent. Thus, in the problem, payments by Piersol were not due until the tenth of the month.

(3) IF WORDS AND FIGURES ARE INCONSISTENT, THE WORDS WILL PREVAIL

One is less likely to make a mistake in writing out a number in words.

THIS AGREEMENT, made on April 13, 19--, between
Robert A. Littlefield, 7023 Paddison Road, Cincinnati,
Ohio, and Sherman Tatum, 316 Third Street, Cincinnati,
Ohio.

Littlefield agrees to furnish all materials and
perform all the work as shown on the specifications
attached hereto entitled "Plans for Landscaping the
property located at 316 Third Street, Cincinnati, Ohio,"
as prepared by Henry Semple, Architect, 400 Central
Avenue, Cincinnati, Ohio. In consideration for which
Tatum agrees to pay Littlefield the sum of $850 upon
satisfactory completion of the work.

Robert A. Littlefield

Sherman Tatum

Contract

(4) WHERE THERE IS A CUSTOM OR TRADE PRACTICE WHICH APPLIES, BOTH PARTIES WILL BE PRESUMED TO KNOW OF IT AND THE CONTRACT WILL BE INTERPRETED IN LIGHT OF THAT CUSTOM OR TRADE PRACTICE

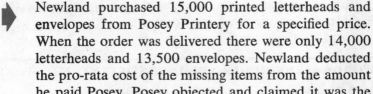

Newland purchased 15,000 printed letterheads and
envelopes from Posey Printery for a specified price.
When the order was delivered there were only 14,000
letterheads and 13,500 envelopes. Newland deducted
the pro-rata cost of the missing items from the amount
he paid Posey. Posey objected and claimed it was the
custom in the job printing industry that the contract
was fulfilled if the order was within ten percent over

or under the amount ordered. If this was true, Newland would have to pay the total amount due.

BEFORE YOU SIGN A CONTRACT...

1. Read it carefully, especially if it has been prepared by the
   other party. The small print is just as much a part of the contract as the large print.
2. Insist that the other party to the contract also sign. If the
   other party cannot write his name, ask him to make his mark
   and have it witnessed.
3. Insist on interpretation of any terms you do not understand.
   If the interpretation given is not what you thought it should be,
   write in such clauses as will make the meaning clear. If in
   doubt, consult your own lawyer before you sign.
4. Be sure that the entire agreement is included in the writing.
   Written contracts should mean what they say. If the clause
   states that the terms of a printed contract cannot be changed,
   make sure that any special agreements are written into it on
   all copies and that such changes are initialed by both parties.
5. When any payments have been made in cash, be sure to get
   a receipt if payment is not acknowledged in the contract. (If
   payments are made by check, indicate the purpose on the face
   of the check. The canceled check will serve as your receipt.)

YOUR LEGAL VOCABULARY

contract under seal   implied contract
executed contract   parol evidence rule
executory contract   simple contract
express contract   Statute of Frauds
formal contract

1. A contract in which the agreement of the parties is spoken or written.
2. A contract that has been fully performed.
3. Contract in which agreement of parties is shown by acts or conduct.
4. A law stating that certain agreements must be in writing to be enforceable.
5. A contract that has not been fully performed.
6. The rule under which a writing cannot be modified or changed by
   prior oral or written agreements or other outside evidence.
7. Written contract that must be in a special form to be enforceable.
8. All contracts that are not formal contracts.
9. A contract to which a seal is attached.

REMEMBER THESE HIGHLIGHTS

1. Unless required by law, contracts need not be in writing.
2. An express contract is stated in words, written or spoken. An implied
   contract is shown by the acts or conduct of the parties.

3. A formal contract is a written contract that must be in some special form. All other contracts are simple contracts.
4. An executory contract is one that has not been fully performed. An executed contract has been completed by both parties.
5. To be enforceable, the following contracts must be evidenced by a writing signed by the party against whom enforcement is sought:
   (a) Contracts to buy and sell goods for a price of $500 or more.
   (b) Contracts to buy and sell real property.
   (c) Contracts that cannot be performed within one year after being made.
   (d) Contracts to answer for the obligation of another.
   (e) Contracts having marriage as the consideration.
   (f) Contracts of an executor or administrator to be personally liable for the debts of an estate.
6. A memorandum of an agreement need not be in any special form, but it must contain all the material facts and be signed by the party against whom the contract is to be enforced.
7. The terms of a written contract may not be changed by parol evidence. However, parol evidence may be used to prove additional terms agreed upon if the writing is clearly incomplete; or to show that a written agreement is not binding because of mistake, fraud, or illegality; or to clarify ambiguous language.

LAW AS PEOPLE LIVE IT

1. Wiley purchased a $300 refrigerator from Buckman, paying $100 down and taking delivery. Is this an executed contract?
2. Beasley orally agreed to pay $550 for a piano, bench, and music cabinet owned by Norton but not to take delivery for sixty days. When Norton attempted to deliver the furniture, Beasley said he had changed his mind about buying it. What rights does Norton have?
3. Hildebrandt was the executor of his brother's estate. His sister was dissatisfied with her brother's will and threatened to sue to break it. Hildebrandt orally agreed personally to give his sister $5,000 if she would not file suit. To be enforceable, is it necessary for Hildebrandt's promise to be in writing?
4. Rowe was admitted to Linville's Hospital as an emergency patient. The next day Linville discussed the cost of the treatment with Rowe's two sons, who told Linville, "Do whatever is necessary to save his life and we will pay you." When Linville presented the bill to the junior Rowes, they claimed the contract was oral and they were not liable because their promise to pay the debt of another (their father) was not in writing. Is that correct?

5. Sparks said to Caswell, "If you marry my daughter I'll deed my farm to you." Caswell did marry Sparks' daughter but Sparks refused to carry out his promise. Does Caswell have any legal rights?

6. Collier and Walker had orally discussed the employment of Collier as sales manager. Walker then wrote Collier offering him a three-year job contract beginning the first of the next month. Collier telephoned his acceptance and reported for work. After six months he resigned and Walker sued him for breaking the contract. Will he succeed?

7. Dana orally promised to leave his house and other property to his cousin, Duncan, if she would live in his home and look after him until he died. Duncan accepted the offer, left her own home, and took care of Dana until his death 15 months later. Dana's children sued to stop the transfer of the property to Duncan, claiming the father's promise had to be in writing and signed by him. Do you agree?

8. Reite purchased a motor scooter on credit from McKenzie for $265 plus certain carrying charges. The written contract provided that the buyer would insure the scooter against loss by fire and theft. The scooter was stolen soon after it was purchased. In defending a legal action to recover the price, Reite claimed that it was orally agreed that the seller would provide the insurance. Can this oral agreement be considered in court?

9. Easton, a contractor, insured his lumber and building materials with Washington County Insurance Company. The contract covered those materials stored in "sheds." Fire destroyed the materials which had been stored in a concrete warehouse and basement. Easton claimed the word "shed" included concrete warehouses. Do you agree?

10. A contest conducted by the Sentinel Publishing Company stated that it was open to all "except employees and their immediate families." Bryant, whose daughter was an employee but did not live with him, entered and won the contest. Sentinel refused to pay Bryant, claiming that he was a member of the immediate family of the employee. Is that correct?

LAW AS COURTS DECIDE IT

1. Lee Wilson & Company negotiated orally with Springfield for the conveyance (transfer of legal title) of Springfield's land. An agreement for the transfer was reached, and this was to have been reduced to writing. However, no memorandum or other writing was signed by either party, and Springfield sold the land to another company. In an action to require Springfield to carry out his promise with him, Wilson claimed the promise to reduce the contract to writing, as required for enforcement under the Statute of Frauds, was sufficient to make the Statute not applicable in this case. What is your opinion?

(Lee Wilson & Company v. Springfield, 230 Ark. 257, 321 S.W. 2d 775)

2. Jack Walker, plaintiff, owned 75 acres of land and orally agreed to sell to Bobby Walker about 38 acres of this land for $100 per acre. Bobby made a payment of $1,076 and, with Jack's knowledge, made many improvements on the land, including erecting a house, digging a well, and planting trees. Four years after Bobby moved onto the land, Jack repudiated the contract and filed an ejectment action against Bobby, claiming that payment in full is required under the Statute of Frauds. Bobby's defense was that, in accordance with Texas law, an oral contract for the sale of land is not within the Statute of Frauds if there is payment of consideration, and possession by the buyer, and if valuable permanent improvements are made upon the land with the consent of the seller. Judgment for whom? (Walker v. Walker, 448 S.W. 2d 171, Texas)

3. Garrison claimed Powers "1800" Restaurant, Inc. owed him $340 for services rendered, and sued both Powers Restaurants and Powers "1800," claiming Powers Restaurants, Inc. had promised to pay the debt. Powers "1800" was in financial difficulty and had assigned all its physical assets to Dale Carter Lumber Company. The secretary of Powers "1800" wrote Garrison explaining this and stating that "all creditors will be paid in due time by Powers Restaurants, Inc." It was this writing upon which Garrison relied in his suit. Is this sufficient to charge Powers Restaurants? (Powers Restaurants, Inc. v. Garrison, 465 P. 2d 761, Oklahoma)

4. Henry Kucks, 81 years old, orally promised Catharina Schlaadt, 76 years old, that if she would marry him, he would leave all of his property to her children by a former marriage. Relying on that promise, Catharina married him. When Kucks died and failed to leave the property as promised, the children of Catharina brought an action against his estate to enforce the promise. Those representing the estate contended that the promise was unenforceable because it was not in writing. Do you agree? (Schlaadt v. Zimmerman, 206 F. 2d 782, Washington)

5. The Farm Air Service, Inc., contracted for fire insurance on the contents of its hangar. The insurance policy included a typewritten clause that the insurance covered "all contents and adjacent to the building within 200 feet . . ." The printed provisions of the policy specifically excluded loss to aircraft. A fire in the hangar destroyed an airplane belonging to Farm Air Service. The insurance company refused to pay for the loss, claiming the contract was ambiguous. Relying on the typewritten clause, Farm Air Service sued the insurance company. Could it collect? (Fidelity-Phenix Fire Insurance Co. v. Farm Air Service, Inc., 255 F. 2d 658)

13 Transfer and Discharge of Contracts

1. *Your parents buy a self-cleaning electric stove on the installment plan and receive a notice to make the payments to the Central Time Loan Co. instead of to the dealer who sold them the stove. Must they do so?*

2. *A friend is under contract to play professional hockey. During the season he is injured in an automobile accident and can no longer play. Is the contract terminated?*

3. *The printer contracted to deliver your school yearbook on May 15, but a strike prevented him from completing the work until August 1. Can the school sue and collect damages for the delay?*

CAN RIGHTS UNDER A CONTRACT BE TRANSFERRED?

Problem: Hermann purchased a small foreign car on the installment plan from Mitchell Motors for $1,650. Because he needed the money immediately, Mitchell transferred his right to the payments to Fletcher Finance Company which in turn advanced to Mitchell the full amount due less a discount charge. Mitchell then directed Hermann to make monthly payments to Fletcher. Must Hermann do so?

Persons frequently have contractual rights or benefits which they wish to transfer to others. Such a transfer of contractual rights is called an *assignment*. The party who makes the assignment transferring his rights is the *assignor*; the one to whom the assignment is made is the *assignee*. Mitchell was the assignor in the problem, and Fletcher was the assignee. When Hermann was notified of the assignment, he was obligated to pay Fletcher. Fletcher could proceed at law to collect the amount due Mitchell from Hermann if necessary.

Unless prohibited by statute, a party may ordinarily assign any rights that he has acquired through contract, provided the <u>perfor-mance</u> (that is, the fulfillment of the agreement) will not be materially changed by the assignment. For example, a right to collect a simple debt is assignable: the duty is fixed and the performance remains the same after assignment. However, rights under a contract are not assignable if they are personal and if the substitution of an assignee would materially change the nature of the performance. Some rights which cannot be transferred include: claims to damages for personal injuries, claims against the United States, rights to personal services, and contracts that involve relations of personal trust and confidence.

Although assignment of contractual rights is usually made voluntarily by the assignor, it may also occur automatically by operation of law. A common example arises when one of the parties dies. Then the dead person's rights under the contract are assigned by operation of law to his personal representative who may ordinarily enforce them. An assignment by operation of law also occurs when a debtor becomes bankrupt and his claims against third persons are assigned by law to a trustee.

Ordinarily, no particular form is required for an assignment. It may be oral or written. Statutes sometimes require certain assignments to be in writing, however.

CAN OBLIGATIONS UNDER A CONTRACT BE TRANSFERRED?

Problem: Gregory contracted with Anderson to take care of her two children during the day while she was at work. When Anderson was unable to carry out the agreement to take care of the children she told Gregory she had transferred the contract to her friend, Frey. Gregory objected and refused to accept Frey. Was Gregory within her rights in doing so?

Although a party to a contract may assign his rights, he may not assign his obligations. A person may, however, delegate or turn over to another for performance his duties under an employment contract when performance does not involve personal skill or special qualifications. Caring for children involves special qualifications and personal skill, and so in the problem Gregory was justified in rejecting Frey. A *delegation of duties* is not an assignment of the contract. The original party to the contract is still obligated or liable for the proper performance of his promises.

It is possible for the party entitled to receive performance under a contract to release the other from his duty to perform and to accept another party in his place. This is neither assignment nor delegation of duties; it is a change of contract. The old contract is abandoned and a new one formed.

WHAT ARE THE RIGHTS OF THE ASSIGNEE?

Problem: Adair, a concert violinist, purchased from Marshall Music Company an Amati violin for $8,000. He paid $1,000 down and agreed to pay the balance in 36 equal monthly installments. Marshall immediately assigned to Thorne its right to collect from Adair. Soon thereafter Adair discovered that the violin was not a genuine Amati and that he had been defrauded. Is he liable to Thorne on his contract?

Courts often say that the assignee "stands in the shoes of the assignor." This means that by assignment he receives exactly the same rights and duties as the assignor had—no more, or less. Therefore, in the problem, Thorne stood in the place of Marshall. Because Adair could claim fraud against Marshall, this same claim was good against Thorne.

December 1, 19--

To: Whitney Williams
3522 E. Roosevelt Dr.
Lake City, LA 70633

Dear Sir:

You are hereby notified that on December 1, 19-- , John Hanchey assigned to this company its right to receive payment due under a contract with you dated September 1, 19-- , for the sale of a washing machine and dryer .

We are enclosing a copy of the assignment for your files. In the future, please send all payments due under the contract to this office.

KRONER COLLECTION AGENCY

John J. Kroner
John J. Kroner, President

Notice of Assignment

To protect his newly acquired rights, the assignee should promptly notify the *obligor* (the debtor or one who owes money or other obligation) of the assignment. This may be done orally or in writing. Until he receives notification, the obligor is justified in believing that he still owes the original creditor, and he will discharge his liability if he pays that creditor. The creditor-assignor is then liable to the assignee for the value of the performance. If the obligor is notified but fails to perform, the assignee may take court action against him.

In making an assignment, the assignor does not undertake to make good if the obligor fails to perform, unless this is specifically required by the contract. He does, however, guarantee that the assigned right is legally enforceable, and that he had a right to assign it.

HOW ARE CONTRACTS USUALLY DISCHARGED?

> **Problem:** Russell loaned Brown $300 to be repaid within three months. When the debt was due Brown did not have the money, but he offered to give Russell a motion picture projector that was worth about $300. Did Brown discharge his contractual obligation by offering to give Russell the projector instead of paying the money?

When a person enters into a contract, he assumes certain obligations. *Discharge of contract,* or termination of these obligations, occurs when the person performs his part of the contract or is released from his responsibilities. Ordinarily, a party performs as he has promised to do. Partial performance does not discharge the obligation.

Failure to perform in accord with the contract terms is known as *breach of contract.* Breach of contract by one party may give the other party the right to treat his obligation as discharged or terminated. When one party terminates a sales contract because of a breach by the other party, the UCC uses the word "cancellation" and provides that the party canceling does not lose his remedy for the breach of the contract by so canceling. He may also have other rights, as discussed in the next chapter.

When a contract calls for payment in money, performance requires the payment of the exact amount due under the terms of the contract. The one to whom the money is owed need not accept anything else. Therefore, in the problem, Russell was under no obligation to accept the projector instead of the payment of $300.

If a check is given in payment of a debt that is payable in money, acceptance of the check merely suspends the debt while the check is being processed for collection. The debt is not discharged until the check is paid by the bank.

When a contract clearly requires performance by a specified date, time is said to be "of the essence." Failure to perform by that date is generally regarded as a breach of contract. When no time is specified, a reasonable time is allowed for performance.

IN WHAT OTHER WAYS MAY CONTRACTS BE DISCHARGED?

Problem: Mims, a landscape contractor, entered into a contract to maintain the lawn of O'Conor's country estate until O'Conor returned from an extended visit overseas. After two years, O'Conor returned. Was the contract with Mims terminated?

Although most contracts are discharged by complete performance, discharge may also be accomplished by: (1) agreement, (2) impossibility of performance, or (3) operation of law.

(1) BY AGREEMENT

At the time the parties agree on the terms of the contract, they may provide for its termination. The original agreement may provide that the contract will terminate: (a) upon a specified date or upon the expiration of a specified period of time; (b) upon the happening or the failure to happen of a specified event (in the problem, Mims' contract to maintain the lawn was terminated by the return of O'Conor); or (c) at the election of either party upon the giving of notice.

The parties may also agree to make changes after the contract has been made. By rescission they may agree to cancel the existing contract entirely, returning any consideration received and placing each party in his original position. Or they may agree that the present contract is not what they want and replace it with a new one. This is discharge by *substitution*. They may also agree to change the performance required by the original contract. An agreement to make such a change is known as an *accord*; performance of the new obligation is called a *satisfaction*. A compromise of a disputed claim or a composition of creditors (Page 161) is an accord, and carrying out the new agreement is the satisfaction. The previous obligation is discharged by an *accord and satisfaction*.

Hardy, an electrician by trade, owed his friend Peters $150. When it became clear that Hardy would not have the cash to repay the loan for some time, the two agreed that Hardy could do some rewiring and new electrical work on Peters' summer home instead of paying the debt in cash. Their agreement to change the performance was an accord. Hardy's completion of the agreed-upon work was the satisfaction. Together, the accord and satisfaction discharged the original contract obligation.

(2) BY IMPOSSIBILITY OF PERFORMANCE

As a general rule, a contract is not discharged when some unexpected event makes performance extremely expensive, difficult, or even impossible for the parties involved. For example, a strike, difficulty of obtaining materials, or some natural disaster such as a flood or earthquake normally does not discharge the contract. The party who fails to perform will be held liable for breach of contract. The parties may, however, expressly provide for the termination of the agreement in the event of inability to perform caused by these or other physical or social forces.

Holmes, who had contracted to supply various airplane parts to Abel's Airport at a cost of $12,686, later defaulted, claiming it was impossible to deliver at the contract price. He stated that the manufacturers had increased their prices, making the cost to him $8,600 more than contemplated. The court held him to the contract. The fact that the contract was no longer economically profitable did not mean it was legally impossible.

There are, however, certain situations in which a contract is discharged under the label of legally recognized impossibility. These are:

(a) **Destruction of the subject matter.** When the performance depends upon the continued existence of some specific thing, the destruction of that thing terminates the contract if the destruction was not the fault of the promisor.

Hitchcock, a famous jockey, contracted to ride the racehorse, Grey Mirage, in the Kentucky Derby. Two days before the race, the horse stumbled during a workout, broke a leg, and had to be destroyed. The contract was discharged.

(b) Performance declared illegal. When a contract which is legal at its formation is later made illegal by statute or administrative decision, the contract is discharged.

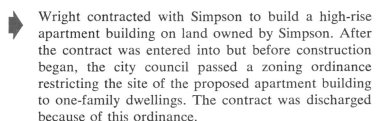

> Wright contracted with Simpson to build a high-rise apartment building on land owned by Simpson. After the contract was entered into but before construction began, the city council passed a zoning ordinance restricting the site of the proposed apartment building to one-family dwellings. The contract was discharged because of this ordinance.

(c) Death or disability. If the contract is personal in nature, the death or the disability of the promisor terminates the agreement.

> Rankins employed Walker for three years to install a computer and supervise its operators. Fifteen months after beginning work, Walker suffered a heart attack and was unable to continue his employment. His obligation was discharged by impossibility.

(d) Act of the other party. If the party to whom an obligation is due makes it impossible for the other to perform, the agreement is terminated.

> Del Pozzo subcontracted to install the air conditioning on a building being constructed by Meyer. The contract provided the air conditioning must be ready by April 1. Because of delays by Meyer, Del Pozzo could not begin work until May 15, the beginning of his busy season. He was within his rights in refusing to do the work and was discharged from his obligation because of Meyer's conduct.

(3) BY OPERATION OF LAW

A contract may be discharged or the right to enforce it may be barred, in effect discharging the contract itself, by operation of law. This happens when the promisor goes bankrupt, or when the time allowed for enforcement of the contract has elapsed under a statute of limitations, as discussed in the next chapter.

Alteration of a written agreement will also usually discharge the agreement by operation of law. *Alteration* is a change in the terms of a contract without the consent of both parties. To discharge the contract, the alteration must be: (a) material, (b) made intentionally, (c) made by a party to the agreement, and (d) made without the consent of the other party.

 Kraft entered into a contract to maintain the elevators in Parker's office building. The contract provided a ten percent discount if the fee was paid annually in advance instead of monthly. After the contract had been signed by Parker, and without his consent, Kraft crossed out the clause referring to the discount. This alteration would release Parker from the contract, if he so chose.

WHAT IS THE EFFECT OF TENDER OF PERFORMANCE?

Problem: Sloan agreed that if he were permitted to use Mills' car for a certain trip he would paint the car on the second day after he returned. When he offered to paint the car on the agreed day, Mills would not permit him to do so because he wanted to use it. Is Sloan's obligation discharged?

An offer to perform an obligation is a *tender*. If the obligation requires the doing of an act, a tender which is made in good faith but rejected without good reason will discharge the one offering to perform. Thus, in the problem, when Sloan offered to perform as agreed and Mills refused, the obligation was discharged. However, an offer by Sloan to paint the car at some other time than that originally agreed upon would not discharge his obligation.

If the obligation is to pay money, the rule is different. Rejection of a proper tender or an offer to pay the money does not discharge

Rejection of a tender of payment of money does not discharge a debt.

the debt or prevent the creditor from collecting at a later date. It merely relieves the debtor of any court costs or future interest that he might otherwise have to pay. To be valid, the tender of money must consist of the exact amount due in *legal tender*—that is, coins or currency of the United States.

A tender of performance, whether by the payment of money or otherwise, must be made without conditions. In some states, such as California, a contract that calls for the payment of money may be discharged, when performance by the obligor is refused, by depositing the amount due in a recognized bank in the name of the creditor.

TO PROTECT YOURSELF . . .

1. Use written contracts, particularly if the amounts involved are large.
2. Prepare all written instruments so that alterations or insertions are difficult or impossible to make without detection. Fill in all blank spaces and have both parties initial any changes that are made in the original writing.
3. Determine—perhaps by checking with the debtor—whether the assignor is subject to any defense that may affect your interest. Remember that the assignee takes only such rights as the assignor has.
4. Don't forget that the assignor does not agree to pay the debt if the third party fails to do so. If you wish him to be liable, he must expressly agree to pay if the obligor defaults, and such agreement must be in writing.
5. Be sure to notify the third party (obligor or debtor) of the assignments as soon as practicable.
6. "Time is of the essence" in many contracts. If such a contract calls for performance by a certain time, failure to perform is usually a breach of contract.
7. Remember that hardship is not impossibility of performance. One who wishes to protect himself against failure to fulfill a contract because of fires, strikes, inability to obtain materials, or similar difficulties, must include a clause in the contract to that effect.

YOUR LEGAL VOCABULARY

accord
accord and
  satisfaction
alteration
assignee
assignment
assignor
breach of contract

delegation of duties
discharge of contract
legal tender
obligor
performance
satisfaction
substitution
tender

1. A transaction by which a party transfers his contractual rights or benefits to another.
2. The action which terminates a contractual obligation.
3. A material change in the terms of a contract, made intentionally by one party without consent of the other.
4. One who transfers his contractual rights.
5. One to whom contractual rights are transferred.
6. An agreement to change the performance required for discharge of the contract, and the performance of the new obligation.
7. An offer to perform an obligation.
8. Coins or currency of the United States.
9. Fulfillment or accomplishment of the contract.
10. Turning over to another one's duties under an employment contract when performance does not involve personal skill or special qualifications.

REMEMBER THESE HIGHLIGHTS

1. A party may generally assign his rights under a contract as long as the performance will not be materially altered by assignment. He does not relieve himself of his contractual obligations by making an assignment. He may, however, delegate his duties when they do not involve his personal knowledge or skill as with artists and professional experts.
2. Ordinarily, an assignment may be oral or written.
3. An assignee acquires only such rights as the assignor has under the contract.
4. Until he is notified of assignment, the obligor is justified in believing that he still owes performance to the original obligee.
5. A contract is ordinarily discharged by performance. The acceptance of a breach of contract may also discharge it.
6. An obligation calling for an act is discharged by a tender of performance that corresponds exactly to the agreement. A tender of payment does not discharge an obligation to pay money; but, if kept open, it relieves the debtor of court costs and future interest charges.
7. Discharge by agreement of the parties may be accomplished by: (a) including provisions for termination in the contract, (b) rescinding the existing contract, (c) substituting a new contract, or (d) making an accord and satisfaction.
8. Difficulty or impossibility of performance arising from the making of the contract generally does not relieve a promisor of his obligation. However, contractual duties may be discharged because of impossibility when: (a) the subject matter is destroyed, (b) a change in the law makes performance illegal, (c) the promisor dies or

becomes disabled and the contract involves personal services, or (d) the other party to the contract prevents performance.

9. The obligation of one party is discharged when a written contract is materially and intentionally altered by the other party without the consent of the former.

LAW AS PEOPLE LIVE IT

1. Orchard Oil Company contracted to sell and deliver 500 barrels of fuel oil each month for one year to Mulholland Mushroom Farm. Orchard delivered the oil for the first two months but did not deliver any during the third month. Mulholland notified Orchard he was canceling the contract because of Orchard's non-performance. Was he entitled to do this?

2. Robinson purchased a set of patio furniture from Polidor and gave his check in payment. The check was dishonored by the bank because Robinson's account had insufficient funds. Has Robinson's obligation to pay been performed?

3. Ponti, a well-known portrait artist, contracted to paint Jackson's portrait for $2,500. Shortly thereafter, the artist was severely injured in an automobile accident. Unable to fulfill his agreement, he asked Bava, an equally competent painter, to do the portrait for him. Is such delegation permitted?

4. Ward owed Engels $400 for merchandise purchased on account. Before the account came due, Ward did $100 worth of electrical work for Engels, and it was agreed that this amount would be deducted from Ward's account. Later, Engels assigned the full $400 debt to Nunn, and the latter gave Ward notice of the assignment. When payment became due, Ward offered Nunn $300 on the grounds that Engels owed him $100 for services. Must Ward pay Nunn $400?

5. Lundy agreed to buy McGill's house trailer for $1,200. When Lundy could not raise the money, McGill agreed to accept a car worth approximately $1,600. McGill waited six months, and when it became clear that the car would not be delivered, he sued Lundy for $1,200. Lundy claimed McGill's agreement to accept the car instead of the money was an accord and satisfaction. Do you agree?

6. Berman, a retail clothier, contracted to buy 1,000 suits, to be delivered on or before April 1, from the Coffey Clothing Company. A strike among the employees of the Coffey Clothing Company made it impossible for the company to fulfill this contract in the time agreed upon. Berman claimed this was a breach of contract and commenced a lawsuit to recover damages. Should he succeed?

7. Casarino, an actor, contracted with Tym to give a TV performance at Tym's TV station on the night of February 4. Illness prevented Casarino from appearing that night. Was the contract discharged?

8. Blair owed Nichols $1,000. Nichols needed the money and assigned the contract to Phillips. He then informed Blair of the assignment by telephone. Is this proper notification of the assignment?

9. Crofoot contracted to prune Pascoe's apple orchard during November. However, Pascoe kept the gates of the road leading to his orchard padlocked so that Crofoot could not enter the orchard. Was Crofoot discharged from his obligation?

10. Van Hunnick agreed to convey an apartment building to Moss for $30,000. Because of a decline in his used car business, Moss was unable either to pay the balance due or to borrow the needed money. When Van Hunnick brought suit against him, Moss claimed impossibility of performance. Would he be released from liability?

LAW AS COURTS DECIDE IT

1. Kyle purchased an automobile from Milliken Chevrolet, Inc. on a conditional sales contract under which the seller retained ownership of the car but the buyer had possession and use of it. Milliken immediately assigned the contract to G.M.A.C. The contract did not comply with the requirements of the state law requiring full disclosure of all costs including extras, registration fees, and insurance; hence, it was illegal. After making two payments to G.M.A.C., Kyle learned of the illegality and stated that he would make no more. G.M.A.C. repossessed the car and Kyle sued to recover its value. In defense, G.M.A.C. claimed it did not know that the contract was illegal when it was purchased, and therefore, was not responsible for the assignor's obligations. Do you agree? (General Motors Acceptance Corporation v. Kyle, 351 P. 2d 768, 54 Cal. 2d 101)

2. O'Brien was employed as President of the National Binder and Chemical Products Corporation on a five-year contract. In his work he developed special processes for the corporation that were extremely valuable trade secrets. His contract provided that he was to work for five years for the corporation and that for five more years he would not work for a competitor of the corporation. After the contract had been in effect for four years, the corporation merged with another corporation and the contract with O'Brien was assigned to the new corporation, Alabama Binder and Chemical Corporation. O'Brien became a vice-president of the new corporation and worked for another year. At that point, the parties were unable to agree on a new employment contract, and O'Brien went to work for a competing company, the Pennsylvania Industrial Chemical Corporation. Alabama sued to stop O'Brien from working for Pennsylvania. O'Brien contended that Alabama had no right to enforce the contract since it was for personal services and not assignable. Do you agree? (Alabama Binder & Chemical Corporation v. Pennsylvania Industrial Chemical Corporation, 410 Pa. 214, 189 A. 2d 180)

3. The defendant, Sunset Packing Company, contracted to purchase Schafer's strawberry crop and to furnish 150-200 laborers to harvest it, beginning June 1. A recruiting fee of $15 per laborer was to be paid by Schafer, who gave Sunset a check for $2,000 as advance payment. Sunset recruited the laborers in Texas, but they went to Idaho to work in the sugar beet harvest. Two days before June 1 Sunset notified Schafer it would be impossible to supply the laborers as agreed but that it would make available 100 laborers from its own labor force if Schafer would pay Sunset an extra $20 per ton of harvested strawberries. Schafer then recruited his own labor force, but at a greater cost, and filed suit against Sunset for $17,880 in lost profits. Sunset claimed that they were discharged from their contractual obligation because of the impossibility of performance. Do you agree with Sunset? (Schafer v. Sunset Packing Company, 474 P. 2d 529, Oregon)

4. On September 26, Nicholas Chouvaldjy paid $8,500 to the Lutheran Home for the Aged under a contract whereby the Home would furnish him living accommodations and care for the rest of his life. The contract was to take effect October 1, although Chouvaldjy had been living in the Home on a month-to-month basis for several months. On September 28, Chouvaldjy died. Did his death terminate the contract? (Gold v. Salem Lutheran Home Association of the Bay Cities, 341 P. 2d 381, 1 Cal. Rptr. 343)

5. On October 20, M. W. Fruit Company contracted with Sissell, a grapefruit grower, to purchase and pick all the marketable grapefruit in Sissell's grove. The written contract provided that "all fruit . . . shall be picked by buyer approximately on or before January 1" of the following year. The fruit company picked 67 tons of grapefruit almost immediately, but there were 45 tons left on the trees. A hard freeze between January 8 and 12 destroyed the unpicked fruit. In defending a suit for damages for the loss of 45 tons of grapefruit, the fruit company claimed its contract was discharged by impossibility because the subject matter was destroyed. Is this a good defense? (M. W. Fruit Company v. Sissell, 371 S.W. 2d 896, Texas)

6. Mrs. Roberta Brown entered into a contract leasing certain property to Jake Mims and giving him the option of purchasing a certain portion of the property for $56,000. Mims kept the only copy of the contract. Six years later, Brown learned that Mims, without Brown's consent or knowledge, had added the name of another party to the contract and had added additional property, terms, and conditions to the option to purchase. Upon learning of the changes in the contract, Mrs. Brown sought to have her obligations under the contract discharged because of the alterations in it. Will she succeed? (Brown v. Mims, 250 S.C. 546, 159 S.E. 247)

14 Remedies for Breach

1. *You are employed to work as a counselor at a youth camp for the entire summer season of six camp sessions. You are dismissed after the first camp session for no fault of your own. Do you have any rights?*

2. *You sell your stereo equipment for $150, with delivery and payment to be made the next week, but the buyer fails to make payment. What are your rights?*

3. *You buy a radio transmitter "guaranteed to have a range of 8,000 miles" under a written contract. In operation you find it to have a range of only 3,000 miles. Do you have any rights against the seller?*

WHO HAS RIGHTS UNDER A CONTRACT?

Problem: Costa's grandfather deposited $5,000 in a trust account in Security Savings and Loan Association with Costa as beneficiary. Under the agreement, Costa could withdraw the money plus the accumulated interest when he entered college or, if he did not go to college, when he was twenty-one years of age. When Costa entered college he tried to withdraw the funds, but Security objected, claiming he was not a party to the contract. Did Costa have any rights?

As we have seen, breach of contract arises when one party fails without legal excuse to fulfill his obligation at the time the performance is due. (Page 186) Breach can also occur when, in advance of the time for performance, one party notifies the other that he does not intend to do what he agreed to do. As a general rule, only parties who have entered into a contract have rights in it even though other persons may gain some advantage from having it performed. There are two important exceptions to this rule:

1. When a contract is made with the primary intention of benefiting a third person, that person is entitled to enforce the agreement; and

2. Most rights that arise under a contract may be transferred to a third person by assignment and may then be enforced by that person.

Costa could therefore collect the money from Security because the contract was made for his benefit. Contracts made specifically for the benefit of a third party may usually be enforced by the beneficiary—the one for whose benefit the contract is made. Life insurance contracts are the most common form of third party beneficiary agreements.

WHAT REMEDIES DOES THE INJURED PARTY HAVE?

Problem: Bostock contracted to roof Misner's house for $1,200, and to finish the work by September 1. On that date Bostock had not even started the job, so Misner arranged with Ritter to do it for $1,600. Does Misner have any rights against Bostock?

When a party to a contract fails to perform his obligation and the other party is injured as a result, the injured party may pursue any one of several remedies. A *remedy* is the means used to enforce a right or compensate for an injury. Remedies may vary with the type of contract, and may differ in effect or result. In the problem, Bostock failed to perform his obligation under the contract. Misner had a choice of several remedies, as discussed below.

Sometimes one party may not wish to enforce a contract or a provision in it. When one intentionally and voluntarily gives up a contractual right, he is said to *waive* his right.

 George rented an apartment to Fleming with a provision that no pets were allowed in the apartment. Fleming brought his canary into the apartment. When George learned of this, he did not require Fleming to get rid of the bird. George waived his right under the "no pet" clause and could not claim breach of contract.

REMEDIES FOR BREACH
OF CONTRACT

1. Rescission
2. Dollar damages
3. Specific performance

---

(1) THE INJURED PARTY HAS THE RIGHT OF RESCISSION OR CANCELLATION

Problem: Kennedy agreed to purchase $1,500 worth of furniture from the Suburban Furniture Company, making the selection from floor samples. Kennedy paid $150 down to bind the bargain. By the time the furniture arrived from the factory, Kennedy had changed her mind about buying it and canceled her order. What rights did the furniture company have?

As you know, if one party breaches the contract, the other party may usually consider his obligation discharged. He need not carry out his part of the contract, and he has the right to be returned to the position that he would have been in had there been no contract. This remedy is the right of *rescission*. Both parties return any consideration they have received, and give credit for what cannot be returned. The entire contract must be rescinded, not just a part of it. It may be done by voluntary agreement of the parties, or by court order at the request of the injured party.

A variation of rescission is called *cancellation*. It exists under the UCC for breach of contract for the sale of goods. The injured party may cancel the contract, returning consideration received, and still retain other remedies such as the right to sue for damages. In the problem, Kennedy's breach of contract gave the furniture company the right to cancel the contract, and to keep as damages the money that Kennedy had paid.[1]

(2) THE INJURED PARTY HAS THE RIGHT TO DOLLAR DAMAGES

Problem: Ormond contracted with Heagan to install some conveyer equipment in his factory according to certain specifications. When the equipment did not work properly, Ormond discovered that Heagan had not followed the specifications. It cost Ormond $25,000 to have the work redone. What rights did Ormond have?

Whenever a breach of contract occurs, the injured party is entitled to be put in the same position he would have been in if the contract had been performed. Typically, this means bringing court action to recover money *damages*. Thus, if there is no performance, or if the performance is faulty or only partially completed, the

---

[1] Under the UCC the amount that may be kept by the seller is limited to 20% of the purchase price or $500, whichever is the smaller. However, the parties may agree to a larger or smaller amount if it is reasonable.

injured party may sue to recover the resulting money loss. In the problem, Ormond could sue Heagan for the $25,000 extra expense which resulted from his failure to follow the specifications.

(3) THE INJURED PARTY MAY COMPEL PERFORMANCE

> **Problem:** Theiss took an option on 60 acres of land from Freeman. When Freeman learned Theiss planned to develop a shopping center on the land, he refused to honor the option. Did Theiss have any rights?

When money damages are not an adequate remedy, a court will sometimes grant the injured party a form of special relief termed *specific performance*. This is an order requiring the defaulting party to perform the contract according to the specific terms agreed upon.

Generally damages are considered to be a sufficient remedy for breach of contract cases involving the sale of personal property. If the property is unique, however, so that it cannot be obtained elsewhere and the loss suffered cannot be measured in money, specific performance may be awarded. This remedy is also generally given when the contract is for the sale of real property, because no two pieces of land are identical. Accordingly, Theiss could maintain an action against Freeman requiring him to fulfill the contract.

Specific performance is ordinarily denied when:

1. There is another remedy that is adequate;
2. The court is not able to supervise performance;
3. The agreement is immoral, fraudulent, or illegal;
4. The contract involves personal service or employment; or
5. Specific performance will work undue hardship on the other party to the contract.

In addition to ordering specific performance of the contract, the court may grant money damages when the defendant's delay in performing has caused a loss.

Specific performance may be required in a breach involving unique property.

HOW ARE DAMAGES MEASURED?

Problem: Eckenrod contracted with Hendry, the owner of an FM radio station, for 13 weeks of radio time to advertise his bookshop. After six weeks Eckenrod canceled the contract for the remaining time. Nevertheless, Hendry continued to broadcast Eckenrod's ad and made no attempt to get other advertising to replace it although this could easily have been done. Was Hendry entitled to recover the cost of advertising Eckenrod's business for the seven weeks after the cancellation?

In awarding damages to a party injured by breach of contract, the court's purpose is to place him in approximately the position he would have been in had the breach not occurred. The amount awarded as damages is usually determined by the extent of the injury. A person is not permitted to increase the damages by continuing to perform his part of the contract after notice of breach or intention to cancel the contract. Thus Hendry, in the problem, could not recover the avoidable costs incurred after Eckenrod canceled the order.

Since failure to perform a duty under contract is in itself a legal wrong, courts will sometimes award *nominal damages* even when there is no actual injury. Nominal damages are granted in recognition of the rights that have been violated, and may consist of a few cents or a few dollars. The plaintiff is usually pleased to have proved his point, or to have established a precedent for the future.

At the time of entering into a contract, the parties may agree upon an amount of money that, in case of default, is to be paid by the one causing the breach to the other party. This sum is known as *liquidated damages*. If the actual damages would be difficult to prove and the amount of liquidated damages is reasonable, courts will enforce such an agreement.

HOW MAY THE INJURED PARTY LOSE HIS REMEDY?

Problem: Simmons had owed Learmonth $500 under an oral contract, and had been in default for ten years. After many unsuccessful requests to get Simmons to pay, Learmonth finally filed suit. Would the courts consider his claim?

Under certain circumstances a remedy for breach of contract will be denied or barred. Thus, a person like Learmonth, who is tardy in pressing his claim or seeking a remedy, may lose his rights. It would be unfair to permit him to wait an unreasonable length of time before bringing suit. Circumstances change, witnesses move, memories fade, records may be lost or destroyed, and there is a greater tendency toward fraud and perjury in proving stale claims.

(1) THE REMEDY MAY BE BARRED BY A STATUTE OF LIMITATIONS

> **Problem:** Owen purchased equipment for her beauty salon and, under a written contract, borrowed $6,000 from Swenson to pay for it. Owen agreed to repay the debt plus interest in monthly installments of $100. The contract also provided that the unpaid balance of the debt would be due immediately if she defaulted on any payment. After making payments for 18 months, Owen failed to pay. Swenson made repeated attempts to collect but never filed suit until more than six years after the last payment had been made. Could he collect?

A creditor may lose his legal rights against a debtor by waiting too long before bringing action on his claim. To prevent persons from being harrassed by actions based on old claims, statutes in all states deny creditors a right of action for damages for a breach of contract after the lapse of a specified time. Such a law is called a *statute of limitations*. If the injured party does not begin an action in court within the prescribed time, the debt is said to be *outlawed* and his right of legal action will be barred. The period of time varies in the different states; and in the same state it may vary according to the nature of the contract. As indicated in the table on page 202, in most states the statute bars an action after six years or less from the time the debt was payable. The statute begins to run from the moment there is a right to sue for a breach or a default of the other party to the contract. Such was the case in the problem above.

In the case of minors and others who lack capacity to contract, allowance is made for their period of incapacity. A minor is given a reasonable time to start the action after he reaches his majority.

Statutes of limitations ordinarily do not discharge debts; they merely bar the remedies of the injured parties. The bar may be waived and the right of action may be revived if the debtor makes a new promise. Since the new promise is a waiver, it need not be supported by consideration. It may be express; or it may be implied, as in the case of a part payment or a payment of interest.

In most states an express oral promise to pay a debt barred by the statute of limitations is sufficient to revive it. However, some

The statute of limitations may bar recovery of a debt.

HI, WILKINS. HAVEN'T SEEN YOU FOR 20 YEARS.

YES, AND I WANT THE $50 I LOANED YOU!

states require such a promise to be in writing before it effectively revives the debt. In most states, partial payment of the debt without an express promise will also revive an outlawed obligation. The period specified in the statute, during which an action must be commenced, begins to run anew from the date of revival of the obligation.

Years Within Which Legal Actions on Contracts Must Be Commenced After Default *

State	Open Book Accounts Receivable	Oral Contracts	Written Contracts	State	Open Book Accounts Receivable	Oral Contracts	Written Contracts
Alabama	3	6	6	Montana	5	5	8
Alaska	6	6	6	Nebraska	4	4	5
Arizona	3	3	6	Nevada	4	4	6
Arkansas	3	3	5	New Hampshire	6	6	6
California	4	2	4	New Jersey	6	6	6
Colorado	6	6	6	New Mexico	4	4	6
Connecticut	6	3	6	New York	6	6	6
Delaware	3	3	3	North Carolina	3	3	3
Dist. of Col.	3	3	3	North Dakota	6	6	6
Florida	3	3	5	Ohio	6	6	15
Georgia	4	4	6	Oklahoma	3	3	5
Hawaii	6	6	6	Oregon	6	6	6
Idaho	4	4	5	Pennsylvania	6	6	6
Illinois	5	5	10	Rhode Island	6	6	6
Indiana	6	6	20	South Carolina	6	6	6
Iowa	5	5	10	South Dakota	6	6	6
Kansas	3	3	5	Tennessee	6	6	6
Kentucky	5	5	15	Texas	2	2	4
Louisiana	3	10	10	Utah	4	4	6
Maine	6	6	6	Vermont	6	6	6
Maryland	3	3	3	Virginia	3	3	5
Massachusetts	6	6	6	Washington	3	3	6
Michigan	6	6	6	West Virginia	5	5	10
Minnesota	6	6	6	Wisconsin	6	6	6
Mississippi	3	3	6	Wyoming	8	8	10
Missouri	5	5	10				

* Note: The UCC provides that actions for the sale of goods must be commenced within four years from the date of the breach of contract.

(2) THE REMEDY MAY BE BARRED BY DISCHARGE OF THE DEBTOR IN BANKRUPTCY

Problem: Nissley, who was hopelessly in debt, saw no way of paying all his creditors. Can Nissley request voluntary bankruptcy?

When a person sees that he is unable to get out of debt, he may apply to the federal court to be declared a *voluntary bankrupt*. A person who takes such a step is usually an *insolvent debtor*—that is, one whose debts exceed his assets. When one becomes a voluntary bankrupt, he places his property under the control of the court where it is used for the satisfaction of his debts. Under state laws, certain assets deemed essential for living may be retained by the bankrupt individual if he so requests. Typically included under this exemption are his home (up to a certain value), personal clothing and effects, basic furniture, tools of his trade, and a car sufficient for transportation. Thus, Nissley could turn his nonexempt assets over to the court and request that he be discharged from his obligations as a voluntary bankrupt.

With certain limitations, the creditors of an insolvent person may have that person declared an *involuntary bankrupt,* provided that the debtor has done any of certain acts harmful to his creditors called *acts of bankruptcy.*

After a person has been declared a bankrupt, a *trustee* is appointed to take possession of his non-exempt property. In some cases the court appoints a receiver to take charge of the assets of the debtor before a trustee is appointed. The duties of the *receiver* are to conserve the assets and protect the rights of the creditors until a trustee can be appointed. The trustee converts the debtor's property into cash and distributes the proceeds proportionally, giving effect to priority of claims and the amount due each creditor.

Most claims against the debtor are discharged by bankruptcy whether or not there was enough money to pay them in full. Certain claims, such as those due for taxes or for alimony and child support, are not discharged by bankruptcy. The bankrupt individual may later acquire enough property to pay his former debts; but he cannot be compelled to pay them unless he voluntarily waives the bar of the discharge of bankruptcy or promises to pay the debt which would otherwise be barred.

HOW MAY A QUASI CONTRACT PROVIDE A REMEDY?

Problem: Reese entered into an oral agreement with Hughes to pay off the mortgage and build a house on Hughes' land in return for a half interest in the land and the right to live in the house until his death. Reese carried out his part of the bargain, but Hughes refused to be bound by the agreement because it was not in writing.

Reese sued to recover the money he had expended. Will he succeed?

One may render a service, pay out money, or deliver goods to another under such circumstances that no remedy exists under contract. For example, enforcement may be barred by the Statute of Frauds. Nevertheless, the law may recognize an obligation known as a *quasi contract,* if justice and good conscience require that one person not get something for nothing from another person unless a gift is intended.

Thus, in the problem, despite the fact that the contract is unenforceable under the Statute of Frauds (Chapter 12), Reese could recover what he had expended under quasi contract.

 If you should pay a merchant money under the impression that you owed it to him, whereas you did not owe him the money, the merchant would be under a duty to return the money to you. Money paid under a mistake of fact may ordinarily be recovered in an action based on quasi contract.

Another illustration of this type of contract is the case of a tradesman who furnishes necessaries to a minor. If the minor refuses to pay, the tradesman cannot recover from the minor for breach of contract, but as we learned in Chapter 9, he can recover the reasonable value of the necessaries furnished. This would be possible on grounds of quasi contract, which is no contract at all, but an obligation imposed by law to avoid injustice.

WHAT IS THE REMEDY FOR INDUCING BREACH OF CONTRACT?

Problem: Curtis entered into a contract with LaMonte to paint a portrait of Curtis' wife as a birthday gift. Pollard then wished LaMonte to paint a mural in his office for a much larger fee and induced LaMonte to break his contract with Curtis. Does Curtis have any rights?

If someone not a party to a contract willfully induces its breach, he commits a tort and becomes liable for damages to the injured party. Since Pollard knowingly and intentionally interfered with Curtis' contractual rights in the preceding problem, he was liable to Curtis for damages. Curtis could also prevent LaMonte from working for Pollard by means of an *injunction,* which is a court order prohibiting a specified act.

WHEN SEEKING A REMEDY FOR BREACH OF CONTRACT...

1. Don't delay. One who "sleeps on his rights" may lose them.
2. If you wish to rescind or cancel your obligation, you must show that the other party breached his agreement in a material way. If you have paid anything, you may be able to recover; if you have performed any service, you are entitled to be compensated.
3. Be prepared to show that you actually suffered loss if the remedy sought is in the form of damages. You must also show that you were able, willing, and ready to perform your part of the agreement unless you have already done so.
4. If you are seeking specific performance, you must show that money damages will not adequately compensate you for the loss suffered. You must also show that you are able, willing, and ready to perform your obligation.
5. For nonpayment of an overdue debt, try to get at least a small payment, because in most states it will prevent the claim from being outlawed for the years specified by the statute of limitations.

YOUR LEGAL VOCABULARY

act of bankruptcy
cancellation
damages
injunction
insolvent debtor
involuntary bankrupt
nominal damages
liquidated damages
outlawed

quasi contract
remedy
receiver
rescission
statute of limitations
specific performance
trustee
voluntary bankrupt
waive

1. Money that is recovered for an injury.
2. Requiring the defaulting party to perform the contract according to the specific terms agreed upon.
3. A statute denying a plaintiff's right of action for damages after a specified time.
4. Avoiding a contract, and being placed in the same position as if there had been no contract.
5. Intentionally and voluntarily giving up a legal right.
6. One whose debts exceed his assets.
7. Damages that are agreed upon when the contract is made.
8. One who applies to the court to be declared bankrupt.
9. The means used to enforce a right or compensate for an injury.
10. A court order prohibiting the doing of a specific act.

REMEMBER THESE HIGHLIGHTS

1. One who is not a party to a contract, as a general rule, has no rights or duties under the contract. However, a third party may sometimes enforce a contract made for his benefit. An assignee may also acquire rights or assume duties under another party's contract.
2. In case of a breach of contract, the injured party has various remedies: (a) he may rescind or cancel the contract; (b) he may recover the amount of his loss, known as damages; and (c) in certain cases, he may be able to require specific performance.
3. After default, the injured party may usually recover the amount already spent in carrying out his part of the contract, but he may not increase the damages.
4. The parties at the time of entering into a contract may agree to the payment of reasonable damages, known as liquidated damages, if actual damages would be difficult to prove in case of default.
5. A remedy for breach of contract may be barred by the lapse of the time period prescribed by a statute of limitations, or by the debtor's discharge in bankruptcy.
6. Although there may not be a binding contract, an injured party may be able to recover under quasi contract.

LAW AS PEOPLE LIVE IT

1. Gibson offered Evans the job of managing his clinic for a period of two years at $15,000 a year. Evans accepted the job but shortly after refused to work, and Gibson then contracted for the services of another manager at a salary of $16,000 a year. (a) Can Gibson rescind the contract with Evans? (b) Can he then sue to recover the loss of approximately $2,000 she caused him to suffer?
2. Peppard entered into a contract with Nesbitt to pave a parking lot for her boutique. The price was $2,400. When Nesbitt failed to perform, Peppard arranged with Richmond to do it for the same price. Peppard then sued Nesbitt for $500 damages for breach of contract. Will she prevail?
3. Gundstrom, a tailor, contracted to make a suit priced at $125 for Bird to wear at a friend's wedding. As part of the contract Gundstrom promised to pay Bird $500 as liquidated damages if the suit was not ready the day before the wedding. Gundstrom failed to meet the deadline and Bird sued him for the $500. Can he collect?
4. Van Sickle contracted to buy 1,000 sheets of quarter-inch fir plywood from Erickson at $3.00 a sheet. Because of a price increase, Erickson refused to honor his contract. Van Sickle promptly purchased the plywood from Wood for $3.60 a sheet and sued Erickson for the difference in his cost. Can he recover?

5. Richey agreed to sell to Donley for $300 an antique desk that had been used at one time by Abraham Lincoln. Richey accepted $50 as a down payment. Later Richey refused to deliver the desk and offered to return the $50 deposit. Donley brought action to force Richey to fulfill the terms of the agreement. Should he succeed?

6. On August 1, 1965, Sullivan purchased furniture from Hartzell, terms 60 days. Sullivan, who had not made any payment on the account, was sued by Hartzell on October 10, 1971. Was Hartzell legally entitled to collect the debt?

7. Henderson owed Sutton $200. Seven years after the debt was due, Henderson paid $75 on the account and promised to pay the balance within 60 days. Henderson failed to pay at the end of the 60 days, and Sutton sued for payment. Henderson pleaded the statute of limitations as a defense. Is this defense valid?

8. Vergara owed several creditors a total of $30,000. Included were West, $2,000, and Kelley, $8,000. Vergara's assets amounted to only $10,000. He paid West and Kelley in full. Could the other creditors force Vergara into involuntary bankruptcy?

9. Grant was asked by Maynard, an elderly man, to live with him and take care of him. Maynard assured Grant that he "would be well taken care of" in his will. Grant did as requested but no provision was made for him in Maynard's will. Does Grant have any rights?

10. Humphreys bought a car from Curtis as a gift for Branyan in recognition of her 25 years of service as Humphreys' employee. Humphreys directed that the title should be registered in Branyan's name. Curtis failed to register the car as directed, and Branyan sought to require him to do so. Will Branyan succeed?

LAW AS COURTS DECIDE IT

1. Kizziar and his wife contracted with Dollar to construct a medical clinic to certain specifications, including a central heating and air-conditioning system "ducted in" to each room. The system was to be large enough to heat and cool the building in a reasonable manner. When the air conditioning system failed to cool the building properly, Dollar proposed that he furnish window air-conditioning units, but the Kizziars refused. When the Kizziars failed to pay the contract price, Dollar sued them for it. The Kizziars claimed that Dollar should pay them damages for failure to provide an adequate system as provided in the contract. Is it your opinion that the window air-conditioning units substantially complied with the contract? If not, what should be the measure of damages? (Kizziar v. Dollar, 268 F. 2d 914)

2. Annie L. Godwin, age nineteen, borrowed $1,410 from Dallas L. Jones and executed a mortgage on certain land left to her by her

deceased father. No payment of interest or on the debt was made for 12 years, and no demand for payment was made during those years. Eleven years after executing the mortgage, Annie told Jones that she did not consider herself bound by it because of her minority and the statute of limitations. In South Carolina the statute of limitations does not bar such actions for 20 years. Should a suit by Jones to collect the debt be successful? (Jones v. Godwin, 187 S.C. 510, 198 S.E. 36)

3. DiFatta leased property to Campagna. The lease provided for the rent to be paid on the first day of each month. If not paid when due, DiFatta could give written notice of the default and if not paid within five days after the notice, DiFatta could cancel the lease. Campagna was late with the October payment. DiFatta gave the notice and Campagna paid within the five-day period. In November Campagna mailed a check for rent to DiFatta on November 5, and DiFatta returned it and brought suit to cancel the lease. DiFatta did not give notice in November and claimed the October notice was sufficient. Do you agree? (DiFatta v. Campagna, 157 So. 2d 633, Louisiana)

4. Lalumia, a bankrupt, had borrowed $528 from the plaintiff and had repaid $212 before being discharged in bankruptcy. His attorney wrote the creditors that "Mr. Lalumia was duly adjudicated a bankrupt on May 31, 1967. He has been troubled by further financial difficulties and will be unable to pay any of his creditors for a period of about six months." The plaintiff relies upon this letter as evidence of Lalumia's promise to pay the debt. Is it? (223 So. 2d 202, Louisiana)

5. In 1950, for a fee of one percent of sales, Cut Price Super Markets contracted to allow Kingpin Foods to use the Cut Price name for ten years, to furnish certain newspaper advertising, and to supply other specified services. The agreement provided for cancellation only if ownership changed, unless Kingpin sold its buildings, fixtures, and inventory to Cut Price. In 1956, Kingpin notified Cut Price that it was rescinding the contract because certain circular advertising had not been paid for. Thereupon Cut Price sued Kingpin for breach of contract, claiming damages. For six years Kingpin had made no claim for refunds, and each year had paid the required franchise fee. In defending the suit Kingpin asked the court to rescind the contract because of failure of Cut Price to pay for the circular advertising. Should the court do so? (Cut Price Super Markets v. Kingpin Foods, Inc., 256 Minn. 339, 98 N.W. 2d 257)

Bailments

UNIT FOUR

There are many times when it is desirable or necessary for you to have someone else's property. A simple example is borrowing a pencil from a fellow student in order to take an exam. There are also times when you may give some article to another for some temporary purpose, such as your coat to the laundry to be cleaned. And there are other times when you may come into possession of lost property belonging to another, as when you find someone's wallet. In each of these cases, the property is to be returned to the owner or disposed of as he directs. The relation is usually, but not always, based on a contract between the parties involved and is called bailment.

Some bailments result in benefit to only one of the parties, as when you loan your neighbor a ladder; others result in benefit for both parties, as when you rent a car.

Bailments are also created when goods belonging to another are transported. Since this is a very common occurrence, we shall study the rights and duties of those who transport goods for hire, known as common carriers. We shall also look at the special rules governing the bailment of the property of guests at hotels and motels.

In the next two chapters, we shall learn some of the rules which govern the relation of bailment, and we shall see how property rights are protected when one person has possession of goods which belong to another.

CHAPTER 15 Mutual Benefit Bailments

1. *You need a car for the senior dance, but yours stops running the day before the event. What legal relationship will arise if you borrow your friend's car for the evening?*

2. *You have your stereo tape cartridge player repaired. Can the repairman keep the player until you pay him for his work?*

3. *A burglar stole some jewels from a hotel guest's room and calmly checked the bag at the hotel checkroom. May the burglar reclaim the bag when he returns later on?*

WHAT IS A BAILMENT?

Problem: To prepare a term paper for class, Barry borrowed six books and a magazine from the public library. What is the legal relation between Barry and the library?

If you loan your ball-point pen to a friend or borrow a book from the library, you are involved in the legal relationship of bailment. Bailments arise in many situations, including:

(1) hire of use (you rent a boat while on vacation);
(2) storage (you place excess furniture in a warehouse);
(3) repair (you leave your damaged motorcycle at a garage to be fixed);
(4) transport (you ship a Christmas gift by air or railway express);
(5) service (you take your suit to a dry cleaner);
(6) security (you leave your watch with a pawnbroker in order to obtain a loan);
(7) sale (a manufacturer sends novelty toys to a retailer to sell, if possible, or return if unsold).

Whenever one party delivers possession of personal property to another, a *bailment* is created. The party who transfers possession of the property is the *bailor*; the one who receives possession is the *bailee*. In the problem, a bailment was created in which the library was the bailor and Barry was the bailee.

In some cases, a person may have charge or use of a thing under the close direction of the true owner, with no interest in it adverse to the owner. This is simple custody, not a bailment. For example, a secretary who uses a company typewriter in her employer's office has custody; her employer technically retains possession.

HOW ARE BAILMENTS CREATED?

Problem: While walking home from school, Tucker saw a dog that appeared to be lost. With a little encouragement, the dog followed him home. Was Tucker responsible as a bailee for the dog?

Bailments ordinarily arise from express or implied agreements. Such agreements are usually contracts, and when consideration is given and received, they are called *mutual benefit bailments*.

On the other hand, you might volunteer to keep and take care of a friend's pet canary while she goes on vacation. Or a neighbor might lend you his power mower without charge. When either the bailee or bailor receives no compensation or benefit from the relation, the bailment is known as a *gratuitous bailment*. Because no compensation is given, no contract is formed.

In certain cases, bailments are created by law when no agreement is possible. Goods that are lost, misplaced, or mistakenly come into the possession of someone other than their owner are usually the subject of such bailments. The finder or receiver of the property is held by the courts to have a bailee's responsibility to the owner. This type of relationship, which is called a *constructive bailment*, is illustrated by the problem. As a finder who voluntarily took possession of the dog, Tucker became the responsible bailee.

WHAT ARE THE CHARACTERISTICS OF A BAILMENT?

Problem: Bauman rented an unfurnished house from Levy Properties, Inc., and obtained furniture from Smith Furniture at a monthly rental fee. Were these bailments?

A bailment has the following characteristics:

(1) THE SUBJECT MUST BE PERSONAL PROPERTY, POSSESSION OF WHICH MAY BE GIVEN TO ANOTHER

Real property such as land or buildings (see Chapter 40) is not bailed; it is leased under different rules of law. The house rental in the problem was a lease between landlord and tenant, as discussed in Chapter 41. Transfer of the furniture was a bailment, between bailor and bailee.

(2) ANYONE WHO HAS POSSESSION OF PERSONAL PROPERTY CAN CREATE THE RELATIONSHIP

Ownership is not necessary. Property may therefore be bailed by an agent or employee (see Unit IX), a custodian, a finder, or even a thief.

(3) THE GOODS MUST BE DELIVERED TO AND ACCEPTED BY THE BAILEE

The transfer is usually actual, as when the bailee drives off in a rented car. Transfer may also be constructive, as when the bailee gets the keys to a car located in a parking lot.

(4) THE IDENTICAL GOODS ARE TO BE RETURNED TO THE BAILOR

The identical goods which have been bailed must be returned to the bailor or some other person designated by him, in the form that has been agreed upon. This may be the same or an altered form.

The identical goods must be returned to the bailor.

SORRY WE LOST YOUR COAT. WILL THIS ONE DO?

HOW IS A BAILMENT TERMINATED?

Problem: Lindsay leased an automobile for one year from Courtesy Cars. Two months later he died. Was the bailment ended?

A bailment may be terminated in the following ways:

(1) BY AGREEMENT OR CONTRACT

When property is rented for a stated time or purpose, the bailment ends when the time passes or the purpose is accomplished. The parties may also, at any time, mutually agree to end the relationship.

(2) BY ACT OF EITHER PARTY

If no specific time is set for the bailment, either party may end it at will; thus, the bailor might simply retake his property peacefully. If either party violates the agreement, the other may elect to end the bailment.

No bailment results without transfer of possession or equivalent.

NOT RESPONSIBLE FOR LOSS

(3) BY DESTRUCTION OF THE SUBJECT MATTER

If the bailed property is destroyed or damaged so badly that it is not fit for the intended purpose, the bailment ends. If the bailee is at fault, he is liable for the loss.

(4) BY OPERATION OF LAW

Death, insanity, or bankruptcy of one of the parties will terminate the relationship if it means that the bailee cannot perform his duties, or if the bailment is one that may be ended at will. Normally, however, if there is a contractual bailment for a fixed period, death or incapacity of a party does not end the relationship. The rights and duties of a deceased party go to the executor of his estate. This would be the rule in the problem.

WHAT IS A MUTUAL BENEFIT BAILMENT?

Problem: To obtain the recommended 10,000-mile servicing, Steinway took his new car to Cardoni, the dealer who had sold it to him. What kind of bailment was created when Steinway left his car with Cardoni?

Bailments are usually classified in terms of who is benefited, as follows:

(1) Gratuitous bailments for the sole benefit of one party;
(2) Mutual benefit bailments for the advantage of both parties.

Unit IV □ BAILMENTS

The most common and important type of bailment is a mutual benefit bailment. Because both bailor and bailee receive consideration, such a bailment is always based on contract. In the problem, the bailor, Steinway, received the benefit of the skill and services of Cardoni's mechanics; the bailee, Cardoni, received the agreed compensation. It was therefore a mutual benefit bailment.

WHAT ARE THE RIGHTS AND DUTIES OF A MUTUAL BENEFIT BAILMENT?

Problem: Morley owned a set of laminated skis which he carelessly left next to a blazing fire. Heat caused the wood to separate at several points and Morley had to take the skis to the Kurt Sports Hut for repair. May Kurt retain the skis until Morley pays for the job?

Although there are several different types of mutual benefit bailment, there are rights and duties common to all. In any bailment, the one holding property has a duty to properly care for and protect it for the bailor. This may mean proper storage of a lawnmower left at a repair shop, exercise and feeding of a dog boarded at a kennel, or careful use of a rented vacation trailer. It also means that if there has been some limitation on the way or length of time the property is to be used, the bailee has a duty to abide by these limitations. Thus, if the bailment is for repair of an automobile, the bailee has a duty to do only the work required or agreed upon; he has no right to drive or use the car for his own personal purposes. And if you rent a bicycle for one hour, you have a duty to return it when that amount of time is up. If a bailee does not take proper care of the property, or uses it in a way not agreed to by the bailor, he becomes liable for loss or damages that may occur.

A bailee also has a duty to return identical property, whether in the same or altered form, to the bailor. This duty is, however, sometimes dependent on the bailor's giving agreed or reasonable compensation to the bailee. When the bailee performs services on the bailed property, he has a right to hold that property until he is paid for his work; Kurt may do so in the problem. This right is known as the *bailee's lien*.

The bailor has certain duties, too. All bailors have a duty to forewarn the bailee of known defects in the property which could cause injury; and a bailor who rents property to others has a duty to provide goods fit for the intended purpose. In the latter case, greater responsibility is placed on the bailor, and he has a duty to inspect the goods for all reasonably discoverable defects before delivering the property to a bailee. In any case, the bailor who does not properly inform the bailee of defects is liable for injuries that result from possession or use of the property. On the other hand, if injury results after the bailee knows or has been properly informed of the defects, he is deemed to have contributed negligence which releases the bailor from liability.

The parties to a mutual benefit bailment may agree that the liability of the bailee be expanded or limited to a specified maximum amount. Generally the parties may also agree that the ordinary bailee shall not be liable for his own negligence. He then remains liable only for any willful or deliberate misconduct.

WHAT IS A BAILMENT FOR STORAGE?

Problem: During the fall harvest, most of the apples picked at Dodd's orchard were immediately placed in the Kickapoo Valley Cold Storage Co. warehouse. When Dodd removed some of the apples three months later, they were spoiled. Kickapoo had carelessly failed to keep the building at the proper temperature. Is Kickapoo liable for the loss?

The placing of goods in a warehouse for storage and safekeeping is a common example of a mutual benefit bailment. A *warehouseman* engages in the business of storing goods for others for a price. Except for those few cases where each unit stored is considered identical to every other unit—as with grain or oil—the warehouseman must return the very same goods he received. He must also maintain his warehouse in suitable condition for the goods he stores. An open shed, while not suitable for some goods, could suffice for bales of cotton. In the problem, Kickapoo was liable for the loss because of its negligence in failing to keep the warehouse in a condition suitable for preservation of the apples.

When he receives goods, the warehouseman issues a *warehouse receipt*. This is a written contract between the bailor who agrees to pay the storage charges, and the warehouseman (bailee) who acknowledges receipt of the goods and agrees to store them. The receipt is also a *document of title* because it is proof of the ownership or control of the goods. For example, a person may store his furniture in a public warehouse while he is building a new house. If during that time he decides to sell the furniture, he may transfer the title to it by simply transferring the warehouse receipt. This is a common method used for transferring title in business transactions. The goods are stored while the owner seeks a buyer or waits hopefully for higher prices. When a sale is finally made, the owner transfers the warehouse receipt. To get his goods, the buyer gives the warehouse receipt to the warehouseman and pays the storage charges due.

 Daniell, owner of a vineyard, stored 50,000 pounds of dried raisins in the Golden Valley Warehouse and received a warehouse receipt. A month later he sold the raisins to Dudley, a broker in Baltimore and gave him the warehouse receipt. Three weeks later Dudley sold the raisins and delivered the receipt to Gage, an exporter. Three months later Gage delivered the receipt to the warehouse, paid the storage charges, and shipped the raisins to Rotterdam.

The deposit of money in a bank is a loan which passes ownership to the bank. It is not a bailment because the bank does not agree to return to the depositor the identical coins or currency received. On the other hand, the delivery of a particular rare coin to a museum for a hobby show is a bailment because the same coin is to be returned to the bailor.

Banks that rent safe-deposit boxes to their customers are bailees for mutual benefit, but not in the ordinary sense. The renter of the box and the bank each have a key, and the box cannot be opened without both keys. Because the bank does not have exclusive possession of the property, some courts hold that the relation is one of landlord and tenant. The bank may allow only authorized persons to have access to the box. It ordinarily has a lien on the contents of the box for the rental charge.

In disputes over damage to cars in parking lots, liability is commonly decided on the basis of whether or not there is a bailment relationship. It is held that the owner continues in possession of his car and has merely rented space if he drives into the lot, parks the car, keeps the key, and can later drive the car away without permission of an attendant. No bailment relationship exists because possession has not been transferred. There is a bailment, however, if an attendant takes possession of the car and gives the owner a claim check which must be surrendered to obtain the car later.

Questions also arise as to whether the bailment of a car or other equipment is a bailment of articles attached or enclosed; such articles may or may not be visible. If the article is normally included, such as a spare tire or auto jack with an automobile, the bailment covers it without regard to the bailee's knowledge of its presence. The question with other contained articles is whether the parties reasonably intended or clearly indicated that they were to be accepted as part of the bailment. If the answer is yes, the accessories are held to be bailed.

Signs in garages and clauses printed on parking lot stubs which restrict the bailee's liability may become part of the bailment contract if the bailor read the notice or was told about the limits at the time the bailment arose.

WHAT IS A BAILMENT FOR HIRE?

Problem: Bohannon rented a house trailer from Cost-Plus Trailers for a week's trip through the Great Smoky Mountains. He was having so much fun he decided to linger on for another week. Then he arranged for Douglas, a newly-found friend, to return the trailer for him. Douglas never did return the trailer. What is Bohannon's liability?

In a bailment for hire, the hirer, or bailee, has the exclusive right to use the property for the purpose and during the time specified in the contract. During that period, not even the bailor or a creditor of the bailor has the right to disturb his possession. The bailee has, however, a duty to abide by the contract terms. If the property is hired for a certain purpose, he has a duty to use it for that purpose only. If the property is to be returned at a specified time, the bailee must return it at that time or be liable for damages. In the problem, Bohannon's unauthorized use of and failure to redeliver the trailer as agreed made him liable to Cost-Plus for both the extra rent and the value of the stolen trailer.

The bailor is entitled to the rent agreed upon at the time the property was hired. This right ends, however, if the property is lost or destroyed through no fault of the bailee. For example, if a person rented an article which was later destroyed in an earthquake, the bailor would have no right to be paid its value or any further compensation for its use.

In a mutual benefit bailment for hire the bailor must furnish goods reasonably fit for the hired purpose. The bailor is obligated to correct all known or reasonably discoverable defects before delivery of the goods to the bailee. He must also inform the bailee of any known, remaining defects. If the bailee is injured or his property damaged because the goods are not reasonably fit for the hired purpose, the bailor is liable. If the bailee has been told about a defect or discovers it himself, yet goes ahead and uses the property and is injured, he is barred from collecting damages. He is held to have assumed the risk, or to have shown contributory negligence.

WHAT IS A BAILMENT FOR WORK AND SERVICES?

Problem: Franklin, a printer, sent 500 copies of a high school annual to Klein's Bindery for binding. A fire broke out in the bindery and all the books were destroyed. Who was liable for the loss?

Whenever a person furnishes goods that are to be serviced or repaired, or materials that are to be made into a finished article, a bailment results. For example, the bailor may deliver goods to a tailor to have a suit made, clothes to a laundry to be washed, or a watch to a jeweler to be cleaned and oiled. If the bailee furnishes some minor materials, such as thread or trimmings for the suit, the relationship is not changed. If the goods are destroyed or damaged and the bailee has exercised reasonable care in their protection, the loss falls on the bailor. Moreover, the bailor must pay for work completed by the bailee at the time the product was destroyed. In the problem, if the fire was not caused by the bailee's negligence, the bailor of the books must take the loss. On the other hand, if Klein had been negligent or deliberately set the fire, he would be responsible.

A bailment of this type involves two relationships: (1) the relationship of bailor and bailee, and (2) the contractual relationship for service or repairs. The worker's duty as a bailee is to exercise reasonable care in protecting the goods; his duty under the service contract is to perform as agreed. The bailee is expected to exercise the skill which a reasonable man should possess before undertaking the work, or the special skill which he holds himself out to possess. In addition to possible liability for injury caused by his negligence or unauthorized use of the goods, the repairman is liable for damages if he fails to make the repairs agreed upon.

WHAT IS A BAILMENT FOR SALE PURPOSES?

Problem: Open Road-Open Skies, Inc. sent Cox a counter display card with 15 new-style fishing lures for his retail sports shop. Although Cox doubted that either his customers or the fish would be interested, he agreed to display the card because he paid nothing and could return any lures not sold. He was to deduct a percentage of each sale for himself and send the balance to the manufacturer. Was Cox a bailee?

Sometimes goods are sent on consignment by a manufacturer or wholesaler to a retailer. A *consignment* is a bailment for sale purposes. Until the goods are sold, ownership remains in the manufacturer or wholesaler (the bailor). The retailer who displays and sells them is a bailee and also, in effect, an agent (Page 451) authorized to sell goods for the bailor. The retailer thus adds to his inventory without buying the goods; the bailor gets his merchandise on the display shelves. In the problem, Cox was a bailee in a consignment.

Bailment for mutual benefit is also created when a merchant sends or leaves goods on approval with a prospective purchaser. The ownership does not transfer to the bailee unless and until he decides to buy. If he rejects the goods, the bailee must return them to the bailor in accordance with the agreement.

CAN A BAILMENT ARISE FROM OTHER BUSINESS RELATIONS?

Problem: Clark went into Foreman's Apparel to buy a sport coat. At the salesman's request, Clark removed his own coat and watched as the salesman placed it on a chair next to the display rack. After trying on a number of coats without satisfaction, Clark looked for his own coat. It was gone. Was the store liable?

Often, a bailment for mutual benefit arises out of other business relations. For example, when one buys an article and gets title but leaves the item with the seller for future delivery, a bailment arises.

If you go into a restaurant and leave your hat with a check girl, a mutual benefit bailment is created and the restaurant is responsible for reasonable care in protecting the hat. No bailment arises, however, if you hang your hat on a nearby hook, or even if a waiter hangs it for you as an act of courtesy. The restaurant does not have possession of the hat as the waiter goes on with his regular duties; you are deemed to be in possession. In a similar manner, Clark retained possession of his coat in the problem. The store was not liable for the loss.

When money is borrowed, personal property may be delivered to the lender as security that the contract will be performed. This creates a particular type of mutual benefit bailment known as a pledge. Upon performance of the contract (that is, repayment of the loan), the bailed property is returned to the bailor. For more about pledges, see Chapter 22.

PRACTICAL POINTERS FOR BAILEES . . .

1. Clearly specify the terms of the contract, preferably in writing, when you accept goods as a bailee for hire, or for storage, repair, transport, service, security, or consignment sale.
2. Before you take possession of or use bailed goods, be certain that you are covered by adequate public liability and property insurance. You are always liable for your own torts, and you could be required to pay damages if you injure someone with the bailed equipment.
3. If you have performed services on bailed goods, do not release them until you are paid for your services or are satisfied that the bailor's credit is good.

PRACTICAL POINTERS FOR BAILORS . . .

1. Because a bailee gets exclusive possession of the bailed goods and may misuse or damage them, try to give your property only to responsible persons.
2. Although a bailee may be liable for willful or negligent conduct which damages your goods, it is wise to carry appropriate property insurance to cover possible losses.
3. Spell out the terms of the bailment contract in writing whenever practicable, and always get a receipt for goods transferred to a bailee.
4. If the bailee is to repair or service the goods, be as specific as possible about prices and work to be done.
5. If you rent a car or other equipment which could be dangerous if in bad condition, inspect it carefully and correct defects before delivery to the bailee.

YOUR LEGAL VOCABULARY

bailee	document of title
bailee's lien	gratuitous bailment
bailor	mutual benefit bailment
bailment	warehouseman
consignment	warehouse receipt
constructive bailment	

1. One who receives possession of personal property belonging to another.
2. One who transfers possession of personal property to another.
3. The relation in which one person is given possession of goods that belong to another.

4. A written contract between one who owns or controls goods and the one who receives and agrees to store them.
5. The right of a bailee to hold goods until paid.
6. A bailment from which the bailor and the bailee each receive some benefit or advantage.
7. Written proof of ownership or control of goods.
8. One engaged in the business of storing goods for profit.
9. A bailment for sale purposes.
10. A bailment in which one party receives no benefit.

REMEMBER THESE HIGHLIGHTS

1. In a bailment, one party—the bailee—has possession of personal property belonging to another, the bailor. The bailee has a duty to return the identical property in the same or altered form, as agreed, to the bailor or someone designated by him.
2. Bailments may be created by contract, informal agreement, or law. Those created by contract are mutual benefit bailments. Those created by informal agreement for the benefit of one party are gratuitous bailments. Those created by law when no agreement is possible are constructive bailments.
3. A bailment does not exist until the property has been delivered to and accepted by the bailee.
4. A bailment may be terminated by agreement or contract, act of either party, destruction of the subject matter, or by operation of law.
5. The bailee is required to use reasonable care in protecting the bailor's property, and to use and return the goods in accordance with the agreement.
6. If one of the parties in a mutual benefit bailment is to service or repair the goods, he has the right to retain possession of the goods until he is paid for his work.
7. In a bailment for hire, the bailor is liable for damages caused by known or reasonably discoverable defects in the property unless he specifically informs the bailee of such defects.
8. A warehouseman engaged in the business of storing goods for hire issues warehouse receipts, is liable for reasonable care only, and has a lien on the goods for reasonable storage charges.
9. A bailment for work or services involves two relationships—that of bailor and bailee, and a contractual relationship for service or repair.

LAW AS PEOPLE LIVE IT

1. Before he left on a two-week vacation, Harcourt asked McNeil, who lived in the adjoining apartment, to pick up his mail from the box

and to accept all packages that might be delivered. McNeil agreed. Was a bailment created when McNeil got the mail or received a parcel for Harcourt?

2. Borowich parked her car in the free parking lot provided by Holiday Supermarket and went in to purchase groceries. When she returned she was shocked to find the car had been stripped of battery, radio, hubcaps, and spare tire. Was Holiday liable as bailee for the loss?

3. During a sale, Sheldon entered Maitland's ready-to-wear shop and found all the clerks busy with customers. She placed her purse under her coat on a counter and, without assistance, went to try on the clothes she liked. When she returned, the purse was gone. Was Maitland's liable?

4. To accommodate a customer, Mello, a gasoline service station proprietor, obtained a two-gallon can of anti-freeze compound from his friend Koontz, who had a competing station across the intersection. Mello promised to return two gallons of the compound when his supply was replenished that weekend. Was a bailment created?

5. Chaplin rented a car from U-Drive under an agreement which said that the car was to be used only in Los Angeles County, California, where the contract was made. An emergency developed and Chaplin drove the car to Seattle. On the way back, the car was badly damaged in an accident that was not Chaplin's fault. Was he liable to U-Drive?

6. Stromberg rented his harvesting machine to Jones for the first two weeks of July. After eight days, Stromberg needed the machine for his own harvest and insisted on taking it back. May he do so?

7. LaRue Jewelers sent samples of five different styles of class rings to Jerry Wilkins, president of the senior class at the local high school. The members of the class were to select the styles they wanted, if any, and the samples were to be returned. What kind of bailment was created? What degree of care was required of Wilkins?

8. Durant owned six palomino horses which he left in Burton's care while he was gone on a three-month, round-the-world cruise. In Durant's absence, Burton traded two of the horses for what he honestly believed to be much better animals. When Durant returned, he was furious. Is Burton liable to Durant for damages?

9. Martin stored his crop of rice in a public grain elevator, obtaining a warehouse receipt in exchange. Six months later he sold the rice to Kellogg. What would Kellogg have to do to get possession of the rice? Would it have to be the same rice which Martin had deposited?

LAW AS COURTS DECIDE IT

1. The Goodyear Clearwater Mills kept employees stationed at the gates to its fenced parking lot. Except for about 30 minutes before and after the time for changing shifts, the gates were kept locked. It

was necessary to get permission of the gatekeeper to park or remove an automobile. No tickets or identification cards were issued. Each employee parked his own car and kept the keys. When Wheeler's automobile was stolen from the parking lot, he contended that Goodyear was the bailee and thus liable for his loss. Do you agree? (Goodyear Clearwater Mills v. Wheeler, 77 Ga. App. 570, 49 S.E. 2d 184)

2. Irving Marsh, a partner in the S. Marsh and Sons Store, Newark, New Jersey, purchased costume jewelry in New York City invoiced at $2,743.70. He carried the package to the Pennsylvania Railroad Station intending to take a train to Newark. When he learned that it would be some time before his train departed, Marsh put the package in a vacant locker, inserted a dime, turned the key, tried the door to see that it was locked, and removed the key and took it with him. Returning 45 minutes later, he inserted the key, opened the locker, and found that the package was gone. The issue is whether the relation of bailment did or did not exist between Marsh and the Locker Company. What is your opinion? (Marsh v. American Locker Co., 7 N.J. Super. 81, 72 A. 2d 343)

3. Defendants were bailors who had rented a tractor and disk (for breaking up soil) to Harper. Harper was informed that the device normally used for raising and lowering the disk was out of order and a hitch lift would have to be used instead. He was also warned that, if overloaded, the hitch lift would cause the front end of the tractor to rear up like a bucking bronco. Harper hired Ellis to use the equipment and told him of the defect. Nevertheless, Ellis overloaded the disk in wet ground and the fourth time the tractor reared up, it flipped over and crushed Ellis badly. Ellis sued the bailors. Are they liable? (Moore v. Ellis, 385 S.W. 2d 261, Texas)

4. Bailey and others deposited bonds worth about $19,500 with the Farmers' Bank for safekeeping. The bank gave them certificate receipts and agreed to return the bonds upon surrender of the certificates. However, the bank sold the bonds and placed the proceeds in an "emergency fund." Later the bank failed and the State Banking Commissioner took over. Some $3,000 was still in the emergency account. Ordinary depositors claim it should be used to pay off all creditors. Bailey and the bondholders claim they are bailors, not creditors, and that the bonds—or proceeds therefrom—belong to them. Who gets the $3,000? (Farmers' Bank of White Plains et al. v. Bailey et al., 227 Ky. 179, 12 S.W. 2d 312)

5. Veech paid 50¢ to park her car in Drybrough's parking lot. She left her fur coat in the car but did not mention it to the attendant. When she returned, the coat was gone. She sued Drybrough, claiming his attendants were negligent. Decide. (Drybrough v. Veech, 238 S.W. 2d 996, Kentucky)

Unit IV □ BAILMENTS

CHAPTER 16 Special Bailments

1. *While at the beach, you find a wallet. Is this a case of "finders keepers," especially if the wallet contains no name?*

2. *While you are on a holiday trip, your fishing gear and camera are stolen from your motel room. Can you hold the motel liable?*

3. *You borrow a snare drum from the school music department. What is your legal responsibility?*

HOW ARE BAILMENTS CLASSIFIED?

Problem: Cushing, who was on a business trip, stopped at the Golden Key Motel for the night. What kind of bailment was created when he left his bags in the assigned room and went out to dinner?

As explained in Chapter 15, all bailments may be classified in terms of which party or parties benefit from the relation. In other words, they may be classified as mutual benefit bailments or gratuitous (sole benefit of one party) bailments.

Bailments may also be classified by whether or not they are based on an agreement. As you know, mutual benefit bailments are always based on legal agreement or contract; and gratuitous bailments, while lacking consideration, are always based on informal agreement between parties. But one type of bailment is not based on agreement because it cannot be. This is the constructive bailment, which occurs when possession of lost property is taken by someone other than the owner. In this case the law, rather than agreement of parties, creates the relation.

Last, bailments may be classified as ordinary and extraordinary. *Extraordinary bailments* are those in which the bailee is held to an unusually high standard of care for the bailed property, as when the bailee is a hotel or common carrier. All other bailments are ordinary. In the problem, Cushing's rental of the motel room resulted in an extraordinary bailment of his luggage.

Chapter 15 dealt with the most common and important of bailments—the ordinary mutual benefit bailment—which is based on contract, benefits both bailor and bailee, and creates certain rights and duties for each party. Bailments which differ basically from this common type include: (1) those which benefit only one party (gratuitous bailments); (2) those which are not based on agreement (constructive bailments); and (3) those extraordinary bailments in which a different and higher degree of liability is placed on the bailee.

WHAT BAILMENTS BENEFIT ONE PARTY ONLY?

Problem: Burley left on a week-long camping trip in a house trailer which belonged to his neighbor, Simenson. Simenson refused to accept any rental payment, and Burley promised to return promptly on the following Monday so that Simenson could leave on his own vacation. However, the fish were biting so eagerly that Burley delayed his return by two days. Simenson meanwhile left in a rented trailer. Must Burley reimburse Simenson for the rental charges?

(1) BAILMENTS FOR THE SOLE BENEFIT OF THE BAILEE

When one borrows goods from another and does not have to pay for their use, the bailment is for the sole benefit of the bailee. Certain responsibilities arise from this relationship. A bailee-borrower is entitled to use the goods only as agreed to by the lender. If he uses them in violation of the agreement, he is liable to the bailor-lender for damages. In the problem, Burley must pay Simenson the rental charges incurred.

A bailee is always required to exercise due care to protect the bailed property, and is liable for loss or damage if he does not. The

Borrowing is an example of a bailment for the sole benefit of the bailee.

SOMEDAY I'M GOING TO BUY SOME GARDEN TOOLS.

degree of care required varies with the nature of the goods and the circumstances of the bailment. If the bailment is for the sole benefit of the bailee, it is normally reasonable to expect him to be more careful than if it is for the sole benefit of the bailor. Obviously, proper

Unit IV ☐ BAILMENTS

care would differ for a load of coal and a case of diamonds. It would differ in crowded cities and deserted country places. It would change if crime was rampant in the location of the bailment, or if peace and order prevailed.

When the bailment is for the sole benefit of the bailee, the bailor is obligated to inform the bailee only of those defects of which he is actually aware. If the bailor does not do this and the bailee does not discover the defects himself, the bailor will be liable for any injury that results.

(2) BAILMENTS FOR THE SOLE BENEFIT OF THE BAILOR

Problem: When Rogan left for six months of duty in the National Guard, he left his motorcycle with Phillips for storage and safekeeping. Without Rogan's knowledge or consent, Phillips rode the cycle frequently, claiming he was keeping it "hot" until his friend returned. Did Phillips have this right?

When one gives possession of his goods to another for his own convenience and does not pay for the service, it is a bailment for the sole benefit of the bailor. Again, certain responsibilities arise.

One who gratuitously accepts the goods of another may not use them unless it is necessary to preserve the goods, or unless he has the permission of the bailor to do so. Accordingly, Phillips violated his duty as a bailee. Rogan had a right to sue him for any loss he may have suffered from the improper use of his motorcycle.

When the bailment is for the sole benefit of the bailor, he is obligated to inform the bailee of known defects. Because he alone is receiving a benefit, the bailor is also obligated to make a reasonable examination of the goods to discover possible hidden defects, and to inform the bailee if any are discovered. Failure to inform the bailee of known or reasonably discoverable defects makes the bailor liable for any injuries that result.

WHAT ARE CONSTRUCTIVE BAILMENTS?

Problem: Olsen, an employee of a small city hotel, found a jade and gold ring on the sink in the public washroom. Kwong, the owner, had reported his loss to the hotel manager and clearly described the ring. Olsen had heard that "possession is nine-tenths of the law" and claims that as finder he is entitled to keep the ring. Is he right?

(1) BAILMENTS OF LOST ARTICLES

An article of personal property is lost when the owner has involuntarily parted with the item and does not know where to find it. A person who finds a lost article is not obliged to take possession of it. If he does, however, courts usually hold that he becomes a bailee for the sole benefit of the bailor, that is, the one who lost the article. If he takes possession with no intention of seeking the true owner, he may actually be guilty of a form of larceny.

Finding a lost article results in a constructive bailment.

The finder who takes possession of goods has certain responsibilities even though the bailment is for the sole benefit of the bailor. He must exercise care reasonable to the nature of the goods and the circumstances surrounding their discovery. This may mean reporting the find to appropriate private authorities or to the police. In some states, it may be necessary to advertise for the owner. After a reasonable or prescribed time has elapsed and other statutory requirements have been met, the finder becomes the owner if the true owner has not come forward to claim the property. In some states, the finder must sell the property at public auction. He keeps the proceeds and may himself acquire title if he is the highest bidder. If the owner does appear, he normally must reimburse the finder for reasonable expenses incurred in advertising and in caring for the goods. Some states require that he pay the finder a reasonable reward.

If property is found in a building open to the public and the circumstances indicate that it was intentionally placed where found but forgotten by the owner, the finder is not entitled to take possession. He must deliver the property to the manager, for it is assumed that the owner will probably remember and return seeking his property. Articles left on planes, trains, and buses are commonly held to be mislaid and not lost; thus, the finder should turn them in to the carrier. In the problem, Olsen would be required to give the ring to the hotel manager for delivery to Kwong.

(2) BAILMENTS BY NECESSITY

> **Problem:** Robert J. Mills has a completely unrelated friend, Robert J. Mills, who lives in another section of the same city. They sometimes receive each other's mail, and parcels are incorrectly delivered to one or the other. What is the duty of the recipient when a package belonging to the other is received?

Occasionally personal property comes into one's possession without any voluntary act on his part. During a flood, for example, personal property belonging to one person may be washed up on the land of another. If the latter takes possession of the property, he is required to take care of it for the owner. Likewise, a person, such as either Robert J. Mills in the problem, is generally required to take care of goods that are mistakenly left or placed in his possession through no fault of the owner. This involuntary type of bailment is sometimes known as *bailment by necessity*.

WHEN IS A HOTEL A BAILEE?

> **Problem:** Nash and his wife lived permanently at the Surfspray, a seaside motel-hotel, and paid a monthly rent. When Cooper visited them for a week, he rented a separate room on a day-to-day basis. During this time, luggage belonging to Cooper and jewelry belonging to Nash were stolen from their rooms. Was the hotel liable?

A *hotelkeeper* (formerly known as an *innkeeper*) is a person who operates a hotel, motel, tourist home, or similar business, and holds himself out as receiving all transients who arrive in proper condition (e.g., not drunk) and who are willing and able to pay for their accommodations. In the past, travelers were especially vulnerable to theft. The common law thus gives the hotelkeeper an insurer-like liability for property brought into the hotel by a guest; as such, he may be totally liable for loss or damage. Today, however, conditions are better and most states limit his legal liability. The hotelkeeper must exercise reasonable care, but usually he can make his own rules for safeguarding costly property. Thus, he may post a notice that if he is to be responsible for valuables, such as jewelry or money, they must be deposited in the hotel safe. By statute or contract, dollar limits may also be placed on the hotel's liability.

A *boardinghouse keeper* is one who furnishes living accommodations to permanent residents, not to transients or travelers. He has neither the special rights nor extraordinary liability of a hotelkeeper.

If a hotel has both transient and permanent residents, it has the status of boardinghouse as to permanent residents, and that of hotel as to transient guests.

A hotelkeeper has common-law liability only for luggage and other property brought into his hotel by a *guest,* or transient. In the problem, Cooper was a guest and the hotelkeeper was responsible for his loss unless state statutes limited his liability. Persons like the Nashes, who make their permanent residence at a hotel, are not guests in the legal sense. To them, the hotelkeeper has only the liability of a boardinghouse keeper, that is, of an ordinary bailee in a mutual benefit bailment. Nash and his wife were boarders, and the hotelkeeper was not liable for their loss unless he had failed to exercise reasonable care.

Although rooms are often rented on credit, a hotelkeeper may demand that payment be made in advance. If he does not collect in advance, he may retain all the goods rightfully in the guest's possession—except clothes actually being worn—until he is paid. This right is known as the *hotelkeeper's lien* and may even be asserted against goods owned by third parties, such as sample merchandise belonging to the employer of a traveling salesman. If the hotelkeeper is not paid, the lien allows him to sell the goods at a public sale.

WHEN IS A COMMON CARRIER A BAILEE?

Problem: Lawson owned a fleet of trucks which he used to make local deliveries for several department stores in his city. Was he a common carrier?

One who transports passengers or goods any distance by any means—including train, plane, truck, bus, ship, and taxi—is a *carrier*. When goods belonging to others are transported, a bailment exists. The bailor who delivers goods to the carrier-bailee for shipment is called a *consignor,* or shipper. The one to whom the goods are shipped is the *consignee*. Carriers are classified as common, contract, and private.

(1) COMMON CARRIER

A *common carrier* undertakes, for hire, to transport passengers or goods for anyone who applies for its services. A common carrier is not a bailee of passengers because, as you recall, only personal property can be the subject of a bailment. However, a passenger's baggage is bailed when checked or delivered into the possession of the carrier.

A common carrier does not insure the safety of its passengers, nor is it liable for injuries which result from the passenger's own negligence. In providing for their security, however, the carrier is duty-bound to exercise the highest degree of care and skill consistent with practical operation.

A common carrier of goods is an extraordinary bailee because of its high, insurer-like liability for goods received for immediate shipment and in transit. Generally if there is loss or damage to the goods, the carrier is absolutely liable. There are some exceptions, as noted in the following section. Also, a carrier may limit its liability by agreement with the shipper. For higher liability, higher rates are generally charged.

(2) CONTRACT CARRIER

A *contract carrier* may select its customers, and transports goods or passengers under individual contracts. In the problem, Lawson was a contract carrier, with the rights and duties of an ordinary mutual-benefit bailee.

(3) PRIVATE CARRIER

A *private carrier* is one who carries his own goods, or members of his own organization, exclusively. A fleet of trucks owned by a supermarket, for example, is operated as a private carrier. No bailment relationship is involved.

WHAT ARE THE DUTIES OF A COMMON CARRIER?

Problem: Cambria Caustics, Inc. requested Transcontinental Airlines, a common carrier, to transport one hundred 5-gallon glass jars of a chemical which was highly corrosive to metals. The airline refused to accept the shipment unless the jars were shielded from possible breakage by wooden crates which in turn had to be wrapped in rubber bags to catch any leakage. Must Cambria comply?

A common carrier is generally required to: (1) serve all persons without discrimination, provided the goods are fit for shipment and lawful; (2) receive and transport the type of goods it holds itself out to carry; (3) furnish adequate transportation facilities, including proper facilities for storage of goods before and after shipment; (4) follow directions given by the shipper; (5) load and unload goods delivered to it (although the shipper or consignee may assume this duty by custom or contract); (6) deliver the goods to the consignee or his agent. In the problem, Cambria must comply in order to make the goods fit for shipment.

Proper place of delivery depends upon custom and may be changed by contract. Motor carriers (trucks), airlines, and often railways commonly offer door-to-door service for pick up and delivery of shipments, especially in large cities. In both cases, the carrier has the primary duty of properly loading its vehicles and is liable if injury results from a careless job. With railroads, the proper place has ordinarily been the freight depot of the carrier, but deliveries to the consignee's address are now becoming the usual practice in many places. Custom has placed upon the consignor the burden of loading, and upon the consignee that of unloading, goods shipped by rail in carload lots. The carrier normally loads and unloads less-than-carload lots.

If the consignee is required to pick up his shipment, the common carrier becomes liable only as an ordinary bailee after the consignee has been notified and a reasonable time has elapsed. In effect, the carrier becomes a warehouseman in a bailment for storage.

When a carrier accepts goods, it issues a *bill of lading* to the shipper. This document (a) acknowledges receipt of the goods, and (b) states the terms of the contract. Some bills of lading are negotiable; that is, they can be transferred by the holder's indorsement and delivery to another party. These are known as *order bills of lading* because the goods are deliverable only upon the order of the consignee. The order bill of lading must be surrendered to the carrier in order to get delivery of the goods.

WHAT ARE THE RIGHTS OF A COMMON CARRIER?

Problem: A railroad transported a large box of tools and other personal belongings to New York for Easton. It refused to release the box until paid for its services. Easton said he needed the tools in order to work and earn enough to pay the charges, and he demanded credit. Was the carrier obliged to deliver the box before receiving payment?

Rates charged and services rendered by interstate railroad, bus, and truck companies are regulated by the federal Interstate Commerce Commission. The Civil Aeronautics Board regulates the airlines. For intrastate carriers, state regulatory agencies perform similar functions. In exchange, the carriers receive special rights to serve certain communities.

ng the rights of the common carrier are those to: (1) enforce
ble rules and regulations for the conduct of its business (for
e, rules stating how goods must be packed); (2) demand
nsation for its services as allowed by law; (3) charge *demur-*
es for use of its equipment when the consignor fails to load or
the consignee fails to unload within a reasonable length of time;
(4) enforce a *carrier's lien,* which permits it to retain possession of
the goods until the charges for transportation and incidental services
are paid. In the problem, the railroad was not required to release the
box to Easton until paid for its services.

ARE EXTRAORDINARY BAILEES LIABLE FOR ALL LOSSES?

Problem: A train with a boxcar load of furniture belonging to Webster was derailed by a tornado in Kansas.
There was extensive damage. Was the railroad, a common carrier, liable?

Although hotelkeepers and common carriers are generally held to
be absolutely liable for loss or damage to goods they possess as
extraordinary bailees, there are several important exceptions. Neither
is liable for injuries or losses it can show were caused by one of the
following:

(1) AN ACT OF GOD

An *act of God* is an act of nature that man cannot reasonably
foresee and avoid. Such things as earthquakes, tornadoes, flash
floods, or unusual storms are considered acts of God. If a carrier
or hotelkeeper is able to avoid a loss by proper care and foresight,
it is liable for losses that result from its failure to do so. The
tornado in the problem would be considered an act of God. If the
carrier were warned of the tornado's approach in time to move the
goods to safety, it would be liable if it failed to do so.

(2) ACT OF A PUBLIC ENEMY

A *public enemy* may be a member of the armed forces of a foreign
country with which our nation is at war. The term also includes
saboteurs of such a foreign country. Acts committed by mobs, rioters,
strikers, or robbers are not acts of a public enemy; hence, they do not
relieve the carrier or hotelkeeper of responsibility for injuries.

In some instances, a carrier may have an express agreement inserted into the contract (the bill of lading) exempting it from liability
for loss caused by riots and strikes.

(3) ACT OF PUBLIC AUTHORITY

A loss occurs by an act of public authority when goods are taken from the carrier or hotelkeeper under legal process. Examples are the seizing of contraband goods by officers of the law, or the taking of goods that have become injurious to the public health or that are legally claimed by a third party. In such cases, the carrier or hotelkeeper is not liable, but must notify the bailor.

(4) FAULT OF THE SHIPPER OR GUEST

The carrier or hotelkeeper is not liable for a loss that results from the bailor's carelessness, such as improper packing or loading by a shipper. Furthermore, if the value of the goods is fraudulently concealed, the bailee may be relieved from liability.

(5) INHERENT NATURE OF THE GOODS

Losses caused by the inherent nature of the goods include: decay of fruit or other perishables; evaporation, fermentation, or unavoidable leakage; spontaneous combustion; and injuries inflicted by animals upon themselves or one another.

USE SPECIAL CARE IN SPECIAL BAILMENTS . . .

1. If you alone benefit from the bailment, a high degree of care is expected of you. If you are the bailee, use the goods only as agreed and protect them from possible loss or harm. If you are the bailor, make a careful examination of the goods for defects that could cause harm and inform the bailee if any are found. Remember that you are liable for damages that result from failure to perform these duties even though the bailment is an informal one without consideration.
2. When you find and take possession of something of value belonging to another, you become a constructive bailee. Comply with local statutes, or otherwise act reasonably in caring for the property and seeking the true owner.
3. After you check in at a motel or hotel, read any rules posted in your room regarding limits on the hotelkeeper's liability for loss of your property. Act appropriately, as by checking valuables at the front desk.
4. When you travel by carrier, you remain responsible for clothing and small baggage which you retain in your possession. Guard it. Moreover, the carrier may limit its liability for baggage you check. If you want greater protection, request and pay for the additional coverage from the carrier.
5. When you ship goods by common carrier, pack, address, and label properly (e.g., "FRAGILE" or "THIS SIDE UP"). Again, check the limits of the carrier's liability, and if you want greater protection, request and pay for the additional coverage.

YOUR LEGAL VOCABULARY

act of God
bailment by necessity
bill of lading
boardinghouse keeper
carrier
carrier's lien
common carrier
consignee
consignor

contract carrier
demurrage
extraordinary bailment
guest
hotelkeeper (or innkeeper)
hotelkeeper's lien
order bill of lading
private carrier
public enemy

1. An act of nature which man cannot reasonably foresee and avoid.
2. One who furnishes living accommodations to permanent residents.
3. The right of a carrier to keep possession of the goods until the charges for transportation and incidental services are paid.
4. A document that must be surrendered to the carrier by the consignee to get delivery of the goods.
5. One who undertakes, for hire, to transport goods or passengers for anyone who applies.
6. One who regularly offers living accommodations to transient persons.
7. A document issued to the shipper by the carrier as a receipt and contract for transportation.
8. One who delivers goods to a carrier for shipment.
9. A fee charged for delay in loading or unloading freight cars.
10. A carrier who transports his own goods or personnel exclusively.

REMEMBER THESE HIGHLIGHTS

1. A bailment for the sole benefit of the bailee is created when the bailee borrows another's goods without being required to pay for their use.
2. A bailment for the sole benefit of the bailor is created when the bailee takes possession of the goods as a favor to the bailor.
3. A constructive bailment is created by law when a finder takes possession of lost goods, or when one person comes into the possession of the goods of another by accident or mistake.
4. Hotelkeepers and common carriers, as extraordinary bailees, have insurer-like liability for bailed property under the common law. However, statute or contract often limit this liability.
5. Hotelkeepers and common carriers may demand payment in advance. If a bill is unpaid, a hotelkeeper may retain all goods rightfully in the guest's possession, except clothes being worn, as security for the payment. The common carrier has a similar lien against goods shipped.
6. Common carriers enjoy monopolistic advantages, but their rates and standards of service are subject to regulation by federal, state, and local government agencies.

7. A bill of lading acknowledges receipt of goods and states the terms of the shipping contract. If it is a negotiable or order bill of lading, it must be surrendered to the carrier in order to get possession of the goods.

8. A common carrier of passengers must exercise the highest degree of care consistent with practical operations in providing for their safety. However, it is not an insurer of their safety.

9. Neither a hotelkeeper nor a common carrier is liable for certain losses, such as those caused by an act of God or the inherent nature of the goods.

LAW AS PEOPLE LIVE IT

1. Cabot borrowed a lawn edger from his neighbor, Phelps. The edger's circular blade was defective although Phelps did not know this. While Cabot was using the edger, the blade snapped and a piece of metal lodged in Cabot's eye, blinding him. Was Phelps liable for the injury?

2. Wiley borrowed an airplane without charge from the Valley-Hi Fly Club. In violation of federal regulations, Wiley flew into a heavy cloud formation. He destroyed the plane when he crashed into the hillside. In the lawsuit which followed, Valley-Hi contended that Wiley was liable for the loss. Was Valley-Hi correct?

3. Zellerbach operated a motor court and catered to the tourist trade. Eaton, who was driving to Texas with his wife and infant child to seek work at an oil refinery, stopped at the court for the night. Eaton and his wife liked the town and he found a job in a local factory. He promptly made arrangements with Zellerbach to live in the cabin at a special rate on a month-to-month basis. Was Zellerbach a hotelkeeper in this relation?

4. While riding on a bus, Macklin opened the window and carelessly extended his arm to test the temperature. Just as he did so, a truck with a wide load came by and struck his arm, even though the bus was on its side of the highway divider strip. Was the carrier liable for Macklin's injuries?

5. Novak inherited an old, 26-foot fishing boat. He delivered it to Parnell's Shipyard, located on the ocean front, and contracted for a thorough overhaul for $1,250. After the work had been completed, but before Novak picked up the boat, a tidal wave destroyed the shop and all the boats in the immediate vicinity, including Novak's. Is Parnell liable for the loss? Must Novak pay the $1,250?

6. The Mercury Moving Company was a common carrier engaged in the transportation of household furniture and personal effects. Because of Mercury's reputation for speed, Poletti sent them an order for the shipment of twenty reels of heavy construction cable to a city it served. Could Mercury refuse to carry the cable?

7. Olmstead was the consignee of goods carried by a railroad company. He was promptly notified when the goods arrived at their destination, but he did not have room for them in his store at the time. Three weeks later the goods were destroyed in a fire of undetermined origin through no negligence of the railroad. Olmstead now sues the railroad for the value of the goods and refuses to pay the transportation charges. Decide.

8. When Mr. and Mrs. George Melton returned to their hotel room after a big night "on the town," it was well past midnight. Because of the hour, neither bothered to take Mrs. Melton's diamond necklace and earrings to the hotel office for safekeeping, even though a sign in their room said that valuables should be checked to hold the management responsible. Before dawn, a burglar broke into the room and stole the jewels. The Meltons claimed the hotel should make good their loss because it was too late to check the jewels when they returned on the night of the theft. Are they correct?

9. A carload of plywood was shipped under an order bill of lading to De Lockey. Zahn bought the full shipment from De Lockey for cash and received a signed receipt which described the goods. May Zahn now claim and get the goods from the carrier?

10. A large shipment of canned fish was being transported by railroad from Seattle to Atlanta. In Chicago, federal agents seized and destroyed the entire shipment because it was part of a production lot tainted with poisonous botulism. Was the railroad liable to the shipper for this loss?

LAW AS COURTS DECIDE IT

1. While a guest at the Kentwood Hotel, Brown had the Lines Music Company deliver a radio to his room under the pretense that he was interested in buying. Brown then persuaded the music company to leave the radio with him so that he could try it out and reach a decision as to buying. Shortly thereafter Brown checked out of the hotel and informed the manager that he was leaving the radio until he paid his bill. When the music company returned for the radio, the hotel contended that it had an unpaid hotelkeeper's lien against the radio. Was the hotel correct? (Lines Music Co. v. Holt, 332 Mo. 749, 60 S.W. 2d 32)

2. Holt shipped by railroad twenty-three mares from Rosebud, Montana, to Fort Worth, Texas. While en route, the young range animals were injured as the result of fighting and kicking among themselves. Holt brought an action against the carrier to recover damages. Was he entitled to judgment? (Holt v. Edwards, 140 S.W. 2d 318, Texas)

3. Gonzalez was found semi-conscious or in severe shock in a wrecked automobile. His abdominal injuries had apparently been inflicted with a knife. At the hospital, before emergency surgery and while the

investigating police officer was still present, attendants made a routine search of his clothing to learn his identity. Some marijuana was found which led to a later charge of illegal possession of narcotics. The question arose whether the hospital was a bailee of the clothing and other belongings, since Gonzalez was in no condition to make a contractual agreement. Decide. (People v. Gonzalez, 182 Cal. App. 2d 276, 5 Cal. Reptr. 920)

4. In the hope that he would buy the car, Pettinelli Motors loaned a 1960 Cadillac, worth $3,100, to Morreale for a road test. Morreale permitted his supervisor, Faust, to drive the car, and Faust was killed in a one-car accident with the vehicle. Pettinelli salvaged the wreck for $400 and sued Morreale for the difference in value. If this was a bailment for the sole benefit of bailee, requiring Morreale to use great care, he would be liable for the slightest negligence in his use and care of the car. What kind of bailment was it? (Pettinelli Motors, Inc. v. Morreale, 242 N.Y.S. 2d 78, 39 Misc. 2d 813)

5. Federal employees improperly loaded six airplane engines on a truck belonging to Savage, a common carrier. Savage employees were negligent in accepting the load so poorly secured, and in failing to correct the obvious defects. Moreover, the truck driver, who knew the condition of his load, carelessly rounded a curve. One engine fell off and killed the driver of an oncoming vehicle. At the trial, a question arose as to who has the duty of properly loading a common carrier truck. Decide. (United States v. Savage Truck Lines, Inc., 209 F. 2d 442)

Sales

UNIT FIVE

Probably the most common type of contract entered into is the contract to purchase goods—goods to eat, to wear, and to use for work and play. A purchase to a buyer is, of course, a sale to a merchant or other seller. With so many sales taking place daily and involving millions of people and many thousands of different products, it is no wonder that certain rules have been developed to protect both sellers and buyers. As a consequence, most sales are usually completed routinely with no special difficulties and with few lawsuits.

In this unit, we shall examine the rules which help to make all this orderly commercial exchange possible. We shall see that the law of contracts as it applies to sales has been liberalized and simplified by the Uniform Commercial Code in line with present attitudes concerning consumer protection, trade practices, and customs.

In many cases the law requires that sellers guarantee certain minimum standards of quality and performance. Nevertheless, there are many precautions which must be taken by the consumer if he is to protect himself against poor merchandise or service.

Should either party to a transaction fail to perform as agreed, the other party has certain rights of action or remedies for breach of contract.

CHAPTER 17 Nature of the Sales Contract

1. *When the baseball coach shifted you from catcher to outfielder, you traded your catcher's mitt for a fielder's glove owned by a friend. Was this a sale?*

2. *A young couple selects matching wedding bands from a catalog in a jewelry store. They agree to pay in full on delivery. Has a sale been made?*

3. *A package of assorted foreign postage stamps is delivered to you by mail, together with a bill for $3. You never ordered the stamps. Must you pay if you keep them?*

WHAT IS A SALE?

Problem: Carter bought a new set of tires for his pickup truck from Colgate, a franchised dealer. At the same time he agreed to buy a panel truck when the new models appeared five months later. Were both of these agreements governed by the law of sales?

A *sale* is a transfer of ownership or title to goods for a consideration called a price. Carter's purchase of the tires was a sale because ownership was transferred at the time of the transaction. His agreement to buy a panel truck at a later date was not a sale. It was a *contract to sell* because ownership would pass in the future. Both agreements were governed by the law of sales, which applies both to present sales of goods and to contracts to sell goods at a future time. In both cases the seller is known as the *vendor*, the buyer as the *vendee* or purchaser.

In many situations, a contract will be primarily for personal services and any goods supplied are merely incidental. For example, when a dentist provides a set of artificial teeth, or a plumber repairs a leaking faucet with a new washer, the relationship is not regarded as a sale. Neither do such services as the "selling" of insurance or of tickets to a show or athletic event qualify as sales transactions under the UCC; they are governed by the general law of contracts or by other special rules. On the other hand, when an electrician sells and installs a room air-conditioner, there is a sale because the labor or service is a minor part of the transaction.

WHAT IS THE EFFECT OF TRANSFERRING OWNERSHIP?

Problem: When Kidwell inherited a million dollars, he went on a spending spree. He bought dozens of suits he never used, a car which he deliberately wrecked, expensive furniture which he quickly tired of and gave away, and crystal champagne glasses which he smashed in his fireplace. Could he be legally stopped from using his goods so wastefully?

It is important to know the difference between a sale and a contract to sell because, generally, both burdens and benefits go with ownership. When one person sells, or transfers ownership of goods to another, he says, in effect, "I hereby transfer to you the legal right to use, control, and dispose of these goods."

Ownership carries valuable rights. Generally one may use his goods as he pleases; he may even destroy them, as in the problem. A rise in value or other gain, such as birth of puppies to a dog he owns, is his as the owner. However, ownership also involves certain duties and burdens. The owner may be taxed in proportion to his holdings. His freedom to use his property may be limited by government regulations for the common good, as by speeding and zoning laws. He has the problems of protection and maintenance. If his property is cared for improperly or used in a manner which interferes with the rights of others, he may be liable for resulting torts. (Page 79) In some cases this responsibility may extend to the use of his goods by another person. For example, in some states the owner of an automobile is responsible for injuries arising out of the operation of his car by another person who has his permission.

An owner of goods must also bear any loss that occurs when his goods deteriorate because of the action of the elements—rain, heat, cold. He loses when they are destroyed, stolen, lost, or damaged without the legal fault of any person, unless they were covered by proper insurance. For example, if a storm damages or destroys camping equipment that you own, you sustain the loss.

In spite of all this, ownership does not always determine who shall take losses. As will be discussed in Chapter 19, the UCC sometimes places risk of loss on someone other than the owner.

DOES THE LAW OF CONTRACTS APPLY TO SALES?

Problem: Libby bought a Polaroid-type camera from Owens' Photo Shop for $79.95. He gave it to his niece as a graduation gift. Were contractual relations involved in both acts?

A sale is the most common type of contract. In general, the law of sales applies the law of contracts to the buying and selling of tangible personal property. Libby's purchase of the camera was a sale. It included all the essentials of a contract: competent parties, genuine and mutual assent, legality, and consideration. Libby's gift to his niece, on the other hand, created no contract because it was a gift, or a transfer of ownership without consideration.

Like other contracts, a sales agreement may be oral, written, or implied from actions, such as a buyer's taking an item from a self-service display of merchandise. Note, for example, how merchants often sell candy and other items through vending machines. The placing of goods in such machines constitutes a standing offer to sell to anyone inserting the required amount of money.

The Uniform Commercial Code has in certain respects liberalized and simplified the law of contracts as it applies to sales. In some cases, the UCC treats all buyers and sellers alike. In others, it treats merchants separately from the occasional or casual seller. A *merchant* is a person who deals in a particular kind of goods, or otherwise holds himself out as having special knowledge or skill in a certain type of sales transaction. A *casual seller* is anyone who does not meet this definition. Thus, you would be considered a casual seller if you sold your private automobile, but a used-car salesman selling the same car would be considered a merchant. In general, the UCC holds merchants to a higher standard of conduct than the casual seller. Merchants are also usually subjected to higher taxation and closer regulation by the government.

Under the UCC, a sales contract may be made in any manner, and it suffices if the parties by their actions recognize the existence of a contract. This is true even though a court might not be able to determine precisely when the contract was made, and generally even though one or more terms are left open.

The Code also adds another proper way of accepting an offer to buy—the seller may simply ship the goods.

 McCloud Modern Bakery sent an order to Golden Grain Mills in which it offered to buy a carload of flour. Golden Grain could have sent an acceptance. Instead, it shipped the flour. A contract resulted.

Under the Code, an offeror may expressly state that his offer to buy or sell goods must be accepted exactly as made or not at all.

Otherwise the offeree may accept and still add an important new term to the contract. You will recall that in most contracts this would void the original offer and be a counteroffer. (Page 116) By the law of sales, however, the new term is included in the contract if the offeror accepts it. This he may do by words or conduct.

If both parties are merchants, the new term automatically becomes part of the contract if the offeror fails to object promptly. However, the new term must not materially or importantly change the offer.

Comparison of Sales with Similar Transactions

Transaction	Type of Property Involved	Is it a Contract?	Is Ownership Transferred?	Is Possession Transferred?
Sale	Goods (Tangible Personal Property)	Yes	Yes	Usually yes
Contract to Sell	Goods	Yes	No	Usually no
Barter	Goods	Yes	Yes	Usually yes
Conveyance	Real Property	Usually *	Yes	Usually yes
Lease	Real Property	Usually *	No	Yes
Negotiation	Negotiable Instruments	Usually *	Yes	Yes
Assignment	Contract Rights	Usually *	Yes	No, but written contract may be delivered to assignee
Bailment	Personal Property	Usually **	No	Yes
Gift	Personal or Real Property, or other valuables	No	Yes	Usually yes

* May be a gift.
** May be gratuitous.

WHAT IS THE CONSIDERATION IN A SALE?

Problem: Grant ordered 300 tons of copper for his foundry from Panamint Mines, Inc. Deliveries were to be in 12 equal monthly installments, and the price was to be the market price as of the first of each month. Was this an enforceable sale?

Both a sale and a contract to sell require a consideration known as the *price*. In return for the price, or a promise to pay the price, the seller transfers his ownership or title to the goods.

The price is usually fixed in the contract, or the parties may merely indicate how the price is to be set at a later date. There was an enforceable sale in the problem because the price could be determined each month from published market figures. Ordinarily, even if nothing is said about the price, a contract results if all other essentials are present. In such case the buyer is required to pay the price that is reasonable for the goods. What is reasonable depends upon the circumstances.

The price may be made payable in money, goods, or services. If it is made payable wholly or partly in goods, each party is considered a seller of the goods which he is to transfer. When the parties merely exchange or trade goods, the contract is a sale known as a *barter*.

 Reynolds paid $2,000 and gave his old car in trade for a new convertible sedan which he bought from Mellon Motors. The law regards Reynolds as seller of his used car, and Mellon Motors as seller of the new sedan.

WHAT IS THE SUBJECT MATTER OF A SALE?

Problem: Taft bought Scovill's bookshop, paying $40,000 as follows:

Land and building	$20,000
Equipment and inventory of books	15,000
Accounts receivable	5,000
	$40,000

Was this transaction governed by the law of sales?

The subject matter of a sale or a contract to sell must be tangible personal property, or goods, such as a jet transport plane, a box of oranges, a hair dryer, toys, or clothing. In general, *goods* means all things which are movable at the time they are identified as the subject of the sales contract. These include growing crops and the unborn young of animals, but do not include such personal property as money (except rare currency and coins which are more than a medium of exchange), or intangible property such as a patent or copyright, rights to money or other things (such as a life insurance contract or a check). Goods do not include real estate, such as land and buildings. Although in everyday speech we may refer to this as a sale, the transfer of title to real estate by deed is properly known as *conveyance* and the agreement of sale that precedes the conveyance is governed by other laws. (Chapter 40) Transfer of most contract rights is made by assignment, and special rules apply. (Chapter 13) In the problem, the land and building were real property and were conveyed to Taft by Scovill. The equipment and inventory of books were goods, and their transfer was governed by the law of sales. The accounts receivable were contract claims against debtors, and they were assigned to Taft.

WHAT RESTRICTIONS ARE PLACED ON SALES?

Problem: Gehrig was experiencing great pain but could not reach his doctor. He therefore asked his friend, Simmons, the neighborhood pharmacist, to sell him some strong medicine containing codeine which normally required a doctor's prescription. Could Simmons legally make the sale?

The creation or performance of a sale or a contract to sell must not involve any illegal act. Statutes in all states prohibit certain kinds of sales. For example, the sale of fireworks may be banned completely, and handguns may be sold only under prescribed conditions. Some sales made on Sundays or legal holidays may be declared illegal. Certain other sales may be illegal when made by persons not properly licensed.

The performance of a sale must not involve an illegal act.

An illegal sale or contract to sell cannot be enforced by court action. If the contract is performed, courts normally will not help either party to cancel or get other relief. Indeed, any party guilty of a related crime may be prosecuted. On the other hand, if one party is an innocent victim, as in a fraudulent sale, he may recover what he had transferred to the wrongdoer.

Some sales restrictions are the result of controls on products involved. Many drugs may be legally sold only to persons who have a physician's prescription. Frequently only registered pharmacists may make such sales, and they are then required to keep accurate records. In the problem, Simmons could not legally make the sale despite the emergency. Other products may be legally sold only if they are correctly packaged and labeled, or, as is the case with meat, have been inspected and stamped. Laws of this type were discussed more fully in Chapter 4.

MUST DELIVERY AND PAYMENT BE MADE AT THE SAME TIME?

Problem: Buford bought Christmas gifts for his wife and children during the Gold Bond Department Store's "Lay-Away Sale" in October. He was to take delivery around December 22, and agreed to pay before January 31 of the next year. Did he own the gifts in October?

In the ordinary situation, in which the buyer selects and purchases goods in a store, the title to the goods passes to him at the time of the transaction although delivery or payment or both do not take place until later. The buyer's duty is to pay; the seller's duty is to transfer possession. Generally neither is obliged to perform until the other does. Thus, unless it is otherwise agreed or is the custom of the trade, the seller may retain the goods until the buyer makes payment in full. Similarily, if the buyer does not get all the goods, he may refuse to pay the price. Normally payment and transfer of possession take place simultaneously at the seller's place of business. The buyer is entitled to a receipt when he pays.

To encourage business, however, most sellers extend credit to qualified buyers, including other business firms. Some retailers do most of their business selling to customers who use credit cards or charge accounts, or arrange to pay the price in installments. (Unit VI) Thus, the buyer may get both title and possession before payment. In the problem, assuming the goods were set aside for Buford at the time of the sale, he got title in October, possession in December, and paid for the goods in January.

MUST UNORDERED GOODS BE PAID FOR?

Problem: Typo Press, Publishers, began to send D'Amico monthly issues of their magazine for teenagers shortly after her 13th birthday. Then they billed her for $6 for a year's subscription. Is she obliged to pay?

Aggressive sales promoters sometimes send goods to prospective buyers even when nothing has been ordered. Postal regulations make the mailing of such unordered merchandise an unfair method of competition. The mailer may not thereafter send bills or dunning letters, and the recipient may treat the unordered merchandise as a gift. Thus, in the problem, D'Amico could keep the magazines and use or dispose of them as she saw fit, without any obligation to Typo Press.

In some states, statutes also cover unordered goods which are sent deliberately but not through the postal system. In such states, the recipient may keep and use the goods without payment. In most states, however, although the recipient is not obliged to accept or return the goods, if he does use them—and they have not been delivered by mail—he is legally obligated to pay the asked price.

A seller cannot evade these rules by writing a new prospect that certain goods will be sent unless the seller is otherwise instructed. Because the offeree is not obliged to do anything, his silence is not an acceptance.

IN SALES, BE INFORMED AND AWARE . . .

1. During your lifetime you will probably enter into more sales (usually as buyer, but often as seller) than any other type of contract. It will pay you to know the law of sales.
2. In some cases, bailment may be preferable to sale. Learn your rights and duties for this and other sale-like transactions: contract to sell, conveyance, lease, negotiation, assignment, barter, and gift.
3. Your best protection against sales fraud is the integrity of the seller as reflected in his established reputation.
4. Your best protection against shoddy merchandise is knowledge of goods and their value, coupled with careful comparison shopping.
5. When you make a major purchase, review your insurance for appropriate coverage against possible resulting loss, or liability to others.
6. For important sales, be sure to have written contracts covering all significant points signed by both seller and buyer.
7. If you receive unordered goods through the mail, you may keep and use them as your own with no obligation to the mailer.

YOUR LEGAL VOCABULARY

barter
casual seller
contract to sell
conveyance
goods

merchant
price
sale
vendee
vendor

1. A consideration in money, property, or services, given in return for the transfer of title to goods.
2. The buyer or purchaser.
3. A non-professional seller.
4. The exchange or trading of goods.
5. The seller.
6. A transfer of ownership of goods for a consideration called a price.
7. A transfer of title to real property.
8. A contract agreement to transfer ownership of goods at a later date.
9. One who deals in a particular kind of goods or otherwise holds himself out as having special knowledge or skill in a certain type of transaction.
10. Tangible personal property that is movable.

REMEMBER THESE HIGHLIGHTS

1. Sales of goods—both present sales, and contracts to sell—are governed by a combination of basic contract law and special UCC provisions on sales. Transfers of ownership of other types of property, such as intangible personal property and real estate, are governed by different sets of rules.
2. Both benefits and burdens go with ownership or title to goods, but ownership does not always determine who will take losses.
3. Merchants are generally held to a higher standard of conduct than casual sellers by the UCC.
4. It is not essential to specify the price in a sales contract. When not specified, the price becomes what is reasonable in the given circumstances. Normally the prevailing market price is used if available.
5. Neither payment nor delivery is essential for transfer of title or ownership.
6. Illegal contracts and contracts to sell cannot be enforced through court action by either party. Under proper circumstances, an innocent party may get relief, however.

LAW AS PEOPLE LIVE IT

1. Coleman, a gun collector, sells a sawed-off shotgun to Hawkins in a state where it is illegal to own or deal in such weapons. Hawkins now refuses to pay or to return the gun. May Coleman get relief in a court?
2. The Mallory Mill sells a quantity of standard aluminum ingots (bars) to Goldenberg. Their contract is complete in all respects except that it fails to state the price. Is it a valid agreement, enforceable in court?
3. Ford was scheduled to graduate from Roosevelt High in June. In March, he agreed to sell his mechanical drawing set to Lopez when the semester ended. Ford spoke of the transaction as a sale. Was it?

4. Harasaki, who was skilled in mathematics, tutored Barrow's schoolboy son in calculus as a friendly gesture. The son received an A for the course but Harasaki refused any payment. Barrow finally persuaded him to accept a beautiful set of bronze bookends. Was this a sale?
5. Galvin opened a Christmas tree lot to help finance his college education. He claimed he was a casual seller, because the lot was a temporary seasonal operation which had no other employees and only a small inventory of trees which he had cut down himself. Was he a casual seller?
6. Litton was admitted to the "Million Dollar Round Table" because he sold that much life insurance in one year. At the celebration dinner, his friend and closest rival, Baines, jokingly said, "Litton hasn't made a single sale—and I can prove it!" Is he right?
7. McDowell sold a battery-powered portable TV set "in good working order" to Tobin for $50. Then Tobin refused to pay until he'd had an opportunity to test the set by using it for a few hours. McDowell refused to deliver the set until he received his money. Who is right?
8. Laurel maintains that when you buy candy from a vending machine, there cannot be a sale because only one person is involved: the buyer. "No agreement, no sale," he says. Is he correct?
9. Employees of the Malcolm Manufacturing Company set up a canteen on the premises. Using volunteer help, it sold sandwiches and other refreshments, at cost, as a convenience to the workers. Those in charge claimed the canteen should pay no sales tax because transactions made at cost were not sales. Is this true?
10. Novak mailed a book to Arnold together with a letter stating that if Arnold wished to keep the book, he should send Novak $9.95. If, however, he did not wish to keep the book, he should return it within ten days. Arnold liked the book and used it, but did not remit the price to Novak. Could Novak require Arnold to pay for the book?

LAW AS COURTS DECIDE IT

1. Roto-Lith mailed an order to Bartlett for a drum of adhesive emulsion to be used in making cellophane for wet-pack spinach. Bartlett replied with an acknowledgment and an invoice, both of which expressly excluded all warranties and said "If these terms are not acceptable, Buyer must notify the Seller at once." Roto-Lith did not object, but later sued for damages when the emulsion proved unsatisfactory. Is Bartlett liable? (Roto-Lith, Ltd. v. F. P. Bartlett & Co., 297 F. 2d 497)
2. Bowen, a patient in the defendant's hospital, died after receiving a transfusion of blood which did not properly match his own. The hospital was not negligent. Dibblee, administrator of Bowen's estate, claimed the hospital had sold defective goods—the blood—and in

doing so had breached a warranty of fitness for intended use and should pay damages. Was this a sale of goods, hence subject to warranties? (Dibblee v. Dr. W. H. Groves L.D.S. Hospital, 364 P. 2d 1085, Utah)

3. In a single, undivided contract, a supplier agreed to supply and also to install $19,000 worth of equipment in Balon's restaurant. Balon paid $500 down but the agreement said nothing about when the balance was due. When the supplier began to make delivery and install the equipment, he demanded an additional $10,000. Balon refused to pay until the job was completed, and the supplier sued for the full price. Must Balon pay before the equipment is installed? (Balon v. Hotel & Restaurant Supplies, Inc., 433 P. 2d 661, Arizona)

4. Canonsburg Pottery Company in Pennsylvania agreed to deliver two carloads a week of three patterns of dinnerware for a period of a year at specified prices to S. R. Taylor Company in Boston. In defending an action for damages for breach of contract, the pottery company claimed that there was no contract, and that the agreement was indefinite and incomplete. It stated that there was no mutual assent because no time of payment was specified. Was that a good defense? (Newspaper Readers Service v. Canonsburg Pottery Co., 146 F. 2d 963)

5. Rudnick Bros. sold certain goods to Johnson & Co. under a contract which provided that the seller would pay the sales tax amounting to $529.93. The New York City sales tax law provides that the tax is to be paid by the buyer, collected by the seller, and paid to the city. Johnson paid the amount due for the goods but refused to pay the sales tax. Thereupon Rudnick sued him for it. Must he pay? (Rudnick Bros. Inc. v. Johnson & Sons, Inc., 186 N.Y.S. 2d 169)

CHAPTER 18 Form of the Sales Contract

1. Your father contracts to buy a second car for the family—a used, two-door sedan priced at $595. Must the contract be in writing to be enforceable?

2. Under an oral sales contract, a local factory receives and uses only 100 gallons of sulfuric acid out of an order for 3,000 gallons which cost well over $500. Must it accept the balance?

3. Newlywed friends of yours contract to have drapes custom-made for several large picture windows in their new home. The price is $750. Must this contract be in writing to be enforced?

HOW DOES THE STATUTE OF FRAUDS APPLY TO SALES?

Problem: Hogan agreed to buy a standard design cabin cruiser from Nautical Needs, Inc., for $6,750. He alone signed the contract which called for delivery in 90 days. Nautical now refuses to go through with the deal unless he'll agree to pay an additional $1,000. Can Hogan hold them to their original agreement?

Sales or contracts to sell, like other contracts, are generally valid and enforceable whether oral, written, or implied from the conduct of the parties. However, under the Statute of Frauds (Chapter 12), certain important types of contracts must be in writing to be enforceable in court. In sales of goods, if the price is $500 or more, there must be some writing which indicates that a contract for sale has been made between the parties. Moreover, it must be signed by the party against whom enforcement is sought, or by his authorized representative. In the problem, Hogan cannot hold Nautical because it had not signed the contract. However, Nautical can hold Hogan to his original offer if it so desires.

WHAT TYPE OF WRITING IS REQUIRED?

Problem: Using his own order blank, Hobart mailed a signed offer to Millard's lumberyard to buy 400 sheets of plywood. Millard phoned his acceptance, the parties orally agreeing at the time on price ($1,600) and time of delivery. Before shipment, Hobart changed his mind and claimed he was not bound because the contract was not in writing. Is he right?

In good business practice, both parties sign if a written contract is used. It shows good faith. Moreover, they cannot foresee which party may need the aid of a court to enforce the agreement.

A full contract need not be written to satisfy the Statute. All that is required is that some signed writing exist which gives the court reason to believe that a contract to sell or a sales agreement has, in fact, been made. A quantity of goods involved must be stated; although the stated quantity need not be accurate, the contract is not enforceable beyond the amount shown in the writing. Details as to time, price, and performance need not be included since these can be determined orally in court. The writing can be done at any time. In the problem, Hobart was wrong because his written, signed offer was a sufficient writing to satisfy the Statute of Frauds.

There is nothing illegal or fraudulent as such about contracts which do not comply with the Statute of Frauds. Failure to satisfy the requirements of the Statute simply means that the contract cannot be enforced in a court of law. Most contracts are voluntarily performed by the parties and there is no need to so enforce them.

WHAT IS MEANT BY "PAYMENT," "RECEIPT," AND "ACCEPTANCE" IN SALES?

Problem: Sanchez telephoned an order to Holmes' Building Supply for a certain quantity of drainage tile priced at $985. The tile was delivered, but when Sanchez checked the shipment later that day, he decided it was not quite what he had wanted. He immediately notified Holmes of his refusal to accept the goods, but Holmes insisted the contract was binding. Sanchez refused to pay and Holmes sued for the price. Who won?

In the law of sales, price may consist of anything, such as money, services, or goods, that is agreed upon by the parties as consideration. *Payment* is the buyer's performance of his obligation by delivery of the price according to the agreement, and the seller's acceptance thereof. Although a check does not discharge the debt until it is cashed, it is considered sufficient as payment for the purpose of the Statute unless the seller insists on cash. If all or part of the price is payable in realty, real property law governs that part of the agreement.

Receipt of goods means that the buyer takes physical possession or control of them. Receipt may be constructive, as when one gets the keys to a car or a warehouse receipt for the goods. *Acceptance of goods* means that the buyer agrees that the goods he has received are satisfactory goods. This is evident when he uses or resells them or otherwise treats them as his own. It may be shown by the buyer's failure to reject the goods within a reasonable time after they have been delivered and he has had a reasonable opportunity to inspect them.

Receipt of the goods alone is insufficient to make an oral contract binding under the Statute of Frauds; both receipt and acceptance are necessary. This fact should be noted carefully, since a person may receive goods without accepting them. This was true of Sanchez. He received the goods but did not accept them because he promptly exercised his right to reject. Normally if goods are properly delivered and conform to the contract of the parties, the buyer is bound. Here, however, the Statute of Frauds enabled Sanchez to avoid his obligation.

WHEN IS A SIGNATURE OR WRITING NOT REQUIRED UNDER THE STATUTE?

Problem: The Four-Square Appliance Company telephoned a rush order to McNeil Labs, Inc., for $1,700 worth of miniature electronic circuits of a standard design. The next morning McNeil sent a letter confirming the sale, signed by the sales manager. McNeil is clearly bound under the Statute of Frauds. Is Four-Square also bound?

One important exception to the requirement of signing is limited to oral contracts made between merchants. In such cases, one of the merchants may send a written confirmation to the other within a reasonable time after the agreement is made. If the receiving merchant does not object in writing within ten days, the writing is sufficient to bind both merchants. In the problem, Four-Square would be bound unless it gave written notice of objection within ten days after receiving the letter from McNeil.

There are four other situations in which all persons may, without a writing or signature, enforce an oral contract for the sale of goods at a price of $500 or more. These are as follows:

(1) THE BUYER HAS PAID FOR THE GOODS IN FULL AND THE SELLER HAS ACCEPTED PAYMENT

If the buyer has paid for part of the goods, the oral contract is enforceable only as to those goods which have been paid for, and then only if a fair division or apportionment can be made. If no division of the goods can be made, the contract is not enforceable.

 At a yard sale of his farm equipment, Smyth sold a used mowing machine to Braun, who paid $1,750 cash. Before Braun returned with a truck to pick up the machine, Smyth resold and delivered the machine to an innocent third party who had paid a higher price. Although he cannot recover the machine from the other buyer, Braun is entitled to a full refund plus damages for breach of oral contract by Smyth.

(2) THE BUYER HAS RECEIVED AND ACCEPTED ALL OF THE GOODS

Again, if he has received and accepted only some of the goods, the oral contract is enforceable only as to those received and accepted.

 Nolan visited Swenson's Paint Shop and orally ordered 100 gallons of Apple Green paint for his apartment house. The paint, priced at $6 a gallon, was to be charged to his account and delivered the following Monday. Nothing was signed. Nolan took one five-gallon can home with him, but his wife was displeased with the color and he disliked the way it went on. Nolan is within his rights in refusing to accept the balance of the order. There was a binding receipt and acceptance only of the five gallons.

An oral contract for specially made goods is enforceable.

MARY JONES
SEAMSTRESS
WEDDING GOWNS
A SPECIALTY

(3) THE GOODS ARE TO BE SPECIALLY MANUFACTURED FOR THE BUYER, AND ARE NOT SUITABLE FOR SALE TO OTHERS IN THE ORDINARY COURSE OF THE SELLER'S BUSINESS

Such a contract may be canceled by the buyer, however, if it is prior to the seller's making either a substantial beginning in manufacturing the goods, or commitments to others to obtain them.

(4) THE PARTY AGAINST WHOM ENFORCEMENT IS SOUGHT ADMITS DURING THE COURSE OF THE LEGAL PROCEEDINGS THAT HE MADE THE ORAL CONTRACT

 Krisler was sued by the seller, Morris, for breach of an oral contract to sell 300 sides of prime beef. The contract should have been evidenced by some writing and signature to be enforceable under the Statute of Frauds. In his testimony during the trial, Krisler admitted that there had been an oral agreement, but said that it was for only 150 sides. Consequently, Krisler is bound to perform or pay damages for breach of contract for that reduced quantity of goods which he admitted ordering.

HOW IS A BILL OF SALE USED?

Problem: On all sales of costly, large equipment such as stoves and hi-fi sets, Levinson's Department Store gave the buyer a bill of sale instead of a cash register receipt. The bill of sale listed seller, buyer, date, price, and serial number, and was signed by a representative of the store. How did this policy help protect Levinson's customers?

A *bill of sale* is written evidence of the transfer of ownership or title to goods. Such a document is sometimes required by statute, as in the case of automobile sales. If signed by the seller, it can satisfy the requirements of the Statute of Frauds for a writing.

A bill of sale may help protect owners and creditors from theft and fraud. It may also make resale of the property easier by providing the owner with some evidence of his ownership. When goods are lost or stolen, the document can be used to prove title if they are recovered by the police. If the owner borrows money using the goods as security, he can better assure the creditor of his ownership. Of course, other persons may have acquired claims against the goods since the bill of sale was issued, and dishonest persons may forge

Know All Men by These Presents:

That Texas Television, Inc., of Bay City, Texas————

Five Hundred Sixty-Five ($565.00)————*in consideration of*
Dollars, to William Ransom, President, Texas Television, Inc., *paid by*
Billy A. Turnage, Bay City, Texas————
the receipt of which is hereby acknowledged, does—hereby **grant, bargain, sell,**
transfer, and deliver *unto the said grantee———the following described goods and*
chattels, to-wit: One Monarch Color Television Set; Model R-5-Mo5141

To have and to hold *the same unto the said grantee——, ———*his———*heirs,*
executors, administrators, and assigns forever.
And *the said* Texas Television, Inc.————

does—hereby covenant with the said Billy A. Turnage, his————

heirs, executors, administrators, and assigns, that Texas Television, Inc. is—
the true and lawful owner——of the said described property hereby sold, and has—
full power to sell and convey the same; that the title, so conveyed, **is clear, free, and**
unincumbered; *and further, that* Texas Television, Inc. will **warrant and**
will defend *the same against the claim or claims of all persons whomsoever.*

TEXAS TELEVISION, INC.————

by William Ransom, President.

In Witness Whereof, *the said*
Texas Television, Inc., by
William Ransom, President,
has———*hereunto set* his hand———*this*
———sixteenth———
day of ———January———, 1972 .
Signed, and delivered in presence of

H. A. Richardson

T. E. Smith

Bay City, Texas

Bay City, Texas

Bill of Sale

such documents to help dispose of stolen goods. In the problem, however, it is clear that Levinson's policy benefits its customers in many ways.

WHAT IS REQUIRED IN A BULK TRANSFER?

Problem: Because of illness, Berrie, the owner, was arranging the sale of his restaurant, complete with supplies and fixtures, to his former manager, Moody. What special requirements must be met in such a sale of the entire business?

Bulk transfer refers to the transfer of a major part of the goods of a business (materials, supplies, merchandise, or other inventory) in one unit rather than individually or in small lots. If a substantial part of the equipment is sold with the inventory, it too is considered part of the bulk transfer.

The Bulk Transfer Law is meant to protect creditors against the occasional dishonest merchant who might otherwise sell out secretly, keep the proceeds, and disappear. If this happens, the creditors still have a claim against him for breach of contract and possible fraud. But it is usually easier to locate the goods and proceed against the person presently in possession.

In addition to the usual rules governing sales, the law calls for notice to the seller's creditors before the bulk transfer is made. The seller, or transferor, is required to list his creditors; the buyer or transferee, is required to notify those creditors of the forthcoming transfer of ownership, and to pay their claims or make other arrangements with them. Failure of the buyer to comply means that the creditors can make their claims against the inventory and equipment after the new owner is in possession. The bulk buyer must also give fair value for the assets of the business or the sale may be set aside as a fraud against the creditors. In the problem, Berrie as seller and Moody as buyer must comply with the bulk transfer law.

An innocent third party purchasing goods in good faith from a bulk transferee gets good title. But if the third party pays no value or knows the merchant failed to comply with the notice law, the creditors can recover the purchased goods.

IN MAKING A SALES CONTRACT . . .

1. Don't overlook the writing and signing requirements of the Statute of Frauds when the price of the goods is $500 or more.
2. Insist that at least the quantity, and preferably all important terms of the agreement, be included in the memorandum of sale.
3. Be sure that the other party signs the contract or memorandum and gives you a copy. He may properly require that you sign, too.
4. Remember that the parol evidence rule applies to sales and contracts to sell as well as to other contracts.
5. Don't forget that you are bound by an oral contract to the extent that you have accepted delivery of the goods or have paid for them.
6. Get a receipt or bill of sale marked "Paid" when you pay the price.
7. Put your contracts in writing even when not required by the Statute of Frauds if, for you, relatively much time, money, or detail is involved.

YOUR LEGAL VOCABULARY

acceptance of goods   **payment**
bill of sale   **receipt of goods**
bulk transfer

1. The buyer's performance of his obligation by delivery of the price, and the seller's acceptance.
2. The sale of a major part of the goods of a business in one block.
3. Written evidence of the transfer of ownership.
4. Taking possession or control of goods by the buyer.
5. The buyer's agreement that the goods he receives are satisfactory.

REMEMBER THESE HIGHLIGHTS

1. Unless otherwise provided by statute, a sale or contract to sell may be oral, written, or implied from the conduct of the parties.
2. To be enforceable, a sale or contract to sell goods for a price of $500 or more must be evidenced by a writing which at least specifies a quantity of goods involved, and is signed by the party against whom enforcement is sought or his representative. Exceptions to the requirement of a writing exist when:
   (a) The buyer has paid for the goods, in full or in part;
   (b) The buyer has received and accepted the goods, in full or in part;
   (c) The goods are custom-made for the buyer and are not readily resalable;
   (d) The party seeking to avoid the contract admits during the legal proceedings that he made the oral agreement.
3. Price may consist of anything, such as money, services, or goods agreed upon by the parties as consideration.
4. Payment is the buyer's performance of his obligation by delivery of the price and the seller's acceptance thereof.
5. There is a receipt of goods when the buyer takes physical possession or control of them. There is acceptance of the goods when the buyer agrees that the goods he has received are satisfactory.
6. Notice of a bulk transfer of the inventory and equipment of a business must be given creditors of the seller before the sale takes place.
7. A bill of sale provides evidence of the transfer of ownership of goods.

LAW AS PEOPLE LIVE IT

1. Seltzer ordered 1,500 pine Christmas trees from Van Veer for $2,400. There was no writing. After the first load of 300 trees had been delivered, Seltzer decided his lot was too poorly located to sell all the

trees ordered. He therefore canceled the balance of the order. Is he liable to Van Veer for the price of the balance?

2. Cutter orally agreed to sell a set of barbell exercising weights to Merckel for $35. Later Merckel refused to complete the deal, claiming there must be a written agreement. Was Merckel right?

3. Fairbanks orally agreed to buy two electric guitars and a matched set of drums from Kern. The price was $750, payable with an imported Swiss watch and $500 cash. Fairbanks paid in full, but Kern decided to reactivate his rock group and refused to deliver the instruments. He claims their oral agreement is not enforceable. Is he right?

4. After completing a telephone conversation with Wolley, a fellow merchant, Gable wrote him as follows: "Thanks for the order. This memo confirms our oral agreement for your purchase of 40 of our Model 7X valves at a total price of $8,000. Delivery in 30 days." Wolley never replied, but two weeks later he canceled the order. May he do so without liability to Gable?

5. Form-Fashioned Shirts, Inc. agreed to sell to the Sterling Department Store chain 1,000 dozen men's T-shirts, each with a Sterling label, and packaged in Sterling boxes. Could such an order be canceled?

6. Under an oral contract with LaRue's Boutique, Wayne's Cabinet Shop built 12 display cases, each designed and painted to resemble a different flower. When LaRue refused to accept and pay for the cases, Wayne sued. Should he be granted judgment?

7. Tomich, a patron of the arts, contracted to buy a Picasso print from the Zeiss Gallery for $900. He signed an agreement to buy and was to make payment and take delivery after the print had been framed. Before then, however, Zeiss decided not to sell. Is he bound to do so?

8. Morgan and Clarke made an oral contract for the sale of an antique brass bed, at a price of $550. Later, they both signed a memorandum which gave the essential details of their agreement. Nevertheless, Morgan breached the contract and defended his action by stating that the memo was signed after the contract had been made, and was not effective. Is this true?

9. Tompkins bought the entire business of Macon's Variety Store. Macon owed $17,000 to his trade creditors on accounts payable. The creditors were not notified of the bulk transfer. What can they do when they discover what happened?

10. Gorky was approached by a stranger who offered to sell him an expensive Swiss watch for a bargain price because he said he was unemployed and "needed money more than time." The stranger showed Gorky a bill of sale indicating that he had bought the watch from Taylor's Jewelers a year before. He also showed his driver's license to prove his identity. Should Gorky rely on this evidence?

LAW AS COURTS DECIDE IT

1. Williamson orally agreed to sell two milk vats to Martz for $1,600. The buyer paid $100, but later repudiated the entire contract. The seller then resold the vats at a loss of $800 and sued for damages, claiming the partial payment had made the oral contract enforceable. Was he correct? (Williamson v. Martz, 11 Pa. D & C 2d 33)

2. Purvis was general contractor for construction of the Science Pavilion at the Seattle World's Fair, at a contract price of more than $3 million. He made a written subcontract with Associated Sand & Gravel to do the pre-cast concrete work at a cost of over $1 million. All details were agreed upon except the cost of certain duct materials. Associated later bought the necessary ducts for about $9,400 and asked Purvis to pay for them. Purvis refused, claiming their contract was defective, even though it was written, because it did not specify the price of the ducts or who would pay for them. Was Purvis right? (James P. Purvis v. U.S.A. for Associated Sand & Gravel, Inc., 344 F. 2d 867)

3. Rubin, by telephone, ordered 60,000 red, green, and blue hula hoops from Consolidated Pipe Co. The same day Rubin wrote a letter of confirmation stating, "As per our telephone conversation of today, kindly enter our order for the following: 60,000 Te-Vee Hoops made of rigid polyethylene tubing, 39¢ each." When Consolidated did not reply or deliver the hula hoops, Rubin sued for damages. Consolidated contended that it was not bound under the UCC. Do you agree? (Rubin v. Consolidated Pipe Co., 396 Pa. 506)

4. The plaintiff, Malaquias, was injured by Novo and as a result was awarded damages of $3,887.50 against him. Novo owned a small store and service station, which he sold to Ferreira soon after the legal action was filed against him. (Consideration received was settlement of an alleged debt of $6,000.) Notice of this sale was not given to Novo's creditors as required by the Bulk Transfer Law. Subsequently Malaquias was unable to collect the amount of the judgment from Novo, because Novo had disposed of his principal asset, his business. Malaquias therefore sued to have the sale of Novo's business set aside or canceled. If this were done, the business would become available to pay the judgment. Should the court set aside the bulk sale? (Malaquias v. Novo, 138 P. 2d 729, California)

5. The New York Bondstone Corporation orally contracted with the Young Lumber Company to furnish certain window frames at a cost of $544.87 for an alteration job. The window frames were of specified sizes and dimensions, and had to be made up specially for the corporation's use. When the corporation refused to accept and pay for the frames, the lumber company sued. Should it win? (Young Lumber Co. v. New York Bondstone Corporation, 179 N.Y.S. 2d 45)

CHAPTER 19 Ownership and Risk of Loss

1. A color television set is delivered to your home on a seven-day-approval. Everyone in the family approves the set, but your mother decides it is too expensive. May she return it to the seller?

2. You order a fishing rod and reel from a mail-order house, paying the price in advance. If the shipment is lost en route, who takes the loss?

3. A classmate sells you a dictionary which he has, unknown to you, stolen. Are you now the legal owner because you were innocent and paid a fair price?

WHO MAY TRANSFER OWNERSHIP TO GOODS?

Problem: A part-time employee of the Monarch Manufacturing Company stole a set of valuable measuring gauges and sold them to Squibb, an innocent buyer. When Squibb read about the theft in the local newspaper, he returned the gauges to Monarch but demanded the price he had paid. Must Monarch pay?

The owner is generally the only one who has a legal right to transfer the title to his goods. It follows, therefore, that a buyer ordinarily does not get a better title than the seller has to give. One who buys stolen goods gets possession but not title because a thief cannot transfer valid ownership. As discussed in Chapter 16, even the finder of a lost article must attempt to find the true owner before he can acquire title.

In the problem, the thief did not own the goods or have authority to sell them. He therefore gave no title or other rights to Squibb. Moreover, Monarch is not obligated to pay Squibb for the return of its own property.

The general rule that a buyer does not acquire a better title than that possessed by the seller has some exceptions. Four of these exceptions are:

(1) A PERSON AUTHORIZED TO DO SO MAY TRANSFER A BETTER TITLE THAN HE HAS

One may validly sell what he does not own if he has been authorized by the owner to do so. Salesclerks in retail stores are so authorized (Chapter 32), as are auctioneers (Page 272), or sheriffs when they sell goods under court order. (Page 102)

(2) A FRAUDULENT BUYER MAY TRANSFER A BETTER TITLE THAN HE HAS

If an owner is induced by fraud to sell his goods, the buyer obtains a voidable title. (Page 123) Upon discovering the fraud, the victimized seller may cancel the contract and recover his goods unless an innocent third party has already given value and acquired rights in them. Such a third party is known as a *good faith purchaser*. Thus, a fraudulent buyer with voidable title may transfer valid title to a good faith purchaser.

(3) A HOLDER OF A NEGOTIABLE DOCUMENT OF TITLE MAY TRANSFER A BETTER TITLE THAN HE HAS

Certain documents of title are closely identified by the law with the goods they represent. Examples are negotiable warehouse receipts and negotiable bills of lading. (Unit IV) The holder of such documents may transfer ownership to the goods. (Page 216) Even though the holder has obtained the document improperly, he may negotiate the document to an innocent third party and thus give good title to the goods it represents.

(4) A SELLER WHO KEEPS POSSESSION OF THE GOODS HE HAS SOLD MAY TRANSFER A BETTER TITLE THAN HE HAS

A buyer sometimes allows a seller to retain possession of the purchased goods temporarily. If the seller then sells and delivers such goods to an innocent second buyer who has no notice of the first sale, the second buyer gets a valid title.

 When their new home was almost finished, the Lenbacks bought a specific set of new living room furniture from Frederic's Fine Furniture Shop. Assuming that he could get replacement goods in time, Frederic resold the Lenbacks' furniture to Kayser, a good faith purchaser who took immediate delivery. Kayser obtained a valid title. If Frederic is unable to replace the set, Lenbacks may sue him for conversion.

WHAT IS REQUIRED FOR TRANSFER OF OWNERSHIP?

Problem: Kim, who was preparing for the Junior Prom, could not decide which of three formal gowns to buy from Roxanne's Dress Shop. At her request, the manager set all three aside until the next day when her mother would be able to come in with Kim to decide. That night a fire of undetermined origin destroyed the store and its contents. Must Kim pay for the dresses which were set aside?

Before ownership in them can pass, goods must be both existing and identified. Goods are *existing goods* when they are physically in existence and their ownership is in the seller. They exist even though something remains to be done to put them in a deliverable condition, as, for example, trimming excess fat from sides of beef. Goods are *identified goods* when they have been selected and designated for the particular contract. This may involve separating them from a larger group or mass, and marking, crating, or otherwise relating them to this contract. The selection or identification is often made mutually by the seller and the buyer, but may be made by either, or by some third party mutually agreed upon. In the problem, there was no intent to buy all three gowns, and no selection had been made of the one to be bought. Since the goods were not identified, ownership and risk of loss remained in the seller.

Unless goods are both existing and identified, they are *future goods*. Any contract for the sale of future goods is a contract to sell, and neither ownership nor risk of loss passes at the time of the agreement.

An important exception to the process of identification is made for *fungible goods*. These are goods of a homogeneous or essentially identical nature in which, by nature or trade usage, each unit is regarded as equal to every other unit in the mass. Wheat or coal of a given variety and grade, or thousands of cases of identical canned fruit in a warehouse would be examples. In many states, ownership and risk of loss in fungible goods pass at the time of the agreement and without identification or separation. The buyer becomes the owner of an undivided portion or share of the mass. Moreover, a bailee, such as a warehouseman, may mix different lots of a given fungible without violating his normal duty to keep the goods he receives separate.

WHEN DOES OWNERSHIP TRANSFER?

Problem: Luzak, of Warsaw, ordered $25,000 worth of advanced scientific testing equipment from Douglas, a

Boston exporter. It was agreed that title and risk of loss would pass "when all necessary permits" were obtained. The U.S. government granted an export license; the Polish government granted an import license. However, when the equipment reached Warsaw, the Polish government refused to grant a permit to exchange Polish currency into dollars to pay for the order. May Douglas retain his goods?

In most sales, the seller is paid, the buyer gets the proper goods, and there are no complications. This is true, for example, when you enter a grocery store, pick out a box of cookies, and buy it. But geographical separation of the parties, and delays in production, delivery, or payment may result in a time interval between performance by the seller and payment by the buyer. Destruction or damage to goods during that time, whether in transit or otherwise, may lead to confusion, argument, and litigation.

By agreement, the parties may clearly specify just when title is transferred and risk of loss shifted from seller to buyer. In the problem, Douglas could retain his goods because a necessary permit had not been obtained. Sometimes trade usage answers these questions; the parties are bound by the trade custom if they do not agree otherwise. But when there is no agreement on the matter and no binding trade usage, the Uniform Commercial Code provides some helpful rules.

The two most critical questions are:

1. When does title pass?
2. When does the risk of loss transfer from buyer to seller?

Ownership usually carries with it the risk of loss; but the law of sales sometimes imposes risk of loss irrespective of ownership, as discussed in the next topic.

In all cases of transfer of title below, and of transfer of risk of loss in the following section, it is assumed that the parties have made no contrary agreement. Note that neither time nor method of payment affects the outcome.

(1) WHEN SELLER DELIVERS DOCUMENT OF TITLE

If the seller is to perform by delivering a document of title, such as a warehouse receipt or bill of lading, title passes when and where the document is delivered.

 Hokawa bought 50 bushels of Red Delicious apples from Jansen. The apples were in a public cold storage warehouse. Title passed when Jansen delivered the warehouse receipt to Hokawa, since in such transactions the parties ordinarily understand or agree that the seller will deliver the warehouse receipts rather than the stored goods.

No. __613__   Date:_Dec. 13, 1972_

FIELDING COLD STORAGE COMPANY
3000 River Road
Trenton, New Jersey

This is to certify that this company , as warehouseman, holds subject to the order of_J. Y. Jansen_, the following: 50 Bushels Red Delicious apples

Storage rate:_one dollar_ ($_1.00_) Dollars per day.

FIELDING COLD STORAGE COMPANY

per. R. K.

Warehouse Receipt

(2) WHEN SELLER DELIVERS GOODS

If the seller is to perform by delivery of the goods rather than by delivery of a document of title, title passes at the time and place of contracting.

 Baker's Nursery bought 2,500 fifty-pound sacks of weed-free steer manure from Sunnyvale Farms. Baker was to load and remove the goods in his own truck. Title passed at the time of the contract.

(3) WHEN SELLER SENDS THE GOODS

If the sales contract requires or authorizes the seller to send the goods, but he is not obliged to deliver them at the destination, title passes to the buyer at the time and place of shipment.

 The Red River Unified School District ordered 1,000 reams of duplicating paper from the Shasta Mills Co. It specified shipment via the Great Northern Railway. Title passed upon delivery to the carrier.

(4) WHEN SELLER DELIVERS GOODS AT DESTINATION

If the contract requires delivery at the destination, title passes when the goods are tendered there.

Lipton ordered an inboard, gasoline-powered marine engine for a sloop he was building at his seashore yard. The seller was required to deliver the engine at the yard. Title therefore passed when such delivery was made.

Tender of delivery requires that the seller put the proper goods at the buyer's disposal, and also notify the buyer so he can take delivery. The manner, time, and place for tender are determined by the agreement and the UCC. This is discussed in Chapter 21.

WHEN DOES RISK OF LOSS TRANSFER?

Problem: Slovak had stored 200,000 pounds of No. 1 Idaho Russet potatoes in Zabel's cold storage warehouse. On Dec. 17, Slovak sold 25,000 pounds to Ruffing. On Dec. 20, Slovak notified Zabel, who issued a negotiable warehouse receipt to Ruffing for 25,000 pounds. On Feb. 15, Ruffing paid the storage charges and ordered shipment of the potatoes to Baltimore. On Feb. 16, Zabel shipped the goods. When did the risk of loss transfer to the buyer, Ruffing?

Risk of loss transfers from seller to buyer at various times, depending on whether the seller is to deliver the goods to a carrier, or whether the goods are held by a bailee (such as a warehouse) and are not to be moved.

(1) WHEN SELLER SHIPS GOODS BY CARRIER

When the contract requires or authorizes the seller to ship the goods to the buyer by carrier, two possibilities exist:

(a) If the contract does not require that the seller deliver the goods at a particular destination, the risk of loss passes to the buyer when the goods are delivered to the carrier.

O'Neal ordered 50 ten-speed men's bicycles for his cycle shop from the Ranger Company. The bicycles were to be shipped to the buyer by Southern Pacific Railway. Risk of loss transferred to O'Neal when Ranger delivered the cartons of bikes to the railroad. Later, when the bicycles were damaged in a derailment, O'Neal took the loss (unless he was able to prove the carrier was at fault).

(b) If the contract does require the seller to deliver the goods at a particular destination, risk of loss passes to the buyer at the destination upon tender of delivery even though the goods are still in the possession of the carrier.

 Creative Coatings Corporation sold an order of roofing paper to Rosa's Building Supply Co., to be delivered to Rosa's warehouse in Memphis, Tennessee. When the carrier's truck arrived with the goods, Rosa asked the driver to return in three days because there was no place available to park the trailer, and no clear storage space in the building. If the roofing paper was lost or damaged during those days, Rosa would take the loss. Risk of loss had passed to him upon the initial tender of delivery by the carrier.

(2) WHEN GOODS ARE HELD BY A BAILEE

When the goods are held by a bailee for the seller and are to be delivered to the buyer without being moved, three possibilities exist. The risk of loss passes to the buyer:

(a) On his receipt of a negotiable document of title covering the goods;

(b) When the bailee acknowledges the buyer's right to possession of the goods;

(c) After his receipt of a non-negotiable document of title or other written direction to a bailee to deliver the goods, subject to certain limitations.

In the problem on page 267, the risk of loss passed to Ruffing on Dec. 20, when Zabel issued the negotiable warehouse receipt.

The most frequently used negotiable documents of title are the order bill of lading issued by common carriers, and the negotiable warehouse receipt issued by warehousemen. By the terms of a negotiable document, the goods are to be delivered to the bearer of the document or to the order of a named party. Such persons, also known as holders, can transfer ownership of the goods by transferring the documents. If a holder is named in the negotiable document, he must indorse as well as deliver the document in order to transfer it to a third party.

It is the common practice of businessmen to use the shipment term *F.O.B.*, which means "free on board." Where the seller is in Denver and the buyer in Buffalo, "F.O.B. Denver" means the seller agrees to deliver the goods no further than the freight station in Denver. Title and risk of loss transfer to the buyer at that point. If the terms are "F.O.B. Buffalo," the seller must deliver the goods at Buffalo and the risk of loss remains with him until such delivery takes place. In the absence of contrary arrangements, the buyer pays the transportation charges in the first example, and the seller in the second.

(3) WHEN NOT COVERED ABOVE, ON RECEIPT OF GOODS

In any case not covered above, the risk of loss passes to the buyer on his receipt of the goods if the seller is a merchant. If the seller is not a merchant, it passes on mere tender of delivery.

Vanessa ordered three sets of sheets and pillow cases during a "white sale" at the Rex Department Store. She used her credit card and asked that the goods be delivered to her home. Because Rex is a merchant, the risk of loss passes to Vanessa when she receives the goods.

WHEN DO INSURABLE PROPERTY INTERESTS TRANSFER?

Problem: Polar-Pack, Inc. is a food manufacturer. In a contract with Morley, Polar-Pack agreed to produce and to place the Morley brand label on a quantity of fast-frozen peas. The peas were processed, packaged, and set aside in cartons with the Morley label in the Polar-Pack cold storage warehouse. Did Morley have the right to insure the goods against possible loss?

The buyer obtains a special property interest in goods at the time of their identification to the contract; this special interest gives him the right to buy casualty insurance on the goods. As you recall, the physical act of identifying goods usually takes the form of setting aside, marking, tagging, labeling, boxing, branding, or in some other way indicating that certain goods are to be delivered or sent to the buyer in fulfillment of the contract. Thus, in the problem, Morley had an insurable interest. If the goods already exist and have been identified, the property interest arises when the contract is made.

The buyer also has the right to: (a) inspect the identified goods at a reasonable hour; (b) compel delivery if the seller wrongfully withholds delivery; and (c) collect damages from third persons who take or injure the goods.

WHEN DO OWNERSHIP AND RISK OF LOSS TRANSFER IN PARTICULAR TRANSACTIONS?

Problem: Karasian was auctioning an antique Persian rug. There was spirited bidding, but when no one would offer more than $1,800, Karasian withdrew the item, saying it would be a bargain at twice that price. May he legally do this?

Certain transactions, because of their frequent use or individualized rules, merit specific consideration.

(1) CASH AND CARRY SALES

When the buyer in a sales contract is a consumer who pays cash and takes immediate delivery, title passes to him at the time of the transaction. Risk of loss passes upon his receipt of the goods from a merchant seller, and on tender of goods by a non-merchant seller.

The seller may insist on payment in legal tender. Checks are commonly used but are not legal tender; thus, acceptance of a check by the seller is not considered payment until the check is paid at the bank.

(2) SALES ON CREDIT

The fact that a sale is made on credit does not affect the passing of title or risk of loss. A *credit sale* is simply an agreement calling for payment for the goods at a later date. Ownership and risk of loss may pass even though the time of payment is delayed.

(3) C.O.D. SALES

Goods are often shipped "collect on delivery," or *C.O.D.* The carrier is instructed to collect the price and transportation charges upon delivery, and to return this amount to the seller. If the buyer does not pay, the goods are not released to him. Thus, the seller retains control over possession of the goods until the price is paid, but ownership and risk of loss transfer upon delivery to the carrier just as though there was no C.O.D. provision. In a C.O.D. arrangement, the buyer loses a right he might otherwise have to inspect the goods before payment.

(4) SALE OR RETURN

When goods are delivered to the buyer in a *sale or return,* the ownership and risk of loss pass to the buyer upon delivery, but he has a right to return the goods and related title to the seller. Unless otherwise agreed, if delivered goods may be returned by the buyer even though they conform to the contract, a transaction is a sale or return when the goods are delivered primarily for resale. Such a transaction is a true sale, but if the buyer returns or offers to return the goods within the fixed or a reasonable amount of time, ownership passes back to the seller. The goods must be in substantially their original condition. Normally goods held on sale or return are subject to the claims of the buyer's creditors, who can seize the goods under court order if such action proves necessary to collect payment.

 Apollo Toys for Adults, Inc. devised a three-dimensional chess game which retailed at $19.95. Martin's Men's Shop accepted a shipment of 12 sets on sale or return consignment in November. Only one set was sold during the entire holiday season and so Martin returned the 11 remaining sets. Apollo had to accept them.

(5) SALE ON APPROVAL

When goods are delivered to the buyer on approval, on trial, or on satisfaction, the ownership and risk of loss do not pass to him until he decides to buy. The prospective buyer may reject for any reason. This type of transaction, in which goods are delivered primarily for the buyer's use, is known as a *sale on approval.* Keeping the goods beyond the time agreed upon or beyond a reasonable time without giving the seller notice of rejection is an approval and acceptance.

 Under an agreement for sale on approval, Rickey delivered a one-volume science encyclopedia to Murray with the understanding that he had ten days during which to decide whether or not to keep the book. Two weeks later the book was damaged by water from a leaking air-conditioner. The loss was Murray's; risk of loss had passed to him at the end of ten days since he had not rejected the book.

(6) SALE OF AN UNDIVIDED INTEREST

Sometimes there is a sale of an undivided interest in goods. This differs from a sale of fungible goods. The sale of an undivided interest is a present transfer of a fractional share of the ownership in an article or in the total quantity of goods involved.

> Sampson sells a one-third interest in his Piper Cub airplane to Burke and another one-third to Buretti. They will all use the plane according to a mutually acceptable schedule. There is no intent to dismantle the plane into three equal parts. Sampson has thus transferred an undivided one-third interest in the plane to each of his friends, along with a one-third share of the risk of loss. Thus, as the plane depreciates, each will bear one-third of the loss.

(7) AUCTIONS

An *auction* is a sale to the highest bidder. When the auctioneer decides that no one will bid any higher for the goods on sale, he closes the bidding by letting his "hammer fall" or by other appropriate signal. In doing so he accepts the bid on behalf of the owner of the goods, and ownership passes to the buyer.

An auction is a sale to the highest bidder.

Auction sales are "with reserve" unless explicitly announced in advance to be without reserve. This means that if nothing to the contrary is stated in the conditions of the sale, an auctioneer may withdraw the goods any time before he announces completion of the sale. In the problem on page 270, nothing was said about the sale being without reserve, and Karasian may legally withdraw the item and not sell it to the highest bidder.

CAVEAT VENDITOR—LET THE SELLER BEWARE . . .

1. Ownership will not necessarily prevent transfer of title to your goods contrary to your wishes when:
   (a) you have authorized someone to sell the goods for you (he may violate your instructions);
   (b) you have been defrauded in a sales transaction and have given a voidable title to the wrongdoer (he can transfer good title to a good faith buyer);
   (c) someone has wrongfully obtained possession of a negotiable warehouse receipt or a negotiable bill of lading for your goods (he can give good title by negotiating the paper);
   (d) you have allowed the person who sold to you to keep possession of your goods (he can sell them again).

   Be alert to such possibilities.

2. It is generally wise to identify goods to the sales contract and to complete performance promptly. Delay may lead to complications.

3. If in doubt, specify in a written contract precisely when title to goods sold is to transfer and when the risk of loss is to shift to the buyer.

4. Insure against losses for damage to goods when the risk of loss has not yet transferred to the buyer.

5. When the buyer's credit is questionable, sell for cash or on a C.O.D. basis.

6. Assure yourself of the integrity and financial responsibility of buyers before selling them goods on credit, and especially when selling on terms of sale or return, or on approval.

7. In preference to a bulk sale at a loss, sometimes an auction sale may generate a higher return for goods which must be sold.

YOUR LEGAL VOCABULARY

auction
C.O.D.
credit sale
existing goods
F.O.B.
fungible goods

future goods
good faith purchaser
identified goods
sale on approval
sale or return

1. Goods that are physically in existence with ownership in the seller.
2. A sale in which the buyer has a right to return ownership to the seller within a reasonable or fixed amount of time.
3. Goods that have been selected and designated for a particular contract.
4. A sale in which payment for the goods takes place, by agreement, at a future time.
5. A sale in which goods are delivered to the buyer on trial.

6. Goods of which each unit by nature or trade usage is treated as equal to every other unit in the mass.
7. An innocent buyer who has given value and acquired rights in goods.
8. A sale to the highest bidder.
9. Goods not identified or not in existence.
10. Collect on delivery.

REMEMBER THESE HIGHLIGHTS

1. Generally the owner is the only one who can legally transfer title to his goods. Exceptions are made for a person who: (a) is authorized by the owner to sell his goods; (b) has obtained title to the goods by fraud; (c) is the holder of a negotiable document of title; (d) is a seller who has retained possession of sold goods.
2. Before ownership in them can pass, goods must be both existing and identified.
3. Ownership and risk of loss pass in accordance with the agreement of the parties, or as determined by trade usage. In other cases, title and risk of loss pass in accordance with UCC rules.
4. A special, insurable property interest is transferred to the buyer at the time of identification of the goods to the contract.
5. In cash and carry sales, title passes when the goods are exchanged for legal tender. If a check is used, the payment is conditional until the check is paid.
6. C.O.D. terms by a seller do not affect the time of transfer of ownership or of risk of loss, but do reserve control of the goods to the seller until payment is received.
7. At an auction, title passes when the auctioneer signifies his acceptance of the bidder's offer.

LAW AS PEOPLE LIVE IT

1. Ashton, of Pensacola, Florida, ordered 50 outdoor barbecue grills from the Chef Supreme Company of Los Angeles, California, terms F.O.B. Los Angeles. The grills were properly packed and shipped via common carrier truck, but were damaged in transit. Chef Supreme demands the sales price from Ashton; he refuses to pay until they replace the damaged items. Is Ashton liable for the full price?
2. Aiken sold a quantity of oak firewood to Grossman. Nothing was said about delivery to a carrier or transfer to a bailee. The goods were set aside and were ready for delivery when they were destroyed by a fire of unknown origin. Who takes the loss?
3. The Daily Journal bought certain rolls of newsprint paper from the Finlandia Forest Corporation. Because the newspaper company lacked

storage space, it was agreed that the goods would remain where they were then stored—in a public warehouse. Finlandia was to deliver a negotiable warehouse receipt. Before it did so, a boiler explosion caused extensive damage to the warehouse and its contents. The warehouse company was found not negligent. Who sustains the loss of the paper?

4. On August 1, Garrison, in New York, ordered 5,000 pounds of hops from Gorini, in Yakima, Washington. The hops were to be dried, baled, and shipped by rail to Milwaukee, Wisconsin, on or before September 30. When does title transfer to Garrison?

5. When Metcalf was about to move, he held a "garage sale" of goods he no longer needed. He sold a large, cross-cut saw to Lerski, having forgotten that he had borrowed the tool from Swift a year before. Did Lerski become the owner?

6. Dickory bought an imported sports coupe from Sproule, a friend who was not a merchant. When Sproule tendered delivery, Dickory asked him to store the car in his garage until he, Dickory, returned from a business trip. Before Dickory returned, Sproule's garage burned down, completely destroying the car. Dickory now refuses to pay for the car, saying he never received it. Must he pay?

7. Karp was wanted for questioning in a burglary investigation by the police. To raise money in order to leave town, he sold his expensive Japanese camera to Amke, then to Barker, and then to Canson, all three of whom acted in good faith and were unknown to each other. Each time, Karp collected half the purchase price and promised delivery after he could get the leather carrying case and extra lenses. Finally, he sold the camera to Dryden, another good faith buyer, on the same terms. Dryden paid half the price, but only after getting the camera. Who owns the camera now?

8. Burdette agreed to display a varied assortment of fireworks in his drugstore for two weeks before July 4 under a sale or return contract with Dante's Inferno Novelty Co. Almost half the goods were still on his counters on July 5. Must he pay for them?

9. Roote bought a color television set on approval from Handy-Andy Appliance Shop, with the privilege of return within a week. Thieves broke into Roote's apartment when he was at work three days later and stole the TV. Roote now refuses to pay for the set, claiming he intended to return it anyway. Must he pay?

10. When Goodrich went out of the retail jewelry business, he held an auction which was announced to be without reserve. At the sale, Miller was the only bidder on a valuable diamond necklace. He made one bid, offering a price which was perhaps 5 percent of the true value. Was the auctioneer legally obliged to let him have the item at the bargain price?

LAW AS COURTS DECIDE IT

1. Ninth Street East, Ltd. was a Los Angeles clothing manufacturer and the plaintiff in this action. It sold $2,216 worth of clothing to Harrison, a retailer in Westport, Connecticut, terms F.O.B. Los Angeles. The seller shipped the goods via common carrier truck. When they arrived, Harrison's wife asked the truck driver to deliver the goods inside the store. He refused and left with the goods which were later mislaid or lost. Harrison refuses to pay. Is he obliged to? (Ninth Street East, Ltd. v. Harrison, 259 A. 2d 772, Connecticut)

2. Novak Business Machines was a retail company which sold Olivetti office machines. When Novak's business failed, a trustee took over his assets for the benefit of his creditors. However, Olivetti had already removed machines it claimed it owned because they had been sold to Novak on consignment. The trustee now asks the court to order return of the machines, claiming the relation was a sale or return and title had passed to Novak. Must Olivetti return the machines? (In Re Novak, Md. Cir. Ct., Harford County, June 13, 1969)

3. Consolidated Chemical Industries purchased three heat exchangers at a cost of $12,500 from Falls Industries in Cleveland. The contract specified that after identification, the machines were to be crated securely and delivered at the destination without breakage, to the Consolidated plant in East Baton Rouge. Because they were not crated securely, the exchangers were badly damaged in transit. Consolidated refused to accept them, and Falls sued, claiming risk of loss had passed when the goods were delivered to the carrier. Do you agree? (Falls Industries, Inc. v. Consolidated Chemical Industries, Inc., 258 F. 2d 277)

4. Hickman, Williams & Company entered into an agreement to sell a quantity of pig iron to the Lukens Steel Company of Coatesville, Pennsylvania. Under the terms of the contract, the seller was required to deliver the goods F.O.B. Coatesville. The pig iron was shipped by the seller, but was lost when a boat operated by Murray Transportation Company dumped the cargo into the Hudson River. In an action brought by the seller against the transportation company to recover damages, it was contended that risk of loss was on the buyer, Lukens Steel Company, at the time of the dumping. Do you agree? (Hickman, Williams & Co. v. Murray Transp. Co. 31 F. Supp. 820)

5. Henry Donnell stole three bales of cotton from the Geneva Gin and Storage Co. and sold it to J. P. Rawls. Rawls paid him the market price for the cotton without knowing or having any reason to know that it had been stolen. In an action by the Geneva Gin and Storage Co. it was contended that title to the cotton had not passed to Rawls by the transaction with Donnell. Was this contention sound? (Geneva Gin and Storage Co. v. Rawls, 240 Ala. 320, 199 S. 734)

CHAPTER **20** Warranties and Product Liability

1. *You buy a new suit and are soon displeased with the color, the fit, the style, and the price. Can you claim a breach of warranty?*

2. *A friend buys a pair of canvas "sneakers" with rubber soles. Within a week of normal use, the soles come loose. Has he any legal rights?*

3. *You enter a hardware store and tell the salesman, "I need something to remove old varnish from a table." The salesman states that a product called Strippo is just what you need, but when you apply it, nothing happens. Is the seller liable?*

WHAT ARE EXPRESS AND IMPLIED WARRANTIES?

Problem: Murphy's Year-Round Comfort Service persuaded Bennett to buy an air-conditioner for his house by telling him it would keep all rooms at 72° F or lower even on the hottest summer days. If the unit failed to do so, would Bennett have any rights against Murphy?

To persuade a customer to buy his product, a seller may say, "This refrigerator will need no repairs for five years!" When such an assurance of quality or promise of performance is explicitly stated by the seller of goods, it is an *express warranty*. In many cases, the law requires that sellers provide certain minimum standards of quality and performance even if no explicitly stated promises or representations are made at the time of the sale. Warranty obligations so imposed by law are *implied warranties*.

A warranty may relate generally to the quality or condition of an article; for example, it may be a statement that "This rebuilt engine is mechanically as good as new." Or it may be limited to some particular fact about the goods, such as "This brand of baseball bat is used in the major leagues," or "This particular television set will bring in Channel 18 if used with an outdoor antenna." In the problem, Murphy made such an express warranty and is liable for its breach.

An express warranty may be oral or written. It may even be implied from conduct, as when a buyer asks for an adhesive that will mend broken porcelain and the seller selects and hands him a tube of a particular cement. If the contract is written, the warranty must be included in the writing or it will probably be excluded from the agreement by the parol evidence rule. (Page 176) When the warranty is made after the sale, it may be oral even though the sales contract was written.

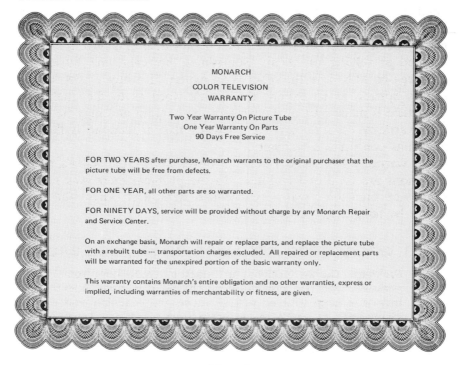

MONARCH

COLOR TELEVISION
WARRANTY

Two Year Warranty On Picture Tube
One Year Warranty On Parts
90 Days Free Service

FOR TWO YEARS after purchase, Monarch warrants to the original purchaser that the picture tube will be free from defects.

FOR ONE YEAR, all other parts are so warranted.

FOR NINETY DAYS, service will be provided without charge by any Monarch Repair and Service Center.

On an exchange basis, Monarch will repair or replace parts, and replace the picture tube with a rebuilt tube --- transportation charges excluded. All repaired or replacement parts will be warranted for the unexpired portion of the basic warranty only.

This warranty contains Monarch's entire obligation and no other warranties, express or implied, including warranties of merchantability or fitness, are given.

Warranty

Most express warranties are given before or at the time of the sale. The price serves as consideration for the goods and the warranty. However, a warranty or any other term may be added to a sales contract later by mutual agreement, and no new consideration is required.

ARE SELLERS' CLAIMS ALWAYS WARRANTIES?

Problem: Morris told Berkowich, his customer, that the sewing machine he was selling him was the private brand of a leading American manufacturer and was made in New Jersey. While inspecting the machine before purchasing, Berkowich observed a stencil on the underside

which read "Made in Hong Kong by A.K.C., Ltd."
A.K.C., Ltd. is an independent foreign firm. Does Berkowich have any rights against the seller?

Sellers often exaggerate the merits of the goods they are trying
to sell. The making of such statements as "best on the market" or
"built to the toughest specifications" is known as sales talk, or *puffing.* Such words are not warranties or statements of fact. They are
merely personal opinions or judgments of value, and buyers are not
justified in relying on them. Sometimes, however, the buyer has
good reason to believe the seller is an expert. If a buyer asks for the
seller's opinion as an expert, the seller's word as to the quality of
the article is made part of the basis of the bargain and may be taken
as a warranty. A statement by a jeweler that a diamond is flawless
may thus constitute a warranty.

No warranty is created when the buyer knows the seller's representations are false or fraudulent. In the problem there was neither
fraud nor breach of warranty because Berkowich knew the facts
before he bought the sewing machine.

WHAT WARRANTIES ARE MADE BY ALL SELLERS?

Problem: Carola bought an electric typewriter from
Mickelle, who had previously purchased it in good faith
from a stranger. Later police traced the machine and
identified it as part of a lot stolen from the Arden Town
Office Supply Company. It was returned to Arden Town.
Does Carola have any rights against Mickelle?

Certain warranties are made by all sellers, whether they are merchants or casual traders. There are five such warranties:

(1) WARRANTY OF TITLE (Implied)

To protect the buyer of goods, the law requires the seller to
warrant that he has the right to sell the goods and that the title transferred is good. These warranties are excluded only by specific
language or by circumstances which should tell the buyer that the
seller may not have good title. An example of such circumstances
would be a sheriff's sale of goods seized under process of law in
which a third party may have an interest. In the problem, Carola has
a cause of action against Mickelle for breach of the warranty of
title. Mickelle would have a similar right against the thief who sold
him the machine, but this would be difficult to enforce.

(2) WARRANTY AGAINST ENCUMBRANCES (Implied)

By the very act of selling, every seller normally warrants that the goods shall be delivered free of all liens or *encumbrances* (creditors' claims) of which the buyer is not aware at the time of contracting. This is not a warranty that the goods are free of encumbrances at the time of the sale, but that they shall be free at the time of delivery. The distinction is important; it enables a seller who has not paid in full for the goods to avoid a breach of the warranty by paying off any outstanding claims before delivering the goods. This clears the lien.

(3) WARRANTY OF FITNESS FOR A PARTICULAR PURPOSE (Implied)

A buyer often makes known to the seller the purpose for which the goods are required. If the buyer then relies on the skill and judgment of the seller in selecting the goods, the seller is required by law to provide goods that are reasonably fit for the indicated purpose. Failure to do so gives the buyer a right of action for breach of warranty.

 Rhodes was in charge of supplies for an oil exploration party preparing to spend a full year in the Canadian Arctic. Creative Plastics sold him a large supply of plastic boots after he had explained his need for boots that would hold up under the extremely low temperatures expected. If the boots cracked and tore in cold temperatures, Rhodes would have a right of action for breach of an implied warranty of fitness for his particular purpose.

This warranty does not arise when the buyer himself selects the goods, or when the buyer orders the goods according to specification, or when because of testing or for other reasons, he does not rely upon the skill and judgment of the seller. However, the warranty may exist even though the buyer has asked for goods by a patent or brand name, provided he relies upon the seller in the actual selection and the seller knows the purpose for which the goods are required. On the other hand, if the buyer insists in getting goods of a particular brand, he obviously is not relying on the seller's knowledge and there is no warranty of fitness for a particular purpose.

(4) WARRANTY OF CONFORMITY TO DESCRIPTION, SAMPLE, OR MODEL (Express)

When a description of the goods, or a sample or model is made part of the contractual agreement, there is a warranty that all the goods supplied shall conform to the description, sample, or model—whichever is used. This is true even if the words "warrant" or "guarantee" are not used in the contract, and even if the seller did not have any specific intention of making a warranty.

 When the Capital City High School ordered new uniforms for its marching band from the Rex-Rite Company, a sample uniform designed and sewn by the school's Home Economics Department was included as part of the agreement. The manufacturer is obliged to provide goods which measure up to its warranty of conformity to sample.

(5) WARRANTY OF CONFORMITY TO SELLER'S STATEMENT OR PROMISE (Express)

A seller will frequently make a statement or promise which constitutes an express warranty. Regardless of the type of seller involved, it is binding as a warranty if it is made part of the basis of the bargain of the parties.

 When Shaw sold a quantity of colored chalk to the Los Rios School District, he said the chalk was non-irritating and non-toxic. Actually the dust caused many students to sneeze and some broke out in skin rashes. The school district could take action against Shaw for breach of express warranties.

WHAT ADDITIONAL WARRANTIES ARE MADE BY MERCHANTS?

Problem: Following specifications provided by the buyer, Newman, Stout built a special office machine which would collect pages of typewritten material in order. Unknown to either party, Burton held a patent on such a machine. Burton sued Stout and collected damages. Can Stout recover from Newman?

In warranties, as in other matters, merchants are held to higher standards of performance than are occasional, amateur sellers. In addition to the five warranties above which are made by every seller, the merchant seller makes the following:

(1) WARRANTY AGAINST INFRINGEMENT (Implied)

Unless the parties agree to the contrary, a merchant seller who regularly deals in goods of a certain kind impliedly warrants that the goods he sells shall be delivered free of the rightful claim of any third party by way of infringement. This means there should be no third party who has a copyright, patent, or similar legal protection on the item, unless, of course, he has given permission to use his idea. However, if the buyer furnishes specifications to the seller which lead to a claim of infringement, the buyer is under an obligation to compensate the seller for any loss suffered. Accordingly, in the problem, Stout can recover from Newman.

(2) WARRANTY OF MERCHANTABILITY (Implied)

When a merchant makes a sale of goods in which he customarily deals, he impliedly warrants that the goods are *merchantable*—that is, as marketable or useable as such goods normally are. The buyer may be another merchant buying to resell, or he may be a consumer buying to use. This warranty of merchantability covers the six situations described below, and may extend to others based on usages of the trade or course of dealing between the parties.

The primary warranty of merchantability is (a) that the goods are fit for the ordinary purposes for which such goods are used. Thus, a radio must bring in broadcasts, soap must clean, and a brick-cutting machine must cut bricks. If the goods are fungible, like grains, (b) they must be of fair average quality. They need not be the best, but they must not be sub-standard. In any event, goods sold (c) must be acceptable in the trade under the contract description. Buyers must not balk at accepting them. Within variations permitted by the sales agreement, (d) they must run of even kind, quality, and quantity. And if required by the agreement, (e) they must be adequately contained, packaged, and labeled. Finally, (f) they must conform to any promises or affirmations of fact made on the label or container.

Any warranty protection that is customary in the trade is included under the implied warranty of merchantability. For example, the seller of a pedigreed dog or other animal is expected to provide papers to prove the animal's lineage.

The warranty of merchantability may continue to protect the buyer beyond the time of sale or time of transfer of risk of loss. Such loss would be the case if the subsequent use or performance of the product indicates that it was not merchantable when delivered.

When a buyer has examined the goods, sample, or model before contracting, or if he refuses to examine, there is no implied warranty of merchantability as to those defects which a reasonable examination would have revealed.

 Larson buys a bolt of cloth marked down in price because of a flaw in the weave which is obvious upon examination. He cannot return the goods claiming a breach of warranty of merchantability.

The warranty of merchantability extends to food sold for human consumption, which must be wholesome and fit for use as food. It also includes foods and drinks that are sold and served to be consumed on the premises, such as in restaurants and drive-ins. Drugs and prepared remedies for human use must be sound and wholesome, too. You may recall from Chapter 4 how both criminal and civil liability may be imposed for violations of the Federal Food, Drug, and Cosmetics Act.

MAY WARRANTIES BE EXCLUDED?

Problem: The Quill and Pen Stationery Shoppe held a sale of shopworn and damaged goods, and boxes of stationery with sheets or envelopes missing. All items were advertised "as is." Langdon bought several items at the reduced prices but after examining them more closely at home, decided he had been gypped. He demanded his money back, claiming a breach of the warranty of merchantability. Is he entitled to a refund?

A seller may sometimes be anxious to sell his goods without being obligated by warranties. He may know the goods are defective and be willing to sell them at reduced prices. Or perhaps he fears that too many claims of possible breach may be made if a warranty is given on new designs. Whatever his reason, a seller, like the stationery shop in the problem, may legally exclude all warranties. He simply makes no express warranties and uses appropriate language to exclude implied warranties.

Note, however, that as a matter of public policy, courts will not allow manufacturers of new products to disclaim liability for injuries caused by defects in their products.

 An auto manufacturer gave a new-car warranty which limited recovery to replacement of defective parts and necessary labor. It stated that the warranty was "in lieu of all other warranties, obligations, and liabilities." Garland bought one of the cars. As she was driving at a normal highway speed shortly after, the steering wheel spun out of her hands and the car crashed. The auto manufacturer was held liable for her injuries and for replacement of the wrecked vehicle.

To exclude or modify the broad warranty of merchantability or any part of it, the seller must mention "merchantability" in his *disclaimer* (notice of exclusion); if the notice is in writing it must be conspicuous. To exclude or modify any implied warranty of fitness, the exclusion must be in writing and conspicuous. A statement such as this would suffice: "There are no warranties of merchantability or fitness which extend beyond the description on the face hereof."

Unless circumstances indicate otherwise, all implied warranties are excluded by expressions such as "with all faults" or "as is," or any language which makes it clear that there are no implied warranties. Thus, Langdon in the problem is not entitled to a refund because he bought the goods "as is."

All implied warranties are excluded by expressions such as "sold as is."

When express warranties are given, they exclude all inconsistent implied warranties except the one for fitness for a particular purpose. No warranty arises as to fitness for use when a casual seller disposes of used or second hand goods as, for instance, when someone in a residential neighborhood holds a garage sale to dispose of assorted used possessions. If the sale is made by a merchant, however, such a warranty may be implied, but only to the degree which is appropriate for the goods involved.

WHAT IS MEANT BY "CAVEAT EMPTOR" AND "CAVEAT VENDITOR"?

Problem: During a vacation trip through New England, Stapleton visited many antique shops and bought several sets of what she thought was early American glassware. When she returned to her home in New York City, an expert told Stapleton the glasses were "excellent modern replicas of the real thing." Can she get her money back by returning the goods?

As already noted, a person who buys goods that he has inspected or had the opportunity to inspect may not complain later of defects that could have been detected by ordinary inspection. The maxim applied in such a case is *caveat emptor*—a Latin phrase meaning "Let the buyer beware," one of the oldest principles of the common law. According to caveat emptor, if one gets the "worst of the bargain" because of his own carelessness or failure to investigate and examine the goods before he buys, he has no one to blame but himself. This assumes, of course, that there has been no fraud on the part of the seller. Thus, Stapleton could not get her money back because no warranties were breached, nor had the sellers fraudulently claimed the glass was authentic early American glassware.

Caveat emptor has been counterbalanced in modern times by the maxim *caveat venditor*—"Let the seller beware." The variety of warranties implied by the law to benefit buyers, the many laws which have been enacted for the protection of consumers (Chapter 4), the expanding rules of product liability discussed in the next section—all have been useful in improving the situation of the buyer.

The UCC declares the general rule that every contract or duty under the Code imposes an obligation of good faith in its performance or enforcement. *Good faith* is defined as honesty in the conduct or transaction. Moreover, for merchants, good faith requires observance of reasonable commercial standards of fair dealing.

WHAT IS PRODUCT LIABILITY?

Problem: Kiernan was driving along a country highway in his new car at a legal speed of 60 m.p.h. The brakes (part of the original equipment) suddenly and unexpectedly locked. He lost control of the car and overturned in the ditch along the side of the road. The car was beyond the express warranty period time limit, and it cannot be shown that the manufacturer—United Motors, Ltd.—was negligent in producing the car, yet the brakes were defective. Is United Motors liable to Kiernan for his injuries?

Marketing of mass-produced goods today commonly involves a succession of sales. Goods are transferred from manufacturers or producers to wholesalers or distributors, then on to retailers, and finally to consumers. The manufacturer and the consumer do not contract with each other. Moreover, the goods are often complex, or have strange chemical components, and the user cannot be expected to test them personally; he must trust his suppliers.

At common law, all warranty liability was dependent upon a contract between the parties. Only the buyer could sue and he could proceed only against his immediate seller, not against the middlemen or distant manufacturer. The buyer and seller were parties to the same contract; they were said to be in *privity of contract*. Courts denied an injured party the right to sue anyone with whom he was not in privity of contract. The UCC broadens the common law rule so that all injured persons who are in the buyer's family or household, including guests, may sue. Moreover, courts in most states have abandoned the requirement of privity of contract and permit the injured to sue sellers, middlemen, and manufacturers.

Today, if a manufacturer or producer makes inaccurate or misleading factual statements in his advertising or labels, he is held liable for resulting injuries to consumers. If the goods are defective or dangerous the maker is similarly liable for resulting harm. In either case, not only the manufacturer or producer, but also middlemen and the immediate supplier may be liable. This responsibility or *product liability* may be based on warranty, fraud, negligence or, increasingly, on a theory of strict tort liability.

The manufacturer and others in the chain of supply may be held liable for a defective product.

A manufacturer is expected to make his product safe for the purpose for which it is intended. This requires care in design and fabrication, including inspection and testing not only of its own product, but also of ingredients and components made by others. It may call for the giving of a warning notice of dangers in use of the product. On the other hand, there is no liability if the product is used for a purpose for which it was not intended, or which could not reasonably be foreseen. Likewise, liability may be barred if the product had been altered by the user (e.g., lengthening a ladder by adding wooden strips to its legs) or if the injured person is himself found guilty of improper conduct which caused the accident (e.g., driving on a defective tire after discovering the defect, or taking an overdose of medication).

To prove negligence in manufacture, which may have taken place months or years before in some distant factory, presents insurmountable difficulties for many plaintiffs. The trend of product liability law in many states, therefore, is to hold the manufacturer and others in the chain of supply strictly liable if someone is injured because of a defective condition in the product. The liability is imposed without regard to whether there is any breach of warranty, or negligence, and without reference to privity. In the problem, if Kiernan brought his action in a state which recognizes strict liability, United Motors would be liable.

"CAVEAT EMPTOR"—BUYER, BEWARE . . .

1. Don't take everything that is said by the seller as a warranty; he may just be puffing.
2. When appropriate, tell the seller what use you intend to make of the goods; if he has superior knowledge and you rely on his advice, he must satisfy the warranty of fitness.
3. Request express warranties in definite written terms when in doubt. This helps avoid later disputes as to their meaning or very existence. If the seller refuses to warrant the goods, go elsewhere, or realize that the risk of defects falls on you.
4. Use special care in buying goods "as is." Inspect to be sure you are willing to take them without the benefit of express or implied warranties as to quality.
5. Remember that your best protection as a buyer is to do business with reputable dealers and to buy reputable products.

YOUR LEGAL VOCABULARY

caveat emptor	implied warranty
caveat venditor	merchantable
disclaimer	privity of contract
encumbrances	product liability
express warranty	puffing
good faith	

1. Let the seller beware.
2. A warranty that is explicitly stated.
3. Honesty in the conduct or transaction.
4. Relationship between persons who are parties to the same contract.
5. Liability of manufacturer or producer, wholesaler, and retailer when a defective product causes injury to a consumer or the consumer's property.
6. Marketable or usable as goods of like nature.
7. Sales talk.
8. A warranty obligation imposed by law.
9. Let the buyer beware.
10. Creditors' claims.

REMEMBER THESE HIGHLIGHTS

1. Warranties may be express or implied. Express warranties are frequently promises or statements of fact. Implied warranties are imposed by law.
2. The following warranties are made by all sellers of goods:
   (a) That the seller has a right to sell the goods. (Implied)
   (b) That the goods shall be delivered free of all liens unknown to the buyer. (Implied)
   (c) That the goods are fit for the purpose of the buyer when the buyer relies on the skill and judgment of the seller, and the seller knows of the buyer's intended use. (Implied)
   (d) That goods sold by description, sample, or model will conform to such description, sample, or model. (Express)
   (e) That the goods will conform to the seller's statements or promises. (Express)
3. The following warranties are made only by merchant sellers:
   (a) That the goods are free of infringement claims by third parties. (Implied)
   (b) That the goods are merchantable—that is, fit for the ordinary purposes for which such goods are used, etc. (Implied)
4. The buyer should examine the goods for defects before he makes a purchase because he has no legal right, in the absence of fraud on the part of the seller, to complain of defects that might have been detected by ordinary inspection.
5. Under product liability, the consumer may be protected even though he does not contract directly with the manufacturer who is held responsible for injuries caused by defective products.
6. Product liability may be based on warranty, fraud, negligence, or strict liability.

LAW AS PEOPLE LIVE IT

1. The Plaza Centurion Hotel advertised itself as "The world's most beautiful hotel . . . offering the most elegant service in America." Lowell paid three times his customary room rental to spend a day and night at the Plaza Centurion. He concluded that many other hotels are more beautiful and provide even better service. May he refuse to pay for his room because of a breach of sales warranty?

2. Merlin had sold a color television set to Kempsky who was very unhappy with the way the set performed. Merlin made several service calls without charge to adjust the color controls. During his fourth visit he said firmly, "Now it'll work right for at least a year—I promise." Is Merlin bound by his words?

3. McConnell purchased an antique clock from Benson, not knowing it had been stolen from Hill. When Hill later claimed the clock, McConnell refused to give it up, saying he was a good faith purchaser who had paid fair value. (a) Must McConnell give the clock to Hill? (b) If so, does McConnell have a cause of action against Benson for breach of warranty?

4. Douglas entered Reed's nursery and asked for a 50-pound sack of "Clobber," a brand name weed-killer he planned to use to eliminate narrow leaf devil grass from his lawn. "Clobber" was advertised as "effective, when properly used, against crabgrass and other broad-leaf weeds and grasses." Douglas applied the chemical according to directions but the devil grass survived. (a) He sues the manufacturer, claiming a breach of warranty. (b) He also sues Reed for failure to give him proper advice. Will he win either suit?

5. Byrd ordered a custard-filled French pastry at the Diner's Delight Cafe. He became sick and his doctor diagnosed the illness as ptomaine poisoning from the contaminated custard. Byrd sued the Diner's Delight for damages to cover medical costs, loss of wages while hospitalized, and pain and suffering. Should he collect?

6. Hanly selected two yards of fabric for a dress. When she placed a pattern on the material she was alarmed to discover that it did not fit. She needed at least one more yard, but the store had no more in stock. She demanded a refund because the fabric was not fit for the purpose intended. Is she entitled to a refund?

7. Watkins, a do-it-yourself hobbyist, decided to build his own patio. Sacks of standard "Pyramid" brand concrete mix which he purchased from Urban's Hardware Store had instructions which advised against direct contact with the skin. Watkins had an unusually sensitive skin, but in his haste to finish before the mix hardened, he repeatedly allowed his hands to touch the wet mix. His skin was burned and he developed a generalized allergic rash. Must either Urban or Pyramid pay damages under some theory of product liability?

8. Lubin opened a toy stand at the state fair, offering yo-yos, hula-hoops, jumping ropes, and sets of jacks with balls. He had remembered all were best sellers in years past, but at the fair he sold almost none. Is Lubin's wholesale supplier, Toy Town, Inc., liable to him for a breach of the warranty of merchantability?

9. To get to his cabin in the backwoods, Danforth bought a set of new but oversize tires for his pickup truck. He inflated the tires below the recommended level to make it easier to traverse the rough open country. While driving at high speed, one tire came off the wheel, and the truck crashed into a tree. Danforth sues the tire maker, claiming it is strictly liable. Who wins?

10. While on a vacation trip to Hawaii, Ronni bought a colorful hula skirt and matching blouse. Both were actually made by Wold, Inc., a novelty clothing manufacturer in Chicago. Some time later, at a costume party, Ronni was wearing the outfit when someone accidentally brushed against her with a lighted cigarette. The garments virtually exploded into flames, and she was seriously burned. Would Wold be liable, and if so, on what basis?

LAW AS COURTS DECIDE IT

1. North Pier Terminal Co. wished to sell a used railroad crane, and advertised it as having a 30-ton capacity and being in "good condition." Capital Equipment bought the crane after making a limited but reasonable inspection. Later, when it discovered that the crane would not work, Capital sued to cancel the contract. At the trial, the defendant's foreman testified that the crane was not in good condition at the time of the sale, and that he had never seen it lift more than ten tons. Was there a breach of an express warranty? (Capital Equipment Enterprises, Inc. v. North Pier Terminal Co., 254 N.E. 2d 542, Illinois)

2. While trying on a pair of slacks in a Mode O'Day Frock Shop operated by Goforth, Flippo was bitten by a poisonous brown recluse spider concealed in the slacks. Flippo was hospitalized for 30 days because of the bite. Was Mode O'Day liable to her for a breach of the implied warranty of merchantability? (Flippo v. Mode O'Day Frock Shops of Hollywood, 248 Ark. SCO 1)

3. Greenman was injured when using his Shopsmith brand power tool, a combination saw-drill-lathe, in a state which recognizes the rule of strict product liability. The lathe did not have a proper fastening such as found on other lathes and this caused a piece of wood to fly off, strike, and injure the plaintiff. Notice of a breach of warranty had not been given by the buyer, and there was no evidence of negligence or fraud on the part of Yuba, the manufacturer. Was the

manufacturer nevertheless liable for the injury? (Greenman v. Yuba Power Products, Inc., 377 P. 2d 897, California)

4. The purchasing agent of Eastern Woodworks, Inc. told Kelsbaugh, a partner in a small adhesive manufacturing company, that he needed a quick-drying glue to use in the manufacture of formica table tops. Kelsbaugh said, "I think I have something that may be of some help to you." He left some glue samples which the woodworking company tested for three weeks and found satisfactory. The company ordered ten gallons at $3 a gallon. The glue failed to hold and the formica separated from the table tops in a few weeks. The woodworking company sued the glue manufacturer, claiming breach of warranty of fitness for a particular purpose. Should it receive judgment? (Shay v. Joseph, 149 A. 2d 3, Maryland)

5. Crabbe negotiated with Freeman for the purchase of Freeman's Pontiac station wagon for $1,475. Crabbe, while trying out the car, noted that the odometer showed the mileage to be only 22,000 miles, and was told that this was the actual mileage. Crabbe learned after the sale that the car had been driven more than 50,000 miles and that the odometer had been turned back in error by a mechanic who reported it to Freeman. Moreover, before selling the car, Freeman caused the service records of the car to be destroyed and removed all the lubrication stickers. The value of a Pontiac station wagon driven 50,000 miles was $1,150 instead of $1,425, and Crabbe sued for the difference. Would a plea of *caveat emptor* be a good defense for Freeman, or did Freeman's assertation that the odometer reading was correct constitute an express warranty? (Crabbe v. Freeman, 160 N.E. 2d 583, Ohio)

6. Rogers purchased bottled ingredients for a home permanent. The manufacturer's labels were directed to the ultimate purchaser and stated that the ingredients were safe and harmless when used as intended. Magazine and television advertising also stated that this particular preparation was safe and harmless. In using the ingredients for their intended use, Rogers found them to be harmful. She then brought an action against the manufacturer for breach of an express warranty. The manufacturer denied liability on the ground that it had not sold the product to Rogers. Should the court dismiss her action? (Rogers v. Toni Home Permanent Co., 147 N.E. 2d 612, 167 Ohio 244)

21 Rights, and Remedies for Breach

1. *You buy a felt marking pen that is warranted to write on any surface. In fact, the ink does not adhere to waxed paper you use for wrapping. Can you get your money back?*

2. *Your mother contracts to sell her collection of rare old jazz records, many irreplaceable. Then she changes her mind when you tell her you want them. Can she be compelled to deliver the goods to the buyer?*

3. *You buy a new suit on charge account credit. (a) May the seller keep the suit until the price is paid? (b) If he lets you take the suit, may he repossess it if you don't pay promptly as agreed?*

WHAT ARE THE RIGHTS OF THE BUYER?

Problem: Nelson Cycle Company made a written contract to sell 4,500 of its patented, exclusive-design, collapsible bicycles to Arbin at a price of $50 each. Delivery was to be no later than Nov. 1. In case of delayed delivery, the parties agreed on liquidated damages. The bicycles arrived on Dec. 1. Is Nelson obliged to pay damages as agreed?

Both the buyer and the seller may enforce applicable rights which are specified by valid terms of the contract. Thus, in the problem, Arbin is entitled to collect liquidated damages (Page 200) as agreed, assuming the amount was a reasonable compensation for the breach.

You may wish to refer to Chapter 14 to review the usual rights and remedies available to the parties for breach of contract. Also see pages 253 and 254 for details of the seller's right to be paid and to have the buyer accept the goods.

Unless otherwise agreed, the buyer has certain special rights in a sale or contract to sell. The most important ones are listed below:

(1) EXAMINATION OF GOODS

Problem: Krakow, a general contractor, ordered 800 sheets of plywood from Murphy for use as finish walls in a housing project. Each sheet was to be free of knotholes and other blemishes on one side. The goods were delivered to the job, but the carpenters found blemishes after they had begun the installation. Krakow's foreman made a spot check and concluded that more than 50 percent of the sheets were defective. Krakow promptly notified Murphy. May Krakow return the unused panels at the seller's expense?

When the buyer has not had an opportunity to examine the goods, he is entitled to do so before paying for them or accepting them as conforming to the contract. If the goods are shipped to the buyer C.O.D., however, he must pay for them before inspection, unless the seller has agreed otherwise with buyer and carrier.

If defective goods have not been accepted but are in the possession of the buyer, he may reship to the seller at the seller's expense, or sell the goods and account to the seller for the proceeds. Even an acceptance may be revoked within a reasonable time by giving proper notice, provided the defects are not known to the buyer and could not have been discovered by a reasonable examination prior to acceptance. In the problem, Krakow properly assumed the panels were acceptable when routinely delivered to the job. He acted reasonably when he learned of the defects, and is entitled to return the goods at the seller's expense.

(2) DELIVERY OF GOODS

Problem: When Briggs bought a second-hand combination refrigerator-freezer from Hedge, nothing was said about delivery. Later, Briggs demanded Hedge deliver the bulky unit to his home, protesting that he would have to rent a truck or trailer to move it himself. Must Hedge deliver as demanded?

The seller must deliver possession of the goods to the buyer or to a person designated by him. *Delivery* is the placing of the property at the disposal of the buyer. It must be made in accordance with the terms of the contract. Thus, the parties may decide whether the buyer is to pick up the goods or the seller is to send them, or whether they are to remain in a warehouse and only the warehouse receipt is to be delivered.

(a) Place of delivery. Unless otherwise agreed or determined by trade usage, the place of delivery is the seller's place of business. If he has no place of business, the place of delivery is his residence. If the goods are known by both parties to be at some other place, that is the place of delivery.

Delivery to the buyer does not mean transport to the buyer's home, farm, or place of business unless that is agreed upon or is customary. In the ordinary situation involving consumer goods, the seller is obliged only to make the goods available at his own place of business. Hence, in the problem on page 293, Hedge is not obliged to deliver the refrigerator-freezer. Hedge fulfilled his obligation when he placed the machine at the buyer's disposal.

(b) Quantity and quality to be delivered. The buyer has the right to receive the proper quality of goods and the exact quantity in one delivery. He may refuse to accept a smaller or larger quantity than the contract specifies. If a smaller quantity is delivered, and the buyer knows the seller will deliver no more, he may accept what there is. If a larger quantity than ordered is delivered, the buyer may accept the goods included in the contract and reject the rest. He may also reject or accept the whole, or accept any commercial unit or units and reject the rest. In keeping with common practice, the UCC refers to the *commercial unit* in which businessmen deal. This is any article, group of articles, or quantity which commercially is regarded as a separate unit or whole. Examples would be a particular machine, a suite of furniture, or a carload lot.

 Bell was owner-operator of ten concession stands at an outdoor music festival. He ordered 2,000 pounds of chipped party ice in 50 lb. sacks for the event. Crystal Clear Ice Co. delivered 3,000 pounds in 25 lb. sacks. Bell may accept or reject the whole lot, or accept any commercial unit or units, and reject the rest.

The buyer is not required to accept delivery in installments unless the agreement specifies such delivery, or unless circumstances make it appropriate or necessary, as where the seller's ability to transport the goods or the buyer's storage space is limited.

WHAT ARE THE BUYER'S REMEDIES?

Problem: Gabrielli ordered 12 dozen Italian handbags from Fuller, an importer. The goods were selected from samples Fuller had displayed at a trade show in New York. Gabrielli paid in full in order to get early delivery of the goods. When the handbags arrived, they did not conform to the samples. Gabrielli refused to accept them and demands return of his money. Is he within his rights?

If the seller fails to perform as agreed, he becomes liable to the buyer for breach of contract. This happens when the seller: (a) fails to deliver the goods; (b) repudiates the contract; or (c) delivers unacceptable goods to the buyer. In any of these cases, the buyer may use the remedy or remedies that are appropriate under the circumstances. They include the right to:

(1) ACCEPT, REJECT, OR REVOKE ACCEPTANCE OF DELIVERY

If the goods delivered or the tender of delivery fail in any way to conform to the contract, the buyer may accept or reject the entire quantity of goods, or he may accept any commercial unit or units and reject the rest. If he rightfully rejects the goods, he may recover anything he has paid. In the problem, Gabrielli was within his rights in refusing the goods and demanding return of his money.

The buyer may reject the goods if they do not conform to the contract.

BUT I ORDERED A CASE, NOT A TRUCKLOAD.

The buyer must notify the seller of rejection or breach within a reasonable time. If he does not give prompt and proper notice, he may later be barred from any remedy.

If the goods have been accepted in ignorance of the breach, the buyer may revoke his acceptance and return the goods to the seller. However, a buyer may know of the non-conformity and accept the goods with the reasonable assumption that the seller will correct it by repairing, replacing, or making some price adjustment. If so, he retains his right to revoke acceptance if satisfactory changes are not made. But when goods are accepted with knowledge of the breach and no reason to expect correction by the seller, they cannot be returned.

(2) COVER

The buyer may *cover*. This means that, acting in good faith and without unreasonable delay, he may buy or contract to buy goods to substitute for those he failed to receive from the seller. If the buyer covers, damages for breach consist of the difference between the cost of cover and the contract price.

> Beckett needed a car to get to his new job in the suburbs. He contracted to buy a 1970 Mustang from Logan at an agreed price. Before time for delivery, Logan refused to perform. Beckett immediately bought a comparable car from another dealer but had to pay an extra $200. Logan is liable for the $200.

The buyer's failure to cover does not prevent his choosing another remedy; however, it does limit recovery of consequential damages to those which could not have been avoided by cover. It is a general principle of contract law that an injured party should *mitigate the damages.* This means he should, if reasonably possible, reduce his injuries or losses, or not permit them to increase.

(3) SUE FOR DAMAGES FOR BREACH

The buyer may sue for dollar damages. If the seller repudiates the contract or does not deliver the goods, the amount the buyer is entitled to is the difference between the contract price and the market price at the time he learned of the breach. He may also collect incidental and consequential damages. Incidental damages include such things as reasonable expenses to inspect, transport, and care for goods rightfully rejected, commissions paid to obtain replacement goods, and other expenses caused by the breach. Consequential damages include losses resulting from needs of the buyer which the seller had reason to know when the contract was made, and which cannot reasonably be prevented by cover. Consequential damages also extend to injuries to person or property which result from any breach of warranty.

Where the buyer has accepted the goods and then given notification of nonconformity, the measure of damages for breach of contract is the loss resulting in the ordinary course of events. Ordinarily, in cases of breach of warranty, courts award the difference between the value of the goods as accepted and the value they would have had if they had been as warranted. However, when use of a warranted product causes injury, the victim does not want a few cents or dollars which the product itself may have cost. The consequential damages may be much higher. This would happen, for example, if a

The buyer may sue for consequential damages resulting from breach of warranty.

cleaning fluid—advertised as "harmless to any fabric"—caused permanent splotches when properly used on a given rug.

In any case of breach of contract, the buyer may accept the goods, and claim a deduction of damages from the price because of the breach. This is often done amicably, without litigation, but if necessary the buyer can seek the same relief in court.

(4) CANCEL

The buyer may cancel the contract while retaining all rights of action he may have against the seller, including suit for damages. When the buyer clearly indicates an intention to cancel, he may merely ask for a return to conditions as they were before the sale. The buyer must then restore the seller to his original position as far as circumstances permit, and the seller must return any consideration received.

 Juliano, a sofa manufacturer, contracted to buy certain foam rubber seat padding from the Resilient Rubber Products Co., making a 25 percent down payment on the price. After the first of several planned shipments arrived, it was obvious that Resilient would not be able to perform as agreed because of quality control problems. The company sales manager admitted this. Juliano might have retained the goods and sued for damages, but instead he elected to cancel and to return the first shipment. Resilient must refund the down payment.

(5) RETURN THE GOODS

Generally a buyer in possession of goods which he has rightfully rejected may reship them to the seller at the seller's expense. However, if the goods are perishable or threaten to decline rapidly in value, a merchant buyer has a good faith obligation to try to sell them for the seller's account instead.

(6) RECOVER THE GOODS OR THEIR VALUE

If there has already been a transfer of ownership under the terms of the contract, the buyer, because he is the owner, has a right to get his goods. The action taken to enforce the right to recover goods wrongfully withheld by another is called *replevin*.

If a buyer with the right to recovery no longer wants the goods, he may sue the defaulting seller for their full value. Even when the seller has merely identified the goods to the contract, the buyer has a right to replevin when similar goods are not reasonably obtainable elsewhere.

> While the country was at war and many goods were in short supply, Louis sold a quantity of nails to Desmond. Thereafter Louis refused to deliver, saying he needed the nails himself, and could get a much better price from someone else. Desmond could use the action of replevin to get his goods.

(7) SPECIFIC PERFORMANCE

Ordinarily, the harm caused a buyer by a breach of a sales contract can be offset by payment of money damages. The buyer may retain the money or use it to buy substitute goods. However, when money damages are not an adequate remedy, the court may grant specific performance (Page 199) even though title or ownership has not yet passed to the buyer. This means the seller may be compelled by court order to do what he agreed to do in his contract. If he refuses, he may be held in contempt of court, perhaps being jailed until he complies.

Courts grant specific performance when the subject matter is unique, such as an original work of art, an heirloom, or a famous race horse. You may recall that this remedy is also available in other types of contracts where items of value other than goods are transferred. Examples are parcels of real estate, patents, copyrights, or shares of stock in a closely-held corporation.

> Lindhoff agreed to sell to Norris a painting by the late American artist Jackson Pollock. Later Lindhoff refused to perform. Norris could specifically enforce

the agreement because the painting was one of a kind and could not be obtained elsewhere for any amount of money damages.

(8) RESELL THE GOODS

A buyer may find himself in possession of goods that he has rightfully refused to accept or for which he has rightfully revoked his acceptance. In such case, he may either hold the goods until he is reimbursed by the seller, or resell them. If the goods are perishable or threaten to decline in value rapidly, and the seller has given no contrary instructions, the buyer must make reasonable efforts to resell them for the seller's account. He may deduct from the proceeds of the resale any payments he has made on the price plus his reasonable related expenses. The balance, if any, goes to the seller.

WHAT ARE THE SELLER'S REMEDIES?

Problem: Jayne Rucelle had no cash, but bought a new spring outfit consisting of dress, hat, coat, shoes, and handbag from a branch store of Max of Manhattan. The store manager accepted her application for a credit card, but refused to release the goods until approval could be obtained from the New York headquarters. What seller's remedy was the manager relying on to hold the goods?

Although a buyer cannot breach a warranty because he never makes one, he can hurt the seller by breaching the contract in other ways, such as wrongfully refusing to accept goods he has agreed to buy, or failing to pay for his purchase.

In addition to remedies available under general principles of contract law, the seller may take advantage of one or more of the following. All the remedies listed apply generally when the buyer (a) wrongfully rejects the goods, (b) wrongfully revokes acceptance, or (c) fails to make a payment due on or before delivery. If the breach affects only part of the contract, the remedy applies to the goods directly affected.

(1) WITHHOLD DELIVERY

Even when title has passed to the buyer, the seller may be entitled to retain possession of the goods until he is paid for them. This right is known as the *unpaid seller's lien*. It exists when (a) the sale is made for cash and full payment has not been received; (b) the sale is made on credit but the time period has expired, as when the buyer is given 30 days in which to pay, yet does not call for the goods or pay within that time; or (c) the buyer becomes insolvent—that is, unable to pay his debts as they fall due—before calling for the goods. In the problem, the store manager was using his unpaid seller's lien.

If the goods have already been delivered when the seller learns that the buyer is insolvent, the seller may reclaim possession if it is within 10 days after the buyer received them. This short time limit does not apply if the buyer misrepresented his solvency to the seller within three months of the time of the delivery.

 Crescent Tool & Die Co. had made a credit sale to Doro of a set of steel dies for use in making plastic knives and forks. Before shipment, Crescent received a credit report which said Doro was insolvent; this permitted Crescent to withhold delivery.

The unpaid seller's lien is discharged or ended when the buyer tenders payment. The seller may lose his lien also by (a) delivering the goods to the buyer or letting him acquire them by other lawful means; (b) delivering the goods to a carrier or other bailee for unrestricted delivery to the buyer; or (c) waiving his right, as by extending credit.

(2) IDENTIFY CONFORMING GOODS

If the buyer breaches the sales contract before the goods have been identified, the seller may proceed to identify conforming goods that are in his possession. After making identification, he may sue the buyer for the sales price, or resell and hold the buyer liable for any difference between the contract price and the price received.

If the goods are being manufactured at the time of breach, the seller may complete and then identify them. In other cases, he may want to resell the partially completed goods for scrap or salvage value. He has a duty to take the action which will cause the least increase in damages—that is, to proceed in a commercially reasonable manner.

 Rexford contracted to buy a matched set of custom hardwood furniture for his office from Manleva. Rexford canceled the order when all that remained to be done to the desk and cabinets was the final spraying, polishing, and assembly. Manleva is justified in spending more time and money to complete the furniture. He can then sell it to someone else and hold Rexford liable for any deficiency in the price received.

(3) STOP DELIVERY BY CARRIER OR BAILEE

If the seller discovers the buyer is insolvent when the goods are already in the possession of a carrier or other bailee such as a warehouseman, the seller may stop delivery of the goods regardless of the quantity involved. When the buyer—even though solvent— repudiates the contract or fails to make a payment that is due before delivery, the seller may stop delivery of carload, truckload, plane- load, or larger quantity. For the seller, having the goods is pre- ferable to having a cause of action, perhaps as just one of the many creditors of a defaulting buyer.

 Anton, a food exporter in New York City, ordered a planeload of fresh strawberries from Yakomoto in California. After the plane had taken off, Yakomoto phoned his banker in New York. He learned that Anton had refused to pay 25 percent of the purchase price in cash, or to accept the draft for the balance as agreed in the sales contract. Yakomoto was within his rights when he ordered the air freight carrier to divert the plane to another buyer in Miami.

(4) RESELL

After breach of contract by the buyer, the seller may resell the goods or any part of them in his possession. He is required to act in good faith and in a commercially reasonable manner in reselling them either privately or at a public sale or auction.

If the resale is private, the seller must give the original buyer reasonable notice of his intention. If the resale is public, the seller must give the buyer notice of the time and place of resale unless the goods are perishable or threaten to decline rapidly in value. Even if the seller fails to comply with all the requirements, however, the good faith purchaser at a resale gets a valid title to the goods.

The original buyer may purchase the goods at the resale, but whoever buys, the seller keeps any profit he may make. On the other hand, if the amount realized is less than the original contract price, the defaulting first buyer is liable to the seller for the de- ficiency. Moreover, he must pay incidental damages for new costs incurred. In fairness, if any expenses are saved because of the breach (for example, the cost of transportation avoided when the goods were not shipped), the seller must deduct such amount.

 Fletcher sold his attaché case to Greene for $15, but Greene changed his mind and refused to accept the item or pay for it. After notifying Greene of his intention, Fletcher acted honestly in seeking a new buyer. He finally persuaded Koster to buy the case for $10. Greene still owes Fletcher $5.

(5) RECOVER DAMAGES

When a buyer repudiates the contract or wrongfully rejects the goods, the seller may sue him for damages. Normally the seller is entitled to the difference between the market price at the time and place for tender of the goods, and the unpaid contract price. Any incidental damages are added (such things as the costs of stopping delivery, and costs of care-custody-resale after the breach), and any expenses saved because of the breach are deducted.

(6) SUE FOR THE PRICE

If the buyer does not pay for the goods, the seller may in certain cases sue him for the purchase price and any incidental damages he has sustained. This is true of: (a) goods which have been accepted; (b) conforming goods which were damaged or destroyed after the risk of loss passed to the buyer; and (c) goods identified to the contract, but which the seller has been and probably will continue to be unable to resell at a reasonable price.

When the seller elects to sue for the price, he must hold the goods for the buyer and release them if and when he collects his money under the court judgment. He may still resell the goods before such collection if the opportunity arises, and credit the proceeds to the original buyer.

When the seller cannot sue for the purchase price, he may still sue the buyer for damages for breach of contract.

(7) CANCEL

If the buyer permits a material breach of contract, the seller may cancel the contract and if desired, sue the buyer for damages for its breach.

A TWO-WAY STREET . . .

A sale, like other contracts, is a two-way street: benefits and burdens flow both ways. Both sellers and buyers have rights and duties; both have remedies in case of breach. To help avoid the difficulties which result from a breach of contract, deal only with responsible, reputable parties, whether they are sellers or buyers. Do not promise more than you can perform, and keep your promises.

AS A BUYER:

1. When in doubt about the seller's integrity or about the quality of his product, buy on credit or on other terms which allow you to examine the goods before you pay for them. Returns and adjustments are usually much easier for you if you still have your money.
2. When time is of the essence, say so in the contract, preferably in writing. As appropriate, spell out other details as to mode of transportation, place of delivery, method of packaging, and installment deliveries.
3. If the seller has apparently breached the contract, communicate with him. Give him a fair chance to perform properly.
4. If the seller refuses to perform, consider remedies short of a law suit, e.g., cancel the contract.
5. Generally seek to mitigate, or lessen, the damages. This usually means you cover by buying the goods elsewhere.
6. Litigate only as a last resort. Court action may be costly, and the outcome is uncertain. Nevertheless, it may be desirable and necessary, especially when the remedy sought is specific performance.

AS A SELLER:

1. When in doubt about the buyer's integrity or ability and willingness to pay for goods when due, sell only for cash or on C.O.D. terms. If you have not been paid and a dispute arises, your position is greatly enhanced if you still have the goods.
2. To evaluate prospective customers' finances, use modern credit investigation techniques.
3. If you ship the goods on credit and then learn of the buyer's insolvency, don't hesitate to stop delivery. The added expense and inconvenience are justified when the alternative may be a bankruptcy proceeding in which you receive a small amount for every dollar of your claim.
4. If the buyer refuses to perform, consider remedies short of a law suit, e.g., cancel the contract.
5. Generally seek to mitigate, or lessen, the damages. This may mean you promptly resell the goods, if still in your possession, on the best obtainable terms.
6. Litigate only as a last resort. Court action may be costly, and the outcome is uncertain. Nevertheless, it may be desirable and necessary when the remedy sought is the purchase price.

YOUR LEGAL VOCABULARY

commercial unit   mitigate the damages
cover   replevin
delivery   unpaid seller's lien

1. Placing property at the disposal of the buyer when the sales contract does not require the seller to ship or transport the goods to the buyer.
2. To reduce injury or loss from the defendant's conduct.
3. An action to recover possession of personal property.
4. A right to retain possession of goods as security for the price.
5. Purchase of substitute goods for those the buyer failed to receive from the seller.
6. An article, group of articles, or quantity which commercially is regarded as a whole.

REMEMBER THESE HIGHLIGHTS

1. The seller is under a duty to deliver the goods in accordance with the terms of the contract. When no place of delivery is specified, the place of delivery is usually the seller's place of business.
2. The buyer may insist upon delivery of the proper quantity and quality of goods. Before acceptance or payment, he may examine the goods to determine whether they conform to the contract.
3. If the seller fails to deliver the goods in accordance with the contract, the buyer may (a) accept, reject, or revoke acceptance of delivery; (b) cover; (c) sue for damages; (d) cancel; (e) return the goods; (f) recover the goods or their value if title has passed; (g) bring an action for specific performance if title has not passed and money damages would be an inadequate remedy; (h) resell the goods.
4. When the buyer breaches the contract, the seller may (a) withhold delivery; (b) identify conforming goods to the contract, then sue or resell; (c) stop delivery by carrier or bailee; (d) resell; (e) recover damages; (f) sue for the price; or (g) cancel.

LAW AS PEOPLE LIVE IT

1. Late in September, Lee's Sports Chalet ordered 200 pairs of assorted sizes of ski boots from the McIntosh Company. Delivery was promised no later than November 1, and time was agreed to be of the essence. A strike in October closed the McIntosh plant for three months and no boots were delivered. Is McIntosh liable in a suit for breach of contract?
2. Bancroft, a produce broker in St. Louis, received a trailer-truck load of vine-ripened cantaloupes from Whitney, a grower in California's

Imperial Valley. He had ordered honeydew melons but Whitney had substituted cantaloupes because they were in plentiful supply and had ripened early because of a heat wave. Bancroft refuses to accept the shipment but realizes the goods are perishable and must be consumed soon. What should he do?

3. Cobb ordered a living room suite from a new furniture store in town called Goldfine's. Nothing was said about delivery, but there was a custom in town that delivery would be made without charge within a 50-mile radius. When no goods arrived, Cobb complained to Goldfine and demanded prompt delivery to his home. Was he justified?

4. The Westman Corporation sold on credit and delivered a $2,700 automatic photo-enlarger together with $1,600 worth of supplies to Padgett, a professional photographer. Three days later, the sales manager of Westman learned that Padgett had been insolvent for more than a month. When confronted with this fact, Padgett said he planned to use the goods to increase his revenue and pay all his debts. Westman doubts he can do it and wants the goods returned. Is it legally entitled to get them?

5. Schiller of Oregon sold Blatz of Arizona a train carload of fir tree bark chips to be used as ground cover. When the shipment was on its way, Blatz phoned and said he now realized he couldn't use more than a tenth of a carload. What can Schiller do?

6. Bach sold Kalow $300 worth of insecticide for his crop of corn. The insecticide killed the bugs but it also burned the leaves and destroyed most of the plants even though applied according to directions. Bach admitted something went wrong with the formula and offered to refund the full $300 paid. Is this the limit of his damages?

7. Horne bought a machine for spraying walnut trees from Mellon, who warranted that the spray would reach the tops of the largest trees. In fact, it did not, and Horne complained about the failure. However, he kept the machine and used it to complete all spraying for that season. Then he told Mellon to come and get the sprayer, and to refund the price less a fair rental charge. Must Mellon do so?

8. Kemal, an art dealer, contracted to sell to Perino a painting by the French artist, Dufy, for $125,000. (a) If Kemal refuses to deliver, can Perino force him to? (b) If Perino repudiates the contract, can Kemal force him to pay the price and accept the painting?

9. Alcott agreed to sell his bicycle to Fitz for $35, then changed his mind and refused to deliver. Is Fitz entitled to cover?

10. For its ice cream and candy-making needs, Gay Nineties Confections, Inc. ordered a quantity of blanched almonds from Albert's Wholesale Suppliers. When the shipment and invoice arrived, it was clear that Albert's had supplied premium nuts, but had billed for only the standard grade as ordered. Was this a breach of contract? What should Gay Nineties do?

LAW AS COURTS DECIDE IT

1. Carpenter sold Boyer 500 hundred lb. bags of potatoes at a price of $1,625 for the carload, F.O.B. Naples, Florida. The potatoes were guaranteed to be suitable for processing into potato chips on arrival. They arrived on March 27 and were unloaded on March 29. Some were used on April 2 but were found to be unsatisfactory. Boyer wrote to Carpenter on April 4, saying he refused to pay the price because the potatoes were no good for chips. This letter reached Carpenter on April 8. Must Boyer pay for the goods? (A. C. Carpenter, Inc. v. Boyer Potato Chips, 28 AD 1557, U.S. Dept. of Agriculture)

2. Lanners bought a used airplane from Whitney and the seller gave assurances of its airworthiness. The seller hired an FAA licensed mechanic to inspect the plane and he also certified it to be airworthy. However, during the first 16 days of ownership by Lanners, the plane developed mechanical trouble. Two 100-hour inspections revealed that it was not airworthy and that the inspection order by the seller had not been completed properly. May the buyer cancel and collect damages? (Lanners v. Whitney, 428 P. 2d 398, Oregon)

3. In April, 1957, Fleet purchased on installments an ice cream freezer and a refrigeration unit from the F. W. Lang Co. In September, 1959, Fleet notified the Lang Company that he was revoking his acceptance because the equipment was unstable and wholly unusable for the purposes intended. Did Fleet have the right to revoke his acceptance? (F. W. Lang Co. v. Fleet, 193 Pa. Super. 365, 165 A. 2d 258)

4. Nora Kesinger purchased a used automobile from Burtrum for $1,180, making payments at various times amounting to $1,004.08. Despite repeated demands, Burtrum never delivered a valid certificate of title to the car. Finally, 30 months later, Kesinger canceled the contract. She tendered back the car she had purchased and used during that time, and demanded return of what she had paid. Under the circumstances, could Kesinger cancel the contract? (Kesinger v. Burtrum, 295 S.W. 2d 605, Missouri)

5. After inspecting a sample of soap, House of Price, Inc. placed an order with Kleigman Brothers for 40,000 lbs. of the soap to be shipped in 50-lb. bags. The soap arrived by rail on December 23, and the House of Price had a truckman remove it from the car and put it in a warehouse in its name. On June 5 of the next year, a representative of the House of Price examined the soap and found that it did not comply with the sample. It thereupon notified Kleigman Brothers that it refused to accept. In defending against an action for a return of the purchase price, Kleigman Brothers contended that the buyer's right to cancel the sale because of a breach of warranty had expired. Was this contention sound? (House of Price, Inc. v. Kleigman Brothers, Inc. 126 N.Y.S. 2d 764)

UNIT SIX

Debtors and Creditors

UNIT SIX

Most contracts of businessmen involve the use of credit, and consumers also rely heavily on credit. Essentially, credit means getting goods or services now in exchange for a promise to pay for them later. It may also mean getting a loan of money now in exchange for a promise to repay later.

As a consumer, you use credit if you borrow money to take a vacation, to get a college education, or to buy a house. You use credit if you buy a motorcycle, furniture, or other goods "on time" or under some type of installment sales plan.

We shall learn how creditors protect themselves against the risk that debtors might not pay when due. We shall also see how the government protects debtors against creditors who would collect excessive interest charges.

Finally, we shall take a closer look at what are called secured transactions. The law governs the contract between the debtor and creditor where the latter has some right to specific property of the debtor as assurance of payment. This usually means getting possession of the property and reselling it in case of default.

You can readily see that there are two broad types of credit: (1) when goods or services are sold, and (2) when money is loaned. Unless otherwise stated, the rules discussed in this unit apply to both types of credit.

CHAPTER 22 Credit for Buyer and Borrower

1. *A school acquaintance asks you to lend him some money. Should you require him to promise in writing to pay it back?*

2. *If you buy something "on time," is it enough for the seller to tell you what your monthly payment is?*

3. *When you borrow money from a pawnbroker, you give him some article to assure repayment. May he nevertheless legally charge you higher interest than other lenders do?*

WHO ARE DEBTORS AND CREDITORS?

Problem: Atkinson borrowed $300 from the credit union of the company where he worked. He agreed to repay $25 a month plus interest. What was the relation between Atkinson and the credit union?

Whenever one person or business is in debt to another, the relation between the two parties is that of debtor and creditor. The *debtor* is the one who owes. The *creditor* is the one to whom the debt is owed. The debt is usually payable in money, and ordinarily it is based on contract. It may arise out of a loan, as in the problem in which Atkinson was the debtor and the credit union the creditor. Or it may arise when goods or services are provided in exchange for a promise to pay later.

Much of the discussion in this book is concerned with debtor-creditor relations. Bailments (Unit IV) frequently result in such a relation, as when you rent a car and pay when you return it. Commercial paper such as checks and promissory notes (Unit VII) is evidence of the debtor and creditor relation. An unpaid employee (Unit VIII) is the creditor of his employer.

HOW DO CREDIT CARDS WORK?

Problem: Collins, who often found himself low on gas and short of cash, applied for and received a gasoline credit card. After using it several times, Collins sold his car, bought a bicycle, and laid the card aside. Several weeks later, when he received a $79 bill from the oil company for purchases he had never made, Collins discovered that the card had been lost or stolen. He then notified the company of the loss. Was he liable for the debt?

Today, credit transactions often take place with the use of credit cards. A *credit card* identifies the holder as entitled to buy goods or to contract for services on credit. It is usually made of plastic, is embossed with the holder's name and identification number, and has a place for his signature. Credit cards are used to make billions of dollars of credit purchases annually. They may be good for certain types of expenses (some, for example, are commonly used for travel and entertainment); or their use may be limited to a certain retail store or chain (cards for a local department store or national oil company); or they may be all-purpose cards which cover any type of purchase from any seller who chooses and is authorized to honor them (banks are generally the issuers of this type).

INTERNATIONAL	Fuel for the future!
International Oil Company Credit Card	EXPIRES
489 719 639 04	12 75
	MONTH YEAR
CARLTON J. JONES	
Carlton J. Jones	
AUTHORIZED SIGNATURE	

Credit Card

Application for a card constitutes an offer; acceptance is made when the company expressly approves the application or sends the card. Together, these acts bind the cardholder in a contract relationship with the issuing business, bank, or company. Generally the cardholder is liable for all purchases he makes with the card, or which are made by others with his permission.

Under federal law the cardholder is liable for unauthorized use of his credit card by any other person such as a thief or dishonest

Unit VI □ DEBTORS AND CREDITORS

finder. His liability is limited, however, to $50 and this liability is imposed only if:

1. the cardholder had requested and received the credit card, or had signed or used it or authorized another to do so;

2. the card issuer had given adequate notice of this liability;

3. the card issuer had provided a self-addressed, pre-stamped notification to be mailed by the cardholder in the event of loss or theft of the card;

4. the card issuer had provided positive means of identification;

5. the unauthorized use took place before the cardholder had notified the issuer that such use might occur.

Thus, the loss or theft of a credit card should be reported immediately to the issuer. In the problem, Collins would probably be liable for the charges but only to a maximum of $50.

Most credit card agreements specify rates of interest to be charged on debts not paid within a certain time period, usually 30 days, after receipt of a bill. A typical charge is 18 percent a year. There may be other terms also. As in the case of any contract, one should read the terms carefully and understand them before signing.

WHAT ARE SECURED AND UNSECURED DEBTS?

Problem: Korman borrowed $850 from Linberg. He promised to repay the borrowed money in twelve months, with interest at 7 percent per year, and gave Linberg a $1,000 bond to hold as security for the payment. The bond was to be returned to Korman when the debt was paid. What was Linberg's legal status?

The main concern of the creditor is whether he will be paid when the debt is due. If the amount is small, or if the credit standing of the borrower or buyer is very good, the creditor may be willing to take an *unsecured debt*. This is a simple personal obligation or promise of the debtor, oral or written, such as a charge account at a retail store or an ordinary promissory note. A debt is a *secured debt* when the creditor is given an interest in some kind of property to protect him if payment of the debt is not made. Thus, Linberg was a secured creditor of Korman.

An unsecured debt is supported only by the debtor's promise and by his general ability to pay. Any assets he has pledged specifically for secured debts are not available to his unsecured creditors. Of course, many debts are unsecured, and some people take pride in being able to borrow just on the promise that they will repay. All United States government bonds and many corporation bonds fall into the unsecured category.

The chief difference between a secured debt and one that is unsecured becomes clear in case of default or breach of the obligation. In accordance with the law or the contract, a secured creditor may sell the property that has been put up to secure the debt and use the proceeds to pay the amount due. If the creditor does not have possession of the property at the time of default, as where the property is an automobile in the possession of the buyer, the creditor may repossess and sell the property. Any excess is returned to the debtor, but if there is a deficiency he remains liable for that amount.

An unsecured creditor, on the other hand, would need to sue his debtor for breach of contract in case of default. Upon obtaining judgment, he would take prescribed steps to collect. (Chapter 6) This is costly and time-consuming. Moreover, some debtors may prove to be dishonest and move away without leaving a forwarding address, or they may have no assets that the creditor can take. In some cases, debtors may even avoid some of their obligations by going into bankruptcy. It is certainly better for the creditor if he already has at his disposal some asset of the debtor, such as the bond in the preceding problem.

If the debtor does pay, the debt is discharged. To avoid the possibility of being charged twice, the debtor should request a receipt if he pays in cash. In some states a debtor is not required to pay a debt unless he is given a receipt. If he pays by check, his canceled check when returned to him by his bank serves as a receipt if it bears a notation showing the purpose for which the payment was made.

HOW MAY DEBTS BE SECURED?

Problem: Rogan was anxious to go home from college for the spring break, but had no money for a bus ticket. To obtain the $15 he needed, he left his typewriter, which was worth at least $75, at Eastman's Pawn Shop. If he did not repay the loan with interest within the agreed time, would he lose title to his typewriter?

When a creditor has an interest in specific property as security for the repayment of a debt, there is said to be a *lien* against that property. A lien gives a creditor the right, in case of default, to require sale of the property and to use the proceeds to pay the debt.

Some liens permit the debtor to keep possession of the liened property while the debt is unpaid but not in default. Mortgages on homes are a very common example of this type of lien. As long as the debt is unpaid, the lien remains unsatisfied and prevents the homeowner from having a clear title.

 A lot and building owned by Wesley had a lien against it. If Wesley wished to sell, he would either have to remove the lien by payment of the debt, or the buyer would have to take title subject to the lien. The buyer would not want to do this unless Wesley reduced the selling price by the amount of the lien.

Other liens permit the creditor to have possession of the property while the debt is unsatisfied. You may recall the bailee's lien (Page 215) and the unpaid seller's lien. (Page 299) Another such lien is the pledge.

When personal property is deposited with a creditor as security for the payment of a debt or the performance of an obligation, it is known as a *pledge*. The *pledgor* gives up the property; the *pledgee* receives it. This is a special type of bailment in which the creditor takes possession of the property as a bailee.

 Bradfield needed money to buy a special shipment of shoes for his retail shoe store. He could have sold 100 shares of stock which he owned in a leading U.S. corporation, but he wanted to maintain this ownership as a long-term investment. Instead, he pledged the stock as security for a loan from his bank.

In the pledge, the pledgee may keep the goods until the obligation is performed, but he may not use them without the owner's permission. In the event of default, the pledgee may sell the property after proper notice to the pledgor. Usually the sale must be made at a public auction in order to establish the fair market value of the property. If the amount received, after deducting expenses and interest, is more than the amount of the debt, the excess must be paid to the debtor. If it is less, the deficit must still be paid by the debtor.

A *pawn* is a pledge of tangible personal property, rather than stocks or bonds or other documents of value. A person in the business of lending money at interest, who requires tangible personal property such as jewelry as security, is known as a *pawnbroker*.

Because the business of a pawnbroker makes it easier for thieves to dispose of stolen property, it is regulated by special statutes. These laws usually provide that the pawnbroker must obtain a license, post a bond, and keep accurate records open to police inspection. If stolen goods are found in the pawnshop, they may be seized without compensating the pawnbroker. Ceilings are commonly imposed on the rate of interest that he may charge.

A pawnbroker requires security for a loan.

When one pawns goods, he must be given a receipt known as a pawn ticket. The pawnbroker is required by law to redeliver the goods when the debt is paid with interest due and the pawn ticket is surrendered.

Goods that are pawned must be held for a certain length of time after the loan is due, in some states for a period of one year, before they can be sold. The rights of the parties to the proceeds of the sale are usually the same as in ordinary pledges. In other states, ownership passes to the pawnbroker at the end of a specified time. Thus, in the problem, Rogan could lose title to his typewriter if he failed to repay the loan.

WHAT OTHER PROTECTIONS DOES THE CREDITOR HAVE?

Problem: Hale, who was moving across the country, transacted to sell a valuable grandfather clock to May, who wished to pay the price in monthly payments. Hale did not want to retain possession of the clock, and May had no property of equal value to put up as security. How could Hale be assured that the debt would be paid?

In addition to his rights to repossess and resell the property in a secured debt, or to sue the debtor for breach of contract in an unsecured debt, the creditor has other means available of assuring payment in case of default. While these are usually used to assure payment of unsecured debts, they are equally available to the secured creditor who fears a deficiency or unpaid balance after sale of the security. In the problem, Hale might use one or more of the following:

(1) SURETYSHIP

If a creditor wishes assurance beyond the debtor's word that a debt will be paid, he may get a third party to assume liability. *Suretyship* is a contractual relation by which a third party becomes primarily liable for the debt, default, or obligation of another person if payment or performance becomes overdue. Three parties are involved. The *principal debtor* owes the debt or obligation. The creditor is the one to whom the obligation is owed. The *surety* is the third party who promises to be liable. Since a surety is primarily liable, he may be bound by an oral contract. If he is later required to make good his promise, he has a right to collect from the principal debtor.

> Cantor started a restaurant business and leased the building from Haggerty for three years. When Haggerty insisted upon some security, Cantor got Dart to agree to be liable for the obligation. The principal debtor was Cantor; his surety was Dart; and the creditor was Haggerty. If Dart had to pay anything, he could sue Cantor.

Since suretyship is a contractual relation, the elements of contract must be present. This means that the surety's promise must be supported by consideration, such as an agreement by the creditor to sell goods on credit to the principal debtor. In the example, the lease was consideration for the promises of both Cantor and Dart, since both of them made their promises at the same time the landlord agreed to lease the premises. Had the suretyship arisen later, the lease would be past consideration and some separate new consideration would have to be given to Dart.

Suretyship contracts are discharged in much the same way as other contracts. If the debtor pays, the surety is discharged. He is also discharged if the creditor releases the debtor or alters the obligation, as by extending the time of performance, without the surety's consent.

Pennypacker was surety on a debt owed by Hudson to Jones. When Hudson was unable to pay on the due date, Jones agreed to give him an extra month to raise the money. Because the creditor did this without notifying Pennypacker and getting his consent, Pennypacker was released from his obligation.

(2) GUARANTY

In a *guaranty,* the third party *guarantor* agrees to pay if the principal debtor fails to do so. But unlike a surety, the guarantor is only secondarily liable. This means the creditor must first sue the defaulting debtor and get a judgment that proves to be uncollectable; in a suretyship, such suit is not necessary. A guaranty contract must be in writing to be enforceable under the Statute of Frauds. (Page 173)

 To help Montag finance the building of a house, Hunt signed a guaranty agreement. Under its terms, Timber King Lumber Yard would sell up to $3,000 worth of building supplies to Montag. If Montag failed to pay, Timber King would have to sue him and get a judgment which proved to be uncollectable before pursuing Hunt.

(3) ASSIGNMENTS

Debtors may agree to settle debts by assignment (see Chapter 13) in preference to being sued in court or declaring bankruptcy.

Rush, owner of a neighborhood variety store, bought merchandise for resale on credit from several wholesalers. Business was bad, and he could not pay his bills. His creditors persuaded him to assign to them all of his rights in his store, including the merchandise, fixtures, and debts customers owed him. The creditors, in consideration for the assignment, released Rush from any further payments.

An employee will sometimes assign a portion of his wages or salary to his creditors instead of undergoing a court trial. In some states such assignments must be in writing, and consented to by the employer and the spouse of the employee.

(4) LIENS

Although most liens are created with the consent of the debtor, statutes in all states provide that a creditor may place a lien against the property of a debtor who is in default. Four common types of such liens are: (a) judgment lien, (b) mechanic's lien, (c) tax lien, and (d) garage or repairman's lien.

(a) Judgment lien. When a court orders a person to pay a sum of money, it is said to issue a judgment against him. This was discussed in Chapter 6. When properly entered in the county records, the judgment creates a *judgment lien* against all real property of the debtor located in that county. This lien usually remains until the debt is paid or the statute of limitations bars collection. Of course, the creditor will normally force a foreclosure sale of the property to collect his claim if he is not paid promptly.

 Jantzen sued Kent for injuries suffered in an auto accident caused by Kent's negligence. The court awarded a judgment to Jantzen for $75,000. He promptly recorded it, thus creating a lien against Kent's farm. Kent's automobile insurance company paid Jantzen $50,000 of the damages, the policy limit. Jantzen could have the farm sold by the sheriff unless Kent promptly paid the balance due.

(b) Mechanic's lien. Sometimes a person who has supplied materials or furnished labor for a building or land improvement is not paid. By statute he may ordinarily file a lien against the property for the value of the labor and materials. Such a lien is called a *mechanic's lien*. The holder may foreclose and have the property sold by court order.

(c) Tax lien. When a person fails to pay taxes or assessments levied against his real property, a *tax lien* may be filed against the property. It is usually several years before the property is sold by the government tax collector to satisfy the lien. Meanwhile the delinquent taxes may be paid and the lien removed.

(d) Garage or repairman's lien. The repair of automobiles and other equipment is a major business activity in our highly mechanized country. Those who do the work might be reluctant to start if they did not have the protection of the *garage or repairman's lien* against

If not paid, a repairman need not release the goods.

the personal property which they have repaired or serviced If not paid, the repairman need not release the goods.

WHAT LAWS GOVERN CONSUMER LOANS?

Problem: Bohr owed debts to several stores and was having difficulty making the payments. To protect his credit rating, he borrowed $300 from Homestead Finance Company, and paid off his other creditors. The new loan had an interest charge of 36 percent per year, and was in 12 monthly installments. What is such a loan called?

By one official definition, a *consumer loan* arises when a person (not a business firm) borrows money primarily for personal, family, household, or agricultural purposes, for which he must either pay a finance charge or repay the loan in four or more installments. It is often termed a personal loan. In the problem, Bohr made such a loan because he borrowed money for a personal need and to obtain extra time under a plan of periodic repayment to the loan company. For this privilege he had to pay a high interest charge.

Today when a person borrows money, he usually has a choice of paying the debt in one sum or in installments. Consumer loans are payable "on time," usually in weekly, biweekly, or monthly installments. They are sometimes called signature loans when they are made on the reputation of the borrower and require only his signature. In such cases, the creditor is usually satisfied if the borrower is regularly employed. Larger loans are generally secured by liens against automobiles or furniture, or repayment is guaranteed by an assignment of wages. Because they are so profitable, consumer loans are made by many financial institutions including commercial and industrial banks, credit unions, and personal finance companies.

Banks operate under banking laws, but special statutes have been enacted in most of the states to govern the operation of consumer or personal finance companies. Under these small loan laws, licensed persons or firms are permitted to make personal loans and to charge higher rates of interest than allowed under the usury laws (Page 149) when the amount loaned is not more than a certain sum, in most states less than $1,000. Many states also place a time limit on the loans, usually three years or less. The higher rates are permitted because of the greater relative expense of making and collecting small loans, and because of the added risk involved.

Small loan laws make it more difficult for "loan sharks" to take advantage of persons who find themselves in need of small amounts of money quickly. They (a) require lenders to be licensed and bonded to insure financial responsibility; (b) provide for state supervision of lenders and revocation of licenses for violation of the law; (c) set the rates of interest to be charged, and prohibit other charges; (d) require interest to be figured on the unpaid balance; (e) permit payment before the due date; (f) limit the amounts to be lent at the rates permitted; and (g) regulate advertising and other practices.

WHAT IS THE TRUTH-IN-LENDING ACT?

Problem: Markham and his bride decided to begin housekeeping in an unfurnished apartment. Easy Finance Company was among the sources they used for funds to buy the furniture they needed. Easy gave them a copy of the loan contract showing the cost only as so many dollars per installment. Could they demand further information?

Advocates of consumer rights have long maintained that consumers are not told how much credit really costs. In 1968, Congress passed the Consumer Credit Protection Act. One very important section is known as the Truth-in-Lending Act. It does not set any ceiling on what creditors can charge, but it requires full disclosure of those charges. Whether it be the interest on a consumer loan or the carrying charge on an installment purchase, the creditor must clearly state in writing the total financing charge in dollars. He must also declare the true equivalent annual interest rate.[1] Thus, 1½% a month must be stated as 18 percent a year. In the problem, Easy Finance is obliged to tell the Markhams the total cost of their loan expressed in dollars and cents, showing the actual annual interest rate.

In the first mortgages on homes, that is, a first lien on the property, the lender need not show the total dollar cost of the credit. Because

[1] The annual percentage rate need not be given, however, if: (a) the charge does not exceed $5 on a credit extension of $75 or less, or (b) the charge is $7.50 or less on a credit extension of more than $75.

these loans often last 30 years, the total interest sometimes exceeds the principal even when the rate is reasonable.

Any creditor who willfully and knowingly violates the Truth-in-Lending Act may be fined or imprisoned, or both. He must pay the debtor twice the finance charge (but no less than $100 nor more than $1,000) plus court costs and attorney fees.

USING CREDIT WISELY . . .

1. Establish a good credit rating. In granting credit, most firms consider "the four C's": Character (Does he pay his bills promptly?); Capacity (Is he steadily employed?); Capital (Does he have ample assets?); and Conditions (Is business generally sound? Is the purpose of this loan sound?).
2. In applying for credit, always be completely accurate and honest. Any immediate advantage gained by misleading a creditor will generally lead to trouble. Credit information about customers is exchanged freely by stores and other creditors and lenders.
3. When you move to a new locality, notify creditors and ask the local credit bureau to relay your credit report. Many credit bureaus throughout the country exchange information.
4. If you put up property as security for a debt, be sure it is returned or properly released when the debt is paid. Otherwise you may later have difficulty selling the property or using it as security again.
5. Pay your debts promptly. If for good reason, such as illness or unemployment, you cannot do so, discuss the problem with your creditors before the debt is due. They will usually grant extensions of time.
6. Handle your credit cards with the care you give your cash. If you lose a card, promptly notify the issuer. If you no longer want a card, cut it in two and burn it.
7. The prudent person should avoid costly small loans except in emergencies. To appreciate the wisdom of saving before you spend, instead of the opposite, determine the small loan rates charged in your state. Now compare them with the low interest rate you could have earned had you planned ahead and earned interest on a deposit of your money in a bank or other savings institution. Add the two rates. The total, in effect, is the true cost of the small loan to you.
8. Buying on credit can prove to be a very expensive habit. The cost of credit itself should always be weighed against the advantage of immediate possession. Even more important, the total cost of the item should be weighed against your future income or assets. Remember, credit is not extra money; it is only an advance of money you will have in the future. If you outspend your future income or assets, or spend it on luxuries when you need it for necessities, you will be in trouble.

YOUR LEGAL VOCABULARY

consumer loan
credit card
creditor
debtor
garage or repairman's lien
guarantor
guaranty
judgment lien
lien
mechanic's lien
pawn

pawnbroker
pledge
pledgee
pledgor
principal debtor
secured debt
surety
suretyship
tax lien
unsecured debt

1. A debt supported only by the debtor's promise and ability to pay.
2. One to whom a debt is owed.
3. Personal property deposited with a creditor as security for the payment of a debt.
4. One who agrees to become primarily liable for the debt of another if such person should fail to pay his debt when due.
5. A pledge of tangible personal property as security for a debt.
6. A loan for personal, family, household, or agricultural purposes which is repaid in installments or with a finance charge.
7. An interest in specific property of another as security for a debt.
8. A contractual relation by which one person becomes secondarily liable for the debt of another if such other defaults.
9. A lien filed against real property for unpaid-for labor or materials.
10. One who lends money at interest requiring tangible personal property as security for the money.

REMEMBER THESE HIGHLIGHTS

1. When one owes money to another, a relation of debtor and creditor exists.
2. A credit card binds cardholder and issuer in a contract relationship. In case of loss or theft of a card, the cardholder is generally liable for unauthorized purchases up to a limit of $50 unless the issuer had been previously notified.
3. A debt may be secured or unsecured. If secured, the debtor gives the creditor an interest in specified property until the obligation is performed. If unsecured, the creditor has a claim only against the general assets of the debtor.
4. When secured debts are in default and are not paid in full by proceeds from sale of the property pledged or otherwise made available as security, and when unsecured debts are not paid, the creditors may take legal action to recover from other assets of the debtor.

5. A creditor may seek and obtain greater assurance of payment of the debt through suretyship, guaranty, assignment, or a lien in appropriate cases.

6. The surety, in agreeing to answer for the debt of another, assumes a primary liability that is essentially the same as that of the debtor's. The guarantor is liable secondarily only after the creditor has exhausted his remedies against the debtor.

7. A lien gives the creditor an interest in specified property of the debtor until the debt is paid or the property is sold to pay the debt.

8. Goods or documents representing property rights may be delivered to the creditor as security for a loan. This creates a pledge and gives the creditor a lien, which he may enforce by sale of the goods or the documents in case of default. Upon performance of his obligation, the pledgor has a right to the return of his property.

9. One may borrow money through a consumer loan. Such loans are regulated by small loan laws, and are made by lenders licensed for that purpose. An interest rate substantially higher than the maximum normally permitted by usury laws is charged legally on such loans.

LAW AS PEOPLE LIVE IT

1. When Kapela opened a copying and duplicating shop, he (a) bought $600 worth of paper from Paper Products, Inc., terms, 2/10, n/30 (he could deduct a 2 percent discount if he paid within ten days, but must otherwise pay the full net price within 30 days); (b) using his bank credit card, bought a typewriter from Metro Office Machines; (c) leased a large automatic copying machine from Korox, Inc., rent payable at the end of each month of use; (d) bought three manually operated duplicating machines on a 24-month installment purchase plan from Korox which permitted the seller to repossess the machines if payments were in default; (e) borrowed $1,000 from the City Bank to meet current expenses, giving as security for repayment a U.S. Treasury bond. Which of the transactions were debtor-creditor relations? Which were unsecured? Secured?

2. De Voto loaned $5,000 to Crossland for use in his business. Crossland signed a note promising to repay the loan, with interest, over the following three years. He also signed and gave De Voto a mortgage on his home as security. De Voto claimed the mortgage gave him a lien and the right to occupy and possess the home until the loan was paid. Was he correct?

3. Tupper ran up a $50 bill for gasoline at Campus Service and was unable to pay it. Rather than be sued for the debt Tupper arranged for his employer to pay the service station $10 from his wages every two weeks. What kind of transaction was this?

4. Fite owed $1,750 for furniture he had purchased from Garfield. When Fite failed to pay, Garfield became concerned and asked Fite to get a surety to stand good for his debt. Weller readily agreed to act as surety but when Garfield asked him to pay he refused. Could Garfield compel Weller to pay for Fite's debt?

5. Moran, a contractor, agreed to build a house for Vitorio. He purchased most of the lumber and materials on open account from the High Sierra Lumber Company. As the house was being built, Weaver noticed its many modern features and offered Vitorio $22,500 cash for it. Vitorio accepted the offer on the day that it was finished. When Moran failed to pay the lumber company, it filed a mechanic's lien against the house. Could this lien be enforced by selling the house even though Weaver had already paid Vitorio in full?

6. Hiakawa, in need of funds, took his reflex camera to Jeffer's Loan Company, a licensed pawnbroker. Hiakawa received $30 and a ticket that permitted him to redeem the camera within a year upon repayment of the loan and interest. Hiakawa was unable to repay the loan until more than a year later, and the pawnbroker had, in the meantime, sold the camera. Did Hiakawa have any recourse?

7. Hubbard borrowed $300 from Open Door Finance Company, a licensed small loan company. When he learned he was being charged 36 percent interest a year, he refused to repay the loan, claiming usury. Was his claim valid?

8. Alsop gave Ryun his Bell Oil Company credit card for use on a cross-country trip by auto. Contrary to Alsop's expectations, Ryun bought not only gas and oil with the card, but also a new set of tires and a battery. Is Alsop liable to the Bell Oil Company for the full amount?

9. Astair loaned Coates $2,000 and took title to Coates' car as security for the loan. Unlike many such lenders, Astair failed to require collision insurance on the car. Later Coates was forced off the road by a hit-and-run driver and the car was totally demolished. Is Coates still liable to Astair for the amount of the loan?

10. Paar owed the Barrymore Variety Store $37.50 for goods purchased. He paid the bill with his personal check after noting the purpose on the face of the check. The check was indorsed and cashed by Barrymore and returned to Paar properly canceled. Barrymore now bills Paar again for the same obligation. What should Paar do?

LAW AS COURTS DECIDE IT

1. Swan-Finch Oil Company borrowed $500,000 from Canuck, Inc., and as security pledged 1,000 shares of stock in Olean Industries. The loan agreement said that in case of default, the lender could sell the stock, and might itself buy the shares. When the oil company failed to pay its debt, Canuck did buy the stock. However, there was no

evidence that any reasonable attempt had been made to arrive at a fair value for the stock or that it had been offered for sale to anyone else. The trustees for the oil company claimed that Canuck, as the pledgee, was obliged to conduct a bona fide sale. Do you agree? (Pettit v. Olean Industries, Inc., 266 F. 2d 833)

2. Whittemore permitted Forsythe to pawn Whittemore's jewelry with Luftig, a licensed pawnbroker, for a loan of $2,000. Luftig, believing that the jewelry belonged to her, gave Forsythe a pawn ticket made out in her name. Three months later Forsythe sold the pawn ticket to another dealer for $185. This dealer paid Luftig the $2,000, surrendered the pawn ticket, and redeemed the jewelry. A few months later Whittemore learned what had happened and sued Luftig, claiming he should have delivered the pawn ticket to her because she owned the pawned goods. Luftig contended that he was required by law to give the pawn ticket to the pawner, Forsythe, and to deliver the pawned articles to whoever tendered the amount due along with the pawn ticket. Was he? (Whittemore v. Luftig, 320 Mass. 211, 68 N.E. 2d 591)

3. Gray purchased a duplex in Florida from Temco Builders on Dec. 10, 1956. Soon thereafter Temco became bankrupt and several creditors who had furnished labor and/or materials were not paid. On Feb. 21, 1957, Penzi Tile Company filed a mechanic's lien for work completed on Nov. 19, 1956. Wright Electric Company and Dawkins Plumbing filed mechanics' liens on March 19, 1957, for work also done in November. This was an action seeking to foreclose on the property to satisfy the liens. In Florida a mechanic's lien must be filed within three months after the last material has been furnished or labor performed by the claimant. Would the court uphold the validity of the liens? (Gray v. L. M. Penzi Tile Co., 107 So. 2d 621, Florida)

4. Richardson owed an attorney a fee of $400. To secure payment of the debt, Richardson pledged a ring worth $1,250. The attorney assigned the debt and the security to Gourlie, who gave the ring to his wife. After the death of Gourlie, Richardson tendered $400 to Mrs. Gourlie and demanded the ring. Mrs. Gourlie refused, saying it had been purchased from the attorney. Richardson paid the $400 into the court and brought action against Mrs. Gourlie to recover the ring. Should he succeed? (Richardson v. Gourlie, 40 So. 2d 553, Florida)

5. When Timberlake became a distributor for the J. R. Watkins Co., his wife, Stella, agreed in writing to be surety for claims of the company against her husband up to $3,000. After Timberlake failed to pay certain amounts due, Watkins sued him and his wife as surety. She claimed she could not be liable because there was no tripartite relationship which is essential for a suretyship. She said her husband was not involved since he owed nothing to Watkins at the time she signed the suretyship agreement. Was this a valid defense? (Timberlake v. J. R. Watkins Co., 209 N.E. 2d 909, Indiana)

CHAPTER 23 Secured Transactions

1. *You consider buying a used convertible advertised in the newspaper. How can you be sure some third party doesn't have a creditor's claim against the car?*

2. *You are buying a matched set of drums on installments. Do you have the right to sell the drums before you have paid for them in full?*

3. *A color TV set is sold on an installment plan. Does the seller have the right to retake it if the buyer does not keep up the payments?*

WHAT IS A SECURED TRANSACTION?

Problem: The Hallmacks, young newlyweds, bought a matched set of living room furniture from Golden's Department Store under a 36-month conditional sales contract. When the goods were paid for in full, they would get clear title. Was this a secured transaction?

As explained in Chapter 22, a creditor holding an ordinary debt may sue the debtor if he fails to pay when due. If all goes well, he should eventually recover what is owed him out of the debtor's general assets. However, the debtor may have many ordinary creditors with similar claims, and the rights of one are no better than those of any other. To reduce his risk, a creditor may insist that specific property owned or being bought by the debtor be made security for payment of his claim. As a secured creditor, he now has priority over all other creditors as to that property which is the security. This is true even if the debtor goes into bankruptcy. If there is any default, recovery can generally be made by selling the security to someone else.

The right in property that the creditor acquires by such an agreement is termed a *security interest*. A *secured transaction* is any transaction by which a creditor is given a security interest in personal property. He may be given actual possession of the property, as in a pledge, or other property may be allowed to remain in the possession of the debtor. The property involved is called *collateral*.

In the secured transaction, the borrower or buyer on credit is still called a debtor, but the Uniform Commercial Code refers to the lender or credit seller as the *secured party*. An agreement between the parties which creates or provides for a security interest as protection for the creditor is a *security agreement*. Thus, in the problem, the Hallmacks were debtors in a secured transaction in which Golden was the secured party or creditor. He retained a security interest in the collateral until he was paid in full. If the Hallmacks failed to make a payment or otherwise breached the contract, he could repossess and resell the furniture.

Secured transactions are governed by the Uniform Commercial Code. Formerly, these transactions had many different names, including conditional or installment sales, inventory liens, pledges, assignments, and chattel mortgages. The Code has not abolished these names or made them illegal. They may still be used, but the transaction must satisfy the requirements of a secured transaction under the Code. The Code does not apply to other forms of security devices such as real estate mortgages or contracts of suretyship.

 Audiocon, Inc. sold an intercommunications system to Winkler under a conditional sales agreement. Because of high installation costs, Audiocon also took a chattel mortgage on an automatic copying machine owned by Winkler. The UCC treats various forms of security agreements in the same way. Thus, the names of the two agreements were of no consequence.

WHAT ARE THE TYPES OF SECURED TRANSACTIONS?

Problem: Hanford, who needed money to pay a life insurance premium, borrowed $95 from his brother and gave him an IOU for the amount. Was this a secured transaction?

Secured transactions in personal property may be divided into two major classes: (1) those in which the creditor has possession of the collateral, called pledges; and (2) those in which the debtor has possession of the collateral.

(1) POSSESSION OF COLLATERAL BY THE CREDITOR (PLEDGE)

The pledge is an oral or written agreement that personal property be held by the creditor as security for a debt. (Page 313) It may be property being bought by the debtor, or it may be property put up as security for a loan of money. No pledge was created by Hanford in the problem because his IOU was merely a written acknowledgment of his debt and was not regarded as property. Therefore, this was not a secured transaction.

Upon default of the debtor in a pledge, the creditor has a right to sell the property. The creditor applies the proceeds of the sale to the debt. Any surplus is returned to the debtor; any deficit remains an obligation of the debtor.

(2) POSSESSION OF COLLATERAL BY THE DEBTOR

Secured transactions in which the debtor has possession of the collateral are to his advantage because they enable him to use the goods before he has paid for them or before he has repaid his loan. Often he can work with the collateral, thus earning money to help meet his obligation when due.

Petropolis opened a food shop he called Pete's Pizza Parlor. The Standard Restaurant Supply House sold him the equipment under a security agreement, with a $5,000 down payment and a $15,000 balance to be paid over 36 months. Here the debtor would use the collateral in running his pizza parlor, thus raising the money to pay for the equipment.

It is this type of secured transaction which enables a consumer to buy an automobile, a movie camera outfit, or other expensive items on credit. He gets immediate possession and use of the goods, although the seller or finance company has the right to take them back if he fails to pay. In a similar manner, a merchant can buy his stock of goods on credit and sell them routinely to his customers. Thus, he gets money to pay his creditor-seller, who retains a security interest in his inventory, while permitting its item by item resale to individual customers.

In an auto loan, the title may be retained by the creditor for security.

DON'T BE TOO ENVIOUS. MOST OF THE NEW ONES STILL BELONG TO THE FINANCE COMPANY.

This type of secured transaction is not limited to buying on credit. It is also used in borrowing money. Suppose one wants to borrow funds from a bank. By giving the bank a security interest in his car, his promise to repay is strengthened by the car's value. If the bank approves the loan, which it is very likely to do with this added security, he has obtained the desired money and still has the use of his car.

In all secured transactions other than pledges, the security agreement must (a) be written, (b) be signed by the debtor, and (c) contain sufficient information to reasonably identify the collateral.

WHAT ARE THE CREDITOR'S PROBLEMS WHEN THE DEBTOR HAS POSSESSION?

Problem: Weaver Truck Sales sold Mann a highway tractor-trailer, accepting an older truck as the down payment and retaining a security interest in the tractor-trailer for the amount of the unpaid balance. Later Mann defaulted in his monthly installment payments. What could Weaver do?

Although the buyer or borrower benefits by keeping possession of the collateral, the creditor faces two serious problems. First, if the debtor fails to make payments as required, the creditor must get possession of the property so that he can sell it to raise money to pay off the debt. This is what happens when a finance company repossesses an automobile bought on credit. In the problem, Weaver may take possession of the tractor-trailer, provided it is able to do so without a breach of the peace. If Mann resists, Weaver will have to get a court order directing an officer to take possession.

Second, since the property is in the possession of the debtor, there is the danger that he might damage, encumber, or dispose of it in a way which would harm the creditor. The Code makes detailed provision for the protection of the creditor in such cases.

Neither of these two problems arises in the case of a pledge, for the creditor has possession of the property all of the time. His possession prevents damage to the goods and bars third persons from getting any superior rights in them through acts of the debtor.

 Hubbard has a security interest in Lydick's rotospader, kept on the latter's ranch. If Lydick needs more money, he may give another lender a second security interest subordinate to Hubbard's claim. Or he may sell his rights in the tool. Usually the security agreement would require that Lydick obtain Hubbard's permission before moving the rotospader from the location specified in the agreement. However, the UCC declares invalid any restriction on Lydick's right to sell his equity.

HOW IS COLLATERAL CLASSIFIED?

Problem: The Sofspun Yarn Makers, Inc. owned 10,000 pounds of raw wool stored in its warehouse. Needing money to meet a payroll, it applied to the New England Bank for a loan. The bank made the loan, taking a security interest in the wool. What kind of collateral is the wool?

In determining what steps must be taken to protect the creditor when the debtor has possession, all property used as collateral is classified as either tangible or intangible. Collateral which consists of tangible property is known as goods, and is further classified as (1) consumer goods, (2) farm products, (3) inventory, or (4) equipment.

(1) CONSUMER GOODS

Goods to be used primarily for personal, family, or household purposes are *consumer goods*. Usually they are durable goods which are not consumed rapidly (like food), and can thus be repossessed.

(2) FARM PRODUCTS

When the debtor is engaged in farming operations, crops, livestock, and the unmanufactured products thereof (such as ginned cotton or milk), as well as the supplies produced or used in the farming operations are *farm products*.

(3) INVENTORY

Goods held for sale or lease, raw materials and materials in process, and goods to be consumed in performing service contracts or in operating a business are classified as *inventory*.

In the problem, Sofspun was engaged in a business. The wool was classified as inventory because it was raw material of that business.

(4) EQUIPMENT

Goods (other than consumer goods, farm products, and inventory) that are to be used primarily in business, in farming, in a profession, by a government unit, or by a nonprofit organization are classified as *equipment*.

| OFFICE SUPPLY | OFFICE | AT HOME |

The classification of goods may change depending on their use.

Goods can be in only one of these four classes at a given time. Their classification may change, however, if their use changes. For example, a television set, when owned by a dealer, is inventory; when used in a remote control factory inspection system, it is equipment; when taken home by you, it becomes consumer goods.

The second major classification of collateral—*intangible property*—has no significant value in itself, but represents real value in rights to money, goods, or performance. It is generally evidenced by documents or writings, and includes the accounts receivable of a business, the rights to performance under a contract (Page 109), bills of lading (Page 232), warehouse receipts (Page 216), commercial paper (Unit VII), bonds, or stocks. (Unit XII)

HOW IS THE CREDITOR PROTECTED?

Problem: Triple-A Appliance Service sold a portable dishwasher on an installment plan to Plumley for use in his home. The seller retained a security interest and filed a financing statement. Before the machine was paid for, Plumley sold it to Garcia, a purchaser in good faith who knew nothing about Triple-A's security interest. Can Triple-A enforce against Garcia its security interest in the dishwasher?

When the creditor has possession of the collateral, as in the case of a pledge, no additional steps are required to protect him. His very possession is notice to any possible subsequent buyer or creditor of the debtor that a security interest may exist. The creditor who has possession is said to have a *perfected security interest*. However, when the debtor has the goods, it may be necessary for the creditor to file what is called a financing statement (Page 333) in order to protect, or perfect, his interest. Filing gives notice that a security interest in specific property exists. The place of filing is specified by the UCC and depends on the nature of the collateral. The UCC favors central filing, usually with the Secretary of State in the state where the transaction occurs.

If the creditor repossesses the collateral upon default, his act of taking possession perfects his security interest even though he has not filed.

When tangible property is used as collateral, the procedure for perfecting the creditor's security interest varies with the classification of the goods.

(1) CONSUMER GOODS

Filing is not required to protect the seller's purchase money security interest in consumer goods against other creditors of the buyer. *Purchase money* here refers to the unpaid balance of the price when the purchaser does not pay cash. This rule relieves retail merchants, who sell many thousands of articles on installment plans, of what would be a heavy burden in paperwork and in payment of filing fees.

Filing would be required if the consumer already owned the goods and was simply borrowing against them as security. Filing is also necessary even in purchase money deals if the seller wants protection against a third person who might innocently buy the goods for his personal, family, or household use from a dishonest debtor. Such a buyer of consumer goods acquires clear title if there is no filing. On the other hand, if there is a filing, the third person is bound by the security interest. This is true even if he has no actual knowledge of its existence.

In the problem, Garcia did not get good title because Triple-A had filed a financing statement and all persons are deemed to have constructive knowledge of this fact. Triple-A can enforce its security interest by repossessing the dishwasher. It may do so without compensating Garcia, who must pursue Plumley to get his money back.

In the case of automobiles, some states provide that instead of filing as above described, a security interest is perfected by noting its existence on the certificate of title to the automobile.

(2) FARM PRODUCTS

A security interest in farm products is perfected by filing, or by taking possession of the products upon default. This applies both as to farm products bought on credit, and those put up as security for a loan.

(3) INVENTORY

A security interest in inventory is perfected by filing, or by taking possession of the inventory upon default. This is true whether the inventory is bought on credit, or put up as security for a loan. But since inventory is purchased by businessmen for the very purpose of reselling, a person buying from such a debtor in the ordinary course of business will get clear title even though he knows of the security interest. For example, if you buy a stove at an appliance store, you get title to it free of the security interest held by the unpaid manufacturer who originally sold it to the store on credit. An exception to the above rule is made for farm products bought from a farmer.

 Schmidt's Shoe Store bought 300 pairs of shoes on credit from the Fashion-Fit Shoe Company, the manufacturer. Fashion-Fit retained a security interest and filed a financing statement covering the goods. Nevertheless, Schmidt's is free to sell the shoes to consumers for cash or on credit. The cash customer gets good title immediately. The credit customer also gets good title immediately unless the seller retains a security interest, in which case the buyer must first pay for the goods.

(4) EQUIPMENT

A security interest in equipment is perfected by filing, or by taking possession of the equipment upon default. This applies whether the equipment is bought on credit, or put up as security for a loan. If the equipment is a motor vehicle, the exception of a notation on the certificate of title may apply. Another exception is made in the case of farming equipment having a purchase price of $2,500 or less. In such case, no filing is required to perfect the seller's purchase money security interest against other future creditors. However, if the seller has not filed, a third person who buys the equipment from the debtor in ignorance of the original seller's security interest takes the property free of that interest if he makes the purchase for his own farming use.

As with goods, the procedure used in perfecting a security interest in intangible property varies with the classification of that property. A security interest in accounts receivable or contract rights which cannot be possessed in a physical sense must be perfected by filing unless the transaction does not cover a significant part of the debtor's accounts or contract rights. For documents, such as bills of lading and warehouse receipts, the creditor may either take possession or file. To perfect a security interest in instruments, such as promissory notes, stock certificates, or bonds, possession by the creditor is essential. It should be noted that there are other detailed rules governing these transactions that are not of great concern to us.

WHAT MUST BE FILED?

Problem: In return for a loan of $5,000, Hope signed and delivered to Adams a note secured by a security agreement covering his cabin cruiser. Can Adams perfect his security interest by filing a copy of the note and the agreement?

As we have seen, a financing statement must usually be filed to protect and perfect a security interest. This paper is distinct from the original contract or security agreement between the parties.

UNIFORM COMMERCIAL CODE — FINANCING STATEMENT — UCC-1

This FINANCING STATEMENT is presented to a filing officer for filing pursuant to the Uniform Commercial Code.   3 Maturity date (if any):

1 Debtor(s) (Last Name First) and address(es)	2 Secured Party(ies) and address(es)	For Filing Officer (Date, Time, Number, and Filing Office)
Hope, Phillip 116 Broad Street Jacksonville, FL	John Adams 406 Madison Avenue Jacksonville, FL	

4 This financing statement covers the following types (or items) of property:

16-Foot Cruise Master Cabin Cruiser

Check ☒ if covered: ☐ Proceeds of Collateral are also covered   ☐ Products of Collateral are also covered   No. of additional sheets presented:

Filed with..........

By: _Phillip Hope_   By: _John Adams_
Signature(s) of Debtor(s)   Signature(s) of Secured Party(ies)

Filing Officer Copy — Alphabetical   *This form of financing statement is approved by the Secretary of State.*
STANDARD FORM—UNIFORM COMMERCIAL CODE—UCC-1

Financing Statement

A *financing statement* is a brief, written notice of the existence of a security agreement. It must include (1) the names, addresses, and signatures of both the debtor and the creditor; and (2) a statement indicating the types or describing the items of collateral. If crops or property attached to buildings or land are involved, the land where such property is located must also be described. If the security agreement extends to products to be derived from the original collateral or proceeds from the resale of such collateral, that fact must be stated. The security agreement may be filed in place of the financing statement if it meets these same requirements.

Any description that reasonably identifies the property is sufficient, even though it might be necessary to ask questions to determine just what property was intended. It is not essential to have a detailed description or to include serial numbers, although confusion and disputes may often be avoided by giving greater detail than is technically required.

> A financing statement described the collateral as a "custom-built, motorized, apple-sorting machine." This description would probably suffice even though it does not give the maker's name or brand, style, serial number, capacity, dimensions, color, weight, or age. Listing additional details would, however, be helpful in avoiding confusion or possible lawsuit.

The purpose of the financing statement is to give warning to third persons who might be interested in buying the collateral, lending money against it, or extending other credit to the debtor. If careful, they will check at the appropriate government filing office for information about any financing statement involving the particular debtor with whom they propose to deal.

In the problem, the note and security agreement were signed only by Hope and therefore did not meet the requirement that a financing statement be signed by both parties. Filing a paper that does not substantially comply with the requirements or filing in a wrong office has the same effect as not filing at all. It does not perfect the security interest.

WHAT ARE THE RIGHTS OF THE DEBTOR AFTER DEFAULT?

Problem: The Coles bought a new washer-dryer combination for their home for $500. They were allowed $150 trade-in on their old washer, and agreed to pay the balance at $50 per month. The appliance dealer retained a security interest in the new machine. After making four payments, the Coles defaulted. The dealer repossessed and wanted to retain the washer-dryer in settlement of the unpaid balance. Could he do this?

Even though he is in default as to payment or performance of the security agreement, the debtor does not forfeit all of his rights. For example, he may pay all that he owes and redeem the collateral any time before the creditor has disposed of it or contracted for its disposal. Or the debtor may demand that the creditor sell the collateral and apply the proceeds of the sale to the payment of the debt if (1) the collateral is consumer goods, and (2) the debtor has paid at least 60 percent of the debt. In the problem, the Coles had paid $150 in the form of their old washing machine, and $200 in cash. Because the washer-dryer they bought was a consumer good, and since the total paid was more than 60 percent of the price, the Coles had the right to demand that the new washer-dryer be sold. They would then be entitled to the surplus or be liable for the deficit, depending upon the amount realized from the sale.

WHAT ARE THE RIGHTS OF THE CREDITOR AFTER DEFAULT?

> **Problem:** Ackerman sold Harvey a matched set of golf clubs for his personal use. Harvey was to make monthly payments, and Ackerman retained a security interest in the set. When Harvey defaulted after paying 30 percent of the purchase price, Ackerman repossessed the clubs, noted that they had hardly been used, and decided to retain them in full settlement of the balance due. Must he notify Harvey?

After default by the debtor, the secured creditor may take possession of the collateral. He may do this without legal proceedings, provided he does not breach the peace. Once he has the collateral, the creditor may sell, lease, or otherwise dispose of it. The proceeds of disposition are applied first to the reasonable expenses of retaking, holding, preparing for resale, and reselling, as well as to payment of reasonable attorneys' fees and other legal expenses incurred. What remains of the proceeds then goes to pay off the secured debt. In some cases, other creditors may have subordinate or secondary security interests in the collateral, and these are now paid off if proper claims have been made. Finally, if any surplus remains it goes to the debtor; if there is any deficiency, the debtor is obligated to pay it unless otherwise agreed.

 Waters defaulted in his contract to buy a camper for his pick-up truck from McCall's Trailer Village. McCall had retained a security interest and now repossessed the camper. The balance due on account was $200; expenses of repossession and resale were $75; the resale price was $175. Waters still owes McCall the $100 deficiency.

As an alternative to resale, the secured creditor may retain the collateral in full settlement of the debt. Written notice must be given to the debtor and, except in the case of consumer goods, to any party known by the secured creditor in possession to have a security interest in the collateral, as well as to any other party who has filed a financing statement to that effect. If the debtor or any other person entitled to receive notice objects in writing within 30 days, the creditor must dispose of the collateral in a "commercially reasonable" manner. This generally means public or private sale. If the proceeds fail to equal the balance due, including all costs of repossession and resale, the debtor is liable for the deficiency unless otherwise agreed. In the unlikely event that a surplus exists, it belongs to the debtor.

In the problem, Ackerman must notify Harvey of his intention to accept the golf clubs in full settlement of the balance due. If Harvey does not object in writing within 30 days, Ackerman becomes the owner; if Harvey objects, the clubs must be resold.

SUGGESTIONS FOR BUYER OR BORROWER IN A SECURED TRANSACTION...

1. Be sure you understand the entire security agreement before you sign it. If you have any doubts, have your lawyer, banker, or other counsel examine the form and explain it to you.
2. Never sign any contract with blank spaces to be filled in later. Draw lines in any blank spaces not used.
3. Know what any charges are for, especially service charges; ask for a detailed listing if it is not offered.
4. Find out if there are any penalties for late payment of installments or discounts for making payments before they are due.
5. Include express warranties or other promises of the seller in the written contract to avoid later difficulty of proof under the parol evidence rule.
6. Always get a copy of the agreement.

YOUR LEGAL VOCABULARY

collateral
consumer goods
equipment
farm products
financing statement
intangible property
inventory

perfected security interest
purchase money
secured party
security interest
secured transaction
security agreement

1. Goods to be used primarily for personal, family, or household purposes.
2. Right of creditor in specific property acquired by security agreement.
3. The lender or credit seller in a security agreement.
4. Condition which exists when the creditor is in possession of the collateral, or when a financing statement or equivalent is filed.
5. Goods held for sale or lease, raw materials and materials in process, and goods to be consumed in operating a business.
6. The transaction in which a creditor is given a security interest in personal property to protect him against the default of the debtor.
7. The amount of money necessary to finance the unpaid balance of the purchase price of consumer goods.
8. Any personal property in which the creditor has a security interest to protect him from default by the debtor.
9. A brief, written notice of the existence of a security agreement.
10. Property which has no significant value in itself, but which represents real value in rights to money, goods, or performance.

REMEMBER THESE HIGHLIGHTS

1. Secured transactions are of two major types: (1) those in which the creditor has possession of the collateral (called pledges), and (2) those in which the debtor has possession.
2. Property used as collateral is known as (1) goods, and (2) intangible property. Goods are classified as (a) consumer goods, (b) farm products, (c) inventory, or (d) equipment. In perfecting a security interest, proper classification is important.
3. A security interest may be perfected by the creditor having or taking possession of the collateral, or by the filing of a financing statement. An exception may apply in the case of a motor vehicle; some states provide that such a security interest is perfected by a notation on the certificate of title.
4. The financing statement identifies the parties and the goods, and gives notice that a security interest in specific property exists. Usually the financing statement and security agreement are separate writings, although the security agreement may be filed in place of the financing statement if it meets the same requirements.
5. After default, the debtor may (a) pay all he owes and redeem the collateral any time before the creditor arranges to dispose, or actually does dispose of it; or (b) under certain specified circumstances, demand that the collateral be sold and the proceeds applied to the payment of the debt.
6. Upon the debtor's default, the creditor may (a) take possession of the collateral if necessary, and sell or dispose of it; or (b) propose to retain it, in settlement of the debt.

LAW AS PEOPLE LIVE IT

1. Wheeler borrowed $50 from a friend, agreeing to repay $5 each week. Although the agreement was informal and oral, he gave the friend his high school graduation ring to hold until the debt was paid in full. Did the friend have a perfected security interest in the ring?

2. Ward, needing money for a surgical operation, mortgaged his ten-speaker stereo to the Benevolent Finance Company. Would Benevolent have a perfected security interest in the stereo at the moment it handed the money to Ward?

3. Burton, owner and operator of the Burton Bargain Buggies used car lot, purchased two color television sets on installment, one for his home and one for his showroom. How would they be classified?

4. Bolar owned a farm with a herd of 50 Holstein cows. He leased the adjoining farm and wanted to buy more cattle. How could he use both the old and the new herd to finance the increase?

5. Louden, a rancher, stored 5,000 bushels of wheat in a public elevator and borrowed money from a bank, giving a security interest in the grain. (a) How was the grain classified? (b) How would the grain be classified if Louden sold it to a milling company for processing into flour, and the miller borrowed money on the same collateral? (c) When the flour is finally made into bread and sold to a consumer, is it likely to be used as collateral?

6. Tomasoff, a public accountant, purchased an automobile from Starr Auto Sales for travel to and from clients' offices. In addition to signing a chattel mortgage, Tomasoff joined with Starr in executing a financing statement which was filed the same afternoon. Did Starr hold a perfected security interest in the automobile?

7. Colby took advantage of a special "no down payment" sale at the Camera Studio and purchased a home sound movie projector to show films of his recent African safari. Colby signed a sales contract agreeing to pay $5 each week and giving the seller the right to repossess upon default. Colby and the Camera Studio then executed a financing statement which was never filed. After making three payments, Colby sold the projector to Stedman who purchased it for home use without knowledge that it had not been paid for in full. Could the Camera Studio repossess the projector?

8. The Deep South Appliance Outlet decided to meet competition by selling for a small down payment and low weekly payments. Although most of the sale items would be classified as consumer goods in the hands of the buyers, the company always filed a financing statement. In preparing these statements, the manager insisted that each must show (a) the sales price, (b) the amount added for the carrying charge, (c) the amount subtracted for the down payment, and (d) the unpaid balance. Was the manager correct?

9. Maurer, engaged in a corn-hog farming operation, bought a used farm tractor for $2,000, executing a security agreement to pay $200 down and $75 per month to Osler. No financing statement was filed. Maurer planted the corn with the help of the tractor and quit making payments. Without mentioning the unpaid debt, he sold the tractor to Tabb for use in road construction work. Osler then notified Tabb that he held a perfected security interest in the tractor. Was he correct?
10. The Fairdeal Discount Store filed in the proper public office a security agreement signed only by the buyer. Would the filing of the agreement be effective as a financing statement and did it constitute notice to the public that the store held a security interest in the goods?

LAW AS COURTS DECIDE IT

1. The Knudsen Music Co. sold several juke boxes and equipment including "a certain selector mechanism called a Gizmo" to Jack Masterson, retaining a security interest for the unpaid balance. The agreement provided that, in case the goods were repossessed and sold for an amount insufficient to pay the costs of repossession and any unpaid balance, the buyer must pay such deficiency. The Knudsen Music Co. repossessed the machines and brought an action to collect a deficiency under the contract. Was it entitled to judgment? (Knudsen Music Co. v. Masterson, 240 P. 2d 973, Utah)
2. The Popular Finance Corporation loaned money to Willard Drane and was given a security interest in his household furniture. A financing statement was properly filed with the furniture described as follows:

   "1—2 pc. living room suite, wine
   1—5 pc. chrome dinette set, yellow
   1—3 pc. panel bedroom suite, lime oak, matt. & spgs."

   Was this description sufficient to reasonably identify the collateral? (In re Drane, 202 F. Supp. 221)
3. David, Olive, and Albert Dolbow, farmers, purchased a boat from the Wilson Boat Company, making a down payment of $500 and agreeing to pay $9,511.80 in 60 equal monthly payments of $158.53 each. A security agreement was included among the usual provisions of a promissory note. The note was assigned to Atlas Credit Corporation. After five monthly payments, the buyers defaulted and Atlas repossessed and sold the boat. The boat sold for considerably less than the unpaid balance and, in attempting to collect the deficiency, Atlas contended that the boat was properly classified as consumer goods. Was the boat consumer goods? (Atlas Credit Corp. v. Dolbow, 193 Pa. Super. 649, 165 A. 2d 704)
4. On August 22, 1962, Bohannon bought farm machinery on credit from Strange for $750, and Strange was given a security interest in the

machinery for the unpaid balance. Bohannon later borrowed money from Lonoke using the machinery as security, and Lonoke filed a financing statement on September 23, 1962. On January 16, 1963, Strange filed his financing statement. Which creditor has priority, Strange or Lonoke? (Lonoke Products Credit Association, 379 S.W. 2d 17, Arkansas)

5. The Midas Coin Co., which dealt in coins for collectors, executed a security agreement giving its bank a security interest in all United States coins in its inventory. This was done to secure payment of debts Midas owed the bank. No financing statement was filed, but the bank took possession of the coins. Later, Midas went into bankruptcy and the bankruptcy trustee claimed the coins for all the creditors. Were the coins money, hence available to all the creditors; or were they goods, and therefore collateral to be retained by the bank? (In re Midas Coin Co., 264 F. Supp. 193)

6. In July 1963, Chavez bought a guitar and amplifier for his night club work and executed a security agreement for the debt to Strevell, the seller. The security agreement was filed as a financing statement, but it contained neither the signature nor the address of the creditor, Strevell. Chavez later traded the guitar for a new model and then pawned it and the amplifier with May, a pawnbroker. When Chavez defaulted on his original debt, Strevell claimed the right to take the items away from the pawnbroker. Decide. (Strevell-Paterson Finance Co. v. May, 77 N.M. 331, 422 P. 2d 366)

UNIT SEVEN

Commercial Paper

UNIT SEVEN

We are all familiar with the usefulness of money—it replaces the need for barter, it can be kept indefinitely and used when it is needed, and it is backed by the federal government. There are also some disadvantages in using money—it can be lost or stolen, it does not give proof of payment of a debt in itself, and it is difficult for the government to adjust the supply of money to satisfy the needs of the people.

To meet these problems and others, commercial paper has been devised to represent money even though it has no value in itself. You and your parents have undoubtedly used forms of commercial paper in the past. In this unit, you will learn about the different types of commercial paper and how they can be useful to you.

We shall discuss various types of commercial paper such as checks, drafts, and notes. While commercial paper is like an ordinary contract in many ways, we shall see it also differs in some ways.

One of the advantages of commercial paper, also known as negotiable instruments, is that it circulates freely, that is, it can be easily transferred from one person to another. Of course, there are rules which govern the transfer, and there are certain rights and liabilities of holders of the instruments. We shall study these rules to be able to use commercial paper efficiently and safely.

24 Nature and Kinds

1. *You buy a hi-intensity desk lamp from a mail-order house in Chicago for $9.98. Why would you pay by check rather than send cash?*

2. *You plan to spend six months in Europe on a foreign study program. Should you take U.S. dollars or your checkbook along to pay for purchases?*

3. *If you loaned your neighbor $1,000 to be repaid perhaps a year or more in the future, you could rely on his oral promise to repay. An IOU would improve your situation. A promissory note would be better. To receive assets as security for repayment, along with the note, would be best. Why?*

WHAT IS COMMERCIAL PAPER?

Problem: After Wilver had selected supplies for the new school year in the neighborhood stationery shop, he was embarrassed to find that he had left his wallet at home. His friend, Ennis, loaned him the money in exchange for a paper on which Wilver wrote "IOU $6.75" and signed his name. Is this a commercial paper?

Commercial paper is the name the Uniform Commercial Code gives to certain properly written orders or promises to pay money which can be passed freely from one person to another. Such documents, also known as *negotiable instruments,* are widely used in personal and business transactions. They are contracts, and as such are governed by the law of contracts as well as by their own special rules.

Some instruments—checks and drafts—serve as convenient substitutes for money. Others—promissory notes—may create credit for the maker. If the seller is willing, a buyer may give his note, or promise to pay at a future time, rather than paying cash. All negotiable instruments contain a promise or order to pay money; thus, the IOU written by Wilver in the problem was not commercial paper. An *IOU* simply acknowledges in writing that a debt is owed.

The word "negotiable" refers to the transferable quality of commercial paper. Much of its unique value lies in the fact that it is more easily transferred than ordinary contract rights. Moreover, a party to whom commercial paper is transferred may acquire rights greater than those of an ordinary assignee. As we shall see, negotiable instruments can be used with great convenience and safety.

HOW DO NEGOTIABLE INSTRUMENTS DIFFER FROM ORDINARY CONTRACTS?

> **Problem:** Hyster built a concrete driveway for Baird who paid him with a promissory note for $750, payable with interest in six months. After a few weeks of normal use, however, the driveway developed large cracks, and Baird did not want to pay Hyster for the job. Hyster had already transferred the note to Lilly, an innocent third person who paid a fair price for it. Must Baird pay Lilly the value of the note when it comes due?

Negotiable instruments differ from ordinary contracts in three ways: (1) method and effects of transfer; (2) importance of writing and delivery; and (3) need for consideration.

(1) METHOD AND EFFECTS OF TRANSFER

Ordinary contracts are transferred by assignment (Chapter 13) and the assignee gets no more than the assignor has to give. Thus, if I assign to you my right to be paid $100 by a debtor, you get the $100 reduced by any valid claim the debtor may have against me.

Negotiable instruments may be assigned like ordinary contracts. But they may also be negotiated, in which case an innocent new holder gets the rights of the transferor free of most defenses the debtor could raise. If the note in the problem had been assigned, Baird could have raised the defense of breach of contract against Hyster or his assignee. But since the instrument was negotiated, that defense could not be used against Lilly, the innocent holder. Baird must pay Lilly when the note comes due. He may then take action against Hyster for breach of contract in the faulty construction of his driveway.

It is this transferable quality of commercial paper which encourages businessmen to accept it freely without elaborate investigation of all the circumstances surrounding each instrument's creation. In most cases there are no complications, but if there are, the innocent holder is protected.

Commercial paper may be negotiated in several ways. Perhaps the most common way is for the *holder* (the party who has physical possession of an instrument which is payable to his order or to bearer) to write his name on the back of the paper and deliver it to the intended recipient. When a person does this, he is said to *indorse* the instrument, and is called the *indorser*. The one to whom he transfers the instrument by indorsement is the new holder or *indorsee*. Indorsement is essential to the negotiation of an instrument payable to the order of a named person.

(2) IMPORTANCE OF WRITING AND DELIVERY

Unlike many other agreements, a negotiable instrument is not effective until it is both in writing and delivered. Delivery first takes place when the writer gives physical possession of the instrument to the new owner or his agent; in doing so, he is said to issue the paper. Delivery is then also required for each subsequent transfer.

Mogul, a busy executive, dictated into his office recording machine the full content of a valid negotiable promissory note payable to Lothrop. Until Mogul's secretary transcribes the information into written form, Mogul signs it, and it is delivered, it is not effective as a promissory note.

An exception arises when an instrument which is ready for negotiation wrongfully comes into the hands of another without delivery. For example, it may be stolen. In such a case the wrongdoer cannot enforce the paper, but an innocent third party who subsequently takes it for value may do so.

(3) NEED FOR CONSIDERATION

Lack or failure of consideration between the original parties to the instrument may be shown just as in the case of any other contract. However, if the instrument is transferred to an innocent third person who has given value for it, lack or failure of consideration between the original parties does not affect the rights of that third person.

WHAT IS A PROMISSORY NOTE?

Problem: Sewell owned the land and building in which he opened a new boat and marine supply company. Because of the nature of the business, he soon needed to raise cash to pay for inventory and meet expenses during the off-season winter months. A friend told him: "Convert your building into cash!" How could Sewell follow this advice without selling the building?

A *promissory note* is a written promise by one person to pay a certain sum of money to another. For example: "I promise to pay to the order of William Mitchell the sum of $1,000. (Signed) Stewart Riley." A promissory note is better evidence of the obligation than an oral promise, and, unlike the simple IOU, may have the advantage of negotiability.

Promissory notes initially involve only two parties: the maker, and the payee.

MAKER: One who executes or makes a promissory note is the *maker*. He promises to pay.

PAYEE: The party to whose order the promissory note is payable is the payee.

```
$ 1,000. 00                              February 26        , 19 —
             Four years and six months        after date, for value received
                                             I            promise to pay to
                        Melvin T. Mays                           , or order,
at  Pacific Coast Bank, Santa Cruz, California
the sum of  One Thousand and  00                                    dollars
                              100
with interest thereon, at the rate of Six (6)  per cent per  Annum    from date until paid.

                      Frank Seymour
                      2133 - South 10th Street
                      Santa Cruz, CA 95060
```

Promissory Note

In addition to the usual, simple promissory note, there are several other types of notes issued for special purposes. These include collateral notes, mortgage notes, judgment notes, and bonds.

When property is pledged to secure performance of a note and this fact, together with a description of the property, is recited on the face of the note, the instrument is a *collateral note*. The property pledged in collateral notes is usually in the form of documents of title, such as stocks. The note typically provides for the sale of the security if the note is not paid when due. If real estate is the security for the payment, the note is a *mortgage note*. In the problem, Sewell could borrow funds by signing a mortgage note and giving a mortgage on the land and building as security for repayment.

When a note authorizes the holder to have a court judgment entered against the maker if he fails to pay, without notice to the maker, the instrument is a *judgment note*. In states where permitted, this provision enables the holder to get judgment speedily without the formality of a court trial. However, the defendant may sometimes petition the court to open the judgment so that he may present a defense.

Bonds are long-term notes issued in return for money borrowed, usually by government agencies and private corporations. Typically, bonds are payable ten or more years after issue; some are not payable for 50 years or longer. Corporate bonds are generally secured by a mortgage or deposit of collateral. If the bonds are unsecured, other than by the general credit of the issuer, they are called *debentures*. Most government bonds are debentures.

To erect a new high school building, for example, a school district might sell 1,000 debenture bonds to as many investors, each bond having a face value of $1,000 and paying interest of 6 percent annually until maturity in 20 years. At the time of the sale, a *trust agreement* is prepared, in which a trustee is named to represent all the bond holders in dealings with the school district. The trustee brings any legal action which may prove necessary to obtain payment of the bonds. Also, when property is pledged as security, the trustee takes possession on behalf of all bond holders.

WHAT IS A CERTIFICATE OF DEPOSIT?

Problem: Texarkana Petroleum Co. was accumulating earnings in anticipation of the expansion of its refinery, planned to start in about a year. The company treasurer wanted to earn some interest on the money, yet be sure it would be available to pay for building costs after 12 months. What should he do?

A *certificate of deposit* is a written acknowledgement by a bank of receipt of money, with a promise to repay it. It is payable

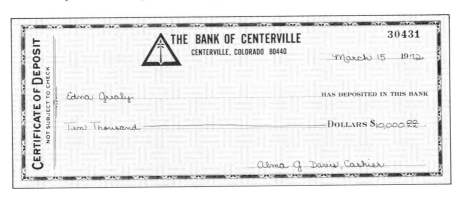

Certificate of Deposit

with interest sometime in the future, usually after a year. Both business firms and individuals use C.D.'s, as these instruments are called, when they have money they will not need for some length of time. In the problem, the Texarkana treasurer should buy certificates of deposit which mature in a year. If the money is needed sooner, he can negotiate the C.D.'s to others for cash.

The bank is prohibited by federal law from paying out the deposit in whole or in part before maturity. Thus, it is free to lend the funds to others for the full period and can afford to pay interest on the C.D. from its own earnings. Contrast this to ordinary checking accounts, on which no interest is earned and from which all funds can be withdrawn on demand. Ordinary savings accounts earn interest if the money is left on deposit, and the bank may lend the money to others. However, banks normally permit the withdrawal of such savings at any time upon presentation of the deposit book.

WHAT ARE DRAFTS AND CHECKS?

Problem: McCullough had closed his checking account at the Continental Divide National Bank but still had a checkbook with unused checks. He was deeply in debt and desperate. Realizing that only the bank knew he had closed the account, he wrote and cashed or got merchandise for seven checks from local stores. Then he left town with no intent to return or to reopen the account. Can the storeowners who took the checks collect from the bank?

A *draft* is a written order by which one party directs another to pay a certain sum of money to a third party. For example: "To Frederick Lanman. Pay to the order of Sam Baker the sum of $500. (Signed) Martin Miller."

$500.00   Nashville, Tennessee   January 15, 1972

To Frederick Lanman
Pay to the order of Sam Baker
the sum of Five hundred 00/100 ———————————————— dollars

                        Martin Miller

Draft

Regular drafts are sometimes described in terms of the time of payment. If the draft is payable at sight or on demand—that is, when it is presented to the drawee by the holder—it is a *sight draft*. The drawee may pay immediately if he is willing to honor the draft. The example on page 348 is a sight draft.

If a draft is payable at a specified time, or at the end of a specified period after sight or after the date of the draft, it is a *time draft*. When it is payable a number of days or months after sight, the draft must be presented to the drawee for acceptance (the drawee's promise to pay the draft when due) in order to start the running of the specified time. When the draft is payable a number of days or months after date, the time starts running immediately from the date of the instrument.

A *check* is a special form of draft by which a depositor directs his bank to pay money to a third party.

The usual purpose of issuing a check is to pay a bill or to withdraw money from the bank. A draft, on the other hand, is usually used to collect a bill. Both checks and drafts initially involve three parties: the drawer, the drawee, and the payee.

DRAWER: One who executes or draws the check or draft is the *drawer*. He orders that payment be made.

DRAWEE: The party directed to pay the draft or check is the *drawee*. In the case of a check, the bank is the drawee.

PAYEE: The party to whose order the draft or check is made payable is the *payee*.

A check differs from a draft in these ways:

(1) A BANK IS ALWAYS THE DRAWEE OF A CHECK

RB&T
RICHMOND BANK AND TRUST CO.

No.
90-205
1211

May 17 19 —

Pay to the Order of *Robin Wayne* $ *75 00*

Twenty-five and 00/100 Dollars

Bruce Grayson

⑈1211⑈0205⑈ ⑈65⑈855⑈038⑈

Check

(2) A CHECK IS PROPERLY DRAWN AGAINST FUNDS THE DRAWER IS SUPPOSED TO HAVE ON DEPOSIT IN THE BANK

The right to issue checks arises from a contract between the bank and a person who deposits funds in the bank for that purpose. The bank is in debt to the depositor for the amount, and it agrees to honor properly drawn checks as long as sufficient funds remain on deposit to pay them. If a party deliberately issues a check and knows no funds will be available when it is presented at the bank, he is guilty of a crime. In the problem on page 348, McCullough acted criminally. His checks will not be honored by the bank. The store owners must pursue McCullough or take the loss.

(3) A CHECK IS ALWAYS PAYABLE ON DEMAND

Because checks are convenient and safe, they are widely used instead of coin or currency to pay debts both in person and through the mails. If a check is lost or stolen, the drawee bank can be notified to *stop payment*—that is, not to cash the check if it is

Checks are both convenient and safe.

YOU WON'T GET ANY MONEY FROM ME.

I CARRY ONLY CHECKS.

presented for payment. Then a duplicate can be safely issued. If the check is made payable to the order of the intended payee, no one else may legitimately cash it. Also, unlike money, a delivered check which is accidentally destroyed or lost can be replaced by the drawer. The drawer might require the payee to post a bond to assure reimbursement if the original check is in fact presented later by some innocent indorsee, who collects.

 LaPerna owed Bailey Auto Service $47.54 for two new tires, and mailed a check for the amount. When Bailey billed him again, LaPerna phoned and learned that his check never arrived. He can tell his bank to stop payment on the first check, and then he can issue a replacement.

WHAT ARE THE SPECIAL DRAFTS AND CHECKS?

Problem: Vasquez, of Seattle, ordered a new steam table for his Taco Shoppe. The manufacturer, located in St. Paul, Minnesota, wanted cash or equivalent before he shipped. How should Vasquez pay for his purchase?

Various forms of drafts and checks have been devised for special purposes. They include:

(1) CERTIFIED CHECKS

A person to whom a personal check is tendered may fear that it will not be paid because of insufficient funds in the bank account of the drawer. He may therefore demand a certified check. A *certified check* is a personal check drawn on a bank by a depositor, but accepted by the bank in advance of payment. The bank sets aside sufficient money from the drawer's account to pay the check when it is presented, and it certifies this fact by appropriate notation, usually on the face of the check. Vasquez, in the problem, could have used a certified check.

(2) CASHIERS' CHECKS

A check that a bank draws on its own funds is a *cashier's check*. Such checks are used by banks to pay their own obligations. They may also be used by persons who wish to send remittances but who have no personal checking account, or for some reason do not wish to use their personal checks. A cashier's check would have been a satisfactory way for Vasquez to pay for his purchase.

Cashier's Check

(3) BANK DRAFTS

A draft drawn by a bank on funds that it has on deposit with another bank is a *bank draft*. Actually a bank draft is a check drawn by a bank on another bank. Banks use these drafts in their own transactions. Sometimes, when a person or a business firm wishes to send a sizable sum to someone who may not wish to accept an ordinary check, he may buy a bank draft from a bank. This would be another possibility open to Vasquez.

(4) MONEY ORDERS

Money orders are issued by post offices, banks, and express and telegraph companies for use in transferring money or making payments over great distances, usually by mail. They serve the same purpose as checks, whether or not they are issued by banks. A money order might have been used by Vasquez.

(5) TRAVELERS' CHECKS

Hotelmen and retailers around the world understandably prefer to take checks only from persons they know and can trust. At the same time, travelers are reluctant to carry cash on journeys. To meet the needs of both the traveler and the merchant who serves him, *travelers' checks* have been devised. Travelers' checks are drafts drawn by a reliable financial organization on itself or its agent, and may be purchased by travelers from banks and other institutions. At the time they are purchased, the buyer signs his name on each check. When he wishes to cash one of the checks, perhaps thousands of miles from home in a place where he is a stranger, he writes in the name of the payee and again signs his name on the check in the presence of the payee who can compare the signatures. The payee is usually willing to take the travelers' check because he knows and trusts the drawee bank or issuing company. Thereafter, the payee may transfer the travelers' check in the same manner as other checks.

HOW ARE NEGOTIABLE INSTRUMENTS DISCHARGED?

Problem: Buckbee held a note for $500 signed by Lomas as maker. On the due date, Lomas offered Buckbee a truckload of watermelons worth more than $500 as payment instead of cash. Must Buckbee accept, and if he does, is the instrument discharged?

Negotiable instruments are ordinarily discharged by payment, but there are several other methods as well.

(1) DISCHARGE BY PAYMENT

A note is usually paid by the maker; a check is usually paid by the bank on which it is drawn; and a draft is usually paid by the drawee. The terms of the instrument must call for payment in money, and payment must be made in money unless the holder is willing to accept something else. For instance, he may voluntarily take another negotiable instrument in payment, or he may accept other kinds of property. In the problem, Lomas could not compel Buckbee to accept the load of watermelons in payment for the note even though their value was greater than the $500 due. But if Buckbee did accept such substitute payment, the instrument would be discharged.

The one paying a negotiable instrument should obtain possession of it at the time payment is made. If the holder keeps the instrument, he might falsely claim he has not been paid and demand a second payment. Or he might be able to negotiate it wrongfully to an innocent third party who then could be entitled to payment. If the instrument is paid in part, an appropriate notation should be made on the paper showing this fact.

 Nettleton was the maker of a note payable to Landa and due the following December. In June, Landa was hard-pressed for cash and agreed to accept 75 percent of the face value in full settlement. Nettleton paid and Landa said he would destroy the note when he returned to his office. Instead, he negotiated it to Allyn, an innocent party who paid for it in good faith. In December, Nettleton would be obliged to pay Allyn. His relief, if any, is in an action against Landa.

If the bank or other party who is obligated to pay the negotiable instrument when it is due fails or refuses to do so, the instrument is said to be *dishonored*. Sometimes the holder may then look to one or more other parties for payment.

(2) DISCHARGE BY CANCELLATION

A negotiable instrument is also discharged by cancellation. *Cancellation* consists of any act, such as intentional destruction of the instrument, that indicates an intention to cancel the obligation.

 To help Daly meet his expenses while in college, his uncle, Corcoran, loaned him $1,500 and took a promissory note as evidence of the debt. On graduation day, Corcoran congratulated Daly, put a match to the note, and used the burning paper to light 50¢ cigars for both of them.

(3) DISCHARGE BY ALTERATION

A fraudulent and material alteration of an instrument by the holder will discharge the obligation of all prior parties. Thus, if a holder changed the rate of interest payable on a note from 7 percent to 9 percent, neither the maker nor any persons who have previously indorsed it would be obligated to pay the note. The maker or drawer is, however, still bound to make payment in accordance with the original terms if the instrument later comes into the hands of an innocent holder.

 Kaiser had issued a note to Balbo for $1,000 with interest at 7 percent. Balbo changed the rate to 10 percent and negotiated the instrument to Ormond, an innocent purchaser. Ormond could collect $1,000 with only 7 percent interest.

COMMERCIAL PAPER CAN BE AS GOOD AS MONEY, IF YOU . . .

1. Learn now how to use it properly.
2. Prepare and sign it with the realization that it may have significant value; handle it with appropriate care.
3. Use care in accepting commercial paper. Although proper negotiation protects an innocent new holder against certain defenses of the debtor, there is no absolute guarantee of payment.
4. Make certain that the other party's credit is good when you lend money in exchange for a note or bond. Assure yourself that he will repay when due and, if practicable, get some security for repayment, such as collateral or a mortgage.
5. Do not normally accumulate large surplus balances in a checking account where they earn no interest for you. Consider transferring such surplus funds into certificates of deposit, or place them in a savings account.
6. Use the stop payment feature on your checking account to keep your bank from paying out on lost or stolen checks.
7. Consider using a certified check, cashier's check, or a money order if a creditor is hesitant about accepting your regular check.
8. Carry large sums of money in the form of travelers' checks when traveling far from home.
9. Be sure that it is noted on the paper when you make a partial payment of a negotiable instrument such as a note. If you pay in full, have it marked paid and get the instrument.
10. Do not make material alterations in commercial paper you hold. Even if the debtor consents, it is best to get a new instrument.

YOUR LEGAL VOCABULARY

bank draft
bond
cancellation
cashier's check
certificate of deposit
certified check
check
collateral note
commercial paper
debenture
dishonor
draft
drawee
drawer
holder
indorse

indorsee
indorser
IOU
judgment note
maker
money order
mortgage note
negotiable instrument
payee
promissory note
sight draft
stop payment
time draft
travelers' check
trust agreement

1. The party directed by the drawer to pay a draft or check.
2. A written promise by one person to pay a certain sum of money to a third party.
3. A special form of draft by which a depositor orders his bank to pay money to a third party.
4. A note for which property such as another note, stocks, or bonds is pledged as security.
5. The party to whose order a negotiable instrument is payable.
6. A special kind of draft drawn by a reliable financial organization on itself, and signed by the purchaser at the time of purchase and again at the time of cashing.
7. One who executes a promissory note.
8. A draft payable on demand, or when it is presented to the drawee by the holder.
9. One who signs his name on the back of a negotiable instrument.
10. One who has physical possession of a negotiable instrument which is payable to him or his order.

REMEMBER THESE HIGHLIGHTS

1. Commercial paper consists of four important types of negotiable instruments: promissory notes, certificates of deposit, drafts, and checks.
2. To transfer a negotiable instrument, the holder may assign it as he would an ordinary contract, or he may negotiate it. Negotiation to an innocent third party cuts off defenses against payment which might be raised if the instrument were an ordinary contract.
3. Notes and certificates of deposit are promises to pay money. Two parties are initially involved: the maker who promises to pay, and the payee who collects.

4. Drafts and checks are orders directing others to pay money. Three parties are initially involved: the drawer who gives the order to pay, the drawee who gets the order, and the payee who collects.

5. A check differs from a draft in that (a) a bank is always the drawee of a check, (b) the check is drawn against funds the drawer has on deposit in the bank, and (c) a check is always payable on demand.

6. Various forms of checks and drafts have been devised for special purposes. They include: certified checks, cashiers' checks, bank drafts, money orders, and travelers' checks.

7. When a holder signs his name on the back of a negotiable instrument before transferring it to someone else, he is said to indorse the instrument.

8. A negotiable instrument is dishonored when the party who is obligated to pay it fails or refuses to do so.

9. Negotiable instruments are usually routinely discharged by payment when due. However, they may also be discharged by cancellation, alteration, and other methods.

LAW AS PEOPLE LIVE IT

1. Ormont imported a large supply of natural hair women's wigs from France and sold them to Sikorsky. Sikorsky paid in part with a note payable to the order of Ormont in six months with interest at 6 percent. To get cash sooner, Ormont indorsed and negotiated the note to the order of Hardee. Identify the parties.

2. Crocker prepares an instrument which looks like a proper note in all respects, but is unique in that in it he promises to pay to the order of Crutcher, the payee, a five-lb. bar of pure silver. Is it a negotiable instrument?

3. You are executor of James Hyatt's estate. Among his possessions you find a paper which reads, "This will acknowledge my legal duty to pay James Hyatt $5,000." It is dated and signed by Farrington. What is the nature of this instrument?

4. Gelman executed the following instrument. Identify the instrument and the parties.

> Green Bay, Wisconsin
> June 1, 1972
>
> On September 1, 1972, I promise to pay to the order of Barney Bibb one thousand dollars ($1,000).
>
> _Roscoe Gelman_
> Roscoe Gelman

---

5. Comberi executed the following instrument. Identify the instrument and the parties.

Kansas City, Kansas
January 15, 1972

Thirty days after date pay to the order of Dorthea Mears the sum of fifteen hundred dollars ($1,500) with interest at the rate of 5% per annum.

To: Otis Beecham
      1812 Arden Way
      Tulsa, OK 74103

Angelo Comberi
Angelo Comberi

---

6. Identify the following instrument and the parties.

San Francisco

SECOND BANK

No.

11-13
1210

Nov 15 _____ 19 —

Pay to the
Order of *G'wat Yong Ming* _____ $ *300.00*

Three hundred & 00/100 _____ Dollars

Tom Fong

⑆1210⑈0013⑆ ⑈456⑈2222⑈

---

7. Hunter wrote a check for $121.75 to Starflash Specialties, a mail-order house. After two months had passed with no word from Starflash, Hunter assumed the check had been lost in the mail. He drew a duplicate check and promptly stopped payment on the first. Starflash in fact received both checks. Because of clerical confusion, it deposited both instruments and Hunter's bank honored both. The bank now insists that Hunter should seek recovery from Starflash. Is this right?

8. A grease fire spread from the kitchen of Luboff's Caterers and destroyed the building and its contents. Included were ten checks received that day from customers, for a total value of $715.87. May Luboff recover under his fire insurance policy for these checks?

9. The Sprawlings Sporting Goods Corporation, like most business firms, used credit extensively. What type of commercial paper will it probably use for each of the following situations?

    (a) to borrow $25,000 from a local bank for three months to buy inventory for summer sales.

    (b) to borrow $100,000 from a large Cleveland bank for three years, to be used as working capital.

    (c) to borrow $500,000 from a Boston insurance company to pay for a new store building.

(d) to borrow $3,000,000 for 25 years from the general public for expansion of operations in Canada and Latin America.

10. Martine wanted to order some 2x3 foot poster size photo blow-ups as advertised by Glamorous You, Inc. of Los Angeles, in a national magazine. The ad expressly said "send no cash or personal checks. No C.O.D. orders accepted." How should Martine pay?

LAW AS COURTS DECIDE IT

1. Northside Building & Investment Company, Inc. executed a note in the face amount of $4,800 payable to the order of Citizen's Bank. The note was later simply delivered to the Finance Company of America as collateral for a loan. In a dispute over whether a certain defense would be good against the Finance Company, it was necessary to decide whether the instrument had been negotiated. Negotiation would make the Finance Company an innocent holder with special rights. What is your opinion? (Northside Building & Investment Co., Inc. v. Finance Co. of America, 119 Ga. App. 131, 166 S.E. 2d 608)

2. The New Britain Bank held a note signed by Horgan as maker. The bank sent a notice to Horgan apparently increasing the interest rate by ½ % for the amount calculated to be due for three successive dates. No evidence was offered to show fraudulent intent. Horgan refused to pay the note, claiming it had been discharged by alteration. Do you agree? (New Britain National Bank v. Baugh, 31 A.D. 2d 898, 297 N.Y.S. 2d 872)

3. Blayton was president of a trucking company which was behind on rental payments for equipment leased from Mason. On Nov. 4, when Mason threatened to sue, Blayton gave his personal check for $3,000 to cover the amount due, and asked him to withhold action until Nov. 6, when the company would be able to pay. On Nov. 6, the company failed to pay and Mason deposited Blayton's check. It was dishonored because Blayton had stopped payment, claiming there was no contract in writing, as required by the Statute of Frauds, to bind him. (a) Was the check a sufficient contract? (b) Was Mason justified in stopping payment? (Mason v. Blayton, 119 Ga. App. 203, 166 S.E. 2d 601)

4. Hewitt was hit by a truck driven by Messer. Later, Messer signed and delivered his promissory note to Miss Hewitt in exchange for her promise not to sue for personal injuries. She kept her promise and did not sue. In an action to collect the note, Messer contended that it was unenforceable because there was no consideration. Was he correct? (Messer v. Hewitt, 98 Ga. App. 498, 106 S.E. 2d 61)

5. Burnett delivered his $90.20 check to Windle, who wrongfully raised the check to read $14,000. If Windle sues on this check, how much can he recover? (Kansas Bankers Surety Co. v. Ford County State Bank, 184 Kans. 529, 338 P. 2d 309)

CHAPTER 25   Form and Content

1. *The figures in an otherwise normal note read $50,000, but the words state "Five hundred and no/100 dollars." Is it a valid negotiable instrument, and if so, for how much?*

2. *To settle a debt owed to Hoffman, a 90-year-old eccentric recluse, the young Neilson gave a promissory note for $10,000 payable in the year 2001, with interest. Neilson assumed he'd never have to pay. Is he correct?*

3. *As a publicity stunt, a steel company held a contest and gave a prize of $1,000 in the form of a check. The check had all the necessary writing engraved in large lettering on a thousand-pound bar of stainless steel. Was the check a valid negotiable instrument?*

WHAT IS A NEGOTIABLE INSTRUMENT?

Problem: Brooks Blettner wrote the following memo, and planned to give it to his nephew, Robert Scholl, as a Christmas surprise:

> I promise you a new car of your choice costing no more than $4,000 when you graduate from high school.
>
> December 25, 1972   *Brooks Blettner*

Is this a negotiable instrument?

To be negotiable, an instrument must be:

(1) in writing and signed by the maker or drawer;
(2) an unconditional promise or order;
(3) payable in a sum certain in money;
(4) payable on demand, or at a definite time; and
(5) payable to bearer or to someone's order.

The memo in the problem is not a negotiable instrument. Although it is in writing and signed by the maker, it fails to meet other requirements. It is not an unconditional promise because it is payable only if Robert Scholl graduates from high school. Neither does it promise a sum certain although it names a maximum amount. It is not payable on demand or at a definite time—Robert just might not graduate at all. Nor is it payable to bearer or to the order of a named person. At most, the writing merely shows an intention to make a conditional gift.

WHAT ARE THE REQUIREMENTS FOR NEGOTIABILITY?

> **Problem:** The Delta Fruit Farm, Inc. employed large numbers of high school students as pickers during the apple harvest. To save time in preparing payroll checks, G. Keith Silex, the secretary-treasurer, signed all of them with a rubber stamp which read: "Delta Fruit Farms, Inc., by G. Keith Silex, Secretary-treasurer." Were the checks validly signed?

(1) WRITING AND SIGNATURE

Commercial paper must be in writing; thus, it is subject to the parol evidence rule. (Page 176) It must also be signed by the maker or drawer with the intent that it create a legal obligation.

The writing may be done entirely in ink or on a typewriter, or it may be a printed form with the terms written or typed in. Pencil may be used but the impression is not durable and may invite alteration. Legally, any medium may be used for surface and inscription provided the end result is recognizable as a writing. If there is a conflict between provisions written by hand and those typed or printed, the handwriting prevails (Page 177) on the theory that it is more likely to reflect the true intention of the party. Similarly, typewritten terms prevail over printed.

The San Francisco Bank

No. 11-57
1210

April 12 19___

Pay to the Order of _Henry Schnepp_ $ 75.50/XX

Seven and 50/100 _____ Dollars

Chr. DeKalb

⑆ 1210⑆0057⑈ ⑆ 1423⑆0210⑈

If the San Francisco Bank honored the above check at all, it would pay $7.50 because the amount expressed in words prevails over the amount in figures. When there is a large discrepancy, the bank is likely to consult the drawer of the check before paying.

Any medium can be used for surface and inscription if the end result is recognizable.

The form of the signature is generally immaterial as long as the person intends it to be his complete signature on the instrument. Thus, the maker or drawer may sign his name by means of a rubber stamp, as in the problem. This may not be wise, however, since such signatures can too easily be duplicated and used by a dishonest person. On the other hand, business firms and government agencies which periodically prepare checks for thousands of payees commonly use printed signatures; to do the job by hand would be unduly burdensome. Special printing and watermarked paper, as well as perforation of the paper where critical items (amount, signature) appear, tend to discourage misuse by unauthorized persons. Moreover, the risk of loss usually rests on the party who honors the check if the drawer's or indorser's signature is in fact a forgery.

A trade or assumed name is effective if it is intended as one's signature. One person may legitimately sign another person's name if he is authorized to do so. (Page 175) Or an individual who cannot write because he is illiterate or crippled may sign his "mark," such as an "X." It is commonly required that another party place the name of the signer next to the mark, and also sign as witness.

The place on the instrument where the signature appears is generally immaterial. Although the lower right-hand corner is the usual place, a signature in the body or elsewhere is sufficient as long as the signer's status as maker or drawer is clear.

 Ben Block executed the following instrument in his own handwriting:

"On demand, Ben Block promises to pay to the order of Grant Tyson the sum of three hundred and seventy-five dollars ($375)."

Block's signature included at the beginning is valid and the instrument is a negotiable note.

(2) UNCONDITIONAL PROMISE OR ORDER TO PAY

Problem: Lucretia Houston inherited an apartment building but found it difficult to insist that her tenants pay their rent when due. One tenant, Van Bularney, was six months behind in his rent when Miss Houston gave Mike Pershing an instrument reading as follows:

"To Van Bularney. Dear Mr. Bularney, Pay to Mike Pershing or his order six hundred dollars on sight. Please. Sorry about this."

It was properly signed "Lucretia Houston" and was dated. Was this a draft?

A negotiable instrument must contain a promise, if it is a note, or an order, if it is a draft or check. No particular words are necessary. In all cases, however, payment must be promised or ordered unconditionally; that is, the obligation must be absolute. A note or writing which simply acknowledges a debt—a letter or a simple IOU, for example—is not a promise to pay. Neither do words which merely make a request qualify as an order to pay. However, the use of courteous language and words like "please" with an otherwise unconditional order do not change its effect. The gentle language of Miss Houston in the problem did not prevent the instrument from being a draft.

A promise or order to pay only upon the happening of a certain event, out of a certain fund, or "subject to" any other agreement, is conditional and not negotiable.

 When Brownell gave Martone a note payable out of the first month's net proceeds from the sale of petroleum to be produced at a wildcat oil well then being drilled, the instrument was not negotiable. Oil might never flow from that well.

However, if the fund is indicated merely for convenience and the general credit of the drawer is committed to the payment, the instrument is negotiable. This would be the case when a draft tells a bank to charge a particular account only as a matter of convenience in record keeping.

Sources of payment are not excluded by the reference to the account. Likewise, commercial paper is negotiable even though it states its consideration or says that the promise or order is made or the instrument matures in accordance with a stated transaction.

 J. Frank Vickers drew a check on the Tamiami State Bank payable to Amos Jones for $3,500. On the face of the instrument Vickers wrote "Payment for brick-work at 761 San Ramon Way, as per agreement of 2/12/72." The check is negotiable.

(3) SUM CERTAIN IN MONEY

Problem: In executing a promissory note, Mirlova promised to pay to the order of Feldmarshall in Chicago, Illinois, "10,000 Russian rubles." Did the designation of payment in a foreign currency render the note nonnegotiable?

A negotiable instrument must call for the payment of a sum certain in money. *Money,* for this purpose, is any medium of exchange which is acceptable as currency either in the United States or in any foreign country at the time the instrument is made. Thus, an instrument collectible in the United States but with the amount expressed in Russian rubles—or any other foreign currency—is negotiable. Normally a conversion is simply made to the number of American dollars which the designated number of foreign currency units will purchase on the day the instrument is payable. If the instrument specifies a foreign currency as the medium of payment, the instrument is payable in that currency.

The promise or order to pay money must not be linked with a promise or order to do anything in addition to the payment of money. An instrument payable in a designated number of bales of cotton would be a valuable contract but not a negotiable instrument. An instrument requiring the payment of money along with the cotton, or giving the payee an option of the money or the cotton, would also be nonnegotiable.

Certain provisions may be included in the instrument without destroying its negotiable character. In fact, they usually tend to make the instrument more appealing to prospective holders. Thus, a sum of money is not considered uncertain if the instrument specifies payment (a) with interest or discount; (b) by installment, per-haps with an *acceleration clause* which makes the entire balance due and payable if any installment is missed; (c) with bank charges for exchanging one national currency into another; or (d) with costs of collection and reasonable attorney's fees in case the instrument is not paid at maturity. The last provision is especially important in notes for comparatively small amounts, because the party liable might otherwise delay or refuse payment on the assumption that the holder couldn't afford to hire an attorney to collect so little money.

(4) PAYABLE ON DEMAND OR AT A DEFINITE TIME

> **Problem:** Vila issued a note to his niece which read as follows: "I promise to pay Toni Tomar or her order $1,000 on her wedding day." It was signed "Gregory Vila" and dated. Was it negotiable?

A negotiable instrument must be payable on demand or at a definite time. In other words, it must be payable at a time certain to arrive, and not at a time that depends upon an event that may or may not occur. It is possible that someday a man will land on Mars, but a note payable at such time would not be negotiable. It is probable that Toni, in the problem, will marry someday, but because she might not the note is not negotiable. Even if and when she does marry, the note remains nonnegotiable because its character is determined at the time it is issued and cannot be changed by later events.

An instrument is *payable on demand* (a) if it is expressly made payable "on demand," "at sight," or "on presentation"; or (b) if no time of payment is specified, as in the case of a check.

| $ 1,250.00 | San Antonio, Texas | March, 10 | 19 72 |

On demand ——————————————————————— Pay to the

order of ___Volney Fentress___

Twelve hundred fifty and no/100 ——————————— Dollars

To: Stewart Swigert   ACME AUTO REBUILDERS

 43 Bubbling Well Lane By: Tilden Pigott

 San Antonio, Texas 78209

Instrument Payable on Demand

An instrument is *payable at a definite time* when it is payable:

(a) on a fixed date, or on or before a fixed date—e.g., "On February 1, 1973," or "On or before February 1, 1973"; or

(b) at a fixed period after a stated date or after sight—e.g., "30 days after Labor Day, 1974," or "90 days after sight"; or

An acceleration clause may make the entire balance due if any installment is missed.

(c) at a definite time subject to acceleration, e.g., "On October 1, 1985, but if any annual interest payment is not made when due, then at the option of the holder, the principal is due and payable at the time of such default."

 Flagstead was holder of a note payable to him by Varetta ten years after date. Interest was fixed at a rate of 6½ percent per annum and was due on January 15 and June 15; if any interest was not paid when due, the entire principal became due. When Varetta failed to pay the interest after two years, Flagstead was entitled to the face amount of the note.

An instrument is not payable at a definite time if payable at a fixed time after the death of a particular individual or the happening of any other certain-to-happen event where the time of the event is unknown.

(5) PAYABLE TO ORDER OR TO BEARER

Problem: Corey signed and dated a note which read: "I promise to pay to Margaret Tash five hundred dollars ($500) on demand." Was the instrument negotiable?

To be negotiable an instrument must contain *words of negotiability;* that is, it must be made payable to order or bearer.

An instrument is *payable to bearer* (or *bearer paper*) when payable:

(a) to "bearer," or "the order of bearer"; or
(b) to "(a specified party) or bearer"; or
(c) to "cash," or "the order of cash," or any other designation such as "payroll" or "expenses" which does not identify a specific payee.[1]

---

[1] Although not of immediate concern here, an instrument also becomes bearer paper when the last or the only indorsement is in blank.

An instrument is *payable to order* (or *order paper*) when it is payable to the order of a specified party. This means that it is payable to the particular party or to anyone to whom he orders it paid. It may read "Pay to the order of Roger Reneker" or "Pay to Roger Reneker or order." If the instrument reads only "Pay to Roger Reneker," it is not negotiable. Thus, the note signed by Corey in the problem was not negotiable.

Order paper may be payable to the order of one person, two or more persons jointly, or one of several persons. Thus, a check made payable "to the order of Sam or Jane Speidel" could be cashed by either of them, while one made payable "to the order of Sam and Jane Speidel" would require the indorsement of both. An order instrument may be made payable to the holder of a certain position or office; it may say, for example, "Pay to the order of the Principal of Central High School." It may also be properly made payable to an estate (e.g., of a deceased person), a trust (e.g., for a minor), or a fund (e.g., the Community Chest). In such cases, the paper is actually deemed to be payable to the order of the representative of the estate, trust, or fund.

WHAT PROVISIONS ARE IMMATERIAL?

Problem: Is the following instrument negotiable?

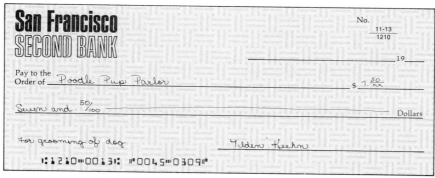

An instrument need not be dated to be negotiable. In the absence of a date, the instrument is regarded as having the date of the day on which it is made and delivered to the payee. If the date is essential to the meaning of the instrument—for example, a draft payable "thirty days after date"—any holder who knows the true date may write it in, making the instrument negotiable. The instrument may be *antedated* (using an earlier date) or *postdated* (using a later date) provided this is not done to defraud.

The instrument need not state the value given or the fact that any value has been given for it, although it is not uncommon to find such words as "for value received" included. On the other hand, although a statement identifying the consideration given for the instrument—as in the problem—has no effect on its negotiability, it may be useful because the canceled check can then serve as a receipt. A draft may contain a provision that the payee, by cashing or indorsing, acknowledges full satisfaction of an obligation of the drawer.

An instrument may state that there is collateral for the obligation. A provision in the instrument which provides for sale of any collateral or security pledged to assure performance of the instrument does not destroy its negotiability; indeed, it may tend to make the paper more acceptable because the holder feels more secure.

WATCH YOUR FORM . . .

1. Form is sometimes as important as substance or content in commercial paper. The rules are precise and strict; follow them.
2. When preparing a negotiable instrument, it is generally wise to:
   (a) Use ink, not pencil, for all writing;
   (b) Be consistent in the way in which you sign your signature;
   (c) Complete all blanks or draw lines through those which are not applicable;
   (d) Use standard printed forms available from attorneys, banks, and stationery stores;
   (e) Consult a lawyer before adding terms or conditions or deleting them from standard forms used in important transactions;
   (f) Be sure the instrument is payable only in money;
   (g) Avoid postdating or antedating checks; if nothing else, such acts may cause confusion and difficulty in negotiation;
   (h) Be sure the instrument is payable to the order of a specified party or to the bearer.
3. When you issue a demand instrument, realize that the paper is immediately collectible even though the holder might not press for prompt payment. Be prepared to pay.
4. Place some reminder on your calendar to meet all payments of interest and principal on commercial paper you have issued when it becomes due. Default can lead to added expense (e.g., attorney's fees), may necessitate early payment of the full principal (if there is an acceleration clause), and can have a negative effect on your credit standing.
5. When you are the payee of commercial paper, especially promissory notes, include a clause for payment of reasonable attorney fees by the maker in case of default.
6. An instrument which is lacking in some essential required for negotiability may still be a valuable contract or creditor's claim.

YOUR LEGAL VOCABULARY

acceleration clause
antedated instrument
money
payable at a definite time
payable to bearer (bearer paper)

payable on demand
payable to order (order paper)
postdated instrument
words of negotiability

1. "Pay to Donald Milligan or order."
2. An instrument with a date later than the date of issue.
3. "Pay to the order of" and "Pay to bearer."
4. A medium of exchange which is acceptable as currency in the United States or in any foreign country at the time the instrument is made.
5. "Payable at sight."
6. An instrument with a date earlier than the date of issue.
7. A clause making the entire balance due upon default.
8. "Pay to Donald Milligan or bearer."
9. "Payable on or before June 16, 1973."

REMEMBER THESE HIGHLIGHTS

1. To be negotiable, an instrument:
   (a) must be in writing and signed by the maker or drawer;
   (b) must contain an unconditional promise, if it is a note, or an unconditional order, if it is a draft or check;
   (c) must call for payment of a sum certain in money;
   (d) must be payable on demand or at a definite time; and
   (e) must be payable to the order of a specified party or to bearer.
2. In conflicts between provisions written by hand and those typed or printed, the handwritten version prevails. Amounts expressed in words also prevail over figures.
3. Although the order or promise of commercial paper to pay money must be unconditional, certain terms, including the following, may be added without destroying negotiability:
   (a) to charge a particular account as a matter of convenience or record keeping;
   (b) to collect interest;
   (c) to be paid in installments;
   (d) to accelerate payment of principal in case of default;
   (e) to require payment of reasonable attorney fees in case of default;
   (f) to identify the consideration received or to be given for the instrument;
   (g) to identify collateral pledged as security for payment, and to provide for its sale in case of default.

LAW AS PEOPLE LIVE IT

1. P. Jameston Lifflander was a talented young actor, aspiring to stardom in the entertainment world. His agent advised him to use a stage name, and soon he was signing autographs and checks as "Ricky Roco." Would such a signature prevent his checks from being negotiable?

2. Wainwright signed an instrument which contained the words "Pay to the order of Angelo Forziatti or bearer." Was this instrument payable to order, or to bearer?

3. Matsuda negotiated to sell 3,000 juniper evergreen bushes to Kwong, but they could not agree on the price. They signed a contract which covered all terms but left the price to be determined by Warren Browne, an experienced nurseryman. Kwong signed a note stating: "I promise to pay to the order of George Matsuda, on demand, whatever amount Warren Browne decides is a fair price for 3,000 juniper bushes sold to me this date by the payee." Was this instrument negotiable?

4. Leezer signed a note which read: "I promise to pay to the order of Curtis Cranfill $2,500." In a dispute which arose later, it was argued that the instrument could not be negotiable because it was not dated, and no time of payment was given. Do you agree?

5. Levering signed a note payable "to Buckner and Birdwell, General Contractors" for constructing a garage. The note was transferred for value by proper indorsement and delivery to Kirkpatrick, who claims to be the innocent holder of a negotiable instrument. Levering refuses to pay, claiming the garage is defective, and he need not pay since the note is an ordinary contract, not a negotiable instrument. Is he correct?

6. Calvin Massie, who was 96 years old, signed a paper addressed to the prospective executor of his estate, Charles Sutton. It read "Pay to the order of Bryan Dahlgren five thousand dollars ($5,000) thirty days after my death." Was the paper a negotiable instrument?

7. Sutherland prepared what appeared to be a valid promissory note for $1,000 payable to the order of his lifelong friend, Burnett. However, he placed the note in his safety deposit box and it was not found until after Sutherland had suffered a fatal heart attack. Could Burnett collect the $1,000 promised by the instrument from Sutherland's estate?

8. Sorenson owed Rockdale $350 and the debt was long past due. After much pleading and threatening of a lawsuit by Rockdale, Sorenson signed and dated a paper which read: "I promise to pay Ralph Rockdale or his order $350 with interest from this date at 6 percent per year, on July 1, 1973, or as soon thereafter as I am financially able to do so." Was Rockdale's situation improved thereby?

9. A note read: "On December 25, 1975, I promise to pay to the order of Emile Le Blanc 100,000 French francs at Prairie Du Chien, Wisconsin." It was signed by Courtney Cowan. Was it negotiable?

10. Hellman was paid monthly, receiving his salary check on the 1st. On Dec. 23 his checking account balance was down to $25, but he wanted to buy his wife a new pair of skis as a Christmas gift and the price was $99.50. Knowing he'd replenish his checking account with a $600 deposit on Jan. 2, he explained the situation to the seller and bought the skis with a check dated Jan. 3 of the following year. The store's bookkeeper mistakenly presented the check for payment on Dec. 24 and it was dishonored. Is Hellman guilty of a crime or breach of contract?

LAW AS COURTS DECIDE IT

1. In each of two promissory notes, these words appeared: "This note evidences a borrowing made under and subject to the terms of a loan agreement dated Jan. 3 . . ." Were the notes negotiable? (United States v. Farrington, 172 F. Supp. 797)

2. In payment for the remodeling of their home, the Zimmermans gave a promissory note to Master Homecraft Company in the amount of $9,747. The note contained unused blanks for installment payments and did not specify a maturity date. The Zimmermans now say they should not be liable on the note because it is impossible to determine from its face the amount due or the date of maturity. Decide. (Master Homecraft Co. v. Zimmerman, 208 Pa. Super. 401, 22 A. 2d 440)

3. On May, 1963, Ferri executed a note promising to pay $3,000 to Sylvia's order "within ten years after date." Two years later, Sylvia demanded payment, and when refused, sued Ferri. Is the instrument due at a definite time, and if so, when? (Ferri v. Sylvia, 100 R.I. 270, 214 A. 2d 470)

4. Mrs. O'Brien of the Bronx, New York, executed and delivered a promissory note for $915, payable to the order of her daughter, Katherine, "thirty days after the sale of my property on Mapes Avenue." After the property was sold, an action was brought to recover on the instrument, whereupon it was contended that the note was not negotiable. Do you agree? (O'Brien v. O'Brien, 16 N.Y.S. 2d 799)

5. The Havana Canning Company issued a check for $125 to George Wells, dated June 7. In the lower left-hand corner the drawer added the words "For berries to be delvd. us June 8th." In an action on the check by an indorsee, Havana contended that the notation was a condition thereby making the check nonnegotiable. Was it correct? (First Bank of Marianna v. Havana Canning Co., 142 Fla. 554, 195 So. 188)

26 Transfer

1. *You receive a scholarship check from a local service club at an awards dinner. In the confusion of well-wishers who flock around you, the check is lost or stolen. If someone forges your name and cashes the check, do you take the loss?*

2. *In a room with ten persons (A through J) each owes one other party present $10. No one has more than one claim for $10. How can one check payable to bearer be used to settle all ten claims or debts?*

3. *You indorse your payroll check with "Pay to the order of Bank of America. For Deposit Only" and your signature. Then you mail it to the bank where you have a checking account. What happens if it is lost in the mails?*

HOW ARE NEGOTIABLE INSTRUMENTS TRANSFERRED?

Problem: Karl Vatter drew a check payable to the order of Olga Kirlov and delivered it to her. What must Olga do to transfer the check to Alice Getz?

Without proper transfer, a negotiable instrument loses much of its unique value and appeal. It is merely assigned like any other contract, and the assignee gets only the rights of his assignor. With proper transfer or *negotiation,* however, the *transferee* (the party receiving the instrument) becomes a holder; as such, he may obtain rights superior to those of his *transferor* (the party making the transfer). Negotiation to an innocent holder cuts off most of the defenses which the party obligated to pay the instrument might otherwise have. These defenses are explained in the next chapter.

Negotiation requires either (1) indorsement and delivery of the instrument, or (2) delivery alone, depending on the nature of the paper.

(1) ORDER PAPER REQUIRES INDORSEMENT AND DELIVERY

The only way commercial paper payable "to order" may be negotiated is by indorsement and delivery. Because the check in the problem is payable to the order of Olga Kirlov, Kirlov must indorse and deliver it to Getz in order to transfer it properly. If Kirlov neglects to indorse the paper, delivery will transfer only the rights of an assignee. However, Getz would then have the right to request and require Kirlov's indorsement.

If someone receives a check in which his name is misspelled, he need not return it for correction. He may either indorse it with his correct name or in the way in which it appears on the paper, or both. A transferee who takes the instrument for value may insist that it be indorsed both ways.

(2) BEARER PAPER REQUIRES DELIVERY ONLY

Commercial paper which is payable to bearer may be negotiated by delivery alone; the bearer simply hands it to another party.

In practice, it is customary for banks and other transferees to require an indorsement when receiving negotiable bearer paper. The indorsement gives added protection to the holder, who can pursue the indorser if the instrument is not paid.

WHAT ARE THE FORMS OF INDORSEMENT?

Problem: Smith enlisted in the U.S. Navy and expects to be away from home for three years. He owns a promissory note made payable to his order by Jones. Smith plans to transfer the instrument to Williams for value but wants to have no further involvement with the paper or its collection. What indorsement should he use?

An indorsement may be (1) blank, or (2) special. Either kind may also be (3) qualified or unqualified, or (4) restrictive. In all cases, the indorsement will appear somewhere on the instrument, ordinarily on the back.

(1) BLANK INDORSEMENT

Problem: Arlo Chapman paid Milton Dopmann for his month's rent by indorsing his pension check to Dopmann in blank, and handing it to him. On his way home by bus, Dopmann lost his wallet containing the check to a pickpocket. The thief promptly bought goods with the check at the Speedy Service Center, which accepted it in good faith. Speedy can collect on the check. What should Dopmann have done to protect himself?

A *blank indorsement* does not specify a particular person to whom the instrument is transferred. It is usually a simple signature. Because it is easy and fast, the blank indorsement is very common. It is satisfactory and safe for the indorser if value is immediately received, or if the instrument is deposited in a bank at the time of indorsement. If not, a blank indorsement can invite a loss, because it transforms an order instrument into a bearer instrument which even a thief can cash.

The indorsee who receives paper with a blank indorsement may protect himself by writing above the signature of the blank indorser a statement that the instrument is payable to him or his order. This converts the blank indorsement into a special indorsement and restores the order status of the paper. In the problem, Dopmann could have written or printed the words, "Pay to Milton Dopmann," just above Chapman's signature. Then only Dopmann could have collected on the check.

Blank Indorsement

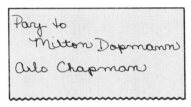

Blank Indorsement Converted to Special Indorsement

(2) SPECIAL INDORSEMENT

Problem: In exchange for some shares of corporation stock, Howard Milbank received from Jon Barksdale a note for $15,000 payable to his order. Milbank wanted to mail the note to his creditor, Dean Floreen, in settlement of a debt. For his own protection before Floreen got the note, and for Floreen's protection thereafter, how should Milbank indorse the instrument?

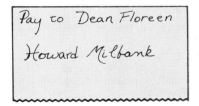

Special Indorsement

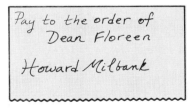

Special Indorsement

In a *special indorsement,* the indorser makes the instrument payable to a designated party, or to that party's order. Words of negotiability are not required. Thus, the words "Pay to" or "Pay to the order of" are equally effective; an instrument indorsed in either way is order paper. To be negotiated again, it must be indorsed and delivered by the indorsee.

In the problem, Milbank should use a special indorsement. Then if the note is lost in the mails, there is little reason for the drawer to hesitate to replace it; as order paper, it is nonnegotiable without Floreen's indorsement. Floreen, too, is protected from loss or theft while he holds the note.

If an instrument is payable to bearer on its face, it may be changed to order paper by special indorsement. Later, it may be changed back to bearer paper by a blank indorsement. The last authorized indorsement determines its character.

(3) QUALIFIED INDORSEMENT

> **Problem:** Charles Youngblood was an agent for John Menk Enterprises. When he received a check from a customer made out in his own name, Youngblood indorsed it to Menk Enterprises, and qualified the blank indorsement with the words "Without recourse and without warranties." What is the legal effect of such indorsement?

A *qualified indorsement* qualifies or limits the obligation that is ordinarily undertaken by an indorser. It releases the indorser from liability to pay if the paper is not paid by the maker or drawee when due. The indorser writes the words "Without recourse," or an equivalent such as "Not liable for payment," over his signature.

Without Recourse

Charles Youngblood

Qualified Blank Indorsement

Pay to
John Menk Enterprises
Without Recourse
Charles Youngblood

Qualified Special Indorsement

Although a qualified indorsement clearly rejects liability for payment, it does not relieve the indorser of liability for certain warranties. To be completely divorced from liability, the indorser must add the words "Without warranties."

In the problem, Youngblood was released both from liability for payment and from warranty liability. Ordinarily a transferee would be unlikely to give value for paper if the transferor refused to be liable in any respect. In the problem, however, Menk readily accepted the check because, as head of the company, he would have to idemnify his agent, Youngblood, for any loss incurred in the course of the agency anyway. (Page 471) In the opening problem on page 372, Smith should try to get Williams to accept the note with a similar indorsement. Williams might refuse, or might pay less for the paper because of the added risk.

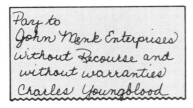

Qualified Special Indorsement
with
Disclaimer of Warranties

(4) RESTRICTIVE INDORSEMENT

Problem: When Forster received a paycheck payable to his order, he indorsed it "For deposit only" and signed it. Does this protect him against possible loss if the check is stolen?

A *restrictive indorsement* specifies the purpose of the indorsement, or prescribes the use to be made of the money proceeds from the paper. An indorser may thus impose conditions on payment. Although such conditions would destroy the negotiability of the instrument if included on its face, they do not prohibit further negotiation when made by an indorser. However, a future holder may be required to see that the funds he pays for the instrument are applied in accordance with the indorsement.

Restrictive indorsements include:

(a) Indorsement for deposit or collection. A restrictive indorsement such as "for deposit" actually converts the instrument into bearer paper even if the word "only" is added. Thus, in the problem, Forster is not protected against possible loss. Preferably, the indorser should include a special indorsement, as "Pay to the Merchants Bank, for deposit." Then the instrument retains its status as order paper. Of course, no difficulties normally arise if the paper is delivered directly to a bank.

(b) Indorsement for benefit of indorser or another. This type of restrictive indorsement includes those made to the indorsee as agent or trustee. For example, "Pay to Frank Nolan, agent, on account of Timothy Brennan, principal," or "Pay to Waldo Macklin, guardian, for benefit of Linda Cass, ward."

(c) Conditional indorsement. A conditional indorsement is made to be effective only upon satisfaction of a specified condition; for example, "Pay to the order of Brooks Stoddard, provided he finishes painting my house by December 31, 1972. Robert Swanson."

WHAT IS THE LIABILITY OF UNQUALIFIED INDORSERS?

> **Problem:** Roger Babb made a promissory note for $2,400 payable in six months to the order of Sam Richmond and gave it to him. (a) Richmond transferred it by blank indorsement to Byron Cort for some goods. (b) Cort in turn specially indorsed it to Noel Paynter. (c) Paynter passed it on to Adam Sivage with a qualified blank indorsement. (d) Sivage transferred it to Floyd Wooley using a restrictive indorsement which read "Pay to Floyd Wooley after completion of garage under construction at 1211 Jefferson Way, Burbank, California." The garage is finished and the note is now due, but Babb is insolvent and cannot pay. What is the liability of each of the indorsers?

An *unqualified indorser* (any indorser who does not limit his obligation by making a qualified indorsement) is normally bound to pay any subsequent holder of the instrument the face amount if the drawee or maker fails to do so. In the problem, only Paynter used a qualified indorsement, and is therefore not liable on the contract. All the others who indorsed without qualification are liable, and the holder, Wooley, can sue any of them. Among themselves, however, the unqualified indorsers are liable in reverse order. That is, if Sivage paid, he could proceed against Cort, who made the indorsement just prior to his. Ultimately, in the normal course of events, Richmond would hold the instrument and pursue Babb.

An indorser who does not qualify his liability (i.e. does not add the words "without warranties") also makes five warranties:

(1) That he has good title or the authority to transfer the instrument;

(2) That all signatures are genuine, signed in person or by an authorized agent;

(3) That the instrument has not been materially altered;

(4) That he has no knowledge of any insolvency action against the maker or drawer (or acceptor, if the instrument has been accepted, as explained on page 398);

(5) That there are no defenses (Chapter 27) of any type that are good against him.

The warranties of the unqualified indorser extend to all subsequent holders who take the instrument in good faith. One who transfers bearer paper by delivery alone makes, to his transferee, exactly the same warranties as the unqualified indorser.

WHAT IS THE LIABILITY OF QUALIFIED INDORSERS?

Problem: Stauffer executed a check payable to the order of Greeley, who indorsed it in blank and gave it to Bench. Bench transferred the instrument "without recourse" to Jardine. When Jardine presented the check for payment, it came back from the bank stamped "Insufficient Funds." Would Jardine be able to collect from anyone?

One who transfers a negotiable instrument by a qualified indorsement, as Bench did, merely transfers the rights that he has in the instrument. He does not undertake an obligation to pay the face amount of the instrument if persons primarily obligated to pay fail or refuse to do so. Accordingly, Jardine had no recourse against Bench, but he could collect from Greeley.

One who negotiates an instrument by qualified indorsement is not, however, entirely free from responsibility. He makes the same warranties as an unqualified indorser, with the exception of the warranty that there are no defenses against him. Instead, he only warrants that he knows of no defense which is good against him. The warranties he makes extend to all subsequent holders who take the instrument in good faith. As mentioned earlier, to free himself of all warranty liability, he must add to his indorsement the words "without warranties."

WHAT IS THE EFFECT OF A FORGED INDORSEMENT?

Problem: Armour accepted Ditter's check in payment for a sleeping bag. The check, made payable "to the order of C. K. Armour," was subsequently lost. The finder indorsed the instrument with a forgery of Armour's signature and used it in making a purchase at Bill's Boot Shop. Who takes the loss?

When one person signs the name of another without his permission, and with intent to defraud, he commits a forgery. (Chapter 5) A forged indorsement on an instrument payable to order generally has no effect and does not pass title. Thus, in the problem, Bill's Boot Shop would have no rights to the check and must take the loss unless it can find the forger and recover from him. This is true even when, as here, the taker paid value and acted in good faith with no knowledge of the forgery.

Signing another's name without permission and with intent to defraud is forgery.

The rule is different in the case of bearer paper because it can be negotiated by delivery only, and so no forgery need be involved. Thus if Ditter's check in the problem had been a bearer instrument, made payable to cash, or if it were an order instrument and Armour had indorsed it in blank, Bill's Boot Shop would have received good title and been able to collect.

In some cases, however, a forgery of a payee's name will be effective. Suppose a dishonest employee fraudulently gets his employer to sign a check made payable to a real person—a customer, for instance—and the employee has no intent to deliver the check to such a person. Or, suppose one person impersonates another, and tricks the maker or drawer into issuing an instrument to him, made payable to the person he is impersonating. In either case the dishonest person may then forge the payee's signature as indorser, and get value for the check or note from some innocent person.

In these cases the loss will fall upon the maker or drawer—the only party who, by exercise of greater care, might have prevented the loss from occurring. One who makes or draws an instrument could and should use caution in selecting and supervising employees, and in identifying the person to whom he delivers a check or note.

WHAT IS AN ACCOMMODATION PARTY?

Problem: Baskin was new in the city. When he made a down payment on a house, he asked his employer, Felton, to indorse the check for him as a courtesy. Otherwise the seller, Hilliard, would refuse to accept it. What if any, was Felton's liability on the check?

Sometimes a person who desires to borrow money or to cash a check is not well known in the community or has not established credit. To make his instruments acceptable, he may arrange—as in the problem—for someone who is known and has a good credit rating to sign the paper with him. Such a signer is an *accommodation party*, whether he signs as a favor or for some consideration. He may sign as a maker or drawee, or as an indorser, as did Felton.

An accommodation party is liable to all subsequent holders of the instrument who give value for it. He is not liable to the party he accommodated. In the problem, Felton made himself liable to Hilliard in the event the check were dishonored when presented to the drawee bank for payment. He would also be liable to any subsequent holder, but not to Baskin.

WHEN YOU WANT TO TRANSFER COMMERCIAL PAPER, REMEMBER . . .

1. When commercial paper is made payable to your order, do not indorse it until you are ready to deliver it. When you deliver it, be sure to indorse properly.
2. Different forms of indorsement serve different purposes. Understand the four basic forms, with variations, and be prepared to use them appropriately. When in doubt, use the special form.
3. Generally do not issue bearer paper or convert order paper into bearer paper (by blank indorsement) unless you expect to get value for it immediately. Bearer paper is so similar to cash that it can too easily be misused by unauthorized persons.
4. If you receive a negotiable instrument which is bearer paper because of a blank indorsement, you can make it payable to your order by adding the words of special indorsement above the indorser's signature.
5. Even commercial paper payable to your order should be handled with reasonable care. If it is lost or stolen before indorsement, you may be faced with delay, inconvenience, and some cost in obtaining replacement paper from the issuer.
6. Do not lend your name to commercial paper as an accommodation party unless you are prepared to pay the full amount of the instrument. Although you are not liable to the party you accommodate, you are liable to pay the holder if the accommodated party fails to do so.

YOUR LEGAL VOCABULARY

accommodation party
blank indorsement
negotiation
qualified indorsement
restrictive indorsement

special indorsement
transferee
transferor
unqualified indorser

1. An indorsement consisting only of the signature of the indorser.
2. The party delivering the negotiable instrument.
3. An indorsement that makes the instrument payable to a particular party or to his order.
4. The party receiving the negotiable instrument.
5. An indorsement that qualifies or limits the obligation ordinarily undertaken by an indorser.
6. A person who signs or indorses to lend credit to another person.
7. An indorsement which conditions the use of the money proceeds from the paper.
8. Any indorser who does not limit his obligation by making a qualified indorsement.
9. A special form of transfer which makes the transferee a holder.

REMEMBER THESE HIGHLIGHTS

1. Instruments payable to order may only be negotiated by indorsement and delivery; those payable to bearer may be negotiated by delivery alone.
2. There are four forms of indorsement: blank, special, qualified, and restrictive.
3. The blank indorsement should not be used unless one deposits the instrument at the same time, or unless value is immediately received from the indorsee.
4. One who transfers a negotiable instrument by an unqualified indorsement is normally bound to pay any subsequent holder the face amount if the drawee or maker dishonors the instrument.
5. The unqualified indorser warrants (a) that he has good title or the authority to transfer, (b) that all signatures are genuine, (c) that there are no material alterations, (d) that he knows of no insolvency actions against the maker, drawer, or acceptor, and (e) that there are no defenses good against him. The qualified indorser makes the same warranties except that under (e) he limits the warranty against defenses to those actually known by him.
6. A forged indorsement on an instrument payable to order generally has no effect and does not pass title.
7. An accommodation party is liable to all subsequent holders of the instrument who give value for it. He is not liable to the party accommodated.

LAW AS PEOPLE LIVE IT

1. Heston negotiated a check to Tommy Tuckett by blank indorsement. Tuckett inserted these words above Heston's signature: "Pay to the

order of Tommy Tuckett." Now Heston claims Tuckett has made a material alteration which voids the instrument. Is this true?

2. Swearingen indorsed a promissory note to Fernando Sanchez "without recourse." Is he therefore free of all possible liability to Sanchez and any subsequent holders with respect to the instrument?

3. Rexford Reynolds figures his time is worth $10 an hour. Since a visit to the Provident State Bank takes at least an hour, plus transportation costs, he does most of his banking business by mail. How should he indorse the checks he mails in for deposit and why?

4. Paul Petro receives a check in which his name is misspelled to read "Pal Peero." What should he do when he indorses it for deposit or transfer?

5. Penny Damone received a promissory note for $500 payable to bearer. She indorsed it "to Lee Van Wert or order." Was the note properly negotiated when Van Wert simply delivered it to Lawrence Evans in exchange for merchandise?

6. Earnshaw received a paycheck payable to his order for $682 from his employer, Paddock. The following day he reported his check as lost, misplaced, or stolen before it had been indorsed. What should Paddock do?

7. Stetson indorsed a draft "without recourse" and delivered it to Lampman. On the day it came due, the drawee refused to pay Lampman, after proving that the signature of the drawer (a certain Alexander Copeland) was a forgery. Lampman sued Stetson for payment. Must Stetson pay?

8. Granger was starting a new business and needed cash. He finally persuaded the Fidelity Bank of Commerce to lend him $10,000 against his equipment. However, the bank insisted that his prominent friend, De Koonig, or someone of equal financial means, indorse the note which Granger signed. De Koonig agreed, and indorsed the instrument. What is his liability?

9. Irene Platten was about to go on a shopping trip. She signed a personal check, and made it payable to "Cash," with the idea that she'd fill in the amount after she found out how much money she'd need. Was this an intelligent thing to do?

10. Leonard Peal gives Thomas Walton a note payable to his order in exchange for a used cement mixer mounted on a truck. Walton warranted all mechanical parts of both truck and mixer to be in good working order. When Peal tried the rig for the first time, the mixer jammed because some concrete from an earlier load had not been properly removed. Peal phoned Walton but learned that Walton had already transferred the instrument to Hull, an innocent person who gave value. Walton had neglected to indorse it, however. Does Peal have a defense good against Hull when the latter tries to collect?

LAW AS COURTS DECIDE IT

1. Temarantz applied to the Security Bank for a loan in order to buy Tomasek's car. The loan was made when Temarantz signed a promissory note and Tomasek signed as co-maker in order to accommodate Temarantz. Later Temarantz resold the car, and defaulted on his loan. Was Tomasek liable to the bank on the note? (Security National Bank of Long Island v. Temarantz, N.Y.S.C., N.Y.L.J., March 17, 1969)

2. The Coppersmiths executed and delivered four promissory notes to the order of Elliott. Elliott in turn indorsed the notes to Whitehurst, but kept them in her possession in order to collect interest on them while she lived. They were found by her executor after death. Now both the executor and Whitehurst claim to own the notes. Who should get them? (Cartwright v. Coppersmith, 222 N.C. 573, 24 S.E. 2d 246)

3. McBerry signed and delivered a promissory note payable to the order of William C. Stepp. Stepp indorsed the note as follows: "I hereby transfer my right to this note over to W. E. McCullough. (Signed) William C. Stepp." He then delivered the note to McCullough. In an action to collect, the question arose as to whether this was a qualified indorsement or a special indorsement. Decide. (McCullough v. Stepp, 91 Ga. App. 103, 85 S.E. 2d 159)

4. The Shorts signed and delivered a $10,000 promissory note payable to the order of Ella B. Ward. Ward indorsed the note "Without recourse on me pay to the order of Eleanor H. Leekley. (Signed) Ella B. Ward," and delivered the note to Leekley. The Shorts defaulted in paying the note, whereupon Leekley contended that Ella B. Ward was liable because of warranties. Was this contention sound? (Leekley v. Short, 216 Iowa 376, 249 N.W. 363)

5. Obie received a check drawn to her order by the Atlanta Federal Savings & Loan Association, Inc. for $2,000. She transferred it to Jett for valuable consideration but neglected to indorse it. When the drawee bank refused to pay the check because it was not indorsed, Jett sued Atlanta and Obie. Are they liable? (Jett v. Atlanta Federal Savings and Loan Association, Inc., 104 Ga. App. 688, 123 S.E. 2d 27)

6. Young, an employee of the General American Insurance Company, caused his company to issue 20 checks over a two-year period with a total value of $24,600. The checks were made payable to a policyholder named Becker, without his knowledge or consent, and were purported to be the proceeds of loans against life insurance policies Becker owned. Actually Young cashed the checks or deposited them for his own use at the plaintiff bank. After the crimes were discovered, the question arose as to whether General American was liable on the checks. Was it? (Delmar Bank of University City v. Fidelity and Deposit Co. of Maryland, 300 F. Supp. 496)

27 Rights of Holders

1. *Your aunt paid a traveling salesman $100 by check for a bolt of Scottish tweed cloth which never arrived. Can she stop payment of the check?*

2. *Shortly after his 16th birthday, Paige bought a late-model used car. After receiving Paige's $750 promissory note in payment, the dealer transferred the note for value to an innocent third party. If Paige later returned the car, would he still be obligated to pay the note?*

3. *Someone steals your book of blank checks, forges your signature to several of them, and passes them in trade. Will they be charged to your checking account at the bank?*

WHO IS A HOLDER IN DUE COURSE?

Problem: Dawson, a used car dealer, sold a car to Phipps after telling him that the engine had been overhauled. He took a check in payment. Bateman, his mechanic, witnessed the sale and said nothing although he knew he had merely tuned the engine. Dawson then indorsed the check to Bateman as his month's salary. Was Bateman a holder in due course?

An ordinary holder of commercial paper normally may: (a) transfer it, as with other contracts; (b) negotiate it; (c) enforce payment of it; or (d) discharge it upon receiving payment or satisfaction. Exceptions are made in some cases. For example, a thief who has stolen paper may collect its face value, but this does not discharge the instrument; the face value is still owed to the true owner. Likewise, if an instrument is restrictively indorsed, it is not discharged if paid in a manner which fails to comply with the restriction. In seeking to collect, the ordinary holder faces all the defenses which confront any assignee seeking to enforce an ordinary contract. (Page 183)

On the other hand, as you know, holders who take negotiable instruments under certain conditions obtain rights superior to those of the transferor. Such privileged holders are known as holders in due course. To qualify as a *holder in due course* (HDC), one must first be a holder; that is, he must be in possession of bearer paper, or of order paper issued or properly indorsed to him or his order. In addition, he must take the negotiable instrument:

(1) IN GOOD FAITH AND FOR VALUE

He must act in good faith, that is, with honesty. Consider, for example, a company which consistently defrauds customers in door-to-door sales. It may take promissory notes in payment and promptly transfer them to a finance company which knows of its fraudulent practice. In such a case, neither firm would be acting honestly and the finance company could not qualify as a HDC.

He must give value. Although courts normally do not test the adequacy of value given, the amount paid must not be so slight in comparison to the value received that it is evidence of fraud. If one gets a $1,000 note in exchange for $100 in cash, for example, fraud might reasonably be suspected.

(2) WITHOUT KNOWLEDGE OF DEFENSE AGAINST, DISHONOR OF, OR CLAIMS TO THE INSTRUMENT

He must not have actual knowledge of facts that would constitute a defense in an action brought against any party to the instrument, or of a claim of ownership by any third party, or of a dishonor of the instrument that has occurred. In other words, to qualify as a HDC, he must not know facts which indicate that the instrument may not be payable according to its terms.

The holder is deemed to have notice of such possible defenses if he has received information which would cause a reasonably careful man to investigate the instrument before accepting it. Mere grounds for suspicion do not constitute notice, however. Thus, the holder would have notice if the instrument contained any signs of alteration, but not if it were merely postdated. Notice received after he has acquired the instrument does not alter a HDC's status.

In the problem, Bateman could not be a holder in due course because he knew of a valid defense which the drawer of the check, Phipps, had against Dawson.

(3) WITHOUT KNOWLEDGE THAT THE INSTRUMENT IS OVERDUE

Simple examination of an instrument due on a certain date generally reveals whether it is overdue. If it is payable on demand, the problem is more difficult because the instrument matures within a reasonable time after it is issued, and what is reasonable depends upon the circumstances of the particular case. An instrument payable in installments is overdue if a single installment has not been paid when due.

If the fact that an instrument is overdue is not apparent from the paper itself, a good faith purchaser for value who has no notice that the instrument is overdue may still become a holder in due course. This could happen if someone altered an instrument, changing the due date from the 5th to the 15th of the month. One could become a holder in due course on or before the 15th if the alteration was not known or apparent to him as a reasonable man.

 When Courtney bought a gold wrist watch from Friendly Finance Jewelers, he signed a note payable over three years. Default in any monthly installment payment of principal and interest accelerated the due date of the entire balance. After eight months, Courtney lost his job and missed two payments. The seller accelerated the due date of the note. Courtney failed to pay and Friendly Jewelers negotiated the note to Swift who had no knowledge of the acceleration. The instrument is not regarded as overdue and Swift may qualify as a HDC.

One who takes an instrument after a holder in due course is called a *holder through a holder in due course*. He (as well as anyone who may follow him) ordinarily has the same rights as the HDC, even though he receives the instrument as a gift or knows of some defense. Of course, he must not be a party to any fraud or illegality affecting the instrument.

WHAT ARE LIMITED DEFENSES?

Problem: Marberry gave Kamm $50 cash and a note for $600 in payment for a motorcycle after Kamm assured him that the odometer reading of 5,200 miles was true. Later, Marberry learned that it had been set back from 25,000 miles, and he determined not to pay the note because of the fraud. However, Kamm had already transferred the note to O'Doul, a HDC. Must Marberry pay O'Doul?

Negotiable instruments are normally enforceable according to their terms, and the great majority are routinely paid when due. Sometimes, however, the party who is called upon to pay may have a legitimate reason for not doing so. This reason—his legal defense—may be good against everyone if it qualifies as a universal defense. More likely, it will be a *limited defense* which may be good against everyone except a holder in due course.

Limited defenses include:

(1) SIMPLE CONTRACT DEFENSES SUCH AS LACK, FAILURE, OR ILLEGALITY OF CONSIDERATION

Thiotis contracted with Marovich for a shipment of imported handmade wooden benches, and paid him by accepting his time draft for $7,850. Marovich indorsed the draft to Hornblower, a holder in due course. The benches were never delivered because of difficulties Marovich had with Yugoslavian trade regulations. Nevertheless, Hornblower can enforce the instrument against Thiotis. If the draft had not been negotiated to a HDC, Thiotis' limited defense of lack of consideration would have been good. Now he must pay the draft, and then take action against Marovich for breach of contract.

(2) FRAUD IN THE INDUCEMENT

Drick defrauded Rockwell when he sold him a domestic "oriental" rug which he intentionally misrepresented to be a genuine Kerman made in Iran. Rockwell paid by check upon delivery, but stopped payment shortly after when his neighbor advised him that the rug was a fake. Drick had already indorsed the check to Charles, a holder in due course. Thus, Rockwell's defense of fraud in the inducement was cut off, and Charles could enforce the check against him. Had Drick not transferred the check to a HDC, Rockwell's defense would have been good.

A similar result would follow in the problem on page 385, where Marberry must pay O'Doul, a HDC, and seek recovery from Kamm. A buyer should not place the blame for his carelessness in dealing with a dishonest seller upon an innocent third party who acquires the commercial paper used in the transaction.

(3) INCAPACITY (OTHER THAN MINORITY)

During a New York City business trip, Lemmon impressed his seven companions at an exclusive night club by paying for all charges with a personal check. The following morning, when reminded of his costly generosity, Lemmon immediately telephoned the club. He told the club manager that his ability to reason was severely impaired by even a single drink, and he had several drinks that evening. Normally, when not under the influence of alcohol, he would not have signed the check. He admitted, however, that he could recall the circumstances and his desire to impress his friends. The club had already transferred the check to a pastry supplier, a HDC. Lemmon's incapacity would be no defense against the HDC; he presumably knew he was making a contract, and the circumstances made the contract possibly voidable but not void.

(4) ORDINARY DURESS OR UNDUE INFLUENCE

 Lombardelli, the elderly immigrant owner of a small neighborhood candy store, was visited by Carey, a member of the local crime syndicate. Carey demanded that Lombardelli sign a $500 promissory note for "protection." Lombardelli refused, but was too frightened to go to the police. That evening, a small fire was discovered and quickly extinguished in the store's back room. When Carey appeared the next morning at the store, he informed Lombardelli that if he did not sign the note, the next fire would completely destroy the building. Lombardelli immediately signed the note and Carey transferred it to his employer, who then transferred it to Winquist, a HDC. Lombardelli claimed that he should not have to pay the note because it was made under duress which rendered the transaction voidable. Although this defense would have been valid against Carey or his employer, it was not good against Winquist, the innocent holder. Lombardelli must pay.

(5) PRIOR PAYMENT OR CANCELLATION

 Bowden owed Crown $4,500 on a five-year note with interest at 10 percent. The note could be repaid early without penalty, and so, to save interest, Bowden paid it off after only three years. He received a receipt from Crown, but foolishly neglected to have him mark the note "Paid" and to pick it up. Crown then indorsed the note to Templeton, a HDC, for a loan of $4,000. Crown planned to pay off the loan and reclaim the note before it matured, but he suffered business reverses and failed to do so. When the note came due, Templeton, as holder in due course, could enforce it against Bowden. Bowden's defense of prior payment was good against Crown, but not against a HDC such as Templeton.

(6) CONDITIONAL DELIVERY

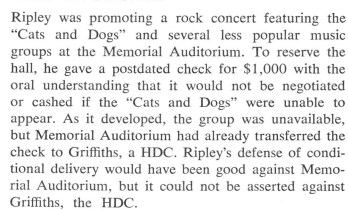

Ripley was promoting a rock concert featuring the "Cats and Dogs" and several less popular music groups at the Memorial Auditorium. To reserve the hall, he gave a postdated check for $1,000 with the oral understanding that it would not be negotiated or cashed if the "Cats and Dogs" were unable to appear. As it developed, the group was unavailable, but Memorial Auditorium had already transferred the check to Griffiths, a HDC. Ripley's defense of conditional delivery would have been good against Memorial Auditorium, but it could not be asserted against Griffiths, the HDC.

(7) NONDELIVERY OF THE INSTRUMENT

Hemphill, the treasurer of Ambrosia Box Lunches, Inc., worked late one night. He carelessly signed but failed to fill in two blank checks and left them on his desk. They were stolen by Leonard, a casual friend of the night watchman who made the rounds with him that night. Leonard filled in names and amounts and transferred the checks, one to a holder in due course and one to an ordinary assignee. Ambrosia had a limited defense of nondelivery good against Leonard and the ordinary assignee, but not against the HDC.

(8) UNAUTHORIZED COMPLETION

Harriman ordered some cam kits and other high-performance auto parts by mail from the Bargain Loft in Miami. Because he wasn't sure of several prices, he sent his signed check with the amount left blank and no top limit placed on its value. The owner of the Bargain Loft dishonestly filled in the blanks for an amount which was at least three times the proper price, and negotiated the check to Paine, a HDC. Such unauthorized completion is a valid defense against the Bargain Loft, but not against a HDC.

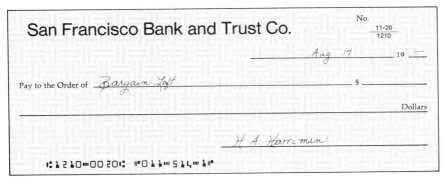

(9) THEFT

 Ashforth, a dishonest bookkeeper of the Allied Columbia Trading Company, was in charge of receipts from customers. He developed a practice of taking for himself occasional checks received by the company and made payable to "Cash." Ashforth would cash the checks at the bank where drawn or transfer them to innocent retailers around town in exchange for money or merchandise which he retained. When his supervisor learned of the practice, the company could not recover from those parties who had honored the checks because they were holders in due course and theft is a limited defense ineffective against them.

WHAT ARE UNIVERSAL DEFENSES?

Problem: Alston and Burdock, partners, were discussing the problem of collecting a note for $15,000 owned by their firm and signed by Cronin as maker. Alston insisted that if they act promptly when the note comes due, the only way Cronin could avoid the obligation would be to go bankrupt, or to disappear, or to die, in any case with insufficient assets to pay this debt. Burdock said there are other possible barriers to collection. Who was right?

Some defenses—known as *universal defenses*—are valid against all parties including holders in due course. Thus, in the problem, Burdock was right. Commercial paper may prove uncollectible not only for the reasons which Alston gave but also when any one of the universal defenses is validly raised. These defenses include:

(1) MINORITY AND LACK OF CAPACITY TO CONTRACT

Minority is a universal defense good even against a holder in due course. It does not matter whether the minor's contracts are void or voidable. Thus, a minor who signs a note may refuse to pay as promised. In most states he would, of course, be required to return any consideration he had received.

Insanity, intoxication, or other contractual incapacity is a universal defense only if its effect is to make a contract void; if it only renders the contract voidable, the defense is limited as discussed on page 118. All contracts of a person judicially declared insane are void, for example.

(2) ILLEGALITY

If the law declares void an instrument made in connection with certain conduct, the defense of illegality may be used against any holder. In most states, for example, a negotiable instrument given in payment for a gambling debt is void.

(3) FORGERY OR LACK OF AUTHORITY

When one person forges the name of another with intent to defraud, the forgery is a universal defense good against all holders. If the intent to defraud is lacking, as where an agent signs his principal's name without authority to do so, no crime is committed but the effect on third parties is the same: no holder can collect from the supposed drawer of such an instrument.

Prior parties not agreeing to material changes may be discharged from liability.

(4) MATERIAL ALTERATION

Suppose a dishonest holder fraudulently and materially alters a negotiable instrument by changing the maturity date, the amount due, the rate of interest, or the place of payment. Prior parties who have not agreed to such changes are generally discharged from liability on the instrument as altered. (They are, however, liable according to its original terms if the instrument is in the hands of a holder in due course. Thus, if the amount payable on a check is boosted from $15 to $150, the HDC could still collect $15.)

(5) FRAUD AS TO THE NATURE OF ESSENTIAL TERMS

If trickery is used in such way that a careful person does not know and has no reasonable opportunity to learn the nature or essential terms of the document he is signing, he can set up a defense of fraud against all holders. For example, a celebrity might sign his autograph on a blank sheet of paper and a dishonest person might print and write a promissory note around it. Or, the signer might not be able to read because he is illiterate in English, or has broken his glasses, and the person planning to defraud gives him a false explanation of the essential terms, or stealthily substitutes one instrument for another before the signing.

(6) DURESS DEPRIVING CONTROL

If the person executes or indorses a commercial paper under conditions of duress which make the transaction void, the duress may be raised as a universal defense. Such might be the case if, after threatening to kill a party unless he signs the instrument, a gang beats him until the pain is unendurable and he signs.

YOUR LEGAL VOCABULARY

holder in due course (HDC)   limited defenses
holder through a HDC   universal defenses

1. A holder who takes an instrument for value, in good faith, and without notice that it is overdue or that there are any defenses, claims, or dishonor as to the instrument.
2. Defenses that are valid against any holder including a holder in due course.
3. One who takes an instrument after a holder in due course.
4. Defenses that may be valid against any holder except a holder in due course.

FOR YOUR PROTECTION . . .

1. It is better to be a holder in due course than an ordinary holder. Therefore, generally:
   (a) Acquire instruments only in good faith;
   (b) Pay value, unless a gift is intended;
   (c) Don't accept an instrument when you know it has been dishonored, or that there are other claims to it, or that some defense exists against payment;
   (d) Don't accept overdue instruments;
   (e) Don't accept altered instruments.
2. If you receive paper as a holder from the maker or drawer, you minimize the possibility of a limited defense being used against you when you try to collect if you generally:
   (a) Properly perform your part of the underlying contractual bargain;
   (b) Commit no fraud in inducing the other party to contract or to sign the instrument;
   (c) Avoid dealing with persons who may lack capacity to contract, such as minors, unless a responsible person also signs the instrument as an accommodation party;
   (d) Never threaten or use duress or undue influence in connection with the instrument or the underlying contract;
   (e) Refuse to accept delivery of instruments subject to conditions, or if conditions are present, comply with them;
   (f) Refuse to accept incomplete instruments; or if there are blanks, fill them in only in strict compliance with the intent of the issuer;
   (g) Never steal an instrument or tolerate any dishonesty or illegality in connection with it;
   (h) Never materially alter an instrument;
   (i) Stay alert to the possibility that the person who deals with you may be a forger;
   (j) Surrender the instrument when you are paid.
3. Be careful about accepting a negotiable instrument from anyone you don't know. Require identification, but remember I.D. cards can be stolen or forged. Generally it is helpful to require indorsement in your presence; this permits comparison of signatures. Sometimes you can help to protect yourself by insisting that an accommodation party known to you also sign the instrument as maker or indorser. It may also be wise to place a dollar limit on the instruments which you are willing to accept.

REMEMBER THESE HIGHLIGHTS

1. To be a holder in due course one must take an instrument for value, in good faith, and without notice that it is overdue or that there are any defenses, claims, or dishonor as to the instrument.
2. Limited defenses are (a) simple contract defenses such as lack, failure, or illegality of consideration; (b) fraud in the inducement; (c) incapacity (other than minority); (d) ordinary duress or undue

influence; (e) prior payment or cancellation; (f) conditional delivery; (g) nondelivery; (h) unauthorized completion; and (i) theft. Limited defenses are not good against holders in due course.

3. Universal defenses are (a) minority and lack of capacity to contract; (b) illegality that renders a contract void; (c) forgery or lack of authority; (d) material alteration; (e) fraud as to the nature or essential terms; and (f) duress depriving control. Universal defenses are good against all, including holders in due course.

LAW AS PEOPLE LIVE IT

1. On her first wedding anniversary date, Susan Marshall received as a gift from her uncle, Orville Heather, a promissory note for $400 payable to her order four years later on the day of her fifth anniversary. Susan needed the money immediately, and so she indorsed the note to Beegley, a HDC. Beegley in turn indorsed it to Fuller for fair value. Fuller happened to know the note had originated as a gift. On the due date, Uncle Orville refuses to pay Fuller, saying there was no consideration for his original promise. Must he pay Fuller?

2. Hanley owed Nichols $1,700 for a snowmobile which Hanley had purchased the year before. Nichols had received only $200 in partial payment, and was becoming extremely exasperated. When he met Hanley in a restaurant one day, Nichols loudly demanded cash or a signature on an interest-bearing note "here and now or I'll haul you into court and sue you for all you've got!" Hanley signed but now refuses to pay the note, claiming duress. Is this a valid defense?

3. The following instrument was indorsed in blank by Burdette and delivered to Brunie on November 10, 1972. Did Brunie become a holder in due course?

```
                              Portland, Maine
                              July 1, 1972

On December 30, 1972, I promise to pay Leroy Burdette

three-hundred dollars ($300) with interest at 5%.

                        Ronald Lyon
                        Ronald Lyon
```

4. Dr. Joseph Bottsford, a dentist, purchased an imported X-ray machine for his office from the Clinical Supply Co. He paid for it with a promissory note payable in monthly installments for the following three years. Although he duly made the first payment, a dispute over the machine's performance arose immediately after delivery. Bottsford was on the verge of a lawsuit to compel removal and replacement of the machine, or restitution of the money he had paid to date. Anderson,

manager of the Tri-City Union Bank, knew of this dispute when he bought the note at a discount from Clinical Supply. Is Tri-City a HDC?

5. Margot received a signed check from Bliss in which the amount had been carelessly left blank. His friend, Magee, persuaded Margot to substantially increase the amount which should have been inserted, and then to indorse the note over to him. He promised to share the illicit gain with Margot. Was Magee a holder in due course?

6. Morrison was payee of a negotiable note for $250 made by Chilson. The instrument was not paid when due and after patiently waiting two more months, Morrison sold it to Garfinkel at a substantial discount. Is Garfinkel a holder? A holder in due course?

7. De Groot, who was a properly appointed sales agent of Lange Laboratories, found a used panel truck for sale at a bargain price. Knowing his employer needed such a vehicle, he agreed to buy it for Lange, giving in payment a check signed "Lange Laboratories by Albert De Groot, Agent." He actually had no authority to make purchases and Lange refused to ratify his contract. Is it nevertheless liable on the check?

8. Stone gave Webster his check for $275 in payment for a used freezer which Webster said was in good working order. When Stone installed the box in his garage, it didn't work. He removed the back panel and discovered that the motor and compressor had been removed. (a) Does Stone have a defense against Webster on the check? (b) Is Stone's defense good against any HDC to whom Webster might negotiate the check?

9. Ronson, who looked older than his age of 17, opened a bank checking account. To attend a senior prom, he rented a tuxedo for $20, rented a car for $25, bought a corsage and a bottle of perfume for $35, and paid for all with checks. The date was a big disappointment, so he stopped payment on all the checks the morning after the prom. Is his minority a valid defense?

10. Arkin drew a draft on Broos payable to Crowther in 36 months. Broos accepted the draft as drawn. Shortly after, Crowther urgently needed money. He erased the "3" to make the instrument appear to be due in six months. He also added a requirement for interest to be paid at 10 percent per year. The alterations would be obvious to any prudent man, but DuPont bought the instrument from Crowther without question. Is Broos liable to DuPont on the instrument?

LAW AS COURTS DECIDE IT

1. An aggressive salesman for Crystal Clear, Inc. sold Woods a water softener and induced her to sign a judgment note in payment. He told her she was not obligated to buy the machine but that it was to be given to her for "advertising." She was to get $50 credit against the price for each name of a prospective customer which she supplied. As was its custom, Crystal promptly transferred the note to the American

Plan Corporation with which it was in a close and continuing relationship. American was thus charged with knowledge of Crystal's fraudulent methods. When Woods defaulted on payments on the note, American Plan sued her, claiming it was a HDC. Was it? (American Plan Corporation v. Woods, 16 Ohio App. 2d 1, 240 N.E. 2d 886)

2. On May 14, Perkins drew a check payable to Stauropoulos and post-dated it May 16. The payee cashed it on May 14 at the National Currency Exchange. Perkins later dishonored the check and claims that National could not be a HDC because the instrument was postdated. Do you agree? (National Currency Exchange, Inc. #3 v. Perkins, 52 Ill. App. 2d 215, 201 N.E. 2d 668)

3. Redding drew a $500 check payable to the order of Hymowitz in payment for plumbing supplies. Hymowitz immediately wrote a blank indorsement on the back of the check. Because Redding insisted that the plumbing supplies be delivered quickly, Hymowitz left the check lying on the counter, went into his office, and called the drawee bank. When he learned that the check was no good, Hymowitz returned and found both Redding and the check were gone. Redding indorsed the check below the signature of Hymowitz and cashed it at Gimbel Brothers, Inc. The drawee bank refused to pay the check, and Gimbel Brothers promptly notified Hymowitz. Would Hymowitz be required to pay Gimbel Brothers? (Gimbel Brothers, Inc. v. Hymowitz, 160 Pa. Super. 327, 51 A. 2d 389)

4. Bluiett received a payroll check for $185.59 from the Silver Slipper Gambling Hall and Saloon. She indorsed it in a manner permitting any subsequent holder to cash it, and foolishly left it on a dresser in her home. The next day she discovered that it was missing along with other items. On the same day, Freddie Watkins used the check to buy two tires from Western Auto, and received the balance of $112.35 in cash. He was later arrested and charged with obtaining money from Western Auto's owner under false pretenses. This offense requires that the accused intend to cheat or defraud the person from whom the money is obtained, and that such person sustain injury or damage. Should Freddy Watkins stand trial for the crime as charged? (Watkins v. Sheriff of Clark County, Nevada, 85 Nev. 246, 453 P. 2d 611)

5. The office manager of the Farmers Union Livestock Commission signed a check that was left blank as to date, amount, and the payee. He then placed the instrument in a safe. After the office had been closed, an employee opened the safe and stole the instrument. He filled in the blanks, making the check payable to himself for $102.85. The instrument came into the possession of Gust Pavilis, an innocent purchaser for value. When Pavilis brought an action to recover on the instrument, the Commission contended that it was not liable because of nondelivery of an incomplete instrument. Do you agree? (Pavilis v. Farmers Union Livestock Commission, 298 N.W. 732, South Dakota)

CHAPTER 28 Liability of Parties

1. *Your father receives a promissory note for $5,000, payable on demand and indorsed by a well-to-do business-man. When the note is presented to the maker for payment, he truthfully says that he cannot pay because he has practically no assets. Moreover, he reveals that he plans to file for bankruptcy. If your father fails to take certain action, he'll get nothing. What must he do?*

2. *You are the maker of a promissory note. Are you discharged from liability if the holder doesn't present the instrument to you for payment?*

3. *Your friend, Larsen, is the holder and payee of a 90-day sight draft payable to his order and drawn against Hooper with whom he refuses to deal. You tell Larsen to present the draft to Hooper for acceptance — or have someone do it for him — or he will never collect his money. Is this true?*

WHO ARE THE PRIMARY AND SECONDARY PARTIES?

Problem: Hewlett is the holder of a check made payable to his order by Grover, and drawn on the local Midtown Bank. If Grover, the primary party, closes his account before the check can be presented for payment, can Hewlett collect from the bank as a secondary party?

The liability of parties to commercial paper is either primary or secondary. A *primary party* is so-called because he is primarily liable; that is, he is liable before anyone else to pay the holder of the instrument. The maker of a promissory note and the drawee who accepts a draft are primary parties.

In the normal case, the maker or drawee pays the instrument and the matter is closed. But sometimes the holder cannot collect from the primary party; perhaps he is insolvent, or bankrupt, or has died leaving insufficient assets, or has simply disappeared. If the holder acts promptly, he may then seek payment from secondary parties if any are available; *secondary parties* are liable only in the event that the primary party fails or refuses to pay the instrument. The drawer of a check or draft, and the indorsers of a check, draft, or promissory note, are secondary parties.

A drawee bank which serves as a depository for funds and which normally honors checks properly drawn on those funds is not liable as a primary or secondary party if the amount on deposit proves insufficient. In such case, it rightfully refuses to accept checks drawn on the deficient account. Thus, in the problem, Hewlett may not collect from the bank.

WHAT IS REQUIRED TO FIX LIABILITY OF SECONDARY PARTIES?

Problem: Shuman gave Blyth a check. Blyth indorsed it to Corcoran, a holder in due course. When Corcoran presented the check for payment, the bank refused to pay because Shuman had insufficient funds. What should Corcoran do?

If the holder is to collect from secondary parties, the law requires that he take two critical steps:

(1) Properly present the instrument to the primary party for acceptance or payment. If it is dishonored, then

(2) Give due notice of dishonor to the secondary parties.

In the problem, Corcoran will want to fix liability on the secondary party, Blyth. Since the instrument has already been presented and dishonored, Corcoran should give notice of dishonor to Blyth. Shuman also remains liable, but he may be unable to pay.

(1) PRESENTMENT

A holder may not pursue secondary parties for payment until he makes certain that the primary party will not pay. *Presentment,* either for acceptance or for payment, is the holder's way of determining the primary party's intentions.

Presentment must be made within a reasonable time after issue if the instrument is payable on demand; it must be made on or before the due date if it is payable at a definite time. If it is payable after sight, the instrument must be negotiated or presented for acceptance within a reasonable time.

An instrument may be presented by mail or through a clearing house (a place set up by banks where mutual claims are settled). Usually, however, presentment is made at a place specified in the instrument. If none is specified, it may be made at the place of business or residence of the primary party.

Any demand for acceptance or payment is sufficient to meet the requirements of proper presentment. However, the party to whom presentment is made may require that the person making the presentment (a) identify himself (he must be the holder or one authorized to act for him); (b) exhibit the instrument; (c) present it at the place specified in the instrument, or if none is specified, at a reasonable place; (d) give a signed receipt on the instrument itself for the amount of any payment made; and (e) surrender the instrument, and give a signed receipt thereon, if full payment is made.

 Mitchum was the holder and payee of a draft drawn by Kidder against Hamill, payable on sight. To save time, Mitchum telephoned Hamill and was told by him that the draft would not be accepted. This was sufficient presentment. Hamill's dishonor of the draft allowed Mitchum to proceed against secondary parties.

Failure to present the instrument properly, as normally required, is excused if (a) waived by the secondary party; (b) the drawee or maker cannot be found with reasonable efforts; (c) the primary party has died or gone into insolvency proceedings, has already refused to pay; or (d) the secondary party has no reason to expect that the instrument would be paid if properly presented.

(a) Presentment for acceptance. A holder who wants to know whether the primary party will pay the instrument may present it to him for acceptance in advance of the time it is due. *Acceptance* is the promise of the drawee to pay the instrument according to its terms. It must be written on the draft itself, and include the signature of the drawee. The signature alone is enough, but usually "Accepted" and the date are also written.

Generally only drafts are presented for acceptance. Although any draft may be presented for acceptance, such presentment is not required to charge the drawer or indorsers of a draft, except in three limited situations:

(1) where necessary to fix the date of payment, as when a draft is payable "thirty days after sight";
(2) where the draft itself states that it must be presented for acceptance; or
(3) where it is payable somewhere other than the drawee's place of business or residence.

Accepted Draft

The drawee is not required to accept or dishonor the draft immediately upon presentment. He may hold the draft until the close of the business day following presentment without dishonoring it. This gives him time to examine his records, and to determine carefully whether to accept.

(b) Presentment for payment. Presentment for payment is required whenever the holder wishes to fix the secondary liability of the drawer, or of any unqualified indorser of a note, draft, or check. It is all that is required for promissory notes, since the maker has already agreed or promised to pay. It is the only presentment normally required for checks, and for drafts due on sight. Even time drafts ultimately require presentment for payment, unless previously dishonored by nonacceptance.

Presentment of demand instruments must be made within a reasonable time after issue. When a check is drawn and payable in the United States, it is presumed that (a) thirty days is a reasonable time for presentment to a drawer, and (b) seven days after indorsement is a reasonable time as to an indorser. Thus, a check should be negotiated or presented for payment within thirty days. Otherwise the drawer may have a defense if, for example, the bank fails after that date. And to hold an indorser liable if the check bounces—that is, is dishonored—it should be presented for payment within seven days after his indorsement. If the holder of a check waits longer than the indicated time limits, he has the burden of proving in court that the longer time was reasonable.

(2) NOTICE OF DISHONOR

After proper presentment and dishonor, notice must be given to any indorsers of the instrument, and to the drawer in the case of a draft or check. The notice may be oral or written, and must identify the instrument and state that it has been dishonored. Oral notice may be given face-to-face or by telephone. In good practice, it should be confirmed in writing. The proper mailing of a written notice constitutes giving due notice even when it is lost en route.

Notice must be given before midnight of the third business day after dishonor. Neither Saturday nor Sunday is counted. Thus, if an instrument is dishonored on Wednesday, the holder has until midnight Monday to give notice. Delay in giving notice of dishonor is excused under the same circumstances as delay in making presentment. In certain special cases, no notice is required.

If a draft is dishonored by nonacceptance, the holder may proceed immediately against the indorsers and drawer to get his money. He need not again present the instrument for payment when due.

 Bradley was payee and holder of a draft drawn by Carney on O'Leary, dated January 19, and due ten days later. Bradley presented the draft for acceptance to O'Leary, the drawee, on January 20. On January 21, O'Leary said he would not accept it. Bradley asked him to reconsider, and on January 22, O'Leary said he just could not afford to pay the draft that month. At this point Bradley should give due notice of dishonor to the drawer, Carney. He can take legal action against him immediately to collect if he wishes, and need not wait until the date of maturity of the instrument, nor present it for payment to the drawee.

It is not uncommon, however, for the holder of a dishonored check or other negotiable instrument to present it again for payment at a later date. A storekeeper may keep a customer's check that has been dishonored for a few days, and then present it to the bank again in hopes that the drawer will have put sufficient funds in his account to cover the amount. However, failure to give due notice when the instrument is first dishonored will discharge the liability of secondary parties. Then if the instrument is not paid on its second presentation to the drawee or maker, recovery from secondary parties will also be blocked.

WHAT IS A PROTEST?

Problem: Gwinn was the holder in due course of a draft drawn by Worthington, of London, England, on Wertheim, a drawee in Boston. The instrument was dishonored by non-payment when due. What must Gwinn do to protect his right to collect from Worthington?

The notice of dishonor required to hold secondary parties must sometimes be in the form of a protest. A *protest* is a formal written notice that the instrument was properly presented and that it was dishonored. It may be made by a notary public, U.S. consular official, or other person authorized to certify a dishonor.

Is this what is meant by a "formal protest" of a dishonored note?

Any dishonored negotiable instrument may be protested if the holder so wishes. A protest is required, however, only when a draft is drawn or payable outside of the United States or its territories. Thus, in the problem, Gwinn should formally protest the dishonor to Worthington in London. When protest is required and not made, the drawer and indorsers are released from liability on the instrument.

When the words "No protest" or the letters "N.P." appear on an instrument, it means that the indorser has waived the right to demand protest or even ordinary notice of dishonor if the instrument is dishonored.

WHAT ARE THE OBLIGATIONS OF THE PARTIES?

Problem: Folberg owed Dempsey close to $5,000 for merchandise purchased. Dempsey owed Watkins, his lawyer, $1,800 for legal services. To pay this debt, Dempsey drew a sight draft on Folberg for $1,800 payable to the order of Watkins. When Watkins presented the draft to Folberg for payment, however, it was dishonored. What choices are available to Watkins?

Whenever commercial paper is used to pay a debt, the original debt is suspended until the paper is due, or until presentment for payment of demand paper. If the paper is dishonored, the holder—

such as Watkins in the problem—has the choice of suing on the paper or on the underlying debt. The liability of parties for payment is as follows:

(1) MAKER

A maker is primarily and unconditionally liable to pay the note according to its terms. Presentment may be made to him but it is not necessary since the obligation is established and accepted by the maker at the time he executes the note. The holder may sue immediately upon the note becoming overdue. Normally only the running of the statute of limitations relieves the maker of this obligation and during the statutory period for the state—commonly six more years (Page 202)—the holder may sue and get judgment against him.

 Mason owed Parsons $350 on a promissory note, due on the first day of the year. The note had passed through the hands of five holders, all of whom had indorsed it without qualification. Hammer, a HDC, was the holder on the due date. He failed to present the instrument for payment to Mason, and thus lost all claim against Parsons and the five other indorsers. However, Mason is primarily liable and must pay unless Hammer fails to collect or sue during the four-year period allowed by that state's statute of limitations.

(2) DRAWEE

A drawee is liable to the holder only when the instrument has been properly presented by the holder, and accepted for payment by the drawee. Thus, he is not liable to the holder for refusing to accept a time draft, or refusing to pay a sight draft or check.

Of course, if the drawee had contracted with the drawer to accept the draft, and then refused to do so, he would be liable for breach of contract. Accordingly, a drawee bank must honor all checks properly drawn to the limit of the drawer's funds on deposit. Theirs is a contract relationship.

(3) DRAWEE-ACCEPTOR

A drawee who has made acceptance is primarily and unconditionally liable for the payment of the draft according to the terms of his acceptance. He is known as the *acceptor*. His liability in that respect is identical with that of the maker of a note.

(4) DRAWER

A drawer is secondarily liable. By executing the draft, he agrees to pay the amount of the draft to the holder if the drawee dishonors the instrument upon presentment, and if he receives proper notice of the dishonor.

 Michel owed Lorraine $500 for a snowmobile. He drew a demand draft on Maree, who owed him more than that sum, and made it payable to Lorraine. The draft was dishonored upon presentment to Maree. Lorraine failed to give Michel proper notice of the dishonor and so he was not liable as drawer on the instrument. Michel may still be liable to Lorraine on the underlying debt for the snowmobile, however.

(5) INDORSERS

An unqualified indorser of a check or draft has greater obligations than the indorser of a note. Both have a secondary liability if the instrument is not paid when due and proper steps are taken to fix liability on secondary parties. But the unqualified indorser of a draft also has secondary liability for payment if the drawee fails to accept the instrument when it is presented.

TO HELP YOU COLLECT ON COMMERCIAL PAPER . . .

1. If a primary party fails to pay an instrument when due, the holder may still be able to collect from a secondary party if there is one on the instrument. When feasible, therefore, get responsible secondary parties to sign commercial paper before you acquire it.
2. Even a secondary party will not be obligated to pay upon default of the primary party unless the holder:
   (a) Properly presents the instrument to the primary party for acceptance and/or payment; and,
   (b) If dishonored, properly notifies the secondary party within the short time allowed by law.
   If you are a holder, be sure to complete these vital chores with promptness and precision.
3. Generally even when not required by the terms of the instrument, present drafts for acceptance as soon as acquired. This forces the drawee to disclose his intent to accept or willingness to pay and enables you, as holder, to seek other relief sooner if necessary.
4. For holders, it is helpful to have commercial paper carry the words "No protest." This makes it unnecessary to give secondary parties the usual prompt notice of dishonor which is otherwise so essential.

YOUR LEGAL VOCABULARY

acceptance	primary parties
acceptor	protest
presentment	secondary parties

1. Promise of the drawee to pay the instrument, as signified by his signature (and usually by the word "accepted" along with the date).
2. The maker of a promissory note, and the drawee who accepts a draft.
3. A formal written notice by a notary public that an instrument was properly presented and dishonored.
4. The drawer of a check or draft, and the indorsers of a check, draft, or promissory note.
5. The first step required in fixing liability of secondary parties; the holder's way of determining the primary party's intentions.
6. A drawee who has agreed to pay the draft according to the terms of his acceptance when it is due.

REMEMBER THESE HIGHLIGHTS

1. The maker of a promissory note and the drawee who accepts a draft are primary parties. The drawer of a check or draft, and the indorsers of a check, draft, or promissory note, are secondary parties.
2. If a holder is to hold secondary parties liable for payment, he must (a) properly present the instrument to the primary party for acceptance or payment. If it is dishonored, then he must (b) give prompt notice of dishonor to secondary parties.
3. Presentment for payment is required on all instruments whenever the holder wishes to fix secondary liability. Presentment for acceptance is required only for certain kinds of drafts.
4. Notice of dishonor may be oral or written, and must be given to secondary parties before midnight of the third business day after dishonor.
5. The maker of a note unconditionally agrees to pay the note according to its terms.
6. The drawee is not liable on a draft until the instrument has been properly presented by the holder, and accepted for payment by the drawee. After acceptance, the drawee is primarily liable.

LAW AS PEOPLE LIVE IT

1. Hughes was HDC of a note executed by Schwartz and indorsed by the payee, Motto, as well as by Reiss. It was payable at the main office of the Manhattan Mercantile Bank. On the due date, Hughes presented the note to Schwartz at his business address. When Schwartz refused to pay, Hughes gave Motto and Reiss due notice of dishonor. Are they liable?

2. Duffy indorsed and delivered to Farrell, a HDC, a demand note for $125 which Singley had made in a state where the statute of limitations for written contracts is six years. Farrell mislaid the note and forgot about it until cleaning out his desk nine years later. He then presented it for payment. Is either Singley, the maker, or Duffy, the payee-indorser, liable on the instrument?

3. Burger was payee of a time draft drawn on Clark. When he presented it for acceptance, Clark simply wrote his name across the face of the instrument. On the due date, Clark claimed he was an indorser and not an acceptor. Is this correct?

4. On January 15, Kiley drew a time draft on Burke, payable in six months to Jacoby. Jacoby indorsed it that same day to Runyan. Runyan never presented it for acceptance, but did make proper presentment for payment on July 15. Burke refused to make payment. When duly notified of the dishonor, Jacoby refused to pay, claiming the instrument should have been presented for acceptance in January. Kiley was solvent then but now is seeking discharge in bankruptcy. Is Jacoby right?

5. Paxton gave Hanna a check for $175 which Hanna indorsed to Pepper, a HDC, in payment of a debt. Pepper promptly deposited the check but it was dishonored by Paxton's bank. He phoned Paxton and was re-assured when Paxton told him to deposit the check again in ten days, after payday. Pepper did this, but the check was again dishonored. This time he gave Hanna notice of dishonor. Is Hanna liable?

6. Adkins held a note which was dishonored. He immediately mailed proper notice of the dishonor to the two indorsers, Barrett and Aber-crombie, but for some unknown reason the letters never arrived. When Adkins sent out follow-up inquiries about two weeks later, Barrett and Abercrombie denied liability on the grounds that they had failed to receive proper notice of dishonor. Are they right?

7. Among the papers found in Burnham's safe-deposit box after his sudden death in mid-July was a promissory note signed by Tanner, and indorsed by Minelli, a millionaire highway contractor. Tanner had gone bankrupt in June. The note had been due the preceding January, but to help his friend Tanner's faltering credit, Burnham had not even presented the note for payment. Is it worth its face value now?

8. Farbwerke Kramer, a German dye maker based in Frankfurt, West Germany, drew a draft on Betner, an importer in Baltimore, Maryland. The draft was payable to the order of Brackett in New York City, and the letters "N.P." were printed prominently on its face. After proper acceptance by Betner, Brackett negotiated the draft to Hunnicutt, a HDC When Hunnicutt presented it to him for payment, Betner could n pay. Must Hunnicutt protest the dishonor because Farbwerke Kra is located in Frankfurt?

9. On August 27, Arman received a draft from Bassett which wa on Castle, payable one year from date. (a) Must Arman p draft to Castle for acceptance? (b) Would your answer be the same if the draft were "payable 30 days after sight?"

10. Arcaro held a promissory note made by Barrett and indorsed by Coffey. On the due date, Arcaro did not bother to present the instrument for payment because he had heard that Barrett was insolvent and was not paying his debts as they came due. In fact, Barrett was simply paying creditors who were most insistent and holding off payment to all others. Is Arcaro justified in giving Coffey notice of dishonor and demanding payment from him?

LAW AS COURTS DECIDE IT

1. Norris J. Temple drew a draft on Maurice E. Temple payable to the order of Hazel Lawless as follows: "Maurice E. Temple, Please pay to the order of Hazel Lawless $351.50, three hundred fifty-one dollars and 50/100. Norris J. Temple." When Lawless presented the draft to Maurice E. Temple for acceptance, he wrote his name on the instrument and nothing more. Would the drawee's signature alone constitute an acceptance? (Lawless v. Temple, 254 Mass. 395, 150 N.E. 176)

2. Doran bought cattle from Friddle and Heathcoate, and in settlement gave certain checks drawn on the Bank of Magazine. Heathcote contacted the cashier of the bank, and the bank orally agreed to pay Doran's checks. Could the bank be held on its oral acceptance? (Bank of Magazine v. Friddle, 179 Ark. 53, 14 S.W. 2d 238)

3. Browne signed promissory notes which were indorsed by the defendant. When Browne dishonored the notes, notice was properly sent to the defendant by certified mail, return receipt requested, addressed to him at his residence. The letter was returned by the post office unopened with "refused" written across the envelope. Had proper notice of dishonor been given? (Durkin v. Siegel, 340 Mass. 445, 165 N.E. 2d 81)

4. Howard loaned the Hotel Bonaza of Las Vegas some $215,000. In exchange, he took two promissory notes executed by the hotel corporation, with defendant Wolf as co-maker, and two notes executed by the hotel but only indorsed by Wolf. The notes were defaulted; Wolf claimed ned only as an accommodation and with the understanding that he held personally liable and that recourse was to be solely Wolf liable? (Howard v. Wolf, New York County, N.Y.L.J., March 28, 1968, p. 14) st her drawee bank in favor of a third party the check in blank and the Bank of Tifton ., partly in cash and partly as a credit to his of Tifton presented the check for payment at eturned because payment had been stopped by vertheless liable for the amount of the check to 115 Ga. App. 555, 155 S.E. 2d 451)

Employment

ARCON PROD.
PERSONNEL DIR.

ACCIDENT
REPORT

SOWINSKI INDUSTRIES
J. SOWINSKI, PRES.

UNIT EIGHT

Sooner or later you will probably get a job and become an employee—almost everyone does. Perhaps you already hold a part-time job, or you expect someday to be self-supporting or a family "breadwinner" with a full-time position. Whether an employee is a minor working casually and part-time, or an adult with a full-time, career position—each is involved in a legal, contractual relation with his employer.

We shall first examine how employment contracts are made, and what rights and obligations are assumed by each party—employer and employee. Then we shall see how government has stepped into the employment relation and set protective controls—minimum wages, maximum hours, and suitable conditions—for the benefit of the worker. Such regulations are a relatively new development; it was in 1938 that the Fair Labor Standards Act was passed, marking the end of "oppressive child labor" and setting the first "minimum wage" at 25¢ per hour. Workers have also gained the right to form and join labor unions, and to bargain collectively with employers over the terms of their employment.

Finally, we shall see how a system of laws called "workmen's compensation" has been developed to deal with injuries, disease, and death occurring in the course of employment.

CHAPTER **29** Contracts of Employment

1. *You accept a job as a stenographer. You can type but you cannot take shorthand. Would your employer be justified in discharging you?*

2. *You are employed as a shipping clerk and you make a serious mistake that costs your employer $400. He severely reprimands you in front of the other employees. Are you justified in quitting your job?*

3. *While working part-time at the Park Lane Bowling Alley, you accidentally drop a bowling ball on a bowler's foot. Are you liable for his injuries?*

WHAT IS EMPLOYMENT?

Problem: Gregory and his son were loading his refrigerator on a pickup truck to move it to the son's apartment. Gregory asked his neighbor, Perkins, to help him. Perkins did. Was Perkins an employee?

Whenever a person or a business firm (the *employer*) hires the labor of another (the *employee*), a relation of *employment* is created. Employment is a form of contract and therefore must include all the essential elements of a contract. (Unit III) In the problem, the relation of Gregory and Perkins was not one of employment because Perkins was merely doing a favor. There was no intent to enter into a contract. (Page 110) In a contract of employment, the employee agrees to do work under the direction and control of the employer; the employer agrees to pay salary or wages.

Although we often speak of "employing" or "hiring" someone for a certain purpose, we are not necessarily creating a legal relation of employment. When you make a contract with someone to do a particular job, as to put a roof on your house, but do not direct or control his actions, he is an *independent contractor* and not an employee. The power of the employer to exercise direction and control distinguishes an employee from an independent contract decides for himself how he shall provide the goods or service ised.

HOW ARE CONTRACTS OF EMPLOYMENT MADE?

Problem: Wright asked Durham, the manager of the Deluxe Supermarket, if he needed part-time help. Durham said he could use him as an extra to work when business required it or some other employee was absent. Durham suggested that Wright report ready to work at 4 p.m., Friday. Was there a contract of employment?

As in the case of other contracts, the employment agreement may be express or implied, oral or written. Whether express or implied, the consent of both parties is required to establish the relation.

Many of the terms of the employment and regulations under which the employee is to work may be implied or are not agreed upon before a worker is actually hired. For example, some firms deduct 25 or 50 cents each time an employee is late. Some firms withhold one or two weeks' wages so that employees will not quit without notice. In some states, laws have been passed regulating such rules or preventing them from being enforced against workers without their consent. In the absence of any statute or agreement to the contrary, however, an employee must abide by company rules or lose his job.

The terms of most contracts of employment are partly express and partly implied. The express portions of the contract proposed in the problem were that Wright would work as an extra employee, depending on when his services were needed, possibly beginning the next Friday at 4 p.m. The pay, the days, hours of work, and even the duties were implied. A definite length of time of employment was neither stated nor implied, and therefore, his employment could be terminated at any time. In the absence of contrary statutes or possible union agreement, all the terms of an employment agreement are not expressly stated. Nevertheless, the courts will enforce the contract if employment is clearly the intent of the parties.

Although individual contracts of employment are usually oral, in some instances they are not enforceable unless they are in writing. We have seen, for example, that when a contract cannot be performed within a period of one year from the date of the making, the agreement must be evidenced by a writing to be enforceable under the Statute of Frauds. (Page 171) This rule applies to contracts of employment.

 Belden was appointed President of Consolidated Books, Inc. and orally agreed to stay for four years. Belden was discharged after two years, and sued to collect damages for breach of contract. He lost. Because the contract could not be performed within a year, to be enforced, it would have to be in writing and signed on behalf of the corporation.

Unlike contracts made between an employer and an individual employee, express contracts made between an employer and a group of employees are always in writing. When the terms of employment are agreed to by representatives of the workers in negotiations with the employer or his representative, the agreement is a *collective bargaining agreement*. The representative is chosen by employees at an election held under the authority of federal or state statute. Commonly, it is a labor union which is selected.

A *labor union* is an organization of workers whose purpose is to further the interests of its members, especially in dealing with employers. Workers in many industries and many public employees are represented by labor unions in contractual negotiations regarding such things as: job classifications; wages for regular work and overtime; hours of work; requirements for employment (such as experience and union membership); pensions; health, safety, and working conditions; method of hiring; causes for discharge; seniority rights; and methods of settling disputes.

WHAT ARE THE RIGHTS OF THE EMPLOYEE?

Problem: Slater hired Hatfield as a deliveryman, but there was nothing to deliver. He reported each day for several days, and was finally laid off without being paid. Could Hatfield require Slater to pay him for the days he reported to work?

In general, the duties and rights of the parties arise from the contract. Some are implied, however, and within recent years many of the rights of employees such as safe and reasonable working conditions have been prescribed by statute and administrative regulations as discussed in Chapters 30 and 31 of this unit. Other rights also arise by custom. Some common rights of employees are:

(1) COMPENSATION

Obviously this right is at the heart of the employment relation. The amount of *compensation* (wage or salary paid for labor or services) may be express or implied; it may be fixed and definite, as a weekly or monthly salary; it may be conditional upon production, "piece work," or the amount of sales; it may be on a time basis, as per hour or day; or it may be a combination of these and other terms. Failure by the employer to pay the agreed or implied compensation gives the worker the right to abandon the job. There is no legal obligation to pay an employee extra for overtime unless required by contract, custom, or statute. Tips belong to the worker unless otherwise agreed.

The right to compensation depends upon the employee's proper discharge of his contract obligations. In the absence of agreement to the contrary, if an employee holds himself ready to perform the service required by the contract, he has performed his part of the agreement and is entitled to his pay. Thus, if Hatfield were ready, willing, and able to work, Slater was obliged to pay him even though he was given nothing to do.

Statutes in most states require certain industries to pay wages monthly, semimonthly, or even weekly in some cases. In most states, when one's employment is terminated, the wages due must be paid at that time or within a specified period. In some states, if an employer does not pay wages that are rightfully earned, the employee may obtain help in collecting them from the state labor commissioner or other state official.

By law and by agreement, deductions may be made before the salary in wages is paid. Social security payments (Chapter 38) and federal income taxes must be withheld and paid directly to the government. By agreement, deductions may be made for other purposes, such as union dues (Chapter 30), insurance, and U.S. savings bonds.

(2) SAFE WORKING CONDITIONS

Problem: Kirby was employed as a painter in Clifford's Body Shop. The exhaust fan in the painting department broke and the fumes were not drawn off. Kirby reported this to his employer. If Clifford failed to have the fan repaired, what were Kirby's rights?

An employee is entitled by law to reasonably safe working conditions, tools, and equipment. This means they must not be harmful to his health, safety, morals, or reputation. If the employer does not provide safe working conditions, the employee may quit his
ᵀn the problem, Kirby had this right. If an employee suffers
,cause of the unsafe working conditions, he has additional
hich will be explained in the next chapter.

(3) REASONABLE TREATMENT

Problem: Hallowell contracted to work as a timekeeper for Mullens' Paving Company during the three summer months. In his second week on the job, Hallowell made a serious error and Mullens, infuriated, struck and injured Hallowell's foot with a shovel. Hallowell quit his job. Was he within his rights?

An employer is required to treat his workers in a reasonable manner. If he assaults an employee (Chapter 5), that employee may quit his job without liability for damages resulting from breach of the employment contract. Thus, Hallowell was within his rights. If Mullens had insulted, rather than assaulted him, Hallowell normally would have no right to quit and could be held liable for breach of contract if he did. As a practical matter, however, employers seldom sue workers who quit in violation of their contracts. Such action would hurt relations with other workers, and probably would not produce much in the way of damages.

(4) AGREED-UPON DUTIES

Problem: Tate was hired as a waitress at Clear Lake Resort for the summer season. When she reported for work, she was told she would have to work as a room maid. She refused and returned home. Could she be held for breach of her agreement?

When the employer insists upon the performance of services not contemplated in the agreement, as in the problem, the employee may rightfully withdraw from the employment. The employee may not, however, abandon the employment merely because of the severity of the work or the unpleasantness of the task if within the scope of the job for which he was employed.

WHAT ARE THE RIGHTS OF THE EMPLOYER?

Problem: Dana employed Gibson as a welder. Dana required all welders to wear protective helmets and goggles while working. Gibson, who had unusually long and thick hair which made it difficult to wear the helmet, refused to do so. Was Dana within his rights in discharging Gibson?

An employer clearly has the right to expect an honest day's work for the wages he pays. But he has other rights too, including:

(1) OBEDIENCE

An employee has the duty to obey reasonable orders and comply with reasonable rules. He agrees, usually by implication, that he will carry out the lawful and reasonable commands and rules of his employer, including the reporting of accidents and the using of prescribed safety devices. In the foregoing problem, the company would be within its rights in discharging Gibson because the rule was reasonable and lawful and he had refused to obey. An employee may not be required to do anything that is illegal, immoral, or contrary to public policy, however. Nor may he be required to perform duties not covered by his contractual agreement.

(2) REASONABLE SKILL

> **Problem:** Jensen was employed by Forrester as a computer programmer. Jensen had operated a sorting machine, but knew nothing about programming. Would her employer be justified in discharging her?

Unless he is a trainee, a person who enters into a contract to work for another implies that he possesses to a reasonable degree the skill, experience, or knowledge that will be necessary to perform his duties. The employer will not be compelled to retain the employee or to pay damages for discharging him if the employee does not perform reasonably well the services he claimed he could do and for which he was employed. Thus, in the problem, Forrester would be justified in discharging Jensen.

(3) LOYALTY AND HONESTY

> **Problem:** Blaine, assistant to the president of Oak Hill Products, had confidential information that his company was going to make an offer to purchase a certain plot of land for $50,000, but would be willing to pay as much as $80,000. He told this to the owners of the land who agreed to give him half of any amount over $50,000 they received. Oak Hill learned of Blaine's action, dismissed him, and sued him for damages. Was the company within its rights?

In entering into a contract of employment, an employee impliedly agrees not to engage in any activities contrary to the interests of the employer. He is liable if he commits or aids in the commission of a fraud upon his employer, as when he lies about his education or experience in order to get the job. If he, like Blaine, reveals confidential information concerning the employer's business, he may be justifiably discharged. He may also be liable for damages. Although an employee is not required to use or even praise the products of his employer, he is bound to do nothing that will harm his employer's business.

An employer has the right to expect an honest day's work for the wages he pays.

(4) REASONABLE PERFORMANCE

> **Problem:** Despite many warnings and reprimands, Pindel, an employee of Burke, continued to take hour-long coffee breaks. Disgusted with his behavior, Burke fired Pindel one day when some important work did not get done because of the long break. Was Burke within his rights?

"An honest day's work" for one's pay is recognized by the law. Hence, an employer like Burke in the problem is justified in discharging an employee who refuses or is unable to carry out, or who habitually neglects, his part of the agreement. An occasional failure to perform his duties, however, is ordinarily not sufficient grounds for dismissal. On the other hand, an employee may be justifiably discharged if he becomes unable to perform because of illness or injury.

IS THE EMPLOYER LIABLE FOR ACTS OF EMPLOYEES?

> **Problem:** Barnhart, an electrician for Elson Electric Contractors, was sent to repair some mixing machines at Clary Chemical Company. He did the work in a negligent manner, ruining the machines and causing several thousand dollars' damage. Was Elson liable for the loss?

If an employee, acting within the scope and in the course of his employment, injures another person, the employer is liable for the damages. It is immaterial that the employer did not authorize the act. Thus, in the problem, Elson was liable for the damage Barnhart caused. Even though an employee intentionally causes damage, in some states the employer may be held liable if the employee has acted with the intention of furthering his employer's interests.

The fact that the employer is liable for the torts of his employee does not relieve the employee from personal responsibility for such acts. Furthermore, if an employee commits a tort not in the course of his employer's business, he alone is liable for any injuries that he may cause.

HOW IS THE EMPLOYMENT CONTRACT TERMINATED?

Problem: Keck hired Spillers as a nurse and companion. After four months, Keck died. Was Spillers' contract terminated?

Contracts of employment are terminated in the same way as other contracts. (Chapter 13) The usual method is by performance. In the problem, the contract was terminated by impossibility of performance as a result of the death of Keck.

You recall that breach of contract is cause for terminating it. When an employer fails to fulfill his obligation to the employee, thereby breaching the contract, the employee may be justified in quitting or abandoning his job before expiration of the agreed time without liability for breach of contract. Similarly, if the employee fails to live up to his obligations, the employer may treat the contract as broken and discharge the employee without liability for breach of contract. In both cases, the breach must be material. By law, employers do not have the right to discharge workers for union activities. Neither does the employee have a right to neglect his duties to engage in union activities.

WHEN YOU BECOME AN EMPLOYEE...

1. Before you go to work, tactfully learn as much as you can about the job: hours, pay, duties, dress, and "fringe benefits."
2. Don't abuse the privilege of taking breaks for rest and refreshments. It could lead to your discharge.
3. Remember that in addition to competent performance of your duties, you owe your employer loyalty, honesty, and obedience.
4. Remember that you are personally responsible for your own negligent acts even though the injured party may also be able to recover from your employer.

YOUR LEGAL VOCABULARY

collective bargaining agreement
compensation
employee
employer

employment
independent contractor
labor union

1. An organization whose purpose is to promote the interest of employees.
2. One who hires the labor of another.
3. An agreement in which the terms of employment are made by the employer and representatives of the workers.
4. A relation in which one hires the labor of another.
5. Wage or salary paid for labor or services.
6. One who contracts to do something for another, but is free of his direction and control.
7. One who works under the direction and control of another.

REMEMBER THESE HIGHLIGHTS

1. Employment is a form of contract, and therefore must include all the essential elements of a contract.
2. An employee is distinguished from an independent contractor by the fact that an employer has the power to exercise direction and control over the employee's work. An independent contractor decides for himself how he shall provide the contracted-for goods or services.
3. Contracts of employment may be express or implied, oral or written. Those made between an employer and an individual employee are usually oral, and the terms partly express and partly implied. Those made between an employer and a group of employees or their representatives are always in writing and the terms usually express.
4. Among the common rights of the employee are (a) compensation, (b) safe working conditions, (c) reasonable treatment, and (d) agreed-upon duties.
5. An employer has the right to require an employee to (a) follow directions and obey reasonable rules, (b) perform his duties in a competent manner, (c) be loyal and honest, and (d) work conscientiously.
6. An employer may be liable for injuries to third parties which result from acts of his employees within the scope and in the course of their employment. The employee also has personal responsibility for such acts.
7. A contract of employment is terminated in the same way as other contracts. Material breach of contract by the employee is cause for his discharge by the employer. The employee is justified in quitting his job if the employer does not fulfill his part of the agreement.

LAW AS PEOPLE LIVE IT

1. Beatty, a college student, asked his neighbor, Rudy, if he could have a part-time job. Rudy said, "Come in and fill out an application." Was there a contract of employment?
2. Wilder hired Hummel to do yard work and odd jobs around her house on Saturdays at $1.75 an hour. After six weeks she told Hummel she

did not need his services any longer. Was there an implied contract that he had a job every Saturday?

3. Postle went to work for Hightower Brick Company. His pay was $100 a week, but his paycheck was for only $82.50. Postle complained and was told that deductions were made for federal income tax, social security, and union dues. Was the employer entitled to make these deductions?

4. Alberts was the night clerk at the Indian Inn. He had several duties besides covering the desk and was not allowed to sleep while on the job. On several occasions the manager of the Inn found Alberts asleep and warned him. If this continued, would the manager be justified in discharging Alberts?

5. Wallace, a warehouseman for Bubbly Bottling Company, was seriously injured in an automobile accident and was unable to do heavy lifting as required or to perform his other duties. Was the employer obligated to keep him on his job?

6. Deveraux contracted with Wagner, an architect, to draw up plans and specifications for a new clinic he wished to build. Wagner, as remuneration, was to receive six percent of the contracted cost of the building. Was this a contract of employment?

7. Ingold, the owner of Seventh Avenue Service Station, directed Hobbs, an employee, to put re-refined oil into the unlabeled oil jars displayed for sale. Hobbs, who knew the law required that re-refined oil be so labeled for sale to the public, refused to do so. Was his disobedience grounds for his discharge?

8. Ransom, a chemist for Belknap Photo Labs, had access to several secret formulas that were the basis of the successful business of the Labs. He quit his job and went to work for a competing company that soon after began marketing similar competing products. Could Belknap prevent Ransom from revealing its secret formulas?

9. Winterbourne, a stockboy for Daugherty Department Store, was delivering some racks of suits to a department and negligently shoved a customer against the escalator, injuring her. Was the store liable?

10. Egenolf signed a contract to teach during the academic year for a certain salary at a new private school. After six months the school ran short of funds and reduced Egenolf's salary $100 a month. Egenolf quit. Was he justified in doing so?

LAW AS COURTS DECIDE IT

1. McCarty, a plasterer by trade, was telephoned by Soden, the Director of the Recreation Commission, about patching some plaster in a building used by the Commission. McCarty agreed to do the work and to bring his own tools, but said the Commission would have to furnish the scaffolding, mortar box, helpers, and materials. McCarty was to be paid

by the hour. When McCarty reported to work, Soden showed him the jobs to be done. Although he could have given McCarty instructions as to how he wanted the work done, Soden did not. McCarty began work, assisted by two Commission employees who mixed the mortar and carried it to McCarty on the scaffold which was furnished by the Commission. Soon after, McCarty fell from the scaffold and sustained serious injuries. In a legal action that followed, the question arose as to whether McCarty was an independent contractor, or an employee entitled to workmen's compensation. Which was he? (McCarty v. Great Bend Board of Education, 195 Kans. 310, 403 P. 2d 956)

2. Smith was employed as an embalmer in Baue's funeral parlor in St. Charles, Missouri. He was paid a weekly salary, and the term of his employment was indefinite. After working for a little over a year, Smith joined the Embalmer's Union. Baue refused to deal with the union and, after attempting to persuade Smith to quit the union and become a partner in the business, Baue discharged Smith. Smith sued Baue for reinstatement. The Missouri Constitution provided that "employees shall have the right to organize and bargain collectively through representatives of their own choosing." There was no problem under federal law. Can Smith get his job back? (Smith v. Arthur C. Baue Funeral Home, 370 S.W. 2d 249, Missouri)

3. Lerche, an actress skilled in playing emotional dramatic parts, but with no experience in comedy, was employed by the Essanay Film Manufacturing Co. to do dramatic acting. When notified that she had been cast for a comedy called the *Black Cat Comedy,* she protested to her employer and was given a notice of dismissal. Was the company justified? (Essanay Film Manufacturing Co. v. Lerche, 267 F. 353)

4. Sylvia was the owner of land onto which several large boulders rolled during a road construction job of the Thomas Brothers Corporation. Sylvia demanded their removal. Clark, construction superintendent for Thomas Brothers, started to remove the boulders, but was stopped by Sylvia who said she had changed her mind. During the argument which ensued, Rego appeared and loudly demanded that Clark leave the boulders where they were. A quarrel followed, and Clark wrongfully struck Rego, breaking his jaw. Rego sued Clark's employer, Thomas Brothers, for damages. Should he succeed? (Rego v. Thomas Brothers Corporation, 340 Mass. 334, 164 N.E. 2d 144)

5. Horton, operator of a taxicab business, employed Woodall as a driver. Jones, who was crippled, engaged the cab driven by Woodall. When she arrived at her destination, her crippled condition and the presence of several packages caused Jones to temporarily lay her purse on the seat as she left the cab. When Woodall noticed this, he slammed the door and drove rapidly away with the purse. Jones then sued Horton for the value of the purse and the $440 which it contained. Should she recover from Horton? (Horton v. Jones, 208 Miss. 257, 44 So. 2d 397)

CHAPTER **30** Government Regulation of Employment

1. *An adult man, a woman, and a boy of 17 are employed by the same firm to do the same type of work. The man is paid $10 a week more than the woman, the boy gets $5 a week less. Is this legal?*

2. *You plan to work on weekends and for the three months of your summer vacation. Will you need a work permit?*

3. *A worker tells you that he is helping to organize a union at his place of employment. May his employer discharge him for such activities?*

HOW IS EMPLOYMENT REGULATED?

Problem: Minsky was employed as a custodian in an automobile factory which shipped its products all over the nation and the world. Was his job subject to state or federal employment law, or both?

Dual sovereignty was established in our country by the Constitution, which gave the federal government certain specified powers, and reserved all other powers to the states and to the people themselves. Dual sovereignty continues today, with the federal government and each of the 50 states exercising powers of government. Even with the introduction of uniform laws, such as the UCC, differences of law between states, and between states and the federal government, exist.

The regulation of trade is one of the areas where federal and state governments are both involved. Under the U.S. Constitution (Art. 1, Sect. 8) Congress has the power ". . . To regulate Commerce with foreign Nations, and among the several states . . ." Commerce among the several states, or between persons in two or more states, is called *interstate commerce*. If the trade is conducted entirely within one state, it is called *intrastate commerce,* and is subject only to the laws of that state.

As the U.S. Supreme Court has come to interpret more liberally the words creating the federal powers to regulate trade, the states have—in effect—lost some of their former sovereign power in that area. In a representative case, the Supreme Court declared that federal power over interstate commerce ". . . includes the power to regulate the local incidents thereof, including local activities in both the States of origin and destination, which might have a substantial and harmful effect upon that commerce." (Heart of Atlanta Motel, Inc. v. United States, 379 U.S. 241) Such words clearly give the Congress very broad powers to legislate for business, including rules applying to employers and workers in firms which produce goods sold across state borders.

Typically the Congress passes statutes which give the federal departments of the government, or specified administrative agencies, the duty and power to enforce the law. They in turn draw up detailed administrative regulations or rulings. If a person or company violates one of its regulations, the agency may investigate, and after a public hearing, it may issue an order to the offending party. The defendant may appeal to the courts for review, but the courts usually uphold the administrative agency because it is composed of experts in the field. These important agencies are discussed further in Chapter 45.

Congress has also enacted statutes which regulate certain matters exclusively, such as the maximum lengths of railroad trains which are permitted in interstate commerce. At the other extreme, even though it might have legislated, in some areas it has chosen not to do so. For example, Congress has deliberately left the regulation of life and casualty insurance to the states. Finally, in certain areas such as labor-management relations and employment conditions, both federal and state legislation exists. Possible conflicts between the two have been minimized because most industrial states have followed the federal example and have enacted labor laws which are carbon copies of the federal laws, although limited to intrastate commerce. If a true conflict between state and federal jurisdiction arises, generally federal law prevails.

Thus, either at the federal or the state level, and sometimes at both, laws exist which deal with such matters as:

(1) minimum wages and maximum hours of work;
(2) protection of children and women against improper work;
(3) the right to get a job without regard to race, color, religion, sex, national origin, or advanced age;
(4) training of apprentices in some crafts;
(5) proper working conditions and compensation for injury suffered on the job (Chapter 31);

(6) security payments in case of unemployment caused by discharge or disability, or by retirement in old age (Chapter 38);

(7) the right of employees to "form, join, and assist" labor unions, and to bargain collectively with employers over wages, hours, and conditions of employment.

In the problem, Minsky's job was subject to both state and federal laws.

WHAT IS THE LAW AS TO WAGES AND HOURS?

Problem: Colacino was employed during the summer as a fruit packer by the Del Prado Fruit and Nut Company. She worked 44 hours a week and was paid $2.00 an hour. How much did she receive each week?

The federal government has enacted the Fair Labor Standards Act (known as the Wage and Hour Law) to provide minimum wages and maximum hours for all employees considered to be under federal jurisdiction. Minimum wages as of 1972 are $1.60 an hour ($1.30 for agricultural workers), and maximum hours which can be worked at regular rates of pay are 40 per week (no daily maximum). This means that the minimum pay for a full week is $64. If more hours than the maximum allowed at regular rates are worked in one week, one and one-half times the regular rate must be paid for all overtime. Thus, in the problem, Colacino's weekly wage was $92, consisting of $80 for regular time and $12 for the time over 40 hours, figured at the rate of $3 an hour. Over the years, as the cost of living has gone up, Congress has raised the minimum wage. When the law was first passed as a depression remedy in 1938, the minimum wage was 25¢ an hour.

The wage and hour requirements of the law do not apply to executives, professional workers, or outside salesmen; nor to employees of certain small enterprises, such as service stations, newspapers, small hotels and restaurants; nor to employees in such industries as small-farm agriculture and fishing. The hour provisions apply only partially to workers in seasonal industries and to certain other groups. The wage provisions do not apply to handicapped workers, learners, apprentices, messengers, or students in retail and service firms or in agriculture, provided their employers have obtained permission to pay less from the United States Department of Labor.

WHAT ARE CHILD-LABOR LAWS?

Problem: Tucker, age 17 and a recent high school graduate, found a summer job working the swing shift (4 p.m. to 12 midnight) on a saw machine in a lumber mill. Could he accept the job?

The federal government and every state have child-labor laws. The federal law is part of the Fair Labor Standards Act. Although these laws vary, they are all based on the principles that early years are better used for education in a free society; that certain heavy work is harmful or dangerous for young bodies; and that child labor at low wages takes jobs from adults. Usually these laws regulate the conditions and types of employment available to those under age 16 or 18. For example, some states require that all minors under 18 who work must do so in the period between 5 a.m. and 10 p.m. Moreover, the job must not be classified as hazardous. If these particular laws were in effect where Tucker lived, he would not be allowed to accept the job.

While the specific laws may vary, their provisions commonly set the maximum number of working hours in a day, prohibit night work, prescribe the grade in school that must be completed, set the required age for certain hazardous occupations, and establish whether a child who is working is required to attend a continuation school on a part-time basis.

 Marjorie Tsukamoto, age 17, knows of a job that is available as a flower maker in a novelty shop. In her state, she may not be employed until she (a) has received a work certificate from the superintendent of schools, (b) has enrolled in a continuation school to attend four hours a week until she has reached age 18 or graduated from high school, and (c) has presented a physician's statement certifying that she is in good physical condition. After she is employed, she will not be allowed to work at night, more than 8 hours in any one day, or more than a total of 48 hours in any week.

Agricultural work, domestic work, and such jobs as baby-sitting, golf caddying, bowling alley pin-setting, delivering papers, and helping parents in nonhazardous work are usually, but not always, exempted from state child-labor laws.

The federal law forbids labor of children under 16, except those engaged in the above-mentioned activities, and those who are actors in motion pictures, theatrical productions, radio, or television. In addition, children between 14 and 16 may be employed in occupations other than mining, manufacturing, and processing, if the employment is confined to periods that will not interfere with their schooling, health, or well-being. Examples of such jobs would be office and clerical work; retailing work—selling, cashiering, modeling, advertisement drawing, window trimming, comparison shopping, price marking, packing and shelving; running errands and making deliveries by foot, bicycle, or public transport; garden maintenance (without use of power mowers); soda fountain work; and gasoline station work (without use of pits or racks).

In occupations found by the U.S. Secretary of Labor to be hazardous, the minimum employment age is 18. In this category are jobs in mining coal and other minerals; logging and lumber production; slaughtering and meat packing; roofing; wrecking, demolition, or excavation work. Also barred to minors under 18 are jobs that involve operating power-driven hoists, motor vehicles, power-driven wood-working and metal forming, punching, or shearing machines. The minor may not work in the manufacture of brick, tile and like products, or of explosives and explosive components; nor may he work where he is exposed to radioactive substances, or where the task involves the use of circular saws, bandsaws, or guillotine shears.

The minimum age for employment in hazardous occupations is 18.

I DON'T CARE IF YOUR MOM DOES SAY YOU CAN REALLY WRECK A HOUSE, YOU HAVE TO BE 18 OR OLDER.

ACME WRECKING CO. JOB APPLICATIONS HERE

Where state child-labor laws have higher standards than the federal act, the state laws apply to children in all industries within that state. Most states require full-time school attendance between the ages of 7 and 16. A few states start at 6 (Hawaii, Michigan, New Hampshire, New Mexico, New York, Ohio, and Utah); some start at 8 (Arizona, California, Pennsylvania, and Washington). At the other end, the young person may quit school at 14 if he lives in Delaware, but in some states he must wait until he is 17 (Maine, New Mexico, Pennsylvania, and Texas) and in another group he must continue his formal education until he is 18 (Ohio, Oklahoma, Oregon, Utah, and Washington). In most of the states there are statutory exceptions.

For employment during school hours, an equal number of states (23) specify the ages of 14 and of 16 as the minimum. All of the states place a limit on the number of hours which a young person may work, and the hours of school are often combined with the hours on the job while school is in session. A common maximum is 48 hours of work in one week, the standard in 24 states. However, the limit ranges from 18 to 54 hours a week for persons under 16. Eleven states place no special limit on the work hours of those between 16 and 17, but most retain controls, and most states require a work permit if the individual is under 16 or 18.

WHAT LABOR LAWS SPECIFICALLY AFFECT WOMEN?

Problem: Johnson, a widow and sole supporter of her five children, was employed on the production line of United Auto Body. Although Johnson was eager to work overtime, she found the company never allowed her more than one hour extra, while male co-workers had put in as much as 8 or 10 hours overtime in a single day. On the bulletin board one day she saw a notice issued by the Equal Employment Opportunity Commission stating that it was unlawful for an employer "to discriminate against any individual with respect to his compensation, terms, conditions, or privileges of employment, because of such individual's race, color, religion, sex, or national origin." Was Johnson being unlawfully discriminated against?

The federal government and all the states have enacted laws designed especially to protect women workers. These statutes may actually regulate working conditions, wages, and hours of work. Or, they may create commissions whose job is to issue regulations setting more detailed standards for such things as lighting, ventilation, and temperature; rest and lunch periods; rest rooms, first aid and sanitary facilities; and elevator service. Frequently the same working conditions that apply to girls and women apply to boys under 18 years of age.

All states except Alabama, Delaware, Florida, Hawaii, Indiana, Iowa, Nebraska, and West Virginia have statutes or regulations specifically limiting the hours of work for women in business or industry. Often these provide that women may work not more than 48 or 54 hours in any one week, or 8 or 9 hours in any 24-hour period, except in cases of emergency or in certain industries. Generally executive and professional women and those employed as domestic workers are exempt from such hour requirements.

In recent years, however, the question has arisen as to whether such "protective" laws are actually more discriminatory than protective. Included in the Civil Rights Act of 1964 was the law which Johnson, in the problem, saw posted on the bulletin board. Enforcement of this fair employment practice law may soon replace most of the special laws which have been passed for the protection of women. Our changing technology and new attitudes on women's rights have led the Equal Employment Opportunity Commission to rule that laws which limit women to certain jobs at certain hours actually discriminate against rather than protect them. They may be barred from a particular job only if there are "peculiar requirements" which truly make it unsuitable for women.

The move against discrimination is also evidenced by the Federal Equal Pay Act, which provides for equal pay for equal work without regard to age or sex of the worker. This means there can be no discrimination in pay for jobs where the performance requires equal skills, effort, and responsibility, and where working conditions are similar. Exceptions are made where wages are based on seniority, a merit system, or quantity or quality of production. The Federal Equal Pay Act, as part of the Fair Labor Standards Act, applies to those workers in enterprises affecting interstate commerce.

Most states have laws that assure women workers a minimum wage. All but 11 [1] states have adopted *equal-pay laws,* which provide that wage rates for women shall be the same as those paid men for the same work.

Special regulations in some states take care of particular problems. For example, premium wages may be specified in the case of *split shifts* in which the worker's hours are divided.

 Cora was a waitress at the Delightful Drive-In. She was required to work from 7 to 9 a.m., 11 a.m. to 2 p.m., and 5 to 8 p.m. six days a week. Even though her hours did not exceed the maximum, she might be entitled to more than the minimum wage.

[1] States which have not yet adopted such laws are Alabama, Delaware, Iowa, Kansas, Louisiana, Mississippi, New Mexico, North Carolina, South Carolina, Tennessee, and Virginia.

WHAT LAWS GOVERN LABOR-MANAGEMENT RELATIONS?

Problem: Benvenuti, an employee of Graphic Arts Press, Inc., was not a member of the union. In an election held by the employees of Graphic Arts, the union was selected as the collective bargaining representative of the employees. Benvenuti did not like the contract the union made. He proceeded to try to make his own contract with the company for a higher wage than others were paid for similar work. Did he have this right?

The National Labor-Management Relations Act of 1947 (known as the Taft-Hartley Act) provides for collective bargaining between employers and employees in businesses engaged in interstate commerce, except railways and airlines which are governed by separate legislation. The Labor-Management Reporting and Disclosure Act of 1959 (Landrum-Griffin Act) regulates certain relationships between the individual union member and his own union such as voting rights and procedures, disclosure of financial information, and relations between unions. Several states have similar acts to govern employment of an intrastate nature. Both the federal and state acts set up machinery to enforce the rights given workers and employers and to settle disputes between them.

The federal labor relations legislation does the following:

(1) IT GIVES EMPLOYEES THE RIGHT TO ORGANIZE

Employees may organize into unions and bargain collectively with their employers, through representatives of their own choosing, for wages, hours, and working conditions.

The employer is not obliged to bargain over such things as product prices, designs, or quality, which are strictly management matters even though they do affect company ability to pay wages. The legislation does not require workers to join a union unless the employer has agreed to have a union shop; in the *union shop,* non-union employees may be hired, but they must join the union within a stated maximum period, usually thirty days. The *closed shop,* in which a worker must belong to the union before he can be hired, is prohibited. Moreover, employees cannot be dismissed from their jobs if they are not permitted to join the union or if they are expelled from it for any reason other than nonpayment of dues. Two types of "shop" not specifically mentioned in the labor legislation are the open shop and the agency shop. The *open shop,* in which the employment agreement either does not refer to union membership, or expressly declares that persons may be hired without regard to union membership, is of course permissible. The *agency shop* is a variation of the union shop; in this type of shop, employees are not required to join the union, but if they do not, they must pay the union the same amount as the dues paid by union members. A few states prohibit the agency shop.

(2) IT SETS UP THE NATIONAL LABOR RELATIONS BOARD

This board administers the rights and duties given to both workers and employers by the Act.

The employees and their union representatives, as well as the employers, are entitled to take part in the hearings before the Board and may dispute any order of the Board in the federal courts.

(3) IT DETERMINES THE MANNER OF SELECTING A SPOKESMAN

It prescribes that, after a secret vote of the workers supervised by the National Labor Relations Board, the representative named by a majority of the employees shall be the exclusive spokesman for all the employees in making employment contracts and dealing with the employer.

Thus, Benvenuti, in the foregoing problem, could not make an individual employment contract with his employer. Employees as a group, however, have the right to reject representation by any union.

For six weeks, union organizers conducted an intensive campaign to get workers of the Classic Brick and Tile Company to join the union. Pickets carried placards which read "CLASSIC IS UNFAIR TO ORGANIZED LABOR," even though the company paid the union scale wage or higher in all categories of work. An election was finally held under the auspices of the National Labor Relations Board to determine whether the union should have the exclusive right to represent the workers in making the contract of employment with the company. By an overwhelming margin, the workers rejected the union. Under N.L.R.B. rules, the union may not picket or call for another election for at least one year thereafter.

(4) IT GIVES EMPLOYERS THE RIGHT TO SUE UNIONS

Employers may sue for damages resulting from violations of collective bargaining agreements or unfair labor practices.

(5) IT DEFINES UNFAIR LABOR PRACTICES

It declares certain actions of employers and of unions to be "unfair labor practices."

WHAT ARE UNFAIR LABOR PRACTICES?

Problem: During her lunch hour and after work, Bergen was an organizer for a labor union in the glove factory where she worked. Her employer said he paid better than union scale wages and did not want to deal with any union. He fired Bergen because of her organizing efforts. Was he legally permitted to do so?

Certain acts of unions and employers are prohibited by the labor-management legislation and are described as *unfair labor practices*. These acts are forbidden in an effort to compel both employers and unions to respect the rights of employees.

(1) UNFAIR LABOR PRACTICES BY EMPLOYERS

Under the National Labor-Management Relations Act, employers may not:

(a) Interfere with the rights of employees to organize or join unions, and to bargain collectively through representatives of their own choosing.

(b) Contribute financial or other support to a union, or dominate its formation or administration.

(c) Discriminate in the hiring, demoting, discharging, and working conditions of an employee to encourage or to discourage union membership. Union shops are permitted, however. Accordingly, in the problem, Bergen's employer was guilty of an unfair labor practice. He might be required to reinstate her and pay wages she lost while barred from her job.

(d) Discharge or discriminate against an employee because he has filed charges or given testimony against the employer under the Act.

(e) Refuse to bargain collectively in good faith with the union which is the representative of the employees.

In addition, employers may not threaten to *blacklist* employees who are union members by placing their names on a list of undesirables sent to other employers with the purpose of making it difficult for them to find work. Employers may not threaten to stop operations, replace workers with machines, or move the factory, just to avoid unionization.

> Carrillo and Burdette were trying to get their fellow workers to join a union. Their employer, Cassidy Clothiers, threatened to fire them and to blacklist them by sending their names to a trade association for distribution to other employers as known "trouble makers." The employer was guilty of two unfair labor practices.

(2) UNFAIR LABOR PRACTICES BY UNIONS

Certain activities of labor unions are also unfair labor practices. Unions may not:

(a) Attempt to force employees to or restrain employees from organizing into unions, or interfere with their right to bargain collectively. Of course, if a majority of the workers select a union, all are bound by its contracts with the employer.

(b) Attempt to cause an employer to discriminate against an employee for any reason other than his failure to pay initiation fees and dues to the union.

(c) Refuse to bargain collectively in good faith with the employer.

(d) Require payment of an excessive or discriminatory fee for initiation into the union.

(e) Attempt to force an employer to pay for services not performed or not to be performed (*featherbedding*).

(f) Patrol alongside the premises of the employer for union purposes (*picket*) after the employer has lawfully recognized another union, or anytime during the 12 months after the picketing union has lost a valid election.

(g) Engage in certain kinds of boycotts and strikes. Most strikes and boycotts by private employees are not illegal if conducted without violence. Generally strikes of public employees are prohibited.

A *strike* is a stoppage of work to force an employer to give in to union demands. Its counterpart is a *lockout* which occurs when an employer closes down to resist union demands or to induce the union to agree to the employer's proposals.

A *boycott* is basically a refusal to have anything to do with the products or services of an employer. In the *primary boycott,* which is legal, a labor dispute leads to the employees' refusal to buy their employer's products. Typically it is accompanied by a strike and picketing. If the employees attempt to cause the suppliers and customers of the employer to refuse to have business dealings with him, it is known as a *secondary boycott*. It need not be accompanied by picketing, but often is. The secondary boycott is generally illegal.

State laws vary considerably from the federal act. But where the matter involves interstate commerce, the federal government has jurisdiction and its laws prevail.

A number of states have enacted *right-to-work laws,* which prohibit compulsory union membership and ban the union shop as well as the closed shop.

WHAT DO OTHER LABOR LAWS PROVIDE?

Problem: Kleinsmith was drafted into the United States Army. After his release from the service, he wished to return to his former job, but his employer told him his job was now held by another and refused to rehire him. What, if any, were Kleinsmith's rights?

Most states, as well as the federal government, have many other laws which regulate certain employment practices.

(1) INDUSTRIAL HOME WORK

Nearly half the states regulate the kind of manufacturing work that may be done in the home, including the ages of those who do the work and the conditions in the home.

(2) FAIR EMPLOYMENT PRACTICES

As we have seen, the federal government and all the states have laws which specifically protect women workers. (Page 425) The federal government (for firms in interstate commerce with 25 or more employees) and all but 13 of the states [2] also forbid an employer to discriminate in hiring, training, promoting, or discharging workers because of race, color, religion, or national origin. Discrimination is prohibited, moreover, in amount of compensation and working conditions. Unions may not exclude persons from membership because of race, color, religion, sex, or national origin.

[2] All except Alabama, Arkansas, Florida, Georgia, Louisiana, Mississippi, North Carolina, North Dakota, South Carolina, South Dakota, Tennessee, Texas, and Virginia.

The federal government and 25 states [3] prohibit discrimination on the basis of advanced age—meaning the ages from 40 to 65. An employer may not fire or refuse to hire or otherwise discriminate against a worker simply because of his age. Exceptions are made for valid occupational needs. For example, airline pilots must be under age 60, and bridge and skyscraper workers must have special physical qualifications.

(3) SERVICEMEN

The Military Selective Service Extension Act of 1950 requires that men who have been drafted, or who have enlisted or been re-called to active duty must be re-employed after discharge from the service unless their employment at the time of induction was temporary.

Upon honorable separation, the veteran must still be able to do his former work. If a service-connected disability makes this impossible, he is entitled to a job with duties he can perform. The veteran must not have been away for more than five years, and he must apply for re-employment within 90 days after discharge. Hence, Kleinsmith in the problem must be re-employed.

(4) CONVICT LABOR

To protect workers and employers from unfair competition by those who would use cheap labor, the federal government and most states either prevent or regulate the use of convict labor in competition with private business. Typically convicts may produce goods, such as license plates and textile products, for use only by government agencies. This is a type of legal discrimination. Ex-convicts may also have difficulty in finding work after their release from prison. Many employers consider such persons untrustworthy, and they are not obliged to hire them even if they are otherwise qualified.

(5) TIME OFF TO VOTE

More than half the states provide that workers must be given sufficient time off with pay, at a time convenient to the employer, to vote in regular primary and general elections. Today, however, since working hours are shorter, and polls open earlier and close

---

[3] All except Alabama, Arizona, Arkansas, Florida, Georgia, Iowa, Kansas, Kentucky, Minnesota, Mississippi, Missouri, Montana, Nevada, New Hampshire, North Carolina, Oklahoma, South Carolina, South Dakota, Tennessee, Texas, Utah, Vermont, Virginia, West Virginia, and Wyoming.

later on election days, this type of legislation is not so important as it once was.

(6) MEDIATION AND CONCILIATION

Both the federal government and most of the states have organized services designed to help prevent strikes and to settle labor-management disputes by voluntary methods. When collective bargaining breaks down or becomes deadlocked, a government representative may try to bring the parties together and settle their differences. He is a mediator or conciliator, and has no power to compel agreement.

(7) CONTROL OVER WAGES

Kickbacks of wages, that is, refunds by an employee to his employer as a condition of keeping his job, are prohibited whenever one is employed on a job being done under contract to the federal government.

(8) APPRENTICESHIP PROGRAMS

In many skilled trades, such as machine building, construction work, and printing, the means of entry for young people is through an *apprenticeship program*. Typically the individual starts as a beginner or apprentice, progresses to the level of ability of a journeyman, and finally attains the status of a master craftsman. He works on regular jobs under the direction of a master craftsman, and often attends formal classes in technical schools. Most states have such programs which are usually conducted in close cooperation with unions and employers.

(9) OCCUPATIONAL SAFETY AND HEALTH

The Federal Occupational Safety and Health Act of 1971 imposed comprehensive regulations which govern such matters as safe walking surfaces, fire protection, work platforms and ladders, hazardous materials, protective equipment, safety signs, first aid and medical services, storage and handling of industrial materials, tools, and machinery. The act does not apply to the construction, coal mining, or maritime industries where special laws exist. Nor does it extend to agriculture, research facilities, or white collar work in offices. Where state or local regulations are more demanding, they remain in effect; for example, on elevator safety and boiler operation.

IF YOU ARE AN EMPLOYEE, REMEMBER . . .

1. Neither employers nor unions may legally discriminate against you because of your race, color, religion, sex, national origin, or advanced age. If you feel you have been discriminated against unfairly, consult an attorney, your union officer, your state or federal labor or employment office, or your state or federal legislative representative for advice or assistance.
2. You and your fellow employees generally have the legal right to organize into unions and bargain collectively with your employer.
3. An employer may not legally discharge you for engaging in a lawful strike. To do so makes him guilty of an unfair labor practice.
4. If you belong to a union, you have a right to vote for your officers in secret elections and to regularly receive accurate information on union finances and activities.

IF YOU ARE AN EMPLOYER, REMEMBER . . .

1. It is generally illegal to discriminate against employees or prospective employees because of race, color, religion, sex, national origin, or advanced age. You may still discriminate, or select, train or promote on such grounds as appropriate educational preparation for particular work, and the time and type of experience possessed.
2. Unions are legal. If they represent your workers, your cooperation with them may provide benefits for all parties involved.
3. You may not discharge or otherwise discriminate against your workers for their decision to join a union.
4. You are obliged to bargain collectively in good faith with representatives of a union which was chosen by a majority of your workers, but you are not obliged to make any concessions.

YOUR LEGAL VOCABULARY

agency shop	lockout
apprenticeship program	open shop
blacklist	picket
boycott	primary boycott
closed shop	right-to-work law
equal-pay law	secondary boycott
featherbedding	split shift
interstate commerce	strike
intrastate commerce	unfair labor practices
kickbacks	union shop

1. Certain acts which violate laws governing relations between labor and employers.
2. A shop in which all employees must belong to the union, but not necessarily before they are hired.
3. A stoppage of work to force an employer to yield to union demands.

4. A patrol, usually made by union members alongside the premises of the employer, during a labor dispute.
5. Requiring an employer to pay for services not performed and not to be performed.
6. A law requiring that wage rates for women shall be the same as those paid men for the same work.
7. A report exchanged by employers, listing workers who are unwanted because of their union activities and making it difficult for them to get work.
8. A refusal by employees engaged in a labor dispute to buy the employer's products.
9. A shop in which a worker must belong to the union before he can be hired.
10. A shift in which the worker's hours are divided.

REMEMBER THESE HIGHLIGHTS

1. The federal government has the power to regulate the employment of those employed in enterprises engaged in interstate commerce, or the production of goods for interstate commerce. The state governments have similar power over intrastate commerce.
2. With certain exceptions, workers considered to be under federal jurisdiction must be paid a minimum of $1.60 an hour for 40 hours of work in any one week, and time and one-half for all hours worked over 40.
3. All states and the federal government restrict the employment of children and have laws designed especially to protect workers who are minors or women.
4. The rights of workers to organize and join labor unions; to bargain collectively with employers; to strike; to secure jobs without regard to race, color, religion, sex, national origin, or advanced age are among those protected by law.
5. Certain acts of employers and of labor unions are "unfair labor practices" and are prohibited by law.

LAW AS PEOPLE LIVE IT

1. Archer, 13 years old, worked as a golf caddy at the Wiltshire Country Club. During the summer vacation he was offered a job operating the riding power mower and helping unpack and shelve goods in the golf pro's shop. Could he be legally employed at these jobs?
2. Eckerd, who was 17, had often helped his father slaughter and dress hogs, sheep, and cattle for home use on the family farm. He therefore felt qualified to work that summer in the Halbach Meat Packing Company plant in town. Could Halbach hire him?

3. Funland Shows, Inc., a traveling carnival, advertised in the "Help Wanted — Male" column of a newspaper for a roustabout who would run a game of chance and also help to set up and disassemble the show's large tents. Nancy Beau wanted to travel and applied for the job. Will Funland be violating the law if it rejects her because of her sex?

4. Kutzer, who had worked as a driver for Hound Dog Bus Lines for 15 years, received a higher wage than Woodruff who had just joined the company. Their work was identical. Could Woodruff complain that Hound Dog was violating the Federal Equal Pay Act?

5. De Lour represented his union in the annual contract negotiations with the employer, Regina Crown Sales Co. De Lour insisted on including in the contract a 5 percent across-the-board price boost on all products to permit a 10 percent wage boost. Was this a proper demand?

6. When a national union sent organizers to try to persuade his workers to join the union, Garner called three of his most trusted employees to his office. He urged them to organize a new union limited to company employees, and offered to provide the union with office space and free time for officers. He gave the men $1,500 to buy printed notices and refreshments for an organization meeting. Was Garner's action legal?

7. Vogel was proud of his reputation as an honest but tough bargainer. After being elected president of his union, he was selected to bargain with the employer over a new labor contract. Vogel met the company representative, Gish, and said "We want a 25 percent wage boost for all workers. That's our first and last word." When Gish said the company couldn't afford that much, Vogel walked out saying, "I'll return when you're ready to say yes." For two weeks he has refused to return and now the workers are planning to strike. Are Vogel and the union guilty of any violation of the law?

8. Adair started work with Dynamic Products as a clerk, and never worked more than 40 hours without getting time and a half wages for overtime. He was promoted to foreman, then supervisor, and finally to an executive position as plant superintendent. His base salary is $50,000. Can he claim time and a half when he works his customary 10 to 20 hours overtime?

9. Pitney had been convicted of passing bad checks to pay for drugs and had been confined in the state penitentiary for three years. When he got out he found that many employers refused to hire him because of his criminal record. Is such discrimination legal?

10. On the day of the general election, Heitsman requested an hour's time off from work, at the employer's convenience, in order to vote. The foreman, Bohr, disagreed with his political views and refused the request. During a slack period, Heitsman went out to vote with two fellow workers who had received permission from Bohr. When he returned, Bohr fired him. Can Heitsman compel the employer to reinstate him?

LAW AS COURTS DECIDE IT

1. A local union whose members were all white required that new applicants for membership be related to and recommended by a present member, and also be approved by a majority vote. Were these rules legal under the Federal Fair Employment Practices Law? (Vogler v. McCarty, Inc., U.S.D.C., E. Louisiana, 65 LRRM 2554)

2. During a labor dispute, television technicians who were on strike picketed the station without success. Then they distributed 5,000 hand-bills which made a sharp, disparaging attack on the quality of the station's programs. For this their employer fired them. They sought relief from the National Labor Relations Board. Must they be rehired? (N.L.R.B. v. Local 1229, I.B.E.W. 346 U.S. 464)

3. Greenwood, member of the Hotel and Restaurant Employees and Bar-tenders International Union and active in soliciting fellow employees to join the union, was discharged by the management of the Sansome House where she had been employed as a waitress. At the time of the discharge Sansome did not know that she was a member of the union nor that she had solicited other employees to join the union. When the Pennsylvania Labor Relations Board ordered her reinstated, the case was transferred to the courts. Sansome contended that it could not have discharged Greenwood for union membership or union activities because it did not know she was a member. Aside from this restriction, it claimed it had the right to discharge any employee for good cause or no cause at all. Was the contention of Sansome correct? (Pennsylvania Labor Relations Board v. Sansome House Enterprises, 378 Pa. 385, 106 A. 2d 404)

4. Stein was employed in a supervisory capacity by the Gordon Brothers Manufacturing Company. He was instructed by the president of the company not to work more than the standard 40 hours in any one week. Nevertheless, unknown to his employer, Stein spent additional hours on the job. He thereafter brought an action to recover for wages at time and a half under the Fair Labor Standards Act. Should he be successful? (Stein v. Gordon Brothers Manufacturing Co., 43 F. Supp. 249)

5. Local 395 of the Oil Workers' Union represented the employees of Standard Oil Company at its refinery in Cleveland, Ohio. Local 346 represented the Standard employees at a refinery at Toledo, Ohio. The Company and Local 395 had reached complete agreement on the terms of a new contract, which had been ratified by the membership. However, the officers of Local 395 refused to sign the contract until the Company had agreed to a contract with Local 346. The National Labor Relations Board found this conduct by Local 395 to be a violation of its obligation to bargain in good faith. Was the Board correct? (Standard Oil Company v. N.L.R.B., 322 F. 2d 40)

CHAPTER 31 Protection of Employees

1. The school custodian is injured when some lockers fall on him. What rights does he have?

2. An attendant in a service station negligently leaves a tire on the floor. Later, carrying a battery, he stumbles over the tire, falls, and breaks his leg. Is his employer liable?

3. During a coffee break in the company cafeteria, a fellow employee negligently spills hot coffee on you, causing severe burns which require medical attention. Is the company liable?

WHAT PROTECTION DO EMPLOYEES HAVE?

Problem: Carson was employed as a welder by the Cromer Steel Fabricating Company. The state regulations provided that an employer must furnish welders with a special type of goggles to prevent injury, and Cromer did so. If Carson seriously injured his eyes because he forgot to wear the goggles one day, would he be able to recover any of the costs of medical care or lost wages from the company?

As we have seen in the preceding chapter, the federal government and all the states regulate the rights and working conditions of employees. Many of these statutes and regulations govern health and safety.

One type of modern employee protection involves on-the-job safeguards like those discussed in Chapter 30. Laws and regulations prescribe in detail minimum standards for sanitation, lighting, ventilation, and fire protection of the working space. They require safeguards for those who work with machinery, including guardrails, fencing, and eye and face protective devices for certain workers such as welders. They also call for employers to provide adequate first-aid facilities.

But employee protection means more than just safeguarding against accidents and injury. It also means providing a system which compensates workers or their dependents when, in spite of safeguards, they are injured or killed while on the job. Laws which deal with this type of protection and specify what benefits shall be received by workers or their dependents are commonly *workmen's compensation laws*. These laws would apply to Carson in the problem. His employer would almost certainly carry workmen's compensation insurance which would—in spite of the fact that Carson had been careless—pay medical expenses and some portion of income lost during the period of disability.

It is significant that only within the twentieth century has it been deemed necessary to protect workers from injury, safeguard their health, require medical care for those injured while working, and continue payment of a portion of their wages while they are off work. Before this time, workers had to depend on the protection of the common law, which we shall see has become inadequate in today's industrialized society.

HOW DOES WORKMEN'S COMPENSATION DIFFER FROM THE COMMON LAW?

Problem: Hogan, a butcher at the Wayside Market, was badly cut by a cleaver that slipped while he was using it. Was the employer liable?

The employer's liability for work-related injuries, diseases, or death, is governed both by statute and common law. In all cases the injury, disease, or death must have occurred in the course of employment from a risk of that employment. But while protection under the common law is still based on who is at fault, workmen's compensation laws generally provide compensation for any injury received, regardless of fault. Thus, in the problem, the liability of the employer would depend on whether he was in a state governed by common law, or one that required him to provide workmen's compensation coverage.

Only a minority of today's workers must depend on the common law to protect them if they are injured in the course of their employment. Frequently included in this minority are workers engaged in agriculture [1] or domestic work, and *casual laborers* (those who do not work for the employer regularly). In fewer than half the states, an employer must also have a minimum number of workers, usually four or five, to be required to come under the terms of the act; it is

---

[1] Agricultural workers are covered by workmen's compensation in Alaska, Arizona, California, Connecticut, Florida, Hawaii, Kentucky, Louisiana, Maine, Massachusetts, Michigan, Minnesota, New Hampshire, New Jersey, New York, Ohio, Oregon, South Dakota, Vermont, Wisconsin, and Wyoming.

likely, however, that he will do so voluntarily. Those who do depend on the protection afforded by the common law must usually, if injured, take legal action to recover damages.

There may, of course, be a policy of insurance obtained by the employee, the employer, or the owner of the premises on which the employee is working. In that case, some payment may be made to the injured worker without legal proceedings. Many employers, although not required by law to cover their workers, do so by carrying workmen's compensation insurance or other liability insurance.

Today, most gainfully employed workers and their dependents are partially protected against the financial losses caused by injuries, diseases, or death through workmen's compensation laws or special employer liability acts. Railways and other common carriers

Casual workers are not generally covered by workmen's compensation.

engaged in interstate commerce are governed by the Federal Employers' Liability Act and the Safety Appliance Act. Longshoremen and harbor workers are also covered by a special federal act. Because of changes in our industrial system and a realization that the cost of injury is a cost of production, such laws have largely taken the place of the common law rights, risks, and duties.

WHAT ARE EMPLOYERS' COMMON-LAW DUTIES?

Problem: Creighton, a warehouse employee for Lorton Storage, was crushed when an overloaded floor of the building collapsed. Was Lorton liable for Creighton's injuries under the common law?

In the absence of statutes, an employer is liable under the common law for injuries to his employees caused by his failure to:

(1) FURNISH A REASONABLY SAFE PLACE TO WORK

What is a reasonably safe place depends, of course, on the nature of the business and other circumstances. For hazardous occupations such as erecting the steel framework for a skyscraper, the employer is obviously unable to provide the degree of safety appropriate for a retail sales job in the completed building. In the problem, Lorton violated his common-law duty of furnishing a reasonably safe place in which to work and would be liable for Creighton's injuries.

(2) PROVIDE REASONABLY SAFE TOOLS, MACHINERY, AND EQUIPMENT WITH WHICH TO WORK

This does not mean, however, that the employer must furnish the best or latest equipment obtainable.

(3) EMPLOY A SUFFICIENT NUMBER OF FELLOW WORKERS

It is the responsibility of the employer to have enough workers to carry out the job.

The employer is responsible for employing a sufficient number of employees.

(4) GIVE ADEQUATE INSTRUCTIONS WITH RESPECT TO THE RISKS OF THE JOB UNLESS THE DANGERS ARE KNOWN OR SHOULD BE KNOWN TO THE WORKER

Hernandez, an artist, was employed by Cavanaugh to paint some murals on the wall of a building. He cautioned Hernandez about the dangers of working on the scaffolding and showed him how to control the pulley ropes, but failed to point out to him the danger of stepping back. Hernandez did step back to get a better perspective, and, of course, fell to the ground. In a legal action against Cavanaugh, Hernandez claimed that the employer did not warn him about the risk of stepping back. The court, in rejecting this defense, said some risks are so obvious that the employer is under no duty to even call attention to them, and certainly under no duty to instruct employees in avoiding them.

WHAT ARE THE EMPLOYEE'S COMMON-LAW RISKS?

Problem: Selby, a salesman in a shoe store, needed a box that was on a high shelf. Instead of using a sturdy stepladder that would have reached the top shelf, Selby climbed up on the lower shelves, fell, and broke his wrist. Was his employer liable under the common law?

Under the common law and in the absence of statutes, an employee assumes three risks. An employer who is sued because of the injury or death of an employee may use as a defense any one of these common law risks of the employee:

(1) INJURIES TO WHICH HIS OWN NEGLIGENCE HAS CONTRIBUTED

If an employee fails to exercise ordinary care in the performance of his duties, he cannot hold his employer liable for any injuries which result. This may be true even though the employer has not fulfilled all of his own duties. For example, if an employee fails to pay attention to where he is going, and falls into a manhole that has negligently been allowed to remain uncovered, the employer is not liable for any injuries sustained. The employee's own carelessness has contributed to the accident. Thus, in the problem, Selby's employer would not be liable at common law because his broken wrist was caused by his own negligence.

(2) INJURIES DUE TO THE ORDINARY RISKS OF THE INDUSTRY

Most jobs entail risks. Some, such as those around machines with stamping or cutting action, involve greater hazards than others, such as those in an office. At the common law, an employee assumes the usual risks of his occupation.

A worker assumes the risks of the job at the common law.

(3) INJURIES DUE TO THE CARELESSNESS OR NEGLIGENCE OF FELLOW WORKERS

 Perez, an employee of Riverbank Laundry, was adjusting the valve on a pressing machine when Abston, another employee, carelessly turned on the steam and Perez was badly scalded. Under the common law, the laundry was not liable for the injury because it resulted from the negligence of a fellow worker. Perez might be able to take action against Abston.

HOW DO WORKMEN'S COMPENSATION LAWS PROTECT EMPLOYEES?

Problem: Clagett was a member and employee of a musical group known as the Cut Ups. During a performance, Todd, another member of the group, removed Clagett's chair while he was standing. Clagett was badly injured by falling to the floor when he thought he was going to sit down. Was the employer liable for Clagett's injuries?

Workmen's compensation laws, in effect, abolish the common-law risks of the employee and related defenses of the employer by providing a system of compensation for workers injured in the course of their employment regardless of fault. They also provide benefits for the surviving family in case of the worker's death. Under workmen's compensation, the common-law question of employee risk, negligence, or fault has been replaced by two fairly simple tests:

(1) Did the injury, disease, or death arise out of and occur during the course of employment?

(2) What is the extent of the employee's injury?

In other words, if the worker is injured or killed while on the job, he or his dependents will be paid according to a schedule based on the severity of the injury. The worker forfeits benefits only if he intentionally injures himself, or is hurt because he is in an intoxicated state. Benefits may be reduced, however, when injury results from the employee's own misconduct.

In the problem, Clagett's employer would not be liable under the common law because Clagett assumed the risk of injury caused by a fellow employee. His only recourse would be against Todd, who was at fault. If Clagett's position were covered by workmen's compensation, however, the question of who was at fault would not be raised. He was injured during the course of his employment, and his medical expenses and a portion of his wages would be paid for the number of weeks specified by the workmen's compensation statute.

Workmen's compensation laws are either compulsory or elective. Under elective laws, the employer has the option of rejecting the coverage. In case of rejection, however, he loses his common-law defenses that the employee (1) was negligent, (2) had assumed the ordinary risks of the job, or (3) was injured because of the carelessness or negligence of fellow workers. Thus, even in elective states most employers decide to come under the act. Employees in elective states may also reject coverage, but again, this is rarely done. Certain types of employers are not required to protect their employees or themselves with workmen's compensation insurance, but they may do so voluntarily. Others, although they might want to elect coverage, are not eligible. For example, in some states neither the employer nor members of his family are covered by workmen's compensation in the case of sole proprietorships or partnerships. (Chapter 43)

The total cost of coverage is paid by the employer, who usually carries workmen's compensation insurance either with the state or with a private insurance company. Workmen's compensation plans are generally administered by a state department of labor, or a special commission or board such as New York's Workmen's Compensation Board or an Industrial Accident Commission.

WHAT BENEFITS DOES WORKMEN'S COMPENSATION PROVIDE?

> **Problem:** Rollins, a lineman for Intercity Power Company, carelessly touched a 50,000 volt line and was killed instantly. If Rollins is covered by workmen's compensation, what benefits will his dependents receive?

Although all states and the District of Columbia have workmen's compensation laws, the requirements and benefits vary. In case of death covered by workmen's compensation, benefits are typically paid to surviving dependents either for a specified time or until the widow remarries or the children reach 18 years of age. The amount of compensation payable to the family, as in the case of Rollins in the problem, will depend on the employee's average earnings prior to his death, and the state in which he lost his life. The family will also receive an amount for funeral expenses. In case of injury, the maximum weekly payments are limited to a percentage of the employee's average earnings prior to disability. There is a waiting period before income benefits are paid, but if the disability continues beyond the waiting period, back payments are made to the date of injury.

Workmen's compensation laws usually provide a minimum benefit as well as a maximum benefit. Costs of medical treatment, hospitalization, and necessary appliances such as an artificial limb are paid for. Most states also pay for retraining if an accident makes it impossible for the worker to resume his former job. This is called *vocational rehabilitation*. In order to be eligible for compensation under most acts, an injured worker or his representative must give his employer notice of the injury within ten days of its occurrence.

All states include either all or specified industrial or occupational diseases under workmen's compensation. If the worker was negligent in contracting the disease, however, the amount of compensation may be reduced.

AS AN EMPLOYER...

1. Be aware of and follow all statutes and regulations governing the health and safety of your employees.
2. In the absence of statutes, be sure to employ a sufficient number of workers and give them adequate instructions of job risks.
3. Provide your employees with a safe place in which to work with safe tools, machinery, and equipment.
4. Consider the advantages of employee coverage under workmen's compensation laws if coverage is optional.

AS AN EMPLOYEE...

1. Follow all safety precautions and use all safety devices prescribed for your job.
2. Recognize the risks which you must assume under the common law, and be prepared to deal with these risks.
3. Be aware of the benefits to which you are entitled under workmen's compensation laws if you are covered.

YOUR LEGAL VOCABULARY

casual laborer   workmen's compensation laws
vocational rehabilitation

1. Laws that in effect abolish the common-law defenses of the employer and provide a system of compensation for workers injured in the course of employment.
2. One who does not work regularly for the employer.
3. Retraining an injured worker in new skills.

REMEMBER THESE HIGHLIGHTS

1. At common law an employer is liable for injuries to or death of his employees caused by his failure to provide (a) a reasonably safe place in which to work, (b) reasonably safe tools, machines, and equipment, (c) a sufficient number of competent fellow workers, and (d) adequate instructions with respect to the risks of the job.
2. At common law an employee assumes the risk of injuries due (a) wholly, or in part, to his own negligence, (b) to the ordinary dangers of the job, and (c) to negligence of fellow workers.
3. Workmen's compensation acts provide protection to covered employees for injuries arising out of and in the course of employment, regardless of fault, unless they are due to the intentional act or intoxication of the injured person.
4. Nearly all employees — except domestic and casual workers, employees of very small firms, and some agricultural workers — are covered by workmen's compensation laws.
5. Workmen's compensation for injury includes payment of medical and hospital expenses, partial reimbursement of wages while the employee is unable to work, and possible vocational rehabilitation. In the case of death of the worker, payment is made to his dependents.

LAW AS PEOPLE LIVE IT

1. Kester was hired by Moonglow Drive-In Theater to carry a banner in a parade advertising the theater. While carrying the banner he was injured by an automobile. Was Moonglow liable?
2. Ennis, a fry cook in Skelton's Eatery, was burned when some grease caught fire. What would determine whether Skelton was liable for Ennis' injuries?
3. Boggliata had a small shop in which he made gift items and souvenirs from fine woods. His only employee, Nettleton, operated a bandsaw that was several years old. When the bandsaw broke, injuring him, Nettleton sued Boggliata for failure to furnish safe tools. Boggliata proved that such equipment, although not the latest or most modern, was widely used, generally safe, and satisfactory for its purpose. Was Boggliata liable?
4. Cherry was a packer at Pumphrey Pickle Plant. The nature of the operation usually caused the cement floor to be wet or covered with water or brine. At one time wood platforms were provided for the packers but these had been removed. One day Cherry was injured when he slipped on the floor. He sued Pumphrey claiming under the common law he failed to provide a safe place to work. As a defense Pumphrey claimed the injury was the result of one of the risks of the job. Who should prevail?

5. Winston hired Strong to apply anhydrous ammonia, a fertilizer, to the soil on his farm. Winston said to Strong, "Be careful when you handle this stuff, it might burn you," but he did not explain how to handle the tank or hose or what to do if he sprayed himself with it. The hose got out of control and sprayed Strong in the face, blinding him in one eye. He sued Winston under the common law, claiming he was not properly instructed in how to handle the equipment. Do you agree?

6. AAAA Warehouse was equipped with an old fashioned freight elevator that had a manually-operated gate on each floor. Each employee using the elevator operated it himself. When the elevator reached a floor the employee had to raise the gate and was supposed to lower it after he got off. Bibbero, a supervisor delivering a message to Dotson, stepped off the elevator after raising the gate but did not lower it because he intended to get back on immediately. While he was talking with Dotson the elevator was moved to another floor. After completing his conversation, Bibbero returned to the elevator, failed to note that it had been moved, stepped into the shaft and fell to his death. What was the liability of the employer under common law? What would it be if he were covered by workmen's compensation?

7. Grivas was on a ladder repairing an electrical outlet for his employer, Marshall Medical Supply Co., when Velardi, another employee, kicked the ladder as he went by causing Grivas to fall and break his back. Distinguish between Grivas' rights under the common law and under workmen's compensation.

8. Owens was chauffeur for Morgali and drove him to the airport to catch a plane. On the way back to Morgali's home Owens was injured in an accident with a hit-and-run driver. What were Owens' rights against Morgali?

9. At the end of his shift, Kitano left his place of employment, got into his automobile, and started home. Within one block of the factory, he was injured in an accident at a railroad crossing. If his employer carried workmen's compensation insurance, would it cover Kitano's accident?

10. Hubbell was drunk when he arrived at work, but his foreman did not notice his condition. Hubbell started his machine, and promptly injured his arm. Was he entitled to workmen's compensation benefits?

LAW AS COURTS DECIDE IT

1. Norbert Crow, the unemancipated 14-year-old son of the vice-president and general manager of the appellant Corporation, was killed by a tractor while working for the Corporation during the summer vacation. He had no work permit and was paid irregularly by his father who was not reimbursed by the Corporation. His job usually required answering the telephone, weighing materials, and at times loading materials on trucks. When the parents were awarded death and burial benefits by the

Industrial Accident Commission, the Corporation appealed the award. The issue was whether Norbert Crow was an employee at the time of the accident despite the fact that the workmen's compensation law provided that members of a family are not so considered and that Norbert had no work permit. What was the court's decision? (Harry Crow and Son, Inc. v. Industrial Accident Commission, 18 Wis. 2d 436, 118 N.W. 2d 841)

2. Milburn was an independent contractor clearing some land for Mc-Donald, defendant in this action. Milburn hired Lupton for a job that was to take about one day, and Lupton was seriously injured while working. He claimed benefits from McDonald, who had workmen's compensation insurance, on the theory that Milburn, who did not have such insurance, was only a sub-contractor. McDonald claimed that Lupton was merely a casual laborer and therefore, under the law, not entitled to workmen's compensation benefits. He claimed, moreover, that Lupton was Milburn's employee, not his. Should Lupton be awarded judgment? (Lupton v. McDonald, 241 Md. 446, 217 A. 2d)

3. Liptak was employed by Karsner to do household work. On several occasions while working in the basement laundry room, she stumbled over a sewer clean-out plug, which extended about two and a half inches above the concrete floor. One day, in so doing, she fell and suffered injuries. In an action brought against Karsner to recover damages under the common law, it was contended that Karsner failed in his duty by not giving warning concerning the danger. Do you agree? (Liptak v. Karsner, 208 Minn. 168, 293 N.W. 612)

4. St. Alexandre, a shipping clerk for the Texas Company, temporarily left his work and sustained a serious arm injury while removing a cap from a soft-drink bottle. The company furnished the cooler and the ice at a convenient location, and each employee paid for his own soft drink. It was an approved custom for the employees to take a "break" and have a soft drink. Did St. Alexandre's injury occur while he was "at work"; that is, did it occur "in the course of his employment"? (St. Alexandre v. Texas Company, 28 So. 2d 385, Louisiana)

5. Jewell Bonds, widow of Willie Jollif, and her children were seeking death benefits under the state workmen's compensation law of Louisiana. The facts showed that Jollif was a timber cutter for Robert Fallin, and worked at a considerable distance from his home. Without the consent or knowledge of Fallin, Jollif took Fallin's pick-up truck from the lumber camp and drove home one weekend to take money to his family. On the return journey the truck overturned and Jollif was killed. Was his wife entitled to workmen's compensation benefits? (National Surety Corporation v. Bonds, 275 F. 389)

Agency

UNIT NINE

You have probably never realized that most of our business and many of our personal activities are carried on by agents, and that you have probably both been an agent and appointed an agent yourself. Agency is truly one of the most common and important of legal relations.

The agency relation is always a triangular affair involving (1) the agent, (2) the one for whom and on whose behalf he is acting, called the principal, and (3) the third party with whom the agent is dealing.

The usefulness of agency can be seen in the case of the owner of a large business. If the law required him to be present every time a contract was made or a transaction occurred which affected his business, he would be severely limited. But with the use of agents to make contracts and carry out transactions for him, he can expand his business and operate widely without extensive travel by himself, using their talent and time. Obviously, agency is indispensible in our modern business world.

You may have noticed that an agent is similar to an employee. In Chapter 32, we will examine some of the similarities and differences of agents and employees. We will also see who may be an agent, how he is appointed, and what acts he can and cannot do.

Chapter 33 includes a discussion of how an agent gets his authority to act for and on behalf of another. Finally, we shall learn about the particular duties and responsibilities of all three parties in the agency relation.

CHAPTER 32 Creating an Agency

1. *The driver of a car disabled on the highway flags you down and asks that you send a tow truck from the next town. Will you be liable if the disabled car leaves before the tow truck arrives?*

2. *You know your buddy is looking for a pair of fiberglass skis. When you come across a "good buy," you decide to put a down payment on them for your friend. Is he now liable for the balance?*

3. *While you are on duty as manager of the baseball team at the local recreation center, City Sporting Goods delivers five dozen baseballs. Will the center be bound by your signature on the receipt?*

WHAT IS AN AGENCY?

Problem: Haller worked at the Hilltop Service Station. His duties included selling gasoline, oil, and accessories, and collecting for them or making out credit tickets. He was also responsible for cleaning windshields, checking tires, lubricating cars, changing oil, and keeping the premises clean. Was Haller an agent or an employee?

In the preceding unit we learned that one who does work for another person under his direction and control, such as typing letters, packing groceries, or repairing radios, is an employee. But there are other kinds of workers who carry out business transactions by making contracts for others whom they represent. A person who acts for and on behalf of another in dealing with third persons is an *agent*. The one for whom he acts, and from whom his authority comes, is the *principal*. When the agent is authorized to act for the principal in dealings with third persons, the relation of *agency* exists.

In the agency relation, the principal is liable to third persons for the acts of his agent when the agent is acting within the authority given him. The proper signing of the principal's name by the agent is the same as if the principal himself had signed.

 When Wilson bought a mini-bike from Wheels, Inc., the salesman signed and gave him a card which entitled him to have the motor adjusted any time within three months of purchase. If the salesman changed jobs or was out of the shop when he returned, Wilson could look directly to the owner of Wheels, Inc. to have the adjustment made. The signature of the salesman, an agent, was as binding on the owner, his principal, as if the owner had signed himself.

Many workers are both employees and agents. Although they may be called employees, they are also agents if they are authorized to represent their employers in contractual dealings with third parties. They have powers, responsibilities, and obligations not possessed by other employees. Haller, in the problem at the beginning of this chapter, was both an employee and an agent. Haller was acting as an employee when he was dispensing gas and oil, cleaning the windshield, checking tires, and performing similar duties. When he was making contracts of sale by and on behalf of his employer— that is, when he was receiving money or credit cards in payment for goods or services—he was an agent. In relations with their employers, both agents and ordinary employees are considered employees, and have all the rights as discussed in the preceding unit.

The title of "agent" does not always mean that a person is one in fact. Some manufacturers appoint "selling agents," or dealers who buy their products and resell them. Many companies also have "agencies" which deal exclusively in that company's products. Although the owners of such businesses are called "agents," they are really independent contractors.

The owner of this "Auto Agency" is really an independent contractor.

WHO MAY BE A PRINCIPAL?

Problem: Brooks, a minor, wished to sell his surfboard. He agreed to pay Filart ten percent of the price, which was

$100, if he would sell the board for him. Filart agreed, but after he had found a buyer, Brooks decided not to sell, claiming that as a minor he had no power to appoint an agent. Was Brooks correct?

Anyone who is legally competent to act for himself may be a principal and act through an agent. This is because the authorized acts of the agent are, legally, the acts of the principal. For the same reason, one who is not competent to act or contract cannot escape that incompetency by appointing an agent.

A minor, as you recall, has limited capacity to contract. (Chapter 9) He may, like Brooks, appoint and act through an agent. Such an appointment and the contract made by the agent with the third party may be avoided by the minor himself, however, to the same extent as any other contract he might make would be avoidable. Thus, Brooks was wrong about his power to appoint an agent, but within his rights in refusing to sell his surfboard.

WHO MAY BE AN AGENT?

Problem: Berger, age 16, was employed as a campus sales representative by the Varsity Shop. Was Berger competent to act as an agent?

Anyone may be an agent, regardless of whether he is competent to act for himself. This is because the agent is only a representative, not one of the contracting parties. Thus, minors and other persons who have a legal or natural incapacity to act for themselves may act for others, and principals who choose these persons as their agents may not renounce their acts because of such incapacity. In the problem, Berger could act as sales agent for the Varsity Shop. His sales would be as binding on the shop as if the owner himself had made them.

It must be remembered, however, that an incompetent person's promise to act as an agent is no more enforceable than any other promise he may make. Although he may bind the principal to third persons, he is not liable to the principal for his failure to do so.

To protect the public against incompetent service in selected fields, most states require agents in such fields to be licensed by the state. Licensing usually requires passing a professional examination. Persons who propose to work as insurance agents, real estate agents, securities brokers, and auctioneers are commonly required to obtain a license.

HOW ARE AGENCIES CREATED?

Problem: Zenovich, who was throwing a party that night, asked her friend, Burns, to pick up 500 balloons and charge them to Zenovich's account. Who would be liable for the charge?

In general, no one may act as an agent for another person unless he has been given authority or power to do so. Most agencies are created by contract, but the essential element is the principal's consent to have the agent act as such.

Often, like Zenovich, you may ask someone to represent you with no thought of paying him for the service. When the agency is not based upon contract, it is a *gratuitous agency*. The authority of a gratuitous agent is just as effective as the authority of an agent appointed by contract. The legal effect of Burns' charging the balloons was the same as if Zenovich herself had picked them up and agreed to pay for them.

An agency may be created by:

1. Appointment;
2. Appearance;
3. Ratification; or
4. Necessity.

(1) APPOINTMENT

Problem: Stafford wrote Mitchell, instructing him to purchase a certain champion Scottish terrier named Tam 'o Shanter. Did Mitchell become Stafford's agent for this purpose?

An agency is usually created by an express appointment. No particular language is necessary; any words that convey the intention of the principal suffice. Ordinarily the appointment is made orally and informally, but it may also be made in writing. If written it may be informal, as in a telegram or a letter giving instructions; or it may be formal, as in a carefully drafted contract. In the preceding problem, Mitchell became Stafford's agent, with power to bind Stafford to perform the purchase contract.

In some instances, the appointment of an agent is required by statute to be in writing. For example, authority to sell land for a principal must usually be in writing. If the appointment is for more than one year or is to end later than one year from the date of the agreement, the Statute of Frauds requires that it be in writing to be enforceable. In some states, an agent's appointment must be in writing if he is to enter into any written contract on behalf of his principal. A written document by which an agent is appointed and his powers defined is called a *power of attorney*.

Know All Men by These Presents:

That I, William H. Harrington ————————————————————————
——————————————————————————————— of Cincinnati ————

County of Hamilton —————, State of Ohio —————————————
have made, constituted and appointed, and by these presents do make, constitute and
appoint James Symington ————————————————————————————
——————————————————————————————— of Cincinnati ————

County of Hamilton —————, State of Ohio —————————————
my true and lawful attorney   in fact, for me and in my name, place and stead,
to manage, operate, and let rental properties in the City of

Cincinnati, County of Hamilton, State of Ohio—————————————

giving and granting unto my said attorney   full power and authority to do and perform
all and every act and thing whatsoever requisite and necessary to be done in and about
the premises, as fully to all intents and purposes as I might or could do, if personally
present, with full power of substitution and revocation; hereby ratifying and confirming
all that my said attorney —— or his   substitute ———— shall lawfully do, or cause to be
done, by virtue hereof.

In Witness Whereof,   I have hereunto set my hand this ___tenth___ day
of ___October___, 19 72 .   *William H. Harrington*

Signed and acknowledged in presence of:

___Ann Peppin___

___Donna Guarino___

Power of Attorney

(2) APPEARANCE

Problem: Hart drove into Mayne's Motors with the intention of trading his car for another one. The only person around was Blair who was seated at the salesman's desk. He had been left in charge by Mayne, with instructions to answer the telephone and ask any callers to wait until Mayne returned from the bank. Blair, upon learning of Hart's purpose, suggested that Hart look around at the cars while he test drove the old car for appraisal purposes. Blair drove Hart's car off the lot and never returned. Would Mayne be liable for the value of Hart's car?

An "agency" may sometimes result from the appearance created by the "principal." This is not a true agency, because there has been no consent or contract. Nevertheless, if an action on your part leads others to reasonably believe that a particular person is your agent, you will be held liable to them for the actions of the apparent agent. Since the principal is the source of authority in an agency, such authority must always come, or appear to come, from his words or acts; it can never arise from the words or conduct of the agent. In the preceding problem Mayne's conduct, in allowing Blair to take charge of the office, reasonably led Hart to believe that Blair was his agent with authority to appraise his car. When a person misleads another into thinking that a particular person is his agent, he will generally be barred from denying the apparent agency. This is sometimes called *agency by estoppel*: Mayne's conduct stops him from claiming he did not appoint Blair as his agent.

(3) RATIFICATION

Problem: Matley was a collector of antique snuff boxes. His friend Rogers discovered a particularly rare one at Lord's Curio Shop and bought it, making a down payment of $20 in Matley's name but without his knowledge. Could Matley be held liable for the balance due?

When a person without real or apparent authority pretends to act as the agent of another, or when one who is really an agent exceeds his authority, he does not bind the person for whom he assumes to act. However, if the supposed principal later expressly or impliedly assents to the act, he is bound. He impliedly assents, for example, by knowingly accepting the benefits of the act. This subsequent approval is ratification as discussed on page 127. In the above problem, Matley could ratify the action of Rogers by notifying Lord of his willingness to complete the purchase, or by paying the balance due. Of if he chose, Matley could refuse to ratify the purchase, and Rogers then would be liable to Lord.

For the ratification to be valid: (a) the third person must have believed that he was making a contract with the principal by dealing with his agent; (b) the principal must have full knowledge of all material facts; (c) an intent to ratify must be shown; and (d) ratification must be of the entire act, not just of those parts that may benefit the principal.

(4) NECESSITY

Problem: Following a quarrel at home, Scott's 16-year-old son decided to move out. Although his parents encouraged his return home, the young Scott rented a room from Carter and said his father would pay the rent. Would the father be obliged to do so?

In a few instances, an agency may be created by necessity. A husband is bound to support his wife and minor children. If he fails to supply them with necessaries, the law gives them power to pledge his credit for such purchases, even against his will. With this exception, their mere relationship usually does not give a wife or children power to bind the husband or father by contract. As in other cases of agency, their ability to act for the husband or father must be authorized. Accordingly, Scott, in the foregoing problem, would not have to pay the rent for his son's room. The son had not been authorized to contract for his father, and the room was not a necessary because he was furnished one at home.

Under unusual and emergency circumstances, however, an agent or employee is authorized to do reasonable and appropriate acts which are not within the scope of his ordinary authority.

ARE THERE ACTS WHICH AN AGENT MAY NOT PERFORM?

Problem: Clifton appointed Fadiman his agent for the sale of his annual crop of strawberries. Fadiman made the sales, but delegated to Lyon the confirming of orders and preparing of invoices. Could he delegate these duties?

One may generally do through an agent anything that he has a legal right to do for himself. However, an agent may not appoint a subagent unless the subagent's duties are of a mechanical or routine nature, as in the problem, or unless the appointment is justified by sudden emergency or a well-known custom. Also, one is not allowed to act through an agent in performing certain uniquely personal acts or public duties.

(1) PERSONAL ACTS

Problem: Thomas, a very busy man, was subpoenaed as a witness in a legal action. Because he planned to be out of town the day of the trial, Thomas briefed his assistant, Glenn, on the matter and appointed Glenn to represent him in the court. Could Thomas do this?

Certain acts that are personal in nature must be performed by the individual himself. They may not be done through an agent. Examples of such acts are voting in an election, taking an oath of office, serving a jail sentence, making a will, and performing military duty. In addition, an agent may not delegate to a subagent the making of any contract which requires his own personal discretion or judgment. In the problem, the act could not be delegated because it required the presence of Thomas himself.

(2) ILLEGAL ACTS

> **Problem:** Spencer wished to promote a shopping center on land that he owned, but the City Planning Commission refused to grant permission. Spencer authorized his real estate agent to offer the chairman of the Commission a ten percent interest in the proposed center if he could persuade the Commission to approve the plan. Could the agent collect his fee?

Acts that one may not lawfully do himself may not be done through another. Hence, if it is unlawful for you to buy alcoholic beverages yourself, you may not buy them through an agent. In the problem, since Spencer could not legally appoint an agent to bribe a public official, the agent could not legally demand his fee. In fact, both men could be prosecuted as criminals in such a case. As discussed in Chapter 10, agreements of unlicensed businessmen are not enforceable. Thus, it is illegal for an agent who is required to be licensed to act as agent without that license.

WHAT ARE THE KINDS OF AGENTS?

> **Problem:** Hopper was appointed general manager of the Kenwood Country Club. What kind of an agent was he?

(1) GENERAL AGENTS

A *general agent* is authorized to transact all of his principal's business of a particular kind, or all of his principal's business at a given place. Unless the principal places a special limitation on a general agent's authority, the agent has the power to transact all of the business necessary for the operation of the particular kind of business in which the principal is engaged. Hopper was a general agent; unless limited by his principal, he had power to hire and fire employees, pay them, buy supplies, maintain the buildings, grounds and equipment, settle complaints, and do all other acts necessary for the operation of the Club.

(2) SPECIAL AGENTS

A *special agent* is appointed to do some specific act or acts, or to transact certain business affairs. A department store employee who is authorized to adjust customer complaints is a special agent. The authority of a special agent is much narrower in scope than that of a general agent, and persons dealing with such an agent must recognize that he has limited authority.

An *auctioneer* is a special agent who sells property to the highest bidder at a public sale. He acts as the representative of the owner in making the sale.

A *broker* is a special agent who may negotiate contracts without having possession of the goods, or who may simply bring parties together for the purpose of negotiating contracts. A real estate agent who finds buyers or renters for property is a broker.

A *factor* is a special agent who sells property that has been delivered to him by the principal for that purpose. A commission merchant who receives goods from a producer to sell on a commission basis is a factor.

MOST BUSINESS IS CONDUCTED THROUGH AGENTS . . .

1. If you act as an agent, have a clear understanding of the extent of your authority. Then don't let your enthusiasm, pride, or ambition allow you to exceed it by claiming more authority than you have. Such behavior could cost you money as well as your job.
2. Use great care if you appoint an agent, especially a general agent. Remember, unless you place a special limitation on his authority, the general agent has power to bind you and your assets to any and all contracts necessary for the operation of your particular business.
3. It is usually desirable to put in writing the appointment of an agent and the extent of his authority, so that there will be no misunderstanding.
4. In selecting an agent, never forget that you, the principal, are liable for what he does within the scope of his authority.
5. Remember, if your agent does what you authorize him to do, such as find a buyer for your property at an agreed price, he is entitled to be paid even if you don't accept the offer.

YOUR LEGAL VOCABULARY

agency
agency by estoppel
agent
auctioneer
broker
factor

general agent
gratuitous agency
power of attorney
principal
special agent

1. One who acts for and on behalf of another in dealing with third persons.
2. A written document appointing an agent and defining his powers.
3. A relation in which one person is authorized to act for another in dealings with third persons.

4. An agent who may bring parties together for the purpose of negotiating contracts.
5. Being barred or stopped from denying an agency because of one's conduct or action.
6. One who authorizes another to act for him.
7. An agent who is authorized to transact all of his principal's business of a certain kind.
8. A special agent who sells to the highest bidder at a public sale.
9. An agent who is authorized to transact certain business only.
10. An agency not based on contract.

REMEMBER THESE HIGHLIGHTS

1. The relation of principal and agent exists when one person authorizes another to act for and on behalf of him in dealings with third parties.
2. Any legally competent person may be a principal. Any person authorized by the principal may be an agent.
3. An agency may be created by (a) appointment, (b) appearance, (c) ratification, or (d) necessity.
4. One may do any lawful business act through an agent. The legal effect of the act of an agent is usually the same as if the principal had performed the act himself.
5. Certain acts that are personal in nature, such as voting or serving a jail sentence, may not be performed through an agent.
6. A general agent transacts all of his principal's business of a particular kind or at a given place. A special agent is authorized to perform some specific act or acts, or to transact certain business affairs.

LAW AS PEOPLE LIVE IT

1. Seymour employed Gurke as his cook. When Gurke complained about the defective condition of certain kitchen utensils, she was told by her employer to purchase whatever new ones she needed and to charge them to Seymour's account. Was Gurke an agent?
2. Mrs. Strickland sent her 9-year-old daughter, Pam, to the store for a carton of milk. Could Pam act as her mother's agent?
3. Nathan gave Bailey some money and asked him as a favor to get him two tickets to a professional hockey game, and two lottery tickets on the outcome of the game. Was an agency established?
4. Klinsky was a door-to-door salesman for Lacy, a vacuum cleaner manufacturer. Klinsky, without authority from Lacy, took a typewriter from Lacy's office and sold it to Cardenas. Could Lacy recover the typewriter from Cardenas?
5. Slaten wrote a letter to Garfinkle authorizing him to arrange for the shipment of 1,000 grapestakes he had purchased from Leland. What kind of agent was Garfinkle?

6. LaRue, without authority but stating that he was Casilli's agent, placed a "package deal" order with the Swinging Stereo Company for a complete stereo setup and a five-year membership in the company's record club. When the stereo was delivered, Casilli was thrilled with its beauty and quality, but felt that LaRue had promised to pay too much for the records. He thereupon notified the Stereo Company that he was ratifying the act of LaRue as to the stereo, but rejecting his act to the records. Could Casilli do this?

7. Jenkins' 17-year-old daughter, Vicki, thought she needed a new formal, but Jenkins disagreed and refused to buy one for her. Vicki, nevertheless, bought a dress at the Mod Shop and charged it to her father. Did this make Vicki her father's agent?

8. Hashisaki gave Parker $5,000 to invest for him in a piece of real estate which Parker would select. Parker became ill and was unable to carry out the assignment, so he asked Mello to select the property and complete the arrangements. Was Hashisaki bound by Mello's acts?

9. Blankenship arranged with Fields, as manager, to collect the rent and make all contracts for the maintenance of an apartment building he owned. What kind of an agent was Fields?

10. Patrick engaged Barker to manage his hardware store. Barker hired Fern to work for one week to help him clean the store, arrange stock, and take inventory. When Patrick learned of this, he refused to pay Fern for his services, claiming that Barker had no right to hire him. Can Fern require payment from Patrick?

LAW AS COURTS DECIDE IT

1. Nissan Motor Corporation appointed McKnight its Denver area agent and dealer for the sale of Datsun automobiles. McKnight purchased automobiles and parts from Nissan and sold them as he desired and at prices he set without any control from Nissan. In this action, the question arose as to whether an agency existed. What is your judgment? (United Fire and Casualty Company v. Nissan Motor Corporation, 164 Colo. 42, 433 P. 2d 769)

2. Walker left his trailer to be sold on consignment at the lot of Pacific Mobile Homes. There was present only one salesman, Henderson, who agreed to try to sell the trailer. Henderson, who described himself as manager, took Walker into the office where he prepared and signed a form entitled "Trailer Consignment Agreement" which he took from the desk. Later the trailer was sold for $1,500, and Walker received three payments totaling $209.41. When the payments stopped, Walker made inquiry and found Henderson had disappeared with the money. He thereupon sued Pacific Mobile Homes, claiming Henderson was its agent with authority to accept and sell the trailer. Pacific's president testified that the salesman on the lot had no authority to complete a sale,

and that he, as president, had to sign all sales documents. He also said that the company forbade its salesmen to take trailers on consignment, and that all were familiar with this policy. Did Henderson have authority to take the trailer and sell it? (Walker v. Pacific Mobile Homes, Inc., 68 Wash. 2d 347, 413 P. 2d 3)

3. Amplo sued Joseph DiMauro for the cost of necessaries supplied by her to DiMauro's wife. DiMauro's defense was that he and his wife had separated; he stated that he had published a notice in a newspaper saying that he would not be responsible for her debts. If the state law makes a husband liable for his wife's necessaries, does she have authority as his agent to bind him for necessaries not otherwise provided? (Amplo v. DiMauro, 52 Misc. 2d 810, 276 N.Y.S. 2d 817)

4. Shenson contracted with the Fresno Meat Packing Co. to slaughter some cattle. The meat packing company, as agent of Shenson, also agreed to make a claim in its own name to the federal government for payment of a subsidy and to remit the proceeds to Shenson. The reason for this arrangement was that Shenson himself was not eligible under the law to be paid the subsidy. After payment of the subsidy was received, the meat packing company refused to pay it to Shenson as agreed. Would Shenson be successful in a legal action to require the company to pay it to him? (Shenson v. Fresno Meat Packing Co., 96 Cal.App. 2d 725, 216 P. 2d 156)

5. R. C. Cochram was instructed by the owners of the Hamcock Ranch to buy certain fruit trees and plants from a Texas nursery unless he could save money by purchasing them elsewhere. Violating his instructions, Cochram placed the order with Ira Chambers at an invoice price of $100 above that of the Texas firm. Upon receipt of the trees, the Ranch owners complained about the price but caused the trees and plants to be planted. In an action to collect the invoice price, Chambers contended that the planting of the trees and plants constituted ratification of the unauthorized act. Do you agree? (Chambers v. Aycock, 15 So. 2d 150, Louisiana)

6. Ruth Cuffman and Elizabeth Blunkall had been attending the neighborhood movie theater together. The theater gave away prizes to those attending who held winning tickets. One evening a new automobile was to be given away, but Elizabeth was unable to attend. Ruth suggested that she take Elizabeth's ticket for the drawing; and if her ticket won the car, Elizabeth would get the car. Elizabeth's ticket won the car, but the regulations stated that the tickets were not transferable and the holder must be present to win. In a suit to gain possession of the car, Elizabeth claimed Ruth was her agent. Do you agree? (Cuffman v. Blunkall, 22 Tenn. App. 513, 124 S.W. 2d 289)

CHAPTER **33** Duties and Liabilities

1. A friend moving from town leaves his tape recorder for you to sell. You would like to buy it yourself. May you?

2. A friend asks you to purchase an electric guitar for him on credit. Who will be liable for payment?

3. You accept a registered letter addressed to your employer. How should you sign for it?

WHAT POWER DOES THE AGENT HAVE?

Problem: While on a trip around the world, Martin left his vacation trailer with his neighbor, Williams, and gave him authority to rent it for $40 a week. Instead of renting it, Williams sold the trailer to Sebastian. Upon his return, Martin demanded the return of the trailer from Sebastian. Was he within his rights?

When a person deals directly with the principal, there is no doubt about the principal's right to make decisions or about his liability. But when one deals through an agent, doubts may arise. Does the agent have the power he claims to have? What will happen if he does not? One who deals with an agent should, for his own protection, learn the extent of the agent's power or authority; for generally, if the agent exceeds his authority, the principal will no longer be liable. In the above problem, it was Sebastian's responsibility to learn the extent of Williams' authority. Martin was not liable, and was within his rights in demanding the return of the trailer.

The extent of the agent's power to act for the principal depends upon the authority given him. Such authority may be express, implied, or apparent.

(1) EXPRESS AUTHORITY

Problem: Frederick gave Rich a power of attorney, specifying as his duty the management of the Casa del Rey Nursing Home. What kind of authority was this?

When a principal specifically appoints an agent, as Frederick did with the power of attorney in the problem, the agent has *express authority*. Express authority may be oral as well as written, however.

If your mother sent you to the store with oral instructions to charge a box of stationery to her account and in her name, you would have express authority.

(2) IMPLIED AUTHORITY

Problem: Delgado authorized Winters to have repairs made on a building that had been damaged by a hurricane, but gave him no money. Was Winters authorized to charge the cost of the repairs to Delgado?

An agent also has authority to do anything that is reasonably necessary or customary to carry out the duties expressly authorized. Such authority is *implied authority*. A special agent with authority only to take orders has no implied power to collect payment. But when a principal authorizes an agent to purchase goods without furnishing the funds to pay for them, the agent has implied authority to make the purchases on credit. In the problem, Winters had implied authority to charge the cost of repairing the building to his principal.

(3) APPARENT AUTHORITY

Problem: Hyde stored his grand piano in Waterson's Warehouse. Desiring to sell the piano, Hyde gave the warehouse receipt to Laird, but directed Laird to check with him regarding the price before selling the piano. Laird found Namoth who offered what Laird thought was a good price, so he sold the piano and transferred the warehouse receipt to Namoth. Can Hyde recover the piano on grounds that Laird exceeded his authority?

In some cases where there is neither express nor implied authority, the principal will nevertheless be barred from denying the existence of an agency. This is true when the principal's acts or conduct reasonably lead third persons to believe that a certain person is his agent. Such authority, arising from the conduct of the principal, is *apparent authority* (or ostensible authority).

In the problem, Hyde's act of giving the warehouse receipt to Laird made it appear that Laird had authority to sell the piano. Because of this apparent authority, Hyde is barred from recovering the instrument.

WHEN IS THE PRINCIPAL LIABLE?

Problem: Friedman authorized Milton, his agent, to sell a bankrupt stock of toys for cash only. Milton sold the goods to Rudy's Stores for 25 percent cash and the balance on credit. Friedman ratified the sale. Must he deliver the goods?

As long as an agent acts within the scope of the authority given by his principal, the principal is liable to the third party for performance of any contract made in his name. He is also liable when, as in the problem, he ratifies the unauthorized acts of his agent. Thus, Friedman must deliver the toys to Rudy.

When an authorized agent does not disclose the identity of his principal, the third party may generally elect to hold either the principal or the agent, but not both. An exception is made for contracts under seal and negotiable contracts such as notes and checks that are made in the agent's name alone; in those cases, the agent alone is liable. Normally to bind his principal and avoid personal liability, an agent will sign the name of his principal to a contract along with his own name and words indicating that he is signing as agent.

If torts or fraudulent acts are committed by an agent who is acting within the scope of his authority, or if they are ratified, the principal is liable to third parties for such acts. For example, if an agent defrauds a customer while selling something to him, the principal is liable for any damages that result. The agent, himself, is also liable for harm caused by his torts or fraudulent acts.

 Price, credit manager of Apex Industries, wrongfully took possession of Agnew's truck while attempting to collect a past-due account from him. Apex Industries was liable to Agnew for damages because Price, its agent, had committed the tort of conversion. Price is also liable for the wrongdoing.

Usually the principal is not liable for an agent's crime unless he authorized or ratified it. As an exception to this rule, the principal is generally liable for the illegal sale, by his agent, of intoxicating liquor or adulterated foods. Thus, the principal would be liable if his agent, a bartender, would illegally serve liquor to a minor.

A principal is deemed to have received notice or information that is given to an agent by a third party. In other words, knowledge by the agent or notice to him is the same as knowledge by the principal or notice to him.

WHAT IS THE EFFECT OF AN AGENT'S WARRANTIES?

Problem: Wright was an agent of the Magic Door Company, which sold a radio-operated garage door with the usual one-year warranty. Strand, a customer of Wright's, was unwilling to buy and could only be persuaded to do so when Wright substituted the words "five-year warranty" for the original "one-year warranty." Did Wright have authority to alter the written contract?

In dealing with an agent, it is important for the buyer to determine by what authority the agent gives warranties for the goods that he is selling. Since an express warranty is based on contract, an agent must have authority to give it. Most courts hold that an agent has implied authority to give whatever express warranties are usual in his type of business. A purchaser, therefore, cannot safely assume that an agent has any authority to make an express warranty beyond those usually given in the trade. Thus, since Wright had no authority to alter the contract, Strand would have no recourse or right of action against Magic Door for a breach of warranty. He would, however, have a right of action against Wright.

WHEN IS AN AGENT LIABLE TO THIRD PERSONS?

Problem: Tomerlin, who was authorized to sell advertising space on the inside pages of *Futura* magazine, signed an unauthorized advertising contract promising QED Corporation the outside back cover of the April and May issues of the magazine. When such advertising did not appear, QED claimed it lost $50,000 in sales. Who was liable for the alleged loss?

As we have seen, a principal is liable on contracts made by his agents within the scope of their authority. The agent may, however, become personally liable to the third party in any one of the following ways:

(1) BY ACTING WITHOUT AUTHORITY

When a person without authority acts as if he were the agent of another, or when an agent exceeds his authority, he becomes liable to the person with whom he is dealing. An agent, like Tomerlin, in the problem, is liable when he falsely warrants his authority.

(2) FOR NONDISCLOSURE OF PRINCIPAL'S IDENTITY

In the case of a simple contract, if the authorized agent does not disclose the identity of his principal, the third party can generally hold either the agent or the principal liable. In the case of formal contracts where the identity of the principal is undisclosed, the agent alone is liable to the third party.

Quality Cleaners authorized Marsella to buy ten acres of land as a site for a new building without revealing its name as the buyer. Marsella contracted to buy the necessary acreage from Brewster. If Quality Cleaners failed to carry out the contract, Brewster would have a right of action against Marsella; or, if he chose, he could sue Quality Cleaners when and if he learned that it was the principal. If Marsella had given Brewster a promissory note signed by himself for the price of the land, Brewster could look only to the agent (Marsella) for payment of the note.

(3) BY AN EXPRESS AGREEMENT

By an express agreement, an agent may make himself personally liable to a third party for the breach of a contract made for his principal.

The agent may be liable for his personal guarantee.

IF YOU WILL SIGN THIS CONTRACT, I WILL GUARANTEE THAT OUR COMPANY WILL DELIVER THE GOODS IN 30 DAYS.

PRESIDENT

(4) FOR RECEIVING MONEY BY MISTAKE

An agent is liable to a third person for money paid by mistake to the agent for his principal, if the money has not already been turned over to the principal in good faith.

 Blanda, not knowing that his wife had paid her $100 dental bill, saw the dentist's receptionist at the bank and paid her also. When Blanda discovered his error, he notified the dentist, who had not yet received the money. The receptionist was liable.

(5) FOR COMMITTING WRONGFUL ACTS

An agent is liable for any wrongdoing committed within the scope of his employment, as well as outside of it. The fact that he is acting as the agent of another and under the latter's direction is immaterial.

Pitt was directed by his employer, Marsh, to repossess an unpaid-for color TV from Hitch's home. Although Hitch tried to prevent it, Pitt and his helper forced their way into the home and seized the TV. They were guilty of the tort of trespass, and along with their principal, Marsh, were liable to Hitch.

WHAT DUTIES DOES AN AGENT HAVE?

Problem: Schmidt gave Herring an antique Chinese vase to sell for him at the highest possible price. Herring, an antique collector himself, bought the vase but did not reveal that fact when he paid Schmidt. If Schmidt discovered the deception, could he avoid the contract?

Because an agent derives his authority from his principal, he has certain obligations to him. In many respects, the agent's duties are the same as those of an employee. But because an agent acts in the place of his principal, greater trust and loyalty are demanded of him than of an employee. Within the scope of his authority, his words legally are the words of the principal, and his acts legally are the acts of the principal. His utmost good faith is required.

An agent owes four duties to his principal:

1. Loyalty;
2. Obedience;
3. Care and skill; and
4. Accounting.

(1) LOYALTY

One of the agent's most important duties is that of loyalty to the interests of his principal. This means an agent must not only inform the principal of anything that affects his interests, but also that he may not benefit personally from transactions completed in connection with the agency, other than to receive his agreed-upon compensation. Indeed, the agent should avoid placing himself in a situation where he might be tempted to place his own interest above that of his principal. Any profits that the agent may make in the exercise of his duties belong to his principal. Also, an agent may not buy from or sell to himself without obtaining the approval of his principal. If he does so, as in the problem, the principal has the right to avoid the contract.

An agent may not secretly represent another person in a transaction that he is performing for his principal unless both parties are informed and give their consent. Otherwise, the agent would have conflicting duties and could not be loyal to both.

(2) OBEDIENCE

Problem: Cannon authorized Lanier to sell his snowmobile for cash only. Lanier sold the vehicle, but accepted the buyer's personal check, which was dishonored when it was presented for payment. Must Cannon suffer the loss?

Another duty of the agent is to obey the lawful instructions of his principal if they are reasonably within the scope of his employment. An agent is liable for damages that result from failure to follow instructions, or to act only within the limits of his authority. Thus, Lanier, not Cannon, was liable in the problem. However, an agent is not bound to follow instructions to do an illegal or an immoral act.

(3) CARE AND SKILL

Problem: Klein owned the Miramar Motel, and hired Gross as manager. Although a safe was provided, Gross kept the rental money in an unlocked desk drawer in the office until it was banked. One weekend $600 was stolen. Could Gross be held liable?

In performing a transaction for his principal, an agent is required to exercise the degree of care and skill that a reasonably prudent man would use in a similar situation. His failure to do so renders the agent liable to his principal for any loss or injury sustained. Thus, Gross could be held for the loss because he was careless in his handling of the rental money.

(4) ACCOUNTING

Problem: Patterson, who often donated animals to the city zoo, sent his agent, Getz, to Africa to buy an elephant. He gave Getz $4500 for travel and other expenses, but insisted that he keep exact records of his expenditures and report them upon return. Must Getz do this?

An agent like Getz must account to his principal for all money and property of the principal that come into his possession. The agent must promptly notify the principal of the receipt of money belonging to the latter, and he must make an accounting of the money within a reasonable time.

The agent is required to keep his money and property separate from those of his principal. If he mixes his property with that of the principal in such a manner that they cannot be separated, all the property may be claimed by the principal. Money held by the agent should be deposited in a bank in the name of the principal. If the agent deposits it in his own name and the bank fails, he is liable for any loss.

WHAT DUTIES DOES A PRINCIPAL HAVE?

Problem: Kenneth signed an agreement with Wilcox appointing him to sell his antique car. If Wilcox found a buyer ready, willing, and able to buy the car, he was to receive a commission of six percent of the price. Wilcox found Shaw who was ready, willing, and able to buy the car, but Kenneth refused to enter into a contract with him. Was Wilcox entitled to his commission?

A principal has many of the same obligations to his agent that an employer has to his employee. Failure of the principal to fulfill these obligations gives the agent the right to abandon their agreement. In addition to complying with all of the terms of the agency contract, the principal is generally required to provide:

1. Compensation;
2. Reimbursement; and
3. Indemnity.

(1) COMPENSATION

Whether an agent is entitled to compensation depends upon the express or the implied agreement between the principal and the agent. In the problem, there had been an express agreement that Wilcox would be paid if he found a ready, willing, and able buyer. Thus, Wilcox had earned his commission even though Kenneth refused to enter into a contract with Shaw. Not all agents are entitled to be paid—obviously a gratuitous agent expects no compensation for his services. However, if one appoints an agent who normally is paid for his services, he is liable for the usual or reasonable fee even though no mention is made of compensation.

(2) REIMBURSEMENT

Problem: Blaine Manufacturing Company authorized its agent, Thomas, to ship a specially constructed packaging machine to its Elmira factory by chartered airplane. Thomas had to pay for the flight in advance. Must Blaine repay Thomas?

The principal is under a duty to reimburse, that is, repay the agent for disbursement and expenses necessary for the proper discharge of his duties. Thus, Blaine must repay Thomas. The agent may not, however, recover disbursements made for illegal purposes or for expenses incurred through his own negligence or fault.

(3) INDEMNITY

> **Problem:** Ascot, while traveling in his capacity as agent for the Jolly Gym Equipment Company, picked up a hitchhiker who robbed him of all his personal funds and valuables. Would the company be required to indemnify him for the amount of his loss?

An agent is entitled to *indemnity* from his principal for any losses or damages he sustains in executing any authorized, lawful act; that is, he is entitled to have the loss made good. However, the loss must result directly from the execution of his authority. An agent, like Ascot, who is robbed of his own money while on a journey for his principal would have no justifiable claim for indemnity.

HOW MAY AN AGENCY BE TERMINATED?

> **Problem:** Logan entered into a one-year contract with Shelbourne to be his buying agent in Chicago. After six months, Logan became dissatisfied with Shelbourne's performance and terminated the agency. Was he entitled to do so?

The relation of principal and agent may be terminated in the same ways as the relation of employer and employee. The usual way is by performance, or in accordance with the terms of the agreement. Agencies created by contract may be terminated like other contracts. (Chapter 13)

The agency also may be terminated at any time by either the principal or the agent. The principal terminates the relation by revoking the agent's authority. Accordingly, Logan could revoke Shelbourne's authority. He would, however, be liable to Shelbourne for breach of contract. The agent can simply quit or can notify the principal in a more formal manner that he renounces the agency relation. However, if an agent wrongfully terminates the agency before the expiration of the agency contract, the principal is entitled to damages arising out of the breach of contract.

Power to terminate does not exist, however, when the agent has a financial interest other than his commission or compensation in the agency. This is an *agency coupled with an interest.*

> Copeland borrowed some money from Pettit to construct a small office building which he leased to various tenants. As security for the loan, he appointed Pettit as his agent to collect the rent and apply 75 percent of it to reducing the loan. Pettit's agency was coupled with an interest, and could not be terminated until the debt was repaid.

An agency is also ordinarily terminated upon the death, insanity, or bankruptcy of either the principal or the agent. In most states, however, this is not true when the agency is coupled with an interest. Thus, in the case of Copeland and Pettit, the death of either party would not terminate the agency.

There is no difference between the way a gratuitous agency may be terminated and the way an agency created by contract may be terminated. There is, however, a difference in the remedies that are available for wrongful termination. Ordinarily, a gratuitous agent cannot recover any damages if his authority is revoked; nor can a principal normally recover any damages from a gratuitous agent if the latter abandons the agency.

IS NOTICE TO THIRD PERSONS REQUIRED?

Problem: Drake was manager of the Brix Tower, with authority to do what was necessary to rent, maintain, and operate the large office building. The owners of the building discharged him, but before he left and after his authority was terminated, Drake contracted with Harris to paint all the corridors and public places in the building. Harris had been engaged at various other times to do painting and had not been informed that Drake was no longer manager. After completing the job, Harris submitted his bill to the owners of the building. Are they obliged to pay?

When the authority of an agent is terminated by the principal's voluntary act, the principal should promptly notify third persons who have previously dealt with the agent. If the principal does not give such notice, the agent continues to have power to make binding contracts between the principal and such third persons. In the above problem it was held that the owners of the Brix Tower would be bound by the contract that Drake negotiated with Harris, and must pay the contract price.

IF YOU ARE A THIRD PERSON DEALING WITH AN AGENT, REMEMBER THAT . . .

1. One who deals with an agent should learn the extent of the agent's authority unless he is willing to look solely to the agent for recovery in case of loss.
2. If you pay an agent money, be sure that he has authority to accept it, and a receipt with the name of the principal on it.
3. If you are in doubt about an agent's authority, contact his principal, or make all checks payable to the known principal.

IF YOU ARE AN AGENT, REMEMBER THAT . . .

1. When you sign anything, you should make it unmistakably clear that you are signing as an agent. Always write the name of your principal first, then add "by" and your signature, followed by word "agent."
2. If your principal instructs you not to reveal his name to third persons, you should have it clearly understood and agreed that your principal will indemnify you for any legal liability you incur.
3. You must avoid placing your interest above that of your principal, or appearing to do so.
4. If you handle your principal's money or other assets, you should keep them separate from your own.

IF YOU ARE A PRINCIPAL, REMEMBER THAT . . .

If you discharge your agent, you should protect yourself by notifying those with whom the agent has been dealing in your name.

YOUR LEGAL VOCABULARY

agency coupled with an interest   implied authority
apparent authority (or ostensible authority)   indemnity
express authority

1. Authority necessary or customary to carry out duties expressly authorized.
2. An agency in which the agent has a financial interest beyond his compensation or commission.
3. Authority by specific appointment.
4. A right to have a loss made good.
5. Authority arising from the misleading conduct of the principal.

REMEMBER THESE HIGHLIGHTS

1. One who deals with an agent should, for his own protection, learn the extent of the agent's authority, which may be express, implied, or apparent.

2. A principal is liable to third parties for contracts made within the scope of the agent's authority, except negotiable instruments or sealed documents made in the agent's name alone. He is also liable for wrongful or fraudulent acts of his agent done while the agent is acting within the scope of his authority.
3. Knowledge by an agent is binding upon the principal if it concerns the business conducted through the agent.
4. An agent may become liable on contracts for his principal by exceeding his authority, by concealing the identity of his principal, by express agreement, or by making a sealed contract or negotiable instrument in his own name. He is also liable for his wrongful acts even though he is acting for his principal.
5. An agent owes his principal loyalty, obedience, care and skill, and an accounting for all of the principal's money and property that come into his possession.
6. A principal owes his agent compensation, reimbursement, and indemnity.
7. In the ordinary agency, both principal and agent have the power to terminate the agency at any time.
8. Death, insanity, or bankruptcy of either the principal or the agent terminates the ordinary agency.

LAW AS PEOPLE LIVE IT

1. Vincent Paving Company wrote to Bragg authorizing him to purchase 20 tons of gravel needed for a road construction contract but giving him no money to pay for it. How would you classify Bragg's power?
2. Church authorized Armer to sell his motorcycle at the highest price possible, but for not less than $800. Armer received an offer of $1,000 from Leigh, but nevertheless sold the cycle to his buddy Guardino for $800. When Church learned of this, he attempted to collect $200 from Armer. Would he succeed?
3. Shimizu, a peach grower, was under contract to deliver his entire crop to Delta Cannery. Travis, a field agent for Delta, scheduled the peaches to be picked and delivered to the cannery during the third week of July. But, in accordance with the trade custom, if the crop ripened earlier or later, and the cannery was notified, they accepted the crop. An early season caused the peaches to ripen two weeks early. Shimizu reported this to Travis who failed to notify the cannery. When the peaches were delivered to the cannery two weeks ahead of schedule, the cannery refused to accept them. As a result, Shimizu lost most of the value of the crop. Was Delta liable for the loss?
4. Marblehead Industries authorized Spreckles to purchase an emergency supply of fuel oil for one of its factories without disclosing the name of his principal. Spreckles ordered 25,000 barrels of oil from Canyon Oil

Unit IX □ AGENCY

Company and signed the order in his own name, "H. S. Spreckles," but had the oil shipped to Marblehead. When Marblehead did not pay for the oil, Canyon sued Spreckles. Would they succeed?

5. Harvey was a sales agent for Elphinstone Encyclopedia. He was authorized to take orders, and, when the encyclopedias arrived, to deliver them and collect the first payment. He sold a set to Bruce, who signed the order blank which stated, "Pay no money now. First payment of $50 due when you receive the books." Nevertheless, Harvey collected $50 as a down payment. He pocketed the money and disappeared. Could Bruce recover the amount he paid from Elphinstone, or have it applied as the first payment?

6. While Harmon, a salesman for the Highway Supply Company, was driving a company car on a business trip, he struck and injured a pedestrian at a street intersection. The pedestrian sued the Highway Supply Company for damages resulting from his personal injuries. Was the company liable?

7. Brink appointed Jewett as his agent to sell Brink's car for $600. By skillful bargaining, Jewett sold the car for $750. Jewett paid $600 to Brink and kept the extra $150. When Brink later learned the facts, he demanded that Jewett give him the extra profit. Jewett claimed that since he had given Brink the price asked for, the $150 belonged to him. Could Brink hold Jewett liable for $150?

8. Anderson engaged Washburn to act as his agent in the sale of electrical appliances. Without Anderson's knowledge, Washburn decided to sell electrical appliances for the Edco Sales Company, a competitor, during his spare time in order to increase his earnings. Did Washburn have the right to work for Anderson's competitor without obtaining Anderson's permission?

9. Carpenter was employed by the Stokes Implement Company as a traveling salesman. The company provided Carpenter with a car and paid him $125 per week and traveling expenses. Through no fault of Carpenter, the car was damaged by a hit-and-run driver and Carpenter paid $70 to have it repaired so that he could continue his work. Was the company legally obligated to pay Carpenter for this expense?

10. Deep Spring Life Insurance Company terminated the employment of Brown, a collection agent. The company did not notify those from whom Brown was collecting. Rothchild and Larmon paid Brown as they had in the past. Would this be considered payment to the company?

LAW AS COURTS DECIDE IT

1. Robert Beckett appointed Gieb as agent to sell his automobile, and delivered to him a certificate of title signed in blank. Without disclosing his principal, Gieb sold the car to Datko, a minor, who paid the full purchase price of $1,500. When the minor later demanded a return of

his money from Gieb, Gieb told him about Beckett. He contended that he was not personally liable and that Datko must look to the principal, Beckett, for his money. Was this true? (Datko v. Gieb, 113 N.E. 2d 672, Ohio)

2. E. L. Getz was the financial agent of his father-in-law, William H. Patterson. During the period of the agency, certain checks, notes, and bond coupons came into the hands of Getz. After the death of Patterson, his wife, Agnes S. Patterson, brought an action against Getz for an accounting. Was Getz under a duty to account for the money and property of Patterson which came into his possession? (Patterson v. Getz, 166 Ore. 245, 111 P. 2d 842)

3. The defendant, Marsh, rented a farm in Vermont belonging to Ufford who lived in New York. The agreement provided that Marsh was to pay as rent "one half the proceeds and products of operating the farm ... and each to pay his half of the expenses," but Marsh was not to have any authority to obtain credit in Ufford's name. Marsh arranged to purchase on credit needed supplies and seed from Johnson. Marsh told Johnson that he had rented Ufford's farm, that checks from the sale of milk were being sent to Ufford who had agreed to see that the bills were paid. Johnson made no inquiry of Ufford nor did he see the lease. When the bills were not paid, Johnson sued both Marsh and Ufford, claiming that Marsh was Ufford's agent. Was that the case? (Johnson & Co. v. Marsh, 111 Vt. 266, 15 A. 2d 577)

4. Weaver and the Minnesota Liquid Fertilizer Company entered into an agreement whereby the company leased certain equipment to Weaver, and Weaver agreed to sell the company's products in the Farmington, Minnesota, area. The company's name appeared on the equipment for sale and on additional equipment owned by Weaver. The company's president and its sales manager visited Weaver's operation on many occasions. In some of the company's sale brochures, Weaver was listed as "Lessee Manager" of the Farmington operation. The lease did not expressly create an agency relationship. Lindstrom did certain repair work on the equipment at Weaver's request and on his statement that he was the agent for the company. When the company refused to pay Lindstrom, he sued the company. Who should win? (Lindstrom v. Minnesota Liquid Fertilizer Company, 264 Minn. 485, 119 N.W. 2d 855)

5. The manager of a retail butcher shop owned by Serges borrowed $3,500 from David for use in the butcher shop. Serges claimed that the manager had no authority to borrow money. Nevertheless, Serges made payments of $200 and told David upon several occasions that the full sum would eventually be paid. Was Serges liable? (David v. Serges, 373 Mich. 442, 129 N.W. 2d 882)

UNIT TEN

Insurance

UNIT TEN

Life is full of risks. The uncertainties of the future are constantly with us, and we spend much of our time planning to cope with these risks. The law itself is a means of avoiding or reducing some of these risks, as we have learned. Chapters 22 and 23, for example, dealt with risks involving credit.

Some of the most serious financial risks that a person faces are those arising from possible loss of his home from fire, injury and damage resulting from an automobile accident, and legal suit for a tort; and everyone knows the financial problems that arise when death takes the wage earner of a family. The uncertainty of loss in cases like these may be lessened by insurance.

Insurance is an arrangement by which we transfer and share the chance or risk of loss with others. After developing a basic vocabulary that will enable us to understand the nature of insurance, we shall study some of the legal principles affecting all types of insurance including the concept of insurable interest, and the necessity for good faith in dealing with insurance companies. Because of the many different kinds of insurance, each with its own peculiarities, it will be possible to examine in detail only a few, such as fire, liability, automobile, and life insurance. We shall also learn some aspects of government regulation of this socially significant industry.

Finally, we shall look at an increasingly vital subject—social insurance—including unemployment compensation, health coverage, and other social security benefits.

CHAPTER 34 Nature of Insurance

1. *You buy a car from a person who has just renewed his insurance on it. Will the insurance be transferred to you along with the title to the car?*

2. *Knowing that a neighbor is ill of an incurable disease, a friend applied for life insurance on the neighbor's life. Will the application be accepted?*

3. *An applicant for fire insurance fails to reveal that he has received various threats that his house would be bombed. Would the insurer be liable?*

WHAT IS INSURANCE?

Problem: Lindquist insured his $20,000 home against possible loss by fire with Atlantic Standard Insurance Company. Later, a fire did $3,000 damage to the home. How much could Lindquist collect?

Insurance is a contract in which one party (usually a company) promises to pay another a sum of money if the latter experiences a specified loss. It may be an agreement to pay a specified amount of money upon the occurrence of a certain event. Or it may be an agreement to indemnify another for whatever loss or damage occurs as a result of specified perils, such as fire or theft. To *indemnify* means to make good, or to pay the party for the actual loss or damage he has incurred.

The written contract of insurance is the *policy*. The maximum amount to be paid in the event of loss is the *face value* of the policy. The party who agrees to pay or indemnify is the *insurer*. The party who is protected is the *insured*.

The consideration for a contract of insurance is the *premium*. The possible loss arising from injury to or death of a person, or from damage to property from a specified peril, is called the *risk*.

In the problem, Lindquist was the insured; the company was the insurer; the amount that Lindquist paid for the insurance was the premium; and the possible loss arising from fire was the risk. The obligations and rights of the parties are set forth in the policy. If

Lindquist has proper coverage, his insurance company will indemnify him for his loss; that is, the company will either pay him $3,000, or restore or replace the property.

Insurance makes an important contribution to society. By collecting small premiums from many insured persons, the insurer builds a large fund from which he can make payments to indemnify the relatively few policyholders who suffer losses. The risk of most financial losses can be covered by insurance.

WHAT ARE THE KINDS OF INSURANCE?

Problem: Tidwell purchased a new automobile. What kind of insurance does he need to protect himself against possible loss or damages awarded against him in a lawsuit resulting from operation of the car?

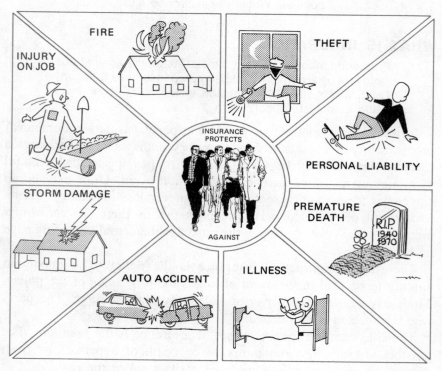

(1) LIFE INSURANCE

This kind of insurance is discussed in Chapter 37. It provides for payment of a specified amount of money upon the death of a person. It often includes other benefits.

(2) MARINE INSURANCE

Marine insurance indemnifies for loss of or damage to vessels, cargo, and other property exposed to the perils of the sea. It is perhaps the oldest type of insurance, dating back to ancient times.

(3) INLAND MARINE INSURANCE

This type of insurance covers property against various perils while it is being transported (other than on the oceans), or wherever it may be located. Inland Marine insurance is discussed in Chapter 35.

(4) FIDELITY AND SURETY BONDING INSURANCE

This form of insurance provides coverage against financial loss caused by dishonesty or failure of one person to perform a legal obligation he has to another. Suretyship contracts (Page 315) are often in the form of surety bonds.

(5) FIRE INSURANCE

Fire insurance protects not only against losses caused by fire, but normally those caused by certain other perils, such as smoke, windstorm, earthquake, rain, and hail.

(6) SOCIAL INSURANCE

This type includes unemployment insurance and old-age, survivors, disability, and health insurance. It will be discussed in Chapter 38.

(7) CASUALTY INSURANCE

Casualty insurance includes coverage for a variety of specific situations in which chance, accident, or negligence may result in loss. Some of the more important types of casualty insurance are:

(a) Burglary, robbery, theft, and larceny insurance protects against losses which result from such acts and, under certain circumstances, from mysterious disappearance of property.

(b) Automobile insurance indemnifies one for losses arising from his ownership and operation of motor vehicles. In the problem, if Tidwell is insured under a suitable casualty policy, almost any loss arising from the operation of his car will be covered. This type is discussed in Chapter 36.

(c) Workmen's compensation insurance is a casualty coverage that was discussed in Chapter 31.

(d) Disability or accident and health insurance is a casualty coverage that reimburses the insured for loss caused by injury or disease. It is frequently sold by life insurance companies as well as by casualty companies.

HOW DOES THE LAW OF CONTRACTS APPLY TO INSURANCE?

Problem: Goldstein purchased an expensive camera and other photographic equipment in preparation for a vacation. He telephoned his insurance agent, Donleavey, and asked that the property be covered against possible loss by fire or theft. Donleavey said, "You're covered; just send me the bill of sale." That night, and before the policy was issued, Goldstein's home was broken into and the camera and other articles were stolen. Was he covered?

Contracts of insurance are governed by the same rules as other contracts. A few points, however, require special mention.

(1) OFFER AND ACCEPTANCE

In an insurance contract, the insured is generally the offeror. He makes an application (the offer) to the insurance company by setting forth the facts requested by the company concerning the risk. On the basis of these facts, and frequently upon further investigation, the insurer determines whether it will accept or reject the application.

Since most insurance companies are corporations and operate through agents, the law of agency (Chapters 32-33) is involved in insurance. Most states require insurance agents to be licensed, and an examination is frequently required.

In property and liability insurance, it is customary for the agent to have power to make a preliminary, oral agreement to insure an applicant. When this is done, a written notation called a *binder* is issued as evidence of the oral contract and the insurance is placed in force immediately. The company reserves the right to cancel the policy after reviewing the facts, unless a loss has occurred. In the problem, Goldstein was covered even though the policy itself had not been issued; he would be able to collect in accordance with its terms.

Even though he represents the insurer, an agent ordinarily has no authority to alter or vary the written terms of the contract.

(2) CONSIDERATION

Problem: Smothers, who was newly married, contracted for some life insurance and also for fire insurance on the furniture and personal effects in his apartment. When must the premiums be paid?

The insurance premium is the consideration given by the insured in return for the insurance company's promise to assume the risk of loss. It is usually paid in advance of the time for which protection is provided. Payment may be made annually, semiannually, quarterly, monthly, or even weekly, depending on what arrangements are made with the insurer.

Life insurance and health and accident insurance are generally not effective until the first premium is paid. Thus, Smothers in the problem would have to pay his life insurance premium in advance, as provided by the policy. Premiums for other kinds of insurance contracts are customarily paid in one lump sum or annually, although many companies allow insureds to pay by installment. Smothers would need to pay the total fire insurance premium in advance for the year unless he had made other arrangements with the insurer.

(3) FORM

Problem: Thele had an insurance policy on his home in Massachusetts. Upon moving to Arizona he claimed the same policy was good on his new house. Is that correct?

A written contract of insurance is usually required by statute. Many states require the use of a standard form of policy, and the printing may not be smaller than a specified size. Even though a standard policy may be used, each state has certain variations in its requirements. Moreover, the location of the property and the kind of protection afforded affects the insurance contract. Accordingly, Thele could not use the same policy when he moved.

WHO MAY BE AN INSURER?

Problem: Provost and Price wished to organize a life insurance business. Could they do so?

Because of its importance to society as well as to the insured, the business of insurance is ordinarily limited to corporations organized for the purpose. In most states, any group or company that deals in insurance is under the supervision of a state insurance commissioner. New applicants, such as Provost and Price, need to get a charter from the state and meet certain requirements before they can start an insurance business.

(1) STOCK AND MUTUAL COMPANIES

A *stock insurance company* has capital stock owned by stockholders who contribute the original capital and share the future profits or losses. A stock company is ordinarily governed by the rules applicable to other corporations as discussed in Chapter 44.

A *mutual insurance company* has no capital stock, and the members are both the owners and the insureds. At periodic intervals they contribute, usually as premiums, to a fund that is used in paying losses and expenses. Because the policyholders are the owners of mutual companies, they are entitled to refunds if losses are low. These refunds, known as dividends, are often used to reduce the premiums charged. Life insurance policies on which dividends are paid are *participating policies*. All mutual company policies are participating. Many stock life insurance companies also issue participating policies.

(2) OTHER TYPES OF INSURERS

Certain lodges and fraternal societies, more than 200 in number, provide life insurance for their members.

In Connecticut, Massachusetts, and New York, life insurance is sold by mutual savings banks. The maximum amount of such insurance that one individual may hold is limited.

State and federal government insurance is also available. For example, Wisconsin issues life insurance to residents of the state under the "State Life Fund." As stated in Chapter 31, workmen's compensation insurance and disability insurance, and certain other forms of casualty insurance, are provided by some states. The federal government also issues insurance of various kinds, such as life insurance to members and veterans of the armed forces, crop insurance to farmers, mortgage insurance to those who lend money for the construction or repair of buildings, deposit insurance to banks and savings and loan associations, and old-age survivors, disability, and health insurance.

WHAT IS AN INSURABLE INTEREST?

Problem: Reimer sold his car for cash to Garmo. Instead of canceling his insurance, Reimer decided to let it run until the policy expired three months later. Two months after Garmo bought the car, it was totally destroyed in a fire.

Reimer placed a claim for the loss with his insurance company. Would he be able to collect?

Anyone who has capacity to enter into a contract may become an insured if he also possesses some financial interest, known as an *insurable interest,* in the life or property.

Without the principle of insurable interest, a contract of insurance would be no more than a gambling agreement or a bet. An agreement without it is invalid because a person who has nothing to lose and everything to gain might be tempted to cause the destruction of the insured property or the death of the insured person so that he would be entitled to the proceeds of the insurance. Thus, Reimer's claim was invalid.

The insured must have an insurable interest.

Insurance is said to be a personal contract; it follows the person and not the property. A policy may be written insuring a specific item and naming an individual as the one who would suffer financial loss if the item were damaged or destroyed. However, if the named individual no longer has an insurable interest in the property at the time of loss, there is no liability under the policy.

(1) INSURABLE INTEREST IN PROPERTY

Problem: When Wesley bought Stewart's farm, he paid one-third down. Stewart kept a mortgage on the farm until it was fully paid. Does he have a right to insure the property?

A person has an insurable interest in property when he would suffer a direct financial loss if the property were damaged or destroyed. He need not be the owner. He may be someone who, like Stewart in the problem, has a security interest in the property. (Chapter 22) In such a case it is possible for several persons to have an insurable interest in the same property. Both a mortgagor and a mortgagee (Chapter 40) have insurable interests; the same is true of a landlord and a tenant. (Chapter 41) Likewise, persons in whose care personal property has been placed—innkeepers, carriers, and ordinary bailees (Chapter 15)—have insurable interests.

 Ellis held a mortgage on a motel owned by Quess. The motel was leased by Frey. Watts was negotiating to purchase the property from Quess. All but Watts had an insurable interest in the property.

For a property or liability insurance policy to be effective, the insurable interest must be in existence at the time of loss. It is possible, however, to obtain coverage on property in which the insured does not have, but anticipates having, an insurable interest. For instance, it is quite common for a shipper to obtain marine insurance coverage on cargo he has not yet purchased for a return trip.

When a house is mortgaged it is common practice for the mortgagee to require, as a condition of the loan, that the mortgagor obtain and pay the premiums on a fire insurance policy containing a mortgage clause. This clause provides that in the case of fire, the mortgagee is paid first, up to the balance of the mortgage.

(2) INSURABLE INTEREST IN LIFE

Problem: Karen Young and Don Adley were engaged to be married. Karen took out a life insurance policy on Don's life. Don died before they were married. Could Karen collect on the policy?

Every person has an insurable interest in his own life. He may also have an insurable interest in the life of another if their relationship is such that he can expect to receive economic benefit from the continued life of the other. A creditor has an insurable interest in the life of his debtor since the debtor represents economic benefit to him. Karen had an insurable interest in the life of Adley because the law recognizes the probable benefit of the continued existence of one engaged person to the other. In like manner, a husband and wife each have an insurable interest in the life of the other and in the lives of their minor children. A sister has an insurable interest in the life of a brother upon whom she depends for support. There may or may not be an insurable interest between an uncle and a nephew, however, because kinship alone does not give an insurable interest.

In life insurance, the insured need not have an insurable interest at the time of the death of the person whose life is insured. But he must have an insurable interest when the insurance is taken out.

WHAT ARE REPRESENTATIONS AND WARRANTIES?

Problem: In his application for fire insurance for his business, Swan stated that he employed a night watchman and would continue to do so. Relying on this statement, the insurance company issued the policy at a reduced rate. Without notifying the insurer, Swan discharged the watchman and did not employ another. When fire damaged Swan's factory shortly thereafter, the insurance company refused to pay for the loss. Was it within its rights?

When a person makes an application for insurance, he is usually given an application form containing questions about the nature of the risk. If the applicant wants property insurance, the form will call for information as to the age, the use, description and condition of the property, as well as its location and value or cost. An application for life insurance calls for such facts as the age of the applicant, any illnesses or accidents that he has had, his occupation and habits, and the health of his parents.

If the statements made by the applicant are used by the insurer in determining whether to accept the application, but are not made part of the final writing, they are called *representations*. A false representation can render the contract voidable only if it is material. However, if statements of past or existing fact made by the applicant are included as part of the final contract of insurance, they are called *warranties*. False warranties make the contract voidable without regard to whether the matter is material. This means that they must be literally true or the policy can be avoided even though the insured honestly believed his statements to be true and acted in good faith. Accordingly, Swan in the problem could not collect on his insurance because he falsely represented that his business would continue to have a night watchman.

Many state statutes ignore the difference between representations and warranties. Courts also look upon warranties with disfavor and whenever possible construe them to be representations. Many policies also contain a clause such as the following: "All statements made by the insured, in the absence of fraud, are construed as representations, not warranties."

WHAT IS THE EFFECT OF CONCEALMENT?

Problem: Schneider applied for a fidelity insurance policy and bond on a new employee, Dennis, the cashier. Dennis had served a prison term for embezzlement but the insurance company was not informed of this fact. Would this affect the contract?

The parties to a contract of insurance are required to act with utmost good faith. Thus, the person applying for insurance has an obligation not only to answer all questions truthfully, but also to volunteer any other facts that may be material to the risk. In insurance, the materiality of a fact can usually be determined by asking: if this fact had been known, would the insurer have issued a policy on the same terms? Failure to disclose such facts, or to speak when there is an obligation to do so, is known as *concealment*. Concealment makes the agreement voidable at the election of the insurer. In this respect insurance contracts differ from almost all other contracts.

In the problem, if Schneider should make a claim of loss covered by the insurance, he would not be able to collect. He had not informed the insurer of a material fact.

In the case of insurance on property, an increase in a hazard, such as a change in location, must be reported to the insurer. Otherwise the insurance is suspended while the hazard is increased.

TO AVOID MISUNDERSTANDINGS...

1. Check coverage of important possible losses periodically. The risk of most financial losses can be covered by insurance.
2. Deal with reputable insurance agents to decrease the possibility of misunderstanding.
3. Contact your insurance agent when you are anticipating a move. Insurance policies may not be transferrable, or changes in the policy may need to be made to be effective in your new location.
4. Be truthful in all insurance applications. False representations may render the contract voidable.
5. Disclose all facts that may be material to the risk. Concealment may also render the contract voidable.

YOUR LEGAL VOCABULARY

binder	mutual insurance company
concealment	participating policies
face value	policy
indemnify	premium
insurable interest	representations
insurance	risk
insured	stock insurance company
insurer	warranties

1. A written contract of insurance.
2. The possible loss arising from death of a person, or from damage to property.

3. A contract whereby one party promises to pay the other a sum of money if the latter experiences a specified loss.
4. A financial interest in property or in the life of a person.
5. The party who agrees to pay or indemnify.
6. Statements of past or existing facts made in applying for insurance.
7. The consideration in an insurance contract.
8. The maximum amount to be paid in event of loss.
9. To make good or pay a party for the actual loss suffered.
10. Written evidence of a preliminary, oral contract of insurance.

REMEMBER THESE HIGHLIGHTS

1. Insurance renders a distinct service to society by collecting small premiums from many insured persons and building a large fund from which those few policyholders who do suffer loss may be indemnified.
2. Insurance contracts and operations are closely regulated by the states.
3. A person has an insurable interest in property when he would suffer a financial loss if the property were damaged or destroyed. The insurable interest must exist at the time of the loss.
4. A person has an insurable interest in his own life, and in the life of another if he can reasonably expect that the death of such person would cause him financial loss. An insurable interest in life need exist only at the time the insurance is obtained.
5. An applicant for insurance must reveal any facts which are material to the risk. If he fails to do so, the insurer can avoid the policy.
6. Statements of fact made in applying for insurance, called representations, can render the contract void only if they are both false and material. Statements included as part of the final contract are called warranties; a false warranty makes the contract voidable even if the matter is not material.

LAW AS PEOPLE LIVE IT

1. Hitchman took out a three-year $20,000 fire insurance policy on his home at a cost of $150. The policy was issued by the Northwestern Insurance Company. Identify: (a) the insurer, (b) the insured, (c) the subject matter, (d) the risk, (e) the face value, and (f) the premium.
2. Hart made application for $30,000 in fire insurance on a duplex he owned. He answered "No" to the question on the application form which asked, "Do you have other fire insurance on this building?" In fact, he had another policy for $25,000 on the same property. In case of loss, would Hart be able to collect on both policies?
3. Gallup opened a doughnut shop and decided to take out insurance covering possible loss by smoke damage, injuries to his employees and customers, and embezzlement of money by the cashier. What kinds of insurance would protect him against these perils?

4. Tooney took out a three-year fire insurance policy on his summer cottage. One year later he sold the cottage to Wilcox for $8,000, and told him it was insured for two more years. One month after this sale, the cottage was destroyed by fire. Wilcox attempted to collect from the insurance company on the unexpired policy. Could he do so?

5. Sharp was about to be married and thought he should have some life insurance. He called Gray, an agent, and told him he would like to have $20,000 coverage. Gray said, "O.K., you're covered; come in and sign the papers when you get back from your honeymoon." While on the honeymoon, Sharp was killed. Could his widow collect?

6. Fanucchi bought Blackburn's pick-up truck for $3,000; he paid $1,200 down, and Blackburn maintained a security interest for the balance due. Soon thereafter the truck was totally destroyed by fire. The question arose whether either Fanucchi or Blackburn had an insurable interest in the truck. What is your judgment?

7. Myers took out an insurance policy on the life of Bock and named himself beneficiary. When Bock died, the insurance company refused to pay on the policy, claiming Myers had no insurable interest. Myers proved he was Bock's uncle. Was he entitled to recover?

8. In an application which was part of his life insurance policy, Garson stated that he was a salesman. In reality he was a guard in a bank. Six months after Garson took out the policy, he was fatally wounded during a bank holdup. Was the insurance company liable?

9. Beck, a minor, had been refused insurance on his automobile because of previous accidents and police citations. He arranged to transfer the title of the car to his brother and to take out insurance in his brother's name. Beck, however, continued to drive the car as he always had. Following an accident the insurance company learned of the situation, denied liability, and sued to cancel the policy. Would it be successful?

10. Halvorson noted an abandoned cannery surrounded by high, dry weeds on a frequently-traveled road, near his home. It occurred to him that the building would easily be destroyed if just one cigarette butt were thrown from a passing vehicle. He therefore decided to insure it against loss by fire. Could he do so?

LAW AS COURTS DECIDE IT

1. State Farm Insurance Company notified Josey that it would not renew his automobile insurance policy after expiration of the present contract. Josey then applied to Allstate Insurance Company. The application blank included the question: "Has any insurer canceled or refused or given notice that it intended to cancel or refuse any similar insurance?" Was Josey obliged to answer "yes" because of his experience with the State Farm Company? (Josey v. Allstate Insurance Company, 252 Md. 274, 250 A. 2d 256)

2. On January 17, Roger Chaney, an agent for United Pacific Insurance Company, ordered a fire insurance policy on some property in Nevada for the defendant, Arley. At Chaney's request, a three-year policy was duly issued and backdated to make the coverage commence January 12. On January 15, a fire had damaged the insured property, and the plaintiff company filed suit to have the policy declared void. The company claimed Chaney and the defendant were in collusion and that Chaney was not acting in good faith in issuing a binder for insurance after the building had been damaged by fire. Do you agree that the policy should be voided? (Arley v. United Pacific Insurance Company, 379 F. 2d 183)

3. In 1933, Ben George died, leaving four minor children, one of whom was Albert George. Ben's sister, Ruth, undertook the care of his children, but in 1934 Albert was committed to a state mental hospital where he remained until his death in 1945. Albert was in the hospital as an indigent patient without means of support. In 1938, Ruth took out a life insurance policy on the life of her nephew, Albert, and paid the premiums until his death. When Ruth tried to collect on the policy at Albert's death, the insurance company refused to pay on the ground that Ruth had no insurable interest in Albert's life. Do you agree? (Commonwealth Life Ins. Co. v. George, 248 Ala. 649, 28 So. 2d 190)

4. Lennon applied for a life insurance policy. He answered "No" to the question "Have you ever had or been told that you had, or been treated for any of the following . . . cancer?" Earlier, a biopsy had been performed on Lennon's larynx. Ten days after applying for the insurance policy, Lennon was operated on to remove the cancerous growth. He did not know it was cancerous. The insurance company was not informed of either of these operations. The policy was issued. Twenty months later Lennon died of cancer of the pancreas. The insurance company declined to pay the death benefit, claiming that Lennon's failure to answer the questions correctly made the contract voidable. Do you agree? (Lennon v. John Hancock Mutual Life Insurance Company, 157 N.E. 2d 518, Massachusetts)

5. Antrell made an offer to purchase a building on the Leech Lake Indian Reservation in Minnesota for $300. He paid $100 cash at the time he made the offer, and received keys to the building from the Tribal Council. Without examining the property, the defendant insurance company issued a policy with a face value of $16,000. Several months after the policy was issued, fire totally destroyed the building. At the time of the loss, Antrell had not paid the balance of the purchase price nor had the title been transferred. The company claims the plaintiff had no insurable interest in the building; if this is true, it is not liable on the policy. What is your judgment? (Antrell v. Pearl Assurance Company, 252 Minn. 118, 89 N.W. 2d 726)

35 Property and Casualty Insurance

1. *Your home is subject to possible loss from many perils including fire, windstorm, vandalism, explosion, and falling aircraft. Is it necessary to take out a separate policy for each peril?*

2. *The inventory and equipment in your father's store are damaged by smoke and water resulting from fire on the roof. Can your father recover for damages under a fire insurance policy?*

3. *You own an original Picasso print worth $15,000 and insure it for full value with each of two companies. If the print is stolen, can you collect the value from both insurers?*

WHAT IS PROPERTY AND CASUALTY INSURANCE?

Problem: While playing golf, Shockley sliced his drive and the ball struck and injured Endicott, who was walking along an adjoining road. Endicott sued Shockley for damages caused by his negligence. What kind of insurance should Shockley have had to protect him?

Property insurance protects the insured against direct loss to real and personal property by such perils as fire, windstorm, and theft. *Casualty insurance* covers losses caused by chance, accident, or negligence. Some casualty losses are to the property of the insured, such as damage to one's automobile resulting from a collision. Others involve injuries to third persons and arise from the tort liability of the insured. In the problem, adequate casualty insurance would have protected Shockley.

The purpose of all property and casualty insurance is indemnification for loss. As you recall, this means that a person who experiences a loss is not permitted to recover more than the actual value of the property at the time it was destroyed or, if the loss is not total, the amount of the damage. This is true even though the insured has policies with more than one company.

 Parker bought a house for $15,000 to which he made improvements costing $3,000. He then increased his insurance to $18,000 and took out policies of $18,000 in each of two companies with the belief that he could collect the amount of any loss from each company. Fire caused $6,000 damage to the building. Parker could collect only the amount of the loss, pro-rated, meaning $3,000 from each insurer.

Insurance companies provide for indemnification of loss for almost any kind of property and against almost any peril that will cause a loss. There may be some exceptions, known as *exclusions*. Losses due to war, invasions, insurrections, and depreciation are common exclusions.

WHAT IS LOSS BY FIRE?

Problem: Brister wrapped her insured diamond ring in a piece of paper tissue and placed it on a table. Her husband, unaware of the diamond inside, threw the tissue into the fireplace and it was burned. The ring was destroyed or lost. Could Brister collect for the loss under his fire policy?

The risk assumed with fire insurance is direct loss by fire, lightning, and removal from premises endangered by fire. In establishing loss by fire, it must be shown that:

(1) THERE WAS AN ACTUAL FIRE, A GLOW, OR A BURNING

The mere scorching or blistering of property by heat is insufficient.

(2) THE LOSS WAS CAUSED BY ACCIDENTAL OR HOSTILE FIRE

An accidental fire is one that was not set or started deliberately by the insured. A *hostile fire,* also known as an unfriendly fire, is one that becomes uncontrollable or that escapes from the place where

In establishing loss by fire, it must be proved that it was caused by a hostile fire.

it is intended to be. To illustrate, damage done by a smoking or overheated stove, or by smoke escaping from a fireplace or pipe, does not arise from a hostile fire unless fire actually escapes from the fireplace, stove, or pipe. Thus, in the problem, Brister could not recover for the loss of her ring because it was destroyed by a friendly fire.

(3) THE HOSTILE FIRE WAS THE DIRECT OR PROXIMATE CAUSE OF THE DAMAGE

Proximate cause is the act, or failure to act, that is the natural and reasonably foreseeable cause of loss or damage. Fire is considered the proximate cause not only of damage by burning but also of losses due to scorching, smoke, water used in extinguishing a fire, broken windows or holes chopped in the roof by firemen, and the hasty removal of goods endangered by fire to a safe place.

 Maxwell's Macaroni Factory caught fire, but quick action by the local fire department saved the buildings. Considerable damage was done by water, however, and the inventory of macaroni was so badly contaminated by smoke that it had to be destroyed. The loss was covered by Maxwell's fire insurance policy because the fire was the direct or proximate cause of the loss.

It is immaterial that a fire results from the negligence of the insured, unless the negligence is so great that it shows a willful destruction of property.

 After dinner one evening, Scott lighted a cigarette and relaxed on the sofa in his living room. He dozed, and the lighted cigarette dropped onto the sofa, setting it afire. Although the fire loss was caused by Scott's negligence, it was covered by the fire insurance on his personal property.

WHAT IS THE STANDARD FIRE INSURANCE POLICY?

Problem: Lyon, who owned a farm and lived on it, bought a second home in town and opened an antique shop. He needed insurance for his farm, his new home, and his shop. Would one policy cover them all?

A fire insurance policy includes the basic, or *standard fire policy,* and one or more *"forms"* which modify the standard policy to apply to the specific type of risk being insured. In all states a standard policy has been adopted which must be used by all insurance companies within the state. In most states this is the New York Standard Fire Policy.

In Lyon's case, the insurer would issue separate policies for each risk. Although the basic policy would be the same,[1] each would be modified by forms to take account of the differences in risks to the home, the farm, and the store. To the policy for his home, a "Dwellings and Contents Form" would be attached. His business policy would include a "Mercantile Building and Stock Form." The "Farm Property—Fire and Extended Coverage Form" would probably be added to the farm policy.

The standard policy and forms may also be modified by *endorsements* or riders. These endorsements [2] are attached to the policy to provide for special and individual needs such as a mortgage clause.

WHAT OTHER PERILS ARE COVERED BY FIRE INSURANCE?

Problem: Risley took out a fire insurance policy on his home, but he also wanted coverage against windstorm and vandalism. Must he take out separate policies for each of these perils?

Difficulty often arises in determining whether a loss was the direct result of fire, lightning, windstorm, explosion, or some other peril. For example, if a truck should crash into a building and explode, causing a fire, it would be hard to tell how much of the loss was caused by the impact of the truck, how much by the explosion, and how much by the ensuing fire. To ease this difficulty, a fire insurance policy may be issued with an *extended coverage endorsement.* This endorsement adds coverage for damage by windstorm, hail, explosion, riot, smoke, aircraft, and vehicles. Risley, in the problem, could obtain the windstorm coverage he wished, and more, by paying an additional premium for extended coverage; vandalism could be included in an optional perils coverage. He could also obtain the desired special coverages separately, or in what is commonly known as a homeowners policy.

---

[1] Some states exempt insurers of farms from using the standard policy.
[2] Compare the spelling of indorsement when referring to a negotiable instrument.

Perils and Losses Insured Against by the Homeowners Policy, Broad Form *

Fire and lightning
Removal from premises
   endangered by other perils
Windstorm
Hail
Explosion
Riot and civil commotion
Smoke
Theft or attempted theft
Water accidentally escaping
   plumbing, heating, air-
   conditioning systems or
   appliances
Rupture of steam or hot water
   heating systems
Vandalism and malicious
   mischief
Aircraft
Vehicles
Weight of ice, snow, or sleet
Falling trees

Falling objects
Freezing of plumbing, heating,
   air-conditioning systems, and
   appliances
Collapse of buildings
Landslide
Glass breakage if part of the
   building
Additional living expenses if
   damage requires insured to
   move from premises
Personal property away from
   premises
Personal property of owner,
   family, and guests
Removal of debris following loss
Replacement cost if insured to a
   specified percentage of value
Medical payments for accident
   occurring on premises
Personal legal liability

* The various coverages listed are subject to exclusions and exceptions, and in some cases to a deductible clause.

Within recent years insurance companies have found it possible to issue package policies which may provide all personal property and liability insurance needed by the average family. These policies have different names, such as "Homeowners," "Comprehensive," "Package," "All-Risk," and "All Physical Loss," because they cover most risks to which a dwelling and its contents are subject. They may include burglary and theft, legal liability, and even losses caused by friendly fires. As with all insurance policies there may be certain exclusions, such as losses caused by termites, earthquakes, floods, and insurrections. Also excluded may be losses which are normally covered by other insurance such as those arising from the ownership and operation of motor vehicles, boats and aircraft, and business activities. "All-risk" policies usually cover losses from all perils except those that are specifically excluded.

WHAT DOES INLAND MARINE INSURANCE COVER?

Problem: Edgar's daughter played the violin, and Edgar had the instrument insured under an inland marine policy known as a musical instrument floater. If the violin was carelessly left on a chair and someone sat on it, would the policy cover the loss?

Inland marine insurance is generally written by fire insurance companies for the purpose of indemnifying for loss to personal property other than automobiles, airplanes, and railroad cars. It was originally developed to cover goods while being transported other than on the oceans, and may still be obtained for this purpose. With time, however, a second type of inland marine insurance has been developed to cover loss to personal property from nearly any cause and wherever such loss occurs. Policies which provide this broad coverage to all of one's personal property, or to specific or scheduled property, are known as all-risk floaters. The term "floater" means that the protection floats with, or follows, the property.

In most states, a policy known as a *personal property floater* is issued when one wishes all of his personal property, wherever located, to be covered against any peril. In cases like Edgar's, individual and separate floater policies may also be issued for certain classes of personal property. Payment would be made for the crushed violin.

It is possible to insure personal property such as one's jewelry and furs, stamp collections, musical instruments, livestock, athletic equipment, wedding presents, and photographic equipment either with an all-risk policy or with policies for specified perils such as fire or burglary. One can also arrange to insure a single piece of personal property, such as an organ or a neon sign. Mail order dealers frequently take out a blanket policy to cover all losses, including breakage and mysterious disappearances of goods shipped. Laundrymen and dry cleaners may take out policies covering possible losses to customers' property in their possession, known as bailee insurance.

Like other all-risk policies, these do not really cover all risks of loss. There are certain exclusions and limitations. Edgar's policy, for example, undoubtedly excluded losses caused by repairing, wear and tear, dampness and extremes in temperature, war, confiscation, and dishonesty of a bailee.

WHAT IS LIABILITY INSURANCE?

Problem: Proxmire, a guest in the Deming Hotel, was seriously injured when a poorly secured mirror fell on him. What rights would Deming have under his liability policy?

Liability insurance, a form of casualty insurance, protects the insured against claims arising from his torts that cause damage to third persons for which he is legally liable. These claims often arise from the operation of automobiles; this is a special kind of liability insurance which will be discussed in Chapter 36. Most business firms and owners of buildings—in fact, anyone who has contact with the public—should carry liability insurance. Assuming that the Deming Hotel was properly insured, in the problem, the insurer would not only defend Deming in a court action for tort, but would also pay any judgment awarded against him, up to the dollar limit of the policy.

Persons engaged in personal services, such as beauty shop operators, and persons rendering professional services, such as hospital operators and physicians, are often covered by liability insurance.

Persons providing personal services usually protect themselves with liability insurance.

This type of insurance is also carried by some television and radio broadcasting companies as a protection against liability for defamation.

Many persons carry liability insurance as a matter of personal protection. For example, if a visitor should trip over a bicycle left in a homeowner's driveway and suffer injury, the insured **owner** would be indemnified if any legal claim resulted in a judgment for damages.

 Shefield's son was bitten by Palmer's pet ocelot and required hospitalization. Shefield sued Palmer for damages. Palmer had personal liability coverage under his homeowner's policy and his insurer defended him in the legal action. The claim was finally settled by the insurer at no cost to Palmer.

Medical payments coverage (Page 496) is also available. It takes care of personal injuries for which the insured need not be legally liable but for which he believes he has a moral responsibility.

 While taking pictures, Lewis stepped backwards, tumbled off Melvin's porch, and sustained a broken back. Melvin was not negligent and had no legal liability to Lewis. However, the medical payments coverage in Melvin's personal comprehensive liability policy could be used to defray Lewis' doctor and hospital bills.

HOW IS A CLAIM MADE?

Problem: LeRoy was getting out of his car in the parking lot of Appling's Appliances when the store's overhead sign fell, injuring LeRoy and damaging the car. What steps must Appling take to be indemnified by his liability policy?

A *claim* is a demand for payment of a loss covered by the policy. All insurance contracts provide that the liability of the insurer is conditional upon receiving notice and proof of loss from the insured.

Notice of loss must be made in the form stipulated by the contract or by statute. It is usually given to the agent who wrote the policy. Most insurance contracts require immediate written notice of loss if it is practicable; if not, loss must be reported within a reasonable time. If legal action is commenced against the insured, immediate notice to the insurer is required. Prompt notice enables the insurer to investigate while the evidence is fresh and witnesses are available, and to take other suitable action.

Proof of loss must be in writing, and must be submitted within 60 or 90 days of the time of loss. This is a sworn statement including information as to origin and time of the loss, value of and damage to the property, injuries suffered, names of any witnesses, and other insurance carried. Accordingly, Appling must both give notice of loss and furnish the insurer with proof of loss. The proof of loss is usually made out on a form supplied by the insurer.

HOW IS A LOSS SETTLED?

Problem: Stansbury's house and contents, insured under a homeowners policy, were destroyed by a tornado.

Stansbury demanded that the insurer replace the property instead of paying the claim in cash. Must the insurer do so?

Unless the policy states otherwise, the insurer promises to indemnify the insured for loss or damage to property to the extent of the actual cash value at the time of the loss. For example, if furniture which is five years old is destroyed, the insurance company is liable for its present value. This does not mean the cost when it was purchased five years earlier or the cost it would take to replace it today; it usually means the replacement cost minus depreciation for age and wear.

All policies provide that the company has the option to repair, rebuild, or replace the property destroyed or damaged with property of like kind and quality. In the problem on page 499, the insurance company, not Stansbury, had the right to select the method of settlement. Therefore, the company could pay Stansbury the amount of the loss in cash, which is customary, or replace the property if it chose.

Policies generally provide that upon settlement of a loss, the insured gives up, and the insurer obtains, the right to recovery from liable third parties. This is known as *subrogation*.

> Willoughby, who was burning trash, negligently allowed the fire to spread, and it destroyed a garage and contents belonging to McMeekin. McMeekin's insurer paid McMeekin's claim and then had the right to proceed against Willoughby for the amount paid out under McMeekin's policy.

Subrogation is closely related to the principle of indemnity. That is, it prevents the insured from collecting more than his actual cash loss. In the example, for instance, if McMeekin's insurer did not have the right of subrogation, McMeekin might collect under the policy and then recover again in a legal action against Willoughby.

HOW IS AN INSURANCE POLICY TERMINATED?

Problem: Fire caused $40,000 damage to Abel's Apartments which were insured for $100,000 under a standard fire policy. The insurer indemnified him for the loss. Did this terminate the policy?

Some kinds of policies provide that payment of a claim for a total loss terminates the policy by completing performance of the contract.

Payment of a partial claim may also reduce the face of the policy by the amount of the claim unless it is a small amount or unless an additional premium is paid. However, this is not true of all insurance. The standard fire policy for dwellings and for business and personal property provides that the full amount of insurance remains in effect despite the payment of any loss. Thus, Abel's policy was not terminated. In many casualty policies, the policy also remains in effect despite the payment of any claims.

 Daniels obtained a $10,000 judgment against Huff, the owner of a campus eating establishment called the Pup Hut, for illness resulting from eating tainted food. Huff was insured for $10,000 under a product liability policy. Payment of the judgment did not reduce the amount of Huff's coverage or terminate the policy.

Property or casualty insurance policies may be terminated by cancellation, or by expiration of the time of the contract.

(1) CANCELLATION

Problem: Acker owned a stamp collection that was insured for $1,000 under an all-risk floater policy. He sold the collection. Could he cancel the policy and recover any portion of the premium?

A policy may be canceled at any time by mutual consent. Statutes and policies usually provide that either party may cancel a policy upon giving notice in accordance with the terms of the contract. The standard fire policy prescribes five days' notice by the insurer to effectively cancel the coverage; other types of insurance may require ten or fifteen days' notice by the insurer. The insured may cancel at any time by giving notice to the insurer.

When a policy is canceled, the insured has a right to demand the return of his share of the unearned portion of the premium if it is not voluntarily tendered by the insurer. The amount varies. When the insurance company cancels a policy, the premium is prorated. To *prorate* means to divide proportionately. For example, if a company cancels a one-year policy at the end of four months, it must return to the insured premiums paid for the eight remaining months. That is, it must return eight-twelfths of the total premiums paid. If the insured cancels the policy, as Acker did in the problem, a part of the premium is returned but the share is less than if the insurance company had canceled it. The amount returned by the insurer is shown in a short rate table in the policy.

(2) EXPIRATION

> **Problem:** Clemente's Cleaners had a comprehensive liability policy that expired at 12:01 a.m. on May 29. At 10 p.m. on May 28 a boiler at the cleaning establishment exploded and injured Williams. At 2 a.m., May 29, Williams died. Would Clemente's policy cover his liability for the death?

Most fire and casualty insurance policies are terminated upon the expiration of the time for which the premiums are paid—usually at the end of one or three years. Some policies are issued for other periods of time. A crop insurance policy is usually issued for a growing season; a rain insurance policy may be issued for one day.

The standard fire insurance policy and most inland marine contracts expire at 12 o'clock noon standard time. Theft, accident, and hospitalization policies generally expire at noon. Most casualty insurance, such as liability and automobile contracts, expires at 12:01 a.m. If a fire or other peril commences during the policy period, and causes damage either before or after the time of expiration, the policyholder is insured. Accordingly, Clemente in the problem was covered for Williams' death.

CAN POLICIES BE ASSIGNED?

> **Problem:** Bauman purchased a home from Day, who had it insured by the Dependable Insurance Company. What should Bauman do about the insurance?

Insurance policies may be assigned, but most provide that the assignment must be approved by the insurer to be valid. To be protected against the perils that might damage his new house, Bauman can apply for a new policy. But he can also arrange with Day and his insurer to have Day's policy assigned to him. The insurer will need to be notified and must assent to the assignment. If he does so, a new contract will be created between Bauman, the assignee, and the insurer. Bauman will settle with Day for the cost of the unused premium.

After the occurrence of a loss, the insured may assign his right to the proceeds of the policy without the consent of the insurer.

YOUR LEGAL VOCABULARY

casualty insurance
claim
endorsement
exclusion
extended coverage endorsement
form
hostile fire
inland marine insurance
liability insurance

notice of loss
personal property floater
proof of loss
property insurance
prorate
proximate cause
standard fire policy
subrogation

1. Coverage against claims for damage caused by one's torts.
2. A fire that is uncontrollable or that escapes from its intended place.
3. A demand for payment of an insured loss.
4. Protection against losses caused by chance, accident, or negligence.
5. A loss specifically listed as not being covered by the policy.
6. An act that is the natural and reasonably forseeable cause of loss.
7. An addition to the standard fire policy giving protection against several other perils.
8. A policy covering movable personal property wherever located.
9. A transfer of the right to recover for loss from liable third parties.
10. A written extension of the standard fire policy to apply to the specific type of risk.

REMEMBER THESE HIGHLIGHTS

1. The purpose of all property and casualty insurance is indemnification. This means that one who suffers a loss may recover only the actual value of the property at the time of the loss, or the amount of the damage if the loss is not total.

2. A fire insurance policy is payable only when an actual, hostile fire or lightning is the direct cause of the loss. The fire policy will protect against other perils if it has appropriate endorsements, such as the extended coverage endorsement.

3. Inland marine insurance is written for the purpose of indemnifying for loss to movable property. It may provide "all-risk" or specified peril coverage for any item or all of one's personal property.

4. Liability insurance is a form of casualty insurance which protects an insured against damage claims arising from his torts and for which he is legally liable.

5. When loss occurs, the insured must normally give notice of loss to the insurer as soon as practicable. Proof of loss must also be submitted by the insured within a specified time from the date of loss.

6. Property and casualty insurance policies are terminated by expiration of the time for which they are written. Both insurer and insured have the right to cancel.

7. A property or casualty insurance policy can be assigned only with the consent of the insurer; proceeds from a loss may be assigned by the insured acting on his own, however.

LAW AS PEOPLE LIVE IT

1. Sheehan's daughter turned on the water in the bathtub and then left to watch television. The forgotten water overflowed, causing extensive damage. What kind of insurance would cover such a loss?

2. An insurance company issued a policy of fire insurance covering Jackson's garage. While Jackson was trying to dislodge some wasps in the garage, he handled some burning paper negligently and set fire to the building. Could he collect on the policy?

3. Dudley used a portable oil heater in a building which was insured against loss by fire. One night the heater was jarred out of adjustment and began emitting heavy smoke that blackened the walls of the room. Would Dudley be able to collect for the damage?

4. During a fire in his home, Buckles and his neighbors moved much of his personal property from the house onto the sidewalk and street. During the confusion, his combination radio-TV-stereo was stolen. Was the loss of this unit covered by his fire insurance policy?

5. Price, a radio-TV repairman, carried some of his tools and parts inventory in his repair truck. What kind of policy could Price take out to protect these items against possible loss?

6. As Thompkins was wheeling her shopping cart down an aisle of Buchanan's Supermarket, the cart collided with a display of bottled soft drinks at the end of the aisle. The eight-foot high display collapsed, and several customers were injured by falling bottles and broken glass. What kind of insurance policy would protect Buchanan if he were held liable?

7. The plate-glass window of Coffey's store was blown in during a windstorm. The insurer wished to replace the glass, but Coffey insisted that he be paid cash for its value. Must the insurer pay?
8. Ronald was injured when an employee of Highsmith's Handyman Shop stumbled and pushed her into a glass display case. Highsmith forgot about the matter and did not notify his insurer until Ronald filed suit six months later. Would this delay release the insurer from liability?
9. "Oklahoma Billy," the world's largest ox, was killed because of the negligence of the carrier while being transported in a trailer for show purposes. He was insured for $10,000 and the insurer paid the claim. Would the insurer be able to collect from the carrier?
10. Following a fire, Baron was paid the face value of his homeowner's policy, $12,000, by the insurer. During the rebuilding, a windstorm did $4,000 more damage. Could Baron collect for the second loss, or had his policy been terminated by payment of the fire loss?

LAW AS COURTS DECIDE IT

1. Weems, who operated a grocery store, was insured under a storekeeper's liability policy. This policy provided that the insurer would pay on behalf of the insured, "all sums which the insured shall become legally obligated to pay as damages because of bodily injury caused by accident and arising out of the ownership, maintenance, or use of the premises." It also provided that written notice of any accident must be given the insurance company "as soon as practicable." Quebe, an employee, was injured on January 31, when someone tossed a lighted firecracker into a truck in which he was working. On May 14, and without any explanation for the delay, Weems notified the insurer of the accident. The insurer disclaimed any liability and sought to be relieved both from liability and from any duty to defend Weems in any legal action by Quebe because of failure to give notice as required by the policy. Should the relief be granted? (Trinity Universal Insurance Company v. Weems, 326 S.W. 302, Texas)
2. The floors in a house owned and occupied by Harvey were covered with wall-to-wall carpeting. Harvey obtained an all-risk personal property floater policy which excluded damage by moths, and damage "occasioned by or resulting from any work thereon in the course of any refinishing, renovating, or repairing process." Fearing possible moth damage to the carpeting, though none had occurred, Harvey employed Nolte to spray the carpeting with a moth preventive. The spraying damaged the carpeting. The insurer claimed it was not liable under the policy. Do you agree? (Harvey v. Switzerland General Ins. Co., 260 S.W. 2d 342, Missouri)
3. Miller, a jewelry dealer, seeks to recover for loss of a ring on a jeweler's block policy, an inland marine coverage which insures against all risks

of loss. In March, Miller gave the ring to Friedman, another dealer, to sell. The next day, Friedman consigned it to a third dealer, Willner. In July, Willner's body was recovered from the East River in New York City. The day before his death Willner had stated that he had the ring "in his pocket," and was still trying to sell it. The ring was not returned either to Miller or to Friedman. Miller requested its return from Friedman, and Friedman tried to locate it, but the ring was never found. The insurance policy stated it insured "against all risks of loss or of damage . . . arising from any cause whatsoever except; . . . Unexplained loss, mysterious disappearance or loss or shortage disclosed on taking inventory." Was the insurer liable? (Miller v. Boston Insurance Company, 420 Pa. 556, 218 A. 2d 275)

4. In 1961, Glens Falls Insurance Company paid the defendant, Perovich, $10,268 to compensate him for the theft of some construction equipment. Later, Glens Falls discovered that in his claim, Perovich had made numerous and material misrepresentations of the value of the stolen goods. The evidence showed that Perovich's original estimate of the loss was $3,500, and that he later told a deputy sheriff that much of the equipment had been recovered. Under the terms of the insurance contract these misrepresentations voided the contract. Should Glens Falls recover the amount paid? (Perovich v. Glens Falls Insurance Company, 401 F. 2d 145)

5. Taff and Hardwick were in an automobile accident that resulted in a $5,000 judgment for Taff. This is an action by Taff to collect the amount of the judgment. The defendant insurance company denied liability because of failure of the insured, Hardwick, to cooperate in defending the action as required in the policy as follows: "Insured shall cooperate with the company and upon the company's request shall attend hearings and trials, and shall assist in effecting settlements, securing and giving evidence, obtaining the attendance of witnesses, and in the conduct of suits." The insurer presented evidence that it unsuccessfully sought to locate Hardwick by letter, telephone calls, and investigators, to cooperate in his defense. Was the insurer released from its obligation to pay the judgment? (Taff v. Hardwick and Empire Fire and Marine Insurance Company of Omaha, 419 S.W. 2d 482)

6. Stewart was injured in a skiing accident on October 12. He was in the hospital five days and released. On November 29, X-rays disclosed a fracture and Stewart reentered the hospital. He had a hospitalization policy with the defendant in this action, but it was terminated for nonpayment of premiums on November 10. The insurance company paid the hospitalization costs until November 10, but on grounds the policy had lapsed, it refused to pay for care after that date. Was the company entitled to stop payments as of November 10? (Intercoast Mutual Life Insurance Company v. Andersen, 75 Nev. 457, 345 P. 2d 762)

CHAPTER 36 Automobile Insurance

1. *While you are driving on a gravel road, a rock cracks the windshield of your sports car. Will your insurance cover the loss?*

2. *Your car is hit from the rear while you are waiting for a signal light to turn green. Your car bumps the car in front of you, causing damage to the trunk and tail lights of that car. Is your insurer liable?*

3. *Your parked car is damaged by a hit-and-run driver. Must you stand the loss?*

WHAT IS THE PURPOSE OF AUTOMOBILE INSURANCE?

Problem: Erickson purchased a pick-up truck. In order to be adequately protected, what insurance coverage should he have?

Automobile insurance has three main purposes:

(1) TO PAY ANY SUMS THE INSURED IS LEGALLY OBLIGATED TO PAY

This includes payment for physical injuries to other people, or for damages to the property of others, which result from the ownership, maintenance, or use of a described motor vehicle.

Insurance which serves this purpose is known as public liability insurance, and most owners of motor vehicles carry it. Erickson, in the problem, should have at least this much coverage. It is for personal injuries or deaths that juries sometimes award damages in the tens of thousands of dollars. Few individuals can afford to pay such claims without the aid of insurance.

(2) TO PAY THE INSURED FOR ANY DIRECT, ACCIDENTAL LOSSES TO THE VEHICLE DESCRIBED IN THE POLICY

Many car owners also obtain collision and comprehensive insurance to indemnify them for the cost of damage to or loss of their own car. It would probably be desirable for Erickson to have comprehensive and, if he can afford it, some form of collision coverage.

If Erickson had purchased his truck on credit, the seller would probably require him to carry property damage insurance to protect the seller's security interest.

(3) TO PAY FOR THE MEDICAL CLAIMS OF OCCUPANTS OF THE INSURED'S VEHICLE WHO ARE INJURED IN AUTOMOBILE ACCIDENTS, WITHOUT REGARD TO FAULT

Medical payments coverage protects the insured, his family, and their guests in case of injuries resulting from automobile accidents. It also makes it less likely that passengers in the insured's vehicle will sue him for negligence (with possible large judgments) if he is at fault in an accident. Erickson should certainly consider carrying medical payments coverage, too.

In addition to private or family automobiles, there are many motor vehicles used in business and government that should or must be insured. Although the needs are basically the same, a greater variety of operations makes the businessman's insurance needs more complex. This chapter deals primarily with the car insurance needs of individuals and families.

WHAT COVERAGE IS GIVEN BY PUBLIC LIABILITY INSURANCE?

Problem: While trying to squeeze into a narrow parking space, Brewster scraped the side of Trotter's car. Trotter insisted Brewster pay him for the damage and then collect from his insurer. Could Brewster do this?

Automobile liability coverage is basically the same as the liability coverage discussed in the preceding chapter. It includes not only payment of damages, but also defense of the insured. Although insurance companies settle many claims out of court, they have a right to have their insured go to trial for a judicial determination of liability and amount of damages. Moreover, the insured is not an agent of the insurer with authority to make settlements. In the problem, therefore, Brewster had no right to make any payment for the damage except at his own expense. His insurer would not be liable to repay him.

In automobile liability insurance, the insurer agrees to pay all claims for which it is legally liable for (a) bodily injury, and (b) property damage. The coverage, generally known as the Family Automobile Policy, extends to all members of the named insured's household and to any others driving the insured's car with permission. In the latter case, the policy makes the driver an additional insured. This is known as the *omnibus clause*. Some companies require policies on cars whose owners are students or members of the armed forces to include an endorsement declaring the coverage void if the car is driven by anyone other than the insured or a member of his family.

Liability insurance also commonly provides coverage for the insured and members of his family when they are operating non-owned vehicles with the owner's permission. This coverage applies to all borrowed or substitute automobiles, including those used when the car described in the policy has broken down or is being repaired or serviced. Also, if one purchases an automobile to replace the one insured, all the coverages under the policy apply to the replacement car for a period of thirty days, or in some policies, until the expiration date.

When one becomes liable for damage or injury while driving a non-owned vehicle, the car owner's policy provides primary coverage; the driver's coverage is in excess.

 Brand was awarded a judgment of $50,000 against Gary, whose car was being operated by Overstreet. Gary had only $30,000 bodily injury insurance. The excess would be paid by Overstreet's insurer.

(1) BODILY INJURY COVERAGE

Problem: Chaney had $10,000/$20,000 bodily injury coverage on his car. As a result of an accident caused by Chaney's negligence, Miller was awarded $6,000 damages, his wife, $13,000, and his daughter $4,000. Was Chaney's liability covered by the policy?

Bodily injury insurance covers the insured against legal liability for bodily injury to and death of other persons. It is usually issued with top limits for each person and for each "occurrence." Today, a common amount of coverage is $10,000 for each person and $20,000 for each occurrence or accident. In the insurance industry's "shorthand," this is called 10/20. By paying comparatively small additional premiums, an insured may have substantially higher limits, such as 25/50, 50/100, 100/300.

In the problem, Chaney's policy would protect him up to a maximum of $10,000 for injuries to or death of one person, and not more than $20,000 for a single occurrence regardless of the number of persons injured or killed. Thus, the insurance carried by Chaney would pay the Miller family only a maximum of $20,000. Miller and the daughter would get the full amount of their judgments but Miller's wife would get only $10,000. Chaney would be personally liable for the other $3,000.

In most states, statutes known as *guest laws* provide that a guest in a car does not have a legal right to sue the driver for damages for injury unless the driver is grossly negligent—driving while intoxicated, for instance—or willfully causes the accident. These laws have been enacted to relieve drivers of the fear and risk of a possible lawsuit if they give a friendly lift to a guest and an accident takes place. They also serve to prevent a guest and owner or driver from secretly agreeing to defraud the insurance company by falsely testifying that the driver was negligent. Such an agreement to defraud is known as *collusion*. A guest is a nonpaying rider. Share-the-ride passengers are considered to be guests. Guests may, of course, sue negligent drivers of other cars who injure them in accidents.

 Jones and Larkins each paid $3 a week to have Moody drive them to and from work. One morning they were injured in an accident caused by Moody's negligence. However, unless Moody showed gross negligence, they could not hold her liable in states with guest laws.

(2) PROPERTY DAMAGE COVERAGE

Problem: Rankin's truck was parked on a steep hill. The brakes did not hold and the truck rolled down the street, jumped the curb, crashed into Dalton's car which was parked in his driveway, and took off a corner of his home, damaging some furniture. In addition to the $1,200 damage to his car, $4,500 to his residence, and $700 to his furniture, Dalton claimed the cost of renting a substitute car while his own was being repaired. Was he entitled to this entire claim?

Automobile liability insurance also covers the insured's legal liability for damages to a third person's property. This *property damage insurance* includes any reasonable amount caused by loss of use of the property. Hence, Dalton was correct in claiming not only the cost of damages to his house, car, and furniture, but also the amount of rental he paid for another car while his was being repaired. A common amount for which property damage liability coverage is written is $5,000, but as Rankin learned, this may not cover the loss. Higher coverage is available for a small additional premium.

WHAT IS MEDICAL PAYMENTS COVERAGE?

Problem: Yaggy, a guest passenger in Benedict's car, was alighting from it when the car started to move and threw her to the pavement. Yaggy suffered a broken arm. Was she entitled to recover medical expenses?

Medical payments coverage is automobile insurance which pays the reasonable medical claims of occupants of a vehicle who are injured in an automobile accident. An occupant is one who is in, upon, entering, or leaving the vehicle. Coverage includes payment of necessary medical, surgical, dental, and X-ray services, and also funeral expenses if death results. Payments are made even though the driver is not negligent or legally liable. Guests like Yaggy in the problem may thus be paid for medical expenses even if a guest law is operative. There is a limit per person, usually $500 to $5,000, but no limit per accident. The expenses must be incurred within one year from the date of the accident, however.

The basic medical payments policy covers the named insured and his family while occupying either an owned or nonowned automobile of any type. Injuries to other passengers are covered if they occur in the insured's own vehicle, or when the insured or a member of his family is driving a nonowned vehicle with the owner's permission. Although this kind of coverage is mainly for car occupants, it also covers the named insured and his family members if they are struck by an automobile while walking, riding bikes, or on roller skates or sleds.

Medical payments coverage provides that when a loss is suffered while the insured is driving a nonowned automobile, the owner's coverage applies first and the insured's coverage serves as excess.

 Appleton borrowed his brother's station wagon to take his son, Bob, and two other boys, Ed and Don Connick, on a camping trip. The car hit a bridge abutment and all four were injured. Appleton's brother had $500 medical coverage per person, and Appleton had $1,000. His medical expenses were $2,000, Bob's were $300, Ed's $800, and Don's $1,300. The first $500 of each claim would be paid by the brother's insurance, and Appleton's would pay the excess. Thus,

$800 of Don's claim, $300 of Ed's claim, and $1,000 of his own claim were paid by Appleton's insurance.

WHAT IS COLLISION COVERAGE?

Problem: Hagan fell asleep while driving and his car crashed into Ramsey's truck and went into a ditch. There was $650 damage to Hagan's car and $900 to Ramsey's truck. No one was injured. How would the damage be settled?

Liability of an insurer under *collision insurance* is limited to direct and accidental loss to the insured's car caused by collision with another object or by upset. Only the actual cash value of the loss is payable. If the insured carries full coverage, the insurer pays the entire amount up to the limit of the policy. More likely, the coverage will be subject to a deductible amount.

The amount deductible varies from $25 to $250, with $50 and $100 being the usual amounts. The deductible amount is applied to each loss that occurs during the policy period; the insured stands the loss up to the deductible amount, and the insurer pays any excess. In the above problem, the $900 damage to Ramsey's truck would be covered by Hagan's liability coverage. The amount Hagan would recover on his own car would depend on the deductible amount in his own collision policy. If it were $100, the insurer would pay $550; if it were $50, the insurer would pay $600.

Premiums are much lower when a deductible is included than when the insurer pays the full amount of collision loss. This is true because most collision claims are for small amounts which are relatively costly for the insurance company to investigate and settle.

In the event of loss from collision or upset, the insured must give notice to the insurer as soon as practicable. Failure to do so may release the insurer from its obligation. The insured also has an obligation to protect the automobile from further loss. Once notice and proof of loss have been properly received, the insurance company has the option of paying for the loss or repairing or replacing the lost or damaged property.

WHAT IS COMPREHENSIVE COVERAGE?

Problem: Coffman drove his new car into a parking garage and told the attendant he was leaving it overnight. When he drove his car out the next morning, he thought something was wrong. On investigation he found that the new engine had been removed and replaced by an old one. Would Coffman's comprehensive insurance cover the loss?

Comprehensive insurance covers all losses to the insured's vehicle from causes other than collision or upset. It includes losses due to such perils as fire, theft, explosion, earthquake, windstorm, hail, water, flood, falling objects, vandalism, and riot. Breakage of glass from any cause is also covered. Thus, comprehensive is an all-risk coverage which would take care of Coffman's loss in the problem. Separate coverages for the various perils can also be obtained, and are usually carried by owners of trucks and other commercial vehicles.

Losses by theft are covered by comprehensive insurance.

Definitions of the various perils covered by comprehensive insurance are the same as for other property insurance. For example, theft includes not only loss of the car or any part of it, but any damage done to the car while stolen, including broken locks.

Theft of car tools and accessories is covered by comprehensive insurance, but loss of clothing and other personal property left in the car is not covered, unless the loss is by fire.

 Turner's car, containing textbooks and a raincoat, was stolen. When the car was recovered, the textbooks and coat were missing, the engine and tires had been removed, and the locks had been smashed. Under his comprehensive coverage, Turner could recover the value of the engine, tires, and locks at the time of their loss, but he could not recover for the loss of either his books or coat.

The policy usually provides that the insured must notify the police in the event of theft. In case of theft, the typical policy also provides that the insurer will reimburse the insured for rental expenses not exceeding $10 a day for 30 days to pay for a substitute automobile or taxicabs.

WHAT IS UNINSURED MOTORISTS COVERAGE?

Problem: Martinelli's car was hit broadside one night by a car that failed to observe a stop sign. Martinelli was killed, his wife was injured, and his car was demolished. Because the driver who caused the accident had no liability insurance and very limited personal assets, Martinelli's wife could not collect damages from him. Did she have to stand the loss personally?

Loss caused by motorists without liability coverage is a serious problem. To protect against it, car owners may carry uninsured motorists coverage as part of their own insurance policy. This coverage allows the insured to collect damages from his own company in the event of loss caused by uninsured and hit-and-run drivers. If Martinelli had this coverage, his wife could collect medical expenses for her injuries and payment for his death. If he did not have this coverage, there would be no recovery. Although a few states also permit payment for property damage, the coverage in most states is limited to bodily injury and death. The maximum limits are based on the requirements of a state's financial responsibility law, as discussed below.

Uninsured motorists insurance is required in a few states, and in several others it must be added to the policy unless the insured specifically rejects it. To collect on uninsured motorists insurance it is not necessary to get a judgment. The settlement is arrived at by mutual agreement or by arbitration. An insured may not collect under this coverage and also from the uninsured motorist.

WHAT ARE FINANCIAL RESPONSIBILITY LAWS?

Problem: Wayne and Alexander were involved in a collision, and each claimed the other was at fault. What would be required of them?

To help deal with the problem of financially irresponsible drivers, all states have enacted financial responsibility laws. These laws either require all cars to be covered by bodily injury and property damage insurance, or provide penalties for drivers who can not show they are responsible financially.

Only three states [1] at present require all cars to be covered by liability insurance. Most states, however, require common carriers of passengers, such as buses and taxicabs, to have such insurance. In some states, other common carriers must also be covered.

Financial responsibility laws require both owners and drivers of cars involved in an accident to furnish evidence of ability to pay damages. Some states require that the driver's license or the car's registration, or both, be revoked following violation of certain traffic laws or failure to show financial responsibility following an accident. Other states require the filing of a standard policy of public liability insurance or the deposit of money or securities following a serious accident in which there is property damage exceeding a specified amount, usually $100, or personal injuries or death. In a few states, if one of the parties admits liability for the accident, the other party is not required to show financial responsibility.

In the problem, since neither party would admit responsibility for the accident, most states would require both to show insurance of $5,000 for property damage and $10,000/$20,000 for personal injuries; or each could deposit cash or securities of the same amounts. They must furnish proof of financial responsibility for possible future accidents. Failure to comply with the requirements results in suspension of the driver's license or the registration or both.

Because of age, poor driving records, traffic violations, or other reasons, some car owners find it difficult to obtain public liability insurance to satisfy the requirements of the financial responsibility law of their state. To enable such persons to comply with this law, an *assigned risk plan* has been devised. A person who has been refused insurance can apply to be assigned to an insurance company that will insure him for the minimum public liability insurance required by the state. The premium, however, is usually much higher than that charged other drivers for similar coverage. Often the insurer will voluntarily insure such a person at regular rates if he has had a clear record for a year.

A recent development being widely discussed is *no-fault insurance*. It is so called because the insured's medical and related expenses up to a specified maximum are paid by the insurer without regard to who was legally responsible for the accident. In this respect, it is similar to workmen's compensation insurance (Page 439) and medical coverage. No-fault insurance applies only to personal injuries (not

---

[1] Massachusetts, New York, and North Carolina. In Connecticut, Maryland, and Rhode Island minors are required to carry public liability insurance.

property damage) and eliminates costly legal actions and delays if the amounts per person are less than those specified, such as $2,000. No payments are made for "pain and suffering." Several states allow or require no-fault insurance, and it is being considered in others.

YOUR LEGAL VOCABULARY

assigned risk plan
bodily injury insurance
collision insurance
collusion
comprehensive insurance
financial responsibility laws

guest laws
medical payments coverage
no fault insurance
omnibus clause
property damage insurance

1. A secret agreement to defraud another.
2. A coverage that pays the reasonable medical claims of occupants of a vehicle who are injured in an automobile accident.
3. Insurance covering loss or damage to the insured's car from all causes other than collision or upset.
4. Statutes requiring that motorists furnish evidence of ability to pay damages in case of accident.
5. Insurance covering the insured's legal liability for bodily injury or death resulting from his operation of a motor vehicle.
6. Insurance covering the insured's legal liability for property damages resulting from his operation of a motor vehicle.
7. An arrangement enabling a person whose application for automobile insurance has been rejected to obtain coverage at a higher cost.

8. Statutes providing that nonpaying riders do not have a right to damages for injuries unless the driver is grossly negligent.
9. Insurance covering the insured's medical and related expenses without regard to who was legally responsible for the accident.
10. Insurance covering direct and accidental loss to the insured's car caused by collision with another object or by upset.

REMEMBER THESE HIGHLIGHTS

1. The basic purposes of automobile insurance are (a) to pay any claims against the insured for injuries to other people or for damage to the property of others, (b) to pay the insured for any direct or accidental losses to his own car, and (c) to indemnify the insured for medical expenses if he or his passengers or family are injured in an automobile accident.
2. Automobile insurance includes public liability (bodily injury and property damage), medical payments, collision, comprehensive, and uninsured motorist coverages.
3. Most policies may be extended to include others who drive the insured car. The insureds are covered when operating cars owned by others, temporary substitute automobiles, and — for a limited period — newly purchased replacement cars.
4. Coverage is available for bodily injury caused the insured by uninsured motorists and hit-and-run drivers.
5. All states require motorists to furnish evidence of their ability to pay damages when they are involved in an accident. For those unable to obtain insurance, assigned risk plans are available. No one need drive without minimal insurance coverage.

LAW AS PEOPLE LIVE IT

1. Poole was injured when he lost control of his pick-up truck on a curve and ran off the road. He was insured for bodily injury and property damage. He sought to collect from his insurance company for his hospital and medical expenses, loss of wages while he was unable to work, and damage to his truck. Will he be able to collect?
2. Bond was sued by Floyd for damages incurred in an automobile accident at a time when Bond's car was being operated by a friend. The friend had permission to drive the car and Bond was insured with public liability insurance by Countrywide Insurance Company. Was the insurer required to defend Bond?
3. Fulbright's automobile liability policy was 15/30; he also had $10,000 property damage and $1,000 medical coverage. While driving under the influence of alcohol, Fulbright side-swiped a bus; the car jumped the curb, struck and injured three pedestrians, and crashed into a store front.

Fulbright suffered extensive injuries and was hospitalized for 60 days. Explain the protection afforded by the policy.

4. While O'Banion was speeding on the open highway, his car skidded on wet pavement, overturned, and rolled down an embankment. Damage was $630. If O'Banion carried $100 deductible collision insurance, for how much would the insurer be liable?

5. Stukey carried comprehensive automobile insurance. While his car was parked near the entrance of a motion-picture theater, a window was broken to gain entry to the vehicle and an expensive camera was stolen. Can Stukey collect on the policy?

6. Kinney and Kaufman were involved in a collision, and Kinney was injured. Neither driver would admit liability. After reporting the accident to their respective insurance agents, what other legal action would be required of the two drivers?

7. When Simpson's car was struck by a hit-and-run driver, the vehicle was damaged and two of Simpson's passengers were injured. What insurance coverage would indemnify the losses suffered?

8. Markle, age 21, had had several automobile accidents and was unable to obtain insurance on his car through the usual channels. What could he do?

9. While Nassa was backing his car out of the garage, he struck a cement wall and damaged a fender. He carried property damage insurance and filed a claim with the insurance company. The company refused to pay, claiming they were not liable. Can Nassa collect?

LAW AS COURTS DECIDE IT

1. Peerless Casualty Company issued a policy insuring Cole against legal liability resulting from operation of his automobile. Cole injured three persons in an accident and, after investigation, the insurer paid their claims voluntarily. Thereafter the company disclaimed liability and sued Cole to recover the payment under a provision in the policy which stated that "the insured agrees to reimburse the company for any payment" for which it would not have been legally obligated. Do you believe Cole should be required to reimburse the insurer for the settlement? (Peerless Casualty Company v. Cole, 121 Vt. 258, 155 A. 2d 866)

2. Rose asked Chapman to take her to the courthouse and also to the neighboring town of Dishman; in return for this favor, she offered to do Chapman's washing for that week. Chapman agreed, saying he also had some business at the courthouse and would like to go to Dishman to look for work. On the way, Chapman needed gas and found he had left his wallet at home. Rose paid for two gallons of gas. On the return trip, Chapman had an accident and Rose was injured. She obtained a judgment against Chapman and filed action against the insurer, Northwest

Casualty Company, to collect. The insurer claimed Rose was a guest and therefore not entitled to liability coverage under the policy. Moreover, the policy excluded coverage while the automobile was being used as a conveyance for hire unless such use was permitted and a premium was paid for the coverage. Should Rose recover? (Rose v. Chapman, 19 Wash. 2d 744, 144 P. 2d 248)

3. On August 22, 1963, a taxi driver named Sharkey, 74 years old, applied to an insurance agent, Bolls, for an assigned risk policy. He was insured for a period of one year by Hartford Accident and Indemnity Company. This policy was renewed the second year and before its expiration Sharkey received notice directing him to pay the premium to his agent and stating that if he did not "Your automobile liability insurance will terminate . . . No further notice will be sent to you." Sharkey paid the premium to Bolls, but Bolls did not remit it to the company or refund it to Sharkey. On December 8, Sharkey asked Bolls to certify to the Mississippi Motor Vehicle Comptroller that he had insurance so that he could get his taxicab license. On December 15, Sharkey was involved in an accident with a Mrs. Harris while driving his taxi. He reported this the same day to Bolls, who notified him that he was not insured. Mrs. Harris sued and obtained judgment against Sharkey who then commenced action against Bolls to recover the amount of the judgment. Should Sharkey win? (Bolls v. Sharkey, 226 So. 2d 372, Mississippi)

4. Crosby had an automobile liability policy with the Travelers Insurance Company in effect when he negligently injured Muncie on October 24. No notice of this accident was given to Travelers until June 20 of the next year. Muncie recovered a judgment against Crosby, who did not pay, and then sued Travelers on the liability policy. Travelers contended that under the policy, notice of the accident had to be given "as soon as practicable." Since notice was not given until eight months after the accident, it claimed to have no liability to Crosby and thus no liability to Muncie. Could Muncie recover from Travelers? (Muncie v. Travelers Insurance Co., 253 N.C. 74, 116 S.E. 2d 474)

5. Vincent Mann borrowed Eschbach's truck with his permission to haul some "stuff" to school, but was to have the truck back before dark. Eschbach believed the "stuff" was a school project of Mann's. Instead, Mann used the truck to gather cardboard boxes for a football rally at Ferndale High School. Eschbach testified that if he had known the purpose he would not have granted the use of the truck. On the fifth or sixth trip to pick up boxes, Mann reluctantly permitted Roddel, who was 15 years of age and had no driver's license, to drive the truck. While Roddel was driving, the truck injured Feathers who was insured by another company. Feather's policy included uninsured motorist coverage. The question in this case is whether, under the circumstances, Eschbach is an uninsured motorist. What is your opinion? (Grange Insurance Association v. Eschbach, 1 Wash. App. 230, 460 P. 2d 690)

CHAPTER 37 Life Insurance

1. *Your father has a $10,000 life insurance policy. Must it be paid in one lump sum upon his death?*

2. *If you allow your life insurance policy to lapse, have you lost all you have paid into it?*

3. *A student who contracts for life insurance fails to mention that his father died of a hereditary disease that is rarely diagnosed before the age of 30. Can the insurance company cancel the contract when it learns of this?*

WHAT IS THE NATURE OF LIFE INSURANCE?

Problem: Shafer, age 17, is debating whether to take out a life insurance policy now or wait until he gets married. What is your advice?

A contract in which an insurer promises to pay a certain sum upon the death of a person is called *life insurance*. Life insurance differs from property and casualty insurance in several ways:

(1) THE EVENT INSURED AGAINST, DEATH, IS BOUND TO HAPPEN

The risk is not whether it will happen, as with property and casualty insurance, but that it will happen at some unknown and possibly premature time in the future.

(2) THERE IS NO POSSIBILITY OF PARTIAL LOSS

The amount payable is the face value of the policy in the case of life insurance.

(3) THE CONTRACT IS NOT ONE OF INDEMNITY

Although potential earning power of the insured can be estimated, it is impossible to place an accurate money value on human life.

(4) THE PREMIUM IS LEVEL

This means that one's premium is the same year after year and cannot be raised as he grows older. Most policies include a savings feature by which a portion of the premium is invested by the company and accumulates compound interest over the life of the policy.

(5) THE PROBABILITY OF LOSS INCREASES EACH YEAR

The likelihood of death increases with age, and premiums increase accordingly; that is, the older the insured at the time he obtains the policy, the higher the premium he will pay. Thus, if Shafer in the problem wishes to pay a lower premium, he should take the policy out now. The premium is lower because the likelihood of death is lower at his age, but he will probably be paying premiums for more years in the future than someone who buys life insurance when he is older.

(6) INSURABLE INTEREST IN A LIFE NEED EXIST ONLY AT THE TIME THE CONTRACT IS MADE

Insurable interest in property, as you recall, must also exist at the time of the loss. (Page 486)

(7) IT IS A CONTINUING CONTRACT

The insurer agrees that if there was an insurable interest and the premiums are paid when they are due, the contract will remain in force. This is a very important feature of life insurance. The insurance company cannot cancel the contract at any time it wishes; only the insured has this right.

(8) A LIFE INSURANCE POLICY MAY BE ASSIGNED WITHOUT THE CONSENT OF THE INSURER

As you recall, consent of the insurer is necessary before a property insurance contract can be assigned.

(9) IN MOST STATES MINORS' CONTRACTS FOR LIFE AND DISABILITY INSURANCE ARE NOT VOIDABLE

This is true if the life or disability insurance is purchased by the minor on himself.

WHAT ARE THE KINDS OF LIFE INSURANCE?

Problem: Weimer contracted for a $10,000, 20-payment life insurance policy. How did this policy differ from other ordinary policies of insurance?

Life insurance is usually classified as (1) ordinary, (2) industrial, and (3) group.

(1) ORDINARY LIFE INSURANCE

In *ordinary life insurance* the contract is made with an individual, and the amount is generally not less than $1,000. There are many kinds of ordinary life insurance policies, but the four most common types are (a) *whole life,* (b) *limited-payment,* (c) *endowment,* and (d) *term.*

(a) Whole life insurance provides that, in return for level premiums paid at regular intervals, the face amount of the policy will be paid upon the death of the insured, or at age 100 when most whole life policies mature. Whole life policies are also known as straight life or continuous premium policies.

(b) Limited-payment life insurance is a kind of whole life policy that provides for the payment of higher premiums during a limited period, usually twenty or thirty years or to age 65, after which the premiums cease. The policy is then said to be "paid-up." Weimer's policy, in the problem, is limited payment insurance. The face value of the policy is paid at the death of the insured, whether it occurs during the premium-paying period or after.

(c) Endowment life insurance is in force for a limited time and provides for the payment of the face value of the policy in the event of the death of the insured within that time. The face value of the policy is paid to the insured if he is living at the end of the specified period.

Ling wished to assure his two-year-old son of a college education. He therefore insured his own life for $10,000 under a 15-year endowment policy. If Ling continued to pay the premiums, he would receive the face value of the policy at the end of 15 years; if he died before that time, his beneficiary would be paid the face amount or it could be left with the insurance company under one of the settlement options ex-plained on page 529.

(d) Term life insurance is a type of insurance in which the insurer is obligated to pay only in the event of death of the insured within a specified period or term, such as five or ten years, or until age 65. The premium is level, and when the term ends the policy expires without further benefits. In this respect term life more closely resembles fire or casualty insurance than any other type of life insurance policy.

Term insurance is relatively inexpensive because it is pure insurance and does not include the additional savings element found in other ordinary policies. It usually does not cover persons after age 65 or 70, however. Sometimes the contract is renewable at a higher premium without a medical examination and before the expiration of the term. It is also possible to obtain a term policy which can be changed or "converted" to an ordinary whole life policy.

(2) INDUSTRIAL LIFE INSURANCE

> **Problem:** Harding, a factory worker, could afford to put $2 a month into life insurance so he contracted for an industrial life insurance policy. Were the benefits any different from those of an ordinary policy?

Industrial life insurance is designed for those who are financially unable to buy ordinary life insurance. The face amount of an industrial policy is low—typically less than $1,000—because premiums are low and also because handling costs are high. Two factors make industrial insurance costly for the insurance company: (1) usually industrial policy premiums are paid weekly or monthly; and (2) they are often collected from door to door.

Industrial policies may or may not have provisions similar to those of ordinary policies. A medical examination is generally not required, for example. Thus, for Harding to learn what his rights are, it will be necessary for him to read his policy. Industrial policies, like ordinary policies, may be whole life, limited-payment life, or endowment.

(3) GROUP LIFE INSURANCE

> **Problem:** As a fringe benefit, Ingles Industries provided a $5,000 life insurance policy for each employee. Dutton quit his job at Ingles. Did he lose all his rights in the life insurance policy provided by the company?

Group life insurance is commonly sold to employers to cover groups of workers. To get maximum pure insurance protection for their workers at minimum cost, employers almost always buy term insurance in group policies. Typical coverage ranges from $3,000 to $10,000 per worker, with the specific amount depending on the worker's salary or classification. The employer is generally considered to be the agent of the employee in making payments so that if the employer fails to pay the group premiums, the insurance will lapse and the insurer is not liable to the employee or the beneficiary.

Employment by the firm is usually the only requirement for participation. Since working groups are usually made up of healthy, active people, no medical examination is required and death claims are low. When an employee leaves the group, he cannot continue his interest in the group policy; but he is commonly permitted to convert it to an ordinary policy within 30 days without taking a medical examination. Thus, if Dutton wished, he could convert and continue to have life insurance protection after leaving Ingles' employ.

WHAT ARE THE RIGHTS OF THE BENEFICIARY?

Problem: Coleman wished to designate his wife as beneficiary of his insurance policy. However, in case she died first, Coleman wished his two children to receive the proceeds of the policy. How could he legally do this?

The party to whom the proceeds of a life insurance policy are payable is the *beneficiary*. The beneficiary may be (1) the insured himself or his estate, (2) a person who takes out insurance on the life of another, or (3) a third person who is not otherwise a party to the contract. Unless the beneficiary is also the party taking out the insurance, he need not have an insurable interest in the life of the insured.

The party to whom the proceeds of a life insurance policy are payable is the beneficiary.

It is also possible to have two or more beneficiaries. They may share equally, or they may be primary and contingent beneficiaries. Thus, in the problem, Coleman could designate his wife as the primary beneficiary and provide that if she died first, the two children would share the proceeds as contingent beneficiaries.

The *proceeds* of a life insurance policy equal the face of the policy less any amount borrowed against it, plus any dividends due. When payable to a living beneficiary, the proceeds of insurance are not subject to the claims of the creditors of the insured.

 When Levering died he owed $10,000 to Stevens. The beneficiary of his $15,000 life insurance policy was his daughter who was entitled to the policy proceeds. Stevens would have to look to the other assets of Levering's estate to pay his claim.

Policies today generally give the insured the right to change the beneficiary by giving the company written notice.

WHAT IS THE LIABILITY OF AN INSURER?

Problem: Sontag was insured under an endowment policy with Southern National Insurance Company. What was the company's liability?

The insurer of life agrees to pay to the insured's estate or to a named beneficiary the amount stated in the policy in accordance with its terms. In an endowment policy such as Sontag's, this means payment of the proceeds to the beneficiary upon the death of the insured, or to the policyholder himself if he is alive at the end of the endowment period. However, life insurance policies sometimes contain provisions that exempt the insurer from liability when death is due to certain causes, such as the crash of an airplane which is not making a regularly scheduled flight. Policies may also provide for exemption from liability in case of the policyholder's death during military service abroad, or at home and abroad.

As in fire insurance, most states have adopted uniform policy provisions which are a part of all ordinary life insurance policies. The following provisions are commonly included in life insurance policies for the protection of the insured:

(1) INCONTESTABLE CLAUSE

Problem: In completing an application for life insurance, Armiger stated that he had never had heart disease. This was not true. After issuing the policy, could the insurer cancel it because of the misrepresentation?

The *incontestable clause* provides that after the policy has been in force for a certain length of time, usually two years, the insurer agrees that fraud or misrepresentation at the time the policy was issued will have no effect upon the performance of the contract.

In the problem, if Armiger died during the first two years the policy was in effect, the company could avoid its obligation. After two years elapse, however, the incontestable clause is in effect and the company may not cancel the contract or refuse to pay the proceeds even though it has relied on the false representation.

(2) DAYS OF GRACE

Problem: Prell's life insurance premium was due on June 10. He got around to paying it on July 6. Was the policy canceled?

Provision is usually made in life insurance policies for 30 or 31 *days of grace* in the payment of the premium. This means that the policy remains in force if the insured pays the premium within 30 or 31 days after its due date. Prell's policy would not lapse if he paid within the grace period. The laws of a few states require the insurance company to send notices of premiums due, and most companies send notices as a matter of courtesy and good business practice.

(3) LAPSE AND REINSTATEMENT

Problem: Beeman had a $20,000 20-payment life insurance policy which he allowed to lapse. A year later he submitted evidence of his good health and paid all of the due back premiums. Must the company reinstate Beeman's policy?

When the insured fails to pay a premium before the grace period expires, the policy is said to *lapse*. This is one method of terminating the contract. Policies usually give the policyholder the right to *reinstate* (to place the policy back in force) within three to five years after lapse provided he is still in good health. The policyholder must also pay, with interest, all premiums due during the lapse.

Most state laws require each policy to contain a reinstatement clause; the standard New York policy, which has been adopted in many states, prescribes such a clause. Thus, in the problem above, the company would reinstate Beeman's policy if he were still insurable, and he would be entitled to have the terms of his contract carried out as if there had been no lapse.

(4) MISREPRESENTATION OF AGE

Problem: Meckling, age 43, gave his age as 39 when he applied for his life insurance policy. If Meckling died, would the company pay his beneficiaries anything?

Misrepresentation of age, while material to the life insurance risk, does not void the policy. The insurer does, however, make an

Misrepresentation of age does not void a policy.

YOU'RE ONLY 45? YOU MUST HAVE HAD A ROUGH CHILDHOOD!

adjustment so the amount of proceeds payable is only that which the premiums paid would have purchased at the insured's correct age. Thus the company, in making a settlement in the problem, would figure the amount of insurance which the premiums Meckling had paid would have purchased for a person 43 years of age. It would then pay the beneficiary that amount.

(5) SUICIDE

> **Problem:** Dobler, who was once a very wealthy man, gradually lost all of his money. In order to provide for his family, he took out insurance on his own life with the intent to commit suicide. Six months after the policy was issued, Dobler took his own life. Was the policy enforceable?

Life insurance policies invariably include a provision that the company is liable only for the amount of premiums paid if the insured commits suicide within one or two years from the date the policy was issued. After that time, the face of the policy is paid; it is presumed that a person would not fraudulently plan a suicide that far in advance. In the problem, therefore, Dobler's beneficiary could not collect the face of the policy but only the premiums that had been paid.

(6) NONFORFEITURE OPTIONS

> **Problem:** Addison, who was in financial difficulty, had a whole life insurance policy that had been in force for 20 years. If he decided to let his policy lapse, would he lose all he had paid in premiums?

Most life insurance has a built-in savings element. To guarantee that this savings element will be used for the benefit of the insured, even in the event of lapse, statutes in all states require the policies to include *nonforfeiture options*. Most policies have several such options, and the insured usually selects one of them at the time of application. Then if he neglects or otherwise fails to pay the premium, the policy can be kept in force. The more common options are: cash surrender value, loan value, automatic premium loan, reduced paid-up insurance, and extended term insurance.

An insured has the right to demand the *cash surrender value* of the policy if he chooses to let the policy lapse. This is the amount of savings and interest accumulated (usually at a modest rate of 2½ percent to 3½ percent a year) in the policy. This sum is also the *loan value* of the policy because the insured may, instead of taking the cash, borrow that amount or any part of it from the insurer by making the necessary arrangements. In the problem, Addison could surrender his policy and take the cash value or, if he preferred, borrow its loan value.

Often a cash surrender or loan value is not available until the policy has been in force for a certain length of time, usually two or three years. This is because much of the first year's premium is paid to the salesman as his commission and other initial costs must be paid by the company. Group policies usually do not have a cash surrender value because they are term.

An *automatic premium loan* keeps the policy in force on its original plan. The policy becomes the security for a loan to pay current premiums; these may later be repaid by the insured, or deducted from the proceeds in case of death or matured endowment. If the policyholder desires to resume payment of premiums, he may do so without the necessity of submitting proof of insurability by a medical examination.

 After the death of her husband, Mrs. Terry found that a $15,000 whole life policy which her husband had carried for ten years, had been allowed to lapse two years previously. Because the automatic premium loan option had been selected by Terry when he took out the policy, it was still in effect and Mrs. Terry collected the face amount of the policy less the premium loan.

The *reduced paid-up life insurance* option provides for the purchase of as much ordinary life insurance as the cash value permits. No further premiums need be paid.

Stuckey, age 27, was unable to keep up the premiums on his $10,000 limited pay life insurance policy, which he had had for 12 years. He decided to let it lapse and take a paid-up policy for the amount listed in the table in his policy. This amounted to $663 per thousand of insurance. There would be no further premium payments, and the company would pay the beneficiary that amount upon his death.

Under the *extended term insurance* option, the cash value of the contract is used to purchase as much term insurance of the same value as possible. If the insured makes no selection of a nonforfeiture option, most insurers automatically use this one. In this way the insured is covered for a specific period of time with the same amount of insurance as in the original policy. No further premiums are required.

In the example above, if Stuckey wishes, he may request that he be covered, as listed in the table, with $10,000 term insurance for a period of 31 years with no further premium payments. At that time the policy will expire.

HOW ARE LIFE INSURANCE CONTRACTS SETTLED?

Problem: When Roberts died, he left a $25,000 life insurance policy. Could the policy be paid in some way other than a single, lump sum?

Upon the death of the insured, notice and proof of death are required by the insurer according to the same general principles discussed on page 499. Proof of death is generally a physician's written statement certifying the date and the cause of death, and an undertaker's certification of burial or other disposition of the body. Proof of age may be required.

An ordinary life insurance policy usually gives the insured or the beneficiary several options as to the way the proceeds of the contract will be paid. These *settlement options* may apply to death proceeds paid to beneficiaries, or to liquidation of the cash value of the contract paid to the insured himself. Most policies provide that the beneficiary may not change the mode of settlement if the insured has previously chosen the one to be followed unless the insured gives the beneficiary the right to change it.

The usual settlement is made by paying the face amount in a single lump sum. Other common settlement options are as follows:

(1) THE INTEREST OPTION

The company retains the proceeds as a principal sum and pays interest to the beneficiary until he asks for the principal.

(2) THE TIME OPTION

The insurer pays equal monthly installments for a given number of years. According to the table in Roberts' policy this would be $129 per month for twenty years, or $163.25 per month for fifteen years.

(3) THE AMOUNT OPTION

The company pays equal monthly installments of the amount specified by the insured or the beneficiary such as $150, as long as the proceeds and the interest thereon last.

(4) THE LIFETIME INCOME OPTION

The proceeds are used to buy an *annuity* which pays the beneficiary a specified sum at regular intervals until he dies.

CAN A LIFE INSURANCE POLICY BE ASSIGNED?

Problem: Browning, a businessman, was in debt to Knox for $5,000 and was unable to pay him. Knox suggested to Browning that he assign to him a $15,000 life insurance policy and thus prevent a legal action for the debt. Could Browning assign his policy?

A policy of life insurance, like any other claim for money, may ordinarily be assigned; written notice to the insurer is usually required in the case of life insurance, however. The policy may be assigned by the beneficiary after the death of the person whose life was insured. It may also be assigned by the insured before his death if there is no restriction imposed by the agreement or by statute. The assignee need not have an insurable interest in the life of the insured. Thus, in the problem, Browning could assign the policy for the purpose of securing the debt. If Browning died before the debt was repaid, Knox would receive only the amount due him; the beneficiary would receive the balance.

WHAT BENEFITS CAN BE OBTAINED FOR DISABILITY?

Problem: Bliss was insured under a $15,000 life insurance policy with a clause providing disability benefits in the event of permanent and total disability. What happens if Bliss is injured and unable to work?

For an additional premium, riders may be attached to the insurance policy which provide for certain benefits payable in event of total permanent disability of the insured. There are two kinds of disability riders. One is a *waiver of premium* rider, which provides that no premiums are required while the insured is disabled. The other pays a cash benefit that is called "disability income."

Disability is usually defined as "incapacity, resulting from bodily injury or disease, to engage in any occupation for remuneration or profit." A total disability that has been continuous for a period specified in the policy, usually not less than four or six months, is presumed to be permanent. Proof of continued disability must be furnished the company from time to time. In the problem, after a waiting period of six months, Bliss' insurance would be kept in force without the payment of any additional premiums. The disability income rider would also assure Bliss a monthly income of a certain percentage of the face amount of the policy as long as he was disabled. Typically, this income is figured as $5 or $10 for each $1,000 of the face amount. Since Bliss' policy was for $15,000, during the period of permanent disability Bliss would receive a monthly payment, probably $75 or $150, in addition to waiver of premiums. Disability benefits coverage is usually terminated if the insured has not become disabled before the age of 55 or 60.

WHAT IS DOUBLE INDEMNITY?

Problem: English's life insurance policy included a double indemnity rider. What was its purpose?

For an additional premium, most insurance companies will include a *double indemnity* benefit in the life insurance policy. Under this provision the insurer promises to pay double (or even triple) the face amount of the policy if the death of the insured is accidental. Policies commonly require that the death result "from bodily injury effected solely by external, violent, and accidental means, independently and exclusively of all other causes and within 90 days after such injury." Some policies also require a visible wound on the exterior of the body, except in cases of death by drowning or asphyxiation.

 Mark Croft had a double indemnity clause in his $10,-000 life insurance policy. During a blinding New

England snow storm, Croft drowned when he mistook a fishing pier for a bridge and drove off the end. The court held it was an accidental death within the meaning of the contract and awarded the beneficiary $20,000, double the face amount of the policy.

The double indemnity coverage generally excludes such causes as suicide, illness or disease, physical or mental infirmity, service in military or naval forces during time of war, and certain airplane accidents. It is also usually inapplicable after age 65 or 70.

NEARLY EVERY FAMILY HAS LIFE INSURANCE, BUT...

1. All policies are not alike. Study your own needs, and select the type or combination of types that will fit them best.
2. Policies differ from company to company. As with other things, it pays to get good advice and shop around when buying life insurance.
3. Every policyholder should study his insurance contract and choose the desirable nonforfeiture and settlement options.
4. Check your policies every few years, or whenever there is any significant change in family, occupation, or financial situation. Be sure the beneficiaries and the options are still what you wish, and that the old coverages and arrangements are still satisfactory.

YOUR LEGAL VOCABULARY

annuity	life insurance
automatic premium loan	limited-payment life insurance
beneficiary	loan value
cash surrender value	nonforfeiture options
days of grace	ordinary life insurance
disability	proceeds
double indemnity	reduced paid-up life insurance
endowment life insurance	reinstate
extended term insurance	settlement options
group life insurance	term life insurance
incontestable clause	waiver of premium
industrial life insurance	whole life insurance
lapse	

1. A contract in which an insurer, in consideration of specified premium, promises to pay a certain sum upon the death of a person.
2. Life insurance which provides for the payment of premiums during a limited period only, after which the premiums cease and the policy is paid up.
3. Insurance that, in return for the regular payment of level premiums, pays the face amount of the policy upon the death of the insured.

4. The party to whom the proceeds of a life insurance policy are payable.
5. The face value of a policy plus any dividends due.
6. The sum of money payable if the policy lapses or is canceled.
7. A provision stipulating that after a policy has been in force for a specified time, fraud or misrepresentation at the time of issue will be ineffective to void the policy.
8. A nonforfeiture option permitting the purchase of as much ordinary life insurance as the cash value permits.
9. Insurance that pays only if death occurs within a specified period.
10. Failure to pay the premium before the grace period expires.

REMEMBER THESE HIGHLIGHTS

1. Life insurance may be classified as ordinary, industrial, and group.
2. The four most common types of ordinary life insurance are whole life, limited-payment, endowment, and term. There are also combinations of these.
3. The beneficiary of a policy may be the insured himself or his estate, a person who takes out insurance on the life of another, or a third person who is not otherwise a party to the contract.
4. Most policies contain an incontestable clause, and provide for days of grace, reinstatement in case of lapse, assignment, and various methods of settlement.
5. In the event a policy lapses, the holder may usually receive the cash surrender value, or elect that a premium loan, reduced paid-up insurance, or extended term insurance be automatically put into effect.
6. For an additional premium, a policy may provide for waiver of premiums in case of disability, for disability income, and for double indemnity.

LAW AS PEOPLE LIVE IT

1. In discussing the merits of insurance, Dennis said to Reece, "All insurance is just alike." Reece claimed life insurance differs in many respects from other insurance. Do you agree?
2. Curtis and Hall disagreed on the relative merits of whole life, limited payment, and term policies. Curtis thought it was foolish to have any but term insurance. What is your judgment?
3. When Alvord died, he owed Henke $10,000. Alvord's wife was beneficiary of his life insurance policy. Henke claimed the proceeds. Would Henke succeed?
4. Dickens was employed by Carter-Abrams Company and insured under the company's group life insurance policy. When he left the company he insisted that he could keep the policy in force by continuing to pay the premiums. May he do so?

5. Morrell had a participating whole life policy and on his application requested that the dividends be retained by the insurer. At his death the beneficiary, his wife, claimed the dividends were part of the proceeds. Was she right?

6. On his application for insurance Kluthe stated he did not have cancer when in fact he knew he did. (a) If Kluthe died the next year would the insurance company have to pay? (b) If Kluthe lived for five years would your answer be the same?

7. McDermott's life insurance premium was due October 12. If he failed to pay the premium by that date, would his policy lapse?

8. In his application for a whole life policy, Whittaker gave his age as 32. At his death 40 years later, the proof of loss birth certificate showed his age was 80. Could the insurer avoid the policy because of the earlier misstatement?

9. Brackenbury has a paid-up limited-payment life insurance policy. He needs funds badly and inquires of you whether the policy can be used to raise money. What would you tell him? What alternatives does he have?

10. Klassen lost his job and was unable to pay the premiums on his $25,000 whole life policy, but he did not wish to cash in the policy. What other options were open to him?

LAW AS COURTS DECIDE IT

1. Jones made application and passed two medical examinations for a life insurance policy with a face value of $43,000, double indemnity, and other benefits. He did not complete the application or pay the premium until later, however, because he was a licensed pilot with his own plane and needed to have a supplemental aviation application. On December 20, Jones offered to give the agent a check in payment of the premium. Instead, at the suggestion of the agent, he signed a note and left the amount blank so that it could be filled in when the cost of the aviation rider was calculated. The agent told Jones he was "technically covered" even though he did not complete and give Jones the conditional receipt (binder) attached to the application. On January 3, the amount of the premium was figured and inserted in the note. The application and medical reports were sent to the Home Office and received on January 5. On January 7, Jones was killed while flying his airplane. On March 15, the insurer denied the application claiming, among other things, that no advance payment had been made so there was no immediate coverage, and that no conditional receipt had been issued as required by the company. Mrs. Jones filed this action to recover the proceeds for the purported policy. Should she be given judgment? (Jones v. John Hancock Mutual Life Insurance Company, 416 F. 2d 829)

2. On January 28, without notifying his employer that he was quitting, Gilby walked off his job with Panhandle Eastern Pipe Line Co. and never returned. His employer had covered Gilby with a $9,000 group policy of life insurance. Despite his wife's efforts to get Gilby to return to work, he did not do so. On March 7 he died from a self-inflicted gunshot wound. Mrs. Gilby filed a claim for the proceeds of the life insurance policy. The policy provided that it was terminated when employment ceased except when the employee was prevented from working because of disability. Judgment for whom? (Gilby v. Travelers Insurance Company, 248 F. 2d 794)

3. Chapman, the insured, had designated his wife as beneficiary on a life insurance policy. Later, without the knowledge of his wife with whom he was living, Chapman properly notified the insurer to change the beneficiary to "Marion K. Mellott, fiancée." A year following the change in beneficiary, Chapman was killed when a tractor overturned on him. His wife demanded the insurance proceeds, claiming her husband had no right to change the beneficiary without her consent. Do you agree? (Chapman v. Prudential Insurance Company of America, 215 Md. 87, 136 A. 2d 752)

4. Thompson took out nine term life insurance policies amounting to $1,055,000 on his wife and named himself as beneficiary. He was a wealthy attorney and was himself insured for $46,000 with his wife as beneficiary. She also expected to inherit $500,000 from her father. Thompson also stated that he had a premonition that his wife was going to have a tragic accident. A year or more after taking out the insurance, Thompson's wife was found stabbed to death. One Dick Anderson was arrested and confessed to the murder. He implicated Thompson and another man, and all three were convicted of the murder. Claiming that conviction in a criminal action does not prevent the convicted person from bringing civil action, Thompson sued to recover on the insurance policies. Should he succeed? (Travelers Insurance Company v. Thompson, 281 Minn. 547, 163 N.W. 2d 289)

5. Boger was an employee of Davis & Sons Construction Company. The company had taken out a group life insurance policy on the lives of its employees, and Boger's beneficiary was his wife. Boger received a certificate showing the terms of the policy. The company deducted a sum from Boger's salary each month to be used with deductions from other employees to pay the monthly premium on the group policy. The company failed to pay the April and May premiums although it had made the deductions from the employees' pay. Boger was unaware that the premiums had not been paid. He died on May 12, after the grace period had elapsed. The insurer refused to pay the death benefits to Boger's wife, and she sued the insurer. Who should win? (Boger v. Prudential Insurance Company, 130 S.E. 2d 64, North Carolina)

CHAPTER **38** Social Insurance

1. You will need a Social Security number when you start working for pay. Where and how can you get one?

2. You know an immigrant widow who speaks no English but who is eligible for survivors insurance benefits. What must she do to obtain these benefits?

3. Your friend loses his job because of a business slump. Must he be willing to accept any new job offered in order to qualify for unemployment compensation?

WHAT IS SOCIAL INSURANCE?

Problem: Ronzani earned $65 a week working as a clerk in a department store. Then she was laid off. Did she have any protection against this loss of income?

Almost all American working people are building future protection for themselves and their families under the Social Security Act. This law provides a variety of benefits including the five broad types listed below:

TYPE	*BENEFIT*
(1) Unemployment compensation	Income for persons laid off from work.
(2) Old-age insurance	Retirement income for workers, age 62 and over, and dependents.
(3) Survivors insurance	Income for widows and dependents.
(4) Disability insurance	Income for disabled workers and dependents.
(5) Health insurance	Hospitalization and medical care for persons over 65.

Unemployment insurance is administered by the states. It is financed by payroll taxes imposed on employers only under federal and state laws.[1] Thus, the amounts payable and the regulations

---

[1] In Alabama, Alaska, and New Jersey, employees are also required to make contributions to the state unemployment compensation funds.

governing their payment vary from state to state. If Ronzani, in the problem, had met the legal requirements of the state where she had been working, she would be entitled to unemployment compensation for a certain length of time after losing her job.

Old-age, survivors, disability, and health insurance is administered by the federal government and financed by means of a federal payroll tax on workers and employers. The workers' taxes are withheld from their pay by the employers as *payroll deductions*. The medical care part of health insurance, which helps pay doctor bills, is a voluntary program; persons over 65 must agree to pay the required monthly premiums in order to participate. Hospitalization, on the other hand, is provided to all who are covered by Social Security.

Before a person begins his first job, he should report or write to the nearest office of the Social Security Administration. This office will assign a number to him and give him a card, called his Social Security Account Number Card, bearing his name, a line for his signature, and the number. When a person's name is changed by marriage, adoption, or court order, a new card is issued showing the new name, but the number always remains the same.

WHO IS ENTITLED TO UNEMPLOYMENT BENEFITS?

Problem: Norton had been employed for five years as inspector in an aircraft factory. When government contracts were cut back, he was discharged. Was he eligible for unemployment compensation?

Unemployment compensation is designed to lessen the financial hardship of losing one's job. An unemployed worker is entitled to such compensation if he meets the requirements of the state law under which he is working. These laws vary somewhat, but in general they require that:

(1) The worker must have been working on a job covered by the state law.

(2) The worker must have been employed by a firm that employed one or more workers on at least one day in each of 20 weeks during the calendar year.

(3) The worker must have received a minimum amount of pay from, or have worked a minimum amount of time on, covered

jobs during the year or two before he lost his job or was laid off.

This usually includes jobs in factories, shops, mines, mills, stores, offices, or other places of business and industry, as well as banks and financial institutions. Railroad workers are covered by a special federal act. Self-employed persons, agricultural and domestic workers, most fishermen, and those employed by charitable, non-profit or religious institutions, and by state or local governments are excluded. In the problem, Norton would no doubt meet the above requirements and be eligible for unemployment compensation.

HOW ARE UNEMPLOYMENT BENEFITS OBTAINED?

Problem: Immediately upon being laid off from his job in a cannery, Chinn applied to the proper state office for unemployment compensation. Could he get it without any lapse of time?

Unemployment benefits are usually figured as a certain percentage of the worker's average wages while he was employed. Thus, the higher the wages, the higher the unemployment benefits. There is usually a weekly minimum which varies from $3 to $25, and a maximum ranging from $40 to $123, for full-time unemployment. These benefits vary from state to state and are subject to increase by the state legislatures as the cost of living increases.

To obtain unemployment benefits, a worker must:

(1) File a claim for the benefits.

(2) Register for a job at a public employment office.

(3) Be able and available for work if a suitable job is offered.

(4) Be totally unemployed for a specified period of time.

The job offered must be one in which the worker is trained or experienced even though it pays less than his former work. It must be within a reasonable distance from his home.

Four states—Connecticut, Delaware, Maryland, Nevada—require no waiting period for benefits in the case of total unemployment. In all others, benefits are payable after a waiting period of one week of total or partial unemployment. In several states, the waiting period may be suspended if the Governor declares a state of emergency due to a disaster. Thus, Chinn would have to wait one week before drawing benefits unless he lived in one of the four states that requires no waiting period. Benefits are payable while the unemployment continues but only up to a certain maximum time which is usually 26 weeks. With assistance from the federal government the time may be extended for as long as an additional 26 weeks if unemployment reaches a specified high level.

If a worker is ill, he cannot collect unemployment benefits in most states; however, he might then qualify for disability insurance provided he meets other requirements. (Page 546)

WHEN ARE UNEMPLOYMENT BENEFITS DENIED?

Problem: Trimble was reprimanded by her employer for frequently taking 30 minutes for her coffee breaks when only 15 minutes were allowed. She was annoyed and quit her job the next day. Was she entitled to unemployment compensation?

Under certain circumstances, an otherwise qualified unemployed person may have his benefits reduced or denied. Typical state rules provide that benefits are partly or completely denied if a worker:

(1) Quits work voluntarily without good cause.

(2) Refuses to apply for, or to accept, suitable work.

(3) Loses his job through a strike or a labor dispute in which he is involved.

(4) Intentionally misrepresents the facts about his situation.

(5) Is discharged for misconduct connected with his work.

(6) Is discharged for theft for which he is later found guilty.

(7) Is attending school full time.

(8) Receives other payments, such as a company pension or social security retirement benefits.

In the problem, Trimble quit her job voluntarily without good cause. Hence, she would be barred from any benefits to which she might otherwise have been entitled.

WHO IS ENTITLED TO OASDHI COVERAGE?

Problem: Foxx attended a state college as a full-time student, but worked three hours a day as a receptionist in the Business Department. Would she be covered by OASDHI and would she pay a social security tax?

Most employees and self-employed persons are entitled to old-age, survivors, disability, and health insurance (*OASDHI*) under the Social Security law. Payments are made to those who qualify and have retired, are disabled, or are survivors or dependents of a retired, disabled, or deceased person. *Old-age insurance* provides monthly insurance benefits for workers and their dependents when the wage earners reach retirement age. *Survivors insurance* provides monthly insurance benefits for dependents when the wage earner dies. *Disability insurance* provides monthly insurance benefits for workers and their dependents if the worker is unable to do any substantial work for pay because he is sick or injured. His ailment must have lasted, or be expected to last, at least one year. Medicare, or health insurance, is discussed on page 547.

Employees not entitled to coverage include: foreign agricultural workers admitted on a temporary basis; employees of foreign governments or of the United Nations (but U.S. citizens so employed may be covered as self-employed); newspaper carriers under 18, and newspaper and magazine vendors over 18 (unless self-employed); railroad and federal employees (they have their own systems); students working for a school, college, or university and regularly attending classes; and state government and political subdivision employees, except by agreement between the state and the United States. Employees of religious, charitable, and educational organizations which are exempt from income taxes are not covered unless the organization elects to bring them under the law. Farm workers are covered if in one year they work for any one employer who pays them at least $150, or employs them for 20 or more days. Domestic workers are covered if they get $50 or more cash wages in a quarter from a single employer. In the problem, Foxx was attending a college with a full schedule of classes and would not be covered.

Unemployment Compensation Requirements and Benefits

State	Minimum Number of Employees and Payroll	Waiting Period (Weeks)	Maximum Weeks of Benefits	Minimum Benefits Per Week	Maximum Benefits Per Week
Alabama	4 in 20 weeks	1*	26	$12	$50
Alaska	1 at any time	1	28	18-23 [1]	60-85 [1]
Arizona	3 in 20 weeks	1	26	10	60
Arkansas	1 in 10 days	1	26	15	63
California	1 and over $100 in any quarter	1	26	25	65
Colorado	4 in 20 weeks	1	26	14	77
Connecticut	1 in 13 weeks	None	26	15-20 [1]	82-123 [1]
Delaware	1 in 20 weeks	None	26	10	65
District of Columbia	1 at any time	1	34	8-9 [1]	73 [1]
Florida	4 in 20 weeks*	1	26	10	54
Georgia	4 in 20 weeks	1	26	12	50
Hawaii	1 at any time	1	26	5	86
Idaho	1 and $300 in any quarter	1	26	17	65
Illinois	4 in 20 weeks	1	26	20	45-65 [1]
Indiana	4 in 20 weeks	1	26	10	45-88 [1]
Iowa	4 in 20 weeks*	1	26	9	64
Kansas	4 in 20 weeks*	1	26	15	60
Kentucky	4 in 20 weeks	1	28	12	60
Louisiana	4 in 20 weeks	1	26	10	60
Maine	4 in 20 weeks	1	26	10	61
Maryland	1 at any time	None	26	10-13 [1]	78 [1]
Massachusetts	1 in 13 weeks*	1	30	18	69-104
Michigan	1 in 20 weeks*	1	26	18 [1]	16-18 [1]/53-87
Minnesota	1 in 20 weeks*	1	26	15	64
Mississippi	4 in 20 weeks	1	26	10	40
Missouri	4 in 20 weeks	1	26	3	57
Montana	$500 in year	1	26	12	47
Nebraska	4 in 20 weeks*	1	26	12	56
Nevada	1 and $225 in any quarter*	None	26	16 [1]	73 [1]
New Hampshire	4 in 20 weeks	None	26	14	75
New Jersey	1 and $1,000 in year	1	26	10	72
New Mexico	1 and $450 in any quarter*	1	30	12	58
New York	1 and $300 in any quarter	1	26	20	75
North Carolina	4 in 20 weeks	1	26	12	56
North Dakota	4 in 20 weeks	1	26	15	58
Ohio	3 at any time	1	26	10-16 [1]	47-66 [1]
Oklahoma	4 in 20 weeks	1	26	16	60
Oregon	1 and $225 in any quarter	1	26	20	62
Pennsylvania	1 at any time	1	30	11	60
Rhode Island	1 at any time	1	26	12-17 [1]	75-95
South Carolina	4 in 20 weeks	1	26	10	56
South Dakota	4 in 20 weeks	1	26	12	47
Tennessee	4 in 20 weeks	1	26	14	55
Texas	4 in 20 weeks	1	26	15	45
Utah	1 and $140 in any quarter	1	36	10	77
Vermont	3 in 20 weeks	1	26	15	74
Virginia	4 in 20 weeks	1	26	18	59
Washington	1 at any time	1	30	17	75
West Virginia	4 in 20 weeks*	1	26	12	71
Wisconsin	4 in 20 weeks*	1	34	21	84
Wyoming	1 and $500 in any year	1	26	10	60

* Some exceptions or special provisions.
1 Includes added benefits for dependents.

In general, *self-employed persons* include owners of unincorporated businesses, partners, independent contractors, farmers, and professional people. Clergymen are permitted to elect coverage as self-employed persons.

HOW DOES ONE QUALIFY FOR BENEFITS?

Problem: Lukens worked steadily for six years for the Careno Candy Company and five years for the Regal Restaurant Supply. Would he be covered under the Social Security Act?

A worker qualifies for benefits when he has worked a required number of "quarters of coverage" in an occupation included under the law. A *quarter of coverage* is a calendar quarter (a three months' period starting January 1, April 1, July 1, or October 1) in which he was paid $50 or more in nonfarm wages. One who is self-employed and has net earnings of $400 or more for the year would receive four quarters of coverage for the year. An agricultural worker receives one quarter of coverage for each $100 in farm wages earned in a year (up to $400). Also, any person who earns the maximum amount ($9,000) taxable for social security during the year gets a full four quarters of credit even if he works only part of the year.

If a worker is insured, he is either "currently insured," "fully insured," or both. Whether he is currently or fully insured governs the benefits which are paid. He is *currently insured* if he has coverage for at least six quarters within the three years before his death. He is *fully insured* only if he has more than six quarters of coverage. No one needs more than 40 quarters of work to be fully insured.

Workers born after 1929 are fully insured according to the following:

If the worker dies when his age is	He will be fully insured with credit for this much work
28 or younger	1½ years
30	2
32	2½
34	3
36	3½
38	4
40 and so on	4½

Note: A person is fully insured if he has credit for ¼ year of work for each year after 1950 up to the year he reaches retirement age or of his disability or death. In counting the years after 1950, a person born in 1930 or later would omit years before he was 22.

In the problem, Lukens would be fully insured because he had more than 40 quarters of coverage.

HOW ARE BENEFITS FINANCED?

Problem: While discussing social security during lunch in the school cafeteria, Neil insisted that the benefits are paid out of federal income taxes and that's why the tax is so high. Was he correct?

The first $9,000 of an employee's earnings or self-employment income is taxed to finance OASDHI. If he is employed, he and his employer share the tax equally. An employee's half of the tax is deducted from his wages each payday. His employer adds his half of the tax and forwards the total to the appropriate U.S. Depository. If the worker is self-employed, he pays his self-employment tax each year at the time he files his individual income tax return. If he is self-employed and his earnings are $400 or more, he must file an income tax return and pay his social security tax even though he is not required to pay an income tax. In the problem above, Neil was wrong. Although social security and income taxes are both based on income, they are separate and distinct taxes.

Most OASDHI benefits are paid from funds received from social security taxes. However, certain costs of the program have been paid from general funds which include income tax receipts. In addition, the federal government uses general funds to provide grants to the states and local governments for welfare payments, medical care, and social services to certain needy persons not covered or inadequately covered by the basic social security program. Those who are helped include persons who are needy and over 65, blind, permanently and totally disabled, dependent children of an unemployed father, or in need of medical care or general assistance. The benefits vary among the states, but all states participate in this program.

Although they can be changed by Congress at anytime, the scheduled social security tax rates are as follows:

Year	Employee	Employer	Self-Employed
1971-72	5.2%	5.2%	7.5%
1973-75	5.65	5.65	7.65
1976-79	5.85	5.85	7.7
1980-86	5.95	5.95	7.8
1987 and after	6.05	6.05	7.9

HOW ARE OASDHI BENEFITS DETERMINED?

Problem: Maitland, who is fully insured under OASDHI, has determined that his average annual earnings since 1950 will be $5,400 at the time he retires at age 65. What will be the monthly benefit payment to Maitland and to his wife, who is aged 62 and not insured?

The exact amount of the monthly benefits payable is determined after the filing of an application for benefits. One can estimate the amount that will be paid, however, because benefits are based on his average monthly earnings as determined from his social security record. The table on the next page shows monthly payments based upon average yearly earnings ranging from $923 or less up to $7,800. Other examples of retirement, survivorship, and disability benefits may be secured from your local Social Security office.

As shown in the table on page 545, Maitland and his wife will receive a monthly benefit payment of $287.10 ($208.80 for Maitland and $78.30 for his wife). These benefits are not taxable as income.

Monthly retirement benefits are provided for workers under OASDHI.

ARE OASDHI BENEFITS REDUCED IF YOU WORK?

Problem: Calister, aged 69, a retired worker receiving monthly benefit checks, works part-time for Mountain States Insurance Company and earns $300 a month in salary. He also gets $2,000 annually in dividends on stock he owns. What effect will this income have on his benefits?

A retired worker, a dependent of the retired or disabled worker, or a survivor who does not earn more than $1,680 a year is eligible for full benefits for all twelve months of the year.

In computing annual benefits for those between retirement and 72 years of age, all income from self-employment and wages is counted. If in a year before a person reaches age 72 he earns less than $1,680, all benefits are generally payable. If he earns between $1,680 and $2,880 in a year by working, $1 in benefits is withheld for each $2 earned over the $1,680. For earnings over $2,880, $1 is withheld for each $1 earned. Thus, in the problem Calister would lose benefits amounting to $1,320 ($600 on salary between $1,680 and $2,880 and $720 on salary above $2,880).

EXAMPLES OF OASDHI MONTHLY BENEFIT PAYMENTS							
Average earnings after 1950 *	$923 or less	$1800	$3000	$4200	$5400	$6600	$7800
Retired worker—65 or older—Disabled worker—under 65	70.40	111.90	145.60	177.70	208.80	240.30	275.80
Wife 65 or older	35.20	56.00	72.80	88.90	104.40	120.20	137.90
Retired worker at 62	56.40	89.60	116.50	142.20	167.10	192.30	220.70
Wife at 62, no child	26.40	42.00	54.60	66.70	78.30	90.20	103.50
Widow at 60	61.10	80.10	104.20	127.20	149.40	171.90	197.30
Widow or widower at 62	70.40	92.40	120.20	146.70	172.30	198.30	227.60
Disabled widow at 50	42.80	56.10	72.90	89.00	104.50	120.30	138.00
Wife under 65 and one child	35.20	56.00	77.10	131.20	181.10	194.90	206.90
Widowed mother and one child **	105.60	167.90	218.40	266.60	313.20	360.60	413.80
Widowed mother and two children	105.60	167.90	222.70	308.90	389.90	435.20	482.70
One child of retired or disabled worker	35.20	56.00	72.80	88.90	104.40	120.20	137.90
One surviving child	70.40	84.00	109.20	133.30	156.60	180.30	206.90
Maximum family payment	105.60	167.90	222.70	308.90	389.90	435.20	482.70

* Generally average earnings are figured over the period from 1951 until the worker reaches retirement age, becomes disabled, or dies. Up to 5 years of low earnings or no earnings can be excluded. The maximum earnings creditable for social security are $3,600 for 1951-1954; $4,200 for 1955-1958; $4,800 for 1959-1965; and $6,600 for 1966-1967. The maximum creditable for 1968-1971 is $7,800 and beginning in 1972, $9,000; but average earnings usually cannot reach these amounts until later. Because of this, the benefits shown in the last column on the right generally will not be payable until later. When a person is entitled to more than one benefit, the amount actually payable is limited to the larger of the benefits.

** Survivors benefits are payable to a widow at any age if she is caring for a child under 18 (or a child 18 or over who became disabled before 18). Unmarried children under 18 (or under 22 if they are full-time students) also qualify for survivors benefits.

Investment income, such as dividends, interest, annuities, pension, or rents for real estate owned as an investment is not counted in figuring benefit deductions. Thus, no deduction would be made in the problem for Calister's investment income from stock owned.

No matter how much one earns in a year, he is eligible for benefit payments for any month in which he neither earns wages of $140 nor renders substantial services in self-employment, e.g., working more than 45 hours a month as a self-employed person. After a person reaches age 72, his benefits are payable each month no matter how much he earns from any source.

WHEN ARE DISABILITY BENEFITS AVAILABLE?

Problem: Kreskie, 32 years of age, had been working in a factory for eight years and was fully insured. He lost a leg and an arm as a result of an accident while on the job. Are disability benefits available for Kreskie?

For a worker to be eligible for disability benefits, he must (a) be under retirement age, (b) be fully insured, (c) have worked at least five years (20 quarters) in a covered occupation during the ten year period ending when he becomes disabled, (d) have a severe and long-lasting disability, and (e) have filed an application for benefits. If he is disabled before reaching the age of 24, he needs credit for only 1½ years of work in the three years before he is disabled. From age 24 to 31, he needs credit for one-half the time between age 21 and the time he becomes unable to work.

Benefits for the disabled's family are also available under Social Security, and are the same as though the disabled worker were 65 and retired. Disabled widows and widowers age 50 or older receive benefits if their disability begins not later than seven years after the death of the insured husband or wife or the end of a widow's right to benefits as a mother caring for her children.

A severe, long-lasting disability is one that prevents the worker from being able to "engage in any sustantial gainful activity." Before any payments can be made it must be established that the condition is physical or mental, is expected to continue indefinitely or result in death, and has lasted for at least 12 months or is expected to last for at least 12 months. The worker must not refuse reasonable medical treatment. The following are ordinarily considered severe enough to meet the test of disability: loss of both arms, both legs or a leg and an arm; heart and lung diseases that cause pain or fatigue on slight exertion; progressive cancer; brain damage that results in loss of judgment or memory; loss of vision, inability to speak, and deafness. In the problem, Kreskie qualified for disability benefits because he was severely disabled, was under 65 years of age, had worked in a covered occupation for more than five of the past ten years, and was fully insured.

If a retired, disabled, or deceased worker has a son or daughter who was disabled before reaching 18 years of age, who has remained disabled ever since, and who is unmarried at the time of the application, such child is eligible for benefit payments. A disabled child does not need a work credit record to be eligible.

If one is disabled, he should promptly file an application for benefits because there is a waiting period of six months before payments can begin. Moreover, the worker's record is "frozen" by such application, and so there can be no reduction in his average monthly earnings because of his forced idleness.

Four states—California, New Jersey, New York, and Rhode Island—also provide benefits for short-term temporary disability of workers. Such benefits compensate for loss of wages caused by illness or injury suffered off-the-job which are therefore not covered by workmen's compensation, ordinary unemployment compensation, or federal disability insurance. In all four states, employees must contribute to the disability compensation fund; in New Jersey and New York employers also contribute. In general, benefits are the same as those for unemployment, although costs of hospitalization may also be covered.

WHAT IS MEDICARE?

Problem: Maytag, age 66, and his wife, age 63, are receiving OASDHI retirement benefits. Now they apply for health insurance. Are they eligible?

Nearly all person age 65 and over are entitled to health insurance— or *Medicare* as it is popularly known—even though they may not be eligible for other OASDHI benefits. In the problem, Maytag is eligible, but his wife will not be eligible until her 65th birthday. The Medicare program consists of two basic plans: (1) compulsory hospital insurance, and (2) voluntary medical insurance.

Hospital insurance benefits help to pay most of the cost of hospitalization, post-hospital care, and certain home health services. The insurance will pay most of the cost of 90 days of care in an approved hospital for each "spell of illness" [2]; the patient must pay only the first $68 [3] of the total bill plus $17 a day for each day from

---

[2] "Spell of illness" is also known as a "benefit period." A benefit period begins when the patient enters a hospital. It ends as soon as he has not been a bed patient in a hospital or facility with skilled nursing care for 60 days in a row. Then a new period can begin.

[3] The Secretary of Health, Education and Welfare sets the exact figure for this "hospital deductible" amount annually. It is based on actual hospital costs during the previous year. The figures given are for 1972; check with your Social Security Office for any later year.

the 61st to the 90th day. Up to 60 additional days of coverage may be added to the basic 90 days in any one spell of illness. However, this lifetime reserve of 60 days may be used only once, and the patient's contribution to the cost is doubled to $34 for each day.

In addition, up to 100 days of extended care in an approved convalescent hospital or nursing home is provided for after a stay of at least three days in a hospital. The first 20 days are paid for by the plan, and the additional 80 days cost the patient only $8.50 a day. The cost will also be paid for 100 home visits per year by visiting nurses or other medical workers after a hospitalization of at least three days.

The benefits of hospital insurance include room and board, ordinary nursing care, drugs, and other items customarily furnished patients. Certain diagnostic services of hospitals are also paid, such as X-rays and laboratory tests for bed patients. The one notable exception is the cost of the first three pints of blood which may be required.

Hospital insurance costs are paid by social security taxes levied equally against employers and employees, and are included as part of the OASDHI taxes. Any deficits are to be paid from general federal revenues.

Medical insurance supplements the hospital insurance and pays for the services of physicians and surgeons, home visits by visiting nurses, and other services. There is a $50 deductible during each calendar year; beyond that, the insurance pays 80 percent of the costs of covered services. These include services of physicians and surgeons wherever performed—home, office, clinic, or hospital. Also included are such services as ambulance charges, X-rays, radium treatments, laboratory tests, surgical dressings, casts, and up to 100 home visits by visiting nurses or therapists (this is in addition to the visits provided for by hospital insurance). Not all medical costs are covered. For example, drugs which are not furnished as part of hospitalization, blood plasma, and special nursing services are not included.

 Stokeley, who was fully covered by Medicare, had a serious spell of illness that required hospitalization. He spent a total of 20 days on two different occasions in the hospital (cost: $1,000), and another 30 days in a convalescent home (cost: $750). His doctor's bill was $650, and ambulance charges were $50. The hospital insurance would pay all but $68 of the hospitaliation costs and all but $85 of the convalescent costs. After the $50 deductible, which

Stokeley must pay, the medical insurance pays 80 percent of the balance of $650, or a total of $520. Thus, total costs were $2,450; Stokeley had to pay $333.

Each person currently enrolled in the medical insurance plan pays a premium of $5.80 per month.[4] An equal amount is paid by the federal government out of general revenues.

A person must apply for Medicare, just as he must apply for all other social security benefits. However, Medicare differs from other OASDHI benefits in that applications must be submitted within three months before or after the month in which one's 65th birthday occurs. Failure to sign up within the prescribed period will result in a six to nine months' delay in protection, and the premium for medical coverage will then cost more.

REMEMBER THIS ABOUT SOCIAL INSURANCE...

1. If you have not already secured a Social Security Account Number Card, do so now. You must have one before beginning your first job.
2. Be informed and aware of the benefits to which you might be entitled as a result of unemployment, disability, or old age.
3. Unemployment benefits may be reduced or denied under certain circumstances. Be sure that you do not jeopardize your rights to unemployment benefits by actions on your part.
4. Should you become entitled to any benefits under Social Security, file an application promptly as there is a waiting period before payments can begin.
5. There are frequent changes in the Social Security law. Keep up-to-date so that you are aware of the costs to you and of the benefits to which you are entitled.

YOUR LEGAL VOCABULARY

currently insured	old-age insurance
disability insurance	payroll deductions
fully insured	quarter of coverage
hospital insurance	self-employed persons
medical insurance	survivors insurance
Medicare	unemployment compensation
OASDHI	

1. Money withheld from worker's pay by employer for taxes or other purposes.
2. A calendar quarter in which a worker has earned $50 or more in non-farm wages.

[4] This is the basic medical insurance premium for the 12-month period starting in July 1972. It is subject to change.

3. Payments designed to lessen the financial hardship of temporary involuntary unemployment.
4. Monthly insurance benefits for workers and their dependents when the worker retires.
5. Monthly insurance benefits for workers and their dependents when a worker sustains a serious, long-lasting disability.
6. Monthly insurance benefits for dependents when a worker dies.
7. Owners of unincorporated businesses, partners, independent contractors, farmers, and professional people.
8. Benefits payable to persons over 65 which cover most of the costs of hospitalization, post-hospital care, and certain home health services.
9. Federal health insurance program which includes both hospital and medical benefits.
10. A person with at least six quarters of coverage within the three years before his death.

REMEMBER THESE HIGHLIGHTS

1. Every employee and self-employed person in covered work obtains a Social Security Card with an account number. This same number is used until the worker retires to assure that his contributions are properly credited.
2. Unemployment compensation provides weekly benefits for a limited time for workers on covered jobs who have been employed a minimum time and have then been discharged.
3. To obtain unemployment benefits, a worker must make proper application, register for a job at a public employment office, be able and available for work on a suitable job, and be unemployed for a specified time.
4. Since unemployment insurance is administered by the states, benefits vary widely.
5. Old-age insurance provides monthly benefits for a worker and his dependents when he retires at age 62 or later.
6. Survivors insurance provides benefits for dependents when the worker dies.
7. Federal disability insurance provides monthly benefits for a worker and his dependents if he has a severe, long-lasting disability.
8. All persons over 65 and covered by social security are entitled to hospital and nursing care at government expense, less a small deductible amount. They are also entitled to most of their medical costs, including fees for physicians and surgeons, if they make a small monthly payment which is matched by the government.
9. Employers and employees share old-age, survivors, disability, and health insurance tax burdens equally. In most states, employers alone pay for unemployment insurance.

LAW AS PEOPLE LIVE IT

1. A nursemaid who had been employed by a family for more than 20 years was discharged when the youngest child started school. Was she entitled to unemployment benefits?

2. Hubbard had been employed for 12 years in a welding business covered by the Unemployment Compensation Act. Upon losing his job through no fault of his own, he put in a claim for unemployment benefits. He thought he would get payments equal to his full-time weekly pay. Would he?

3. Abernathy registered at a public employment office immediately after losing his job. Six days later he accepted an offer of employment. He then claimed unemployment benefits for the time he was out of work. Was his claim proper?

4. McGuire was convicted of stealing a typewriter from his employer and was promptly sentenced to 60 days in the county jail. After waiting one week, McGuire insisted that he was eligible for unemployment compensation. Was he correct?

5. Barrington was a bachelor who had no dependents, and was employed in a covered occupation at an average annual salary of $7,800. He was fully insured. Upon reaching age 65, he retired. What would be his monthly benefit under OASDHI?

6. Brandt was employed and fully insured in a covered occupation at an average annual salary of $3,000. Upon reaching age 65, he retired. At this time his wife was 66 years of age and his children were independent adults. What would be the total amount of the monthly benefit received by Brandt and his wife under OASDHI?

7. Staubach died, leaving a wife 40 years of age and two children of ages 13 and 19. The older child had three more years of full-time college to complete. The younger child married when she reached 18. Staubach had been working in a covered occupation with an average monthly salary of $450. What OASDHI benefit payments would Mrs. Staubach receive each month (a) during the first year after her husband's death? (b) during the fourth year after her husband's death? (c) during the tenth year after her husband's death? (d) during the twentieth year after her husband's death?

8. If there had been six dependent children in the Staubach family, in problem 7, would social security survivors benefits go up proportionally?

9. Garriety, age 68, was qualified for both hospital insurance and the supplementary medical insurance. He entered the hospital for an operation which was the only medical care he had during the year. The hospital room bill for 15 days was $800, and hospital X-ray and laboratory services amounted to $250; drugs administered during his stay cost $300. The doctor's fee was $1,000. How much, and for what items would his health insurance pay?

LAW AS COURTS DECIDE IT

1. Club Hubba Hubba hired some Japanese women and brought them to Hawaii where they were to work as night club entertainers for six months. The Club, which could change their acts, impounded their passports on arrival, gave them room and board and other benefits, and advertised them as the "Hubba Hubba Girls." The girls were not permitted to work for anyone else without the consent of the Club; and if the Club consented, it was compensated for their services and in turn paid the girls. The Club claims they were independent contractors, like most traveling entertainers, and therefore it need not pay social security taxes for them. Was the Club correct? (Hubba Hubba v. U.S. & Evans, 239 F. Supp. 324)

2. Joe Fitzgerald, a laborer, injured his back. Physical therapy did not help, and his doctor recommended injecting oil into his spinal canal for x-rays (myelogram), a painful but non-dangerous procedure. If the result was positive, he said surgery should follow which would require six months for recovery. Joe refused this treatment and claimed disability benefits. Is he entitled to such benefits? (Fitzgerald v. Finch, U.S.D.C., E.D. of Kentucky, #1862)

3. After being employed for nine years as manager of a woman's apparel shop, Grubman was discharged. Her salary had been $90 a week. She filed a claim for unemployment insurance and, during the one-week waiting period for benefits, was referred to a position as a salesperson in a department store. The pay would be $50 a week, and Grubman would be selling goods similar to those sold in the shop she had managed. When she declined the sales position, the Unemployment Compensation Board rejected her claim for unemployment compensation on the grounds that she had refused to engage in suitable work to which she had been referred. Was the Board correct? (Grubman v. Unemployment Compensation Board, 107 A. 2d 186, Pennsylvania)

4. Kossman operated a retail meat business. Although his business continually showed a net operating loss, Kossman paid an old-age, survivors, and disability tax computed at the self-employed rate on a salary which he paid to himself. After paying OASDHI taxes the requisite number of quarters and reaching retirement age, he contended that he was insured and entitled to retirement benefits. Was he correct? (Kossman v. Folsom, 157 F. Supp. 157)

5. Coy died 27 months after having become eligible for retirement benefits under old-age, survivors, and disability insurance. He had never filed an application for retirement benefits. His estate filed an action to collect for each of the 27 months for which he had been eligible and had received no payments. Does the estate have a valid claim? (Coy v. Folsom, 228 F. 2d 276)

Property

UNIT ELEVEN

Over the centuries, one of the most precious human rights has been that of private ownership of property. The right of private ownership of property and its protection is guaranteed by the 5th and 14th Amendments to the U.S. Constitution, and much of this book has been concerned with the acquisition, use, and protection of property.

In our society, the legally protected and closely related rights of freedom of contract and private property are vital to our free enterprise system. Acquiring private property is a strong incentive to creative and energetic effort. The cooperative acquisition of property in the name of the government permits the ownership and use of schools, parks, museums, and libraries which could not be afforded individually. Nevertheless, most property in this country is privately owned. The cooperative nature of acquiring the funds necessary to hold property by large business firms has also helped make our affluent society possible.

We shall study some of the most common ways of acquiring, holding, and disposing of property. We shall also discover that there are responsibilities related to ownership of property including limitations as to its use. We shall take a special look at how land—real property—is transferred, and how many persons simply buy the use of real property through leases in much the same manner as one can buy the use of personal property through bailments. Finally, we shall consider how one's property is disposed of after death. After all, you can't take it with you.

39 **Personal Property**

1. *While on a camping trip in Glacier National Park, you (a) catch some trout; (b) find a wallet, with cash and I.D. cards, on the trail; and (c) pick up an auto tire inner-tube from a gully. Do you acquire property rights in these things?*

2. *A neighbor strongly objects to certain policies of the city government. In protest, he refuses to pay property taxes on his house and lot. What action will the government take?*

3. *You and five friends pool your savings to buy a small single-engine airplane. What form of ownership should you use?*

WHAT IS PROPERTY?

Problem: Guthrie rented his Squaw Valley vacation cabin to Ranlett for three months during the winter ski season. Did Ranlett acquire property under the lease?

When someone speaks of property, you probably think of all the tangible things you see around you: paper, desks, clothing, buildings and the land on which they rest, airplanes in the air, autos on the highways, and boats on the waterways. However, all property is not tangible, just as the study of property is not always concerned with things. The law considers *property* as a group of rights or interests which are protected by law and honored by society. (Chapter 2) Ownership of tangible goods is such a right; but there are rights other than ownership that can be obtained in things both tangible and intangible.

Suppose you own some land, which you rightfully call "property." Ownership gives you assorted rights, including those (a) to possess, use, and enjoy; (b) to dispose of (by gift or sale), consume, or even destroy; and (c) to give away after death. You also have the right to rent or lease your land. If you rent, your tenant also acquires property—that is, a right to use your land. In the above problem, Ranlett acquired a property interest in the cabin.

Rights may also be obtained in intangible things. Important intangible rights are often represented by legal documents: the patent for an invention like color television, the copyright to this book, the franchise or license to sell a leading brand of cola in your home town, the right to collect money under a life insurance policy.

The right to own property is fundamental in our free enterprise system.

Tangible and intangible property can also be conveniently classified as real or personal. *Real property* means rights in land, and includes water and minerals and all things permanently attached to the land, such as buildings and trees. (Chapter 2) It also includes rights closely related to land, such as the intangible rights to drive over your neighbor's land to get to your own. *Personal property* means rights in all other things.

HOW MAY PROPERTY BE ACQUIRED?

Problem: While comparing their wrist watches, some friends explained how each had acquired possession. Allerton had bought his with earnings from a paper route; Bates received his as a graduation gift; Calkins inherited his from an uncle who had died; Darby, a skilled craftsman, had made his own; Egan had found his on the street and had complied with local laws to find the owner, without success. Did each friend have property in his own timepiece equal to that of every other?

Real or personal property is most commonly acquired by contract, gift, or inheritance. In addition, personal property may be acquired by accession, intellectual or artistic labor, finding, or occupancy. Other methods of acquiring real property are discussed in the next chapter. In the problem, each friend had equal property in his own timepiece. The scope of ownership is not affected by how property is acquired.

(1) ACQUIRING PROPERTY BY CONTRACT

Any kind of property may be acquired and transferred, or bought and sold, by contract. Most people acquire most of their property by entering into employment contracts and earning wages or salaries paid in money or in other benefits. Much of this income is used, in turn, to purchase personal property. In fact, so much commercial activity involves the sale and purchase of personal property that a special body of law has been developed over the years to deal solely with such transactions. Sales are discussed in Unit V.

> To earn money for college, Frazer agreed to mow the lawns, and trim and weed the gardens of ten neighbors once a week for three months during the summer. He would thus acquire more than $1,000 by means of contracts with his customers.

(2) ACQUIRING PROPERTY BY GIFT

To be legally valid, a gift must combine an intent to transfer owner-ship with a delivery of the property or of something representing it, such as keys to a car or documents of title to a home. A mere promise to make a gift creates no rights.

> Brandenburg dangled the key to his small imported sports coupe in front of his young niece, Patricia, and said, "You've been doing so well in high school that I'm giving you my little MG." Patricia had no property rights in the coupe because, as yet, there was no delivery.

Sometimes a gift is conditional, as when a young man gives his fiancée an engagement ring. If they mutually agree not to get married after all, or if the girl breaks the engagement, the giver may generally reclaim the gift; if he breaks the engagement, however, she is normally entitled to keep the ring. Another type of conditional gift is made when the donor expects that he may die imminently. He may take his gifts back if he survives or changes his mind before he dies.

For other gifts, such as candy and perfume, no condition is intended by the parties or implied by law. Absolute title passes and the giver cannot demand their return.

(3) ACQUIRING PROPERTY BY ACCESSION

Personal property may be acquired by *accession,* which is the right of an owner of property to an increase in things that he owns.

The increase may be natural or man-made. Thus, farm crops and the young of animals belong to the owner of the land and the animals. When new parts are put into an article, they generally become part of the article being modified or repaired. For example, if a new roller is put in your typewriter, it becomes part of the typewriter and belongs to you. Of course, the repairman has a lien on the machine and may insist on payment before he returns it to you.

If by mistake someone innocently improves another's property, courts seek to do justice by letting the improver keep the property after paying fair value for the original item. Thus, in one case, an

Personal property may be acquired by accession.

innocent trespasser who increased the value of lumber 28-fold by changing it into barrel hoops acquired title to the new goods. A person who innocently buys property from a thief may be compelled to return the stolen goods (Page 262), but he may usually remove anything he has added. However, a thief or willful wrongdoer who improves another's property generally gets to keep nothing if found out.

(4) ACQUIRING PROPERTY BY INTELLECTUAL OR ARTISTIC LABOR

One may acquire personal property rights by original production. An author or inventor has exclusive property rights in his own productions prior to the time of publication or the marketing of the invention. If the author or inventor wishes to retain his exclusive rights thereafter, he may do so for a limited time by properly requesting and obtaining a grant from the federal government.

A grant to an author, an artist, or a composer of the exclusive rights to possess, produce, and publish or otherwise dispose of his intellectual production is a *copyright*. A copyright gives the owner the sole right to make and sell his creation, or to authorize others to do so, for 28 years. At the end of that time he has the privilege of renewal for another 28 years.

DeRose and two friends were young musicians who enjoyed improvising whenever they got together for a jam session. One day Revell heard them and together they put the music down on paper and added lyrics. They could protect the property they had thus created by copyrighting their composition.

A grant of the exclusive privilege to make, use, and sell an invented product, or to authorize others to do so, is a *patent*. A patent is granted for any new and useful process, machine, manufacture, or

Personal property may be acquired by intellectual labor.

THE GREAT AMERICAN NOVEL

composition of matter. It is also given for certain new and distinct varieties of plants. An idea alone is not patentable. A patent is good for 17 years and is not renewable. However, an inventor will sometimes add improvements to the original product and patent them over the years, thus in effect extending the duration of his monopoly.

(5) ACQUIRING PROPERTY BY FINDING

As pointed out in Chapter 16, the finder of property lost by another does not acquire title merely by taking possession. As against all but the true owner, however, he does have the right of possession unless local statutes require that he turn the goods in to some designated authority. If the owner cannot be found within some specified length of time, statutes often make the finder the owner, or provide that he may sell the article at a public auction and retain the proceeds or become the owner himself by purchase. Some statutes provide that the finder is entitled to his expenses and a reasonable reward if the true owner claims his goods.

(6) ACQUIRING TITLE BY OCCUPANCY

Occupancy means acquiring title by taking possession of property which belongs to no one else. A common example is *abandoned property* or personal property that has been discarded by the owner. In such a case the finder who takes possession gets absolute title.

> In response to public pressure to improve the environment, a national container company offered to buy used cans and bottles, regardless of their condition. One Saturday, Gardner and the 25 members of his Boy Scout troop picked up three truckloads of such containers from along the sides of a heavily traveled country road. They acquired property by occupancy and transferred ownership to the container company by sale.

Like abandoned property, wildlife is considered unowned. The first properly licensed person to take possession of a wild animal by killing or capturing it becomes the legal owner.

(7) ACQUIRING PROPERTY BY INHERITANCE

A person may acquire both real and personal property by inheritance from others upon their death. This method of transferring property is discussed more fully in Chapter 42.

WHAT ARE THE FORMS OF OWNERSHIP?

Problem: After graduation from high school, Hartman became an electrical appliance repairman. His wages were good, and his expenses were low because he was a bachelor living at his parents' home. With most of his savings Hartman bought shares for himself in a mutual fund. What form of ownership did he use?

Tenancy is the general name given to the various forms of ownership. One, two, or more persons may hold the title to a single piece of property as follows:

(1) SEVERALTY

When property is owned by one person alone, it is held in *severalty*. In the problem, Hartman held his shares in severalty.

(2) TENANCY IN COMMON

Problem: Pauley, Towle, and Conrad were good friends and co-workers at a local office. While they could not afford a summer home individually, together they were able to buy a cabin at a nearby lake which they agreed to share according to a schedule. What form of ownership would be appropriate for them?

When two or more persons own undivided shares or interests in property, they are *tenants in common*. Their interests or shares may be equal but need not be, and they are undivided in that they are held under a single title. Although all have the right of possession, they can agree to give exclusive use to one or the other at certain times. This is true of all forms of multiple ownership. In the problem, tenancy in common would be the best solution.

Upon the death of any one of the co-owners, his interest passes to his heirs, who then become tenants in common with the other co-owners. In life, any owner may sell his share or interest to one or more other persons, who thereby join the prior owners as tenants in common. The owners may also agree to sell the entire property and divide the proceeds according to their shares. Sometimes such sale or partition is ordered by a court upon petition of an owner in case of dispute, even though it may cause an economic loss.

(3) JOINT TENANCY

> **Problem:** Joseph Gwaltney and his twin brother, John, have never married. Several years ago they bought an eight-unit apartment house as an investment and they now occupy one of the units. In the event either dies, they wish the survivor to get the building. What form of ownership should they select?

The ownership of property by two or more persons equally, but with the right of survivorship, is known as *joint tenancy*. The right of survivorship means that if one of the joint owners dies, the surviving owner or owners get his interest automatically. In the problem, the Gwaltney twins could use this form of ownership. A joint tenant may not give his share to someone else by will, but may transfer it while he still lives; this ends the joint tenancy and makes the new owner a tenant in common.

In some states a joint tenancy between husband and wife is a *tenancy by the entireties*. This differs from the ordinary joint tenancy in that neither spouse acting alone may convey his interest to a third person. Also the creditor of one cannot reach the property; he must be a creditor of both husband and wife to do so.

(4) COMMUNITY PROPERTY

> **Problem:** All the property belonging to Hasbro and his wife was community property. Domestic difficulties developed between the two, and although there was no divorce, the husband made a will in which he left all community property to his nephews and nieces. Could he legally do this?

In eight states [1] where the law was influenced by French and Spanish customs, all property acquired by husband and wife during their marriage is *community property*. Each owns an undivided one-half interest in such property. Property owned by either at the time of marriage, or received subsequently by either as a gift or inheritance, is separate property. It becomes community property only if the owner formally or informally treats it as community property and intermingles it with other community assets. Statutes in some community property states provide for the right of survivorship; in other states, the spouse who dies is permitted to dispose of his half by will, or that portion goes to the heirs. In either case, it is clear that Hasbro in the problem may not legally deprive his widow of at least her half of the community property.

WHAT ARE THE LIMITATIONS ON OWNERSHIP?

Problem: Yardney, who lived alone, loved dogs. She started with a single Collie. It had five puppies which she "simply could not" sell or give away. Within two years, three of the puppies added 17 more to the colony. The resulting noise and odor soon became unbearable to the neighbors. Could they compel Yardney to dispose of most of the dogs?

Certain limitations on ownership are necessary in civilized society. The right of an owner to freely use and dispose of his property is therefore subject to restrictions designed to protect the equally important rights of others.

A person is not permitted to use his property in an unreasonable or unlawful manner that injures another. Thus, in the problem, Yardney could be compelled to correct what amounted to a nuisance. (Page 79)

Under its police power the government may adopt laws for the protection of the public health, safety, morals, and general welfare. This power extends to the use of property. Thus, a city may require that buildings be maintained at a certain level of livability. It may enact zoning laws which restrict certain neighborhoods to residential use, and other laws which prohibit the keeping of livestock in certain sections. It may regulate the purity of food and drugs sold to the public. It may even destroy private property, as, for example, trees in the path of a forest fire. All such laws limit the absolute freedom of owners.

[1] Arizona, California, Idaho, Louisiana, Nevada, New Mexico, Texas, and Washington.

Unit XI □ PROPERTY

All property is liable for the payment of its owner's debts unless specifically exempt by statutes. There are various legal means by which creditors can force a sale of the debtor's property with the proceeds going to pay judgments for overdue debts. (Chapter 23)

To help meet the costs of government, a resident may be compelled to pay taxes based on the worth of the property he owns, or upon his net income. In addition, *assessments* or special levies may be made against real property to pay the cost of improvements such as the initial installation of street lights or sewers.

If a person fails to pay his lawful taxes or assessments, the government may impose a lien on and later sell his property. Proceeds are then applied to the payment of the taxes, and the balance, if any, goes to the former owner. (Page 317)

MANAGE AND USE YOUR PROPERTY WISELY . . .

1. Understand your various property rights and use them intelligently. You may use and enjoy what you own, let others use it, borrow against it, sell it, or give it away.
2. Do not abuse your property rights in any way that injures others. They can take legal action to stop you and may even collect damages for injuries.
3. Protect your property against hazards by suitable care. Protect it against seizure through legal process by paying taxes to the government and debts to your creditors when due.
4. Be alert to the many ways in which property can be acquired. When prices are high, acquiring property by making or growing your own things can be a profitable hobby.
5. If you become a co-owner with someone else, be sure to take title in an appropriate form. Use tenancy in common with strangers and with ordinary associates and friends. Use joint tenancy with a spouse or other persons or members of your family whom you would want to have the full ownership by right of survivorship if you should die.
6. In community property states, be sure to keep separate property separate, with clear independent records, if you do not want it to become community property.

YOUR LEGAL VOCABULARY

abandoned property
accession
assessments
community property
copyright
joint tenancy
occupancy
patent

personal property
property
real property
severalty
tenancy
tenancy by the entireties
tenancy in common

1. A group of rights or interests which are protected by law and honored by society.
2. Ownership of property by two or more without the right of survivorship.
3. Ownership of property by one person alone.
4. The right of an owner of property to an increase in things that he owns.
5. The exclusive right to make, use, and sell an invented product.
6. A means of acquiring title by taking possession of property which belongs to no one else.
7. The exclusive right of an author, artist, or composer to possess, use, and sell his intellectual production.
8. Charges against real property for improvements.
9. A form of joint tenancy by husband and wife where neither may dispose of his interest without the consent of the other.
10. Ownership of property by two or more with the right of survivorship.

REMEMBER THESE HIGHLIGHTS

1. Technically, property means a group of varied rights or interests which are honored by organized society. However, people often use the term "property" for the things themselves — both real and personal, tangible and intangible — in which one may have rights and interests.
2. Property is classified as real or personal. Real property consists of rights in land and things permanently attached to it; personal property consists of rights in all other things.
3. Rights in property may be acquired by contract, gift, accession, intellectual or artistic labor, finding, occupancy, or inheritance.
4. Ownership by one person is tenancy in severalty. Ownership by two or more persons may take the form of joint tenancy or tenancy in common. In some states husband and wife hold property by tenancy by the entireties and in others by community property.
5. All ownership of property is limited: (a) an owner may not use his property so as to injure others; (b) property may be taken for support of the government, and, unless exempt, for the payment of private debt; (c) the owner's use of his property may be controlled by the state.

LAW AS PEOPLE LIVE IT

1. As he watched some workers install a steel beam in a new skyscraper in Manhattan, Professor Lumen said, "That steel started as real property and became personal property. Now the workers are changing it back to real property. Eventually it will again become personal property and then revert to its original status as real property." Essentially he is right. Can you tell why?

2. At an engagement party, Trudy Lannett and Richard Hurst announced their plans to get married in six months, after their graduation from college. While engaged, Richard gave Trudy a series of gifts: a diamond engagement ring, perfumes, candy, and some leather-bound books. Then Trudy eloped with Marco Manelli. Can Richard get his gifts back?

3. Heaston, a student working after hours in the school chemistry lab, discovered a chemical compound for a new plastic. He told no one but continued to perfect his idea at home. Eight months later a staff chemist of Peerless Plastic Products independently came up with the same idea and had it patented. Now Heaston claims royalties because he was first with the idea. Is he entitled to such payments from Peerless?

4. McPherson stole three bushels of peaches from Loblaw's backyard orchard and converted them into a quantity of delicious canned jam worth much more than the raw fruit. After McPherson's arrest, the question arose as to who owned the jam. Decide.

5. Sedgwick, Hooks, and Beaumont were hot rod hobbyists who had equal shares in a drag racer as tenants in common. After a disagreement, Hooks wanted to get out of the arrangement and demanded the engine as his share of the commonly-owned racer. Is he entitled to it?

6. For ten years, Isaacson and his sister, Janette, invested their savings in a 12-unit apartment house, holding title as joint tenants. Then Issacson got married. Shortly after, he was killed in an auto accident. His sister and his widow now are in a dispute over who should get his share of the apartment house. Who should?

7. Hubinger was about to go into surgery for a dangerous heart operation. Realizing that his chances for survival were very slight, Hubinger gave his valuable gold wrist watch to his friend Hyatt, saying, "Take it — I won't be counting time any more." In fact, Hubinger survived and is back at work. May he take his watch back?

8. Jensen was captain of a merchant marine freighter. Because he was forced to spend so much time at sea, he did not marry until after retiring at age 50 and settling in Monterey, California. Over the years, through consistent saving and sound investing, Jensen had accumulated a fortune of about a half-million dollars. Under California community property law, is his wife entitled to half his fortune?

9. Larson was greatly displeased with market prices for crops one season. In a fit of anger he put a torch to several large stacks of hay which he owned and had stored on his farm. All burned to the ground. Is he guilty of arson or any other crime?

10. Cattle on McDonald's ranch in Montana became infected with the highly contagious hoof-and-mouth disease. Government agents quarantined the five-county area where the ranch was located, destroyed all the infected and exposed cattle, and buried them in quicklime. Under what power did the government agents act?

LAW AS COURTS DECIDE IT

1. After some preliminary correspondence, Davies voluntarily sent a recommendation to the Carnation Company concerning a "value and property" she had found in its powdered milk. The idea called for advertising the use of the product for sprinkling into warm or hot liquid foods during cooking. Carnation replied that it was not interested, and that although it had not chosen to advertise this feature, it had previously tested it — which was true. Eight years later, after Carnation began to advertise the product for use with warm liquids, Davies sued for damages. Should she collect? (Davies v. Carnation Company, 352 F. 2d 393)

2. Hamilton and Johnson were tenants in common of a parcel of land. Hamilton wanted to end the relationship and brought a suit for court partition of the property. To force a sale of the property would be inconvenient for Johnson and cause him some loss. Must the court nevertheless order partition? (Hamilton v. Johnson, 137 Wash. 92, 241 Pac. 672)

3. Farm Bureau Mutual Automobile Insurance Co. paid the insured owner of a car when it was stolen, and thus became entitled to his rights. Eventually the car was found in the possession of Moseley, who had bought it in good faith and added certain equipment. The thief had evidently installed a new engine. Who gets the car, the engine, the added equipment? (Farm Bureau Mutual Automobile Insurance Co. v. Moseley, 47 Del. 256, 90 A. 2d 485)

4. Isaac Ettlinger bought two policies of insurance on his life from the Connecticut General Life Insurance Co., one in 1923 for a face value of $15,000, and one in 1929 for $50,000. He named as beneficiaries his daughters by a first marriage. In 1935 Isaac remarried; in 1941 he died. He had paid some premiums over the years with his own money, and some after the marriage with community property. How should the proceeds of the insurance policies be distributed? (Ettlinger v. Connecticut General Life Insurance Co. et al., 175 F. 870)

5. Picard sued United Aircraft Corporation claiming infringement of a patent for a lubricating system used in airplane engines. According to the evidence, another engine with such a system had been developed experimentally by someone else for the U.S. government but was never produced commercially. Does this earlier development prevent Picard from having a valid patent? (Picard v. United Aircraft Corporation, 128 F. 2d 632)

CHAPTER 40 Real Property

1. *Oil is discovered under the land on which your home is built. Can you sell the oil and the land below the surface, yet retain title to your home and the surface land?*

2. *You and your spouse want to move from your apartment into a house. The price is $12,000; all you have in savings and cash received as gifts is $2,000. Can you still buy the house?*

3. *A wealthy aunt conveys to you by warranty deed a 160-acre farm. Other relatives say you cannot have it because you are a minor and moreover you paid no consideration. Are they right?*

WHAT DOES REAL PROPERTY INCLUDE?

Problem: Norberg purchased a lot in the downtown business district, erected a store building on the lot, installed "built-in" recessed lighting fixtures, and bought the right to use the lot next door for access from the side street. What kind of property did he thus acquire?

Real property, which is also called real estate or realty, includes: (1) land, (2) buildings, (3) fixtures, and (4) certain rights in the land of others. In the problem, Norberg acquired real property of each of these four types.

(1) LAND

Problem: A railroad company owns the land used for underground tracks which enter the Grand Central Terminal in New York City. May the railroad sell or lease the air space above the tracks to a real estate developer for construction of a building?

Land is not only the surface of the earth, but also the air space above and whatever is beneath the surface to the very center of our planet. Land also embraces everything of a permanent nature that is attached to the soil—such as perennial grass and trees—and things embedded in the soil—such as minerals, oil, and gases. Annual crops are generally held to be personal property.

An owner of land has a right to the peaceful enjoyment and control of it. Airplanes may fly over his property, but not so low or so often as to interfere unreasonably with his use and enjoyment of the land. If a neighbor's tree has limbs or roots which overhang or extend into his adjoining property, he has the legal right to cut them off at the property line.

Courts have limited the extent of a landowner's rights above the soil in order to allow for the development of aviation and space flight. However, one owns upward a sufficient distance to provide enjoyment of the surface and all the space he can reasonably occupy and use, as by erecting a skyscraper. Thus, in the problem, the railroad could lease or sell the air space above its tracks—something that has, in fact, been done.

(2) BUILDINGS

Problem: The Marshall Brothers' Carnival has ten air-conditioned 5' x 5' ticket booths. The booths are transported on flat-bed trucks and mounted on the ground for every show. Are they real property when on the ground?

Buildings of a permanent nature attached to the land become real property. Although most buildings are intended to be fixed and permanent, they can sometimes be temporary and movable. When they are, as in the problem, they are regarded as personal property.

(3) FIXTURES

Problem: The Sovereign Oil Company leased a corner lot in downtown Boston from Hyatt. A service station was built on the site. When the lease ended 20 years later, Hyatt claimed that the building, the pavement, and the underground tanks belonged to him. Is he correct?

When personal property, such as a fence, is attached to land so that it is regarded as real property, it is a *fixture*. Courts have held that such things as bathroom fixtures, furnaces, built-in bookcases, and elevators are fixtures when their removal would cause damage to the building.

Landlord and tenant, and buyer and seller often become involved in questions of what is to be regarded as a fixture and what as personal property. Such questions may also come up in connection with tax liability and security for borrowed money. The parties may agree to treat all attached items as fixtures or as personal property. But when the parties involved cannot agree and the dispute comes before a court, the judge will usually pose these three questions:

(a) Is the property so attached that it cannot be removed without great damage to itself or to the building—e.g., a central air conditioning system?

(b) Is it specially adapted to and needed for the particular building—e.g., an escalator in a department store?

(c) Most important, did the person who affixed the personal property intend for it to become a fixture—e.g., a costly safe embedded in the concrete floor of a shop?

Real property may include fixtures if their removal would cause damage.

Equipment and materials used by a tenant for business or trade purposes are known as *trade fixtures*. Generally they may be removed when the lease is terminated or the property sold, unless they have become a part of the premises. The following items have been held to be trade fixtures which could be removed: shelving in a store, refrigerators in a hotel, temporary partitions, machinery attached with bolts and screws, and portable garages. However, such things as underground tanks and permanent buildings are part of the realty and may not be removed in the absence of contrary agreement. Thus, Hyatt in the problem was right in claiming the building, pavement, and tanks as his own.

(4) RIGHTS IN OTHERS' LAND

Problem: Vickers owned a long sloping lot on the shore of Lake Winnebago, in Wisconsin. His summer home was built at the top of the lot, next to the access road. When he sold the lower half of the lot to Sykes, the buyer wanted assurance that he could get to his lot. The seller, Vickers, wanted assurance that he could get to the lake. What can be done legally to satisfy both parties?

An *easement* is a right to use the land of another for a specific purpose. It is a type of intangible right to real property which is recognized and protected by the courts. Easements are commonly created for such purposes as automobile driveways, streets, sewer or drainage lines, telephone and electricity wires, and pipelines. In the problem, Vickers could retain an easement in the lot Sykes bought for a right of way to the lake. To satisfy Sykes, Vickers could give him an easement to drive and walk across the upper lot to reach his land.

One may also obtain rights to remove things from another's lands, such as water, gas, wood, or minerals. This is known as a *profit*.

HOW IS REAL PROPERTY ACQUIRED?

Problem: Chilton, a land developer, wanted to buy a full square block in downtown San Francisco as the site for a new hotel. The property was owned by 23 different persons, some of whom refused to sell. Chilton therefore asked the city government to use its power of eminent domain to acquire the entire block and then to transfer it to him. He claimed this was justified because the new hotel was badly needed by the public, and he would pay full cost plus a generous commission. Could the city comply with his request?

Title to real property is not transferred in the same manner or with the same ease and convenience as the title to personal property. The principal ways of acquiring real property today are by (1) deed (in a sale or gift) and (2) wills and inheritance. Other ways are (3) adverse possession, (4) dedication, (5) eminent domain, (6) public grant, and (7) accretion.

(1) DEED

Transfer of title to real property generally takes place with the execution and delivery of a deed. A *deed* is a written instrument by which the owner conveys to another the title to real property. It must be signed by the transferor.

Although a written contract of sale usually precedes delivery of a deed, this is not always true. For example, if a person makes a gift of real property and no consideration is required, there is no contract of sale.

(2) WILLS AND INHERITANCE

Acquiring real property by wills and inheritance is discussed in Chapter 42.

(3) ADVERSE POSSESSION

If a person openly and continuously holds land belonging to another for an uninterrupted period of time (commonly 20 years), he may, if he satisfies statutory requirements, acquire title to it by *adverse possession*. Statutes require that there be (a) continuous, actual, and exclusive occupancy for the statutory period with (b) an open claim of ownership of the land by the occupant (c) which is hostile to the title to the true owner. A tenant, even if he fails to pay his rent, is there by permission. His occupancy does not ripen into adverse possession no matter how long it continues.

If all requirements are met, however, the true owner, having "slept on his rights," ordinarily loses title. This is in keeping with the rationale of the statute of limitations (Page 201) as well as with the public policy encouraging use of land. Moreover, it serves to clear titles when flaws exist in the documents or record of title.

 Upon his death, Morlan's grandfather left him 80 acres of unimproved land in a distant western state where the statutory period for adverse possession was only five years. Morlan did nothing about it until the sixth year when he visited the property while on vacation. To his chagrin he found a stranger named Ferguson on the property. Ferguson had been living on the land continuously for seven years, cultivating it and paying taxes. Ferguson thus acquired title by adverse possession.

By similar uninterrupted adverse use of another's land without his consent for the statutory period, one can also acquire an easement. This may happen, for example, when a landowner does not prevent his neighbor from going across his land to reach a main road for an extended period of time. An easement acquired in this manner is known as a *prescription*.

(4) DEDICATION

When the owner of real property sets it apart for public use, as a street or park for example, he is said to dedicate it. His act is known as *dedication*. The government involved is under no obligation to accept the dedicated property; it may be too costly to maintain, or of little or no use to the public. However, if the dedication is accepted, the land must be held and used for the purpose specified: if it is dedicated to the city for use as a public park, the city generally cannot sell the park at a later date for use as a housing project or other purpose.

 Kegley developed 10 acres as a suburban shopping center. He dedicated a large portion of the land for parking by conveying title to the city for that specified purpose.

(5) EMINENT DOMAIN

Eminent domain is the power of the government to take private property for public use. It is usually exercised only when the owner is unwilling to sell, or unwilling to sell at a price which the government thinks is a fair value. The owner is entitled to fair compensation; if not satisfied with the price offered, he may demand a trial by jury to set a just price. In some cases, the government will purchase an easement rather than full title.

The property must be taken for a public use such as highways, airports, parks, and land for public buildings. Railroads and utilities may also exercise this power for such essentials as land for tracks and switching yards, and for telephone and electric lines. Eminent domain may not be used for other private purposes, even though the public may benefit and a fair price is offered. Thus, in the problem on page 570, the city could not comply with Chilton's request. However, redevelopment of blighted urban neighborhoods may be done by the government under the power of eminent domain; the land is returned to private ownership by sale after the old buildings are razed.

(6) PUBLIC GRANT

The federal government has acquired much land by purchase (for example, the purchase from France under Napoleon that gave us the Louisiana Territory) and by conquest from the Indians and Mexico. Subsequently, the government offered these lands to settlers for "homesteading," a practice which is still allowed in some areas. Usually a "homesteader" must occupy the government land, cultivating or improving it, for a prescribed time; then the land is transferred to the settler by public grant after payment of a small fee.

In the 1800's, the federal government made grants of land to the states for support of land grant colleges. It also subsidized railroad construction by making grants of right of way and of certain adjacent public lands to railroad companies in the West.

(7) ACCRETION

When the action of the water along the shore of a river, lake, or ocean gradually and imperceptibly builds up the land, the addition belongs to the owner of the land. This is known as *accretion*.

 Since the late 1800's, an island ranch in the delta of the Sacramento river near San Francisco has been owned by members of the Schaeffer family. Over the decades, silt has been carried downstream by the river and deposited along the shoreline at certain points. Many acres have been added by accretion.

WHAT ARE THE STEPS IN BUYING REAL PROPERTY?

Problem: Silverman advertised his store, land, and building for sale. When Wagner was shown the property, the two men agreed upon the price and other terms of a contract to sell which were reduced to writing and signed by both parties. Each received a copy. Did Wagner thus become the owner of the property?

Although the steps in the buying and selling of real property vary somewhat from state to state, they are commonly: (1) contract to convey, (2) survey, (3) protection of title, (4) execution of the deed, (5) escrow, and (6) recording the deed.

(1) CONTRACT TO CONVEY

Before conveyance (that is transfer) of title, buyer and seller usually make a contract to convey the property at a future time. It is sometimes called a land contract, and, of course, must be in writing. (Chapter 12) In the problem, Wagner had a land contract; he still needs a deed to become the owner.

(2) SURVEY

To determine its exact boundaries, the property should be surveyed. The result can be compared with the legal description of the property which is usually on file in the office of the county registrar of deeds. The same defined parcel of land may later be transferred again and again without new surveys. This is true, for example, of most city lots improved with houses.

(3) PROTECTION OF TITLE

The buyer of real property wants some assurance that he will get the title which he is paying for and believes he is acquiring. To protect against possible valid claims of others to the same land or parts of it, he may obtain (a) an abstract of title, (b) a policy of title insurance, or (c) a Torrens System registration.

An *abstract of title* is a condensed history of a particular parcel of land. It is abstracted or taken from legal records of the "chain of title" over the years. It includes a summary of all conveyances, recorded liens or encumbrances, and other matters that may affect the quality or extent of the title to the land. If the abstract is accurately made and complete, the buyer may usually rely on the opinion of the attorney who prepared it that the title is valid.

Title insurance, which is now quite common in this country, is an improvement over the abstract. It is appropriate to insure titles because (a) the abstract does not always show every fact that may affect the title; (b) the attorney might give a faulty opinion yet not be liable unless it can be proved that he was negligent (which may be difficult to do); (c) even if the attorney is found to be negligent and liable he may be financially unable to pay resulting damages; and (d) the transferor also might be financially unable to make good on covenants or promises he has made in the deed.

When the title is insured, the pertinent records are examined and maintained by attorneys and other employees of the insurance company. In exchange for a premium, the company agrees to insure that the title is good. This means it will pay the buyer damages suffered because of errors in the public records, and because of certain off-record hazards such as forgery, incompetency of grantors, or lack of delivery in the chain of title.

Under the *Torrens System,*[1] public registration may, at the option of the landowner, replace the usual method of conveyance. After public notice to permit claimants to appear, a court examines the title. If it finds the title is valid, it directs that a certificate of title be issued and filed in the registrar's office. When the property is later conveyed, mortgaged, or otherwise encumbered, the related documents are presented to the registrar for registration, and he issues proper new certificates. Anyone who suffers a loss because of errors made by the registrar is reimbursed from a fund accumulated from registration fees. Generally the system has not proved popular

---

[1] This system is available in Colorado, Illinois, Massachusetts, Minnesota, New York, North Carolina, Ohio, Oregon, Virginia, and Washington. California has repealed its Torrens System statute.

because of added cost, time delay, inadequacy of the fund to cover losses, and the fact that not all adverse claims are cut off by registration.

(4) EXECUTION OF THE DEED

To be valid, the deed must be executed properly and contain certain features. It must name a competent *grantor,* or person who transfers title to real property by sale or by gift. If the property is held in the names of husband and wife, both are grantors and both must sign. It must also name a *grantee* (person to whom property is conveyed) who is capable of holding title. A minor or insane person may be a grantee. There must be a description of the property sufficient to identify it. There must be proper words of conveyance, such as "I quitclaim to. . . ," and there must be proper execution, in which the grantor signs, and in some states seals, the deed. Finally, the deed must be delivered and accepted. The delivery must be made by the grantor or his agent while the grantor is living; other methods of transfer of title are used after the grantor dies.

(5) ESCROW

The seller may give the deed, abstract, or title insurance policy and other papers to a disinterested third party for delivery to the buyer when he performs as promised. The buyer normally gives the third party the necessary money payment together with a promissory note and mortgage for the balance due. Papers so delivered to an attorney, bank, or other neutral third party are said to be delivered in *escrow*.

The third party escrow agent normally prorates, or allocates fairly, the property taxes and fire insurance, if assigned, on the property as of the date of transfer of title. The seller is responsible prior to such date; the buyer thereafter. The escrow agent also prorates rents or other incomes if any are being earned on the property. He may, in accordance with instructions from the parties, require a pest control report to assure the buyer that the building is not infested with termites and that any necessary corrective work has been completed. He sees to it that all necessary documents are available and signed if required. If everything appears to be in proper order, he delivers the deed to the buyer, the payment to the seller, and the note and mortgage to the bank or other lending institution which financed the sale. When appropriate he uses money received from the parties to pay all fees, including the real estate salesman's or broker's commission, attorneys' fees, and recording fees.

(6) RECORDING THE DEED

As soon as a deed is accepted, it should be recorded in the public register of the county in which the land is situated. This gives public notice of the conveyance. When an escrow agent is used, he may record the deed as part of his service, or the title insurance company may attend to this important detail.

If a deed is not recorded by the grantee, it is not valid against innocent third parties who may later pay value for the same property in good faith without notice, or lend money with the land as security.

An unrecorded deed would be good against future claimants who paid no value. For example, it would be good against heirs under the will of a grantor of property if he had sold the same property to another under a deed which was not recorded.

WHAT ARE THE KINDS OF DEEDS?

Problem: Tiffany, in buying a house from Crandall, wanted the seller to guarantee that the house was not subject to any easements. What kind of deed should Tiffany demand?

The two most commonly used deeds of conveyance are the quitclaim deed and the warranty deed.

(1) QUITCLAIM DEED

A *quitclaim deed* effectively conveys whatever interest the grantor has in the property at the time the deed is executed, and nothing more. The grantee thus assumes the risk that the grantor may have a faulty title or no title at all.

 Kerby died without leaving a will. Under the law of the state where he lived, his widow was entitled to one-third of the value of his separate estate. His four adult children shared the remaining two-thirds. Included was the house occupied by the widow. The children wanted their mother to have exclusive title to the property. Therefore each child signed a quitclaim deed conveying his interest to the mother.

(2) WARRANTY DEED

A *warranty deed* conveys whatever interest the grantor has in the property, but also contains statements by which the grantor warrants that certain facts are true or that certain things will be done. This is the type of deed most frequently used. In the problem, Tiffany should require a warranty deed containing a covenant or guaranty that the land is not subject to any easements.

The covenants usually found in a warranty deed are as follows:

(a) That the grantor is the owner of the land.

(b) That if the grantor is the agent of the owner, he has the right or authority to convey.

(c) That the property is not encumbered, as by mortgages or other liens, unless otherwise stated.

(d) That the grantee shall have quiet enjoyment of the property; i.e., that no one with a superior title will disturb his possession.

(e) That the grantor will execute any additional documents that may be needed to perfect the title of the grantee.

WHAT DOES A REAL ESTATE MORTGAGE TRANSFER?

Problem: As an investment, Emery bought a small apartment house from Gordon. He paid 20 percent of the purchase price in cash and borrowed the balance from the Standard Savings and Loan Association, signing a note and mortgage. What rights did Standard acquire?

For most families, the buying of a home is the largest purchase of a lifetime. Moreover, the home is needed most when money is most scarce—when the family is young and the children are growing. Consequently, most homes are bought on credit with a small down payment and the balance due in installments over a period of 20 or 30 years. The house and lot become security for a loan evidenced by a promissory note and a mortgage.

A real estate mortgage (Page 346) is a written agreement that creates an interest in real property as security for an obligation; when the obligation is performed—that is, when the property is paid for—the mortgage ends. The *mortgagor* is the debtor who gives a mortgage as security while retaining possession. The *mortgagee* is the creditor who gets a security interest in the property.

A mortgage has three important characteristics which should be remembered:

(1) If the obligation or debt is not paid on schedule, the mortgagee may have the property sold by court order to satisfy his claim.

(2) The mortgagor has the right to regain the property by paying the amount due within a limited time after default. Even after court sale of the property the mortgagor has a right to redeem it by paying in full, usually within one year.

(3) Upon performance of the obligation, the security interest is terminated.

If the debt is not paid on time, the mortgagee may have the property sold to satisfy his claim.

In the problem, Standard had the right to have Emery keep the property in satisfactory condition, less ordinary wear and tear. The mortgagor may not destroy the property or otherwise impair the security. Commonly the mortgagee will require that fire insurance be carried sufficient to cover his equity as creditor. Not only the land and building existing at the date of the mortgage, but all later additions or improvements become security for the loan. If Emery should default on any payment, Standard can apply to a court to have the property sold (generally by an officer of the court) to repay the loan. This is known as the *right of foreclosure*.

In some states, the *deed of trust* is used in place of a mortgage. This is a deed given by the borrower to a trustee as security for payment of the debt to the lender. Details of the applicable law vary widely, but it is popular with creditors in those states [2] where title to the property goes to the trustee until the debt is paid, and the property can be sold on short notice without foreclosure if the debtor defaults. Moreover, in these states, the debtor does not have a right to redeem the property after its sale.

[2] California, Colorado, District of Columbia, Delaware, Mississippi, Missouri, Tennessee, Texas, Virginia and West Virginia.

WHEN DEALING WITH REAL PROPERTY . . .

1. Whenever personal property is already attached or is to be attached to the land and there is a possibility for future disagreement as to whether it is a fixture, come to a clear understanding before making the contract. Preferably, put the agreement in writing, whether the contract involved is a sale, lease, or mortgage.
2. Sometimes you may be able to enjoy the use of real estate which you need without buying the property. Simply purchase an easement or profit in the land.
3. If you inspect your idle real property at reasonable intervals, you can prevent misuse and forestall loss of title through adverse possession.
4. When the government seeks to take your land by condemnation under its right of eminent domain, consult a lawyer. You have a constitutional right to a trial by jury to determine the fair price that must be paid.
5. Land has a relatively high value. Therefore, when you buy land, it is wise to take appropriate steps to protect your title. Increasingly this means that you will demand a policy of title insurance from the seller.
6. The law generally insists on meticulous compliance with the requirements for valid execution of a deed. An attorney or competent and reliable real estate broker will help you.
7. The services of an escrow agent are usually worth the modest cost involved.
8. Normally demand a warranty deed rather than a quitclaim deed when buying property; it provides added protection.
9. If you are asked to convey property and want to be free of possible obligations, use a quitclaim deed.
10. If you have a choice as a borrower, use a mortgage instead of a deed of trust. A deed of trust gives the holder power to sell your property upon default, with no right of redemption.

YOUR LEGAL VOCABULARY

abstract of title	grantor
accretion	land
adverse possession	mortgagee
dedication	mortgagor
deed	prescription
deed of trust	profit
easement	quitclaim deed
eminent domain	right of foreclosure
escrow	Torrens System
fixture	trade fixture
grantee	warranty deed

1. Personal property attached to land so that it is regarded as real property.

2. A written instrument conveying title to real property.

3. A deed that conveys only the interest the grantor has in real property.
4. A deed that conveys whatever interest the grantor has in real property, and includes covenants that certain facts are true and that certain things will be done.
5. Power of the government to take private property for public use in exchange for just payment.
6. The surface of the earth and whatever is above or beneath the surface.
7. Title acquired by occupying land belonging to another, without the other's consent, for a certain uninterrupted period of time, under prescribed conditions.
8. The person who transfers title to real property.
9. The debtor who gives a mortgage as security.
10. A property right one has in the land of another, such as a right to cross the other's land.

REMEMBER THESE HIGHLIGHTS

1. Real property includes land, buildings, fixtures, and certain rights in the land of others (notably easements and profits).
2. The transfer of title to real property requires certain formalities not necessary in the transfer of personal property.
3. Real property is usually acquired by deed (sale or gift) or inheritance. Other less common ways include adverse possession, dedication, eminent domain, public grant, and accretion.
4. The steps in buying and selling real property are commonly: contract to convey, survey, protection of title, execution of the deed, escrow, and recording of the deed.
5. Deeds and other instruments affecting the title to land should be recorded promptly, for otherwise they may not be valid against innocent third parties who later buy the same land or lend money with the land as security.
6. The two most commonly used deeds of conveyance are the quitclaim deed and the warranty deed.
7. In case of default by the mortgagor, the mortgagee may obtain a court order for the foreclosure sale of the mortgaged property.

LAW AS PEOPLE LIVE IT

1. Neuhoff bought a home from Donson and obtained a warranty deed to the property which included a warranty of quiet enjoyment. On three sides, Neuhoff found noisy neighbors, all with large families of small children, dogs, and loud musical instruments. Neuhoff sued Donson for breach of warranty of quiet enjoyment. Is he entitled to judgment?
2. In a state where the period of adverse possession is five years, Tumico rented a small house for one year from his cousin Petrillo but never paid

the rent. When the lease ended, the Tumico family stayed on without permission and without payment. Petrillo knew Tumico was unemployed and so he did nothing. After four more years of this arrangement, Tumico claimed he owned the house by adverse possession and could not be evicted. Is this the law?

3. Crowley sold a lot to Mulvaney, who thought his realtor had recorded the deed. In fact, the deed was not recorded. After Crowley's death, his executor checked the public records and found the deed still in Crowley's name in the register. He now claims the property for the estate and the heirs. Can Mulvaney keep the lot?

4. According to the county records, Carter was the owner of certain land. Sadler claims the same land by adverse possession, and a court trial is pending to determine who really is entitled to the parcel. Kalvar now offers Carter and Sadler each $2,500 for his interest, if any, in the land. If they both agree to sell, what form of deed would be appropriate?

5. Borgstrom conveyed his home to James by quitclaim deed. After taking possession, James discovered that property taxes had not been paid for three years, a mortgage balance of $2,000 was owed to a bank, and the public had an easement to walk across the lot to reach a playground. Does James have any recourse against Borgstrom?

6. While living in New Mexico, Kirby bought an Iowa farm from Brenehan, getting a warranty deed to the property which included a warranty of quiet enjoyment. When Kirby moved to the farm, however, he found tenants in possession with four months remaining on their lease. Brenehan had never mentioned the tenants. Is he liable to Kirby for damages?

7. Joslyn had been in business at a particular location in Hartford, Connecticut, for many years. When the government Redevelopment Agency sought to buy his land for razing and redevelopment purposes, Joslyn refused to sell. He claimed the proposed purchase was illegal because it was not for a public use since the Agency planned to lease or resell much of the land to private, not public, owners. Can he be compelled to sell?

8. Houghton built a cabin above the snow line in the Sierra Mountains. To assure himself of access during the winter when he planned to go skiing, he offered to dedicate to the county an approach road leading to the main highway. It was 500 yards long and 30 feet wide, and the county snow plows would keep it clear if it were a county road. In all probability, he and his infrequent private guests would be the only persons using the road. Is the county obliged to accept the gift?

9. During a flood which followed heavy rains, the river which formed the boundary between the land of Bibb and Firpo shifted so that it now flows only through Firpo's property. Bibb now claims as his own all the land on his side of the river which formerly included the river bed and some of Firpo's land. Is Bibb entitled to this land?

LAW AS COURTS DECIDE IT

1. K.K. Ash and A.G. Ash executed and delivered a mortgage on certain land in Riverside County, California, as security for a note for $1,000. The value of the land lay chiefly in its timber. The holder of the note and mortgage brought an action against the mortgagors to recover damages arising out of the cutting of some eucalyptus trees growing on the mortgaged property. If the cutting of the trees impaired the value of the security, was the mortgagee entitled to judgment? (Easton v. Ash, 18 Cal. 2d 530, 116 P. 2d 433)

2. Annie E. Peterson and her husband executed an instrument which stated that "this document is to show that we, Annie E. Peterson and Nelson Peterson, have agreed to sell to Nelson Johnson" a specified lot owned by Mrs. Peterson. The instrument recited the consideration and then stated: "Now it is understood that should Johnson pay these notes at maturity, we agree to make him, or as he may direct, a deed to said premises." In an action to recover possession of the lot, it was contended that the foregoing instrument was a deed of conveyance. Do you agree? (Peterson v. Reichman, 93 Tenn. 71, 23 S.W. 53)

3. Plaintiff owned a farm adjoining the Philadelphia Gun Club. Portions of the shot fired at birds during meets fell on the plaintiff's land. This forced his employees to seek shelter and damaged his produce. For nine years the Gun Club paid the plaintiff a yearly compensatory sum, but then the plaintiff refused to renew the contract and sued to end the practice. The Club claimed the shooting had been going on for more than 21 years and therefore it had acquired an easement. Did the Club have an easement? (Digirolamo v. Philadelphia Gun Club, 371 Pa. 40, 89 A. 2d 357)

4. Arizona Coffee Shops bought two lots from Phoenix Downtown Parking Association, executing a mortgage to secure the unpaid balance of $200,000. The note provided for acceleration in the event of default in the payment of interest or principal. All payments were made on time until March 1, 1961, when because of the illness of its bookkeeper, one interest payment was inadvertently missed by Arizona. Phoenix on April 4 began foreclosure proceedings. Arizona immediately tendered the past-due interest but it was refused. Is Arizona entitled to any relief? (Arizona Coffee Shops v. Phoenix Downtown Parking Association, 95 Ariz. 98, 387 P. 2d 801)

5. Fiore secretly executed a deed for certain land to his wife, and left it with his attorney for safekeeping without any further instructions. After Fiore died, the deed was recorded. Now his wife claims the land by virtue of the deed. A son argues that the deed was ineffective and so he is entitled to an interest in the land as an heir. Was the deed effective? (Fiore v. Fiore, 405 Pa. 303, 174 A. 2d 858)

CHAPTER 41 Landlord and Tenant

1. *When your brother goes away to college, he and a friend lease an apartment for the nine-month school year. Must the lease be in writing to be enforceable?*

2. *The water heater in your rented apartment breaks down. Do you have to pay for the replacement?*

3. *A visitor to your rented apartment falls down the stairs in the public hallway because of poor lighting. Are you liable for his injuries?*

WHAT IS A LEASE?

Problem: Ziegler entered into an oral agreement with Fenimore to lease the latter's seashore cottage for the summer season of three months. Later, Ziegler tried to avoid the contract, claiming the lease was not enforceable because it was not in writing. Was he correct?

The relation of landlord and tenant always involves real property. Lease or rental of personal property, you recall (Chapter 15), creates the relation of bailment.

A *lease* is a legal agreement which provides that one person, the *tenant*, shall have exclusive possession and control of the real property of another, the *landlord*. The agreement may be either express or implied. The landlord is also known as the lessor; the tenant is the lessee. *Rent* is the consideration given by the tenant.

Although the term "lease" is often used to designate the writing which establishes the relation, a lease may be oral. Remember, however, that under the Statute of Frauds, leases which extend for more than one year should be in writing; courts will otherwise refuse to enforce them. Because the lease in the problem was for only three months, Ziegler was wrong; the oral agreement was binding.

No particular language is necessary in a lease; but the words used must express an intention that property owned by the lessor be possessed by the lessee. To help avoid disputes later on, however, the lease should state in plain language all important terms of the agreement.

WHAT ARE THE TYPES OF TENANCY?

Problem: Stone leased from Bergman 3,200 acres of cattle-grazing land in an isolated part of Texas. Rent was payable annually, at the end of the calendar year, and was calculated on the basis of the number of cattle which used the land. No time limit was specified. What type of tenancy was created by the lease?

A lease may be made to last for a definite length of time, to be renewable periodically, or to continue until one or both of the parties wish to terminate it.

When a lease is for a definite period of time, such as six months, one year, or ninety-nine years, it is called a *tenancy for years*. Note that it has this name even when the period of the lease is less than one year. In a tenancy for years, the lease may give the tenant an option to renew. Normally he is required to indicate his intention before the lease terminates. If a tenant for years does not renew, but remains in possession after the lease has expired, a *tenancy at sufferance* arises. The landlord may treat such a tenant as a trespasser. However, if he acquiesces to the continued occupancy, as by accepting additional rent, a new tenancy from year to year is generally created. If the old lease was for a year or longer the landlord can hold the tenant for another full year. If the old lease was for less than a year, the landlord can hold the tenant for another full month.

When the tenancy is for a renewable period of time with rent due at stated intervals, it is a *periodic tenancy*. Such a tenancy may be by the week, the month, the year, or any other period of time agreed upon. If the rent is paid by the month, it is referred to as a *tenancy from month to month*. If the rent is paid by the year, as in the problem, it is a *tenancy from year to year*. A periodic tenancy continues for successive time periods until one of the parties ends it by giving proper notice of termination.

When no specific term of the lease is decided upon, the relationship is called a *tenancy at will*, and may be terminated at the will of either party. It continues indefinitely until termination.

WHAT ARE THE RIGHTS AND DUTIES OF A TENANT?

Problem: Ravizo leased a house from Maloney for single family use. To help the family finances, Mrs. Ravizo installed bunk beds on the second floor and took in eight college students as boarders. Maloney claims this violates the lease. Is he right?

The rights and duties of a tenant include the following:

(1) PAYMENT OF RENT

A tenant's most important duty is to pay, when due, the agreed-upon rent. Although rent is usually expressed as a fixed sum of money, it may consist of services or of property, or be a share of the crops of a farm or a percentage of the profits of a business. Leases ordinarily require rental payment in advance, but in the absence of a contract clause or custom to that effect, rent is not due until the end of the term.

Before leasing property in a tenancy for years, landlords some-times require the payment of the first and last month's rent. Thus, if the tenant later fails to make prompt advance payment of the next period's rent, the landlord can use the last month's rent for the month during which legal steps are taken to force the tenant to move. In residential rentals, a "clean-up" or "security" deposit is almost always required. The amount of this deposit is refunded at the end of the leasing period if the property is left as clean and neat as it was when first occupied.

In the absence of a statute or agreement, or of negligence on the part of the landlord, destruction of part of the premises by burning or other cause does not relieve the tenant of the duty to pay the rent. On the other hand, if the property is a total loss or nearly so, the lease is normally terminated and the tenant's duty to pay rent ends.

(2) POSSESSION

A tenant is entitled to exclusive possession of the leased property, and may recover damages if such possession is refused by the land-lord or barred because someone with superior rights is in oc-cupancy.

 Pattison leased a store building to Bernardi for three years, with an option to renew. Because business was poor, Pattison assumed Bernardi would not renew and leased the building to Ishikawa. When Bernardi did renew, Pattison became liable for damages to Ishikawa.

(3) USE OF THE PROPERTY

A tenant may use the property for any purpose for which it is designed or customarily used, or in any manner agreed to in the lease. If a tenant leases land for farming, he has no right to use it for any other purpose, such as mining or motel operation. If he leases a house as a single family residence as did Ravizo in the problem, he may not use the building as a boarding house. In some neighborhoods such action would also violate zoning regulations.

(4) CARE OF THE PROPERTY

A tenant must take reasonable care of the leased property. He must return it in substantially the same condition it was in when the lease began, making all minor repairs as necessary in the absence of agreement to the contrary. Although he is not liable for the wear and tear caused by ordinary use, he is liable for deterioration or destruction caused by his willful misuse or negligence. In modern residential leases, by custom or agreement and sometimes by statute, landlords may agree to make all repairs, even such minor ones as replacing faucet washers and electric fuses.

The tenant is normally under no obligation (in fact, he has no right) to make major structural changes or repairs, or to make improvements without the consent of the landlord. Thus, if windows are broken or a roof develops leaks, repair or replacement is the concern of the landlord. However, the tenant is legally expected to act reasonably. He should take appropriate steps to prevent avoidable damage from wind and rain until the landlord has been notified and can make the needed repairs. Also, if the tenant's negligence or misconduct caused damage requiring major repairs, it is his duty to have the corrective work done.

As a practical matter, the tenant is obligated to notify the landlord when major repairs become necessary, unless the latter learns the facts by other means, as through his own routine inspection or notice by city housing code authorities.

A person injured in a public area of a building must look to the landlord for relief.

When a number of tenants rent portions of a building, as in an apartment house or office structure, the landlord is responsible for the upkeep of the exterior and the public areas. Public areas are those not under the specific control of any one tenant and include common hallways, stairs, and elevators. One who is injured because of the faulty condition of these areas must look to the landlord for relief. On the other hand, if someone is injured because of a tenant's negligence in maintaining a private area, the tenant is liable.

(5) ASSIGNMENT AND SUBLETTING

Unless he is restricted by the terms of the lease, a tenant may assign his lease or sublet all or part of the premises. An *assignment of a lease* takes place when the tenant transfers his entire interest in the lease to a third person. Although the assignee becomes liable to the landlord for the rent and performance of other conditions of the lease, the original tenant also remains liable as a surety (Page 315) and can be made to pay if the assignee does not.

A *subletting* takes place when the tenant leases all of the property to someone else for some of the time remaining under the lease, or part of the property for either all or some of the time remaining. When property is sublet, the original tenant becomes a landlord in relation to the sublessee, but he continues to be directly liable to his own landlord for performance of the lease.

Leases often require prior approval of assignment or subletting by the landlord. Courts have held that the landlord must act in good faith in withholding his consent. An absolute prohibition against assignment or subletting would be contrary to public policy.

WHAT ARE THE RIGHTS AND DUTIES OF A LANDLORD?

Problem: Healy leased a store building from Cherney for one year. After just three months, Healy moved out all his possessions and left town, defaulting on his rent. Cherney did not relet the store. Is Healy liable for the rent for the remaining nine months?

In general, the rights and duties of a tenant are balanced by reciprocal duties and rights of his landlord.

(1) RECEIPT OF RENT

Unless a landlord expressly waives his right and agrees to allow the premises to be used without charge, he always has a right to the agreed rent. If the tenant fails to pay the rent, the landlord may:

(a) Sue for the rent that is due. If a tenant has breached the lease and abandoned the property, the landlord generally is not obliged to relet. He may hold the tenant liable for the rent on the idle premises as it comes due. Thus, in the problem, Healy is liable to Cherney for the full year's rent even if he does not occupy the store. In the alternative, Cherney could relet the premises, and keep all the rent received. If it was less than the amount due, he could hold Healy liable for the deficiency.

(b) Maintain an action to evict the tenant and reenter the property. Breach of the lease by the tenant normally gives the landlord the right to terminate it. (Chapter 14) He may begin an action to force the tenant off the property, called *eviction*. In some states the landlord may include his claim for overdue rent in the same action.

(2) INSPECTION

Generally a landlord has no more right to enter the premises of his tenant than does a trespassing stranger. However, it is very common for the landlord to include a provision in the lease reserving a right to enter, even in the absence of the tenant, for the purpose of inspection and repairs which may be necessary to protect the property, or to show it to prospective tenants or buyers at reasonable times.

(3) CONDITION OF PREMISES

Normally a landlord is not liable for injuries resulting from the defective condition of leased property. He is not obliged to furnish premises fit for any particular purpose or to keep the premises in repair, unless otherwise agreed. A statutory exemption is made in some states when property is leased for human habitation; the landlord is then required to provide and keep the quarters in a condition fit to live in. Also a landlord may be liable for injuries resulting from known defective conditions in the property which are concealed from the tenant.

Under some circumstances the tenant may claim *constructive eviction* and refuse to pay rent. This could happen if the landlord failed to perform certain duties as defined in the lease or imposed by statute. Examples would include failure to make agreed-upon repairs of the premises, and failure to heat or air-condition. If the law requires that the premises be kept in a condition fit for human habitation, an infestation of insects or rodents could amount to constructive eviction. However, the landlord is not responsible for the possibly annoying behavior of neighbors.

An important trend in the law is the enactment of housing codes in large cities which not only govern new construction, but also dictate the condition of old and new quarters used for human habitation. A representative code makes provisions such as these:

(a) There shall be no exposed electrical wiring.
(b) The roof shall not leak.
(c) Every ceiling and wall shall be smooth, free of loose plaster and wallpaper, and easily cleanable.
(d) Outside doors and windows shall have tight-fitting screens.
(e) Every unit shall have a private bathroom.
(f) Gas stoves shall be properly vented and connected.

(4) TAXES

In the absence of contrary agreement, the landlord pays all real property taxes and assessments on the property leased. Long-term leases of commercial property commonly provide that the tenant will pay such taxes and assessments as well as premiums for prescribed fire insurance.

(5) FIXTURES

If a tenant adds fixtures (Page 568) to the property so that they become a permanent part of it, they belong to the landlord. Remember, however, that this general rule does not apply to trade fixtures. Because the problem may provoke disputes, it is desirable for the parties to agree in advance on which additions are to be considered permanent fixtures and which removable personal property.

HOW MAY A LEASE BE TERMINATED?

Problem: Whitney had leased an apartment to Kale in a month-to-month tenancy. On the last day of January, Whitney told Kale he would have to move the next day because the quarters were needed for close relatives who had unexpectedly arrived. Was Whitney entitled to terminate the lease in this manner?

A lease may be terminated in several ways. If it is made for a definite period of time, it terminates at the end of such time. It may also be terminated by agreement before the expiration of the term, as when the tenant surrenders the lease to the landlord, and the landlord accepts. Mere abandonment of the premises without assent of the landlord is not surrender, but a breach of the lease. Any breach by the tenant generally gives the landlord the right to terminate the lease.

In a periodic tenancy, the party seeking to terminate must notify the other party to the lease. There is usually a requirement that this notice be in writing, and given so many days before it becomes effective or before expiration of the term. Time and method may be specified in the lease, but generally are subject to statute; thirty days is typical notice time for a tenancy from month to month. In the problem, Whitney could not terminate the lease on such short notice unless Kale was willing.

If the tenant fails to move out within the time allowed by law, the court may order an officer to evict him by moving all occupants and their belongings out into the street.

IF YOU ARE A TENANT...

1. Written leases generally contain many clauses that protect the landlord. Read with understanding before you sign. If terms are unacceptable, request a change. If refused, go elsewhere.
2. You are not permitted to remodel or change the premises without the consent of your landlord.
3. You may be held liable if someone is injured because of the faulty condition of the premises caused by your negligence. Remember that normally you, the tenant, have the obligation to make necessary minor repairs and to notify your landlord of the need for major repairs. Protect yourself with careful maintenance and with adequate liability insurance.
4. State statutes or local housing codes may entitle you to demand that the landlord provide and maintain premises which are fit for human habitation.
5. Don't forget to give your landlord proper notice of your intention to move if lease or statute requires the giving of notice in order to terminate, as is usually the case in periodic tenancies. Failure to give notice will obligate you to pay additional rent even if you vacate the premises.
6. If you are a tenant in a tenancy for years, be sure to vacate before expiration of the lease. If you stay on without permission, you can be treated as a trespasser or held liable for as long as another full year's rent.

YOUR LEGAL VOCABULARY

assignment of a lease	subletting
constructive eviction	tenancy at sufferance
eviction	tenancy at will
landlord	tenancy for years
lease	tenancy from month to month
periodic tenancy	tenancy from year to year
rent	tenant

1. A legal agreement which provides that the tenant shall obtain possession of the real property of the landlord.
2. The consideration given by a tenant.
3. A periodic tenancy where the rent is paid by the year.
4. The one who is given possession of real property under a lease.
5. A lease that exists for a definite period of time.
6. The tenant transfers his entire interest in the lease to a third person.
7. A legal action taken to force the tenant off the property.
8. The tenant leases part of the property for some or all of the time remaining, or he leases all of the property for some of the time remaining.
9. One who, through a lease, transfers to another exclusive possession and control of his real property.
10. A lease which exists for an indefinite period of time and may be terminated at the will of either party.

REMEMBER THESE HIGHLIGHTS

1. The relation of landlord and tenant always involves real property.
2. A lease may be a tenancy for years, a periodic tenancy (a tenancy from month to month, a tenancy from year to year), or a tenancy at will.
3. Generally the tenant is responsible for paying the rent, making minor repairs, taking reasonable care of the premises, and using the premises only for the purposes agreed upon or for which they are designed.
4. A tenant may assign the lease or sublet the premises unless there is a restriction in the lease which requires prior approval by the landlord.
5. Generally the landlord must deliver possession of the premises, see that the tenant is not deprived of their use by the landlord or anyone else with superior title, and unless otherwise agreed, pay taxes on the property.
6. A lease may be terminated by expiration of the leasing period, agreement of the parties, or at the option of either party upon breach by the other. In a periodic tenancy, either party seeking to terminate must give the other proper notice.

LAW AS PEOPLE LIVE IT

1. Stull and Gordon were partners in a bowling alley. They rented their building from Padden in exchange for 10 percent of the gross proceeds as rent. The partners later became heavily indebted to Cort. He sued them, including Padden as a defendant. Cort claimed Padden was a partner and fully liable as such since he shared in the profits. Is Padden the landlord or a partner?
2. Sharwell rented a house and garage from Malinski. Neither building was covered by fire insurance. While overhauling the engine of his antique

Model A Ford in the garage, Sharwell negligently left a pile of oily rags in a cardboard carton. That night they ignited by spontaneous combustion and destroyed the garage and the house. Is Sharwell liable to Malinski for the loss?

3. La Follette leased an apartment from Wolcott for the nine-month school year. After final examinations were over in June, three days short of nine months, La Follette left for home without notifying anyone. The landlord now demands one month's additional rent because La Follette failed to give notice of termination. Is he liable?

4. Garver was a tenant in Barnham's apartment house. While visiting in Garver's apartment, Fogg slipped on a loose scatter rug on the highly polished floor and broke his ankle. Who is liable for the injuries?

5. Settle leased a small warehouse for five years. After three years, Settle contracted to let Korb occupy the entire premises for a full year. Was this an assignment or a subletting?

6. Margulio rented a house from Hirsch for a year, under a lease which gave the landlord "the right to inspect and show the premises at reasonable times." A month before expiration of the lease, Hirsch brought the first of what became a series of prospective new tenants to see the house. In each case, Hirsch notified his tenant in advance, but after five such visits in one week, Margulio told the landlord "No more!" Is he within his rights?

7. The McGraws leased a house for three years. Early in their occupancy they improved the property by installing curtains, drapes, removable wall-to-wall carpeting carefully installed over the hardwood floors, a motorized outdoor television antenna, and a portable incinerator. With the permission of the landlord, they also replaced the central heating unit with a combination heating and air conditioning unit. May they remove all these things when they leave?

8. Poppich leased a store from Kohl for five years, paying a fixed rental of $600 a month. The landlord paid the real property taxes and assessments. After a year, several public parking lots were opened in the vicinity and the store property was assessed for its share of the cost. Can Kohl force Poppich to pay this new levy since he gets the benefit of the parking lots?

9. To improve his failing health, Craig decided to live in the country and rented a farmhouse from Pingree in Wisconsin. "To get lots of fresh air," Craig left several windows open throughout the year. Rain and snow warped the sills and floor next to the windows. Craig claims this was ordinary wear and tear, considering his condition. Is he liable to the landlord for damages?

10. Baxter opened a hamburger shop in a building which he leased for five years from Geeting. The long hours impaired Baxter's health and after one year he sold the business to Goodwin, assigning the lease as part of

the deal. When Goodwin later defaulted on rent payments, Geeting tried to collect from Baxter. Is Baxter liable?

LAW AS COURTS DECIDE IT

1. Stockton Realty Company rented an apartment to Green in a three-story building which had a washroom and clothesline for use by tenants on the roof. After Betty Reiman, a 14-year-old friend, removed Mrs. Green's clothes from a line, she tripped on some object and fell against a skylight in the roof. The glass was too weak to support her weight and she dropped to the floor below, sustaining injuries. Is the landlord responsible for the condition of the roof, hence possibly liable in damages for the injury? (Reiman v. Moore, 42 C.A. 2d 130, 108 P. 2d 452)

2. Hughes rented an apartment from Westchester Development Corporation for use by his mother for a year commencing October 1. Hughes' mother occupied the apartment until the following April 21 and then vacated it. When Westchester sued for overdue rent, Hughes denied liability. He claimed constructive eviction by the landlord because the apartment was overrun with cockroaches and other insects, and because his mother was frequently disturbed by loud sounds of radios, fights, arguments, and dancing at various hours of the day, night, and early morning. Was this a case of constructive eviction? (Hughes v. Westchester Development Corporation, 64 App. D.C. 292, 77 F. 2d 550)

3. Wallenberg leased certain property from Boyar in a periodic tenancy from month to month, beginning October 1. The rent was payable in advance on the first of each month. On November 27, Wallenberg left without notifying the landlord. Is Boyar entitled to rent for the month of December? (Boyar v. Wallenberg, 132 Misc. 116, 228 N.Y.S. 358)

4. Papallo rented a dwelling from the Meriden Savings Bank. At that time the kitchen ceiling was in poor condition, and shortly thereafter a piece of plaster fell. Papallo mentioned this to an officer of the bank and was promised that the ceiling would be repaired. About a month later a larger piece of plaster fell, striking Papallo and injuring him. When he sued, the bank contended that when the lease was signed it had no duty to repair, and that later there was no consideration to support the bank's promise to repair. Therefore it said it was not liable. Was the bank correct? (Papallo v. Meriden Savings Bank, 128 Conn. 563, 24 A. 2d 472)

5. Oles rented an apartment on the top floor of a three-story apartment building owned by Dubinsky. The bottom step on a back stairway that was used by all the tenants was missing. The second step was supported by a broken and rotted bracket. The second step gave way, causing injury to Miss Oles. Would the landlord be liable? (Oles v. Dubinsky, 231 Mass. 447, 121 N.E. 405)

42 Wills and Intestacy

1. *You wonder what would happen to your cycle, books, stereo, and other belongings if you should die. Who would get them?*

2. *The father of one of your young friends dies without leaving a will. Will your friend receive any share of the estate?*

3. *Your neighbor argues that no one needs a will because the state has laws which say how a deceased person's property shall be distributed. Do you agree?*

WHAT IS A WILL?

Problem: Moore and his young wife were on the deck of a cruise ship during their honeymoon. As they discussed plans for the future, they earnestly assured one another that, "What's mine is yours!" Does this effectively take the place of a will?

The right to decide who shall receive one's property after death is a valuable property right. By using a written document known as a *will,* a person may direct the distribution of his property after his death. If one does not make a will, his property is distributed according to state intestate ("without a will") statutes.

A will takes effect only upon the death of the maker, who is called a *testator.* The document may therefore be changed or canceled at any time during the maker's life. This is fortunate, for time brings changes both in one's assets and in the needs of those to whom he wishes to leave them. As discussed later, a will can be updated from time to time to reflect these changes.

The fact that the existence and contents of a will are proved only after the death of the maker opens the way to false claims under forged documents. This has in turn led to strict rules regarding the preparation and execution of wills. If a will fails to comply with the legal requirements, courts will not enforce it; the deceased person's property is then distributed as if he had made no will.

Ordinarily, a will cannot be made orally. In the problem the statements of the honeymooners would be expressions of their desires or intentions but could not take effect as a will.

Personal property that is left by will is a *bequest* (or legacy); real property, a *devise*. The deceased person who makes the gifts is the *decedent*; those who receive the gifts by will or intestacy are known as *beneficiaries*. Technically, persons who inherit by virtue of an intestate statute are *heirs*.

WHY MAKE A WILL?

Problem: Tinnell wanted to make special gifts of money after death to several friends, a favorite nephew, his faithful secretary, his church, and his college alma mater. He wanted to leave controlling shares of stock in the family business to his oldest son, and a diamond which was a family heirloom to his daughter. He also was determined to set up a trust to take care of a third child who was mentally retarded. Should he make a will?

Many people believe that the limited amount of property which they have does not warrant the trouble and expense of making a will. However, most owners of property who are qualified to make a will can benefit significantly by doing so. The legal fee is usually small; in fact, some attorneys who hope to handle the estate later on will charge nothing.

If there is a will, the decedent's property is distributed in the way he desires. If there is no will, the distribution is made according to intestate laws and the results may be very different. In the problem, for example, if Tinnell did not have a will in which he made the indicated gifts, none of his stated wishes would be realized.

Through a will, a person can direct the distribution of his property after death.

It is often less expensive to distribute property after death with the aid of a will. The testator can name his spouse or other close relative as his personal representative to handle the estate, and let that party collect the fees allowed. He can waive the bond otherwise required by law for a personal representative. By following the advice of his lawyer, he may be able to save many thousands of dollars on estate and inheritance taxes if the estate is large. He may also be able to lessen the possibility of costly litigation among heirs.

Administration of gifts can be simplified by a will. For example, assume that a man dies leaving a wife and two children. If there is no will, one-third of his estate probably goes to his widow and one-third to each of the children. The court will probably appoint the widow as guardian of the estate of the children. As such she will be responsible for taking care of and managing the estate for the children, spending available money as reasonably necessary. She will have to provide a bond assuring faithful performance of her duties, and she will be required to make periodic reports to the court of her stewardship until the children reach adulthood. At that point, if they are normal, they will get control of their share of the estate whether or not they are able to handle it prudently. The time, expense, and annoyance of this procedure could have been avoided by a will which left everything to the wife. If the husband doubted her ability to handle the assets, he could have set up a trust in the will and named a banker or other trustee to manage the estate. He might have given her the interest earned on the assets as income for life, coupled with the right to use the principal if necessary; the trust could have stated that the children would inherit what was left when she died and when they reached certain prescribed ages.

WHAT ARE THE REQUIREMENTS OF A WILL?

Problem: Doran was 82 years old, absent-minded, blinded by cataracts on both eyes, and unable to read or write English. Was he competent to make a will?

A will should ordinarily be prepared by a lawyer, if only to make certain that all legal requirements are met. Assuming that the testator has the necessary *testamentary intent*—that is, that he wishes to dispose of his property after death by means of the will—there are two basic requirements in all states: (1) the testator must be legally competent, and (2) the will must be in writing and signed by the testator. In most states there is also a requirement that (3) the will be witnessed and, usually, signed by the witnesses.

(1) TESTATOR LEGALLY COMPETENT

Generally only persons who are adults, at least 21 years old, may make wills. A number of states have lowered the minimum age to 18, however, and several have gone even lower.

The testator must also have capacity to make a will. He must be able to know at least in a general way (a) the kind and extent of his property, (b) the persons who are "the natural objects of his bounty" or generosity, and (c) what he is doing in making the will—namely, making arrangements to dispose of his property after death. If the testator does not have capacity when he makes the will, the fact that he later acquires capacity does not validate his will. If he had capacity when he made the will, and later lost it—as by going insane—his will remains valid. In other words, capacity to make the will must exist at the time the will is made. In the problem, none of Doran's infirmities or limitations would render him incompetent to make a will.

(2) IN WRITING AND SIGNED

Generally a will must be in writing and signed by the testator. No particular form or words are necessary so long as the testator's intentions are expressed. The document may be printed, typewritten, or handwritten in pencil or ink; or it may be any combination of printing, typewriting, and handwriting. It need not be dated but in good practice always is.

The will must be signed by the testator or by someone for him in his presence and at his express direction. To prevent unauthorized additions to the will, many states require that the signature be placed at the end.

 A will was concluded as follows:

> "Signed this ninth day of June, 1930
>   Jane Taylor
> Executors to serve without bond."

The New York court held that this will was not signed at the end as required by statute. It was, therefore, not admitted to probate. In other states the will is valid down to the signature and any provisions beyond that point are void.

Last Will and Testament

OF

Richard W. Lewis

I, Richard W. Lewis   *of* City of Chicago

County of Cook   *and State of* Illinois

being of sound and disposing mind and memory, considering the uncertainty of continuance in life, and desiring to make such disposition of my worldly estate as I deem best, **do make, publish and declare, this to be my Last Will and Testament;** *hereby revoking and annulling any and all former wills, testaments and codicils whatsoever by me made.*

    First: *I desire that all my just debts and funeral expenses be paid, as soon as possible after my decease.*

    Second: *I give, devise and bequeath* to my wife, Sharon A. Lewis, the balance of my estate remaining after the above debts are paid.

    I Nominate *and appoint* Leo S. Chin, 143 Elm Drive, Chicago, Illinois *the Execut*or *of this my Last Will and Testament.*

    In Witness Whereof, *I have set my hand and seal to this, my* **Last Will and Testament,** *at* Chicago, Illinois *this* first *day of* November, 19 7-.

Richard W. Lewis

    The foregoing Instrument was signed, published and declared by the said Richard W. Lewis *as and for* his *Last Will and Testament, in our presence and at* his *request, and in* our *presence, and in the presence of each other, we hereunto subscribe our Names as Attesting Witnesses.*

Paul Blasdell   *address* 10 Circle Drive, Chicago, Illinois

Alberto Martinez   *address* 5001 W. Harrison St., Chicago, Illinois

Will

(3) WITNESSES

In the states where witnesses are required, a will must ordinarily be witnessed and signed by a minimum of two persons. Some states require three.

Most states which call for witnesses require that they understand they are witnessing the signing of a will. They must all be present and sign in the presence of each other and of the testator, and they must all be present when the testator signs (or acknowledges the existing signature to be his own). In most states a witness who is also a beneficiary under the will is disqualified from receiving the gift. However, if he is an heir he receives the gift up to the amount he would get in case of intestacy. Although the witness must know that he is witnessing the signing of a will, he need not and usually does not know the contents.

After a will has been executed, the original should be put in a safe place. The attorney who drafted it will usually also retain an unsigned copy in his files, and may provide an extra unsigned copy for the testator's use.

WHAT ARE THE SPECIAL TYPES OF WILLS?

Problem: Hewett bought a printed "short form will" at the stationery store, filled in the blanks with pen and ink, and signed and dated the document. Was it a valid will?

In addition to the ordinary formal will, many states recognize three other special types of wills:

(1) HOLOGRAPHIC WILL

A *holographic will* is one that is written entirely in the testator's own hand and signed by him. In some states the will must also be dated in the testator's own hand. No witnesses are required for a holographic will to be valid.

(2) NUNCUPATIVE OR ORAL WILL

A *nuncupative* (or oral) will is recognized in most states as valid for disposal of personal property only, and usually the amount is strictly limited. Generally such a will must be made during the testator's last illness, and one or more witnesses are required. The testimony of the witnesses must be reduced to writing within a specified time. Because of these limitations, oral wills are uncommon.

(3) SOLDIER'S OR SAILOR'S WILL

An oral or written *soldier's or sailor's will* is generally valid for disposing of personal property even though it does not comply with the formalities required for other wills. Although it remains in force after the maker returns to civilian life, he may want to make a new will, especially if he acquires any real property.

In the problem, Hewett's will could not qualify as an ordinary formal will in most states because there were no witnesses; it was not valid as a holographic will because some of the words were not in his own handwriting; and obviously it was neither a nuncupative nor a soldier's or sailor's will.

HOW MAY A WILL BE CHANGED?

Problem: Tappen had a properly prepared ordinary formal will in a state which required witnesses. Several years later, he used pen and ink to change the percentages of his estate going to the beneficiaries. He dated and signed his name next to each change. Were his changes effective?

The testator may revoke his will by defacing, tearing, or destroying it with the intent to revoke it, or by making a new one which replaces it. If he makes a new will, it is customary for the testator to include a clause saying that any and all prior wills are revoked. The clause, and dating of the document, may prevent confusion and litigation after death. Nevertheless, it is possible that a later-dated will which makes gifts that are inconsistent with the first, will alone suffice to revoke the first.

If the testator wants to delete specific provisions of his will, he may do so by crossing them out with the intent to revoke. He should sign and date the changes.

If the testator wants to modify the will by substitution of terms, or change it by addition of new terms, he may do so by interlineation in a holographic will. He may even do so by interlineation in an ordinary formal will in those states which do not require witnesses. But in states which require witnesses, as in the problem, additions are not effective unless made with the same formality required for the original will. In Tappen's will, the old percentages remain in force.

In states which require witnesses, the proper way to change an ordinary formal will is by preparing a *codicil*. This is an amendment to the will which adds to, removes, or otherwise alters some of its provisions. It is executed with the same formality as the will itself.

In most states, divorce of a testator does not revoke his will. Lawyers normally cover this problem by appropriate disclaimers in the property settlement agreement between the parties. A new will is usually an even better solution.

WHAT ARE THE LIMITATIONS ON THE TESTATOR?

Problem: Bendix was a widower with three adult children. The youngest daughter was happily married to a wealthy physician. The son was independently wealthy in a business of his own. The oldest daughter was still keeping house for her father. She had never married in order to care for her invalid mother for more than 15 years. Could Bendix, the father, elect to leave everything to this eldest daughter and nothing to his other children?

Although the law gives extensive power to dispose of property by will, this power is by no means unlimited. State laws vary, but in general some limitations exist.

The rights of creditors may not be defeated by will. One must be "just before he is generous"; lawful debts of the testator are paid by the estate before any other property is distributed.

The rights of a surviving husband or wife may not be defeated by will except with his or her consent. The surviving spouse may elect to accept either what the will provides, or what statutes and case law in the state allow. Otherwise, generally speaking, a testator is not obliged to leave anything to anyone, including close relatives. Contrary to a common erroneous belief, he need not mention a disinherited person, nor bequeath him a nominal sum such as one dollar. However, in some states, if he wishes to disinherit his children, he must either make provision for them while still alive, or explicitly exclude them in his will. Otherwise they take the shares provided them by intestate statutes. Thus, in the problem, by using appropriate language, Bendix could leave everything to his eldest daughter.

Statutes in some states provide that a testator may not give more than a certain portion of his estate to charity. Such laws are traceable to medieval England where the kings did not want too much land to pass into the possession of religious organizations.

WHAT IS INTESTACY?

Problem: Mosbacher, a bachelor, had a superstitious idea that to make a will was to invite disaster. Accordingly, he never made a will, yet he died in an accident at the age of 29. How will his property be distributed?

A person who dies without leaving a will, or whose will is declared invalid, is an *intestate*. The court appoints a personal representative to take charge of such an individual's property, pay his debts including costs of administering the estate, and then distribute the balance in accordance with the intestate statutes.

The laws governing the distribution of the property of the intestate vary among the states. The nature of the property (real or personal) may affect the outcome. In some states, however, if the decedent leaves a wife or husband as well as children, the surviving spouse receives one-third of the property and the balance is divided equally among the children. If there is only one child, the division may be equal. If the children have died and left children of their own, these grandchildren inherit their parents' share of the estate.

If no children survive, the spouse is generally given one half of the estate and the parents of the deceased share the other half. If the parents are dead, their share goes to any of the decedent's surviving brothers and sisters. If any of the brothers or sisters have died but have left surviving children, the share of the parent is distributed to the children who are the nieces or nephews of the deceased.

If the decedent is a single person, his parents get his property. In the problem, Mosbacher's parents get his estate. If neither is alive, it goes to his brothers and sisters. If the decedent is a widow or widower with children, the children share the estate equally.

 Lombard died leaving his widow and two children, A and B. His third child, C, was dead, but he had left two children, X and Y, grandchildren of the decedent. Under the laws of his state, the wife would receive one third of the property and the other two-thirds would be divided among the children, or, in the event any of the children were dead, among the children of the deceased child. The property of the decedent would therefore be divided one third to the wife, two-ninths to A, two-ninths to B, and one-ninth each to X and Y, the children of C. This division is shown in the following chart.

ESTATE OF DECEDENT

$\frac{1}{3}$ to Wife	$\frac{2}{9}$ to Child A	$\frac{2}{9}$ to Child B	$\frac{1}{9}$ to X, Child of C	$\frac{1}{9}$ to Y, Child of C

WHO SETTLES THE AFFAIRS OF THE DECEDENT?

Problem: In his will, Hargrove appointed his wife as the executrix of his estate, naming his brother as an alternate. Under what circumstances would the brother be called upon to serve?

The testator may designate a person to administer the will. This is a valuable right, for such *executor* (*executrix* if a woman) has important duties and is compensated out of the assets of the estate. If there is no will, or if the will does not name an executor, or if the executor is unable or unwilling to serve, the court appoints a personal representative to do the job. Such person is called the *administrator* (*administratrix* if a woman), and the spouse or other close relatives are usually favored. Hargrove, in the problem, properly named his brother as the alternate executor to serve in the event that his wife proved to be unable or unwilling to serve.

Unless the testator has waived the bond in the will, the executor must furnish a bond assuring faithful performance of his duties. The cost of the bond is paid out of the estate. A personal administrator generally is required to give bond, but very commonly, corporate administrators such as bank and trust companies need not because they are presumed to be financially responsible.

After the death of the testator, the will is presented in a *probate court,* sometimes called a surrogate or orphan's court. If the will is found to be valid, it is admitted to probate. If the executor qualifies and is approved, he gathers and protects the assets, files an inventory of the estate, pays all outstanding debts and taxes if any, and distributes the remaining property in accordance with the will. If there is no will, the administrator performs the indicated duties and distributes the remaining property in accordance with the intestate statutes.

The primary duties of the executor (or administrator) are to assemble and preserve the assets and collect any amounts due the estate, and then to pay the just debts of the deceased from the available funds. Priority debts include expenses of the last illness and funeral, and administrative expenses such as fees payable to the executor and his attorney.

SINCE "YOU CAN'T TAKE IT WITH YOU . . ."

1. The right to decide who shall receive your property after you die is a valuable right. Use it by making a will as soon as you have sufficient property to justify such action, and are qualified by law to do so.
2. A will is a technical legal document; failure to prepare it properly may defeat your intentions, lead to law suits, add to costs of probate, increase the tax burden. Consult legal counsel before you act.
3. Your will is an important document; keep it in a secure place. For handy ready reference, use an unsigned copy at your home or office.
4. For large, complex estates, a commercial executor (bank or trust company) is advisable; for small ordinary estates, a spouse or close relative is often preferable.

YOUR LEGAL VOCABULARY

administrator
   (or administratrix)
beneficiaries
bequest (or legacy)
codicil
decedent
devise
executor
   (or executrix)

heir
holographic will
intestate
nuncupative (or oral) will
probate court
soldier's or sailor's will
testamentary intent
testator
will

1. A document completely handwritten by the testator, and signed by him, directing the distribution of his property after death.

2. A signed, written document directing the distribution of property after death.

3. Personal property left by a will.

4. A person who inherits property by virtue of an intestate statute.

5. A formal amendment to a will.

6. A person who dies without leaving a will.

7. A deceased person.

8. A person designated by the maker of a will to administer the will.

9. A person appointed by the court to administer the estate of a decedent.

10. The court in which the will is presented.

REMEMBER THESE HIGHLIGHTS

1. The general requirements of an ordinary formal will for a person with testamentary intent are that it must (a) be made by a competent person, and (b) be in writing and signed by the testator. In most states it must also be witnessed.

2. One must execute a will in the manner required by law and should have qualified legal assistance in doing so.

3. Since a will does not become effective until after the death of a testator, it may be revoked or changed at any time prior to the testator's death.

4. Creditor's rights to be paid just claims, and the rights of a surviving husband or wife to a share of the estate as recognized by law may not be defeated by a will which may attempt to give the property to others.

5. The will may appoint an executor to distribute the property of the deceased according to the terms of the will. When the named executor cannot or will not serve or when the will does not name an executor, or when there is no will, the property is distributed by an administrator appointed by the court.

LAW AS PEOPLE LIVE IT

1. Mulholland was just ten years old when she inherited ten million dollars from an aunt. May she spend the money or give it away in life or after death by will?

2. As required by the law of his state, Virotto signed his ordinary formal will in the presence of two witnesses. While Virotto stepped out of the room momentarily to answer a long distance telephone call, the witnesses signed the will. Was it a valid will?

3. Troxell was a retired high school teacher, 85 years old. He was suffering from a delusion that all of his former students were his own children, and he was determined to leave his estate to help them get started in their careers. Could he do so?

4. After his wife died, Renfro—who had never had any children—decided to leave his entire estate to the non-profit hospital which had cared for his wife on several occasions. Could he do so?

5. Through years of work as a motion picture stunt man, Tobey accumulated a sizable estate. Then he married and made a will leaving everything to his young wife. They were divorced soon after, with no children, and he forgot about the will. Five years later he was killed in a stunt scene, and the will was found among some old letters. Is it still valid?

6. Ballard and Bokum, both 22, were soldiers. Shortly before one night patrol, Ballard told his friend, "I've got a feeling I'm not coming back from this one. Tell my kid brother Tim that he can have my car, and you can have my rifle." The rifle was a standard government issue carbine, but Ballard had kept it in excellent condition. Were his words a valid will?

7. A massive stroke had paralyzed Lockwood but he was evidently unaffected mentally. However, he could communicate only by signaling with weak movements of a finger. Could he make a will?

8. While he lived in New York State, Frame incurred debts of several thousand dollars to three creditors. When they threatened to sue, he moved to another state without leaving any forwarding address. Later he died, and the news was printed in the weekly newspaper in his old home town. The creditors saw the item. Can they collect their debts from Frame's estate?

9. Sanchez checked the intestacy law of his state and decided that the statutory plan of distribution of a decedent's estate was precisely what he wanted. Should he perhaps make a will anyway for other good reasons?

10. During a winter flight in his private plane, Caparios—a bachelor—crashed into an isolated mountain peak and was mortally wounded. Before he died, he evidently scribbled this note on the face of his aerial

map: "I leave all my property to my brother Leo." and signed and dated it. The map was found with his remains in June. Was the writing a valid will?

LAW AS COURTS DECIDE IT

1. In connection with the probate of the will of Ellen Burge, the question arose as to the differences between an ordinary gift in life (inter vivos) or a gift in contemplation of death (causa mortis), and a gift by will. What are the differences? (Starks v. Lincoln, 316 Mo. 483, 291 S.W. 132)
2. Certain heirs contested the will of Jane Hawkins on the ground that she was of unsound mind when she executed her will. They based their claim on the fact that she could not comprehend the provisions of the will in their legal form. Does such inability render a testator incompetent? (Ditton v. Hart, 175 Ind. 181, 93 N.E. 961)
3. When Peace died at the age of 88, four paper writings were found folded together in a seed catalog in his desk. All were entirely in his handwriting; all began with the words "I . . . declare this to be my last will." Each was executed as required by statute, but they were inconsistent with each other and could not be construed as one single will. Only one was dated. Could any of the four apparent wills be admitted to probate? (Peace v. Edwards, 170 N.C. 64, 86 S.E. 807)
4. Gustav Dreyfus used a typewriter to type his own will and then he signed and dated it in his own hand. Was it a valid holographic will? (In re Dreyfus Estate, 175 Cal. 417, 165 P. 941)
5. Krause telephoned Cullinan and asked her to come over with Frizalle to witness a will. When they arrived, Krause said nothing about her will but simply showed them a sheet of folded paper and said, "Here are the pen and ink; sign it." They signed and left. Was this sufficient for a formal will? (In re Krause's Estate, 18 C.A. 2d 623, 117 P. 2d 1)
6. Thompson spent his vacation in the home of a niece, Catherine Nicholson. At the end of his vacation he left the writing which is printed below lying on a table. Mary Agnes and David were Catherine's children. Mrs. Nicholson contended that the writing was a valid will. Do you agree?

"Dear Catherine:

Just a few lines to let you know I am starting to Monaca, and I was very much pleased with the vacation. Catherine, I want you to know you are to get all I have when I die. Tell Mary Agnes and David that Uncle George said hello and give them a big hug and a kiss for me.

I remain as ever,

July 7, 1949   Uncle George Thompson"

(Appeal of Thompson, 375 Pa. 193, 100 A. 2d 69)

UNIT TWELVE

Business Organization

UNIT TWELVE

Within a very few years you, and most of your fellow students, will have completed your formal education. You will then probably seek gainful employment in a full-time job which may become your lifetime career. You may be self-employed in an individual proprietorship, especially if you are a professional such as a doctor or a lawyer, or a small retail store operator. You may eventually see advantages in joining with one or more trustworthy friends in a partnership which permits handling bigger jobs, earning greater rewards, and sharing the responsibilities and work, as discussed in Chapter 43. You may be employed by a sole proprietorship or partnership, but if you are like most privately employed workers in America today, you will probably be employed by a corporation.

Corporations, which carry on most of the business in this country, are discussed in Chapter 44. We shall learn about the organization, ownership, and authority of corporations as well as the rights and liabilities of shareholders who are the owners of the corporation.

It is important and helpful to learn about these legal forms of business which so greatly influence our welfare. Indeed, business firms exert such great influence over our lives that the government has become concerned with how they function. Chapter 45 discusses not only how government regulates business, but also how the lives of all citizens are affected by this regulation.

43 Partnerships

1. *At the end of the school year, a classmate of yours buys more than 100 textbooks from other students. During the summer he cleans and reconditions them. In September he sells them at a profit to incoming students. What legal form of business organization is he using?*

2. *Three partners spend 20 years building their business to where its annual sales exceed a million dollars. Then one of the partners dies. Does the business end?*

3. *One of four partners in a firm of accountants contributed more capital than the others. He also attracts more business and does more work than any of them. Is he legally entitled to a larger share of the profits?*

WHAT IS AN INDIVIDUAL PROPRIETORSHIP?

Problem: Using his own savings, a bank loan, and credit from his suppliers, Huff opened a clothing shop near a college campus. What was the legal form of his business?

The law recognizes three principal kinds of business organization: individual proprietorships, partnerships, and corporations. An individual proprietorship is owned by one person. Partnerships have two or more owners. A corporation is a separate entity in the eyes of the law and may be owned by any number of persons.

When a person, such as Huff in the problem, owns and controls his own business, it is an *individual proprietorship*. The owner enjoys all the profits and suffers all the losses. Businesses that are individually owned and operated are the simplest form of organization and the most numerous, but they do much less business in dollar volume than do corporations. Small neighborhood grocery stores, cafes, and gasoline service stations are often individual proprietorships. Most farmers and professional men also conduct their businesses in this manner.

There are no particular legal requirements for organizing or conducting an individual proprietorship. However, the single proprietor must comply with any laws applicable to the kind of business in which he engages.

Wodehouse opened a franchised "fish and chips" restaurant. He had to obtain a city business license, a state permit for sales tax collections, and a federal number for income tax and social security withholding purposes. In addition his facilities were inspected periodically by the local health department.

In case of breach of contract or tort liability, the owner's individual property as well as his business property may be taken to satisfy any judgment for damages obtained against him in court.

WHAT IS A PARTNERSHIP?

Problem: Arnott and Brading organized and operated the Concordia Convalescent Home. They agreed to share profits and losses equally after paying all expenses. The building was leased from Sheller for rent which was to be 6 percent of the gross revenue. Hassell was hired as resident manager for $200 a month plus 19 percent of the net profits. Are all four men partners in the business?

A *partnership* is an association of two or more persons to carry on as co-owners a business for profit. It is based upon a voluntary agreement by which the persons, called *partners,* unite their capital, labor, or skill in the business. In the case of the convalescent home, Arnott and Brading were partners but the others were not. Neither Sheller nor Hassell owned part of the business, and their sharing of the profits was merely a method of paying them rent and salary.

A partnership appears to operate as a separate unit or legal entity because contracts are made in the firm name. In most states, however, a partnership does not have a legal existence separate from that of the owners. For example, it cannot sue or be sued in the firm name

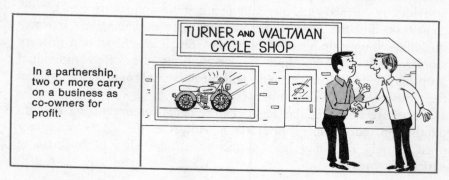

In a partnership, two or more carry on a business as co-owners for profit.

TURNER AND WALTMAN CYCLE SHOP

in many states. Anyone who wishes to bring an action against a partnership in such states must sue the partners jointly and individually. However, the Uniform Partnership Act [1] treats a partnership as an entity for keeping of accounts, holding title to real estate, and certain other purposes.

In many cases, persons join together for promotion of charity or recreation, or in enterprises not organized to earn profits, such as social or fraternal clubs, labor unions, or volunteer fire fighting companies. Such organizations are not partnerships, but are either unincorporated associations or non-profit corporations.

WHAT ARE THE KINDS OF PARTNERS AND PARTNERSHIPS?

> **Problem:** Wickersham was a licensed physician who had been practicing medicine for almost 30 years. Looking forward to retirement, he invited Hensel, who had just completed his internship and residency, to join the office. They agreed to share net profits at a rate of 75 to 25, increasing Hensel's share 5 percent annually as he gained experience until it leveled off at 50-50. Was Hensel an employee or a partner?

A partnership may be formed for any lawful purpose by an express or implied contract. It may be for commercial purposes or for professional ones. In the problem, Hensel was a junior partner in a professional partnership.

It is always desirable to put the partnership agreement in writing. Doing so encourages thoughtful review of the diverse problems of a new business, and helps to avoid future controversies over rights and duties. However, partnership agreements need not be in writing unless required by the Statute of Frauds. As you recall (Page 171), the Statute applies if it is agreed that the firm is to last longer than one year. The formal document containing the terms of the agreement is called the *partnership agreement* (or articles of partnership). A qualified lawyer should be consulted to assist in drafting the document so that intentions of the partners are properly expressed and all important matters are covered.

Partners may be classified as general, silent, or secret. A partner who is publicly active in the operation of the business is a *general*

---

[1] The Uniform Partnership Act is in force in all states except Alabama, Florida, Georgia, Hawaii, Iowa, Kansas, Louisiana, Maine, Mississippi, and New Hampshire.

partner or an active partner. A *silent partner* may be known to the public but takes no active part in management. A *secret partner* is not known to the public but does participate in management of the firm. Both the secret and silent partner are liable for partnership debts.

PARTNERSHIP AGREEMENT

THIS AGREEMENT, made in the City of Baker, State of Florida, on the fourteenth day of February, 19--, between ROGER WILKINS and KENNETH FRYE, both of Baker, Florida.

WHEREIN IT IS MUTUALLY AGREED, AS FOLLOWS:

1. That the parties hereto shall, as partners, engage in and conduct the business of buying and selling musical instruments.

2. That the name of the partnership shall be BAKER MUSIC COMPANY.

3. That the capital of the partnership shall be the sum of Forty thousand dollars ($40,000); and each party shall contribute thereto, contemporaneously with the execution of this agreement, the sum of Twenty thousand ($20,000) in cash.

4. That at the end of each calendar year the net profit or net loss shall be divided equally between the parties hereto, and the account of each shall be credited or debited as the case may be with his proportionate share thereof.

Roger Wilkins
Roger Wilkins

Kenneth Frye
Kenneth Frye

Signed and delivered
in the presence of

R. W. Wesley

Robert Jones

Partnership Agreement

Most states recognize limited partnerships, either under common law principles or under the Uniform Limited Partnership Act.[2] In a limited partnership, certain members, known as *limited partners,* can contribute capital and share profits but cannot exercise any control

---

[2] This act has been adopted by all states except Alabama, Delaware, Kansas, Kentucky, Louisiana, Maine, Oregon, and Wyoming.

over the business. These partners are also "limited" by the fact that their personal liability for debts of the firm is limited to the amount of their investment. In such a firm there must be at least one general partner. This special form can be created only by proper execution and recording of a certificate stating the essential details of the agreement.

If a minor enters into a partnership agreement, he ordinarily loses none of his rights and privileges as a minor. Thus, he can normally plead minority as a defense if sued by a creditor of the partnership. He may also withdraw from a partnership and end the relationship without being liable for breach of contract. There are some states, however, which hold a minor liable on contracts he makes in connection with a business he is in alone or as a partner.

WHAT ARE THE DUTIES OF A PARTNER?

Problem: Popkin and Pextin were partners in a thriving parcel delivery business. Pextin was in charge of the truck fleet. He arranged to replace ten trucks with models from Buffington, a local dealer. The price of $40,000 was fair and competitive. By skillful bargaining and persuasion at a social dinner that evening, Pextin persuaded Buffington to allow him a quantity discount of 5 percent. Pextin now claims the $2,000 discount belongs to him alone because it was an "extra" arranged on his own time. Is he right?

Each partner is required by law or agreement to carry out certain duties in a partnership. Among these duties are:

(1) TO USE REASONABLE CARE

In fulfilling partnership duties required by law or agreement, every partner is expected to use reasonable care. However, he is not personally liable for honest mistakes or errors of judgment.

(2) TO ACT WITH INTEGRITY AND GOOD FAITH

The relationship of the partners is one of utmost trust and confidence. Each partner is duty-bound to act with the highest integrity and good faith in dealing with the other members of the firm. He must in every instance act with strict loyalty to the interests of the partnership. In transactions, he is not permitted to retain any benefits for himself unless, of course, he has the consent of his partners. Thus, Pextin is wrong in his claim to the discount in the problem. All profits or other benefits flowing from firm business properly belong to the partnership.

 In a lecture to his law school class on partnerships, Professor Veritas gave this good advice: "Enter a partnership with greater care than you enter a marriage. Be sure your partner is compatible—you'll be spending a lot of your life together. But he should also be competent and industrious—you'll have to do the work he doesn't, and share the cost of his mistakes. And he'd better be honest and financially responsible—your fortune is on the line for what he does."

(3) TO REFRAIN FROM PARTICIPATING IN COMPETITIVE BUSINESS

Unless there is an agreement to the contrary, a partner may not engage in any other enterprise if it competes with the partnership, or if it prevents him from performing his partnership duties. He may, however, engage in personal activities that result in advantage or profit, as long as the business or the time of the firm is not involved. Thus, a partner in a retail store may spend a reasonable amount of time buying and selling stocks on the organized markets for his personal account, or managing an apartment house he owns as an investment.

(4) TO KEEP ACCURATE RECORDS

A partner may not borrow firm money without the consent of his partners. He has a duty to keep an accurate record of all transactions that he performs for the firm, and to turn over to the firm all moneys and properties belonging to it. He must reveal to the other partners all material facts concerning the operation of the business which come to his attention.

WHAT ARE THE RIGHTS OF A PARTNER?

Problem: While serving as enlisted men in the Navy, Curry and Chan planned a deluxe restaurant which they would open after their discharge. Chan would do all the food and liquor buying and supervise the kitchen; Curry would do everything else. Curry would provide the required capital of $75,000, on which the firm would pay interest. All profits would be shared equally. Would this be a valid partnership?

In general, if the partners agree among themselves regarding their rights, the contract will govern. In the absence of agreement, however, their rights are governed by law. The principal rights are:

(1) RIGHT TO PARTICIPATE IN MANAGEMENT

Each partner has the right to see the account books and to have an equal voice and vote in management of the business. One partner has no more authority than another, even if he has contributed all the capital and does more productive work. In case of disagreement on ordinary management questions, the will of the majority prevails; however, if the matter may involve a fundamental change in the original agreement, the vote must be unanimous. When there is a deadlock among an even number of partners, voluntary or court-ordered dissolution may follow.

The ordinary rule as to sharing management may be changed by agreement. Consequently, each partner may be delegated to operate certain parts of the business, as agreed by Curry and Chan in the problem.

(2) RIGHT TO PROFITS

Problem: Forbush and Upson were partners in a business in which Forbush contributed the capital totaling $100,000, and Upson contributed his skill and time. They agreed to share the profits and losses equally. The business failed and after all assets were sold and used to pay creditors, unpaid debts still totalled $50,000. What is the dollar loss for each partner?

Unless the agreement makes other provisions, both profits and losses are divided equally. Thus, Forbush and Upson must share the loss, $75,000 for each.

$100,000 Capital invested (by Forbush)
  50,000 Unpaid debts
$150,000 Total losses ÷ 2 partners = $75,000
     loss for each.

Of course, if Upson has no assets, Forbush will sustain the full loss.

(3) RIGHT IN PARTNERSHIP PROPERTY

Problem: Amesbury, Findley, and Rice were partners in a floor refinishing service. Unknown to his associates, Rice would mount his own camper cabin on the back of one of the company pick-up trucks every weekend and drive into the country with it on overnight fishing trips. Did he have a legal right to do this?

Partnership property consists of all property originally contributed by the partners, as well as all property acquired for the firm or with its funds. It is held in a special form of co-ownership called *tenancy in partnership*. Each partner is a co-owner of the entire partnership property and not the sole owner of any part of it. For example, if a firm of two partners owns two identical trucks, each partner has a one-half interest in both trucks; one partner may not claim one of the vehicles as his own. Because a partner has no exclusive interest in any firm property, he alone cannot sell or assign his interest in any item belonging to the business. He may, however, sell his entire interest in the firm to another party. Such a person becomes an assignee, not a partner.

Each partner has an equal right to use firm property for partnership purposes, but one partner may not use the property for himself unless the others consent. Accordingly, in the problem Rice was violating the partnership agreement. He had no right to use the company truck for personal pleasure trips without the consent of his partners.

(4) RIGHT TO EXTRA COMPENSATION

Problem: Forth and Bassett became partners in a restaurant supply business. Forth was more energetic than his partner and often worked ten-hour days as well as on week-ends. His efforts paid off and the business prospered. Is he entitled to extra compensation for his extra work?

Even though he supplies more capital, or provides extra services, or is a more productive worker, one partner is not entitled to extra compensation unless all partners so agree. Thus, Forth gets nothing extra for his effort except his regular share of the enhanced profits. Common sense and fairness often dictate that a partner who gives more should receive more—a larger percentage of the profits, rental for use of his land, interest for a loan, or a salary for extra labor.

WHAT AUTHORITY DOES A PARTNER HAVE?

Problem: "The Igloo" was a winter sports retail store featuring ski clothing and equipment. Harnish, one of the three partners, did all the buying. To achieve seasonal balance, but without consulting his partners, Harnish contracted to buy a large quantity of summer camping equipment. When they learned of his act, his partners objected and now refuse to pay for the goods. Are they liable to the seller?

Each partner acts as an agent for the firm and for the other members of the partnership. The law usually implies to each member those powers necessary for the carrying on of business. These include the powers:

(1) TO MAKE BINDING CONTRACTS FOR THE FIRM

Partners may make binding contracts regardless of the folly of the transaction, provided it is within the scope of the business. In the problem, Harnish's partners are not liable. Both Harnish and the seller should have realized that addition of summer camping gear would constitute a fundamental change in operation of the winter sports shop. The contract was beyond the scope of the business as agreed.

(2) TO RECEIVE MONEY OWED TO THE FIRM AND TO PAY OUT MONEY OWED BY IT

All partners are bound by payments received even if a receiving partner wrongfully pockets the money for himself. Each partner may also adjust debts of the firm, and compromise claims the firm has against others.

(3) TO BORROW MONEY IN THE FIRM NAME

A partner may borrow for partnership purposes, give promissory notes, and mortgage or pledge personal property of the firm, when the firm is engaged in commercial trading.

(4) TO SELL

A partner may sell in the regular course of business any of the goods of the business, and give warranties on the goods sold.

(5) TO BUY

Any kind of goods may be purchased by a partner within the scope of the business for cash or credit.

(6) TO DRAW CHECKS

A partner may draw checks for company purposes, and indorse and cash checks payable to the firm.

(7) TO HIRE EMPLOYEES AND APPOINT AGENTS

Partners have the authority to hire and fire employees and agents in carrying on the business.

(8) TO RECEIVE NOTICE OF MATTERS AFFECTING THE PARTNERSHIP

A partner may bind all partners by declarations and admissions even if they are contrary to the best interests of the partnership.

The eight foregoing powers are implied by law, but may be limited by agreement of the partners. If there is an internal agreement to limit powers of certain partners, it is binding on the partners themselves but not upon third parties who are not aware of the limitations. A partner who acts in violation of such an agreement is liable to his associates for any resulting loss. Of course, no partner may bind the firm in contracts which are beyond the scope of the firm's business. Partners engaged in an aerial photography business, for example, are not bound by a contract of one of their number to use the plane for air ambulance service. Likewise, a partner may not discharge his personal debt by agreeing to offset it against one due the firm.

 Williamson, a partner in a firm which builds residences for sale, owed Steinberg $35,000 for a personal debt. Steinberg was willing to accept a home constructed by Williamson's firm to offset this debt. Unless the other partners agreed, Williamson could not legally do this.

As in the case of ordinary agency, the other partners may ratify the action of a partner who has exceeded his authority. The partnership may thus become bound. (Page 456)

WHAT ARE A PARTNER'S LIABILITIES?

Problem: Shapiro and Barron were in the business of selling antiques. They had secretly agreed that Barron would do all the buying because he was a better judge of value. Nevertheless, Shapiro one day had what seemed a once-in-a-lifetime chance to buy a genuine Louis XIV dining set "for a song." He agreed. Is the firm bound?

Among themselves, partners may make any agreement they choose with regard to performance of duties and sharing of liabilities and losses. Third persons, however, may not be aware of such internal agreements. If so, all partners are liable without limit for all obligations of the firm which arise out of contracts made by any partner within the scope of the firm's business. Thus, in the problem, the firm and both partners are bound. If a loss results, Barron could seek recovery because Shapiro had violated their agreement.

A partnership is liable for fraud, negligence, and other torts committed by any partner while engaged in partnership business. As with any employer (Page 415), the partnership is also liable for torts committed by employees while engaged in company business.

When a judgment is obtained against a partnership, the individual property of the members may be seized and sold under process of law for the satisfaction of the debt. The creditors of the individual partners, however, have first claim to such property. If one member is compelled to pay an obligation of the firm, he is entitled to recover a proportionate share from each of the other partners.

A partner cannot escape his responsibility for firm debts by withdrawing. If he does withdraw, he remains liable for all debts incurred while he was a member. A new partner who joins the firm is liable for both old and new debts of the business. However, creditors with claims which arose before he joined the firm cannot seize his individual property; they are limited to his share of partnership property.

HOW IS A PARTNERSHIP ENDED?

Problem: Beatty, Beban, and Ballou were partners in a law firm. They had agreed to stay together for five years, and to decide at the end of that time whether to continue. A heavy debt was incurred to buy furniture and a reference library. Although a good number of clients consulted and retained them, the partners were not paid immediately because most cases did not come to trial until more than a year had elapsed. Beatty became impatient after two years of the relationship and withdrew to enter business with his father. Is he liable in damages to his partners?

Dissolution of the firm occurs when any partner ceases to be associated in the carrying on of the business. The remaining partner(s) then engages in *winding up* or settling and completing all outstanding unfinished business of the firm. *Termination* occurs when the winding up process is completed and the legal existence of the firm is ended.

Partnerships may be ended by (a) action of one or more of the partners, or (b) automatically by operation of law, or (c) by decree of a court upon proper petition.

(1) ACTION OF THE PARTNERS

A partnership may end by agreement of the parties. For example, if the original agreement is for one year, the partnership concludes at the end of that year. Sometimes a firm is organized for a specific purpose, such as the disposal of all the lots in a large subdivision. Sale of the last lot would then end the partnership. Also, as in any contract, the parties may unanimously agree at any time to terminate their relationship.

Withdrawal of any partner dissolves the partnership. If the agreement permits such withdrawal, possibly after some reasonable notice, the withdrawing partner would not be liable to those who remain. If he withdraws in violation of the agreement, however, he is liable. In the problem, Beatty breached his contract and would be liable. Even if it is a *partnership at will* in which a partner may withdraw at any time, he could be liable if his sudden withdrawal did irreparable damage to the firm.

(2) OPERATION OF LAW

Death of any partner dissolves the partnership. This is a serious disadvantage of the partnership form of organization. Wise partners will anticipate this inevitable event and agree upon steps to take when it happens. Perhaps they agree to continue with a new firm which buys out the decedent's share over a period of years. Bankruptcy, a kind of financial death, if suffered by any partner or by the firm also automatically dissolves the partnership.

(3) DECREE OF COURT

The partners can usually arrange for dissolution privately and amicably. In some cases, however, appeal to a court becomes necessary. The judge may order dissolution if one partner has become insane, or is otherwise incapacitated, or is guilty of serious misconduct affecting the business. Also, if continuation is impracticable or if the firm is continuously losing money and there is little or no prospect of success, a court may end the firm's existence.

Dissolution involves a change in the relation of the partners, but it does not terminate the partnership until all affairs are taken care of. When the business is dissolved, the partners retain authority to perform acts necessary to wind up affairs and to complete transactions already started. This could require many months.

Notice should be given to third parties when dissolution arises from the act of a partner or an agreement, and does not involve public proceedings. When notice is required, actual notice must be given to existing creditors and customers, and notice by publication in an appropriate journal must be given to other persons. Failure to give proper notice renders all members of the firm liable for the subsequent acts of a partner committed within the scope of the business, in spite of the fact that there has been a dissolution.

A court may end a firm's existence if there is little or no prospect of success.

Upon the dissolution of a partnership, business creditors have the first right to the assets of the firm. After the obligations of the partnership to creditors have been paid, the remaining assets are distributed to members of the partnership according to their interests.

A BUSINESS OF YOUR OWN? . . .

1. If you want to start a business of your own with minimal difficulty, consider the individual proprietorship form of organization. However, you should have adequate capital, understand business management, be a good salesman, be blessed with physical health and abundant energy, and possess a positive, optimistic outlook.
2. A partnership may result in the sharing of burdens and an increase in the benefits of ownership, but the partners should be compatible, competent, honest, and financially responsible. Select your partners carefully.
3. Even when not required by law, it is best to reduce the partnership agreement to writing in order to anticipate and resolve potential difficulties and disagreements between the partners before they arise.
4. Consider being a limited partner should you wish to be free of the burdens of management or the risk of unlimited liability while sharing in the profits of the business.
5. If you expect to contribute more than the other partners in capital or labor, provide for extra compensation in the partnership agreement. Otherwise, all partners will share equally in the profits (and losses) of the firm.
6. Be sure that the partners and the firm carry adequate public liability and casualty insurance.

YOUR LEGAL VOCABULARY

dissolution
general partner
individual proprietorship
limited partner
partner
partnership
partnership agreement
  (or articles of partnership)

partnership at will
secret partner
silent partner
tenancy in partnership
termination
winding up

1. Partner active in operation of the business and known to the public.
2. A partner who takes no active part in the management of the business but is known to the public.
3. A partner who takes an active part in the management of the business but is not known to the public.
4. A business which is owned and controlled by one person.
5. An association of two or more persons to conduct as co-owners a business for profit.
6. A person associated in a partnership business.
7. A partner whose liability is limited to the amount of his investment.
8. The ownership relation existing between partners.
9. Settling of all unfinished business after dissolution.
10. A type of partnership in which a partner may withdraw at any time.

REMEMBER THESE HIGHLIGHTS

1. Individual proprietorships are the simplest and most numerous form of business organization. The owner makes all decisions, keeps all the profits, and is liable without limit for all losses.
2. A partnership is an association of two or more persons to carry on as co-owners a business for profit. Profits and losses are shared equally unless otherwise agreed, but every partner is liable without limit to creditors for debts of the business.
3. Unless otherwise agreed, all partners have a right to participate in management with equal authority.
4. In dealings with each other, partners are bound to act with the highest integrity and good faith. They must keep each other informed about the business, maintain accurate records, and take no secret profits.
5. Partners own firm property as tenants in partnership. Each may use the property for company business, but not for personal purposes without consent of the other partners.
6. Limited partnership is a special form in which one or more limited partners contribute capital but not services. The financial liability of a limited partner is only the amount of his investment.
7. Partnerships may be terminated by (a) action of the partners, (b) operation of law, or (c) decree of court.

LAW AS PEOPLE LIVE IT

1. Dowd is a student whose father owns and operates the local pharmacy. He says he does not want to follow in his dad's footsteps, and adds: "An individual proprietor is the sole owner of his business, but it really owns him." What does he mean by these words?

2. Jane Cogdill and her sister, June, became business partners and opened a beauty salon. An employee using the wrong dye in the wrong way destroyed most of a customer's hair. Are the partners liable?

3. Merlini and Boomer became partners in a bakery. To avoid the hazard of unlimited liability, they bought a large policy of public liability insurance. Does this eliminate the risk for them?

4. To offer private security patrol service, Grigg and Maxey organized a partnership. Grigg hired Cotler as a guard. Three days later Maxey fired him. Grigg said he planned to rehire Cotler. Maxey said he'd fire him again. If neither partner yields, what happens to the firm?

5. Fordyce, DeSola, and Waldrop became partners to operate an employment agency. In their oral agreement they said nothing about the duration or life of the firm. After a year, however, Waldrop insisted on putting their oral agreement in writing because he believed they were violating the Statute of Frauds. Was he correct?

6. Finch and Solomon were partners in an advertising agency which specialized in public relations. After the first few months, Finch began spending four or five full afternoons every week playing golf at a local country club, usually with the same friends. He claimed to be "practicing what we preach," but income of the firm declined sharply. Solomon thought he was neglecting his work at the office. Was his complaint valid?

7. After undergoing surgery by Doctors Perera and Sleeman, partners, Brickett received their bill for $600. He thought the charge was exorbitant. Perera, without consulting Sleeman, reduced it to $500, which Brickett paid. Was Sleeman bound by Perera's compromise?

8. Cardin and Caron bought 1,600 acres of farmland. They took title as tenants in common and openly expressed the hope to sell the property at a substantial profit in the future. Were they partners?

9. When he entered into a partnership with Lawrie, age 22, Alpert was just 19 years old. Their agreement to operate a dog training (obedience) school was for three years, renewable. After one year, Alpert decided to withdraw and go back to school himself. Was he liable for breach of contract?

10. Fife and Tremaine organized their partnership to operate the exclusive agency franchise for sales and service of a popular imported car in Houston. After several prosperous years, they sold the franchise and all their facilities to a third party. Fife claimed he could take his share of the proceeds and retire. Tremaine said he could not because their

written partnership agreement had five years still to go. Which partner is correct?

LAW AS COURTS DECIDE IT

1. Roberts and Hunt were partners in the practice of law. A client, Powell, turned over to them for collection a promissory note. The partners obtained a judgment and Hunt compromised the claim, collecting $75 in full settlement. However, he kept the money and left the state. Then the firm was dissolved. Is Roberts, the remaining partner, liable to Powell for the sum collected? (Powell v. Roberts, 116 Mo. App. 629, 92 S.W. 752)

2. Owen and Cohen entered into a partnership to run a bowling alley in Burbank. The business operated at a profit for some three months, but bitterness developed between the partners and receipts were declining when Owen sought a court decree for dissolution. He complained that Cohen refused to do any manual work on the premises; humiliated him before customers and employees; wanted to open a gambling room on the second floor; demanded more than the agreed salary of $50 weekly and appropriated additional sums when Owen refused. Should the court decree dissolution? (Owen v. Cohen, 19 Cal. 2d 47, 119 P. 2d 713)

3. Holmes and Darling, partners, operated a sales agency to sell White Rock mineral water. Darling, unknown to Holmes, took orders for other beverages both at the office and while on the road selling White Rock mineral water. When Holmes learned what Darling had been doing, he brought an action for an accounting to the partnership for the commissions on the beverages. Must Darling account to his partner for the commissions? (Holmes v. Darling, 213 Mass. 303, 100 N.E. 611)

4. Sheldon conducted an insurance business. For several years Little managed the business, kept the books, and handled the finances. For his services as manager, Little received one-half of the profits after all expenses had been paid. Did Little's receipt of a portion of the profits prove that he was a partner of Sheldon? (Sheldon v. Little, 111 Vt. 301, 15 A. 2d 574)

5. Carroll and Cross were partners doing business under the firm name of Perishable Air Conditioners. Cotton, an employee of the firm, was severely injured during the course of his employment. Within two months and before Cotton had brought an action, the partnership was dissolved. Although the partnership had been dissolved, Cotton brought an action against the firm and had a summons served on Cross only. Cotton insisted that the dissolution of the partnership did not terminate all of the authority of a partner to act for the other members of the firm. Do you agree? (Cotton v. Perishable Air Conditioners, 18 Cal. 2d 575, 166 P. 2d 603)

44 Corporations

1. *You and several friends, all minors, decide to organize a corporation. May you do so?*

2. *Your father is one of the directors of a large local corporation. It has a very poor year and suffers a substantial loss. Is your father liable along with his fellow directors for the loss to the shareholders?*

3. *Your parents own $10,000 worth of stock in General Motors Corporation. May they visit a GM factory and take in exchange for their stock any new car costing no more than that sum?*

WHAT IS A CORPORATION?

Problem: Dr. Ronald Veeder, a prosperous surgeon, was willing to go into a promising electronic manufacturing business with Hibbott, an engineer. However, the doctor could not devote any time to the business, and he said he didn't want to "sign any blank check" for unlimited liability if the business should fail. What form of business organization would be appropriate?

Most business in this country is carried on by corporations. A *corporation* is an artificial legal being which is granted certain powers. As defined by the Supreme Court of the United States, it is also "an association of individuals united for some common purpose, and permitted by law to use a common name, and to change its members without the dissolution of the association." A corporation is created only by government charter or grant.

There are good reasons for the popularity of the corporate form of business organization.

(1) PERPETUAL LIFE

Since the corporation is a *legal entity,* separate and distinct from its owners and managers, it can outlast them and go on indefinitely.

(2) LIMITED LIABILITY

Creditors normally cannot collect claims from individuals who own shares in the corporation. Thus, although the corporation is liable without limit for its debts, the individual owners stand to lose only the amount they have invested. It is this feature which makes the corporation an appropriate form of business organization for Dr. Veeder and Hibbott, in the problem.

(3) TRANSFERABLE SHARES

An individual shareholder can sell his share in the corporation without getting the consent of other shareholders and without disturbing the company's operation. The new shareholder acquires all the rights which the old shareholder possessed.

(4) ACCESS TO CAPITAL

Because their liability is limited to their investment, many persons—like Dr. Veeder in the problem—are willing to buy shares in corporations. Great sums of money can thus be raised to create giant corporations which engage in large scale mass production and distribution of goods.

(5) PROFESSIONAL MANAGEMENT

Because of its greater financial strength, a corporation is usually able to obtain better professional management than individual proprietorships or partnerships. In the problem, this aspect of the corporate form would also appeal to Dr. Veeder.

HOW ARE CORPORATIONS CLASSIFIED?

Problem: Mayor Bowditch and his council wish to create in their city a permanent non-profit organization to conduct an annual parade and sports event similar to the New Year's Day Tournament of Roses Parade and football game held in Pasadena, California. Can this be accomplished with a corporation?

Corporations are commonly classified as public and private. Public corporations are established by the state for governmental purposes. Incorporated cities, state hospitals, state universities, and colleges are common examples of public corporations. A public corporation would probably serve the needs of the mayor and his council in the problem.

Private corporations are of two types: (1) those which do not distribute profits and are created for social, charitable, or educational purposes—churches, colleges, athletic clubs, fraternal societies, and similar institutions; and (2) those created for the financial profit of their members—businesses of all kinds, such as banks, manu-facturing and merchandising companies, and airlines. In this chapter, we will focus primarily on the private profit-seeking corporation.

HOW IS A CORPORATION ORGANIZED?

Problem: Pruitt scientifically analyzed the job of yard and garden maintenance. Then he devised a plan to do the work efficiently and cheaply using a variety of motorized mechani-cal aids. He convinced Grieg and others to join him in organizing a corporation to offer their service to home-owners. Can they create the corporation by agreement among themselves?

Corporations must be formed under authority of government; un-like partnerships, they cannot be created by simple agreement of participants. Thus, Pruitt and the others could not organize a corporation simply by making an agreement among themselves. They must have state authorization to do so.

Laws of most states require that there be a minimum number of legally competent adult incorporators, generally at least three.[1] Only a minority of the states require that the incorporators be shareholders.

Application for incorporation must be made to the state govern-ment. This is done by preparing and filing *articles of incorporation* which set forth:

(1) The name of the proposed corporation;
(2) The period of duration, which may be perpetual;
(3) The purpose or purposes for which the corporation is or-ganized;
(4) The amount of the capital stock which is to be issued and the number and value of the shares into which it is to be divided;
(5) The location of its initial principal office;
(6) The number of directors or the names and addresses of the persons who are to serve as directors until the first annual meeting of shareholders or until their successors are elected;
(7) The name and address of each incorporator; and
(8) Any other provisions, not inconsistent with law, which may be desired, such as a description of special types of stock which may be issued.

[1] Iowa, Kentucky, Michigan, New York, and Wisconsin permit one or more to incorporate; Mississippi, Nebraska, and South Carolina require only two; Utah requires not less than five; Arizona specifies "any number of persons."

When the application is filed, fees paid, and other conditions met, a *certificate of incorporation* (or charter) is issued by the proper state official, usually the Secretary of State. Corporate existence normally begins at the time the certificate is issued, but it may be postponed until a first organizational meeting is held.

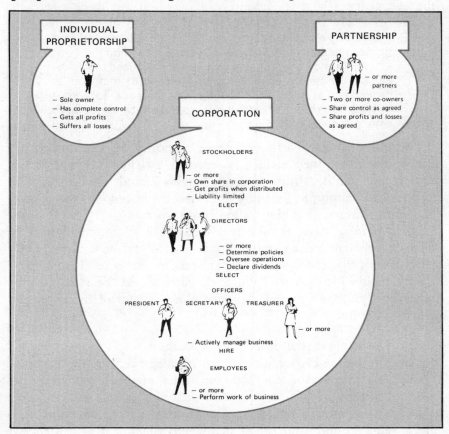

WHAT ARE SHARES OF STOCK?

Problem: "A" is an incorporator of the newly formed Cannonball Trucking Corporation. "B" is a director. "C" is the president. "D" is a shareholder who owns most of the stock. If the corporation buys a truck, who owns it?

Corporations issue small units of ownership known as *shares of stock*. When a person buys one or more shares of stock he becomes a *shareholder* (or stockholder).

A shareholder is issued a *stock certificate* which is evidence of his ownership and rights in the business. Note, however, that stock ownership does not transfer ownership of specific corporate property to the holder. The corporation, as a legal person, remains owner of all corporate property, as in the problem where the Cannonball Corporation owns the truck.

Stock may have a *par value,* which is the face value printed on the certificate. If it does not have a par value, it is *no-par stock,* and is originally sold at a price set by the board of directors of the corporation. When the stock changes hands in later transfers, the price may be much higher or lower. This *market price* will be determined by many factors, including how profitable the corporation has been and promises to be in the future.

Every business corporation has *common stock.* If common stock is the only type issued, its owners have all the votes which control the corporation (one vote for one share), and they receive all the profits declared by the board of directors to be available to shareholders, called *dividends.* In some companies, the common stock is divided into voting and nonvoting shares.

Some corporations issue an additional special class of stock called *preferred stock.* There may be no voting power associated with this kind of stock. However, investors who want greater assurance of earnings are attracted to preferred stock because the holder enjoys priority over common shareholders with respect to dividends. For example, by contract with the corporation, the preferred stockholder may be entitled to receive $10 per share each year before any distribution of profits is made to the common shareholders. Preferred stock may also be *cumulative.* This means that if the $10 is not paid some year, the holder has the right to cumulate or add up all unpaid dividends and to be paid the full cumulated amount before the common stockholders are entitled to receive any dividends. In some cases the preferred stock is also *participating.* For example, in a given year, the fully participating preferred shareholder will receive $10 and the common shareholder will receive an amount equal to that received by preferred. Beyond that, any balance is divided equally between the preferred and the common shareholders.

Upon termination of the business and after all debts are paid, the preferred may receive their investments from assets remaining before the common shareholders get anything.

HOW IS CORPORATE BUSINESS CONDUCTED?

Problem: Sato was a major shareholder, but not an employee or agent, of the Oriental Food Products Company,

Incorporated. He contracted on behalf of the company to
sell a quantity of rice on favorable terms. The corporation
refused to fulfill the contract, claiming that Sato had no
authority to represent the firm. Did Sato have such authority
as a shareholder?

Although a corporation is a person in the eyes of the law, it must
act through human agents elected by the shareholders, appointed by
the directors, or hired by the officers. No shareholder, even if he
owns all the stock, may act for the corporation or bind it by contract merely because he owns stock. In the problem, Sato had no
authority to represent the corporation.

Shareholders control the affairs of a corporation indirectly by
electing the directors. They also have the power to vote on major
issues such as changing the corporation charter. The directors over-
see the corporation and formulate general policies. They delegate to
officers the necessary authority to conduct the day-to-day affairs of
the company. The officers hire other employees, and with their
assistance get the necessary work done.

WHAT ARE THE POWERS AND DUTIES OF DIRECTORS?

Problem: Lumm was a member of the board of directors of
the Muskegon Pump Co., Inc. He expected to be in Europe
at the time of the next regular annual meeting of the board.
Could he arrange to have another member vote for him?

The *board of directors* is the top governing body of the corporation. Most states require that there be at least three directors, but the
actual number and their qualifications will vary, depending both on
local statutes and on the charter and bylaws of the particular
corporation. Statutes sometimes require that directors be shareholders. A few states require that directors be legal adults.[2] Some
say the president of the company must also serve as a director, and
in many corporations all the directors are also officers. In the absence
of provisions to the contrary, anyone may become a director.

Generally the board of directors may enter into any contract to
promote the business for which the corporation was formed. While
its powers are very broad, they may be limited by statute, charter, or
bylaws. The collective and personal judgments of the directors are
deemed necessary in making corporate decisions; thus, a member is
generally not allowed to vote by *proxy*. That is, he may not have

[2] Arkansas, Florida, Georgia, Nevada, New York, Pennsylvania, Tennessee.
Oklahoma requires that directors be legally competent to enter into contracts.

another take his place and vote for him even if he gives the other instructions. In the problem, Lumm could not have another member or other person represent and vote for him at the board meeting.

Directors are liable to the corporation only for losses caused by their intentional or negligent mismanagement; they do not guarantee financial success of the firm. They are expected, of course, to act with due diligence and a reasonable degree of care. They must always seek to advance the best interests of the corporation, and are required to act with a high degree of honesty and good faith.

WHAT ARE THE POWERS AND DUTIES OF OFFICERS?

Problem: Because of his extensive knowledge of pop and rock music and his "feel" for youthful preferences in artists and songs, Dewey was selected by the board of directors of Station KOMS, a corporation, to serve as president and program director. Several stockholders objected and sought a court order for his dismissal because he was only 20 years old. Was Dewey legally qualified to serve as president?

Corporation laws generally provide that the firm must have at least three officers—a president, a secretary, and a treasurer—but it may have as many other officers as the bylaws permit. Officers are usually appointed by the board of directors although they may also be elected by the shareholders. Generally there are no restrictions on the selection of officers; they do not necessarily have to be shareholders or directors, have certain qualifications, or be of a minimum age. Accordingly, Dewey, in the problem, was legally qualified to serve as president.

Since the officers of a corporation are its agents, they are generally governed by principles of agency. Limitations may be imposed by charter and bylaws and by the board of directors. Like the directors, officers are not liable for honest errors of judgment which cause loss to the corporation, but may be held accountable for willful or negligent acts.

WHAT ARE THE POWERS OF A CORPORATION?

Problem: McCurry organized a corporation in which he owned all the stock. His wife and young son were directors with him, and they served as treasurer and secretary, respectively, under his direction as president. If the father should die, would the business survive indefinitely because it was a corporation?

A corporation generally may be formed for any lawful business purpose. Certain powers, described below, are recognized by law as being inherent to corporate existence.

(1) PERPETUAL SUCCESSION

In most jurisdictions, the corporation is the only form of business organization which may be granted the right to perpetual succession. *Perpetual succession* means that, regardless of changes in its membership, the corporation is to exist continuously during the period for which its charter was granted. Although there is a trend to remove any limitation on the life of a corporation, some states still set a maximum number of years. During this time, the death or withdrawal of a member by transfer of his shares has no effect, as such, on the corporations's continued existence. Thus, the death of McCurry in the problem would not legally affect the corporation's existence. Practically, of course, the business may end when its owners decide to end it, or when it fails. This could happen when a key officer leaves, as in the problem, should McCurry die.

(2) CORPORATE NAME

To function as a business unit and to engage in various activities, a corporation must have a name. It may enter into contracts, sue, and be sued in this name.

(3) CORPORATE SEAL

The power to have a seal is inherent in corporate existence, but is insignificant because of the declining importance of seals in the law and business practice.

(4) BYLAWS

A corporation has the power to make its own reasonable internal rules and regulations for the management of its affairs. These rules are called *bylaws*. Bylaws must be consistent with external law, such as state statutes, as well as with the corporation's charter. Those which conflict with such authority are invalid.

Other powers are expressly stated in the corporation's charter, and still others are implied as necessary to carry out the expressly granted powers. Among the implied powers are the rights to:

    (a) Acquire and hold property;
    (b) Borrow and loan money;
    (c) Make, indorse, and accept negotiable commercial paper;

(d) Issue various types of bonds;

(e) Mortgage, pledge, lease, or sell its property;

(f) Buy its own stock, unless, for example, such an act would make it impossible for the corporation to pay its debts or to pay off any superior class of stock;

(g) Acquire and hold stock in other corporations if not in violation of anti-trust laws;

(h) Make reasonable donations or gifts for civic or charitable purposes.

WHAT ARE THE RIGHTS OF SHAREHOLDERS?

Problem: Becket owns 400 shares of stock in a corporation that has 1,000 voting shares. Stukey and Schwingle, who together own the remaining 600 shares, decide to keep Becket from becoming or naming one of the three directors. Can they do so?

Although his status does not give him the right to possess any corporate property or to participate directly in management, the shareholder does enjoy certain important rights and privileges:

(1) THE RIGHT TO EVIDENCE OF OWNERSHIP

A shareholder has the right to have issued to him a properly executed stock certificate as evidence of his ownership of shares in the business. This certificate can normally be transferred by sale or gift to someone else without the consent of other shareholders. In some closely-held corporations, where the owners may want to be able to choose their associates, it may be provided that shares must first be offered to the corporation or to the other stockholders.

(2) THE RIGHT TO ATTEND SHAREHOLDER MEETINGS AND TO VOTE

A shareholder is ordinarily entitled to attend shareholder meetings and to vote. Regular meetings are usually held annually at the place and time designated in the charter or bylaws, and notice of them is usually not required.

A shareholder is usually entitled to as many votes as the number of voting shares of stock he holds. Many states provide for *cumulative voting* in the election of directors. Under this plan, each shareholder has the right to cast as many votes in total as the number of shares of stock he holds multiplied by the number of directors to be elected. The shareholder may cast all his votes for one candidate, or distribute them among two or more candidates. Thus, in the problem, if three directors are to be elected by means of a cumulative voting plan, Becket may cast 1200 votes for one candidate (i.e. 400 shares X three positions). Stukey and Schwingle have a combined voting power of 1800 votes (i.e. 600 shares X three positions). They may elect two directors by dividing their votes and casting 900 for each. If cumulative voting is not in effect, Stukey and Schwingle could keep Becket off the board because he would have only a minority vote.

If a member does not wish to attend meetings and vote personally, he ordinarily has the right of voting by proxy. Most of the millions of Americans who individually own comparatively few shares of stock in various corporations cast their votes in this manner. The management mails them necessary forms which they sign and return, giving directors authority to use their votes on matters other than elections to office. Federal law requires that the proxy form give the shareholder an opportunity to specify by ballot his approval or rejection of particular proposals.

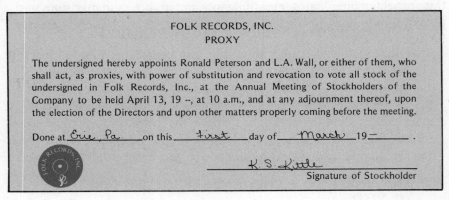

Proxy

(3) THE RIGHT TO INCREASE THE CAPITAL STOCK

Shareholders alone have the right to increase the capital stock of the corporation. When the capital stock is increased, each shareholder ordinarily has a right to purchase additional shares so that he will maintain the percentage of interest in the corporation he had before the increase. This is called the *preemptive right*. It enables him to protect his proportionate interest in past and future profits, as well as his voting power.

(4) THE RIGHT TO A SHARE OF THE PROFITS

Each shareholder is entitled to a proportionate share of the profits which are distributed on his class of stock. Dividends are usually paid in money, but they may be in the form of shares of stock or other property. Even when profits are earned, the board of directors in its sole discretion may decide to retain them for future needs of the company. Very rarely, courts will intervene at the request of stockholders and compel the distribution of dividends when there is an unreasonably large surplus of retained earnings.

(5) THE RIGHT TO SHARE IN REMAINING ASSETS

When a corporation is dissolved, a shareholder is entitled to share pro rata in any assets that remain after all debts have been paid. As noted earlier, if preferred stock has been issued, its holders may have priority in this final distribution.

(6) THE RIGHT TO INSPECT RECORDS AND PROPERTY

A shareholder has the right to inspect, and make appropriate records of the books and the property of the corporation. However, this inspection may be denied unless made at a reasonable time and place. Some states also require that good faith and proper motive be demonstrated.

HOW IS THE CORPORATE EXISTENCE TERMINATED?

Problem: According to its certificate of incorporation, Carnival Row Corporation was created to operate amusement shows and devices at the New York World's Fair for the duration of the Fair. When the Fair ended, how was the corporate existence terminated?

A corporation may be ended by the following:

(1) BY AGREEMENT

A corporation terminates upon expiration of the agreed period of its existence. Thus, the Carnival Row Corporation, in the problem, was automatically dissolved when the Fair ended, as specified in its certificate of incorporation. It may terminate before that time if the members (usually those with a majority of the voting power) voluntarily surrender the charter with the consent of the state.

(2) BY FORFEITURE

The state may bring judicial proceedings for the forfeiture of the charter of a corporation that has been guilty of certain acts. Examples would be fraudulent application for a charter, flagrant misuse of corporate powers, or franchises which have injured the public. This seldom happens.

(3) BY CONSOLIDATION OR MERGER

Two corporations may *consolidate* with the approval of the boards of directors and a majority of the shareholders in each of the corporations involved. In such case, their separate existences cease and a new corporation is formed.

When two corporations *merge,* one corporation absorbs the other. The absorbing corporation continues to exist, maintaining its charter and identity; the other disappears. Again approval must be given by the directors and under certain circumstances by the stockholders of the merging corporations.

MAY A BUSINESS CHOOSE ANY NAME?

Problem: Klock and Perrel were partners who had been doing business for years as Klock and Perrel, Jewelers. When their sons graduated from college and joined the firm, it was decided to add two new stores and to incorporate. Could they still use their former business trade name for the corporation?

The name under which a business is conducted is useful as a matter of convenient identification and important as a matter of goodwill. An individual proprietorship may be known by the name of the owner, a partnership by the name of the partners. A corporation must select a name. It can include the names of real persons, and it is common for partnerships to retain their original name, as in the problem, when they incorporate. The word "Incorporated," or the abbreviation "Inc." is simply added to the former trade name.

Any business may use a fictitious name, for example "Imperial Jewelers." Most states require that when an individual or partnership operates under a fictitious name, it must be formally registered in a designated government office, along with the name or names and addresses of the proprietor or partners. This problem normally does not arise with corporations because of the routine filing of the certificate of incorporation which informs the public of the relevant facts.

There are some limitations on the adoption of a corporate name. One may not use a name which is the same or deceptively similar to one already in use or which may give a false impression. In some jurisdictions, a corporation may not use words such as these in its name: "guaranty," "investment," "state police," "marine corps," "government." Some states will not allow the use of the words "and Company" unless the term represents a partner or unless the business is incorporated.

CORPORATION—VALUABLE AID, BUT NOT A PANACEA . . .

1. The corporate form of organization offers important advantages and should be considered as a possibility for any new business. However, if the success of the business depends on the continued life, talents, and credit of one man, this form becomes unwise.
2. Incorporators who expect the organization to last indefinitely or "perpetually" should consider the corporate form of organization. It should also be considered for public corporations and private non-profit seeking organizations.
3. Since corporations must act through agents to do the work of the business, it is essential that competent personnel be selected.
4. The buyer of preferred stock who desires guaranteed dividends should seek shares with the cumulative feature.
5. Officers of the corporation should be selected with great care since they make most of the decisions and the directors tend to rely on their advice.
6. Although most stockholders routinely sign proxies which give corporate officers control, their voting rights should be exercised in an intelligent manner after studying the annual reports of the corporation.

YOUR LEGAL VOCABULARY

articles of incorporation	market price
board of directors	merge
bylaws	no-par stock
certificate of incorporation (or charter)	par value
	participating stock
common stock	perpetual succession
consolidate	preemptive right
corporation	preferred stock
cumulative stock	proxy
cumulative voting	shareholder (or stockholder)
dividend	share of stock
legal entity	stock certificate

1. A document filed with the state in an application for incorporation.
2. A person who owns one or more shares of stock.
3. An artificial legal person, created by law and having the right to continue in existence without regard to any change of its members.
4. When corporation A and corporation B become corporation C.
5. When corporation A absorbs and eliminates corporation B.

6. Stock which has priority with respect to dividends, and with respect to assets upon termination of the corporation.
7. The governing body of a corporation which determines policies, declares dividends, and hires officers.
8. Evidence of ownership and rights in a corporation.
9. Profits declared available for distribution to shareholders.
10. Authority to act for another; by a stockholder, written authorization designating another person to vote for him at a shareholders' meeting.

REMEMBER THESE HIGHLIGHTS

1. A corporation can only be created by government grant. The organization must be approved by the state which, after review of the articles of incorporation, issues a charter or certificate of incorporation.
2. Corporations are favored as a form of business organization because of advantages of perpetual life, limited liability, transferability of shares, access to capital, and professional management.
3. A shareholder normally has the right to (a) have issued to him a properly executed stock certificate, (b) attend shareholder meetings and to vote, (c) subscribe for increased capital stock in proportion to the shares he owns, (d) a proportionate share of the profits, when profits are distributed, (e) a pro rata share in the assets upon termination of the corporation, and (f) inspect the books and property of the corporation. Certain classes of shares may be non-voting, and some may have priority in the distribution of dividends and capital.
4. The directors ordinarily possess the power to enter into any contract necessary to promote the business for which the corporation was formed. They are liable only for willful or negligent acts which injure the corporation, but must act with a high degree of good faith and in the best interests of the corporation.
5. Officers of a corporation, governed by the law of agency, are not liable for honest mistakes of judgment. Like the directors, they are held accountable for willful or negligent acts which injure the corporation.
6. The powers of a corporation are: (a) those incidental to the existence of a corporation, (b) those expressed in the charter, and (c) those implied to enable the corporation to exercise the express powers.
7. A corporation is terminated by agreement, forfeiture, or by consolidation or merger.

LAW AS PEOPLE LIVE IT

1. Martinson bought and paid in full for 300 shares of stock, par value $25, in the Egret Air Lines, Inc. Was he correct when he said that he couldn't lose more than $7,500 on this investment?

2. Blount organized a corporation to manufacture antibiotic medicines for cattle, and he owned most of the capital stock. All went well until a faulty batch of drugs caused the serious illness or death of more than 3,000 cows. After a series of lawsuits, the corporation was forced into bankruptcy with some $200,000 in debts unpaid. Could Blount be held personally liable for these debts?

3. The Columbia Condiments Company was a corporation which had been in business nationally for many years. Then some former employees filed incorporation papers for a new company called Columbian Condiments, Inc. Should their application be approved?

4. Garoni was a minority shareholder of the Neopolitano Pasta Company, Inc. He obtained a court order permitting him to inspect the company books of account, but the corporate secretary refused to let him make copies of any of the documents. May Garoni make copies of the records?

5. President Pincott of the Anchors-Aweigh Rope Company was having difficulties with his board of directors, and feared they planned to dismiss him after New Year's Day. To gain the favor of the stockholders, therefore, Pincott ordered the company treasurer to send out checks for a special Christmas bonus dividend. Was this legal?

6. Plunkett owned 60 percent of the voting stock of the ZYX Corporation. He was the promoter who conceived the idea of the company, was one of the 3 incorporators, one of the 5 directors, and was named secretary-treasurer of the company. He claimed he knew "what this business needs" and that he could make any contract for "his corporation." Was he entitled to make any contract for the company?

7. Because of poor business judgment by the president and vice-president in charge of sales, the Eureka Hydraulic Jack Company ended the year with a sizable deficit. Were these officers personally liable for the loss?

8. At the time of her death, Litz owned 1,000 shares of stock, valued at $500,000, in a corporation with assets consisting solely of apartment houses. She also owned a modest cottage which she occupied. In her will, she left all her real property to her nephew Arnold, and her personal property to others. Arnold claims the stock as well as the cottage. Is he entitled to both?

9. While driving a truck for the Paramount Piano Company, Inc., Dobson negligently collided with Rieger, who was seriously injured. Dobson owns 75 shares of stock in Paramount, acquired under an employee stock purchase plan. Rieger sued Paramount and Dobson for $300,000 damages. Dobson claims his liability is limited to the value of his shares of stock. Is he right?

10. In a discussion with friends, Wesler insists that a director of a corporation may not also serve as an officer because this would be "a conflict of interest." "Directors select officers," he argued, "and could keep themselves on the payroll as officers this way." Is Wesler right?

LAW AS COURTS DECIDE IT

1. According to the bylaws of the Biltmore Tissue Corporation, when a stockholder dies or desires to transfer his shares while alive, the corporation or the other stockholders shall have a first opportunity to purchase his stock. If this option is not exercised, after 90 days the holder may sell his shares to anyone. When Kaplan, a stockholder who owned 20 shares, died, the corporation's board of directors sought to buy his shares. His executor refused. Can he be compelled to sell? (Allen v. Biltmore Tissue Corp., 2 N.Y. 2d 534, 141 N.E. 2d 812)

2. General Telephone Company of Florida owned more than 1 percent of the stock of Florida Telephone Corporation, and sought to examine the latter's stock records in order to make a list of the names, addresses, and holdings of all shareholders. Florida refused, claiming General intended to gain this information in order to buy their shares and thus get control of the company. Can General get a court order to compel the disclosure? (Florida Telephone Corp. v. State ex rel. Peninsular Telephone Co., 111 So. 2d 677, Florida)

3. Dodge and another were owners of 10 percent of the shares of the Ford Motor Co. They sued the corporation and its board to compel the declaration of a dividend. The Ford Company was very prosperous at the time (1916), having a surplus of almost $112 million and cash and municipal bonds of nearly $54 million. However, Henry Ford wanted to retain the money for expansion, reducing the price of the car from $440 to $360 in order to increase sales from 500,000 to 1,000,000 annually. Can the board of directors be compelled to declare a dividend? (Dodge v. Ford Motor Co., 204 Mich. 459, 170 N.W. 660)

4. Coleman, age 17, became a messenger in a Cambridge bank. The following year he was promoted to bookkeeper. He kept the depositors' ledger and by altering the records he was able to steal a total of $310,143.02 before the bank was forced to close some six years later (in 1910). The president, Dresser, had ignored warnings and evidence of shortages over the years. For example, he had been told that Coleman, whose salary never exceeded $12 a week, had acquired an automobile and other "luxuries." Could the president be held liable for the losses? (Bates v. Dresser, 251 U.S. 524, 64 L.Ed. 388)

5. Mimnaugh purchased 100 shares of stock in the Atlantic City Electric Company, a corporation engaged in the production and sale of electricity. The processes used by Atlantic resulted in the accumulation of ash, which had to be removed at an expense to the corporation. Mimnaugh, as a shareholder, suggested a plan to reduce the expense of the ash removal and demanded pay for his plan. Does a shareholder have a right to manage the business of the corporation? (Mimnaugh v. Atlantic City Electric Company, 7 N.J. Supp. 310, 70 A. 2d 904)

CHAPTER 45 Government Regulation of Business

1. *A friend at work advises you to buy corporation stocks, but only in firms which are listed on the New York or other organized stock exchanges. "Uncle Sam regulates them, and so you can't lose your shirt." Is this true?*

2. *Your cousin claims the federal government is inconsistent because it encourages some monopolies and condemns others. Is he right?*

3. *Because you may have seen some advertisements which are false or misleading, does this mean the laws against them are useless?*

WHAT IS THE LEGAL BASIS FOR GOVERNMENT REGULATION OF BUSINESS?

Problem: In a "rap session," two students, Goral and Parr, were discussing government and business. Parr said, "If a businessman is honest and pays his taxes when due, he can forget all this talk about government meddling in business affairs!" Goral disagrees. Who is right?

Business means producing and distributing goods—from airplanes to zithers—and providing services—from accounting to zoo designing. All of us are involved as consumers; many of us as employees. The field of business is broad and varied. Since its impact on national well-being is so great, government is necessarily concerned with how business operates. As we shall see, Goral, in the problem, was more knowledgeable than Parr. There is a vast amount of government involvement in business affairs, financed, of course, by taxes, fees, assessments, and loans. We have already learned about special rules designed to protect consumers (Chapter 4), borrowers (Chapter 23), employees (Chapter 31), and insureds (Unit X). Here we view the entire field at the federal, state, and local levels to see how government specifically regulates business.

Each state may use its police power to make laws which regulate intrastate commerce, that is, business conducted wholly within that state. Local governments operate under the authority of the state.

Under the police power, statutes are valid if necessary or desirable for the health, safety, morals, or general welfare of the people. Under this power the government may even destroy private property without compensating the owners when such property is a nuisance or threat to the public good.

As we have learned, the federal government has only those powers delegated to it by the states under the U.S. Constitution. However, the U.S. Supreme Court has interpreted the Constitution in a liberal manner which has given the federal government very extensive power over interstate commerce—that is, business between or affecting persons in two or more states. Even laws which some may consider objectionable are binding on all so long as they are constitutional.

WHAT IS THE SCOPE OF GOVERNMENT INVOLVEMENT IN BUSINESS?

Problem: Morales recently graduated from a public business college. He had an old family recipe for barbecued chicken, and decided to use it in a fast-service food shop. With two classmates Morales formed a partnership and began the business. How did government affect his project?

The government does many things which we as individuals need or want but cannot do as readily. The U.S. Constitution authorizes the federal government to enact laws for the common good; state constitutions give state and local governments similar authority. Accordingly, government officials at the federal, state, and local levels may cooperate with, control, encourage, or suppress business practices as needed. Government interacts with business in countless ways, including the following:

(1) CULTIVATING HUMAN TALENTS

Government assists and supports public schools, colleges, libraries, and museums, enabling persons to become more productive workers and more perceptive consumers. In the problem, Morales and his partners were educated in public schools which are supported by local, state, and federal funds. A chef they later hired had been trained in an apprenticeship program conducted jointly by local vocational schools and unions.

(2) MAINTAINING FREE AND FAIR COMPETITION

Government promotes our competitive business system by: legislating uniform laws for formation of corporations and partnerships;

state and local licensing of new business firms; regulating new security issues and stock and commodity exchanges; restraining unfair trade practices and *monopolies* (i.e., where one firm or a small group has such control over the supply of goods as to be able to set the price. The *Sherman Antitrust Act* of 1890 and the *Clayton Act* of 1914 make it illegal to conspire or combine to restrain free, competitive trade, or even to do certain acts which tend to lead to monopoly); preventing false and misleading advertising; and by regulating rates and levels of service provided by water, electric, and gas utility companies. Morales and his friends utilized state partnership laws for their legal form of organization. They obtained a city license for the business, secured a state permit to collect and transmit sales taxes, and had the premises approved by the local fire department for fire hazards and adequacy of exits. The local health department inspected equipment for storage, weighing, refrigeration, and preparation of food, as well as facilities for dishwashing, ventilation, and rest rooms. They used the services of regulated public utilities. Even the neon sign in front had to comply with local regulations as to size, construction, and location. Their business is protected against monopolistic competition.

(3) ENCOURAGING TRAVEL AND TRANSPORT

The use of travel and transport facilities is encouraged by: subsidies or grants in aid; regulation of rates and services of airlines, trucks, buses, railroads, ships, pipe lines; construction and maintenance of highways, airports, harbors and canals; and by regular weather reports. Morales will get supplies by rail and truck, and he and his partners will use highways and airways themselves.

(4) PROMOTING COMMUNICATION

Communication between business and the public is promoted by licensing of television and radio and by a low cost postal service. Morales sent direct mail notices of his grand opening to people in his neighborhood and constantly uses the mail service. He may eventually advertise on radio or television.

(5) PROTECTING MENTAL AND PHYSICAL HEALTH

Government protects the mental and physical health of citizens by: enacting and enforcing pure food and drug laws; inspection of food manufacturing and retailing establishments; control over air, water, and noise pollution; sewage and waste disposal and treatment; establishment of standards for commodities; public clinics and hospitals;

Medicare and Medicaid; free lunch programs for poor school children; and slum clearance and urban redevelopment programs. Morales must maintain sanitation standards prescribed by state and local laws; he uses chickens, dairy products, and other foods inspected under state and federal laws for compliance with standards of quality; and he uses local government waste systems.

(6) STIMULATING RESEARCH AND DEVELOPMENT

Research and development are promoted by: grants for research to schools and companies; encouragement of creativity with patents, copyrights, and trademark registration; projects in government laboratories and on government experimental farms; application of atomic energy; and space travel and communication. Morales serves better quality chickens and other foods because of federal and state agricultural research. He will have legal protection for his distinctive trade name and store design.

(7) SHIELDING AND PRESERVING NATURAL RESOURCES

The preservation of natural resources is provided for by: reservation of vast areas for public parks, forests, and preserves; forest fire fighting, reforestation, and wildlife protection; control of oil and mineral production; and dam construction and flood control. When private land is flooded by dams, the government buys the title under its right of eminent domain. Reclamation of waste land permits additional production of food which middlemen, like Morales, and ultimate consumers buy.

(8) FINANCING NEW BUSINESS AND OLD

Government agencies provide for direct loans, indirect guarantees of private loans, and regulation of the supply of money and credit. Morales and his partners may have received a bank loan guaranteed by the federal government, or a direct loan from the *Small Business Administration,* a federal agency which advises and assists small business firms. Local governments also sometimes give business firms, especially manufacturing companies, free land or tax relief to induce them to locate in the community.

(9) PROMOTING HOUSING AND REGULATING LAND USE

The government is involved in housing and land use through: guarantees of home loans; rent subsidies for low income tenants and interest subsidies for low income home buyers; public housing projects for the poor and the aged; zoning laws and building codes; and rent controls (normally imposed in time of war and acute housing shortage, but sometimes continued in time of peace, as in New York City since World War II). Morales was able to open his shop only on a lot zoned for such commercial use, in a building erected according to prescribed standards with certain space for parking.

(10) SHIELDING THE WEAK AND AIDING THE NEEDY

Government provides for compensation to the unemployed and to workers injured on the job, as well as welfare grants and food stamps to the poor, the blind, the disabled, and the unemployed. Note that such laws benefit a minority at the expense of the majority. They are nevertheless legal because they advance the general welfare of society. If Morales discharges a worker who cannot find a new job, the employee would qualify for unemployment compensation; if injured on the job he would get workmen's compensation.

(11) GUARANTEEING THE RIGHTS OF LABOR

Workers are protected by: laws assuring their rights to organize into unions of their own choice and to bargain collectively with their employers; laws providing minimum wages, maximum hours, and proper conditions of employment; and by social security laws against hazards of income loss from disability, retirement, or death. Recall (Chapter 30) that federal labor laws give workers the right to strike against private employers. The U.S. Supreme Court has held this right has not been given to government employees, however. When Morales hires help they enjoy rights under federal and state laws, and Morales pays special taxes to help pay for social security. He withholds and pays added taxes for the employees' contributions to the plan. He must also post appropriate notices informing his employees of their rights under law.

(12) EXTENDING A HELPING HAND TO MINORITY GROUPS

Civil rights legislation outlaws discrimination because of race, color, sex, religion, national origin, or advanced age. Other laws provide for free legal assistance to the poor. Morales himself may have received special financial and counseling help because of his minority status. As an employer, he may not discriminate in his hiring and promoting practices on any of the forbidden grounds.

(13) ASSURING SAFETY AND SECURITY OF PERSON AND PROPERTY

American citizens are protected by: military forces against potential foreign enemies; police against domestic criminals; firemen against hazards of fire; an elaborate local system of official records of title to real property; federal bankruptcy laws to protect both creditors and debtors; and state probate laws which protect creditors yet assure distribution of assets to proper beneficiaries. Morales' shop is protected by the local police and fire departments. If his business should fail, his creditors would be protected to some extent under the bankruptcy law, and he would be given a fresh start free of most of his debts.

(14) AIDING FARMERS

Agriculture is promoted by: loans to farmers; output controls to prevent surpluses; price controls on milk and other products; research on crops, animals, fertilizers, insecticides, and land use; cooperative marketing plans; subsidized exports; standardization of fruits, vegetables, and grains; and control of injurious insects, plant diseases, weeds, and rodents. Indirectly Morales and his customers get better, cheaper food because of these legally-imposed controls and services.

(15) PROTECTING CONSUMERS

Consumers are protected with a variety of laws as discussed in Chapter 4, including state and local licenses for designated trades and professions. Morales would no doubt need a local license for his food shop and must comply with any applicable laws such as those controlling packaging of food.

(16) PROMOTING ECONOMIC DEVELOPMENT AND FULL EM-PLOYMENT

The economic development of the country is promoted through: tax revisions; monetary controls; price-wage-interest-profit controls in times of economic distress; encouragement of full employment; *tariffs* (i.e., taxes on imports; the Constitution forbids taxes on exports); *embargoes* (laws banning the export of certain goods to specified countries); other controls on our foreign trade; and heavy buying of the output of business (government collectively is the best customer of American industry). Morales' business should benefit from these activities, but it is also restricted by them.

HOW DOES GOVERNMENT REGULATION AFFECT THE ULTIMATE CONSUMER?

Problem: Several years after Allard graduated from a public high school, he bought his first car on time,

got married, moved to the capital city of the state. There
he bought a home for himself and his bride, paying ten
percent down. He became a real estate salesman, while
she found work as a beautician. How were the Allards
affected by government regulation?

The preceding topic indicated how businessman Morales and his
partners were involved with government regulation in many ways.
Reviewing the given list of government functions with yourself in
mind will enable you to identify many government regulations which
affect you directly as a consumer. Indirectly, as a citizen, you are
the intended ultimate beneficiary of all government action.

In the problem with the Allards we can quickly list a number of
government contacts. He and his wife attended local public school
under state compulsory attendance laws; he was licensed to drive
by the state, and his car was also registered; the automobile sales
contract was regulated by state and federal law; his marriage was
regulated by state law; and his house was built under a local *building
code* (which prescribes types of materials to be used, and construction standards). The home was in a neighborhood subject to a local
zoning law which limited use to single residential rather than multiple
residential (duplexes, apartments), commercial (retail stores and
offices), or industrial purposes (warehouses, factories). The home
loan was insured under a federal statute. Both he and his wife were
licensed under state law, after appropriate examinations, to work
as salesman and beautician respectively. In these and many other
ways, the law protects the person and controls his conduct as long
as he remains within the national boundaries. If he is a citizen, this
influence continues even when he travels abroad.

WHAT ARE INDEPENDENT ADMINISTRATIVE AGENCIES?

Problem: The telephone company in your state plans to
boost the rates for all calls. May its management make
the change by simply notifying all customers of the
new schedule of rates?

The impact of government on business is most evident to many
businessmen through the work of *independent administrative agencies*.
These are government bodies, consisting of commissions or boards,
which commonly combine the traditionally separated functions of
the legislative, executive, and judicial branches. They exist at the
local level in such agencies as city planning or zoning commissions,

or airport, park, and school boards. They are to be found at the state level in professional licensing boards and public utility commissions. But they are most prominent and powerful at the federal level, as noted below.

The independent administrative agency is created by the legislature which defines its powers and appropriates money for its support. Usually the chief executive officer (the President or governor) appoints the members and sometimes names the chairman of the board or commission, subject to confirmation by the appropriate legislative body. At the county and city levels, the legislative body (e.g., supervisors or council) frequently makes the appointments. The courts may review decisions of the agency for compliance with the law creating it. However, judges are reluctant to upset agency rulings because the agency members are experts in the technical fields they regulate.

The table below lists some of the major independent administrative agencies at the federal level and provides an idea of their wide range and important influence.

FEDERAL AGENCY	AREA OF ACTIVITY
Atomic Energy Commission (*A.E.C.*)	Atomic energy development, for peace and war.
Civil Aeronautics Board (*C.A.B.*)	Air transport.
Federal Communications Commission (*F.C.C.*)	Radio, television, telephone, and telegraph communications.
Federal Maritime Commission (*F.M.C.*)	Construction and operation of merchant ships on high seas.
Federal Power Commission (*F.P.C.*)	Oil, gas, and electricity production and distribution.
Federal Reserve Board (*F.R.B.*)	Money and credit supply.
Federal Trade Commission (*F.T.C.*)	Unfair competition, monopoly, and product misrepresentation.
Interstate Commerce Commission (*I.C.C.*)	Railroad, bus and truck, and inland waterway transportation.
National Aeronautics and Space Administration (*N.A.S.A.*)	Space exploration.
National Labor Relations Board (*N.L.R.B.*)	Labor-management relations.
Securities and Exchange Commission (*S.E.C.*)	Regulation of issuance of securities, and of securities exchanges where they are traded.

Administrative agencies extend their influence over much of the business world. Various agencies have the power to: set rates and determine service and safety standards for planes, trains, buses, taxis, trucks, ships, and pipe lines; establish rules of collective bargaining for relations between unions and employers; control our atomic energy research and space exploration; regulate our money supply; allocate television and radio channels; and decide whether large companies may merge and how they may advertise. In the problem, the telephone company would have to obtain permission from the public utility commission of the state before rates could be boosted.

Collectively there are more rulings and orders of independent administrative agencies today than published opinions of judges in court cases. The prospect is that independent administrative agencies will grow in importance as society becomes more complex.

A variety of administrative agencies function at the state and local levels. They supplement the work of regular government executive departments and relieve the courts and legislative bodies of much detailed work. Their duties and powers vary widely, but the table below suggests their scope.

STATE AGENCY	AREA OF ACTIVITY
Agricultural Price Stabilization Board	Sets food production quotas and prices.
Alcoholic Beverage Control Board	Grants licenses to sell liquor.
Workmen's Compensation Board	Awards damages for work-related injuries and deaths.
COUNTY AGENCY	**AREA OF ACTIVITY**
Airport Board	Acquires and operates county airports.
Parks and Recreation Board	Acquires and operates parks.
Air Pollution Control Board	Establishes and enforces standards of air purity.
CITY AGENCY	**AREA OF ACTIVITY**
Public Housing Authority	Acquires and operates public housing projects.
Downtown Redevelopment Agency	Condemns and razes slums and redevelops area.
Transit Authority	Operates local bus and rail transit systems.
School Board	Operates public schools.

HOW DO AGENCIES ENFORCE COMPLIANCE?

Problem: The Prescott Broadcasting Company owned and operated a television station in a major metropolitan area under license from the Federal Communications Commission. The F.C.C. ordered Prescott to devote more time to locally-oriented broadcasts (instead of national chain broadcasts) and to allow more time for public-service type shows. If Prescott refused to comply, what could the F.C.C. do?

Independent administrative agencies may enforce compliance with their orders and rulings by using *sanctions,* or penalties, to produce obedience. Often the agency will issue a *cease and desist order*, telling the defendant to stop the forbidden practice.

Various other orders may be issued; fines and penalties may be imposed; property may be seized or withheld; licenses suspended or revoked; damages assessed, or other action required. If the defendant fails to comply with a cease and desist order, the agency must normally seek enforcement by a regular court. If he then fails to comply with the court order, he may be held in contempt of court and fined or imprisoned until he complies.

In the problem, the F.C.C. could revoke or refuse to renew the Prescott license. However, Prescott could request a court review of the order.

GOVERNMENT—SERVANT, NOT MASTER . . .

1. Government serves man, not vice versa. Properly viewed, government is not the opponent of honestly conducted business, but its ally.
2. In his capacity as private individual or business manager, the wise citizen takes full advantage of government services; the prudent citizen obeys all government laws and regulations; the good citizen also participates in government, as voter, observer, and constructive critic.
3. For business manager and consumer-citizen alike, the independent administrative agency is often the most important arm of government. Whenever appropriate, learn what such agencies can do for you.
4. If dissatisfied or aggrieved by action of an administrative agency, you can appeal to the regular courts for review. However, they seldom overrule the decisions or rulings because the agencies are usually staffed by the top experts on the problem.
5. If dissatisfied with the conduct of a business firm which is regulated by an independent administrative agency, you may ask the agency to provide assistance or relief.

YOUR LEGAL VOCABULARY

A.E.C.
building code
C.A.B.
cease and desist order
Clayton Act
embargo
F.C.C.
F.M.C.
F.P.C.
F.R.B.
F.T.C.
I.C.C.

independent administrative
  agencies
monopoly
N.A.S.A.
N.L.R.B.
sanctions
S.E.C.
Sherman Antitrust Act
Small Business
  Administration
tariff
zoning laws

1. National Aeronautics and Space Administration—independent federal administrative agency concerned with exploration of space.
2. Control over the supply of goods to the extent that prices may be set.
3. A penalty imposed to compel obedience to a regulation or order.
4. Atomic Energy Commission—independent federal administrative agency concerned with development of peaceful and military uses of atomic energy.
5. Law banning the export of certain goods to specified countries.
6. Securities and Exchange Commission—independent federal administrative agency which regulates stock issues and stock exchanges where they are traded.
7. A tax on imports.
8. Federal Trade Commission—independent federal administrative agency which regulates business competition and certain trade practices.
9. Government agencies which commonly combine legislative, executive, and judicial powers and functions.
10. Local laws which specify what use may be made of land (residential, commercial, industrial).

REMEMBER THESE HIGHLIGHTS

1. Government and business are closely involved in each other's affairs and mutually dependent upon each other, and consumers benefit from the operation of both.
2. Independent administrative agencies commonly combine the traditionally separated legislative, executive, and judicial functions of government. They have a great influence on business and society through the regulations they make and enforce.
3. Independent administrative agencies exist at all levels of government, but are especially significant at the federal level.

4. Every business firm is affected importantly by legally imposed government regulations and legally provided services. Many business firms also count government departments and agencies among their best customers.

5. Legally prescribed standards of conduct and services determine or affect many human activities—from birth to death, including education, marriage, employment, and recreation.

LAW AS PEOPLE LIVE IT

1. Some 90 competitors who made similar products in the widget-gadget industry organized a trade association which held annual meetings, published a monthly journal, and exchanged routine information on costs of producing and distributing their products. Was any of this activity illegal?

2. At the last national convention of the Widget-Gadget Trade Association held in Las Vegas, Nevada, Winston—president of the largest firm in the industry—and the heads of the four other companies who together did 80 percent of the total industry business, met secretly. All claimed they were suffering from aggressive price-cutting competition. Therefore they shook hands and informally agreed "as gentlemen" to exchange price lists and to maintain the current level of prices for six months. They would meet in Chicago to review the situation. Were they violating any federal laws?

3. When he graduated from high school, Hovey began to cultivate certain types of fruit trees. Soon he was selling them to others. As the years went by he hired researchers to improve the trees, and his business prospered. Within thirty years Hovey was selling more than 90 percent of all the fruit trees of this specialty type. He never bought out any competitor; they simply could not match his quality and price. Was he acting in violation of laws against monopoly?

4. Vandenberg, a cement manufacturer, wanted to expand by selling his product in a big city located in the adjoining state. However, if he added the cost of shipment by truck or train, the price would be too high. Therefore he insisted that the I.C.C. force the carriers involved to reduce their rates "to serve the public." Must they?

5. Corson owned a pick-up truck used in his business. The truck was 12 years old and was not equipped with an exhaust-control device required by a new rule imposed by the state department of motor vehicles. To install the device would cost about $100. Corson refused, saying that was more than the pick-up truck was worth. He claimed the rule was unconstitutional because it would deprive him of the use of his property without due process of law. Is he right?

6. Chellems refused to transmit to the federal government the income taxes he had withheld for his employees, his own personal income tax, and also his corporation's income tax. He said he was a pacifist and objected to the government's spending for military needs as well as for atomic research and space exploration. Can he be compelled to pay?

7. Skaggs brought an action to prevent the government from spending money on relief payments and rent subsidies for the poor. He said this was unfair discrimination against those who paid taxes yet did not qualify for relief. Will he win?

8. A group of "hippies" was disappointed and disillusioned with life as they observed it in the city. They rejected all laws and other forms of social control, and moved into a wilderness area to live like hermits. Are they still protected by and subject to law?

9. Kreeling planned to add an office to his warehouse building. To save money, he decided to have his own employees do all the work during idle time from their duty as mechanics in his shop. Can he do the job as he pleases, using workers who are not skilled in such work?

10. Crawford owned an old riverside paper mill which used large quantities of water. In the manufacturing process much waste was dumped into the river. A new state law required filtration of the waste water to reduce pollution. Crawford objected saying paper makers in other states were not required to install the expensive filtration equipment, and this would place him at a competitive disadvantage because he would have to charge more for his products. Must he comply with the law or close down his plant?

LAW AS COURTS DECIDE IT

1. Under a federal law governing wheat production, Filburn was given a quota. He violated the administrative order by cultivating 11.9 extra acres and harvesting 239 excess bushels of wheat. This made him liable for a penalty of $117.11, which he refused to pay. He claimed the law violated the U.S. Constitution because his production was local, and federal power was limited to interstate commerce. Most of his wheat was used on his own farm to feed his poultry and livestock, to make flour for his family, and to provide seed for the next year. Was the federal government acting properly within its power to regulate interstate commerce? (Wickard v. Filburn, 317 U.S. 111, 87 L.Ed. 122)

2. In 1911, the United States government brought an action against 71 associated companies which were engaged in the oil business under the leadership of John D. Rockefeller. The companies allegedly

made agreements to fix prices, limit production, and control the transportation of oil. At one time they formed a trust and nine trustees managed all the companies. Later, Standard Oil Company of New Jersey acquired a majority of the stock of the other companies and controlled their operations. Did this arrangement violate the Sherman Antitrust Act? (Standard Oil Co. v. U.S., 221 U.S. 1, 55 L. Ed. 619)

3. In television commercials for its "Rapid Shave" cream, Colgate-Palmolive sought to prove the product's "superior moisturizing power." To do so it applied the product to what looked like sandpaper and immediately thereafter a razor appeared to shave the paper clean. In fact, however, to really do the trick would require that the paper soak for 80 minutes. The advertiser actually used a "mock-up" simulation made of clear plexiglass on which sand had been sprinkled. The F.T.C. claimed this was deceptive practice. Was it? (F.T.C. v. Colgate-Palmolive Co., 380 U.S. 379, 13 L.Ed. 2d 904)

4. The city manager and other officials of Phoenix sought to end a business conducted by Engle and Showell without a trial or public hearing. The city had ruled that the business was a public nuisance. The defendants asked the court for an injunction to prevent such action. Should it be granted? (Hislop v. Rogers, 54 Ariz. 101, 92 P. 2d 52)

5. The Stovers objected to high municipal taxes in Rye, New York. In protest, they hung tattered clothing, old uniforms, rags, and scarecrows on lines in their front yard in their "pleasant residential neighborhood." The city passed an ordinance prohibiting the practice without a permit, and then refused to grant a permit. Was the statute and its use a valid exercise of the police power? (People v. Stover, 12 N.Y. 2d 462, 191 N.E. 2d 272)

Glossary

A rich vocabulary is to be found under the heading YOUR LEGAL VOCABULARY at the end of each chapter. The words in those lists are explained in the text and may be found through the use of the index.

A

Abandon: to give up or leave with no intent to reclaim.

Abate: to stop or reduce.

Accessory: one who, though not a direct participant, aids or encourages the commission of a crime.

Acquittal: a judicial discharge; a verdict of not guilty.

Action: the formal demand of one's rights in a court; a lawsuit.

Action of mandamus: civil action, under common law, to force performance by an official.

Affidavit: a written statement, the truth of which is verified by oath or affirmation before a proper official.

Affinity: legal relationship based upon marriage; kindred by marriage.

Affirm: to ratify, confirm, a solemn promise to tell the truth under the penalty of perjury.

Agency shop: a union contract provision requiring that nonunion employees pay to the union the equivalent of union dues in order to retain their employment.

Allegation: a statement to be proven in a legal action; an unsupported claim.

Alibi: proof that one was elsewhere at the time of the commission of the act.

Alien: a citizen of one country residing in another country.

Alimony: an allowance for her support, given by a husband to his wife, after a legal separation or divorce. (In some circumstances, may be given to husband by wife).

Allonge: a paper securely fastened to a commercial paper in order to provide additional space for indorsements.

Ambiguity: an expression whose meaning can be taken in two or more ways.

Annexation: attachment of personal property to realty in such a way as to make it become real property.

Annul: to cancel, destroy, or make void.

Answer: a written statement of the defendant's position.

Anticipatory breach: in a contract, when the promisor refuses to perform prior to the time required, and the refusal is accepted as a breach by the promisee.

Appeal: taking the case to a reviewing court to determine whether the judgment of the lower court or administrative agency was correct.

Appellate court: a court of review.

Appraise: setting the value on, as goods; estimating the amount of a loss.

Arbitration: the settlement of disputed questions, whether of law or fact, by one or more arbitrators by whose decision the parties agree to be bound.

Assent: agree, the act of agreeing.

Asset: an item of one's property.

Attachment: a legal seizure, usually of goods.

Attest: to bear witness to; to certify as to the truth and genuineness of a document.

B

Bad check laws: laws making it a criminal offense to issue a bad check with intent to defraud.

Bankrupt: one in an insolvent condition who has committed an act of bankruptcy; also, one who has been formally declared a bankrupt.

Blue-sky laws: state statutes designed to protect the public from the sale of worthless stocks and bonds.

Bona fide: in good faith, without deceit or fraud.

Breach: the breaking or violating of a right or duty either by doing or failing to do.

Brief: written or printed arguments and authorities furnished by a lawyer to a court.

Business trust: a form of business organization in which the owners of the property to be devoted to the business transfer the title of the property to trustees with full power to operate the business.

C

Capital: net assets of a corporation.

Cause of action: grounds for a lawsuit.

Chattel: an article of personal property.

Circumstantial evidence: circumstances surrounding an event from which facts can be inferred.

Client: one who employs a lawyer.

Code: a systematized collection of laws.

Coercion: the use, or threat of use, of physical force to restrain or force another's actions.

Comaker: a person who with another signs a negotiable instrument on its face and thereby becomes primarily liable for its payment.

Commission merchant: a bailee to whom goods are consigned for sale.

Compromise: a settlement reached by mutual concessions.

Conflict of laws: the body of law that determines the law of which state is to apply when two or more states are involved in the facts of a given case.

Consanguinity: relationship by blood.

Contingent beneficiary: the person to whom the proceeds of a life insurance policy are payable in the event that the primary beneficiary dies before the insured.

Contra: opposite or contrary.

Cooling-off period: a procedure designed to avoid strikes by requiring a specified period of delay before the strike may begin during which negotiations for a settlement must continue.

Cooperative: a group of two or more persons or enterprises that act through a common agent with respect to a common objective, as buying or selling.

Cost plus: a method of determining the purchase price or contract price by providing for the payment of an amount equal to the costs of the seller or the contractor to which is added a stated percentage as his profit.

Custody: the control and possession of property; the authority exercised by a guardian over a ward.

Counterclaim: a claim by a defendant in opposition to or a deduction from the claim of the plaintiff.

Covenant: a mutual agreement in writing.

Cross-examination: the examination made of a witness by the attorney for the adverse party.

D

Declaratory judgment: a procedure for obtaining the decision of a court on a question before any action has been taken or loss sustained. It differs from an advisory opinion in that there must be an actual, imminent controversy.

Decree: a court of equity judgment or order comparable to a common-law court judgment.

De facto: existing in fact, as distinguished from existing in law.

Default: failure to perform something required.

Demurrer: a pleading that may be filed to attack the sufficiency of the adverse party's pleading as not stating a cause of action or a defense.

Deposition: the testimony of a witness taken out of court before a person authorized to administer oaths.

Descent: the passing of an estate by inheritance and not by will.

Directed verdict: a direction by the trial judge to the jury to return a verdict in favor of a specified party to the action.

Discharge: the act by which a person is freed from a legal obligation.

Dismiss: a procedure to terminate an action by moving to dismiss on the ground that the plaintiff has not pleaded a cause of action entitling him to relief.

Divorce: the severing of marriage ties, effected by court judgment.

Docket: a list of actions ready for trial.

Domestic bill of exchange: a draft drawn in one state and payable in the same or another state.

Domicile: that place where a man has fixed his habitation, not for a temporary purpose, but to which whenever he is absent he has the intention of returning.

Due process of law: the right to the regular privileges and protections afforded by constitutions, statutes, and courts.

E

Ejectment: an action for the recovery of real property. Frequently used to determine ownership.

Eleemosynary corporation: a corporation organized for a charitable or benevolent purpose.

Equitable: just, fair, right.

Erosion: the loss of land through a gradual washing away by tides or currents, with the owner losing title to the lost land.

Escheat: the transfer to the state of the title to a decedent's property when he dies intestate not survived by anyone capable of taking the property as his heir.

Estate: the interest or right that one has in property.

Estate in fee simple: the largest estate possible in which the owner has the absolute and entire property in the land.

Estoppel: that which prevents a man from denying or affirming certain facts because they are contrary to a previous claim, admission, or course of action.

Exception: an objection, as an exception to the admission of evidence on the ground that it was hearsay; the exclusion of particular property from the operation of a deed.

Exemplary damages: damages in excess of compensation, given to punish the defendant for the supposed mental anguish caused the plaintiff.

Exoneration: removal of a charge or responsibility; an equity existing between secondary parties and the primary party.

Expert witness: one who has acquired special knowledge in a particular field through practical experience, or study, or both, which gives him a superior knowledge so that his opinion is admissible as an aid to the court.

Ex post facto law: a law that makes a crime an act which was legal when done, or increases the penalty after the commission of a crime.

F

Fiduciary: a relationship based upon trust or confidence.

Foreclosure: a legal proceeding which extinguishes a mortgagor's ownership interest.

Foreign corporation: a corporation incorporated under the laws of another state.

Forfeiture: the loss of some right or privilege.

Franchise: a special privilege conferred by government.

Friendly fire: a fire that does not become uncontrollable nor escape from the place where it is intended to be.

G

Grace period: a period generally of 30 or 31 days after the due date of a premium of life insurance in which the premium may be paid.

Grand jury: a jury that considers evidence of the commission of a crime and prepares indictments to bring offenders to trial before a petty or petit jury.

Gift causa mortis: gift given with the giver's belief of his impending death, which can be revoked upon his survival.

H

Hearsay evidence: testimony, not of what a witness knows personally, but of what he has heard said by others.

Hedging: the making of simultaneous contracts to purchase and to sell a particular commodity at a future date with the intention that the loss on one transaction will be offset by the gain on the other.

Hidden service charge: a service charge not stated as a separate item but included in the total.

Hung jury: a petty jury that has been unable to agree upon a verdict.

I

Immaterial: unimportant; existing but making no difference.

Inducement: that which causes or influences action.

Infant: a person not of full legal age.

Inheritance: property received by an heir.

Instrument: a written document.

Interlineation: a writing between the lines.

International bill of exchange: an instrument made in one nation and payable in another.

Interstate: between two or more states or between places or persons in different states.

Intrastate: wholly within one state.

Invalid: of no legal effect; void.

Issue of fact: a dispute over what happened.

Issue of law: a dispute over the legal effect of what happened.

J

Joint and several contract: a contract in which two or more persons are jointly and individually obligated or are jointly and individually entitled to recover.

Judgment by default: a judgment rendered on the plaintiff's evidence alone because the defendant failed to answer the summons or appear.

Judicial sale: a sale made under order of court by an officer appointed to make the sale or by an officer having such authority as incident to his office.

Jurisdiction: range of court power to hear and determine over a particular defendant, or a given class of cases.

Jurisdictional dispute: a dispute between rival labor unions which may take the form of each claiming that certain work should be assigned to it.

L

Last clear chance: the rule that if the defendant had the last clear chance to have avoided injuring the plaintiff, he is liable even though the plaintiff had also been contributorily negligent.

Leading question: a question which suggests the desired answer to the witness, or assumes the existence of a fact which is in dispute.

Levy: a seizure of property by an officer of the court in execution of a judgment of the court.

Limited partnership: a partnership in which at least one partner has a liability limited to the loss of the capital contribution that he has made to the partnership, and such a partner neither takes part in the management of the partnership nor appears to the public to be a partner.

Litigation: a suit at law for the purpose of enforcing a right.

L.S.: an abbreviation for the Latin words *Locus Sigilli,* meaning the place of the seal.

M

Malice: spiteful or malevolent intent to cause harm; a reckless disregard for law.

Martial law: government exercised by a military commander over property and persons not in the armed forces.

Maturity: the day on which a commercial paper becomes due.

Measure of damages: a principle used to determine the compensation for injuries.

Mediation: the act of a third person to settle the dispute of two contending parties.

Merger of corporations: a combining of corporations by which one absorbs the other and continues to exist, preserving its original charter and identity while the other corporation ceases to exist.

GLOSSARY

Misrepresentation: a false statement of fact although made innocently without any intent to deceive.

Moratorium: a temporary suspension.

Mutual mistake: a mistake on the part of each of the parties having to do with the same matter.

N

Nominal partner: a person who in fact is not a partner but who holds himself out as a partner or permits others to do so.

Nonsuit: abandonment or renunciation of an action by the plaintiff or a decision against him because he was unable to establish a case.

Notary public: a public officer who, among other powers, can present and formally protest commercial paper.

Notice of protest: a formal notice that a commercial paper has been dishonored.

Novation: the discharge of a contract between two parties by their agreeing with a third person that the third person shall be substituted for one of the original parties to the contract, who shall then be released.

O

Oath: a solemn attestation of the truth of that which is asserted.

Obligation: a duty.

Occupation: taking and holding possession of property; a method of acquiring title to personal property which has been abandoned.

Option contract: a contract to hold open an exclusive or first right to buy.

P

Partition: the division of property between co-owners so that each may own his share individually.

Perjury: when under oath, an intentional false statement or the failure to tell what had been promised.

Per se: in, through, or by itself.

Person: a term that includes both natural persons, or living people, and artificial persons, as corporations, which are created by act of government.

Petty jury: the trial jury of twelve. Also petit jury.

Picketing: in labor law, the placing of members of a union, usually with signs, in such a manner as to convey their grievances to others.

Polling the jury: the process of inquiring of each juror individually in open court as to whether the verdict announced by the foreman of the jury was agreed to by him.

Presumption: an inference as to the truth or falsehood of a fact drawn from the existence of other known facts.

Presumption of innocence: the presumption that a person accused of crime is innocent until it is shown that he in fact is guilty of the offense charged.

Pretrial conference: a conference held prior to the trial at which the court and the attorneys seek to simplify the issues in controversy and to eliminate matters not in dispute.

Prima facie: at first sight; apparently true; on the first appearance.

Primary beneficiary: the person designated as the first one to receive the proceeds of a life insurance policy.

Principle: a fundamental truth or doctrine, as a principle of law.

Privileged communication: a communication by a client to his attorney in professional confidence and which the attorney is not permitted to divulge. A few states recognize this privilege in such cases as doctor-patient and priest-penitent.

Privity: joint and private knowledge with another.

Probate: the proof of a will by the proper court.

Process: a writ or order of a court generally used as a means of acquiring jurisdiction over the person of the defendant.

Promoter: one who originates, furthers, and organizes the formation of a corporation.

Proof: the establishment of a fact by evidence.

Pro rata: proportionately; according to interest or share of each.

Public utility: a private corporation that has certain powers of a public nature, such as the power of eminent domain, to enable it to discharge its duties for the public benefit.

Punitive damages: damages in excess of those required to compensate the plaintiff for the wrong done, which are imposed in order to punish the defendant because of the particularly wanton or willful character of his wrongdoing.

Purchaser in good faith: a person who purchases without any notice or knowledge of any defect of title, misconduct, or defense.

Q

Qualified acceptance: an acceptance of a draft that varies the order of the instrument in some way.

Quasi: as though.

Quorum: that number of persons required to be present at a meeting in order to transact business.

R

Real evidence: tangible objects that are presented in the courtroom as proof of the facts in dispute or in support of the theory of a party.

Rebate: a discount; reduction; sometimes handed back to the payer after he has paid the full amount.

Receipt: written evidence that an obligation has been discharged in full or in part.

Redress: to correct; to make right; receiving satisfaction for an injury sustained.

Referee in bankruptcy: a referee appointed by a bankruptcy court to hear and determine various matters relating to bankruptcy proceedings.

Registration of titles: a system, generally known as the Torrens system, of permanent registration of title to all land within the state.

Release: to surrender or relinquish to another a right, claim, or interest.

Remote damages: damages which were in fact caused by the defendant's act but the possibility that such damages should occur seemed so improbable and unlikely to a reasonable man that the law does not impose liability for such damages.

Repudiate: to reject; to renounce a right, duty, obligation, or privilege.

Reservation: in making a conveyance, the making and keeping of a previously nonexistent right, by the grantor.

Restrictive covenants: covenants in a deed by which the grantee and his transferees become obligated to refrain from doing specified acts.

Reversible error: an error or defect in court proceedings of so serious a nature that on appeal the appellate court will set aside the proceedings of the lower court.

Rider: in insurance law, an attached writing that modifies the printed policy.

S

S. S.: abbreviation for the Latin word *scilicet*, meaning to wit, namely, that is to say.

Scope of employment: the area within which the employee is authorized to act with the consequence that a tort committed while so acting imposes liability upon the employer.

Sentence: the judgment of a court in a criminal case.

Severed realty: real property that has been cut off and made moveable, as by cutting down a tree, and which thereby loses its character as real property and becomes personal property.

Short-rate table: a table in an insurance policy showing the amount of the premium that will be returned if the insured cancels.

Signature: a written, printed, typewritten, or rubber-stamped name, sign, or mark written by a person himself, or by his proper agent.

Sitdown strike: a strike in which the employees remain in the plant and refuse to allow the employer to operate it.

Solvency: financially able to pay one's debts.

Special damages: damages that do not necessarily result from the injury to the plaintiff but at the same time are not so remote that the defendant should not be held liable for them.

Stare decisis: the principle that the decision of a court should serve as a guide or precedent and control the decision of a similar case in the future.

Status quo: original position prior to the making of a contract.

Stipulation: a material condition or article in an agreement.

Strict tort liability: liability imposed for harms caused by inherently dangerous goods.

Subscribe: to write under; to sign at the bottom or end of a writing.

Substantial performance: the equitable doctrine that a contractor substantially performing a contract in good faith is entitled to recover the contract price less damages for noncompletion or defective work.

Summary judgment: court judgment, based on written evidence, showing insufficient basis for the claim of the defense.

Supreme law: the United States Constitution is the supreme law in those cases where the power is expressed or implied in the federal constitution. In all other cases a state constitutional provision would be the supreme law. When a conflict arises between the United States Constitution and a state constitution, each is the supreme law in its own area of power.

Syndicate: an association of individuals formed to conduct a particular business transaction, generally of a financial nature.

T

Trade secrets: secrets of any character peculiar and important to the business of the employer that have been communicated to the employee in the course of confidential employment.

Treasury stock: stock of the corporation which the corporation has reacquired.

U

Ultra vires: an act or contract beyond the power of a corporation.

Underwriter: the one who insures another; the insurer.

Undisclosed principal: a principal on whose behalf an agent acts without disclosing to the third person the fact that he is an agent nor the identity of the principal.

Unfair competition: the wrong of employing competitive methods that have been declared unfair by statute or an administrative agency.

Uniform law: any one of a number of proposed laws that have been approved by the National Conference of Commissioners on Uniform Laws.

Universal agent: an agent authorized by the principal to do all acts that can lawfully be delegated to a representative.

Unoccupied building: a furnished building whose inhabitants are temporarily away.

Unwritten law: that portion of the law not found in constitutions, statutes, or ordinances. Most of the "unwritten law" is written in the cases.

V

Vacant building: an unfurnished building.

Venue: the geographic area over which the court presides.

Verify: to fix, determine, or establish a fact by use of a statement under oath.

Versus: (Latin) against. Abbreviated vs. or v.

Vested: fixed; settled; not subject to being defeated; a legal right of present or future property enjoyment.

W

Watered stock: stock issued by a corporation as fully paid when in fact it is not.

Works of charity: in connection with Sunday laws, acts involved in religious worship or aiding persons in distress.

Works of necessity: in connection with Sunday laws, acts that must be done at the particular time in order to be effective in saving life, health, or property.

Writ: anything written.

Z

Zoning law: a regulation, frequently an ordinance, restricting or permitting certain types of improvements or uses of land in specified areas.

Index

of warranty, 294-299; recovery of goods or value, 298; replevin, 298; resell goods, 299; return of goods, 297; specific performance, 199, 298
Bylaws, 632

C

C.A.B. (Civil Aeronautics Board), 648
Cancellation, 198, 353; as limited defense, 387; discharges negotiable instrument, 353; of insurance policy, 482; right of, 297
Capacity to contract, 135; lack of, as universal defense, 390
Capital punishment, 101
Care, as agent's duty, 469; of property, by tenant, 586
Car registration, 42
Carrier, 230; common, 230; common as ordinary bailee, 230; contract, 231; duties of common, 231; duties of common, of goods, 231; duties of common, of passengers, 231; how private and common differ, 231; liability for losses of common, 231; liability of, 233, 234; private, 231; regulation of common, 233; rights of common, 232
Carrier's lien, 233
Car title, 43
Case, how tried, 99
Case law, 9
Cash and carry sales, 270
Cashier's check, 351
Cash surrender value, 528
Casual laborer, 439
Casual seller, 243
Casualty insurance, 192, 481; liability insurance as, 498; types of, 481-482
Cause, proximate, 494
Caveat emptor, 285
Caveat venditor, 285
Cease and desist order, 650
Certificate, stock, 628
Certificate of deposit, 347
Certificate of incorporation (charter), 628
Certificate of registration, 42
Certificate of title, 43
Certified check, 351
Charitable subscriptions, 162
Charity, what testator may give to, 601
Charter (certificate of incorporation), 628
Chattel mortgage, 326
Check, 349; bank is always drawee of, 349; cashier's, 351; certified, 351; how differs from draft, 349-350; illustrated, 349; obligations of parties, 349-350; parties to, 349; presentment required, 350; requirement upon dishonor, 399-401; special types of, 351-352; travelers', 352; use of, 343, 349
Child-labor laws, 423
Citation, 28

Citizen, 15; protection of, 17
Citizenship, 15; gaining or losing of, 15-16; showing allegiance, 17
City agencies, 649; areas of activity, 649
Civil action, 98
Civil Aeronautics Board, 25
Civil law, 73; differs from criminal, 73
Civil rights, 19; equality before law, 22; freedom of self-expression, 20; ownership and protection of private property, 24; personal security, 21
Civil Rights Acts (1964), 426
Claim, 499; compromise of a disputed, 161; for damaged goods, 231, 233-234; how made, 499; insurance, 499
Class action, 52
Clause, acceleration, 363
Clayton Act, 643
Closed shop, 427; banned by right-to-work laws, 431
C.O.D. (Collect on Delivery), 270
Codicil, 600
Collateral, 325; classification of, 329; consumer goods as, 329; equipment as, 329; farm products as, 329; intangible property, 330; inventory as, 329; possession of, by creditor, 326, 330; possession of, by debtor, 327
Collateral note, 346
Collective bargaining, 433; agreements, 411; right to, 411
Collective bargaining agreement, 411
Collision insurance, 512
Collusion, 510
Commerce, interstate, 420; intrastate, 420
Commercial bribery, 77
Commercial paper, 343; held by a HDC, 383; obligations of parties, 401
Commercial unit, 294
Common carrier, 230; as ordinary bailee, 230; claims for damages, 233-234; differ from private, 231; duties of, 231; liability for losses, 233-234; of goods, duties of, 231-233; of passengers, duties of, 230-231; regulation of, 233; rights of, 232
Common law, 5; duties, of employer, 440; how differs from workmen's compensation, 439
Common-law risks, of employee, 442
Common stock, 629
Common torts, 78-80
Communication, promoting, by government in business, 643
Community property, 561-562
Compensation, 411; agent entitled to, 470; as principal's duty, 470; as right, of employee, 411; carriers, 233; partner entitled to, 616; unemployment, 537
Competent party, 135
Competition, maintaining free and fair, 642-643
Complaint (information), 97
Compliance, how administrative agencies enforce, 650

Extortion, 77
Extradition, 89
Extraordinary bailee, liability, 233
Extraordinary bailment, 225

F

Face value, 479; of policy, 479
Fact, material, 125
Factor, 459
Fair Credit Reporting Act, 58
Fair employment practices, 431
Fair Labor Standards Act, 422, 426
Fair Packaging and Labeling Act, 57
Fair trade laws, 56
False advertising, 55
False pretenses, 77
Family Automobile Coverage, 508
Farmers, aided by government, 646
Farm products, 329
Farm Property-Fire and Extended Coverage Form, 495
F.C.C. (Federal Communications Commission), 648
Featherbedding, 430
Federal agencies, 648; areas of activity, 648; Small Business Administration, 644
Federal Bureau of Investigation (F.B.I), 88
Federal courts, 91-92
Federal Employer's Liability Act, 440
Federal Equal Pay Act, 426
Federal Food and Drug Administration (F.D.A.), 59-61
Federal Food, Drug and Cosmetic Act, 57, 59, 64; as regulates adulteration, 60; as regulates misbranding, 60-61; as regulates sanitation, 60
Federal Hazardous Substances Act, 59-60
Federal Trade Commission (F.T.C.), 51, 54, 57
Felony, 75; compounding a, 146
Fidelity and surety bonding insurance, 481
Financial responsibility laws, 514-515
Financing statement, 333; filing of, 333-334; purpose of, 334
Finding, acquiring property by, 559; bailment by, 212, 225, 228
Fire, friendly, 493; hostile, 493; loss by, 493-494
Fire insurance, 481, 493-496; inland marine, 497; protection against other perils, 495-496; standard policy, 495
Firm name, choosing, 636-637
Firm offer, 115
Fixture, 568, 569; added to property, 568-569; trade, 569
Flammable Fabrics Act, 62
Floater, 497; all-risk, 497; personal property, 497
Form, 495; Dwellings and Content, 495; Farm Property-Fire and Extended Coverage, 495; Mercantile Building and Stock, 495; modified by endorsements, 495
F.M.C. (Federal Maritime Commission), 648
F.O.B. (Free on Board), 268
Food adulteration, 60
Food and Drug Administration (F.D.A.), 25, 57; adulteration, 60; misbranding, 57, 59-61; sanitation, 60
Forbearance, 157; may be consideration, 157
Foreclosure, 578; right of, 578
Forfeiture, corporation dissolved by, 635-636
Forged indorsement, effect of, 377-378
Forgery, 77; as universal defense, 390; in contract, 483
Formal contract, 170
F.P.C. (Federal Power Commission), 648
Fraud, 124; as a tort, 74; as to nature of essential terms, as universal defense, 391; collusion as, 510; contracts induced by, are voidable, 124; in the execution or terms of a negotiable instrument, 386, 391; in the inducement, as limited defense, 386; tests for, 124-126
F.R.B. (Federal Reserve Board), 648
Friendly fire, 493
F.T.C. (Federal Trade Commission), 648
Full employment, promoted by government, 646
Fully insured, 542
Fungible goods, 264
Fur Act, 61
Fur Products Labeling Act, 61
Furs, labeling of, 61
Future goods, 264

G

Gambling agreements, 148
Garage or repairman's lien, 317
General agent, 458
General partner, 611-612
General powers of a corporation, implied, 631-633
Gift, 162; acquiring property by, 162, 557; decedent gives, 595
Good faith, 285; of insured, 487
Good faith purchaser, 263
Goods, 245; acceptance of, 254; acceptance of, by buyer, 254; bulk transfer of, 257; consumer, 329; delivery and payment of, 247; delivery of, 247, 293-294; delivery of, by carrier, 230-232; duties of common carrier of, 231-232; exceptions to general rule of transfer of, 262-263; existing, 264; fungible, 264; future, 264; identified, 264; identified, to a particular contract, 264; identified existing, not to be delivered, 300; identified existing, to be delivered, 300; identifying conforming, 300; inherent nature of, 234; misbranding and mislabeling, 57; nonresellable 256;

payment for, 244; proper shipment by carrier, 231; receipt of, 254; recovery of, or value, 298; requirements of Statute of Frauds for sales of, 252-253; retention of, not paid for, 299-300; risk of loss, 267-269; sale or return, 271; stopping delivery of, 301; subject matter of a sale, 241; transfer of ownership, 262; unordered, 247; warranties against encumbrances, 280; warranty for a particular purpose, 280; warranty of merchantability, 282; warranty of title, 279; when ownership transfers, 264-267

Government, agencies, 648; agencies, areas of activity, 648; corporations formed under authority of, 627; how regulation affects ultimate consumer, 646-647; legal basis for regulation of business, 641; restrains monopolies, 643; scope of involvement in business, 642

Government employees, forbidden right to strike, 645

Government involvement in business, 642-646

Government regulation, how affects ultimate consumer, 646-647; legal basis for, of business, 641; of employment, 420-433

Government standards, effect of, 62-63

Grace period, 526

Grand jury, 97

Grantee, 575

Grantor, 575

Gratuitous agency, 454

Gratuitous bailment, 212

Griffin-Landrum Act, 427

Group Life Insurance, 523-524

Guarantor, 316

Guaranty, 316

Guardian, 35

Guest, 230; fault of, 234

Guest laws, 510

H

Hazardous Substances Labeling Act, 57

Health Insurance, 482

Heir, 595

Hire, bailment for, 218-219

Holder, 344; in due course, 385; rights of, 283-291; through a HDC, 385; what must do upon dishonor, 399-400

Holder in due course (HDC), 383; qualifications of, 383-385; rights of, limited defenses, 385-389; rights of, universal defenses, 389-391

Holder through a HDC, 385

Holographic will, 599

Homeowners Policy, broad form, 496

Homesteading, 572

Honesty, employer's right to, 414

Hospital insurance, 547

Hostile fire, 493; as proximate cause, 494

Hotel, as a bailee, 229-230

Hotelkeeper (innkeeper), 229

Hotelkeeper's lien, 230

Hours, of employment, law of, 421-423, 425

Housing, promoting of, by government, 644

Housing code, representative, 589

I

I.C.C. (Interstate Commerce Commission), 648

Identified existing goods, in possession of bailee, 268; not to be delivered, 300; to be delivered, 300

Identified goods, 264

Identity of parties, mistake as to, 130

Identity of subject matter, mutual mistake concerning, 130

Illegal acts, may not be performed by agent, 458

Illegal agreement, 145-153; affecting marriage, 147; effect of, 145; in violation of public policy, 147; in violation of statutes, 152-153; lotteries, wagers and gambling, 148; made without required license, 150; restraining trade unreasonably, 150-152; tending to injure public service, 146-147; tending to obstruct justice, 146; to commit crimes or torts, 147-148; to pay usurius interest, 148; types of, 146; unconscionable, 150; what makes, 145

Illegal contracts, other, 152-153

Illegality, as universal defense, 390

Illegal lobbying contract, 147

Implied authority, 464

Implied contract, 169

Implied powers, of a corporation, 632-633; of partners, 616-618

Implied warranty, 277; excluded, 283-284; imposed by law, 281-283; kinds of, 279-283

Imports, tariffs, 646

Incapacity, other than minority, as limited defense, 386-387

Incompetency, of employee, 414-415

Incontestable clause, 525-526

Incorporation, articles of, 627; certificate of, 628

Incorporator, 627

Incorrigible, 94

Indemnify, 479

Indemnity, 471; agent entitled to, 471; as principal's duty, 471; double, 531; exclusions as exceptions to, 493; insurance loss, 479; insurance provides, 493; subrogation related to, 500

Independent administrative agencies, 647; what are, 647-649

Independent contractor, 409

Indictment, 97

Individual proprietorship, 609-610

Indorse, 345

Indorsee, 345

Joint tenants, 561
Judgment, 101; how satisfied, 102-103; who renders, 101
Judgment lien, 317
Judgment note, 346
Jurisdiction, 91
Jury, grand, 97; trial, 99
Justice of peace courts, 90
Juvenile, 93
Juvenile court, 93

K

Kickbacks, 433

L

Labeling, textiles and furs, 61
Labor, convict, 432; fair employment practices, 431-432; guaranteeing rights of, by government, 645; industrial home, 431; unfair practices, by unions, 430; what are unfair practices, by employers, 429
Laborer, casual, 439
Labor laws, conciliation, 433; convict labor, 432; fair employment practices, 431-432; Fair Labor Standards Act, 426; industrial home work, 431; mediation, 433; National Labor Relations Act and Labor-Management Act govern, 427; provisions of others, 431; servicemen, 432; specifically affecting minors, 423-426; specifically affecting women, 425-426; time off to vote, 432; workmen's compensation, 439-440
Labor-management, relations, laws governing, 427
Labor-Management Act of 1947, 427
Labor-Management Reporting and Disclosure Act (1959), 427
Labor union, 411
Lack of authority, as universal defense, 390
Land, 567
Land contract, 573
Landlord, 583; condition of premises, 588-589; duties of, 587-589; fixtures, 589; receipt of rent, 588; rights of, 587-589; taxes, 589
Landlord's duty, condition of premises, 588; taxes, 589; inspection, 588
Landlord's right, receipt of rent, 587; to evict tenant and reenter property, 588; to fixtures, 589; to sue for due rent, 588
Landrum-Griffin Act, 427
Land use, regulation of, by government, 644
Lapse, 526; of insurance policy, 502
Larceny, 76
Larceny insurance, 481
Law, 4; administrative, 9; as a changing process, 26; business, 10; case, 9; civil, 73; common, 5; conflict of, 8; constitutional, 8; contracts assigned by operation of law, 184; criminal, 73; development of, 5; due process of, 23; enforcement of, 87-90; equality before, 22; equal pay, 426; federal regulating food, drugs and cosmetics, 59; forms of, 6; implied warranties imposed by, 279-283; nature and kinds, 4-11; of contracts, how applies to insurance, 482; operation of, terminating bailment, 214; protecting contracting minors, 136-138; purposes of, 3-4; right-to-work, 431; Roman civil, 6; statute, 8; two great systems of, 6; unconstitutional, 8; uniform, 8; unwritten, 5; violation of, 74; Wage and Hour, 422; what is, 4; where to find, 28; why protects consumer, 50-52; why we have, 3
Law merchant, 10
Law of contracts, applies to insurance, 482-483; applies to sales, 242-244
Laws, bedding, 66; child-labor, 423; consumer loan, 318; consumer protection, 64; equal pay, 426; fair trade, 56; financial responsibility, 514-515; governing employment, 420-433; governing labor-management relations, 427; governing property of intestate, 601-602; guest, 510; labor, specifically affecting women, 425; other labor, 431; right-to-work, 431; state and local, protecting consumers, 64; Sunday, 153; Truth-in-Lending, 319-320; unemployment compensation, 537-538; wages and hours, 422; workmen's compensation, 439
Lease, 583; assignment of, 587; contents of, 583; duties of landlord, 587-589; duties of tenant, 585-587; kinds of, 584; rights of landlord, 587-589; rights of tenant, 585-587; subletting of, 587; termination of, 589-590
Legacy (bequest), 595
Legal action, how started, 87-88, 96-99; years in which, on contracts must be commenced, 201
Legal duties, 15
Legal entity, 625
Legal rate, 149
Legal rights, 19, 26
Legal systems, 87-103
Legal tender, 191
Lessee, 583
Lessor, 583
Liability, for crimes and torts, 82; of accommodation party, 379; of agent, to third persons, 466-468; of drawee, 402; of drawee-acceptor, 402; of drawer, 403; of employer, for acts of employees, 415; of extraordinary bailee, 233-234; of indorsers, 403; of insurer, 525; of maker, 402; of partner, 618-619; of principal, in agency, 464-465; of secondary parties, fixed by

value as, 528; extended term insurance as, 529; reduced paid-up life insurance as, 528

Non-partisan, 26

Nonpayment of wages, 412

Nonperformance, of employee, 415

Nonresellable goods, 256

No-par stock, 629

No protest (N.P.), 401

Note, bond as long-term, 347; collateral, 346; judgment, 346; mortgage, 346; presentment for payment, 399; promissory, 346; special forms of, 346-347

Notice of dishonor, 399-400

Notice of loss, 499

Notice of protest, 401

Notice to third parties, 472

Nuisance, 79

Nuncupative will (oral will), 599

O

OASDHI (old-age, survivors, and disability insurance), 540; availability of disability benefits, 546; cash payments, table of, 545; coverage, 542; determination of benefits, 544; disability, 546-547; finance of benefits, 543; health insurance, 547; Medicare, 547; monthly benefit payments, 545; qualifications for benefits, 542; reduction of benefits by work, 544-546; scheduled tax rates of, 543; who is entitled to coverage, 540

Obedience, as agent's duty, 469; employer's right to, 413-414

Obligation, of acceptor, 402; of drawee, 349; of drawer, 403; of parties, 349; of qualified indorsers, 377; of unqualified indorsers, 376

Obligor, 186

Occupancy, 559; acquiring title by, 559

Occupational Safety and Health Act of 1970, 58

Occupational Safety and Health Act of 1971, 433

Offer, 110; contracts of insurance, 482; defective, 110-112; firm, 115; how ended, 112-114; kept open, 114-115; made by mail or telegraph, 117; requirements of, 110-112; UCC affects, 115

Offer and acceptance, in insurance contracts, 482

Offeree, 109

Offeror, 109

Officers, of corporation, powers and duties of, 631

Old-age insurance, 536, 540

Omnibus clause, 509

Open shop, 427

Operation of law, contracts assigned by, 184; terminates partnership, 620; terminating bailment, 214

Opinion, 124

Option, 114; amount, 530; automatic premium loan, 528; cash surrender value, 528; extended term insurance, 529; interest, 530; lifetime income, 530; loan value, 528; nonforfeiture, 527-529; reduced paid-up life insurance, 528; settlement, 529-530; time, 530

Oral warranties, 277-278

Oral will (nuncupative will), 599

Order, in negotiable instrument, 362

Order bill of lading, 232

Order paper (payable to order), 366; requires indorsement and delivery, 371-372

Orders, money, 352

Order to pay, as requirement for negotiability, 362

Ordinances, 8

Ordinary life insurance, 522-523; endowment, 522; limited-payment, 522; term, 522; types of, 522; whole life, 522

Ostensible authority (apparent authority), 464

Outlawed, 201

Ownership, community property, 561; effect of transfer, 242; forms of, 560-562; joint tenancy, 561; limitations of, 562-563; severalty, 560; tenancy in common, 561; transfer of, of goods, 262; when transferred in particular transactions, 270

Ownership of goods, risk of loss, 267-269

P

Parents, rights and duties of, 37-38

Parks and Recreation Board, 649

Parole, 103

Parol evidence rule, 176

Participating policy, 484

Participating stock, 629

Parties, competent, 135; incompetent, 135; rights and obligations of, in employment contract, 411-416

Partner, 610; active, 612; authority of, 616-618; compensation entitled to, 616; duties of, 613-614; general, 611; implied powers of, 616-618; kinds of, 611-612; liability of, 618-619; limited, 612; rights of, 614-616; right to participate in management, 615; secret, 612; silent, 612

Partner's authority, to borrow money in firm name, 617; to buy, 617; to draw checks, 617; to hire, appoint and dismiss, 617; to make binding contracts for firm, 617; to receive and pay firm money, 617; to receive notice of matters affecting partnership, 618; to sell, 617

Partner's duty, to act with integrity and good faith, 613; to keep accurate records, 614; to refrain from participating in competitive business, 614; to use reasonable care, 613

Partnership, 610; articles of, 611; at will, 620; dissolution of, 619; formation of, 611-613; how ended, 619-621; kinds of, 611; limited, 612; partners in, 610; right in, property, 615-616; right to profits, 615; tenancy in, 616; winding up, 619

Partnership agreement (articles of partnership), 611; minor loses none of his rights in, 613; required to be in writing when longer than a year, 611

Partnership property, partner's right to, 615-616

Partner's right, extra compensation, 616; partnership property, 615; profits, 615; to participate in management, 615

Party, accommodation, 379; primary, 396; secondary, 396; obligations of, in commercial paper, 401

Par value, 629

Passengers, duties of common carrier of, 230-231

Past consideration, 162

Past performance, not consideration, 162

Patent, 559; acquiring property by, 559

Pawn, 313

Pawnbroker, 313

Payable, at a definite time, 364-365; on demand, 364; to bearer, 365; to order, 365-366

Payable at a definite time, 364

Payable on demand, 364

Payable to bearer (bearer paper), 365

Payable to order (order paper), 366

Payee, 349; of negotiable instrument, 346, 349

Payment, 253; discharging negotiable instrument, 353; for goods, 244; of rent, 585; presentment for, 399; presentment for, of draft, 399; presentment for, of note, 399; stop, 350; time of, of negotiable instrument, 364-365; what constitutes, 253-254

Payroll deductions, 412

Perfected security interest, 330

Performance, 183; contracts classified by, 170; contracts discharged by, 186; impossibility of, 188-190; injured party may compel, 199; reasonable, employer's right to, 415; specific, 199

Periodic tenancy, 584; termination, 590

Perjury, 75

Perpetual succession, 632

Personal acts, may not be performed by agent, 457-458

Personal property, 556; bailment of, 212-213; bequest, 595; division of, of an intestate, 601-602; floater, 497; secured transaction, 326; trade fixtures, 569

Personal property floater, 497

Picket, 430

Physical health, protection of, by government, 643

Plaintiff, 98

Pleadings, 98

Pledge, 313; pawn as, 313; secured transaction, 326

Pledgee, 313

Pledgor, 313

Police power, 18

Policy, 479; face value of, 479; insurance, 479; participating, 484; termination of insurance, 500-502

Political rights, 19

Poll tax, 26

Pollution, 35, 649

Possession, adverse, 571

Postdated instrument, 366

Power, implied, of partner, 616-618; of agent, 463-464

Power of attorney, 455

Powers and duties, of directors of corporation, 630-631; of officers of corporation, 631

Powers of corporation, 632-633

Precedent, rule of, 5

Preemptive right, 634

Preferred stock, 629; may be cumulative, 629; may be participating, 629

Premises, condition of, 586-589

Premium, 479; waiver of, 531

Prescription, 571

Presentment, 397; fixes liability, of secondary parties, 397; for acceptance, 398; for payment, 399; required of drafts or checks, 397-399

Price, 244; market, 629; payment of, 253

Price cutting, 56-57

Price-wage-interest-profit controls, 646

Pricing methods, unfair, 56-57

Primary boycott, 430

Primary parties, 396

Principal, 451; debtor, 315; in agency, duties of, 470-471; in agency, liability of, 464-465; who may be, 452-453

Principal debtor, 315

Principal's duties, compensation as, 470; indemnity as, 471; reimbursement as, 470-471

Prior payment, as limited defense, 387-388

Private carrier, 231; differs from common, 231

Private corporations, 626-627

Private property, ownership and protection of, 24-25

Privity of contract, 286

Probate court, 603

Probation, 95

Proceeds, 525; of life insurance policy, 525

Product, warranties, 277-278

Product liability, 286

Profit, 570; partner's right to, 615

Program, apprenticeship, 433

Promise, in consideration, 157; unconditional, as requirement for negotiability, 362

Promissory note, 346; dishonor of, 353; illustrated, 346; negotiable, 346; obligations of maker of, 346; parties involved, 346; presentment for payment, 397-399; special forms of, 346-347

Proof of loss, 499

Property, 555; abandoned, 559-560; acquiring, by accession, 557-558; acquiring, by contract, 557; acquiring, by finding, 559; acquiring, by gift, 557; acquiring, by inheritance, 560; acquiring, by intellectual labor, 558-559; acquiring, by occupancy, 559; acquiring, real, 570-573; acquisition of, by corporation, 633; alteration of, 558; assessment of, 563; community, 561-562; distribution of intestate, 601; forms of ownership of, 560-562; government assures safety and security of, 645; how acquired, 556-560; insurable interest in, 269, 485; insurance, 492; intangible, 330; kinds of, 555-556; landlord, 583; leasing, 583; limitations on ownership of, 562-563; ownership of, 555-556; partner's right in partnership, 616; personal, 556; real, 556, 567-578; rent of, 583; steps in buying real, 573-576; tenant, 583; tenant's care of, 586-587; tenant's use of, 585-586; transfer of, 573-578

Property damage insurance, 510

Property insurance, 492-502

Property ownership, community property, 561-562; joint tenancy, 561; tenancy by the entireties, 561; tenancy in common, 560-561; severalty, 560

Proprietorship, individual, 609

Prorate, 501

Prosecution, 97

Protection of employees, by workmen's compensation laws, 443-444

Protest, 401; notice of, 401

Proximate cause, 494

Proxy, 630

Public authority, act of, 234

Public corporation, 626

Public enemy, 233

Public grant, 572

Public Housing Authority, 649

Public liability coverage, 508-510; bodily injury, 509-510; property damage, 510

Public liability insurance, coverage given, 508

Public policy, illegal agreements in violation of, 147

Puffing, 279

Purchase money, 331

Purchaser in good faith, 263

Q

Qualified indorsement, 374; special form of, 374

Qualified indorser, 377; liability of, 377

Quarter of coverage, 542

Quasi contract, 204; remedy provided by, 203-204

Quitclaim deed, 576

R

Rate, contract, 149; legal, 149

Ratification, 127; agency created by, 456

Real estate mortgage, 577-578; transfer of, 577-578

Real property, 556; abstract of title, 574; acquired by accretion, 573; acquired by adverse possession, 571; acquired by dedication, 571-572; acquired by deed, 570; acquired by eminent domain, 572; acquired by public grant, 572; buildings, 568; contract to sell, 172; conveyance, 245-246; dedication of, 571; deed, 570; devise, 595; division of, of intestate, 601-602; easement, 569; escrow, 575-576; execution of deed, 575; fixtures as, 568-569; how acquired, 570, 573; joint tenancy of, 561; kinds of deeds, 576-577; land, 567; land contract, 573; mortgage on, 577; protection of title, 573-575; recording the deed, 576; steps in buying, 573-576; surveyance of, 573; tenancy in common, 561; title insurance, 574; Torrens System registration, 574; transfer, 573-578; what includes, 567-570

Reasonable skill, employer's right to, 414

Receipt, of rent, 587; warehouse, 216

Receipt of goods, 254

Receiver, 203

Reckless driving, 44

Recognizance, 97

Reduced paid-up life insurance, 528

Registration, car, 42; certificate of, 42; Torrens System, 574

Regulation, government, of business, 641; of employment, 420-422

Rehabilitation, vocational, 445

Reimbursement, agent entitled to, 470-471; as principal's duty, 470

Reinstate, 526

Remedy, 197; barred by bankruptcy laws, 202-203; barred by statute of limitations, 201-202; for breach of contract, 197-199; for breach of warranties, 294-299; for inducing breach of contract, 204; injured party's loss of, 200-203; of buyer, 295-299; of injured party, 197-199; of seller, 299-302; provided by quasi contract, 203-204

Remedy for breach, cancellation, 198; dollar damages, 198; recession, 198; specific performance, 199

Rent, 583; payment of, 583, 585, 588; receipt of, 588

Replevin, 298

Reporter, 28; abbreviations for, 29

Representations, 487

Requirements, unemployment compensation, 541

Rescission, 198

Research, stimulation by government, 644

Restrictive indorsement, 375; types of, 375-376

Revocation, 114; of will, 600
Rider (endorsement), 495; waiver of premium, 530-531
Right, easement, 569; of foreclosure, 578
Right of cancellation, 297; of injured party, 198; under UCC, 198
Right of recession, of injured party, 198
Right of tenant, possession, 585; assignment or subletting, 587; use of the property, 585
Rights, as an individual, 18; civil, 19; in property, 555-556; legal, 19, 26; natural, 19; of assignee, 185-186; of beneficiary, 524-525; of buyer, 292-294; of collective bargaining, 411; of common carrier, 232-233; of creditor, after default, 335-336; of debtor, after default, 335; of defrauded party, 126-127; of holders, 383-391; of holders in due course, 385-391; of labor guaranteed by government, 645; of landlord, 587, 589; of partner, 614-616; of seller, 299-302; of shareholders, 633-635; of students, 39; of the employee, 411-413; of tenant, 584-587; parental, 37-38; political, 26; transfer of contract, 183-184; under contract, 196-197; waiver of, 197
Right-to-work law, 431
Risk, 479; assumed with fire insurance, 493; in life insurance, 520
Risk of loss, when transferred, 267; when transferred in particular transactions, 270-272
Risks, employee's common-law, 442
Robbery, 76
Robbery insurance, 481
Roman civil law, 6
Rule of Naturalization, 16
Rule of precedent, 5
Rules of the road, 44; care required, 44

S

Safe-deposit boxes, 217
Safekeeping, bailment for, 216
Safety, for consumer protection, 62, 65
Safety Appliance Act, 440
Sale, 241; acceptance of, 253-254; auction, 272; barter, 245; bill of, use of, 256; bulk transfer, 257-258; cash and carry, 270; caveat emptor, 285; caveat venditor, 285; C.O.D., 270; comparison with similar transactions, table, 244; consideration in, 244; contract in writing, 253; credit, 270; delivery and payment of goods, 247; effect of not complying with Statute of Frauds, 252-253; fungible goods, 264; future goods, 264; identified existing goods, in possession of bailee, 268; identified existing goods, not to be delivered, 300; identified existing goods to be delivered, 300; identified goods, 264; identifying goods to a particular contract, 264; implied

warranties in, 281-283; law of contracts applies to, 243-244; memorandum, 174-175; of specifically-made goods, 256; of undivided interest, 272; on approval, 271; or return, 271; payment in, 253; price, 244; receipt of, 254; restrictions placed on, 246-247; Statute of Frauds applies to, 252; subject matter of, 245; transfer of ownership in, 262-272; transfer of ownership of goods, 262; transfer of risk of loss, 267-270; with right to return, 271; under UCC, 243; unordered goods, 247-248; vendee, 241; vendor, 241; warranties, in seller's claims, 278-279; warranties in, 277-278
Sale on approval, 271
Sale or return, 271
Sales contract, form of, 168-170; nature of, 241
Sanctions, 650
Sanitation, for consumer protection, 65
Satisfaction, 187; accord and, 187
School board, 649
Scope, of government involvement in business, 642
Scope of employment, 409
Seal, 158; contract under, 170; corporate, 632
S.E.C. (Securities and Exchange Commission), 648
Secondary boycott, 431
Secondary parties, 396; liability of, requirements to fix, 397-400
Secret partner, 612
Secured debt, 311
Secured party, 326
Secured transaction, 325; creditor's problems when debtor has possession, 328; pledge, 326-327; possession of collateral by debtor, 327-328; types of, 326-328
Security agreement, 326
Security interest, 325; in consumer goods, 331; in equipment, 332-333; in farm products, 331; in inventory, 332; perfected, 330; perfected by financing statement, 330
Security of person, assured by government, 645
Selective Service Extension Act of 1950, 432
Self-employed persons, 541
Seller, 241; casual, 243; in sales contract, 241; merchant, 243; remedies of, 299-302; rights of, 299-302
Seller's rights, acceptance of goods by buyer, 299; cancellation, 302; damages, 302; identify conforming goods, 300; payment of goods, 299; resell goods, 301-302; retention of goods not paid for, 299-300; stopping delivery, 301; sue for purchase price, 302; unpaid seller's lien, 299
Selling agent, 452
Servicemen, employment of, 432

Testimony, 100
Textile Fiber Products Identification Act, 61
Textiles, labeling of, 61
Theft, as limited defense, 389; insurance, 481; of negotiable instrument, 383, 389
Third party, assignment of contract rights, 183-184; liability of agent to, 466-467; notice should be given to, on termination of partnership, 620-621; notice to, 472; rights under a contract, 196-197; tenant's liability for injuries to, 587
Time, of payment of negotiable instrument, 364-365
Time draft, 349
Time option, 530
Title, abstract of, 574; acquiring by occupancy, 559; certificate of, 43; conveyance of, 245-246; deed as, to real property, 570; document of, 216; protection of, of real property, 573; Torrens System, 574-575; warranty of, 577
Title insurance, 574
Title of goods, transfer of title to, 262-267
Torrens System, 574-575
Tort, 74; agreement to commit, 147-148; assault, 78; battery, 79; common, 78-80; conversion, 79-80; defamation, 80; fraud as, 74; how differs from crime, 74; liability for, 82; negligence, 80; nuisance, 79; responsibility for, 81; trespass, 79
Trade, agreements, to restrain illegally, 151; agreements to restrain unreasonably, 150-151; valid agreements to restrain, 152
Trade fixture, 569
Trade practices, unfair, 54-58
Traffic controls and signals, 43
Traffic regulations, 43
Transaction, secured, 325
Transfer, bulk, 257-258; insurable property interest, 269; method of, in bailment, 213; method of, of negotiable instruments, 344-345; of insurable interest, in property, 269; of negotiable instruments, 371-372; of ownership, requirements for, 264; of real property, by deed, 570; what does real estate mortgage, 577
Transferee, 371
Transferor, 371
Transit Authority, 649
Transport, encouraging travel and, by government, 643
Travelers' checks, 352
Trespass, 79
Trial jury, 99
Truant, 39
Trust, deed of, 578
Trust agreement, 347
Trustee, 203
Truth-in-Lending Act, 58, 319

U

Unauthorized completion, as limited defense, 388-389
Unconditional promise, as requirement for negotiability, 362
Unconscionable, 150
Unconstitutional, 8
Undisclosed principal, 465
Undivided interest, sale of, 272
Undue influence, 128; as limited defense, 387
Unemployment benefits, forfeited, 539-540; how obtained, 538-539; provisions for, 537-538; when denied, 539-540; who are entitled to, 537-538
Unemployment compensation, 537; requirements and benefits, 541
Unfair labor practices, 429; by employer, 429; by unions, 430
Unfair pricing method, price cutting below cost, 57; price cutting in violation of fair trade acts, 56; representing foods, 56; representing goods or services, 56; representing retail prices as wholesale, 56
Unfair Sales Acts, 57
Unfair trade practice, 54; commercial bribery, 77; false and misleading advertising, 54; games of chance and lotteries, 55; misbranding and mislabeling goods, 57; other, 58; price cutting and unfair pricing methods, 56; selling used articles as new, 57
Uniform Commercial Code (UCC), 8, 10; applies to sales, 243; consideration under, 158-159; demands good faith, 285; filing financing statement, 330-331; firm offer, 115; governs negotiable instruments, 343; installment sale under, 326; offer affected by, 115, 117; payment of goods under, 353; protection of creditor under, 330-334; receipt and acceptance of goods under, 254; rights of cancellation under, 198; rights of secured creditor, 330-334; risk of loss of ownership of goods, 264-269; states adopted, 10; Statute of Frauds, provisions in, 171-174
Uniform Limited Partnership Act, 612
Uniform Partnership Act, 611-612
Unilateral contract, 117
Uninsured motorists insurance, 514
Union, featherbedding by, 430; picket by, 430; strike by, 430; unfair labor practices by, 430
Union shop, 427; banned by right-to-work laws, 431
United States Code (U.S.C.), 28
United States Constitution, bill of rights of, 19
United States Department of Agriculture, 62
United States Marshalls, 88